Anonymous

The Royal Kalendar

and court and city register, for England, Scotland, Ireland, and the colonies

Anonymous

The Royal Kalendar
and court and city register, for England, Scotland, Ireland, and the colonies

ISBN/EAN: 9783337328764

Printed in Europe, USA, Canada, Australia, Japan

Cover: Foto ©Andreas Hilbeck / pixelio.de

More available books at **www.hansebooks.com**

New Edition, corrected to the 8th of February, of

THE COURT and CITY REGISTER;

OR,

GENTLEMAN's Complete ANNUAL CALENDAR,

For the Year 1781;

CONTAINING,

I. New and Correct LISTS of both HOUSES of PARLIAMENT.

II. The COURT REGISTER.

III. LISTS of the ARMY, NAVY, UNIVERSITIES, PUBLIC OFFICES, HOSPITALS, &c.

With many Improvements, and the Addition of some new LISTS.

LONDON:

Printed for J. JOLLIFFE, in *St. James's-street*;
J. WALTER, at *Charing-Cross*;
HINTON, T. CASLON, C. DILLY, J. ROBSON, S. CROWDER, G. ROBINSON, R. BALDWIN, B. LAW, W. NICOLL, W. STUART, E. JOHNSTON, T. LOWNDES, T. LONGMAN, E. JOHNSON, J. RUSSEL, J. ALMON and J. DEBRETT, W. FLEXNEY, and B. COLLINS.

[Price bound, 2s. and with an Almanack 2s. 6d.]

INDEX

Admirals —— 146
    Admiralty Office 134
    ———— Court 135
Africa Comp. of Merch. 213
Agent Victuallers —— 142
Agents to the Army —— 169
Aldermen of London 203
Ambassadors to and from Foreign States —— 92
AMERICA —— 110
Amicable Society —— 216
Amelia, Prss. her Estab. 90
Antiquary Society —— 226
Archdeacons —— 201
Army, List of —— 171
Artillery Company —— 209
Asylum —— 232
Auditors of Land Tax 97
Augmentation Office 105
Bank of England 214
    Bankers, London 214
Bankruptcy, Commiss. of 98
Bartholomew's Hospital 227
Baronets —— 190
Bethlem —— 228
Bishops —— 16
Board of Works —— 85
Bridewell —— 228
British Museum —— 226
British Lying-in Hospital 231
Cambridge Univ. 236
    Capt. of the R. Navy 148
Chamberlain, Ld. his Office 70
Chancellors of Dioceses 201
Chancery, Court of —— 97
Chaplains in Ordinary 77
Charter House —— 227
Chelsea Hospital —— 168
Christ's Hospital —— 228
Cinque-Ports —— 168
Coll. of Doctors of Law 107
College of Physicians 220
Commissioners of Sewers 210
Committee of City Lands 210
Common Council —— 204
Common Pleas, Court of 102
Commons, List of H. of 21

Commons, alphabetically 54
————, their Officers 68
Company for propagating the Gospel in New England 227
Comptrollers of Army 169
Consuls, abroad —— 94
Cornwall, Dutchy of 86
Corporation for Seamen 231
Counsel, King's, and Serj. 105
Cumberland, D. of, his Estab. 89
Customs —— 116
Deans —— 200
    Dispensary for Poor 233
    ———— Inf. Poor 233
Drawing Room in Tower 167
East India Directors 211
    Equitable Assur. Off. 218
Exchequer, Officers of 95
———— Court of 103
Excise Office —— 119
Filazers to Com. Pleas 103
    First Fruits Office 105
Foundling Hospital —— 230
General and staff Off. 169
    Gen. Medical Asylum 232
George's, St. Hospital 229
Gloucester, D. of, his Estab. 89
Governments in America 112
———— Gibraltar, and Minorca, &c. —— 115
———— in Gr. Britain 189
Greencloth, Board of 80
Greenwich, Hospital 139
Gresham College —— 222
Guy's Hospital —— 229
Hackney Coach Office —— 133
Haslar, Hospital at —— 140
Hawkers & Pedlars Office 133
Heralds-College —— 90
Hosp. for Fr. Protestants 228
Housekeepers, &c. —— 74
Houshold, his Majesty's 80
Hudson's-Bay Comp. 213
Jewel Office —— 72
    Imprest Offices —— 96

Insurance Off. against Fire	216
Justices of Wales	105
KING's Bench, Court of	101
King's Kitchen	82
Knights of the Garter	91
——— Bath	91
——— Thistle	92
LAncaster, Dutchy Court	105
— Officers of the Court	106
Laudable Soc. for Widows	225
Laud. Soc. of Annuitants	228
Levee Days	79
Lieutenants of Counties	109
Lieutenants of the Navy	153
Lieutenancy of London	207
Lock Hospital	231
London Lying-in Hospital	231
——— Hospital	230
Luke's, St. Hospital	231
MAGDALEN House	232
Marine Society	232
Marshalsea Court	106
Master of the Horse	84
Master of the Robes	72
Masters and Commanders	151
Medical Society, Lond.	233
Messengers	73
Middlesex Hospital	230
Militia of London	208
Million Bank	213
Minorca	115
Mint	134
Misericordia Hospital	233
Morden's College	131
Music, Band of	73
NAVAL Officers	135
Navy Yards	137
—— Royal, List of	142
ORDNANCE, Civil	164
Ordnance, Military	166
Oxford University	234
PAY of the Army	169
Pay Office, Navy	135
Paymaster of Land Forces.	115

Paymaster of Pensions	97
Peers, House of	1
——, H. of, alphabetically	18
Peers, their Officers	67
Peeresses	16
Penny Post	128
Pensioners, Band of	83
Pipe Office	104
Plymouth Hospital	140
Post Office	123
Preachers at King's Chapel	79
Prebendaries	202
Privy Seal	108
Privy Council	69
Proctors	108
QUEEN's Houshold	87
Queen Anne's Bounty Office	105
RANGERS and Keepers	75
Rect. and Vic. Lond.	223
Registers in Doc. Com.	107
Royal Academy	219
—— Chapels	76
—— Nursery	88
—— Society	222
Russia Company	213
SALT-Office	122
Secretaries of State	110
Senegambia	115
Serj. and King's Counsel	105
Scots Hospital	234
Sheriffs	131
Sick and Hurt Office	140
Sixpenny Receivers-Office	140
Signet-Office	109
Sion-College	222
Small-Pox Hospital	230
Soc. of Artists of Gr. Brit.	219
Soc. for Chr. Knowledge	227
Society for Gospel	227
—for Encouragem. of Arts	218
—for Recovery of drowned Persons	229
Stamp Office	132
South Sea Company	212
Superannuated Officers	147

TALLY Court	96	War Office	115
Tax Office	96	Wardrobe, Removing	72
Tenth's Office	105	———— Great	76
Thomas's St. Hospital	228	Welch Charity	219
Tower of London	163	Westminster-Court	209
Trade, Board of	110	———— Infirmary	229
Tradesm. &c. to the King	74	———— Lying-in Hospi-	
Treasurer of the Chamber	87	tal	232
Treasury	94	———— General Dispen-	
Trinity-house	130	sary	233
Turkey Company	213	Widows and Children of Cler-	
VICTUALLING-Office	121	gymen.	225
		Woolwich Acad. and Lab.	167
WALES, Prince of, his Establishment	87	YEOMEN of the Guard	82

SCOTLAND.

Admiralty Court	244	Great Seal-Office	244
Bank	246	Lyon-Office	245
———— Royal	ibid.	Mint	244
Baronets	240	Officers of State	242
Chancery	245	Peers	237
College of Physicians	245	Police, Establishment of	244
Commissary-Court	244	Post Office	245
Comm. for Fisheries, &c.	245	Privy Seal	244
Court of Session	243	Register Office	245
———— Justiciary	243	Signet	244
———— Exchequer	243	Stamp Office	247
Customs, Salt Duty, &c.	247	Tax Office	244
Excise Office	246	Universities	248

IRELAND.

Artillery and Engineers	265	Deans	270
Bankers	269	Excise	268
Baronets	271	General-Officers	265
Battle Axe Guards	266	Governors, &c.	266
Chancery	260	Imprest Office	268
Clerks of H. of Lords	264	King's-Council	263
College of Physicians	270	Laboratory	266
Commons, House of	254	Ordnance	265
———— Alphab. List of	259	Patentee-Officers	268
Commissioners of Customs	267	Peers	249
———— of Appeals	269	Post Office	269
———— of Works	266	Prerogative Court	264
Counties, Governors of	266	Privy-Council	249
Court of King's-Bench	261	Rangers, &c.	264
———— Common Pleas	262	Stamp Office	268
———— Exchequer	ibid.	State-Officers	264
———— of Admiralty	265	Trinity-College Univ.	269
———— of Delegates	265		

The HOUSE of PEERS.

SPEAKER, ✤ Rt. Hon. EDWARD Lord THURLOW.

☞ *Those with this Mark* ✤ | K. G.---K. T.---or K. B. *Kt.*
are Privy-Counsellors. | *of the Garter, Thistle, or Bath.*
* *Under Age.* | LL.D. *Doctor of Laws.*
† *Don't sit in the House.* | F.R.S. *Fellow of the Royal Society*
[*Roman Catholick Peers.* | *Inclosed thus* [ ] *are their*
‡ *Generally reside in the Country* | *Country Seats.*
b. m. w. batchelor, married, widower.
N. B. *The Scots Peers take Place of all those of the same Rank, created since the Union,* 1707.

PEERS *of the* BLOOD ROYAL, 3.

1762. *Aug. 19. **H**IS Royal Highness GEORGE-AUGUSTUS-FREDERICK, Prince of Wales, Duke of Cornwall and Rothsay, Earl of Chester and Carrick, Electoral Prince of Brunswick-Lunenburgh, Baron of Renfrew, Lord of the Isles, Great Steward of Scotland, and Captain General of the Artillery Company, K. G. *b.*

1764. *Nov.* 14. ✤ His R. H. Wm. Hen. D. of Gloucester and Edinburgh, E. of Connaught in Ireland, Gen. of his Maj. Forces, Col. of the 1st Reg. of Foot Guards, Chanc. of the Univ. of Dublin, Ranger and Keeper of Windsor Forest, and Cranbourn Chace, Ranger of Hampton-Court Park, Warden and Keeper of New Forest, *Hampshire, &c.* and Pres. of the Lond. Infirmary, K. G. [*Cranbourn and Hampton-Court Lodges, and Lyndhurst, Hants.*] *m.*

1766. *Oct.* 22. ✤ His Royal Highness Henry Frederick Duke of Cumberland and Strathern, and Earl of Dublin in Ireland, Ranger of Windsor Great Park, and an Admiral of the Blue Squadron, K.G. [*Gr. Lodge in Windsor Park, and Cannon Park, Hants.*] *m.*

DUKES, 22.

Ric. III. 1483. *June* 28. ‡ Cha. Howard, D. of Norfolk, E. of Arundel & Surrey, Heredit. E. Marshal, Premier D. & E. of Eng. [*Arundel Castle, Sussex, Worksop Manor, Nottinghamsh. Deepden, n. Dorking, Surrey, & Graystock, Cumb.*] *m.*

Edw. VI. 1546. *Feb.* 16. ✤ Edward Seymour, Duke of Somerset, Lord Seymour [*Maiden Bradley, and Seend, Wilts, and Berry Pomeroy, and Totness Castles, Devon.*] *b.*

Cha. II. 1675. *Aug.* 9. ✤ Charles Lenox, D. of Richmond in England, of Lenox in Scotland, and of Aubigny in France, E. of March, Ld. Lieut. and Cust. Rot. of the Co. of Sussex, Lieut. Gen. of his Majesty's Forces, High Steward of the City of Chichester, Col. of the Sussex Mil. and F.R.S. [*Goodwood, near Chichester, Sussex.*] *m.*

1675. *Sept.* 11. ✤ Augustus Henry Fitzroy, Duke of Grafton, Earl of Euston, Hereditary Ranger of Whittlebury Fo-

and Coventry, one of the Governors of the Charter Houſe, and Preſ. of the Small Pox Hoſp. K. G. [*Euſtonhall, Suffolk, and Wakefield Lodge, Northamptonſhire*] m.

1682. *Dec.* 2. Henry Somerſet, Duke of Beaufort, Marquis of Worceſter, Ld. Lieut. of the County of Monmouth, Col. of the Monmouthſh. Militia, and LL.D. [*Badminton, Gloceſterſhire, Troy, near Monmouth*] m.

1683. *Jan.* 10. George Beauclerk, D. of St. Albans, E. of Burford, Hereditary Grand Falconer of Eng. Hereditary Regiſter of the Court of Chanc. L. Lieut. and Cuſt. Rot. of the County of Berks, and High Steward of the Corporat. of Windſor. w.

WILL. III. 1689. *Apr.* 8. ✤ Harry Powlet, D. of Bolton, M. of Winchester, & Premier Marq. of England, Vice-Adm. of the Counties of Southamp. & Dorſ. and an Adm. of the White Squad. of his Maj. Fleet. [*Hackwod, Hants, Bolton-Houſe, Yorkſh. Hook Park, Dorſetſh. & Ealing, Midd.*] m.

1694. *May* 4. ✤ Thomas Oſborne, D. of Leeds, (Viſc. Dumblaine in Scotl.) Marq. of Carmarthen, LL.D. and F.R.S. *Kiveton, Yorkſh. North Mims, n. Hatfield Herts*] K. G. w.

1694. *May* 11. * Francis Ruſſell, Duke of Bedford, Marquis of Taviſtock [*Woburn Abbey, Bedfordſh. Streatham, Surry*] b.

1694. *May* 12. Wm. Cavendiſh, D. of Devonſhire, Marq. of Hartington, Ld. High Treaſurer of Irel. Gov. of the County of Corke in that Kingdom, and Col. of the Derbyſh. Mil. [*Chatſworth, Derbyſhire, and Chiſwick, Middleſex*] m.

Anne. 1702 *Dec.* 14. ✤ Geo. Spencer, D. of Marlborough, M. of Blandford, L. Lt. & Cuſt. Rot. of *Oxfordſh.* Ranger of Wichwood Foreſt, *Oxfordſh.* H. Stew. of the Corporation of *Oxf.* a Gov. of the Chart. H. Preſid. of the Radcliffe Infirm. at *Oxf.* High Stew. of the Corporation of Woodſtock, one of the elder Brethren of the Trinity Houſe, K. G. & LL.D. [*Blenheim H. near Woodſtock, Oxf. & Ealing, Midd.*] m.

1703. *Mar.* 10. Charles Manners, D. of Rutland, M. of Granby, Preſident of the Welſh Charity School, Ld. Lt. and Cuſt. Rot. of Leiceſterſh. and Col. of the Leiceſterſhire Militia. [*Haddon Hall, Derbyſh. Belvoir Caſtle, Lincolnſhire, and Chevely Park, Cambridgeſhire.*] m.

1711 †Douglas Hamilton, D. of Brandon in England, of Chattelherault in France, and of Hamilton in Scotland, Marq. of Douglas, Hered. Keeper of Holyrood Houſe, Keeper of the Palace at Linlithgow, and Caſtle of Blackneſs, and a Captain in the Army. [*Hamilton, Lanerkſh. and Roehampton, Surry.*] m.

HOUSE of PEERS. DUKES. 3

Geo. I. 1715. *July* 29. Brownlow Bertie, D. of Ancaster and Kesteven, M. of Lindsey, Lord Lieut. and Custos Rot. of Lincolnsh. President of the Lock Hospital [*Grimsthorpe,* *Swinstead, and Uffington, Lincolnshire*] m.

716. *July* 6. ✱ William Hen. Cavendish Bentinck, Duke of Portland, M. of Tichfield, one of the Trustees of the British Museum, President of the British Lying-in Hospital, and Medical Asylum, LL.D. and F.R.S. [*Welbeck, Nottinghamsh.*] m.

719. *Apr.* 30. Geo. Montagu, D of Manchester, Vis. Mandeville, L. Lt. Cust. Rot. & Col. of the Militia of Huntingdonsh. H. Stew. of Godmanchester, Collector of the Customs outwards in the Port of *London*, LL.D. [*Kimbolton Castle, Huntingdonshire,*] m.

719. *April* 30. ✱ James Brydges, Duke of Chandos, Marq. of Carnarvon, Ranger of Enfield Chace, H. Steward of the City of Winchester, LL.D. [*Minchendon House, Middlesex, Avington, Hants, and Keynsham Abby, Somersetshire*] m.

720. *June* 13. Jn. Fred. Sackville, D. of Dorset, E. of Middlesex, Vice Admiral of the Coasts, Lord Lt. and Cust. Rot. of the Co. of Kent and City of Canterbury, Col. of the West. Reg. of Kentish Militia, and High Steward of Stratford upon Avon [*Knowle n. Sevenoaks, Kent*] b.

720. *June* 13. Francis Egerton, D. of Bridgewater, M. of Brackley [*Worsley-Hall, Lancashire, Ashridge, Bucks*] b.

Geo. II; 1756. *Nov.* 13. ✱ Henry Fienes Pelham Clinton, Duke of Newcastle, Earl of Lincoln, Lord Lieutenant and Custos Rotulorum of Nottinghamshire, Steward, Keeper, and Guardian of the Forest of Sherwood, and Park of Folewood, in the County of Nottingham, High Steward of East Retford, Auditor of the Exchequer for Life, Comptroller of the Customs in the Port of London, High Steward of Westminster, and President of the Westminster Hospital, K.G. LL.D. and F.R.S. [*Oatlands near Weybridge, Surry, and Clumber Park Nottinghamsh.*] w.

Geo. III. 1766. *Oct.* 22. ✱ Hugh Percy, D. of Northumberland, Earl Percy, Lord Lieutenant and Custos Rotulorum of the Counties of Middlesex and Northumberland, Vice Adm. of Northumberland, Vice Adm. of all America, Presid. of the Middlesex Hospital and Westminster Dispensary, and a Trustee of the British Museum, F. R. S. [*Alnwick-Castle, Northumberland, and Sion House, n. Brentford, Middlesex*] K. G. w.

766. *Nov.* 5. ✱ Geo. Montagu, D. of Montagu, Marq. of Monthermer, Master of the Horse to the King, Gov. and Capt. of Windsor-Castle, Pres. of St. Luke's Hosp. and F. R. S. [*Dean, Northamptonsh. Blackheath in Kent, and Richmond, Surry*] K. G. w.

HOUSE of PEERS. EARLS.

MARQUIS, 1.

Geo. II. 1746. *Apr.* 19. ✻ Char. Watson Wentworth, M. of Rockingham, E. of Malton, (also Earl of Malton in Ireland) Lord Lieut. and Cuſt. Rot. of the Weſt Riding of Yorkſhire, City of York, and County of the ſame, and Cuſt. Rot. of the North Riding, a Gov. of the Charter-Houſe, K.G. and *F.R.S.* [*Wentworth-houſe Yorkſh.*] m.

EARLS, 78.

Hen. VI. 1442. *May* 20.] ‡ Geo. Talbot, E. of Shrewſbury, Ld. Talbot, E. of Waterford and Wexford in Irel. [*Iſleworth, Middleſex, Heathorpe, near Chipping-norton, Oxfordſh.*] m.

Hen. VII. 1485. *Oct.* 27. Edw. Smith Stanley, E. of Derby, L. Stanley, Ld. Lieut. Cuſt. Rot. and Col. of the Mil. of the Co. of Lancaſter [*Knowſley-hall, Lancaſh. & the Oaks near Epſom, Surrey*] m.

Hen. VIII. 1529. *Dec.* 8. ✻ Francis Haſtings, Earl of Huntingdon, Lord Haſtings, *F.R.S.* [*Dunnington Park, near Leiceſter, Ledſtone-Hall, Yorkſhire.*] b.

Edw. VI. 1551. *Oct.* 11. Henry Herbert, E. of Pembroke and Montgomery, L. Herbert, H. Stew. of Saliſbury, and a Lt. Gen. [*Wilton, Wilts*] m.

Jam. I. 1603. *July* 21. Thomas Howard, E. of Suffolk and Berkſhire, Viſc. Andover. [*Aſhted, near Epſom, Surry.*] w.

1605. *May* 4. ✻ James Cecil, E. of Saliſbury, Viſc. Cranburn, (Son-in-law to the E. of Hillſborough) Treaſurer of the King's Houſhold, Ld. Lt. Cuſt. Rot. and Col. of the Militia of Herts, and High Steward of the Bo. of Hertford, [*Hatfield Houſe, Cecil Lodge, and Quickſwood, Hertfordſhire*] m.

1605. *May* 4. Brownlow Cecil, E. of Exeter, Ld. Burleigh, *F.R.S.* [*Burleigh Houſe, Northamptonſhire, near Stamford, Lincolnſhire*] w.

1618. *Aug.* 2. Spencer Compton, E. of Northampton, Lord Compton, Lord Lieutenant and Cuſt. Rot. of the County of Northamp. Recorder of the Town of Northamp. and perpetual Preſident of the Northamptonſh. Infirmary, [*Caſtle Aſhby, Northamptonſh. Compton Vinyates, Warwickſh.*] m.

1622. *Sep.* 14. ✻ Baſil Fielding, E. of Denbigh, V. Fielding, a Lord of the King's Bed-Chamber, Maſter of his Majeſty's Harriers and Fox-hounds, (Earl of Deſmond in Ireland.) [*Newnham Paddox, near Rugby, Warwickſhire*] m.

1624. *May* 29. John Fane, Earl of Weſtmorland, Lord Burgherſh, a Captain in the Northamptonſhire Militia, [*Apethorp, Northamptonſhire, and Brimpton, Somerſetſhire*] b.

Cha. I. 1627. *Mar.* 9. Charles-Henry Mordaunt, E. of Peterborough and Monmouth, Viſc. Mordaunt, [*Dantzey, Wilts, Mount, near Southampton*] b.

1628. *Mar.* 26. George Harry Grey, E. of Stamford, Lord Grey [*Enville-Hall, Stafford. and Dunham Maſſey, Cheſh. m.*]

1628. *July* 12. George Finch, E. of Winchelſea and Nottingham, Viſc. Maidſtone, one of the Lords of the King's Bedchamber, Ld. Lt. and Cuſt. Rot. of the Co. of Rutland, a Major of the 87th Reg. of Foot, and Preſ. of the Aſylum for the Relief of the Infant Poor, [*Burleigh on the Hill, Rutland*] *b.*

1628. *Aug.* 4. Philip Stanhope, E. of Cheſterfield, Lord Stanhope, F. R. S. [*Eythorp, Bucks*] *m.*

1628. *Aug.* 5. Sackville Tufton, E. of Thanet, Ld. Tufton, Hereditary Sheriff of Weſtmorland, and Lord of the Honour of Skipton in Craven [*Hothfield, Kent, Appleby Caſtle, Weſtmorland, and Skipton Caſtle in Yorkſhire*] *m.*

Cha. II. 1660. *July* 12. ✣ John Montagu, E. of Sandwich, V. Hinchingbrook, firſt Lord Commiſſioner of the Admiralty, a Governor of the Charter-houſe, an Elder Brother of the Trinity Houſe, and ranks as a General in the Army, Rec. of the Corporation of Huntingdon and Godmancheſter, LL.D. [*Hinchingbrook Houſe, near Huntingdon*] *m.*

1661. *Apr.* 20. Wm. Anne Holles Capel, E. of Eſſex, Viſc. Malden, Maſter of his Majeſty's Stag-Hounds [*Caſhioberry Park, near Watford, Hertfordſh.*] *m.*

1661. *Apr.* 20. ✣ Frederick Howard, E. of Carliſle, Viſc. Morpeth, Lord Lieut. of Ireland, and Lord Lieut. and Cuſt. Rot. of the Eaſt Riding of Yorkſhire [*Caſtle Howard, near Malton, Yorkſhire*] K. T. *m.*

1662. *Feb.* 15. Henry Scott, E. of Doncaſter, Ld. Scott (D. of Buccleugh in Scotland) Preſid. of the Scotch Hoſp. [*Adderbury, near Banbury, Oxfordſh. Dalkeith, Eaſt Park, and Smeaton, near Edinburgh, & Melroſs, Roxburghſh.*] K. T. *m.*

1672. *Apr.* 23. * Anth. Aſhley Cooper, E. of Shafteſbury, Ld. Aſhley, [*Winbourn St. Giles, Dorſetſhire*] *b.*

1679. *Sep.* 11. Fred. Auguſtus Berkeley, E. of Berkeley, V. Durſley, Conſtable of St. Briavell's Caſtle in the Foreſt of Dean, Ld. Lt. Cuſt. Rot. and Col. of the Mil. of the Co. of Glouc. Cities and Counties of Briſtol and Glouc. Keeper of the Deer and Woods in the Foreſt of Dean, and H. Stew. of the City of Glouc. [*Berkeley-caſtle, Glouceſterſhire.*] *w.*

1682. *Nov.* 30. Willoughby Bertie, E. of Abingdon, Ld. Norreys, High-Steward of Abingdon and Wallingford [*Rycote, Oxfordſhire, and Witham Berks, but near Oxf.*] *m.*

1682. *Dec.* 1. Thomas Noel, E. of Gainſborough, V. Cambden, High Steward of the Corporation of Chipping-Cambden, Glouceſterſhire [*Exton, Rutl.*] *b.*

1682. *Dec.* 6. Other Hickman, Earl of Plymouth, Lord Windſor, Lord Lieut. and Cuſt. Rot. of Glamorganſhire, and F. R. S. [*Hewell-Grange, Warwickſhire*] *m.*

Will. III. 1690. *Apr.* 15. ✣ Rich. Lumley Saunderſon, E.

of Scarbrough, Vifc. Lumley, (Vifc. Lumley, in Ireland) [*Glentworth, Lincolnſh. Sandbeck, Yorkſh. Lumley-Caſtle, near Durham*] w.

1695. *May* 10. ✠ Wm. Hen. Naſſau de Zuleſtein, Earl of Rochford, Vifcount Tunbridge, one of the elder Brethren of the Trinity Houſe, a Governor of the Charter Houſe, Vice-Admiral of the Coaſt, Lord Lieutenant, Cuſt. Rot. and Colonel of the Weſt Battalion of the Militia of the Co. of Eſſex [*Eaſton Suffolk, and St. Oſyth Eſſex*] K.G. w.

1696. *Feb.* 10. * George Keppel, Earl of Albemarle, Vifcount Bury. [*Quiddenham, Norfolk, and Bagſhot Park, Surrey*] b.

1697. *Apr.* 26. Geo. William Coventry, E. of Coventry, Vifc. Deerhurſt, Lord Lieut. and Cuſtos Rot. of Worceſterſhire [*Crome Court, near Worceſter*] m.

1697. *Sep.* 24. ✠ Geo. Buſſy Villiers, E. of Jerſey, Vifc. Villiers [*Middleton Stony, Oxfordſhire*] m.

Anne 1706. *Dec.* 29. Vere Poulett, E. Poulett, Vifc. Hinton, Lord Lieut. and Cuſt. Rot. of the County of Devon, and City of Exeter, Recorder of Bridgewater. [*Hinton St. George, Somerſetſhire, and Twickenham, Middleſex.*] m.

1706. *Dec.* 29. Geo. James Cholmondeley, E. Cholmondeley Vifc. Malpas, Ld. Lieut. and Cuſt. Rot. of the County of Cheſter, and Col. of the Cheſhire Mil. (Vifc. Cholmondeley of Kells in Ireland) [*Cholmondeley, Cheſhire.*] b.

1711. *July* 24. Edw. Harley, E. of Oxford and E. Mortimer, Ld. Harley, a Ld. of the Bedch. to his Maj. Ld. Lieut. of the County of Radnor, a Truſtee of the Britiſh Muſeum, LL.D. and F.R.S. [*Eywood and Brampton Bryan Caſtle, Herefordſhire*] m.

1711. *Sep.* 3. Robert Shirley, E. Ferrers, V. Tamworth. [*Chartley Caſtle, Staffordſh. and Staunton-Harold, Leic.*] m.

1711. *Sep.* 4. Wm. Wentworth, E. of Strafford, V. Wentworth F.R.S. [*Wentworth-Caſt. Yorkſh. Boughton Northamptonſhire*] m.

1711. *Sept.* 5. ✠ William Legge, Earl of Dartmouth, Vifcount Lewiſham, Lord Privy Seal, Preſident of the London Diſpenſary, and Vice Preſident of the Foundling and Lock Hoſpitals, Recorder of Litchfield, LL.D. and F.R.S. [*Sandwell-hall, Stafford, Blackheath, Kent, Woodſham-Hall, Yorkſhire.*] m.

Geo. I. 1714. *Oct.* 15. Cha. Bennet, E. of Tankerville, L. Oſſulſton. [*ChillinghamCaſt. Northumb. & Dawney-court, Bucks*] m.

1714. *Oct.* 15. Heneage Finch, E. of Aylesford, Ld. Guernſey, LL.D. one of the Lords of his Majeſty's Bedchamber, [*Packington, Warwickſh. Aylesford, Kent. Albury near Guildford, Surry*] b.

1714. *Oct.* 15. Rt. Rev. Fred. Hervey, E. of Briſtol, L. Hervey, Biſhop of Derry in Ireland, D.D. [*Ickworth-Lodge, Suff.*] m.

HOUSE of PEERS. EARLS. 7

1717. *Aug.* 3. Henry Yelverton, Earl of Suffex, Vifc. Longueville, Col. of the Northamptonfh. Militia [*EaftonMauduit,
Northamptonfh. Brandon, Warwickfhire, Shedlington, Bedfordfhire, Chefhunt, Hertfordfhire*] m.

1717. *Mar.* 18. George Naffau Clavering Cowper, E. Cowper,
V. Fordwich, a Prince of the holy Roman empire, F. R. S.
[*The Mote near Canterb. and Cole-Green, Hertf.*] m.

1718. *Apr.* 7. Philip Stanhope, Earl Stanhope, Vifc. Mahone,
F.R.S. [*Clevening near Sevenoaks, Kent*] m.

1719. *May* 4. Rev. Robert Sherrard, Clerk, Earl of Harborough, Vifc. Sherrard (Baron Leitrim in Ireland) [*Staple-
ford, Leicefterfhire, Glafton, Rutlandfhire*] m.

1721. *Nov.* 15. Thomas Parker, Earl of Macclesfield, Vifc.
Parker, F.R.S. LL.D. [*Sherborn-caftle, Oxfordfh.*] w.

1721. *Dec.* 21. ❊ George Fermor, E. of Pomfret, L.Lempfter,
Keeper of the lower Parks and H. at Windfor. [*Eafton-
Nefton, Northamptonfhire, and Sunbury Middlefex*] m.

1722. *May* 23. Wm. Graham, E. and Baron Graham of Belford (Duke of Montrofe in Scotl.) Chancellor of Glafgow
Univ. [*Myndock Caftle, Dumbartonfh. Kincairn Perthfh.
and Buchanan in the Highlands*] m.

1722. *May* 24. John Ker, E. and B. Ker of Wakefield (D. of
Roxburgh in Scot.) a L. of his Maj. Bedch. K.T. [*Fleurs,
near Kelfo, Roxburghfh. Broxmouth, near Dunbar, and Old
Windfor, Berks.*] b.

Geo. II. 1729. *Sep.* 16. John Waldegrave, E. Waldegrave,
Vifc. Chewton, Mafter of the Horfe to her Majefty, Col. of
the Coldftream Reg. of Foot Guards, Gov. of Plymouth,
and a Gen. of his Majefty's Forces. [*Naveftock, near
Ongar, Effex*] m.

1730. *May* 24. ❊ Jn. Afhburnham, Earl of Afhburnham,
Vifc. St. Afaph, Groom of the Stole, LL.D. [*Afhburnham
Place, Suffex, Chelfea, Middlefex.*] m.

1731. *Dec.* 8. Tho. Howard, E. of Effingham, L. Howard, Dep.
E. Marfh. of Engl. [*New Grange, r. Rotherham, Yorkfh.*]m.

1741. *Feb.* 6. Geo. Walpole, E. of Orford, Vifc. Walpole,
Ranger of Hyde and St. James's Parks, a Ld. of the King's
Bedch. Ld. Lieut. Cuft. Rot. of Norfolk, and of the City
and County of Norwich, Steward of the Corporation of
Yarmouth, and Col. of the Weft Reg. of the Norfolk Mi-
litia. [*Houghton Norfolk, Haynton Devonfh.*] b.

1741. *Feb.* 9. Charles Stanhope, Earl of Harrington, Vifc.
Peterfham, Lieut. Col. Commandant of the 85th Regiment
of Foot [*Gawefworth, Chefhire, Peterfham, Surry*] m.

1743. *Apr.* 11. John Wallop, E. of Portfmouth, Vifc. Lymington [*Hurftorne near Whitchurch Hants*] m.

1746. *July* 7. Geo. Grevile, E. Brooke, and *Nov.* 27, 1759,
E. of Warwick, Ld. Grevile, Recorder of Warwick [*Warwick Caftle, and Little Ealing, Middlefex*] m.

HOUSE of PEERS. EARLS.

1746. *July* 8. ✤ Granville Levefon Gower, E. Gower, Vifc. Trentham, Ld. Lt. and Cuft. Rot. of the Co. of Stafford, Recorder of Stafford, and a Gov. of the Charter-Houfe, K.G. [*Trentham Hall, near Newcafle, Staffordfh.*] m.

1746. *Aug.* 20. ✤ Jn. Hobart, E. of Buckinghamfhire, Ld. Hobart [*Blickling, Norf. and Marble-Hall, near Richmond, Surry*] m.

1746. *Sep.* 6. William Fitzwilliam, Earl Fitzwilliam, Vifc. Milton (alfo Earl Fitzwilliam in Ireland) [*Milton Northamptonfhire, near Peterborough*] m.

1748. *May* 27. Geo. Edw. Henry Arthur Herbert, Earl of Powys, Vifc. Ludlow, Recorder of Ludlow, Ld. Lt. Cuft. Rot. and Col. of the Militia of the County of Montgomery [*Powys-cafile, near Montgomery*] b.

1749. *Oct.* 18. Geo.Wyndham, E. of Egremont, Ld. Cockermouth. [*Orchard Wyndham, Somerfetfh. & Petworth, Suff.*] b.

1749. *Oct.* 18. Geo. Nugent Grenville Temple, E. Temple, Vifc. Ld. Cobham, Col. of the Bucks Mil. and one of the Tellers of the Excheq. for life. [*Stowe, n. Buckingham*] m.

1749. *Dec.* 1. George Simon Harcourt, E. Harcourt, Vifc. Nuneham, [*Stanton Harcourt, and Nuneham, Oxfordfh.*] m.

1750. *Aug.* 3. ✤ Francis Seymour Conway, E. of Hertford, Vifc. Beauchamp, (L. Conway in Irel.) Lord Chamb. of his Maj. Houfh. Ld. Lt. and Cuft. Rot. of the Co. of Warwick, and of the City of Coventry, Prefid. of the Magdalen Houfe, a Vice Prefid. of St. George's Hofpital [*Ragley, Warwickfhire, Sudbury Hall, Suffolk.*] K. G. m.

1752. *Mar.* 8. Fran. North, E. of Guildford, Ld North, Treafurer to the Queen's Houfhold, H. Stew. of Banbury, a Vice Prefident of St. George's Hofpital. [*Waldersfoare near Dover, Kent, Wroxton-Abbey near Banbury, Oxfordfhire*] w.

1753. *June* 26. ✤ Charles Cornwallis, E. Cornwallis, Vifc. Brome, a Lieut. Gen. of his Maj. Forces, Colonel of the 33d Reg. of Foot, Confta. of the Tower of London, and Ld lt. of the Tower Hamlets, [*Brome and Culford-hall,Suffolk*]w.

1754. *Apr.* 2. ✤ Philip Yorke, E. of Hardwicke, Vif. Royfton, one of the Tellers of his Maj. Excheq. Ld Lt. and Cuft. Rot. of the Co. H. Stew. of the Univ. of Cambridge, and a Truft. of the Brit. Muf. LL.D. & F.R.S. [*Wimple,Camb.*]m.

1754. *Apr.* 3. Henry Vane, E. of Darlington, Vifc. Barnard, Mafter of the Jewel Office, Gov. of the City and Caftle of Carlifle, Ld. Lieut. and Vice Adm. of the County of Durham, and Colonel of the Militia of the Bifhoprick of Durham [*Ruby Cafile, Durham*] m.

1756 *June* 16. Hen. Bellafyfe, E. Fauconberg, L. Bellafyfe, a Ld. of the K.'s Bedch. and Lord Lieut. of the North Riding of Yorkfhire. [*Newborough Hall, Yorkfhire*] m.

HOUSE of PEERS. EARLS and VISCOUNTS.

1756 *June* 17. Hen. Tho Fox, Earl of Ilchester, Ld. Stavordale, [*Redlynch, near Bruton, Somerset, & Melbury, Dorsetsh.*] *m.*

Geo. III. 1761. *Mar.* 18. Wm. West, Earl Delawarr, Visc. Cantalupe, a Capt. in the 2d Reg. of Guards, and ranks as Lieut. Col. in the Army. [*Bolderwood Lodge, Hants*] *b.*

1761 *March* 21. ✱ Wm. Talbot, E. Talbot, Lord Hensol; and, Sept. 29, 1780, Ld. Dinevor, of Dinevor, Carmarthenshire, Ld. Stew. of his Maj. Housh. and LL.D. [*Hensol, Glamorganshire, Aldborough-hall, Essex*] *m.*

1764 *May* 19. Robt. Henley, E. of Northington, Ld. Henley, Mast. of the Hanaper, and one of the Tellers of the Excheq. for Life. K.T. [*Grange, near Alresford, Hampshire*] *b.*

1765 *Sep.* 28. Jacob Pleydell Bouverie, E. of Radnor, Visc. Folkestone, Recorder of Sarum, a Capt. in the Northamptonshire Militia, and perpetual Pres. of the Salisbury Infirmary. [*Longford Castle, n. Salisbury, Wilts, and Coleshill House, near Farringdon, Berks*] *m.*

1765 *Oct.* 5. Jn. Spencer, E. Spencer, Visc. Althorp, High Stew. of St. Albans [*Althorp, n. Northampton, Wimbledon and Battersea, Surry, Hounslow, Midd. St. Albans, Hertfordsh.*] *m.*

1766 *Aug.* 4. John Pitt, E. of Chatham, Visc. Pitt, a Capt. in the 87th Regiment of Foot [*Burton Pynsent, Somersetsh. Hayes, n. Bromley, Kent*] *b.*

1772 *Aug.* 12. ✱ Henry Bathurst, E. Bathurst, Ld Apsley, Pres. of the Council, and a Gov. of the Char. House, [*Cirencester, Gloucestersh. and Fairy Hill, near Chiselhurst, Kent*] *m.*

1772 *Aug.* 12. ✱ Wills Hill, E. of Hillsborough, Visc. Fairford, Sec. of State for the South. Depart. Reg. of the Co. of Chan. in Irel. F.R.S. LL.D. (also E. of Hillsborough in Irel.) [*Hillsborough, Co. of Down, Irel. and Hill Park, Kent*] *w.*

1776 *June* 8. ✱ Tho. Bruce Brudenell, E. of Aylesbury, Ld. Bruce, Chamb. of the Queen's Household, Ld. Lt. and Cust. Rot. of Wiltsh. [*Tottenham, n. Marlborough, Wilts.*] *m.*

1776 *June* 8. ✱ Thomas Villiers, E. of Clarendon, Ld. Hyde, Chancellor of the Duchy and County Palatine of Lancaster, [*Hindon in Wilts, and Grove, n. Watford, in Hertfordsh.*] *m.*

1776 *Oct.* 19. ✱ William Murray, Earl of Mansfield, and Lord Mansfield, Ld. Ch. Just. of the King's Bench, and a Gov. of the Charter-house [*Cane-Wood, Midd.*] *m.*

VISCOUNTS, 14.

Edw VI. 1549. *Feb.* 2. Edw. Devereux, Visc. Hereford, Premier Viscount of England [*Nanteribba, Montgom.*] *w.*

Mary 1554. *Sep.* 2. Anth. Joseph Browne, Visc. Montague [*Cowdry, near Midhurst, Sussex*] *m.*

Ja. I. 1624 *July* 7. Rich. Fienes, Viscount and Baron Say and Sele, LL.D. [*Tattershall, Bucks*] *m.*

Cha. II. 1682 *Dec.* 2. ✱ Geo. Townshend, Visc. Townshend,

10 HOUSE *of* PEERS. Viscounts & Barons.

Mafter Gen. of the Ordnance, Col. of the Queen's Reg. of Drag. Guards, and a Lt. Gen. [*Raynham-hall, Norfolk*] m.
1682 *Dec.* 11. ✤ Th. Thynne, V. Weymouth, High Stew. of Tamworth, one of the Elder Brethren of the Trinity Houfe, K. G. [*Longleat, Wilts.*] m.
Anne 1712 *July* 8. Fred. St. John, Vifc. Bolingbroke and St. John of Batterfea [*Lydiard-Tregozen, near Wotton Baffet, Wilts*] w.
Geo. I. 1720 *June* 23. ✤ Hugh Bofcawen, Vifc. Falmouth, Capt. of the Yeomen of the Guard, and ranks as a General in the Army [*Tregothan, Cornwall*] m.
1721 *Sep.* 10. George Byng, Vifc. Torrington, [*Southill, Bedfordfhire*] m.
Geo. II. 1746 *Feb.* 17. W. Fitzgerald, Vifc. Leinfter of Taplow, (D. of Leinfter, in Ireland) a Priv. Counf. in Irel. and Gov. of the Co. of Kildare [*Car Town, Co Kildare, Irel.*] m.
Geo. III. 1762. *May* 5. Tho. Noel, Vifc. Wentworth, LL.D. [*Wellfborough, and Kirkby-Mallory, near Hinkley, Leic.*] b.
1762 *May* 6. Wm. Courtenay, Vifc. Courtenay [*Powderham Caftle, near Exeter*] m.
1763 *Apr.* 21. Jn. Ward, Vifc. Dudley and Ward, LL.D. Recorder of Kidderminfter [*Himley Hall, Staffordfhire, Teddington, Middlefex, and St. Laurence, n. Canterbury*] b.
1766 *Oct.* 28. Cha. Maynard, Vifc. Maynard, [*Eafton-Lodge near Dunmow, Effex*] m.
1776 *June* 8. Robert Hampden, Vifc. Hampden, F.R.S. [*Hampden-houfe, Bucks; Bromham-hall, Bedfordfhire; and Glynde-place, Suffex*] w.

BARONS, 72.

Edw. I. 1261. ✤ Fran. Dafhwood, Ld Le Defpencer, Premier Baron of England, Ld Lt. & Cuft. Rot. of Buckinghamfh. Joint Poftmaft.-Gen. one of the Vice-Pref. of the Found. Hofp. and of the Medical Afylum, F.R.S. and LL.D. [*Weft-Wycomb, Bucks, and Mereworth Cafile n. Malling, Kent.*] w.
1269 *Dec.* 29. * Edward Southwell, Lord de Clifford [*King's Wefton, near Briftol, Gloucefterfhire*]
Edw. I. 1295 *June* 23. Geo. Nevill, Ld Abergavenny [*Redbroke, near E. Grinftead, Suffex*] w.
1296 *Jan.* 26. Geo. Thickneffe, Lord Audley of Heleigh, [*The Solygon, near Southampton*] b.
1298 Geo. Townfhend, Lord de Ferrars, of Chartley, Lord Bourchier, Lovaine, Baffet, and Compton, eldeft Son of Lord Vifc. Townfhend, [*Tamworth-Caftle, Warwickfhire, and Rifby-Park, near Beverley, Yorkfhire*] m.
1299 *Dec.* 29. Hugh Percy, Lord Percy, (Earl Percy) eldeft Son of the D. of Northumberland, a Lieut.-Gen. and Col. of the 5th Reg. of Foot. [*Stanwick, Yorkfh.*] m.

Thomas Barret Lennard, Lord Dacre [Bel-
n.
May 13. ‡ Charles-Philip Stourton, Lord
urton Cafile, Staffordshire] b.
Aug. 12. John Peyto Verney, Lord Wil-
oke, Lord of the Bedch. to the King, LL.D.
(Compton Verney, Warwickshire] m.
Jan. 19. Henry Paget, Lord Paget of Beaude-
iire, Colonel of the Staffordsh. Mil. LL.D.
ind Beaudefert, both in Staffordshire) m.
13. Henry Beauchamp St. John, Ld. St. John
dford, Northamp. Melckburn, Bedfordshire] m.
'y 21. ‡ Rob. Edw. Petre, Ld. Petre of Writtle
ce, and Writtle Park, Effex] m.
Henry Arundel, Lord Arundel of Wardour
: facred Roman Empire) [Wardour Cafile
all near Colifworth, Lincolnsh.] m.
n Bligh, Ld. Clifton of Leighton Bromfwold,
;h Steward of Gravefend and Milton in Kent
ley in Ireland) [Cobham Hall, Kent] m.
‡ John Dormer, Ld. Dormer of Wenge, ‡
Wenge, Bucks, Ewdfworth, Hants, Grove
arwick] w.
Henry Roper, Lord Teynham. ‡ [Linfted
verfham, Kent] m.
vard Leigh, Lord Leigh, High Steward of the
ord [Stoneleigh Abby, near Warwick] b. ‡
m. Byron, Lord Byron of Rochdale [Newfied
hamshire] m.
Dec. 11. Wm. Craven, L Craven, of Hamfled
ew. of Newbury, Berks. LL.D.[Combe Abby,
arwickfh. Beenham, n. Newbery, Berks,] m.
Hugh Clifford, Lord Clifford of Chudley, ‡
ion.] m.
❀ Francis Godolphin Osborne, (Marq. of
Ld. Osborne, of Kiveton in Yorksh. only Son
Leeds, and Capt. of Deal Cafile, w.
. 10. Edm. Boyle, Ld. Boyle (E. of Corke &
nd) [Marfton, Bigot, n. Frome, Somerfetfh.] m.
Tho. Hay, Ld. Hay of Pedwarden (Earl of Kin-
) Rec. of the T. of Camb. and Chanc. of the
St. Andrew's in Scotland. [Dupplin Cajile,
‡
– Willoughby, Ld. Middleton [Wollaton Hall
am]
ne 9. ❀ Geo. Onflow, Ld. Onflow, a Ld. of his
nber, Ld. Lieut. & Cuft. Rot. of the Co. of

HOUSE *of* PEERS. BARONS.

Surry, H. Stew. of Kingston upon Thames and Guilford, and LL.D. [*Clandon, near Ripley, Surry*] m.
1716 *June* 22. Rob. Marsham, Ld Romney, Pref. of the Society for encouraging Arts and Manuf. Pref. of the Marine Society, LL.D. and F.R.S. [*The Mote by Maidstone, Kent*] w.
1718 *Apr.* 7. Charles Sloane Cadogan, Ld. Cadogan, Master and Worker of the Mint, and a Trustee of the Brit. Mus. [*Caversham Lodge, Oxon, near Reading, Berks*] m.
1723 *May* 27. Peter King, Lord King, [*Ockham, Surry*] m.
Geo. II. 1728 *May* 27. John Monson, Lord Monson, [*Broxburn Bury near Hodsdon, Hertfordsh. South Carlton, and Burton near Lincoln.*] m.
1735 *Jan.* 23. Francis Godolphin, Lord Godolphin, Gov. of the Scilly Islands [*Baylis near Windsor, Bucks*] m.
1741 *May* 9. Tho. Bromley, Lord Montfort, High Stew. of the Town of Camb. LL.D. [*Drayton, Middl.*] m.
1741 *May* 12. Fred. Henry Thynne How, Lord Chedworth [*Chedworth, Gloucestershire*] b.
1742. *April* 20. ✤ Geo. Edgcumbe, Ld. Edgcumbe, Captain of the Band of Gentlemen Pensioners, an Adm. of the Blue, Lord Lieut. and Cust. Rot. of Cornwall, LL.D. [*Mount Edgcumbe, Devon, and Cotbell, Cornwall*] m.
1743 *Dec.* 20. Edwin Sandys, Lord Sandys, a Trustee of the British Museum [*Omberfley Court, Worcestershire*] m.
1746 *July* 5. Matth. Fortescue, Ld Fortescue, High Steward of Barnstaple [*Castle Hill, near South Molton, Devon*] m.
1747 *June* 29. Henry Liddel, Lord Ravensworth [*Ravensworth Castle, Durham*] m.
1749 *June* 12. ✤ Wm. Ponsonby, Ld. Ponsonby, a Trustee of the British Museum, and Vice Adm. of Munster in Ireland (E. of Besborough in Ireland) [*Roehampton, Surry, Sysonby, Leicestershire*] w.
1750 *Mar.* 28. Vere Beauclerk, Lord Vere, one of the Vice Presidents of the Asylum [*Hanworth, Middlesex*] m.
1756 *June* 4. Horatio Walpole, L. Walpole [*Woolterton, Norf.*] n.
1760 *May* 20. ✤ Wm. Petty, Ld. Wycombe, LL.D. Lieut Gen. in the Army, (E. of Shelburne in the K. of Ireland, [*Wycombe, Bucks, Bow-wood Park, near Calne, Wilts*] m.
1760. *May* 21. Henry Bilson Legge, Ld. Stawell, Surveyor of the Customs [*Holte-Forest, near Farnham, Surry*] m.
1760 *May* 22. Lewis Monson Watson, Ld. Sondes, one of the Auditors of the Impreft for Life [*Lees-court, near Feversham, Kent, and Rockingham-castle, Northamptonshire*] w.
Geo. III. 1761 *April* 7. ✤ Tho. Robinson, Ld. Grantham, first Lord of the Board of Trade, m.
1761 *Apr.* 9. Rich. Grosvenor, L. Grosvenor, Pref. of Westmin. Lying-in Hosp. [*Eaton-ball, n. Chest. & Coombe, Surry*] m.

HOUSE of PEERS. BARONS.

1761 *Ap.* 10. Nath. Curzon, Ld Scarsdale, LL.D. [*Keddleston, n. Derby*] m.
1761 *Apr.* 10. Frederick Irby, Lord Boston, a Ld. of his Majesty's Bed-cham. and LLD. [*Hedsor n. Beconsfield, Bucks*] m.
1762 *May* 4. ✣ Tho. Pelham, L. Pelham, Keeper of Great Wardrobe, and Surv. Gen. of Customs in the Port of London [*Stanmere, near Lewes, Holland and Bishopstone, Sussex*] m.
1762 *May* 6. * Henry Richard Fox, Lord Holland, and April 16, 1763, Lord Holland, Baron of Foxley, *b.*
1762 *May* 7. Jn. Ja. Perceval, L. Lovel & Holland of Enmore, (also E. of Egmont in Ireland) [*Enmore Castle, Somerset*] m.
1762 *May* 10. Jos. Damer, Lord Milton, of Milton-Abbey in Dorsetshire, (also Lord Milton of Shrone-hill in Ireland) *Milton Abbey, Dorsetshire*] w.
1762 *May* 10. Edward Hussey Montagu, Ld. Beaulieu, K.B. [*Ditton Park, Bucks, and Beaulieu, New-Forest, Hants.*] m.
1762 *May* 12. George Venables Vernon, Lord Vernon, of Kinderton [*Sudbury, in Derbyshire*; *Newick Park, Sussex*; and *Briton-ferry, Glamorganshire*] m.
1763 *April* 23. Tho. Reynolds Morten, Ld Ducie, of Tortworth, Cl. of the Cr. in the Co. Pal. of Lancaster [*Tortworth, and SpringPark, Gloucestersh. & North-Court, Isle of Wight.*] m.
1765 *July* 16. ✣ Charles Pratt, Lord Camden, of Camden Place, a Gov. of the Charter Ho. Recorder of the City of Bath, and F.R.S. [*Camden Place, near Chiselhurst, Kent*] w.
1765 *Aug.* 15. Henry Digby, Lord Digby of Sherborne in Dorsetshire, Lord Lieut. and Cust. Rot. of the County of Dorset, and of the Town of Poole (Ld. Digby in the Kingdom of Ireland) [*Sherborne Castle, Dorsetshire*] m.
1765 *Dec.* 22. John Campbell, Ld. Sundridge of Coombank in Kent. D. of Argyll in Scotland, Hereditary Master of the King's Houshold in Scotland, a General of his Majesty's Forces, and Col. of the 1st Reg. of Foot, [*Inverary and Campbelltown, Argyllshire, & Rosneath, Dunbartonshire*] m.
1776, *May* 14. Alexander Hume Campbell, (Lord Polwarth) Ld. Hume of Berwick, eldest Son of the Earl of Marchmont in Scotland, [*Wrest, Bedfordshire*] m.
1776, *May* 14. ✣ John Stuart, (Ld Mountstuart in Scotland) Ld. Cardiff, of Cardiff-Castle in Glamorgansh. eldest Son of the E. of Bute, Envoy Extra. and Min. Plenipot. to the King of Sardinia, [*Lemer, near Welwyn, Hertfordshire*] m.
1776, *May* 14. ✣ Edward Hawke, Ld. Hawke, of Towton in Yorkshire, K. B. Vice Admiral of Great Britain, Admiral of the Fleet, Pres. of the Maritime School, and an Elder Brother of the Trinity-House, [*Sunbury, Middlesex, and Scartbingwell-Hall, near Towton, Yorkshire*] w.
1776, *May* 14. ✣ Jeffry Amherst, Ld. Amherst, of Holmesdale in Kent, K. B. Lt. Gen. of the Ordnance, a Gen. in

the Army, Col. of the 2d Tr. of H. Gds. and of the 6cth Reg. of Foot, Commander in Chief of the British Forces, and Gov. of Guernsey [*Montreal, n. Seven Oaks in Kent.*] m.

1776, *May* 14. Brownlow Cuft, Ld. Brownlow, of Belton in Lincolnshire, LL. D. [*Belton, near Grantham, Lincolnshire, and Overstone, near Northampton.*] m.

1776, *May* 14. Geo. Pitt, Ld. Rivers, Ld. Lt. and Cuft. Rot. of the Co. of Southampton, Col. of the Dorfetfh. Militia, and LL. D. [*Stratfieldsay, n. Hartford-Bridge, Hants.*] m.

1776, *May* 14. Nath. Ryder, Ld. Harrowby, of Harrowby in Lincolnsh. [*Streatham in Surrey, & Shiplake in Oxfordsh.*] m.

1776, *May* 14. Thomas Foley, Ld. Foley, of Kidderminfter in Worcestershire, [*Stoke Edith, in Herefordshire*] w.

1778, *June* 2. ❦ Edward Thurlow, Lord Thurlow, of Afhfield in Suffolk, Lord High Chancellor of England, and a Governor of the Charter-Houfe [*Knight's Hill, near Dulwich, Surrey*] b.

1780. *June* 13. ❦ Alex. Wedderburn, Ld. Loughborough, of Loughborough, in the County of Leicefter, Ld. Chief Juft. of the Court of Com. Pleas [*Mitcham, Surrey; and Chesterhall, North Britain.*] m.

1780. *Sept.* 29. William-Hall Gage, Ld. Gage, of Firle, in Suffex, (Vifc. Gage, in the K. of Ireland) Pay-m. of his Majefty's Penfions and Bounties, F. R. S. (*High Meadow, Gloucesterfh. near Monmouth, and Firle, near Lewes, Suff.x.*

1780. *Sept.* 29. James Brudenell, Ld. Brudenell, of Deene, Northamptonsh. next Brother to the D. of Montagu, Maft. of the Robes, and Keeper of the Privy Purfe to his Majefty [*Deene, Northamptonshire.*] m.

1780. *Sept.* 29. ❦ William De Grey, Ld. Walfingham, of Walfingham, in Norfolk, [*Englefield-Green, Staines*] m.

1780. *Sept.* 29. Wm. Bagot, Ld. Bagot, of Bagot's Bromley, Staffordfh. [*Blithfield, near Litchfield.*] m.

1780. *Sept.* 29. Cha. Fitzroy, Ld. Southampton Lt. Gen of his Majefty's Forces, Col. of the 3d. Reg. of Dragoons, and Groom of the Stole to the Prince of Wales [*West Horfly, near Guildford, Surrey, and Highgate, Middlefex.*] m.

1780. *Sept.*29. H. Herbert, Ld Portchefter, of Highclere, in the Co. of Southampton, Couf. to the E. of Pembroke, Col. of the Wiltshire Militia, and LL.D. [*Highclere, Hants*] m.

SCOTS PEERS (16.) *Elected* October, 1780.

Cha. II. 1684 *Nov.* 1. Alexander Gordon, D. of Gordon, Marq. and E. of Huntley, a Capt. in the Army, [*Strathbogy, Aberdeensfhire, Gordon Caftle, Bamffshire*] K. T. m.   4

Will. III. 1684 *Feb.* 3. Ja. Douglas, Duke of Queensberry, Earl of Drumlanrig, Prefid. of the Police, a Ld. of the King's Bedchamb. [*Nidpath, Peeblefh. Barnton, Midlo-*

Anne, 1705, *April* 30. ‡ John Murray, D. Marq. and E. of Athol, Marq. and Earl of Tullibardin, Visc. Glenalmond, Lord Murray, Lord of the Isle of Man, and Keeper of Falkland [*Dunkeld, near the river Tay; Blair Cast. Athol; Tullibardin Castle, Perthsh. and Castleton, Isle of Man.*] m.
1701. *June* 23. William John Ker, Marquis and Earl of Lothian, Earl of Ancram, Baron Ker of Newbottle and Jedburgh, a Maj. Gen. and Col. of the 1st Troop of Horse Guards [*Newbottle, Mid-Lothian*] K. T. m. 2
Jam. III. 1488. *May* 28. ‡ James Cunningham, Earl of Glenca rn, and Baron of Kilmaurs [*Kilmaurs, in Cunningham; and Finlayston, Renfrewshire.*] b.
Jam. IV. 1503. Aich. Montgomery, E. of Eglington, Ld. Montgomery, a Lt. Gen. Col. of the 51st Reg. of Foot, & Gov. of Dumbarton cast. [*Eglington & Androsan, Airsh.*] 2
1509 David Kennedy, Earl of Cassilis, Lord Kennedy, heretable Bailiff of Carrick, [*Cassilis, Airshire*] 2
Jam. VI. 1606 *July* 10. James Hamilton, E. of Abercorn, Ld Paisley, (alsoVisc. Strabane in Ireland, & a Privy Count. there) [*Paisley, Renfrewsh.; Dudingston, near Edinburgh; St. Stephen's Green, Dublin; Witham, Essex*] b. 4
1623 *Sept.* 19. John Stewart, Earl of Galloway, Ld. Gairlies, Ld. Commiss. of the Police in Scotl. [*Galloway Ho. in Wigtounsh. and Gairlies in Stewarty of Kircudbright*] K.T. 2
Cha. I. 1633 *May* 12. Jn. Campbell, E. of Loudoun, Ld. Mauchlin, a Gen. of his Maj. Forces, Gov. of Edinburgh Castle, Col. of the 3d Reg. of Foot Guards, and F. R. S. [*Loudon Castle, Airshire*] b. 8
1633 *June* 19. George Ramsay, Earl of Dalhousie, Lord Ramsay, his Maj. High Commiss. to the Church of Scotland, [*Dalhousie Castle, near Dalkeith, in Mid-Lothian*] 2
1682. *Nov.* 30. George Gordon, Earl of Aberdeen, Lord Haddo [*Haddo House, Aberdeenshire*] m. 2
Jam. VII. 1686. *Aug.* 16. John Murray, E. of Dunmore, Visc. Fincastle, Gov. of Virginia [*Dunm. & Fincastle, Perthsh.*] m. 3
1697 *Apr.* 23. ✠ Hugh Hume Campbell, E. of Marchmont, Lord Polwarth, Keeper of the Great Seal of Scotland, F.R.S. [*Redbraes, Berwickshire*] m. 5
Anne 1703 Niel Primrose, E. of Roseberry, V. Primrose, K.T. [*Barnbougle Castle, W. Lothian, Dalmenie Edinb. Primrose; Mid-Lothian, Bisley in Norf. & Holland-House, Middx.*] m. 5
Jam. VI. 1621 *Aug.* 26. ✠ David Murray, Visc. Stormont, Sec. of State for the Northern Department, Justice General of Scotland, and Keeper of Scoon. [*Scoon, Perthshire, Kumlington Castle, Annandale*] K. T. m. 2

N. B. The Figures after the 16 Scots Peers, shew the Number of Parliaments in which they have sat.

16 HOUSE of PEERS. PEERESSES, & BISHOPS.

PEERESSES in their own Right, by Creation or Descent.

JEmima Campbell, Marchioness Grey, and Baroness Lucas, Lady to the Earl of Hardwicke, (St. James's Square) [*Wreſt-Houſe, near Ampthill, Bedf.*]   May 9, 1740

Charlotte Murray, Baroneſs Strange, of Knokyn, widow of the late Duke of Athol, and Lady of the Iſle of Man [*Caſtleton, Iſle of Man*]   Dec. 29, 1299

Priſcilla Barbara Elizabeth Burrell, Baroneſs Willoughby de Ereſby, in the County of Lincoln, Wife of Peter Burrell, Eſq.   1314.

Mary Stuart, Baroneſs Mount Stuart of Wortley in Yorkſhire, Lady of the E. of Bute [*Montagu Houſe, Yorkſh. South Audley Street*]   April 3, 1761

Heſter Pitt, Baroneſs of Chatham, Lady of the late E. of Chatham,   Dec. 4. 1761

Carolina Townſhend, Baroneſs of Greenwich, limited to her Sons by Mr. Townſhend, Widow, firſt of the E. of Dalkeith, an now of the late Rt. Hon. C. Townſhend-[*Bruton Street, Sudbrook, n. Peterſham, Surry*]   Aug. 19, 1767

Elizabeth Campbell, Baroneſs Hamilton, of Hameldon, in Leiceſterſhire, limited to her Heirs Male, (Lady of the D. of Argyll, and Duch. Dow. of Hamilton) a Lady of the Queen's Bedchamber   May 14, 1776

ARCHBISHOPS and BISHOPS, 26.
With the Sum each See is charged in the King's Books.

✤ HON. Dr. Fred. Cornwallis, Ld. Abp. of Canterbury, (Uncle to E. Cornwallis) Primate of all Engl. Preſid. of Corp. of Sons of the Clergy and of the Society for Prop. of the Goſpel, a Vice Preſident of St. George's Hoſpital, and a Gov. of the Charter Houſe [*Croydon, Surry*] 2682:12:2

✤ Dr. William Markham, Ld. Abp. of York, Primate of England, and Ld High Almoner to his Majeſty [*Biſhopthorp, near York*]   161cl.

✤ Dr. Rob. Lowth, Ld. Bp. of London, Dean of his Majeſty's Chapels Royal, a Governor of the Charter-Houſe, and F. R. S.   [*Fulham, Mid.*] 1000l.

Dr. John Egerton, Ld. Bp. of Durham, Cuſt. Rot. of the Prin. of Durham, firſt Couſin to the Duke of Bridgewater [*Durham Palace, Auckland Caſtle, Durham*]   1821:1:5

Dr. John Thomas, Ld. Bp. of Wincheſter, Prel. of the Order of the Garter, and Clerk of the Cloſet to the King [*Chelſea Farnham Caſtle, Surry, Wincheſter Palace*]   2873:18:1

Rt. Hon. Ld. Jam. Beauclerk, D.D. Ld. Bp. of Hereford, Uncle to the Duke of St. Albans, Brother to Ld. Vere, Vice Preſident of the Aſylum [*Palace at Hereford*]   768

Dr. Edm Keene, Ld. Bp. of Ely [*Ely Pal. Camb.*] 2134:18:6
Sir Wm. Ashburnham, Bart, and D.D. Ld. Bp. of Chichester,
Rector of Gestling in Sussex [*Chich. Pal. Suff.* 677:1:3
Dr. John Hume, Ld. Bp. of Salisbury, Chanc. of the Order of
the Garter, and Brother in Law to the Earl of Kinnoul.
[*Salisbury Palace, Wiltshire*] · 1385:5:9
Dr. Phil. Yonge, Ld Bp of Norw. [*Palace at Norwich*]834:11:7
Dr. Thomas Newton, Lord Bishop of Bristol, and Dean of St.
Paul's] *Bristol Pal. Glsc.* 294:11:0
Dr. Cha. Moss, Lord Bishop of Bath and Wells, Canon of
Sarum, and F.R.S [*Wells Palace, Somersetshire* 533:1:3
Dr. Jonathan Shipley, Ld. Bp. of St. Asaph [*Palace at St.
Asaph, Flintshire*] 187:11:8
Dr. Edm. Law, Ld. Bp. of Carlisle, and Master of Peter House
in Cambridge [*Rose Castle, Cumberland*] · 531:4:9
Hon. Dr. Shute Barrington, Ld. Bishop of Landaff, Canon of
Windsor, and Bro. to Ld. Visc. Barrington. [*Mongewell-
House, Oxfordshire.*] 154:14:2
Dr. John Hinchliffe, Ld. Bishop of Peterborough, and Master
of Trinity College, Camb. [*Peterborough*] 414:17:8
Hon. Dr. Brownlow North, Ld. Bp. of Worcester, second Son to
the E. of Guildford, [*Hartlebury, Worcestersh.*] 929:13:3
Hon. Dr. James Yorke, Lord Bishop of Gloucester, Brother to
the Earl of Hardwicke, Dean of Lincoln [*Palace at
Gloucester*] ,, 315:7:3
Dr. John Thomas, Lord Bishop of Rochester, Dean of West-
minster. [*Bromley, Kent*] 358:4:0
Dr. Richard Hurd, Lord Bishop of Litchfield and Coven-
try, [*Litchfield-Palace, Ecclesball-Castle, Staffordshire*]
559:17:3
Dr. Jn. Moore, Ld. Bp. of Bangor, Archdeacon of Anglesea
and Bangor [*Bangor Palace, Caernarvorshire*] 131:16:3
Dr. Beilby Porteus, Ld. Bp. of Chester, Master of St. Cross
Hospital, and Rector of Hunton, in Kent. [*Palace at Ches-
ter*] 420:13:3
Dr. John Butler, Ld. Bishop of Oxford, Preb. of Winchester,
Archd. of Surry, [*Cuddesden, Oxfordsh.*] 381:11:0
Dr. John Ross, Ld. Bp. of Exeter, Archdeacon of Exeter,
and Vicar of Frome, Somersetshire, F.R.S. [*Exeter Palace*]
Dr. Tho. Thurlow, Ld. Bp. of Lincoln, brother to the Ld.
Chancellor, Rector of Stanhope, in the County of Dur-
ham, and Master of the Temple [*Bugden, Hunt.*] 823:4:9
Dr. John Warren, Ld. Bp. of St. David's, Rector of Elm,
in the Isle of Ely, and of Emneth, in Norfolk, [*Aberguilly,
n. Carmarthen*] - 426:2:1
Dr. George Mason, Ld. Bishop of Sodor and Man, (*Bishop's
Court, Isle of Man*)

The HOUSE of PEERS in Alphabetical Order, with their *Town Residence.*

D stands for Duke, M for Marquis, E for Earl, V for Viscount, L for Lord, Bp. for Bishop.

☞ *The Figures after the Names refer to the Pages on which each Lord is mentioned with his Titles in the foregoing List.*

Abercorn E 15, *Grosv. squ.*
Aberdeen E. 15, *Wimpole-street*
Abergavenny L 10, *Grosv. place*
Abingdon E 5,
Albemarle E 6,
Amherst L 13, *Whitehall*
Ancaster D 3. *Suvile-row*
Argyll D 13, *Argyll-Street*
Arundel of Wardour L 11, *Portman-square*
Ashburnham E 7, *Dover-street*
Athol D 15,
Audley, L 10. *Half Moon-str.*
Aylesbury E 9 *Seymour-place, May Fair*
Aylesford E 6, *Arlington-street*
Bagot L 14, *Upper Brook-str.*
Bangor, Bp 17, *Grosvenor-sq.*
Bath and Wells, Bp 17, *Grosv. pl.*
Bathurst E 9, *Apsley-House, Hyde-Park Corner*
Beaufort D 2, *Grosvenor-sq.*
Beaulieu L 13, *Dover street*
Bedford D 2, *Bloomsbury square*
Berkeley E 5, *Bolton-street*
Besborough E 12, *Cavendish-sq.*
Bolingbroke V. 10,
Bolton D 2, *Southampton-str. Bloomsbury*
Boston, L 13, *Grosvenor-street*
Bridgewater D 3, *Cleveland row*
Bristol E 6, *St. James's-square*
Bristol Bp 17, *Dean's court, St. Paul's*
Brownlow L 14 *Bond-street*
Brudenell L 14, *Portugal-str. Grosvenor-square*
Buccleugh D 5 *Grosvenor sq.*

Bucks E 8, *Old Bond-street*
Byron L 11, *Queen-Ann street*
Cadogan L 12, *Whitehall*
Camden L. 13, *New Burl.-str.*
Canterbury Abp 16, *Lambeth*
Carlisle E 5 *(Ireland)*
Carlisle Bp 17, *Queen-square, Westminster*
Carmarthen M 11, *Grosv.-sq.*
Cassilis, E. 15.
Chandos D 3, *Chandois-street*
Chatham E 9, *Grafton-street*
Chedworth L 12, *Berkley sq.*
Chester Bp 17. *Great George-street, Westminster*
Chesterfield E 5, *S. Audley-str.*
Chichester Bp 15 *Albemarle-st.*
Cholmondeley E 6, *Piccadilly*
Clarendon, E 9 *Up. Grosv. str.*
Clifford L 10, *Spring gardens*
Clifford of Chudley L 11, *Berkeley square*
Corke E 11, *Upper Grosv. str.*
Cornwallis E 8, *America*
Coventry E 6, *Piccadilly*
Courtenay V 10, *Grosvenor sq.*
Cowper E 7, (at *Florence*)
Craven L 11, *Charles-street, Berkley-square*
CUMBERLAND, D 1, *Pallmall*
Dacre L 11, *Bruton-street*
Dalhousie E 15,
Darlington E 8, *Cleveb. S. J. sq.*
Darnley E 11, *Berkley-square*
Dartmouth E 6, *Ch. st. St. J. sq.*
De Lawarr E 9, *Albemarle-str.*
Denbigh E 4, *South-street*
Derby E 4, *Grosvenor square*
Devonshire D 2, *Piccadilly*

A List of the HOUSE *of* PEERS.

ke-street	Hawke, L. 13,
b Audley st.	Hereford V 10 *Chandos street*
ner square	Hereford Bp. 16, *(Hereford)*
street	Hertford E 9, *Grosvenor street*
rg Gardens	Hillsborough E 9, *Han. sq.*
erkeley-str.	Holland L 13,
	Huntingdon E 4 *St. James's Pl.*
bemarle st.	Jersey E 6, *Grosvenor square*
). Grof. str.	Ilchester E 9, *Burlington-str.*
elphi	King L 12, *Dover street*
Conduit str.	Kinnoul E 11,
:man square	Landaff Bp 17, *Welbeck-street*
cadilly	Leeds D 2, *St. James's square*
street	Leigh I. 11.
str. May f.	Le Despencer, L 10, *Hanover sq.*
Grof.-str.	Leinster D 10,
b Audley-st.	Lincoln Bp 17, *Temple*
. James's sq.	Litchfield Bp 17, *Great Russel*
). st. Han. sq.	*street, Bloomsbury*
Seymour-str	London Bp 16, *St. James's sq.*
bole street	Lothian M 15. *Portland-pl.*
Piccadilly	Loughborough L 14, *Lincoln's-*
Chandos-st.	*inn fields*
impole street	Loudoun E 15, *Privy garden*
ton-street	Macclesfield E 7, *Cavendish sq.*
Harley str.	Manchester D 3, *Portman sq.*
harles-street,	Mansfield E 9, *Bloomsbury sq.*
	Marchmont E 15, *Curz. st M. f.*
	Marlborough, D 2, *Pall-mall*
,Up. Grof. st.	Maynard V 10, *Oxford-street*
7, Upper-	Middleton L 11,
	Milton L 13, *Tilney st. May-f.*
Stable yard	Monson L 12, *Albemarle street*
er Grof. str.	Montagu D 3, *Privy garden*
ball	Montague V 9, *Grof.-sq.*
adilly	Montfort L. 12,
Whitehall	Montrose D 7, *Up. Grosv. str.*
Grosvenor sq.	Mountstuart L. 13 *(Turin)*
rietta street	Newcastle D 3, *New palace yd.*
rosvenor-sq.	Norfolk D 1, *St. James's sq.*
een-st. Gr. sq	Northampton E 4, *(abroad)*
	Northington E 9, *Charles-street,*
endish square	*Berkeley-square*
t. James's sq.	Northumberland D 3, *Char. cr.*
able yd. S. J.	Norwich Bp 17, *Up. Grof. street*
Park street	Onslow L 11, *Dover street*

Alphabetical List of the House of Peers.

Orford E 7, *Green-street, Grosvenor-square*
Oxford E 6, *Harley street*
Oxford Bp 17, *Hill-street, Berkeley-square*
Paget L 11, *Spring gardens*
Pelham L 13, *Stretton street*
Pembroke E 4, *Privy garden*
Percy, L 10, *Grosvenor-square*
Peterborough E 4,
Peterborough Bp 17, *Conduit st.*
Petre L 11, *Park lane*
Plymouth E 5, *Bruton street*
Polwarth, L 14, *St. Jam.-sq.*
Pomfret E 7, *Chandois-street, Cavendish-square*
Portchester L 14, *Tenterden-street, Hanover-square*
Portland D 3, *Burlington house*
Portsmouth E 7
Poulett E 6, *Stratford-place*
Powis E 8, *Albemarle street*
Queensberry D 14, *Piccadilly*
Radnor E 9, *Grafton street*
Ravensworth L 12, *St. J. sq.*
Richmond D 1, *Privy garden*
Rivers L. 14, *Hertford street*
Rochester Bp 17, *Deanry, West.*
Rochford E 6, *Up per Harley-st.*
Rockingham M 4, *Grof. sq.*
Romney L 12,
Roseberry E 15, *Holland Ho. K.*
Roxburgh D 7, *Hanover square*
Rutland D 2, *Arlington-street*
St. Albans D 2, *Bolton row*
St. Asaph Bp 17, *Bolton-row, Piccadilly*
St. David's Bp 17, *Gr. Geo. st.*
St. John L 11, *Conduit street*
Salisbury E 4, *Stratford Place*
Salisbury Bp 17, *Hertford street*
Sandwich E 5, *Admiralty*
Sandys L 12, *Portland-place*
Say and Sele V 9, *Jermyn-str.*
Scarbrough E 5, *South Aud. str.*
Scarsdale L 13, *Mansfield street*
Shaftesbury E 5 *Grosvenor sq.*
Shelburne E 12, *Berkley square*
Shrewsbury E 4, *Stanhope str.*
Somerset D 2, *Upper Gros. str.*
Sondes L 12, *Grosvenor square*
Southampton L 14, *Stanhope-street*
Spencer E 9, *St. James's place*
Stamford E 5, *Charles-street, Berkeley-sq.*
Stanhope E 7, *Harley-street*
Stawell L 12, *Upper Seymour-street*
Stormont V 15, *Portland Place*
Stourton L 11, *St. James's sq.*
Strafford E 6, *St. James's square*
Suffolk E 4, *Pall-mall*
Sussex E 7, *Stratford Place*
Talbot E 9, *Lincoln's Inn fields*
Tankerville E 7, *Grosvenor sq.*
Temple E 8, *Pall-mall*
Teynham L 11, *(Lisle)*
Thanet E 5, *Grosvenor square*
Thurlow L. 14, *Ormond-street*
Torrington V 10, *(Brussels)*
Townshend V 9, *Portman sq.*
Vere L 12, *St. James's square*
Vernon L 13, *Park Place*
Waldegrave E 7, *Whiteball*
Wales, Prince of, 1
Walpole L 12, *Bruton street*
Walsingham L 14, *Lincoln's Inn-Fields*
Warwick E 7, *St. James's sq.*
Wentworth V 10, *Savile-row*
Westmorland E 4, *Suckville-st.*
Weymouth V 10, *Arlington str.*
Willoughby de Broke L 11, *Hill street*
Winchelsea E 5, *(Abroad)*
Winchester Bp 16, *(at Chelsea)*
Worcester Bp 17, *Grosvenor-square.*
York Abp 16 *Bloomsbury sq.*

The HOUSE of COMMONS.
SPEAKER,
‡ Rt. Hon. CHARLES WOLFRAN CORNWALL, Efquire.

List of the COUNTIES, BOROUGHS, &c. *in the Order they are called over in the House; with the Names of the Members returned for each, the Places they possess, and their Country Seats.*

Note, *co.* stands for *county*; *bor.* for *borough*; *n.* for *near.*
The Figure after the Name shews in how many Parliaments the Member has served.
Those printed in *Italic Characters* (without any Figure) were new Members at the late General Election.
‖ Privy-Counsellors.   § Chosen since the General Election.
† Voted in upon Petition.

ENGLAND 489.
BEDFORDSHIRE 4.

‡ T. hon. John (Fitzpatrick) earl of Upper-Ossory, in the kingdom of Irel. nephew to the duchess of Bedford and earl Gower, ld. lt. and cust. rot. of this county, and keeper of Rockingham Forest (*Ampthill Park, in this county, Farming-woods, Northamptonshire, and Tentore, Queen's county, in Ireland*) 4

Hon. St. Andrew St. John, *brother to lord St. John Borough of Bedford.*

Sir William Wake, baronet (*Courteen-Hall, Northamptonshire*) 2

Samuel Whitbread, of Cardington, near this borough, esq; father-in-law to lord St. John, and brother-in-law to earl Cornwallis (*Bedwell Park, Herts*) 2

BERKSHIRE 9.

John Elwes, esq; (*Marcham, near Abingdon, and Bucklebury, in this county*) 3

Vinchcombe Henry Hartley, esq; (*Bucklebury, near Thatcham, Berks*) 2

Borough of Reading.

John Dodd, esq; lieutenant colonel of the Berkshire militia (*Swallowfield, near this borough*) 5

Francis Annesley, of this borough, esq; one of the trustees of the British Museum 2

Borough of Abingdon.

John Mayor, esq; (*Langton, near Horn-Church, Essex, Lacy Court, near Abingdon, Berkshire, and Upminster, Essex*)

Borough of N. w. Windsor.

Penyston Portlock Powney, esq;

Hon. John Montagu, only son to Lord Beaulieu (*Ditton Park, Bucks*) 3

Borough of Wallingford.
John Aubrey, esq; son of sir Thomas Aubrey, baronet, LL.D. (*Llantrithyd, Glamorganshire, and Borstall Tower, in this county*) 3
Chaloner Arcedeckne, esq; (Cockfield-Hall, Suffolk)

BUCKS 14.
✤Rt. hon. Ralph (Verney) E. Verney, of the king. of Irel. and F.R.S. (*Ramsgate, Kent, and Middle Clayton, in this county* 5
Thomas Grenville, next brother to earl Temple. (*Wotton Underwood, Bucks.*) 2

Borough of Buckingham.
James Grenville, jun. esq; first cousin to earl Temple 3
Richard Aldworth Neville, esq; of Billingbear, in Berkshire, brother-in-law to earl Temple (*White Knights, near Reading*)

Borough of Chipping-Wycomb.
Robert Waller, esq; (*Huggingdon-house, near this borough*) 4
Rt. hon. Charles Stanhope, lord Mahon, eldest son of earl Stanhope

Borough of Aylesbury.
Anthony Bacon, esq; a merchant in London, and one of the elder brethren of the Trinity House, (*Cyfartha, n. Cardiff, Glamorganshire*) 5
Thomas Ord, esq; Receiver-Gen. of the Dutchy of Lancaster, (Sudbury-Green, near Harrow, Middlesex)

Borough of Great Marlow.
William Clayton, esq; uncle to sir Robert Clayton, and brother-in-law to earl of Pomfret (*Harleyford, near this borough*) 7
Sir John Borlase Warren, bart. master and commander in the navy (*Little Marlow, in this county*) 2

Borough of Wendover.
Richard Smith, esq; a general in the East India Company's service (Chiltern Lodge, near Hungerford)
John Mansell Smith, esq; son of the above member

Borough of Agmondesham.
William Drake, esq; LL.D. (*Shardeloes and Amersham Mount, Bucks*) 7
William Drake, jun. esq; LL.D. son to the other member 3

CAMBRIDGESHIRE 6.
Right hon. Lord Robert Manners, only brother to the duke of Rutland, and a captain in the Royal Navy.
Hon. Philip Yorke, nephew and heir to the earl of Hardwicke, (Hamels, Hertfordshire)

University of Cambridge.
Hon. John Townshend, M. A. second son to lord viscount Townshend

House of COMMONS.

James Mansfield, esq. M.A. his Majesty's solicitor-general, and counsel for this university. 2
Borough of Cambridge.
Benj. Keene, esq. son of the bishop of Ely (*Catley, near Cambridge*) 2
James Warwood Adeane, esq; aid-de-camp to the king, and lieutenant-colonel of the first troop of horse-grenadier guards (Babraham-Hall, near Cambridge, and Chalgrove, Bedfordshire)

CHESHIRE 4.

John Crewe, esq; lieut. col. of the militia of this county, (*Crewe Hall, near Nantwich*) 4
Sir Robert Salusbury Cotton, bart. major of the militia of this county, (*Cumbermere-abbey, near Nantwich*) 2
City of Chester.
Thomas Grosvenor, esq; only brother to lord Grosvenor (*Wimbledon, Surrey, and Walthamstow, Essex*) 5
Richard Wilbraham Bootle, esq; F.R.S. *Latham Hall, near Ormskirk, Lancashire, and Rhode-hall, Cheshire*) 4

CORNWALL 44.

Sir William Lemon, bart. (*Carelew, in this county*) 3
Edward Eliot, of Port Eliot, esq; receiver-general of the dutchy of Cornwall 6
Borough of Dunheved, alias Launceston.
Thomas Bowlby, esq. commiss.-general of muster
§ Hon. Charles George Perceval, brother to the earl of Egmont
Borough of Liskerrett, alias Liskeard.
Samuel Salt, of the Inner Temple, esq; deputy-governor of the South Sea Company 3
Hon. Wilbraham Tollemache, next brother to the earl of Dysert, and cousin to earl Spencer (*Calverley-hall, near Nampiwich, Cheshire*) 3
Borough of Lestwithiel.
Hon. Thomas De Grey, son of lord Walsingham, one of the lords commissioners of Trade and Plantations, and F. R. S. (*Windsor, Berks*) 3
§ George Johnstone, esq. a captain of the royal navy 3
Borough of Truro.
Bamber Gascoyne, esq; one of the lords of the Admiralty, and steward of the borough court of Southwark, (*Barking, Essex, and Childwell, near Liverpool, Lancashire* 5
Henry Rosewarne. esq; *of this borough, vice-warden of the Stannaries of Cornwall.*
Borough of Bodmyn.
Geo. Hunt, esq;(*Mollington, Chesh. and Lanhidrock, n. this bo.*) 6

William Masterman, esq. (Trinity, near this Borough)

Borough of Helston.
Philip Yorke, esq; 2 ⎫
Jocelyn Dean, esq. dead ⎬ A double return.
Lord Hyde 2 ⎭
William Evelyn, esq; 3 ⎭

Borough of Saltash.
Sir Grey Cooper, of Gogar in Scot. bart. joint sec. to the treasury, and King's counsel in the dutchy court of Lancaster, (*Richmond, Surrey, and Worlington, near Newmarket*) 3

✤ Rt. hon. Charles Jenkinson, L.L. D. secretary at War, and clerk of the Pells in Ireland for life, (*Addiscombe-Place, near Croydon, Surrey*) 4

Borough of East Looe.
John Buller, esq; one of the lords of the Treasury, comptroller of the mint, auditor of the dutchy of Cornwall, and recorder of this borough (*Bake, near this borough*) 4

William Graves, esq; a master in chancery (*Thanckes, near this borough*) 3

Borough of Portpigham, or West-Looe.
Sir William James, bart. F. R. S. a director of the East-India Company, one of the directors of Greenwich Hospital, and an elder brother and deputy master of the Trinity-House (*Park Farm-Place, Eltham, Kent*) 2

John Buller, esq; nephew to earl Bathurst, (*King's-Nympton, Devonshire, and Morval, Cornwall*) 3

Borough of Grampound.
Sir John Ramsden, bart. brother-in-law to the marq. of Rockingham and lord Ducie, (Byram, Yorkshire)

Thomas Lucas, esq; president of Guy's hospital (Lee, in Kent)

Borough of Camelford.
John Pardoe, jun. esq; (Layton, Essex)
James Macpherson, esq. (Putney-Common)

Borough of Penryn.
Sir Francis Basset, bart. (Tehidy-Park, in this county, and Imly-Park, Northamptonshire)

John Rogers, esq; (*Penrose in this county*) 2

Borough of Tregony.
John Stephenson, esq; a merchant in London, (*Brentford Butts, Middlesex*) 4

John Dawes, esq; a banker in Westminster

Borough of Bossinney.
Hon. Henry Lawes Luttrell, eldest son of visc. Carhampton, adjutant general to the army in Ireland, a col. in the army, and lieutenant colonel of the 1st regiment of horse 3

House of COMMONS.   25

Hon. Cha. Stuart, lieut. col. of the 26th reg. of foot, and fourth son of the earl of Bute.   2

Borough of St. Ives.
William Praed, esq. (Tyringham-Newport, Bucks)
Abel Smith, esq.

Borough of Fowey.
Philip Rashleigh, esq; (Menabilly, near this borough)   3
Right hon. Molyneux (Shuldham) lord Shuldham, of the kingdom of Ireland, vice admiral of the white   2

Borough of St. Germans.
Edward James Eliot, esq; son of the member for Cornwall, (Port Eliot, Cornwall)
Dudley Long, esq; (Saxmundham, Suffolk)

Borough of Midshall or Mitchell.
Hon. William Hanger, next brother to lord Coleraine   2
Francis Hale, esq; brother-in-law to the right hon. Richard Rigby, (Mistley, Essex)   2

Borough of Newport.
Rt. Hon. James (Maitland) viscount Maitland, eldest son of the earl of Lauderdale
John Cogbill, esq; (Richings, Bucks)

Borough of St. Mawes.
✤ Rt. hon. Robert Craggs (Nugent) earl Nugent, of the kingdom of Ireland, joint vice treasurer of Ireland (Gosfield-Hall, Braintree, Essex)   4
Hugh Boscawen, esq;   2

Borough of Callington.
George Stratton, esq; (Great Tew, Oxfordshire)   2
John Morshead, esq; (Hascomb Place, Surrey)

CUMBERLAND 6.
Sir James Lowther, bart. son-in-law to the earl of Bute, lt. and cust. rot. of the counties of Cumberland and Westmoreland, col. of the Cumberland militia, and an alderman of the city of Carlisle (Lowther-Hall, Westmoreland, the Flat near Whitehaven, and Laleham, Middlesex)   5
Henry Fletcher, esq; a director of the East-India company, (Clea, in this county)   3

City of Carlisle.
Rt. hon. Charles (Howard) earl of Surrey, son and heir to the Duke of Norfolk (Greystock, near Penrith, Cumberland)
William Lowther, esq. a major in the Cumberland militia

Borough of Cockermouth.
John Lowther, esq.
John Baynes Garforth, esq.

DERBYSHIRE 4.
Rt. hon. ld. Richard Cavendish, next bro. to d. of Devonshire
Hon. Nat. Curzon, eld. son of ld. Scarf. (*Kedleston, near Derby*) 3
Borough of Derby.
Rt. hon. George Augustus Henry Cavendish, second brother
 to the duke of Devonshire (*Latimers, Bucks*) 2
Edward Coke, esq; son to the member for Norfolk, (Longford,
 near this town)

DEVONSHIRE 26.
John Parker, esq; neph. to earl Poulett, and col. of the 4th bat-
 talion of the militia of this county (*Saltram, near Plympton, Devonshire*) 4
Hon. John Rolle, bro. to the late ld. Rolle, (*Tydwell in this co.*) 2
Borough of Ashburton.
Charles Boone, esq; one of the proprietors of Crawley's iron
 forges (*Barking-Hall, near Needham-Market, Suffolk*) 5
Robert Palk, esq; late gov. of Madrafs (*Haldon-House, in this co.*) 3
Borough of Tiverton.
Sir John Duntze, bart. (*Rockbere House, near Exeter*) 3
John Wilmot, esq; son of the late lord chief justice of the
 court of Common Pleas (*Berkswell, Warwickshire*) 2
Borough of Clifton-Dartmouth Hardness.
✢ Rt. hon. Richard (Howe) lord viscount Howe, of the king-
 dom of Ireland, a vice-admiral of the red, (*Langar, near Not-
 tingham, and Porter's-Lodge, Hertfordsh.*) 5
Arthur Holdsworth, of this borough, esq.
Borough of Oakhampton.
Richard Vernon, esq, bro.-in-law to earl Gower, one of the clks
 of the Green-Cloth (*Hilton near Wolverhampton, Staffordsh.*) 5
Humphry Minchin, esq. (*Soberton near Droxford, Hants.*) 2
Borough of Honiton.
Sir George Yonge, bart. president of the Misericordia Hos-
 pital (*Escott, near Ottery St. Mary in this county*) 5
Alexander Macleod, esq; (Theobalds, Hertfordshire)
Borough of Plymouth.
Sir Frederick Leman Rogers, bart. (Blackford, Devon)
George Darby, esq; a vice admiral of the blue, and one of the
 lords of the Admiralty
Borough of Beeralstone.
§ Hon. William-Robert (Fielding) visc. Fielding, eldest son
 of the earl of Denbigh, and capt. in the 3d reg. of drag. gds.

Borough of Plympton-Earle.
Sir Ralph Payne, K. B. a clerk of the board of green cloth,
 and late governor of the Leeward islands 2
§ Hon. James Stuart, second son of the earl of Bute, (*Aston, near Stevenage, Herts.*) 3

House of COMMONS.

Borough of Totness.
Sir Philip Jennings Clerke, bart. (*Duddleston-Hall, Shropsh.*) 3
Launcelot Brown, jun. *esq.*

Borough of Barnstaple.
John Clevland, esq; accomptant of the six-penny receivers office, and one of the directors of Greenwich-Hospital (*Tapley near Biddeford*) 3
Francis Bassett, *esq.* lieut. col. of the 2d reg. of the *Devonshire* militia, (Heanton-Court, and Rawleigh, near this borough; Bratton, near Southmolton; and Umberleigh, near Great Torrington)

Borough of Tavistock.
✤ Rt. hon. Richard Rigby, paymaster-gen. of the land forces, master of the rolls in Ireland for life, one of the deputy-rangers of Phœnix Park near Dublin (*Mistleyhall near Manningtree, Essex*) 3
Hon. Rich. Fitzpatrick, junior, bro. to the earl of Upper Ossory, a capt. in the 1st reg. of ft. gds. and ranks as lieut. col. in the army 3

City of Exeter.
Sir Charles Warwick Bampfylde, bart. son-in-law to Sir John Moore, bart. (*Poltimore, near Exeter*) 2
John Baring, esq; (*Mount Radford, near this city*) 2

DORSETSHIRE 20.
Humph. Sturt, esq; LL.D. (*Critchill-House, near Salisbury, Wilts.*) 3
Hon. George Pitt, esq; only son of lord Rivers (*Stratfield-Sea, Hants.*) 2

Borough of Dorchester.
Wm. Ewer, esq; a merchant in London, one of the directors of the Bank, a trustee of Morden College, and treasurer of the Turkey-Company (*Richmond, Surrey*) 3
Hon. George Damer, eldest son of lord Milton (*Milton-Abbey, Dorsetshire*)

Borough of Lyme-Regis.
Hon. Henry Fane, uncle to the earl of Westmorland, and surveyor of the king's private gates, roads, and bridges 3
David Robert Michel, *esq*;

Boroughs of Weymouth and Melcombe-Regis.
✤ Rt. hon. Welbore Ellis, brother-in-law to Hans Stanley, treasurer of the navy, LL.D. F.R.S. (*Twickenham, Middlesex, and Tilney Hall, Hants*) 7
William Chafin Grove, esq; LL.D. recorder of this borough Zeals, *and Chcfinbury, Wilts*) 2
John Purling, esq; (*Bradford Peverel, in this county*) 3

§ Gabriel Steward, of this bor. esq; paymaster of the marines 2
Borough of Bridport.
Thomas Scott, esq; (Shepperton, Middlesex)
Richard Beckford, esq; a West-India merchant, and son of the late alderman and representative of the city of London.
Borough of Shafton, or Shaftsbury.
Sir Thomas Rumbold, bart. (Woodhall, Herts)
Francis Sykes, esq; brother-in-law to lord viscount Galway (Bassildon, near Reading)

Borough of Wareham.
John Boyd, esq.
Thomas Farrer, esq; (Clapham, in Craven, Yorkshire)
Borough of Corff-Castle.
John Bond, esq; recorder of Poole, Dorchester, and Wareham (Grange near Wareham, Dorsetshire) 6
Henry Bankes, esq.
Borough of Poole.
Joseph Gulston, esq; (Corfe-Mullen, Dorsetshire)
William Morton Pitt, esq; (Encombe, in Purbeck, Dorsetshire)

DURHAM 4.
Sir Thomas Clavering, bart. brother to the late sir John Clavering, K. B. (Axwell-Park near Durham) 3
Sir John Eden, bart. brother to sir Robert Eden, bart. (Windlestone, near Darlington, in this county) 2
City of Durham.
John Lambton, esq; a lt. gen. of his majesty's forces, and col. of the 68th regiment of foot (Harraton-Hall near this city) 4
John Tempest, esq; (Wynyard, near Stockton in this county) 3

EBOR, or YORKSHIRE 30.
Sir George Savile, bart. F. R. S. bro.-in-law to the earl of Scarborough, col. of the 1st battalion of Yorkshire West-Riding militia, (Rufford near Mansfield, Nottinghamshire) 5
Henry Duncombe, esq; (Copgrove, in this county)
Borough of Aldborough.
Charles Mellish, esq; S. A. S. Recorder of Newark 2
§ Hon. Edward Onslow, second son of lord Onslow
Borough of Boroughbridge.
Anthony Eyre, esq; (Grove, near Retford, Notts) 2
Charles Ambler, esq; a King's counsel, and solicitor-general to the Queen 3
Borough of Beverley.
Sir James Pennyman, bart. of this borough, and Ormsby-Thornton, Yorkshire 3
Evelyn Anderson, esq; a lieutenant in the king's regiment of light dragoons 3

House of COMMONS.

Borough of Hedon.
William Chaytor, efq; (*Spenithorne, near Bedale, and Croft, near Northallerton, Yorkshire*)   2
Chriſtopher Atkinſon, eſq. a merchant in London, (Hale, Norfolk)

Borough of Knareſborough.
Hon. Rob. Boyle Walſingham, brother to the earl of Shannon, a captain in the royal navy, and a colonel of marines, (*Gainſborough, Lincolnſhire*)   3
Right hon. William (Ponſonby) viſc. Duncannon in Ireland, only ſon of the earl of Beſborough, and ſon-in-law to earl Spencer

Borough of Malton.
Will. Weddell, efq; (*Newby, near Rippon, in this county*)   4
§ Edmund Burke, efq; (*Gregories, near Beaconsfield, Bucks*)   4

Borough of Northallerton.
Henry Peirſe, brother-in-law to lord Monſon (*Bedale, in this county*)   2
§ Edwin Laſcelles, efq; (*Harwood-Houſe, near Wetherby, Yorkſhire*)   3

Borough of Pontefract.
Rt. hon. Robert (Monckton) viſcount Galway, of the kingdom of Ireland.
William Nedham, efq; (*Edwinſtow, Nottinghamſhire*)   3

Borough of Richmond.
✤ Rt. hon. ſir Lawrence Dundas, bart. vice admiral of Shetland and the Orkneys (*Moor Park, Hertfordſhire, Aſkhall, Yorkſhire*)   4
Hon. James (Graham) marquis of Graham, eldeſt ſon of the duke of Montroſe in Scotland

Borough of Ripon.
William Aiſlabie, efq; one of the auditors of the Impreſt for life, and principal regiſter of the Conſiſtory Court of the archbiſhop of York, (*Studley Royal near this Borough*)   8
Hon. Frederick Robinſon, brother to lord Grantham, (Newby, Yorkſhire)

Borough of Scarborough.
Right hon. Geo. (Carpenter) earl of Tyrconnel of the kingdom of Ireland (*the Homme, Herefordſh. Randalls, Surrey*)   3
Hon. Charles Phipps, brother to lord Mulgrave, and a captain in the navy   2

Borough of Thirſk.
Sir Thomas Gaſcoigne, bart. (Parlington, in Yorkſhire)
Beilby Thompſon, efq; (*Eſkricke, near York*)   3

City of York.
Rt. hon. lord John Cavendiſh, third uncle to the duke of Devonſhire, (*Great Billing, near Northampton*)   3

Charles Turner, esq; an alderman of this city (*Kirkleatham Park, in this county*) 3

Town of Kingston upon Hull.

Right hon. lord Robert Manners, great uncle to the duke of Rutland, a general of his Majesty's forces, colonel of the 3d, or prince of Wales's regiment of dragoon guards, and lieut. gov. of Hull (*Bloxholme near Sleaford, Lincolnshire*) 6
William Wilberforce, *esq*; (of this borough, and Wimbledon, Surrey)

E S S E X 8.

John Luther, esq; (*Myles's near Ongar in this county*) 4
Thomas Berney Bramston, esq. (*Skreens, near Chelmsford*) 2

Borough of Colchester.

Sir Robert Smyth, bart. (Beer-Church-Hall, Essex)
Isaac Martin Rebow, of this borough, esq; colonel of the eastern battal. of Essex militia, and recorder of Colchester 5

Borough of Malden.

John Strutt, esq; (*Terling-Place, near this borough*) 2
Eliab Harvey, *esq.*

Borough of Harwich.

Jn. Robinson, esq; LL.D. joint secretary to the Treasury, and col. of the Westmoreland militia, (*Michaelstow, near Harwich, and Sion-Hill, Middlesex*)
Hon. George Augustus North, eldest son of the right hon. lord North, secretary and comptroller of his majesty's houshold, secretary to the chancellor of the Exchequer, and col. of the Cinque Port volunteers 2

G L O U C E S T E R S H I R E 8.

Sir Wil. Guise, bart. (*Rendcomb near Cirencester in this county*) 3
§ James Dutton, esq; (*Shireborne, Gloucestershire*)

Borough of Tewkesbury.

Sir Wm. Codrington, bart. lieut. col. of the southern battalion of the Glouceft. militia (*Dodington near Sodbury in this co*) 6
James Martin, esq; brother to the late member, a banker in London, and one of the directors of the Million Bank 2

Borough of Cirencester.

James Whitshed, esq; brother-in-law to earl Bathurst, (*Hampton-court, Middlesex*) 5
Samuel Blackwell, esq; lieutenant colonel commandant of the northern battalion of the Gloucestershire militia (*Williamstrip near Fairford, and Ampney Park near this borough*) 2

City of Gloucester.

Cha. Barrow, esq; recorder of Tewksbury, LL.D. (*Highgrove, near this city*) 6
John Webb, *esq.* (Cote-House, near Bristol, Gloucestershire)

H E R E F O R D S H I R E 8.

Sir George Cornewall, bart. (*Moccas Court in this county*) 2

House of COMMONS.

✤ Rt. hon. Thomas Harley, esq; alderman and merchant of London, president of St. Bartholomew's hosp. and second brother to the earl of Oxford (*Berrington, near Leemminster, in this county; and Hoolley, near Croyden, in Surrey*)

City of Hereford.
John Scudamore, esq; (*Kent Church, near this city*) 4
Sir Richard Symons, bart. (*Meend near this city*) 3

Borough of Leominster.
✤ Right hon. John (Bateman) viscount Bateman, of the kingdom of Ireland, master of the buck hounds, lord lieut. and cust. rot. of Herefordshire (*Shobdon court in this co.*) 7
Richard Payne Knight, esq; (Downton, Herefordshire)

Borough of Weobley.
John St. Leger Douglas, esq; (*Wilsdon, Middlesex*) 3
Andrew Bayntun, esq; 2

HERTFORDSHIRE 6.
Wm. Plumer, esq; (*Blakesware, and Gilston-Park, in this county*) 4
Thomas Halsey, esq; (*Great Gaddesdon in this county*) 3

Borough of Hertford.
Thomas Dimsdale, esq; of this borough, baron of the Russian empire.
William Baker, esq; (*Bayfordbury, near this borough*) 2

Borough of St. Albans.
John Radcliffe, esq; brother-in-law to the earl of Carlisle (*Hitchin Priory, Herts*) 3
William Charles Sloper, esq brother to Gen. Sloper, and son-in-law to the bishop of St. Asaph

HUNTINGDONSHIRE 4.
Rt. hon. Peter (Ludlow) earl of Ludlow in the kingdom of Ireland (*Great Stoughton near Kimbolton, in this county*) 3
✤ Rt. hon. John (Montagu) visc. Hinchingbroke, eldest son of the E. of Sandwich, and son-in-law to the D. of Bolton, vice chamb. of his Maj. hous. (*St. Neots in this county, and Horton, near Northampton*) 2

Borough of Huntingdon.
Rt. hon. Constantine John (Phipps) lord Mulgrave, of the kingdom of Ireland, one of the lords of the admiralty, a captain in the royal navy, an elder brother of the Trinity-House, and F.R.S. (*Mulgrave Hall, near Whitby*) 3
§ Sir Hugh Pallifer, bart. a vice-admiral of the white, gov. of Scarborough castle, one of the elder brethren of the Trinity-House, and master of Greenwich hospital, (*Chiselhurst, Kent*) 2

KENT 10.
Hon. Charles Marsham, LL.D. eldest son to lord Romney, bro.

ther-in-law to lord Egmont, one of the vice prefidents of the fociety for the encouragement of arts, manufactures, and commerce (*the Mote, near Maidftone*)   3
Filmer Honywood, efq; fon of fir John Honywood, bart. (*Evington, Kent*)   2

City of Rochefter.

George Finch Hatton, efq; coufin to the earl of Winchelfea, (*Eaftwell Park, Kent*)   3
Rob. Gregory, efq; a director of the Eaft India Company (*Walthamftow, Effex*)   3

Borough of Queenborough.

Sir Charles Frederick, K. B. F.R.S. brother-in-law to lord vifcount Falmouth, furveyor general of the Ordnance, and comptroller of the laboratory at Woolwich   7
Sir Walter Rawlinfon, knt. and banker in London, F.R.S. and F.S.A. (*Stowlangtoft, near Bury, Suffolk*)   2

Borough of Maidftone.

Sir Horatio Mann, knt. nephew to the baronet of the fame name (*Bourn Place, near Canterbury*)   2
Clement Taylor, efq.

City of Canterbury.

George Gipps, Efq; an alderman of this city.
Charles Robinfon, efq; recorder of this city, Sandwich, Deal, Dover, Hythe, and New Romney, and a commiffioner of bankruptcy.

LANCASHIRE 14.

Sir Thomas Egerton, bart. (*Heaton in this county*)   3
Thomas Stanley, efq; (*Crofs Hall in this county*)   2

Borough of Lancafter.

Wilfon Braddyll, efq. (Portfield, near Whalley, and Conifhead Priory, near Ulverftone, both in this county)
Abraham Rawlinfon, jun. efq.

Borough of Prefton.

John Burgoyne, efq; a lieut. gen. of his Maj. forces.   3
Sir Henry Hoghton, bart. (*Hoghton Tower and Walton Hall in this county, and Caftle Hedingham, Effex*)   3

Borough or Town of Liverpool.

Bamber Gafcoigne, efq; fon of Bamber Gafcoigne, one of the lords of the Admiralty
Henry Rawlinfon, efq;

Borough of Wigan.

Henry Simpfon Bridgeman, efq; fon to Sir Henry Bridgman, bart. (Wefton under Lizard, Staffordfhire)
Hon. Horatio Walpole, fon of ld. Walpole (Wolterton, Norfolk)

Borough of Clitheroe.

Thomas Lifter, efq; LL. D. major commandant of the York-

shire light dragoons. (*Gisburn Park*, and *Maum-Water-House, near Skipton in Craven, Yorkshire*) 3
John Parker, esq; *brother-in-law to the above Member* (Mansfield, near Settle, Yorkshire)

Borough of *Newton.*
Thomas Peter Legh, esq; (Golborne Park, Lancashire)
Thomas Davenport, *a counsellor at law* (Hindon, Middlesex)

LEICESTERSHIRE 4.

John Peach Hungerford, esq; (*Dingley Hall, Northamptonshire, near Market Harborough*) 2
William Pochin, esq; (Barkby, near Leicester)

Borough of *Leicester.*
Hon. Booth Grey, brother to the earl of Stamford 3
John Darker, esq; treasurer of St. Bartholomew's Hospital (*Gayton, Northamptonshire*) 2

LINCOLNSHIRE 12.

Charles Anderson Pelham, esq; (*Brocklesby, n. Caistor, in this co.*) 2
Sir John Thorold, bart. (*Syston-Park, Lincolnsh.*) 2

Borough of *Stamford.*
Sir George Howard, K.B. LL.D. a general of his majesty's forces, colonel of the 1st reg. of dragoon guards, and governor of Chelsea Hospital (*Stoke Place, near Windsor*) 3
Henry Cecil, esq; nephew to the earl of Exeter (*Burleigh, Northamptonshire, near this borough*) 2

Borough of *Grantham.*
Francis Cockayne Cust, esq; uncle to lord Brownlow, counsel to the admiralty and navy, one of the council to the university of Cambridge, and ranks as a King's counsel (*Cockayne-Hatley, Bedfordshire*) 3
George Sutton, esq; eldest son of lord George Sutton (*Kelham, Notts*) 2

Borough of *Boston.*
Rt. hon. lord Robert Bertie, uncle to the duke of Ancaster, one of the lords of the King's bed-chamber, a general of his majesty's forces, col. of the 2d troop of horse-guards, and governor of Duncannon, in Ireland (*Chisleburst, Kent*) 2
Humphry Sibthorp, esq; LL.D. (*Canwick, near Lincoln, and Skimpans, near Hatfield, Herts*) 3

Borough of *Great Grimsby.*
John Harrison, esq; (Norton Place, near Gainsborough, in this county)
Francis Eyre, esq;

City of *Lincoln.*
Sir Thomas Clarges, bart.
Robert Vyner, esq; (*Gautby, n. Horncastle in this county*)

[D]

MIDDLESEX 8.

John Wilkes, esq; F. R. S. an alderman and chamberlain of
the city of London 4
George Byng, esq; cousin to viscount Torrington (*Wretham
Park, near Barnet, in this county*) 3

City of Westminster.
Sir George Brydges Rodney, bart. rear admiral of England,
and an adm. of the white squadron (*Great Alresford, Hants*) 2
Hon. Charles James Fox, uncle to lord Holland 3

City of London.
Frederick Bull, esq; an alderman of this city (*Wanstead, Essex*) 3
Geo. Hayley, esq; a merc. and ald. of this city (*Bromley, Kent*) 2
Nathaniel Newnham, esq; an ald. of this city (*Tanhurst, Surrey*)
§ John Sawbridge, esq; an alderman of London, and col. of
the east batt. of the Kent militia (*Ollantigh, Kent*) 3

MONMOUTHSHIRE 3.
John Hanbury, esq; (*Pontypoole, near Uske, in this county*) 3
John Morgan, esq; brother to the member for Brecknockshire
(*Tredegar, in this county, and Therrow, Brecon.*) 3

Borough of Monmouth.
Sir John Stepney, bart. his Majesty's envoy extraordinary to
the Court of Dresden (*Llannelly, Caermarthenshire*) 3

NORFOLK 12.
Sir Edward Astley, bart. (*Melton Constable, Norfolk*) 3
Tho. William Coke, esq; (*Holkham Hall, near Wells, Norfolk,
and Longford, near Derby*) 2

Borough of King's Lynn.
Hon. Thomas Walpole, next brother to lord Walpole, a merchant in London (*Carshalton, Surrey*) 2
Crisp Molineux, esq; one of the vice presidents of the Westminster Lying-in Hospital (*Garboldisham in Norfolk, Chippenham in Cambridgeshire, and Thundersley in Essex*) 3

Town of Great Yarmouth.
Rt. hon. Ch. Townshend, esq; cousin to visc. Townshend,
vice-treas. of Ireland, LL.D. (*Honingham, in this county*) 6
Hon. Richard Walpole, second brother to lord Walpole, a
banker in London 3

Borough of Thetford.
Charles Fitzroy Scudamore, esq; deputy ranger of Whittlebury
Forest, and cursitor of the court of Chancery in Ireland
(*Holme Lacey, Herefordshire*) 9
Richard Hopkins, esq; (*Oving, near Aylesbury, Bucks.*) 4

Borough of Castle-Rising.
Robert Mackreth, esq; (*Ewhurst, Hants*) 2

House of COMMONS. 35

John Chetwynd Talbot, esq; nephew and heir to E. Talbot, and son-in-law to the earl of Hillsborough 2
    City of Norwich.
Sir Harbord Harbord, bart. LL.D. (*Gunton, Norf. and Middleton, Lancash.*) 5
Edward Bacon, esq; (*Earleham, near this city*) 7
  NORTHAMPTONSHIRE 9.
Lucy Knightley, esq; (*Fawsley Hall, near Daventry, and Pytchley House, near Kettering, both in this county*) 3
Thomas Powys, esq; (*Litford, near Oundle, in this county*) 2
   City of Peterborough.
Richard Benyon, esq; (*Gidea Hall, Romford, Essex*) 3
James Phipps, esq; *of that city*
   Borough of Brackley.
John William Egerton, esq; son of the bishop of Durham, and a captain in the 7th regiment of dragoons 2
Timothy Caswall, esq; deputy paymaster general of the forces (*Sacomb Park, Herts*) 5
   Borough of Northampton.
Rt. hon. Geo. John (*Spencer*) visc. Althorpe, son of earl Spencer
Geo. Rodney, esq; eldest son of sir Geo. Brydges Rodney, bart.
   Borough of Higham-Ferrers.
Frederick Montagu, esq; (*Papplewick, Nottinghamshire*) 4
  NORTHUMBERLAND 8.
Rt. hon. lord Algernon Percy, second son to the duke of Northumberland, col. of the Northumberland militia, and a vice-presid. of the Middlesex-hospital (*Faucett, in Yorksh.*) 2
Sir Wm. Middleton, bart. (*Belsay Castle, Northumberland*) 2
   Borough of Morpeth.
Peter Delme, esq; brother-in-law to the earl of Carlisle (*Earl Stoke, near Devizes, Wiltshire*)
Anthony Storer, esq; 2
  Town of Newcastle upon Tyne.
Sir Matthew White Ridley, bart. son to the late member (*Blakedon, near Morpeth, Northumberland*) 3
Andrew Robinson Bowes, esq. (Benwell, in this county.)
  Town of Berwick upon Tweed.
Sir John Hussey Delaval, bart. (*Seaton Delaval, and Fordcastle, Northumberland, and Doddington, near Lincoln*) 2
Hon. Jn. Vaughan, bro. to lord Lisburne, a maj. gen. gov. of Fort William in Scotl. and col. of the 46th reg. of foot 2
  NOTTINGHAMSHIRE 8.
Rt. hon. lord Edward Charles Cavendish Bentinck, only brother to the duke of Portland
Charles Meadows, esq. 2

[D 2]

Borough of East Retford.

Right Hon. lord John Pelham Clinton, second son of the duke of Newcastle, a gentleman of the prince of Wales's bedchamber

Wharton Amcotts, esq; (East-Retford, Nottinghamshire, and Kettlethorpe, near Newark, Lincolnshire)

Borough of Newark upon Trent.

Sir Henry Clinton, K. B. first cousin to the d. of Newcastle, commander in chief of the forces in North America, a lieut. gen. col. of the 7th reg. of dragoons, and of the 84th reg. of foot, and gov. of Limerick in Ireland   3

Rt. hon. lord George Sutton, uncle to the duke of Rutland, and col. of the Nottinghamshire militia (Kelham, Notts)   5

Town of Nottingham.

Daniel Parker Coke, esq;   2
Robert Smith, esq; of this town   2

OXON 9.

Rt. hon. lord Charles Spencer, LL.D. next brother to the duke of Marlborough, treasurer of the chamber, and verderer of Whichwood Forest, in this county (Wheatfield, Oxfordshire)   4

Rt. hon. Philip (Wenman) lord viscount Wenman, of the kingdom of Ireland, LL.D. (Thame Park, in this county)   3

University of Oxford.

Sir William Dolben, bart. (Thingdon, Northamptonshire)
Francis Page, esq; LL.D. (Middle Afton, Oxfordshire)   3

City of Oxford.

Rt. hon. lord Rob. Spencer, second bro. to the duke of Marlborough, and one of the lords commissioners for Trade, &c. 3
Hon. Pere. Bertie, only brother to the earl of Abingdon, a captain in the royal navy (Weston on the Green, near Bicester, Oxfordshire, and Yattendon, near Newbury, Berks)   3

Borough of New Woodstock.

Rt. hon. William Eden, esq; bro. to sir John and sir Rob. Eden, and brother-in-law to sir Gilbert Elliot, bart. a privy counsellor in Ireland, and prin. sec. to the lord lieutenant   3

Rt. hon. George Parker, viscount Parker, eldest son of the earl of Macclesfield, a gentleman of the Prince of Wales's bed-chamber.   2

Borough of Banbury.

Rt. hon. Fred. (North) lord North, LL.D. eldest son to the earl of Guildford, first lord of the Treasury, chancellor of the Exchequer, ld. warden and admir. of the Cinque Ports, ld. lieut. and custos rotulorum of Somersetsh. chanc. of the universf. of Oxford, recorder of Gloucester and Taunton, one of the elder breth. of the Trin. ho. gov. of the Turkey comp. pres. of the Foundling Hosp. and of the Asylum, and a

House of COMMONS. 37

governor of the Charter Houfe, K. G. (*Dillington, Somerfetfhire, and Bufhy Park, Middlefex*) 3

RUTLANDSHIRE 2.

Thomas Noel, efq; coufin to the earl of Gainfborough (*Exton,
in this county, and Walcot, in Northamptonfhire*) 8
George Bridges Brudenell, efq; coufin to the duke of Montague, one of the clerks of the Board of Green Cloth(*Ayfton
in this county*) 5

SALOP or SHROPSHIRE 12.

Noel Hill, efq; lieut. col. of the militia of this county, (*Tern,
near Shrewfbury*) 3
Richard Hill, efq; (Hawkeftone, in this county)
Borough of Shrewfbury.
William Pulteney, efq; (*Balls, near Hertford*) 3
Sir Charlton Leighton, bart. (Waltefbury, Salop).
Borough of Ludlow.
Rt. hon. Edw. (Clive) lord Clive of the kingdom of Ireland,
lord lieut. and colonel of the militia of this county, and recorder of Shrewfbury (*Oakley Park, Salop*; *Walcott, near
Bifhop's Cafile, and Claremont, Surrey*) 2
Frederick Cornewall, efq; fon of captain Frederick Cornewall, of the Navy (*Diddlesbury, and Ferry Hall, Salop*) 2
Borough of Bridgnorth.
Thomas Whitmore, efq; (*Apfley, near this borough*) 3
Hugh Pigot, efq; brother to the late lord Pigot, and a vice-admiral of the white 2
Town and Liberties of Wenlock.
Sir Henry Bridgeman, bt. LL. D. (*Wefton, Shrop. Cafile Bromwich, Warwickfhire, and Lever, Lanc.*) 6
§ George Forefter, efq; (*Wil'y, near Bridgnorth*) 4
Borough of Bifhop's Cafile.
Henry Strachey, efq; Storekeeper of Ordnance (*Sutton Court,
near Briftol*) 2
William Clive, efq; brother to the late member 2

SOMERSETSHIRE 18.

Richard Hippifley Coxe, efq; (*Stone Eafton, n. Wells, in this co.*) 3
Sir John Trevelyan, bart. (*Nettlecomb, near Taunton, in Somerfetfhire, and Wallington, Northumberland*) 2
Borough of Taunton.
John Halliday, efq; a banker in London (*Yard-Houfe, near
Taunton, Tilfhead, near Devizes, Wilts*) 2
John Roberts, efq; a colonel in the army
Borough of Ivelchefter.
Peregrine Cuft, efq; a merchant in London, and uncle to
lord Brownlow 4
Samuel Smith, jun, efq; a banker in London

[D 3]

Borough of Milborne Port.
Thomas Hutchings Medlycott, esq;
John Townson, esq;
          City of Wells.
Clement Tudway, of this city, esq; barrister at law   5
Robert Child, esq; a banker in London (*Osterley Park, Middlesex, and Upton, Warw.*)   4
          Borough of Bridgewater.
Benjamin Allen, of this borough, esq;   3
Hon. Anne Poulett, brother to earl Poulett   3
          City of Bath.
Abel Moysey, of Lincoln's-inn, esq; a Welch judge   2
Hon. *John Jefferys Pratt, only son of lord Camden, one of the tellers in the Exchequer*
          Borough of Minehead.
John Fownes Luttrell, esq; (*Dunster Castle, Somerset and Netherway, near Dartmouth*)   2
Francis Fownes Luttrell, esq;
          City of Bristol.
Matthew Brickdale, esq;

SOUTHAMPTON, or HAMPSHIRE. 26.

Robert Thistlethwayte, esq; a captain in the Hampshire militia, (Norman-Court, near Andover, and Southwick-Place, both in this county)
Jervoise Clarke Jervoise, esq; one of the gentlemen of the King's privy-chamber (*Bellmont, near Portsmouth, and West Bromwich, near Birmingham*)   3
          City of Winchester.
Henry Penton, esq; one of the lords commissioners of the admiralty, letter carrier to his Majesty, and recorder of this city (*Eastgate House in this city*)   3
Lovel Stanhope, of this city, esq; uncle to the earl of Chesterfield, a clerk of the board of green-cloth   2
          Town of Portsmouth.
Sir Will. Gordon, K.B. one of the clerks of the board of green-cloth, (*Gerrington-Park, near Loughborough, Leicestershire*) 2
Hon. Robert Monckton, uncle to visc. Galway, gov. of Portsmouth, a gen. in the army, and col. of the 17th reg. of foot 2
          Borough of Newport, in the Isle of Wight.
✤ Sir Richard Worsley, bart. comptroller of his majesty's houshold, gov. of the Isle of Wight, one of the verdurers of the New Forest, col. of the south batt. of Hampshire militia, F.R.S. and A.S. (*Apuldurcomb-Park, in the Isle of Wight*)   2
Hon. John St. John, brother to lord visc. Bolingbroke, surveyor-general of the crown lands,   3

House of COMMONS.

Borough of Yarmouth in the Isle of Wight.
Edward Morant, esq; (*Brockenhurst, New Forest, Hants*) 3
Edward Rushworth, esq; (White Clift Lodge, near this bor.)
Borough of Newton in the Isle of Wight.
Edward Meux Worsley, esq; (*Gatcomb in this island*) 2
John Barrington, esq; son of Sir Fitzwilliam Barrington, bart. (Swainstone, in the Isle of Wight)
Borough of Lymington.
Thomas Dummer, esq; (*Cranbury, Hants*) 3
Harry Burrard, esq; 2
Borough of Christchurch.
Sir James Harris, K. B. minister to the court of Russia.
§ John Frederick, esq; son of Sir John Frederick, bart. (*Burwood-Park, Surrey*) 2
Borough of Andover.
Sir John Griffin Griffin, K. B. a general of his Majesty's forces, col. of the first troop of horse grenad. guards, recorder of Saffron Walden, son-in-law to Mr. Clayton, Memb. for Marlow, (*Audley-End, Essex*) 3
Benjamin Lethieullier, esq; (*Norwell, near this borough*) 3
Borough of Whitchurch.
Right hon. George (Brodrick) viscount Midleton of the kingdom of Ireland, son-in-law to lord Pelham (*Pepper Harrow, near Godalmin, Surrey*) 2
✣ Rt. Hon. Thomas Townshend, cousin to visc. Townshend, (*Frognal, near Foot's Cray, Kent*) 5
Borough of Petersfield.
William Jolliffe, of this borough, esq; (*Petersfield-House, Hayton-Castle, Cumberland, and Chester le street, Durham*) 5
Thomas Samuel Jolliffe, esq; brother of the above member, (Trotton, in Sussex, and Charlton, Somersetshire)
Borough of Stockbridge.
Hon. John Luttrell, third son of visc. Carhampton, and a capt. in the royal navy (*Kimpson, Southampton*) 2
Hon. James Luttrell, fourth son of visc. Carhampton, a lieut. in the royal navy 2
Town of Southampton.
John Fuller, esq; (*Rosehill, Sussex*) 2
Hans Sloane, esq; a commissioner of the board of Trade, col. of the northern batalion of the Hampshire militia, and a trustee of the British Museum (*South Stoneham, Hants*) 3

STAFFORDSHIRE 10.
Sir John Wrottesley, bart. LL.D. brother-in-law to the duke of Grafton, a captain in the 1st reg. of foot guards, with the rank of lieut. col. in the army, (*Wrottesley, Staffordshire*) 3

House of COMMONS.

Right hon. George (Legge) visc. Lewisham, eldest son of the earl of Dartmouth, (*Sandwell, near Birmingham*) 2

Borough of Stafford.
Hon. Edward Monckton, uncle to visc. Galway, and half brother to gen. Monckton
Richard Brinsley Sheridan, esq; (Heston, Middlesex)

Borough of Tamworth.
John Courtney, esq; secretary to the master-gen. of the ordnance, and nephew to the earl of Bute
§ John Calvert, sen. esq; (*Albury-Hall, Hertfordshire*) 6

Borough of Newcastle under Line.
Right hon. George Granville-Leveson (Gower) Viscount Trentham, eldest Son of Earl Gower. 3
Archibald Macdonald, esq; bro. to lord Macdonald, son-in-law to earl Gower, and one of the Welch judges. 2

City of Litchfield.
George Anson, esq; nephew to the late lord Anson, (*Shugborough, Staffordshire*) 2
Thomas Gilbert, esq; comptroller of the King's wardrobe, and paymaster of the pensions to the widows of sea officers, (*Cotton, near Stone, Staffordshire*) 4

SUFFOLK 16.
Sir Thomas Cha. Bunbury, bart. (*Great Barton, near Bury, in this county*) 4
Sir John Rous, bart. (Henham Hall, in this county)

Borough of Ipswich.
Thomas Staunton, esq; (*Sibton Park, Suffolk, and Samford Hall, Essex*) 5
Wm. Wollaston, esq; (*Great Finborough Hall, near this borough, and Shenton Hall, Leicestershire*) 3

Borough of Dunwich.
Sir Gerrard William Van Neck, bart. (*Heveningham, Suffolk*) 3
Barne Barne, esq; (*Sotterley, in this county*) 2

Borough of Orford.
✠ Rt. hon. Francis (Seymour Conway) lord visc. Beauchamp, eldest son to the earl of Hertford, cofferer of his Majesty's household, colonel of the Warwickshire militia, and a privy counsellor in Ireland 4
Hon. Robert Seymour Conway, 3d son to the earl of Hertford, a captain in the 1st regiment of foot guards, and ranks as lieutenant colonel in the army 4

Borough of Aldeburgh.
Martyn Fonnereau, esq; 2
Philip Champion Crespigny, esq; procurator-general to the king, (Burwood, near Cobham, Surrey)

(Burwood, near Cobham, Surrey)
Borough of Eye.
Rich. Phillipfon, efq; a major-general, and col. of the 20th reg. of dragoons   4
Arnoldus James Skelton, efq; brother-in-law to earl Cornwallis
Borough of Bury St. Edmunds.
Sir Charles Davers, bart. (*Rufbrook, Suffolk*)   3
✠ Rt. hon. Henry Seymour Conway, brother to the earl of Hertford, a gen. of his Majefty's forces, gov. of Jerfey, and col. of the royal reg. of horfe guards (*Park Place, near Henly upon Thames, Berks*)   7
SURREY.   14.
Sir Jofeph Mawbey, bart. (*Vauxhall, and Botleys near Chertfey, in this county*)   4
Hon. Auguftus Keppel, uncle to the earl of Albemarle, an admiral of the blue, and one of the elder brethren of the Trinity Houfe (*Bagfhot Park, Surrey, and Elden-Hall, near Thetford, Norfolk*)   3
Borough of Gatton.
Right hon. William (Mayne) lord Newhaven, of the kingdom of Ireland, an Englifh baronet (*Gatton Park, Surrey*) 2
Robert Mayne, efq; brother to lord Newhaven, a banker in Weftminfter   2
Borough of Haflemere.
Edward Norton, efq; barrifter at law, and fon of Sir Fletcher Norton, (Wonerfh, Surrey)
§ Walter Spencer Stanhope, efq; (*Horsforth, near Leeds, and Cannon-Hall, near Barnefley, Yorkfhire*)
Borough of Bletchingley.
Sir Rob. Clayton, bart. one of the vice-prefidents of the Middlefex hofpital (*Merden, near Godftone, in this county*)   3
John Kenrick, efq; clerk of ordnance deliveries
Borough of Reigate.
Hon. John Yorke, fecond brother to the earl of Hardwicke, clerk of the crown in the court of Chancery, patentee for making out commiffions of bankruptcy, and F. R. S.   6
Sir Charles Cocks, bart. clerk of the Ord. (*Dumbleton Glouc.*)   3
Borough of Guildford.
✠ Right hon. Sir Fletcher Norton, Knt. chief juftice in eyre of his Majefty's forefts fouth of Trent, recorder of this borough, LL.D. (*Grantlay, near Ripon, Yorkfhire, and Wonerfh, near this borough*)   5

House of COMMONS.

George Onflow, efq; out ranger of Windfor foreft, and coufin to Lord Onflow, (Ockham near Ripley; and Faxgrove Lodge, near Chertfey, in this county) 4

Borough of Southwark.
Sir Richard Hotham, knt. (Merton-Place, Surrey)
Nathaniel Polhill, efq; (Peckham-Lane, Surrey) 2

SUSSEX. 20.

Rt. hon. lord George Henry Lenox, only brother to the duke of Richmond, a lieut.-gen. of his majefty's forces, and col. of the 25th reg. of foot (*Weft Stoke, in this county*) 4
Hon. Thomas Pelham, eldeft fon of lord Pelham (Stanmer, Suffex)

Borough of Horfham.
Jas. Wallace, efq; his majefty's attorney-gen. king's ferj. in the dutchy court of Lancafter, and att.-gen. and ferj. of the cos. palatine of Durham and Lancafter (*Carleton-hall, Cumb.*) 3
§ Sir George Ofborne, bart. one of the grooms of his majefty's bed-chamb. 2d major of 3d reg. of foot-guards, and mufter-maft.-gen. of the forces in Amer. (*Chickfand, Bedfordfh.*) 3

Borough of Bramber.
Thomas Thoroton, efq; (*Screveton, near Bingham, Notts*) 5
Sir Henry Gough, bart. (*Edghafton, Warwickfhire*) 2

Borough of New Shoreham.
Sir Cecil Biffhopp, bart: (Parham, Suffex)
John Peachey, efq; fon of Sir James Peachey, bart. (*Weft Dean, Suffex*) 2

Borough of Midhurft.
Henry Drummond, efq; brother-in-law to the earl of Northampton (*Wimbleton, Surrey, Langley-Broom, Bucks*) 2
§ Sir Sampfon Gideon, bart. LL.D. bro. in-law to ld. Gage, (*Abingdon-Hall, near Cambridge, and Belvidere-Houfe, near Erith, Kent*) 3

Borough of Eaft Grinfted.
✤ Rt. hon. lord George Germain, uncle to the duke of Dorfet, fecretary of ftate for the colonies, and clerk of the council in Ireland (*Stoneland Lodge, Suffex, and Drayton, Northamptonfhire*) 7
Rt. hon. Sir John Irwin, K.B. lieut. gen. of His Maj. forces, colonel of the 57th regiment of foot, commander in chief of the forces in Ireland, firft commiffioner of His Majefty's barracks, and a privy counfellor of that kingdom 4

Borough of Steyning.
Sir Thomas George Skipwith, bart. (*Newbold-Hall, Warwickfhire*) 3
§ John Bullock, efq; col. of the eaft reg. of Effex militia, (*Faulkburn-Hall, Effex*)

House of COMMONS.

Borough of Arundel.
Sir Patrick Crauford, knt. conservator of the Scotch privileges in the Netherlands
Thomas Fitzherbert, esq; (Stubbington-Lodge, near Portsm.)

Borough of Lewes.
Hon. Henry Pelham, second son of lord Pelham
Thomas Kemp, esq; of this borough.

City of Chichester.
Hon. Wm. Keppel, uncle to the earl of Albemarle, a lt. gen. of his majesty's forces, and col. of the 12th reg. of dragoons 4.
Thomas Steele, esq; (Hampnet, near this city)

WARWICKSHIRE 6.
Sir Robert Lawley, bart. (Canwell, Staffordshire)
Sir Geo. Augustus William Shuckburgh, bart. (Shuckburgh, in this county)

Borough of Warwick.
Hon. Charles Francis Greville, next brother to the Earl of Warwick, one of the lords of the admiralty, and F.R.S. 3.
Robert Ladbroke, esq; a banker in London, son of the late alderman (Idlicote, Warwickshire)

City of Coventry.
§ Sir Thomas Halifax, knt. alderman and banker of London, (Enfield, Middlesex)
§ Thomas Rogers, esq; banker, in London, (Newington-Green, Middlesex)

WESTMORLAND 4.
Sir Michael Le Fleming, bart. (Rydal, Westmoreland) 2
James Lowther, esq; (Aikton, Cumberland) 2

Borough of Appleby.
Philip Honywood, esq; a general of His Majesty's forces, colonel of the 4th regiment of horse, and governor of Kingston upon Hull (Markes Hall, Essex) 5
§ Hon. William Pitt, brother to the earl of Chatham

WILTSHIRE 34.
Charles Penruddock, esq; (Compton Chamberlain, in this co.) 3.
Ambrose Goddard, esq; (Swindon, in this county) 3

City of New Sarum.
William Hussey, esq; (of this city) 4
Hon. Will. Henry Bouverie, next brother to the E. of Radnor 2

Borough of Devizes.
Sir James Tylney Long, bart. nephew and heir to lord Tylney (Draycot, in this county, near Chippenham, and Admiston, near Blandford, Dorsetshire) 4
§ Henry Jones, esq; a merchant, in London

Borough of Marlborough.

Right hon. James (Stopford) earl of Courtown, in Ireland a gentleman of the prince of Wales's bed-chamber, (Beate-Hall, in Cheshire, and Courtown, Wexford, Irel.)
William Woodley, esq;

Borough of Chippenham.

Henry Dawkins, esq; son-in-law to the earl of Portmore, LL.D. F.R.S. and F. S. A. (Standlinch, Wilts)   2
Giles Hudson, esq; a merchant, in London

Borough of Calne.

John Dunning, esq; barrister at law, recorder of Bristol (Neal Ashburton, Devon, and Putney Heath, Surrey)   3
✢ Right honourable Isaac Barré   4

Borough of Malmesbury.

Rt. hon. Arthur (Hill) viscount Fairford, eldest son of the earl of Hillsborough   2
§ John Calvert, jun. esq; (Albury-Hall, Hertfordshire)

Borough of Cricklade.

John Macpherson, esq;   2
Paul Benfield, esq;

Borough of Hindon.

Lloyd Kenyon, esq; chief justice of Chester, and one of the king's counsel (Gredington, in Flintshire, near Whitchurch, Salop, and Marsh-Gate, near Richmond, Surrey)
Nathaniel William Wraxall, esq;

Borough of Old Sarum.

Thomas Pitt, esq; recorder of Oakhampton (Boconnie near Lestwithiel, Cornwall)   5
Pinckney Wilkinson, esq; (Burnham, in the county of Norf.) 2

Borough of Heytesbury.

William A'Court Ashe, esq; a general of his Majesty's forces, and colonel of the 11th regiment of foot   3
§ Francis Burton, esq; barrister at law, and recorder of woodstock

Borough of Westbury.

Sam. Estwick, esq; LL.D. agent for the colony of Barbadoes 2
John Whalley Gardiner, esq; (Roche-Court, n. Fareham, Herts)

Borough of Wotton-Bassett.

Hon. Henry St. John, brother to ld. visc. Bolingbroke, one of the grooms of his Maj. bedchamber, a major-general, and col. of the 36th reg. of foot   2
William Strahan, esq; joint-printer to his Majesty   2

Borough of Ludgarshall.

Rt. hon. Peniston (Lamb) viscount Melbourn of the kingdom of Ireland (Brocket-hall near Hatfield, Herts, and Melbourne, Derbyshire)   3

Geo. Auguſtus Selwyn, eſq; paymaſter of the Board of Works, ſurveyor of the meltings and clerk of the irons in the Mint, and regiſter in the court of Chancery in the iſland of Barbadoes (*Matſon, near Glouceſter*) 6

Borough of *Wilton*.
Right Hon. George *Auguſtus* (*Herbert*) lord *Herbert*, eldeſt ſon of the earl of *Pembroke*
Rt. hon. William Gerard Hamilton, chancellor of the Exchequer and a privy counſellor in Ireland (*Hampton Court*) 6

Borough of *Downton*.
Hon. Hen. Seymour Conway, ſecond ſon of the e. of Hertford, deputy-cofferer of his majeſty's houſhold, clerk of the Hanaper in Ireland, and conſt. of Dublin caſtle 4
Robert Shaftoe, eſq. 2

Borough of *Great Bedwin*.
Paul Methuen, eſq; fa.-in-law to ld. Boſton (*Corſham, Wilts*) 3
Sir Merrick Burrell, bart. one of the directors of Greenwich Hoſpital (*Weſt Grinſtead, Suſſex*) 6

WORCESTERSHIRE 9.
Hon. Edward Foley, eſq; next brother to lord Foley (*Whitley Court, in this county*) 3
William Lygon, eſq; (*Madresfield in this county*) 2

Borough of *Eveſham*.
Sir John Ruſhout, bart. (*Northwick, Worceſterſhire, and Harrow on the Hill, Middleſex*) 3
Charles William Boughton Rouſe, eſq; brother to ſir Edward Boughton, bart. (Rouſe-Lynch, Worceſterſhire)

Borough of *Wich*, or *Droytwich*.
Hon. And. Foley, eſq; ſecond brother to lord Foley (*Newport, Herefordſhire*) 2
Edward Winnington, eſq; only ſon of Sir Edward Winnington, bart. (*Stamford, Worceſterſhire*.) 2

Borough of *Bewdley*.
Right hon. William Henry (Lyttelton) lord Weſtcote, of the kingdom of Ireland, a lord of the treaſury, and high ſteward of this borough (*Hagley Park, near Stourbridge, Worceſterſhire*) 2

City of *Worceſter*.
Thomas Bates Rous, eſq; 2
Hon. *William Ward*, brother to viſcount *Dudley* and *Ward*

BARONS of the *Cinque Ports* 16.

Town and Port of *Haſtings*, in *Suſſex*.
Rt. hon. Henry (Temple) viſc. Palmerſton, of the kingdom of Ireland, LL.D. one of the lords of the treaſury (*Broad-*

[E]

lands near *Rumfey*, *Hants*, and *Eaft Sheen*, *Surrey*) 4
John Ord, efq; attorney-gen. of the duchy court of Lancafter 2

Town and Port of Sandwich, in Kent.
Philip Stephens, efq; fec. to the adm. and to the charity for the benefit of fea-officers widows (*North End, Midd.*) 5
Sir Rich. Sutton, bart. one of the lords of the treafury, counfel to the board of Ordnance, and record. of St. Albans (*Norwood Park, Notts, and Moulfey, Surrey*) 3

Town and Port of Dover, in Kent.
John Henniker, efq; fon-in-law to fir Jn. Major, bart. a merch. in Lond. a direct. of the Lond. Affur. and F.R.S. (*Stratford near Bow, and Newton Hall near Dunmow, both in Effex*) 3
John Trevanion, efq; a merchant in London 2

Town and Port of New Romney, in Kent.
Sir Edward Dering, bart. (*Surrenden near Afhford, Kent*) 4
Richard Jackfon, efq; king's counfel, counfel to the Board of Trade, Bank, and South Sea companies, and one of the counfel to the univerfity of Cambridge 4

Town and Port of Hythe, in Kent.
Wm. Evelyn, efq; capt. of Sangate caftle (*St. Clair in this co.*) 3
Sir Cha. Farnaby, bart. (*Kippington n. Seven Oaks, in this co.*) 4

Town of Rye, in Suffex.
William Dickinfon, efq; (*near Somerton, Somerfetfhire*) 3
Hon. Thomas Onflow, efq; eldeft fon of lord Onflow (*Weft Clandon, near Guildford, Surrey*) 2

Town of Winchelfea, in Suffex.
✣ Right Hon. Charles Wolfran Cornwall, efq; SPEAKER, and chief juftice in Eyre, north of Trent (*Barton Priors near Winchefter*) 3
John Nefbitt, efq; (Winchelfea, and Kefton, near Bromley, Kent)

Town and Port of Seaford, in Suffex.
John Durand, efq; a merchant in London, and one of the elder brethren of the Trinity H. (*Carfhalton, Surrey*) 2
§ Chriftopher D'Oyley, efq; comptroller of the army accounts (*Hampton Court*) 2

WALES 24.

County of ANGLESEA 2.
Rt. hon. Tho. James (Bulkeley) lord vifc. Bulkeley, of the kingdom of Ireland (*Baronhill, near Beaumaris, Anglefea,* 2

Borough of Beaumaris.
Hon. Sir George Warren, K. B. (*Poynton, Chefhire, Widdring-
ton Caftle, Northumb. and Fetcham, Surrey*) 4
County of BRECON 2.
Charles Morgan, efq; lieut. of this co. (*Tredegar, Monmouth-
fhire, Ruperra, Glamorganfhire, Brickendonbury, Herts,
and Treago, Herefordfhire*) 4
Town of Brecon.
Sir Charles Gould, Knt. judge advocate general to the army,
chancellor of the diocefe of Sarum, and LL.D. (*Ealing,
Middlefex, and Stretham, Cambridgefhire*) 2
County of CARDIGAN 2.
Rt. hon. Wilmot (Vaughan) earl Lifburne, of the kingdom
of Ireland, lord lieut. of this county, and one of the lords
commiffioners of the admiralty (*Mambead near Chudleigh,
Devonfhire, Grindon-Ridge near Berwick, and Crofswood in
this county*) 5.
Town of Cardigan.
John Campbell, efq; col. of the militia of this county (Glan-
fraed, in this county, and Stackpole-court, Pembrokefhire)
County of CAERMARTHEN 2.
John Vaughan, efq; lord lieut. and cuft. rot. of this
county (*Golden-grove, Caermarthenfhire*) 2
Borough of Caermarthen.
George Philipps, efq; (Coedgaing, near this borough)
County of CAERNARVON 2.
John Parry, efq; attorney-general of the North Wales circuit,
conftable of Conway Caftle, and fellow of the Antiquarian
Society) (Wernvawr, in this county)
Borough of Caernarvon.
Glynn Wynn, efq; only brother to the Rt. hon. lord Newbo-
rough (*Caernarvon town, in this county*) 3
County of DENBIGH 2.
Sir Watkin Williams Wynne, bart. lieut. and cuft. rot. of Me-
rionethfh. (*Llanverda, Shropfh. and Winftay in this county*) 3
Borough of Denbigh.
Richard Myddelton, efq; lieut. cuft. rot. and col. of the militia
of this co. and rec. of this bo. (*Chirke Caftle, Denbighfh.*) 6.
County of FLINT 2.
Sir Roger Moftyn, bart. lieutenant of this county, and col.
of the militia thereof (*Moftyn, Flintfhire*) 5
Borough of Flint.
Watkin Williams, efq; major of the Shropfhire militia.
(*Penbedw, Denbighfhire, and Erbiftock, Flintfhire*) 2.
County of GLAMORGAN 2.
Charles Edwin, efq; (Lanmihangle, in this county),

[E 2]

House of COMMONS.

Borough of Cardiff.
Sir Herbert Mackworth, bart. col. of the Glamorganshire militia (*Gnoll n. Neath, Glamorgansh. and Buntingdale, Shropsh.*) 4

County of MERIONETH 1.
Evan Lloyd Vaughan, efq; (*Corfygedol, in this county*) 2

County of MONTGOMERY 2.
William Moftyn Owen, efq; (Bryngwyn, in this county)
Borough of Montgomery.
Whitfhed Keene, efq; brother-in-law to the earl of Dartmouth, furveyor of his Majefty's works, and fecretary to the lord chamberlain of His Majefty's houfhold 3

County of PEMBROKE 3.
Hugh Owen, efq; eldeft fon of fir Wm. Owen, bart. lieut. cuft. rot. and col. of the militia of this county (*Orielton in this county, and Bodowen, Anglefea*) 3
Borough of Pembroke.
Hugh Owen, of this borough, efq; 2
Town of Haverfordweft.
Right Hon. William (Edwardes) lord Kenfington, of the kingdom of Ireland (*Johnftone near this borough*) 6

County of RADNOR 2.
Thomas Johnes, efq; (*Croft. Caftle, Herefordsh. and Llanvar, Cardiganshire*) 2
Borough of New-Radnor.
Edward Lewis, efq; (*Downton, near Radnor, and Putney, Surrey*) 2

SCOTLAND 45.

County of ABERDEEN.
Alexander Garden, of Troup, efq; 3

Kintore, Bamff, Cullen, Elgin, and Invecurie.
Staates Long Morris, efq; father-in-law to the duke of Gordon, col. of the 61ft reg. of foot, a major gen. in his majefty's fervice (*Huntley Lodge, North Britain*) 2

County of AIR.
Hon. Hugh Montgomery, efq, brother to the earl of Eglintoun, and a major of the Weft Fencible regiment

Burghs of Irvine, Air, Rothefay, Inverary, and Campbeltown.
Sir Archibald Edmonftone, bart. (*Duntreath, North-Britain*) 4

House of COMMONS.

County of ARGYLL.
✤ Rt. hon. lord Fred. Campbell, next bro. to the d. of Argyle, lord regifter of Scotl. (*Ardincaple, near Dumbarton*) 3

County of BAMFF.
Rt. hon. James (Duff) earl of Fife in the kingdom of Ireland (*Duff-Houfe, Bamffshire*) 4

County of BERWICK.
Hugh Scott, of Harden, in this county, efq; grandfon to the earl of Marchmont.

Burghs of Lauder, Haddington, Dunbar, North-Berwick, and Jedburgh.
Francis Charteris, junior, of Amisfield, efq; nephew to the member for Sutherlandfhire 2

County of CAITHNESS.
John Sinclair, of U.bfter, efq; (Thuro Caftle, in this county)

Wick, Tain, Dingwall, Dornock, and Kirkwall.
Colonel Charles Rofs, of Morangie

County of DUMBARTON.
✤ Rt. hon. lord Fred. Campbell, next bro. to the d. of Argyll, lord regifter of Scotl. (*Coombank, near Seven Oaks, Kent*) 3

Burghs of Dumbarton, Rutherglen, Glafgow, and Renfrew.
John Crauford, efq; chamberlain of Fife (*Achinames and Errol, North Britain*) 2

County of DUMFRIES.
Sir Robert Laurie, of Maxwelltown, bart. ranks as a lieut. col. and is major to the 7th regiment of dragoons 2

Burghs of Dumfries, Sanquhar, Kircudbright, Lochmaben, and Annan.
Sir Robert Herries, knt. a banker in London (Richmond, Surrey)

County of EDINBURGH.
Henry Dundas, efq; lord advocate for Scotland, and one of the keepers of the fignet (*Melville, near Edinburgh*) 2

City of Edinburgh.
William Miller, junior, of Barfkinning, efq; fon of the lord chief-juftice Clerk

County of ELGIN.
Right hon. ld. Wm. Gordon, brother to the duke of Gordon 2

County of FIFE.
Robert Skene, of Hallyards, efq; a major general in England, and adjutant general in Scotland

[E 3]

House of COMMONS.

Burghs of Cupar, Perth, Dundee, St. Andrews, and Forfar.
George Dempster, of Dunichen, esq; secretary to the Order of the Thistle for life 4

Burghs of Kirkaldie, Bruntisland, Kinghorn, and Dysart.
John Henderson, esq; eldest son of Sir Robert Henderson, bart. *(Fordell, and Earl's-ball, both in the county of Fife)* 2

Burghs of Craill, Kilrenny, Anstruther-Easter, Pittenween, and Anstruther-Wester.
Sir John Anstruther, of Anstruther, bart.

County of FORFAR.
Rt. hon. Wm. (Maule,) earl Panmure, of the kingd. of Irel. a gen. of H's Majesty's forces, and col. of the royal N. Brit. dragoons *(Panmure and Brechin-Castle, both in this county)* 8

Burghs of Aberbrothock, Aberdeen, Montrose, Brechin, and Inverbervie.
Adam Drummond, esq; 2

County of HADDINGTON.
Hugh Dalrymple, jun. of Northberwick, esq;

County of INVERNESS.
Hon. Simon Fraser, of Lovat, a lieut. general of his Majesty's forces, and col. of the 71st regiment of foot 4

County of KINKARDINE.
Rt. hon. lord Adam Gordon, of Cuttieshillock and Woodtoun, uncle to the D. of Gordon, gov. of Tinmouth castle, a lieut. gen. of His Maj. forces, and col. of the 26th reg. of foot 4

Stewartry of KIRKUDBRIGHT.
Peter Johnston, of Carnsalloch, esq;

County of KINROSS.
George Graham, esq; (Kinross-house, in this county)

County of LANERK.
And. Stuart, of Craigthorn, in this co. esq; one of the keepers of the signet in Scotl. and one of the lords of trade in Engl. 2

County of LINLITHGOW.
Sir Wm. Augustus Cunynghame, of Livingstone, bart. nephew to the earl of Eglintoun, one of the clerks-comptroller of the board of green cloth *(Livingstone, in West Lothian)* 2

County of CROMARTIE.
George Ross, esq;

House of COMMONS.

Burghs of Inverness, Nairn, Forres, and Fortrose.
Sir Hector Monro, of Novar, K. B. barrack. maft. gen. in Scotl. a maj. gen. in the Eaft Indies, and commander in chief of the company's forces at Madras   3

Counties of ORKNEY and ZETLAND.)
Robert Buckie, of Tankerness, esq;

County of PEEBLES.
Alexander Murray, esq; of Murrayfield, his majesty's solicitor general for Scotland

Burghs of Culross, Dumfermline, Innerskeithing, Queensferry, and Stirling.
James Campbell, esq; a major in the Weft Fencible regiment

County of PERTH.
Hon. Ja. Murray, uncle to the d. of Athol, gov. of Fort William, and col. of a reg. of Highlanders (*Strowan, North Britain*)   3

County of RENFREW.
John Shaw Stewart, of Greenock, esq; youngest son of sir Mich. Stewart, of Black Hall, bart. (Shaw House, Renfrewshire)

County of ROSS.
Lord Macleod, col. of the 73d regiment of foot.

County of ROXBURGH.
Sir G. Elliot, of Minto, bart. counsellor at law, son to the late member   2

County of SELKIRK.
John Pringle, of Clifton, esq;   4

Burghs of Selkirk, Lanerk, Peebles, and Linlithgow.
Sir Ja. Cockburn, of Langton, bart. heretable usher of the white rod (*Petersham, n. Richmond, Surrey*)   3

County of STIRLING.
Thomas Dundas, of Castlecary, esq; only son to sir Lawrence Dundas, bart. (*Upleatham, Yorkshire*)   4

County of SUTHERLAND.
Hon. James Wemyss, of Wemyss, son of the late E. of Wemyss, a lieut. in his Majesty's navy.   4

County of WIGTOWN.
Hon. Keith Stewart, of Glafferton, only brother to the earl of Galloway, a captain in the royal navy   3

Stranrawer, Wigtown, Whithorn, New-Galloway.
William Adam, of Woodstone, esq;   4

An *Alphabetical* LIST of the Counties, Cities, and Boroughs, with the *Pages* where their representatives are to be found.

Bingdon	21	Canterbury	32	Grantham	33
Agmondesh.	22	Carlisle	25	Grimsby	33
Aldborough York	28	Castle-Rising	34	Guildford	41
Aldeburgh	40	Cheshire	22	Hampshire	29
Andover	39	Chester	23	Harwich	30
Appleby	43	Chichester	43	Haslemere	41
Arundel	43	Chippenham	44	Hastings	45
Ashburton	26	Chip. Wicomb	22	Hedon	29
Aylesbury	22	Christ-church	39	Heytesbury	44
Banbury	36	Cirencester	30	Helston	24
Barnstaple	27	Clitheroe	32	Herefordshire	30
Bath	38	Cockermouth	25	Hereford-city	31
Beaumaris	47	Colchester	30	Hertfordshire	31
Bedford-county	21	Corff-castle	28	Hertford-town	31
Bedford-town	21	Cornwall-county	23	Higham Ferrers	35
Bedwin, Great	45	Coventry	43	Hindon	44
Beeralston	26	Cricklade	44	Honiton	26
Berkshire	21	Cumberland-co.	25	Horsham	42
Berwick	35	Dartmouth	26	Huntingdonshire	31
Beverly	28	Derbyshire	25	Huntingdon town	31
Bewdly	45	Derby	26	Hythe	46
Bishop's-castle	37	Devizes	43	Ivelchester	37
Blechingly	41	Devonshire	26	Ipswich	40
Bodmyn	23	Dorsetshire	27	Kent	31
Boroughbridge	28	Dorchester	27	King's-Lynn	34
Bossinney	24	Dover	46	Kingston on Hull	30
Boston	33	Downton	45	Knaresborough	29
Brackley	35	Droytwich	45	Lancashire	32
Bramber	42	Dunwich	40	Lancaster	32
Bridport	28	Durham-county	28	Launceston	23
Bridgnorth	37	Durham-city	28	Leicestershire	33
Bridgwater	38	East-Looe	24	Leicester	33
Bristol	38	East Grinsted	42	Leominster	31
Buckingham-co.	22	Essex-county	30	Lewes	43
Buckingham to.	22	Evesham	45	Lincolnshire	33
Bury St. Edmunds	41	Exeter-city	27	Lincoln	33
Calne	44	Eye	41	Liskerret or Liskeard	23
Callington	25	Fowey	25		
Cambridge-coun.	22	Gatton	41	Litchfield	40
Cambridge-univ.	23	Gloucestershire	30	Liverpool	32
Cambridge-town	23	Gloucester-city	30	London	34
Camelford	24	Grampound	24	Lostwithiel	23

Ludlow	37	Petersfield	39	Surry	41
Ludgarshall	44	Plymouth	26	Suffex	42
Lyme Regis	27	Plympton-Earle	26	Tamworth	40
Lymington	39	Poole	28	Taviftock	27
Maidftone	32	Pontefract	29	Taunton	38
Malden	30	Portfmouth	38	Tewkfbury	30
Malmefbury	44	Prefton	32	Thetford	34
Malton	29	Queenborough	32	Thirfk	29
Marlborough	44	Reading	21	Tiverton	26
Marlow, Great	22	Retford	36	Totnefs	27
Melcombe Regis	27	Richmond	29	Tregony	24
Midhurft	42	Reigate	41	Truro	23
Middlefex	34	Ripon	29	Wallingford	22
Milborne Port	38	Rochefter	32	Warwickfhire	43
Minehead	38	Romney, New	46	Warwick	43
Mitchell	25	Rutlandfhire	37	Wareham	26
Monmouthfhire	34	Rye	46	Wells-city	38
Monmouth	34	Salop-county	37	Wendover	22
Morpeth	35	Saltafh	24	Wenlock	37
Newark onTrent	36	Sandwich	46	Weobley	31
Newcaftle under Line	40	Sarum, New	43	Weftbury	44
		Sarum, Old	44	Weft-Looe	24
Newcaftle on T.	35	Scarborough	29	Weftminfter	34
Newport, Hants	38	Seaford	46	Weftmorland	43
Newport, Corn.	25	Shaftsbury	28	Weymouth	27
Newton, Lanc.	33	Shoreham	42	Whitchurch	39
Newtown, Hants	39	Shrewfbury	37	Wigan	32
Norfolk	34	Somerfetfhire	37	Wilton	45
Northallerton	29	Southampton-co.	38	Wiltfhire	43
Northamptonfh.	35	Southampton-to.	39	Winchelfea	46
Northampton	35	Southwark	42	Windfor	21
Northumberland	35	Staffordfhire	39	Winchefter	38
Norwich	35	Stafford	40	Woodftock	36
Nottinghamfhire	35	Stamford	33	Wotton-Baffet	44
Nottingham, to.	36	Steyning	42	Worcefterfhire	45
Oakhampton	26	Stockbridge	39	Worcefter	45
Orford	40	St. Albans	31	Yarmouth, Great	34
Oxfordfhire	36	St. Germans	25	Yarmouth, Bor.	39
Oxford-univerfity	36	St. Ives	25	Yorkfhire	28
Oxford	36	St. Mawes	25	York City	29
Penryn	24	Sudbury	41	WALES	46
Peterborough	35	Suffolk	40	SCOTLAND	48

AN ALPHABETICAL LIST
OF THE
House of COMMONS, &c.

Those printed in *Italic Characters*, were new Members at the General Election 1780.
§ Chosen since the General Election.
† Voted in upon Petition.
N. B. *Where the Place of Residence is left blank, they are chiefly out of Town; but any Gentleman sending an Account of the Residence or Removal of any Member, it shall be carefully inserted.*

Names.	Where chose.	Town-Residence.
ADAM, William	Stranrawer, &c.	Chesterfield-street
Adeane, Ja. Warw.	*Cambridge*	*Harley-street, Cav.-sq.*
Aislabie, William	Ripon	Grosvenor-square
Allen, Benjamin	Bridgewater	Parliament-street
Althorpe, Viscount	*Northampton*	
Ambler, Charles	Boroughbridge	Queen's-square
Amcotts, Wharton	*East Retford*	*Suffolk-street*
Anderson, Evelyn	Beverley	Arlington-street
Annesley, Francis	Reading	Upper Grosvenor-str.
Anson, George	Litchfield	St. James's-square
Anstruther, Sir John	*Craill, &c.*	*Halfmoon-street*
Arcedekne, Chaloner	*Wallingford*	*Harley-street*
Ashe, Wm. A'Court	Heytesbury	Park-street
Astley, Sir Edward	Norfolk	Wimpole-street
Atkinson, Christopher	*Heyden*	*Park street*
Aubrey, John	Wallingford	Hamilton-street
Backie, Robert	*Orkney & Zetland*	
Bacon, Edward	Norwich	Bruton-street
Bacon, Anthony	Aylesbury	Copthall-court
Baker, William	Hertford	Hill-street
Bampfylde, Sir Ch. Warwick }	Exeter	Halfmoon-street
Bankes, Henry	*Corff Castle*	
Baring, John	Exeter	St. Alban's-street
Barne, Barne	Dunwich	Temple
Barré, Rt. hon. Isaac	Calne	Manchester-buildings
Barrington, John	*Newton, Hants*	*James-st. Bedford-row*
Barrow, Charles	Gloucester	Howard-street, Strand
Bassett, Sir Francis	*Penryn*	Portland-place
Bassett, Francis	*Barnstaple*	Pall-mall
Bateman, Viscount	Leominster	Park-lane

An Alphabetical List of the HOUSE OF COMMONS. 55

Names.	Where chose.	Town-Residence.
Bayntun, Andrew	Weobly	Portman-street
Beauchamp, Viscount	Orford	Stanhope-str. May-fa.
Beckford, Richard	Bridport	Sackville-street
Benfield, Paul	Cricklade	Grosvenor-place
Bentinck, ld. Ed. Ch.	Nottinghamshire	Charles-st. Berk.-sq.
Benyon, Richard	Peterborough	Grosvenor-square
Bertie, lord Robert	Boston	Mortimer-street
Bertie, hon. Peregrine	Oxford city	Pall-mall
Bishopp, Sir Cecil	Shoreham	St. James's-street
Blackwell, Samuel	Cirencester	Wellbeck-street
Blake, Sir Patrick	Sudbury	Charles-st. Cavend. sq.
Bond, John	Corff Castle	Parliament-street
Boone, Charles	Ashburton	Soho-square
Bootle Rich. Wilbr.	Chester	Bloomsbury-square
Boscawen, Hugh	St. Mawes	Halfmoon-street
Bouverie, hon. W. Henry	New Sarum	David-street
Bowes, And. Robinson	Newcastle	Grosvenor-square
Bowlby, Thomas	Launceston	Park-street
Boyd, John	Wareham	Great George-str. West.
Braddyll, Wilson	Lancaster	Grosvenor-street
Bramston, Th. Berney	Essex	Clifford-street
Brickdale, Matthew	Bristol	Delahay-street
Bridgeman, Henry Simpson	Wigan	St. James's-square
Bridgman, Sir Henry	Wenlock	St. James's-square
Brown, Launcelot	Totness	Lincoln's-inn New-squ.
Brudenell, Geo. Brid.	Rutlandshire	Great George-street
Bulkeley, Viscount	Anglesea	Berkeley-square
Bull, Frederick	London	Leadenhall-street
Buller, John	Eastlooe	Privy-gardens
Buller, John	Westlooe	Lincoln's-inn-fields
§ Bullock, John	Steyning	
Bunbury, Sir Tho. Charles	Suffolk	Whitehall
Burgoyne, John	Preston	Hertford-street
§ Burke, Edmund	Malton	Charles-st. St. Ja.-sq.
Burrard, Harry	Lymington	Conduit-street
Burrell, Sir Merrick	Bodmin	Great George-street
§ Burton, Francis	Heytesbury	
Byng, George	Middlesex	Berkeley-square
§ Calvert, John	Tamworth	Portman-square
§ Calvert, John, jun.	Malmsbury	
Campbell, L. Fred.	Dumbartonshire and Argyllshire	Craig's-court, Charing-cross

2

An Alphabetical List of the HOUSE OF COMMONS.

Names.	Where chose.	Town-Residence.
Campbell, John	Cardigan	Harley-street
Campbell, James	Culross, &c.	Adelphi
Cafwall, Timothy	Brackley	Davis ftr. Berkley-fq.
Cavendish, Lord John	York	New-ftr. Spring-gard.
Cavendish, Lord Rich.	Derbyshire	Savile-row
Cavendish, Lord G. Aug. Henry	Derby	Hertford-ftr. May Fa.
Cecil, Henry	Stamford	Harley-street
Charteris, Francis	Lauder, &c.	Lower Grofvenor-ftr.
Chaytor, William	Heyden	Parliament-street
Child, Robert	Wells	Berkeley-fquare
Clarges, Sir Thomas	Lincoln	Tylney-street
Clavering, Sir Tho.	Durham County	Bruton-ftreet
Clayton, Sir Robert	Blechingley	Hill-ftreet
Clayton, William	Great Marlow	
Clerke, Sir Phil. Jenn.	Totnefs	Knightfbridge
Clevland, John	Barnftaple	Savile-row
Clinton, Lord J. P.	East Retford	New Palace-yard
Clinton, Sir Henry	Newark	(in America)
Clive, Lord	Ludlow	Berkley-fquare
Clive, William	Bishop's Caftle	Arlington-ftreet
Cockburn, Sir James	Selkirk, &c.	Charlotte-ft. Bloomf.
Cocks, Sir Charles	Ryegate	Cavendish-fquare
Codrington, Sir Wm.	Tewkefbury	Davies-ftreet
Cogbill, John	Newport, Cornw.	Wimpole-ftreet
Coke, Thos. Will.	Norfolk	Hanover fquare
Coke, Dan. Parker	Nottingham	Temple
Coke, Edward	Derby	
Conway, Rt. hon. H. S.	St. Edmondfbury	Warwick-ftreet, Charing-crofs
Conway, Hon. H. S.	Downton	Stanhope-ftreet
Conway, Hon. R. S.	Orford	Upper Brook-ftreet
Cooper, Sir Grey	Saltafh	Parliament-ftreet
Cornewall, Sir Geo.	Herefordfhire	Stanhope-ftreet
Cornewall, Fred.	Ludlow	Lincoln's-inn
Cornwall, Rt. Hn. C. Wolf. SPEAK.	Winchelfea	Privy-gardens
Cotton, Sir R. S.	Chefhire	
Courtney, John	Tamworth	Brainfton-ft. Marylebo.
Courtown, Earl	Marlborough	Halfmoon-ftreet
Coxe, Rich. Hippif.	Somerfetfhire	Clerges-ftreet
Craufurd, Sir Patrick	Arundel	Piccadilly
Crauford John	Dumbarton, &c.	Grafton-place
Crefpigny, Philip Champion	Sudbury, & Aldeborough, Suff.	Old Palace-yard, Weftminfter
Crewe, John	Chefhire	Grofvenor-fquare

An Alphabetical List of the HOUSE OF COMMONS.

Names.	Where chose.	Town-Residence.
Cunynghame, Sir Will. Auguftus }	Linlithgowfhire	Queen-ftr. May-fair
Curzon, Hon. Nat.	Derbyfhire	Somerfet-ftreet
Cuft, Peregrine	Ilchefter	Great George-ftreet
Cuft, Fra. Cockayne	Grantham	Lincoln's-inn
Dalrymple, Hugh	*Haddingtonfhire*	*Bruton-ftreet*
Damer, hon. George	Dorchefter	
Darby, George	*Plymouth*	*Cavendifh Square*
Darker, John	Leicefter	St. Barthol. Hofpital
Davenport, Thomas	*Newton, Lancafh.*	*Serjeants Inn*
Davers, Sir Charles	St. Edmondfbury	Hanover-fquare
Dawes, John	*Tregony*	*Sackville-ftreet*
Dawkins, Henry,	Chippenham	Portman-fquare
De Grey, Hon. Tho.	Leftwithiel	Upper Harley-ftreet
Delaval, Sir J. H.	Berwick	Hanover Square
Delme, Peter	Morpeth	Grofvenor fquare
Dempfter, George	Cupar, &c.	Berners-ftreet
Dering, Sir Edward	New Romney	Mansfield-ftreet
Dickenfon, William	Rye	Queen-Anne-ftreet
Dimfdale, Baron	*Hertford*	*Lincoln's-inn-fields*
§ D'Oyly, Chrift.	Seaford	Charles-ft.Berkley-fq
Dodd, John	Reading	Audley-fquare
Dolben, Sir William	*Oxford Univerfity*	*Charles-ftr. Cav.-fq.*
Douglas, Jn. St. Leger	Weobley	Pall-mall
Drake, William	Agmondefham	Grofvenor-fquare
Drake, William, jun.	Ditto	George-ftr. Hanov. fq.
Drummond, Henry	Midhurft	Pall-mall
Drummond, Adam	Aberbrothock, &c	Golden-fquare
Dummer, Thomas	Lymington	Mortimer-ftreet
Duncannon, Vifc.	*Knarefborough*	*Cavendifh Square*
Duncomb, Henry	*Yorkfhire*	
Dundas, Sir Lawrence	Richmond	Arlington-ftreet
Dundas, Thomas	Stirlingfhire	Hertford-ftreet
Dundas, Henry	Edinburghfhire	Savile-row
Dunning, John	Calne	Lincoln's-inn
Duntze, Sir John	Tiverton	Pall-mall
Durand, John	Seaford	Lime-ftreet
§ Dutton, James	Gloucefterfhire	
Eden, Sir John	Durham County	Downing-ftreet
Eden, Rt. Hon. Will.	Woodftock	(Ireland)
Edmonftone, Sir Arch.	Irvine, &c.	Argyll-ftreet
Edwin, Charles	*Glamorganfhire*	

F

58　An Alphabetical List of the HOUSE OF COMMONS.

Names.	Where chose.	Town-Residence.
Egerton, Sir Thomas	Lancashire	St. James's-street
Egerton, John Wm.	Brackley	Albemarle-street
Eliot, Edw. James	St. Germains	Spring-gardens
Eliot, Edward	Cornwall	Spring-gardens
Elliot, Sir Gilbert	Roxburghshire	Park-st. Westminster
Ellis, Welbore	Weymouth, &c.	Little Brooke-street
Elwes, John	Berkshire	Welbeck-street
Estwick, Samuel	Westbury	Berkley-st. Portm. sq.
Evelyn, William	Hythe & Helstone	Charles-str. Berk.-sq.
Ewer, William	Dorchester	Lincoln's-inn-fields
Eyre, Anthony	Boroughbridge	Clifford-street
Eyre, Francis	Great Grimsbey	Cecil-street, Strand
Fairford, Viscount	Malmsbury	Bruton-street
Farrer, Thomas	Wareham	Pall Mall
Fane, Hon. Henry	Lime Regis	Berners-street
Farnaby, Sir Charles	Hythe	Pall-mall
§ Fielding, visc.	Beeralston	
Fife, Earl of	Bamffshire	Whitehall
Fitzherbert, Thomas	Arundel	Bond-street
Fitzpatrick, Hon. Rd.	Tavistock	Audley-square
Fleming, Sir Mich. Le	Westmorland	St. James's-square
Fletcher, Henry	Cumberland	Southampton-row
Foley, Hon. Edward	Worcestershire	Bentinck-street
Foley, Hon. Andrew	Droitwich	Park-street
Fonnereau, Martyn	Aldborough, Suff.	Charlot.-str. Bloomsb.
§ Forester, George	Wenlock	St. Alban's-street
Fox, Hon. Ch. James	Westminster	St. James's-street
Fraser, Simon	Invernessshire	Downing-street
Frederick, Sir Charles	Queensborough	Berkeley-square
§ Frederick, John	Christchurch	Savile-row
Fuller, John	Southampton	Welbeck-street
Galway, Viscount	Pontefract	Hill-street
Garden, Alexander	Aberdeenshire	Half-moon-street
Gardiner, John Whal.	Westbury	
Garforth, John Baynes	Cockermouth	Brook-street
Gascoigne, Sir Thomas	Thirsk	Piccadilly
Gascoyne, Bamber	Truro	Admiralty
Gascoyne, Bamber, jun.	Liverpool	Admiralty
Germain, Lord Geo.	East Grinstead	Pall-mall
§ Gideon, Sir Sampson	Midhurst	St. James's-square
Gilbert, Thomas	Litchfield	Queen-str. Westminstr.

| Crewe, John | Cheshire | Grosvenor-square |

An Alphabetical List of the HOUSE OF COMMONS.

Names.	Where chose.	Town-Residence.
Gipps, George	Canterbury	
Goddard, Ambrose	Wiltshire	Savile-row
Gordon, Lord Adam	Kincardineshire	Golden-square
Gordon, Ld. Will.	Elginshire	Green-park Lodge
Gordon, Sir Will.	Portsmouth	Curzon-str. May-fair
Gough, Sir Henry	Bramber	Bruton-street
Gould, Sir Charles	Brecon	Horse-guards, Whith.
Graham, Marquis	Richmond	*Upper Grosvenor-st.*
Graham, George	Kinrosshire	*Sackville-street*
Graves, William	East Looe	Inner Temple
Gregory, Robert	Rochester	Berners-street
Grenville, Tho.	Bucks	St. James's-street
Grenville, James, jun.	Buckingham	Conduit-street
Greville, Hon. Charles	Warwick	Saint James's-square
Grey, Hon. Booth	Leicester	Charles-str. Berk.-sq.
Griffin, Sir John } Griffin	Andover	New Burlington-street
Grosvenor, Thomas	Chester	Cavendish-square
Grove, Wm. Chafin	Weymouth, &c.	Somerset-street
Guise, Sir William	Gloucestershire	Seymour-place
Gulston, Joseph	Poole	*Pall-mall*
Hale, Francis	St. Michael	Whitehall
Halliday, John	Taunton	Parliament-street
§ Hallifax, Sir Tho.	Coventry	Birchin-lane
Halsey, Thomas	Hertfordshire	Jermyn-street
Hamilton, W. Ger.	Wilton	Arlington-street
Hanbury, John	Monmouthshire	New Bond-street
Hanger, Hon. Wm.	St. Michael	Pall-mall
Harbord, Sir Harbord	Norwich	Albemarle-street
Harley, Thomas	Herefordshire	Aldersgate-street
Harris, Sir James	Christchurch	*(Abroad.)*
Harrison, John	Great Grimsby	*Clarges street*
Hartley Winch- } combe, Henry	Berkshire	Soho-square
Harvey, Eliab	Malden	*Clifford-street*
Hatton, Geo. Finch	Rochester	Portman-square
Hayley, George	London	Goodman's-fields
Henderson, John	Bruntisland, &c.	New-palace-yd. West.
Henniker, John	Dover	Savage-gardens
Herbert, Lord	Wilton	*Privy-garden*
Herries, Sir Robert	Dumfries &c.	*St. Mary Axe*
Hill, Noel	Shropshire	Sackville-street
Hill, Richard	Shropshire	*Wimpole-street.*

F 2

An Alphabetical List of the HOUSE OF COMMONS.

Names.	Where chose.	Town-Residence.
Hinchingbroke, Visc.	Huntingdonshire	Mansfield-street
Hoghton, Sir Henry	Preston	Upper Brook-street
Holdsworth, Arthur	Dartmouth	
Honywood, Philip	Appleby	Charles-str. Berk.-sq.
Honywood, Filmer	Kent	Bolton-street
Hopkins, Richard	Thetford	Bruton-street
Hotham, Sir Richard	Southwark	Fludyer-street
Howard, Sir George	Stamford	Grosvenor-square
Howe, Viscount	Dartmouth	Grafton-street
Hudson, Giles	Chippenham	Basingball-street
Hungerford, J. P.	Leicestershire	New-str. Spring-gard.
Hunt, George	Bodmyn	Seymour-place
Huffey, William	New Sarum	Buckingham-street
Hyde, Lord	Helstone	Upper Grosvenor-str.
Jackson, Richard	New Romney	Southampton-build.
James, Sir William	West Looe	Gerrard-street, Soho
Jenkinson, Charles	Saltash	Parliament-street
Jervois, Jerv. Clarke	Hampshire	Hanover-square
Johnes, Thomas	Radnorshire	Hertford-str. May-fair
Johnston, Peter	Kirkudbright	Lincoln's-inn
§ Johnstone, George	Leftwithiel	Kensington Gore
Jolliffe, William	Petersfield	Little Argyll-street
Joiliffe, Tho. Samuel	Petersfield	Ditto
§ Jones Henry	Devizes	
Irwin, Sir John	East Grinstead	Piccadilly
Keene, Whitshed	Montgomery	Stable-yard, St. Ja.
Keene, Benjamin	Cambridge	Charles-str. Berk.-sq.
Kemp, Thomas	Lewes	Adelphi Hotel
Kenrick, John	Blechingly	Berners-street
Kensington, Lord	Haverfordwest	Jermyn-street
Kenyon, Lloyd	Hindon	Lincoln's-inn-fields
Keppel, hon. Augustus	Surrey	Audley-square
Keppel, hon. William	Chichester	Dover-street
Knight, Rich. Payne	Leominster	
Knightley, Lucy	Northamptonsh.	Grosvenor-square
Ladbroke, Robert	Warwick	Parliament-street
Lambton, John	Durham city	New Bond-street
§ Lascelles, Edwin	Northallerton	Portman-square
Laurie, Sir Robert	Dumfriesshire	Oxenden-street
Lawley, Sir Robert	Warwickshire	Hollis-st.Cavendish-sq.
Legh, Thomas Peter	Newton, Lancash.	
Leighton, Sir Charlton	Shrewsbury	Cleveland-court, St. J.
Lemon, Sir William	Cornwall	Great George-street
Lenox, Lord George	Sussex	Privy-garden

An Alphabetical List of the HOUSE OF COMMONS. 61

Names.	Where those.	Town-Residence.
Lethieullier, Benj.	Andover	Seymour-place
Lewis, Edward	New Radnor	Charles-ſtr. Berk.-ſq.
Lewiſham, Viſc.	Staffordſhire	St. James's ſquare
Lisburne, earl	Cardiganſhire	Admiralty
Liſter, Thomas	Clitheroe	George-ſtr. Han.-ſq.
Long, Sir Ja. Tylney	Devizes	Groſvenor-place
Long, Dudley	St. Germains	Piccadilly
Lowther, Sir James	Cumberland	Charles-ſtr. Berkley-ſquare
Lowther, James	Weſtmorland	Queen-ſtr. May-fair
Lowther William	Carliſle	Berkeley-ſquare
Lowther John	Cockermouth	Ditto
Lucas, Thomas	Grampound	Albemarle-ſtreet
Ludlow, earl	Huntingdonſhire	Groſvenor-ſtreet
Luther, John	Eſſex	Portland-place
Luttrell, hon. Hen. Lawes	Boſſinney	Leiceſter-ſquare
Luttrell, hon. James	Stockbridge	Pall-mall
Luttrell, hon. John	Ditto	Ryder-ſtreet
Luttrell, John Fownes	Minehead	Harley-ſtreet
Luttrell, Fran. Fownes	Minehead	Middle Temple
Lygon, Wm.	Worceſterſhire	Edward-ſtr. Port.-ſq.
Macdonald, Arch.	Newcaſt. under L.	Adelphi
Mackreth, Robert	Caſtle Riſing	Cork-ſtreet
Mackworth, Sir Herb.	Cardiff	Cavendiſh-ſquare
Macleod, Alexander	Honiton	
Macleod, Lord	Rofsſhire	
Macpherſon, John	Cricklade	Mancheſter-buildings
Macpherſon, James	Camelford	Mancheſter-buil. Weſt.
Mabon, Lord	Chipping Wycombe	Harley-ſtreet
Maitland, Viſcount	Newport, Cornw.	
Mann, Sir Horatio	Maidſtone	Groſvenor-ſtreet
Manners, Lord Robert	Kingſton upon H.	Groſvenor-ſquare
Manners, Ld. Rob.	Cambridgeſhire	
Mansfield, James	Cambridge	Temple
Marſham, Hon. Cha.	Kent	Arlington-ſtreet
Martin, James	Tewkeſbury	Whitehall
Maſterman, William	Bodmyn	Red-lion-ſquare
Mawbey, Sir Joſeph	Surrey	Groſvenor-ſtreet
Mayne, Robert	Gatton	Jermyn-ſtreet
Mayor, John	Abingdon	Abingdon-ſtreet
Meadows, Charles	Nottinghamſhire	Clifford-ſtreet

F 3

An Alphabetical List of the HOUSE OF COMMONS.

Names.	Where chose.	Town-Residence.
Medlycott, T. H.	Milbourn Port	
Melbourn, Lord	Luggershall	Piccadilly
Mellish, Charles	Aldborough	Manchester-square
Methuen, Paul	Bedwin	Lower Grosvenor-st.
Michel, David Robert	Lime Regis	
Middleton, Sir Will.	Northumberland	Golden-square
Midleton, Viscount	Whitchurch	Hill-street
Miller, William	Edinburgh	Sackville-street
Minchin, Humphry	Oakhampton	Wimpole-street
Molyneux, Crisp	King's Lynn	New Palace-yard
Monckton, hon. Rob.	Portsmouth	Bruton-street
Monckton, hon. Edw.	Stafford	St. Alban's-street
Monro, Sir Hector	Inverness, &c.	Jermyn-street
Montagu, Hon. John	Windsor	Dover-street
Montagu, Frederick	Higham-Ferrers	Hanover-square
Montgomery, Hugh	Airshire	
Morant, Edward	Yarmouth	Park-lane
Morgan, Charles	Breconshire	Great George-street
Morgan, John	Monmouthshire	Abingdon-street
Morris, Staates Long	Kintore, &c.	Harley-street,
Morshead, John	Callington	Somerset-st. Portm.sq.
Mostyn, Sir Roger	Flintshire	Bruton-street
Moysey, Abel	Bath	Lincoln's-inn-fields
Mulgrave, Lord	Huntingdon	Admiralty
Murray, Hon. James	Perthshire	Manchester-buildings
Murray, Alexander	Peeblesshire	Bridge-street, West.
Myddelton Richard	Denbigh	Berkley-square
Nedham, William	Pontefract	Seymour-Place
Nesbitt, John	Winchelsea	Aldermanbury
Neville, Rd. Aldworth	Buckingham	Mount-street
Newhaven, Lord	Gatton	Stratford-place
Newnham, Nathaniel	London	Paper-build. Temple
Noel, Thomas	Rutlandshire	New Bond-street
North, Lord	Banbury	Downing-street
North, hon. G. A.	Harwich	Ditto
Norton, Sir Fletcher	Guildford	Lincoln's-inn-fields
Norton, Edward	Haslemere	Middle Temple
Nugent, Earl	St. Mawes	Great George-street
Onslow, George	Guildford	Bridge-street.
Onslow, Thomas	Rye	Harley-str. Cav.-sq.
§ Onslow, Edward	Aldborough	
Ord, John	Hastings	Lincoln's-inn-fields
Ord, Thomas	Aylesbury	Upper, Harley-street

5

An Alphabetical List of the HOUSE OF COMMONS. 63

Names.	Where chose.	Town-Residence.
§ Osborne, Sir Geo.	Horsham	Charles-st. Berk.-sq.
Owen, Hugh	Pembrokeshire	Grosvenor-street
Owen, Hugh	Pembroke	Russell co. Clevl.-sq.
Owen, William	*Montgomeryshire*	*Grovesnor-square*
Page, Francis	OxfordUniversity	Pall-mall
Palk, Robert	Ashburton	Bruton-street
§ Pallifer, Sir Hugh	Huntingdon	
Palmerston, Viscount	Hastings	Park-str. Westminster
Panmure, Earl	Forfarshire	Chesterfield-street
Pardoe, John	*Camelford*	*Bedford-row*
Parker, John	Devonshire	Sackville-street
Parker, John	*Clitheroe*	
Parker, Viscount	Woodstock	Cavendish-square
Parry, John	*Carnarvonshire*	*Lincoln's-inn-fields*
Payne, Sir Ralph	Plympton	Grafton-street
Peachey, John	Shoreham	Wimpole-street
Peirse, Henry	Northallerton	Harley-street
Pelham, Ch. Anderson	Lincolnshire	Arlington-street
Pelham, Hon. Henry	*Lewes*	*Stretton-street*
Pelham, Hon. Thomas	*Sussex*	*Stretton-street*
Pennyman, Sir James	Beverley	South Audley-square
Penruddock, Charles	Wiltshire	Soho-square
Penton, Henry	Winchester	Admiralty
§ Perceval, Hon. C.G.	Launceston	
Percy, Lord Algernon	Northumberland	South-Audley-street
Phillips, George	*Carmarthen*	
Phillipson, Richard	Eye	New-str. Spring-gar.
Phipps, hon. Charles	Scarborough	Harley-street
Phipps, James	*Peterborough*	*New Bond-street*
Pigot, Hugh	Bridgnorth	Park-place, St. Jam.
Pitt, Thomas	Old Sarum	Park-lane
Pitt, Hon. George	Dorsetshire	Hertford-street
Pitt, William Morton	*Poole*	*Arlington-street*
§ Pitt, Hon. William	Appleby	
Plumer, William	Hertfordshire	Cavendish-square
Pochin, William	*Leicestershire*	*St. James's-street*
Polhill, Nathaniel	Southwark	Southwark
Poulett, Hon. Anne	Bridgewater	Albemarle-street
Powney, Penniston *Portlock*	*Windsor*	*Parliament-street*
Powys, Thomas	Northamptonsh.	Albemarle-street
Praed, William	*St. Ives*	*St. James's-street*
Pratt, hon. John Jeff.	*Bath*	*New-Burlington-str.*
Pringle, John	Selkirkshire	St. Martin's-lane

An Alphabetical List of the HOUSE OF COMMONS

Names.	Where chose.	Town-Residence.
Pulteney, William	Shrewsbury	Piccadilly
Purling, John	Weymouth, &c.	Portland-place
Radcliffe, John	St. Albans	Upper Grosvenor-str.
Ramsden, Sir John	Grampound	Pall-mall
Rashleigh, Philip	Fowey	Northumberland-str.
Rawlinson, Sir Walter	Queenborough	Lincoln's-inn-fields
Rawlinson, Henry	Liverpool	Great George-street
Rawlinson, Abraham	Lancaster	
Rebow, Isaac Martin	Colchester	Duke-street, Westm.
Ridley, Sir Mat. White	Newcastle	Strand
Rigby, Richard	Tavistock	Pay-office, horse gds.
Roberts, John	Taunton	Margaret-st. Cav.-sq.
Robinson, John	Harwich	Parliament-street
Robinson, Charles	Canterbury	Lincoln's-inn, O. Buil.
Robinson, Frederick	Ripon	Whitehall
Rodney, Sir G. B.	Westminster	(Abroad)
Rodney, George	Northampton	Stafford-street
Rogers, John	Penryn	Old Palace-Yard
Rogers, Sir F. L.	Plymouth	Pall-mall
§.Rogers, Thomas	Coventry	Cornhill
Rolle, John	Devonshire	
Roscwarne, Henry	Truro	St. James's street
Ross, George	Cromartyshire	Conduit-street
Ross, Charles	Wick, &c.	
Rous, Thomas Bates	Worcester	Harley-street
Rous, Sir John	Suffolk	Wigmore-street
Rouse, C. W. B.	Evesham	George-st. Hanover-sq.
Rumbold, Sir Thomas	Shaftesbury	
Rushout, Sir John	Evesham	Savile Row
Rushworth, Edward	Yarmouth	New Bond-street
St. John, Henry	Wotton Bassett	Park-lane
St. John, John	Newport	Strutton-street, Picc.
St. John, St. Andrew	Bedfordshire	
Salt, Samuel	Liskeard	Inner Temple
Savile, Sir George	Yorkshire	Leicester-fields
§ Sawbridge, John	London	New Burlington-st.
Scott, Thomas	Bridport	Coleman-street
Scott, Hugh	Berwickshire	Sackville-street
Scudamore, Cha. Fitz.	Thetford	Albemarle-street
Scudamore, John	Hereford	Stafford-street
Selwyn, Geo. Aug.	Luggershall	Cleveland-row
Shaftoe, Robert	Downton	
Sheridan, R. B.	Stafford	Great Queen-street

An Alphabetical List of the HOUSE OF COMMONS.

Names.	Where chose.	Town-Residence.
Shuckburgh, Sir G. A. W.	Warwickshire	Welbeck street.
Shuldham, Lord	Fowey	Craven-street
Sibthorp, Humphry	Boston	Parliament-street
Sinclair, John	Caithness	Park-street, Westmin.
Skelton, A. J.	Eye	Poland-street
Skene, Robert	Fifeshire	Haymarket
Skipwith, Sir T. Geo	Steyning	Clifford-street
Sloane, Hans	Southampton	Southamp.-st.Bloom
Sloper, Wm. Charles	St. Albans	Audley-square
Smith, Richard	Wendover	Harley-street
Smith, John Mansell	Ditto	Ditto
Smith, Abel	St. Ives	Parliament-street
Smith, Samuel, jun.	Ilchester	Aldermanbury
Smith, Robert	Nottingham	Lombard-street
Smyth, Sir Robert	Colchester	Grafton-street
Spencer, Lord Cha.	Oxfordshire	Grosvenor-place
Spencer, Lord Robert	Oxford city	Berkeley-square
Stanhope, Lovel	Winchester	Grafton-street
§Stanhope, Walter Spencer	Haslemere	Haymarket
Stanley, Thomas	Lancashire	
Staunton, Thomas	Ipswich	Abingdon-street
Steele, Thomas	Chichester	New Bond-street
Stephens, Philip	Sandwich	Admiralty
Stephenson, John	Tregony	Scots-yard, Bush.-la.
Stepney, Sir John	Monmouth	Bury-street
§ Steward, Gabriel	Weymouth, &c.	Abingdon-street
Stewart, John Shaw	Renfrewshire	St. James's-street
Stewart, hon. Keith	Wigtownshire	Cleveland-square
Storer, Antony	Morpeth	Portugal-st.May-Fair
Strachey, Henry	Bishop's Castle	Park-street
Strahan, William	Wotton Basset	New-street, Fetter-la.
Stratton, George	Callington	Hereford-street
Strutt, John	Malden	Fludyer-street
Stuart, Hon. Charles	Bossiney	Cavendish-square
§Stuart, Hon. James	Plympton	
Stuart, Andrew	Lanerkshire	Berkeley-square
Sturt, Humphrey	Dorsetshire	St. James's-square
Surrey, Earl	Carlisle	St. James's square
Sutton, Lord George	Newark	Grosvenor-street
Sutton, Sir Richard	Sandwich	Berners-street
Sutton, George	Grantham	Grosvenor-street
Sykes, Francis	Shaftesbury	Upper Brook-street
Symons, Sir Richard	Hereford	Bolton-street

66   An A'phabetical List of the HOUSE OF COMMONS.

Names.	Where chose.	Town-Residence.
Talbot, John Chetw.	Castle-Rising	Up. Brook-street
Taylor, Clement	Maidstone	
Tempest, John	Durham City	Wimpole-street
Thistlethwayte, Robert	Hants	Queen Anne-street
Thompson, Beilby	Thirsk	Cavendish-square
Thorold, Sir John	Lincolnshire	Ditto
Thoroton, Thomas	Bramber	Knightsbridge
Tollemache, Hon. Wilbraham	Liskeard	New Norfolk-street
Townshend, Charles	Yarmouth, Norf.	Stanhope-street
Townshend, Thomas	Whitchurch	Albemarle-street
Townshend, Hon. John	Cambridge Univ.	Pall-Mall
Townson, John	Milbourn Port	Cony-court, Gray's Inn
Trentham, Viscount	Newcastle under Line	Whitehall
Trevelyan, Sir John	Somersetshire	Half-moon-street
Trevanion, John	Dover	Charles-str. Caven. sq.
Tudway, Clement	Wells	Wimpole-street
Turner, Charles	York	Grosvenor-street
Tyrconnel, E. of	Scarborough	Hanover-square
Van Neck, Sir G.W.	Dunwich	Piccadilly
Vaughan, Hon. John	Berwick	(Abroad)
Vaughan, John	Caermarthensh.	Brooke-street
Vaughan, Evan Lloyd	Merionethshire	Glouceft.co. St. Ja.str.
Verney, Earl	Bucks	Curzon-street, May-F.
Vernon, Richard	Okehampton	St. James's-place
Upper Ossory, E. of	Bedfordshire	Grosvenor Place
Vyner, Robert	Lincoln	Conduit-street
Wake, Sir William	Bedford	Hill street
Wallace, James	Horsham	Lincoln's-inn-fields
Waller, Robert	Chipp. Wycomb	Half-moon-street
Walpole, Hon. Tho.	King's Lynn	Lincoln's-inn-fields
Walpole, Hon. Rich.	Yarmouth, Norf.	Spring Gardens
Walpole, Hon. Horatio	Wigan	
Walsingham, Hon. Robert Boyle	Knaresborough	Stratford-place
Ward, Hon. William	Worcester	Park-street
Warren, Sir George	Beaumaris	Grafton-street
Warren Sir Jo. Borlase	Great Marlow	Q Ann-str.Cav.-squa.
Webb, John	Gloucester	Mortimer-st. Cav. sq.
Weddell, William	Malton	Upper Brook-street
Wemyss, Hon. James	Sutherlandshire	Cha. str. St. Jam.-sq.
Wenman, Viscount	Oxfordshire	
Westcote, Lord	Bewdley	Berners-street
Whitbread, Samuel	Bedford	Portman-square

Names.	Where chose.	Town-Residence.
Whitmore, Tho.	Bridgenorth	Wimpole-street
Whitshed, James	Cirencester	New Burlington-str.
Wilberforce, William	Kingston upon Hull	New Bond-street
Wilkes, John	Middlesex	Princes-court, Westm.
Wilkinson, Pinckney	Old Sarum	Hereford-street
Williams, Watkin	Flint	Adam-street, Strand
Wilmot, John	Tiverton	Bedford Row
Winnington, Edward	Droytwich	
Wollaston, William	Ipswich	Wimpole-street
Woodley, William	Marlborough	Mansfield-street
Worsley, Edw. Meux	Newtown, Hants	Welbeck-street
Worsley, Sir Richard	Newport, Hants	Stratford Place
Wraxall, William	Hindon	Grosvenor-place.
Wrottesley, Sir John	Staffordshire	Hertford-street
Wynn, Glynn	Caernarvon	Berkeley-square
Wynne, Sir W. Williams	Denbighshire	St. James's-square
Yonge, Sir George	Honiton	Stratford Place.
Yorke, Hon. John	Reygate	Berkeley-square
Yorke, Philip	Helstone	Park-st. Grof.-sq.
Yorke, Hon. Philip	Cambridgeshire	Bond-street

CLERKS and OFFICERS of the House of PEERS.

AShley Cowper, Esq; Clerk of the Parliaments.
Samuel Strutt, Esq; Clerk Assistant.
Matthew Robert Arnott, Esq; Reading Clerk and Clerk of the Private Committees.
Mr. Crofts, Clerk of the Journals.
Other Clerks in the office, Ed. Parratt, F. Wm. Feary, Ja. Hamilton, Wm. Walmsley.
Mr. Edward Blackstock, Copying Clerk.
Sir Francis Molyneux, Knt. Gent. Usher of the Black Rod.
Robert Quarme, Esq; Yeoman Usher.
DOOR-KEEPERS.
Mr. Copeland, Mr. Dennis, Mr. Hodges, Mr. Sutherland, Mr. Leuzan, Mr. Waterhouse, and Mr. Randall.
HOUSEKEEPER.
Mr. Robert Robe, Keeper of the Stole-Room.
Necessary Woman, Mrs. Hickson

Officers of the House of Commons.

John Hatsell, esq; Clerk of the House of Commons (*Cotton Garden, Old Palace Yard*)
John Ley, esq; Clerk Assistant (*St. Margaret's-street, Westminster*)
George White, esq; Clerk of Committee of Privileges, and Clerk of the Select Committees for trying Elections
John Rosier, esq; Clerk of the Fees
Hardinge Stracey, esq;
    His Deputy, Mr. Tho. Parker,
George White, esq;
    His Deputy, Mr. G. White, jun. } Clerks without Doors, attending Committees.
Edward Barwell, esq;
    His Deputy, Mr. Nath. Barwell
Robert Gunnell, esq;
    His Deputy, Mr. Henry Gunnell
Hardinge Stracey, esq; } Clerks of the Ingrossments
Mr. David Jones
John Benson, esq; Clerk of the Journals and Papers
Edward Colman, esq; Serjeant at Arms
John Clementson, esq; Deputy Serjeant at Arms
The Reverend Mr. Cornwall, Chaplain
Samuel Dunn, esq; Secretary } to the Speaker
Mr. Mann Trainbearer
Charles Bathurst, Lockyer Davis, Benjamin White, and John Nichols, Printers of the Votes
Mr. Henry Hughs, Printer of the Journals, &c.
Mr. S. H. Babb delivers out the Votes to Members
Mr. Joseph Pearson } Door-keepers
Mr. Godfrey Barwell,
Mr. John Bellamy, House-keeper
Mr. William Whitham
Mr. Charles Williams } Messengers
Mr. Guy Wood
Mr. Richard Taylor
Mr. Thomas Baker, Lower Door-keeper,

[63]

His Majesty's Most Honourable PRIVY-COUNCIL.

Those marked thus ˣ *are Members of Parliament.*

DUKE of Gloucester
    Duke of Cumberland
Archbishop of Canterbury
Lord Chancellor
Archbishop of York
Earl Bathurst, Lord President
E. of Dartmouth, Lord Privy Seal
Duke of Somerset
    Richmond
    Grafton
    Bolton
    Leeds
    Marlborough
    Portland
    Chandos
    Newcastle
    Northumberland
    Montagu
Marquis of Rockingham
Marquis of Carmarthen
Earl Talbot, Lord Steward
Earl of Hertford, Ld Chamberl.
    Huntingdon
    Salisbury
    Denbigh
    Sandwich
    Carlisle
    Scarborough
    Rochford
    Jersey
    Kinnoul
    Breadalbane
    Marchmont
    Bute
    Pomfret
    Ashburnham
    Gower
    Buckinghamshire
    Temple
    Cornwallis
    Hardwicke

Earl of Hillsborough
    Ailesbury
    Clarendon
    Mansfield
    Besborough
ˣEarl Verney
Earl of Shelburne
ˣEarl Nugent
Lord George Cavendish
    ˣCharles Spencer
    ˣFrederick Campbell
    ˣGeorge Germain
    Loughborough
Viscount Townshend
    Weymouth
    Stormont
    Falmouth
    ˣHowe
    Barrington
    ˣBateman
    ˣHinchingbrook
    ˣBeauchamp
Lord Mountstuart
    ˣNorth
    Bishop of London
    Le Despencer
    Onslow
    Edgcumbe
    Grantham
    Pelham
    Camden
    Hawke
    Amherst
    Walsingham
ˣCharles Wolfran Cornewall, Speaker of the House of Commons
ˣSir Fletcher Norton
ˣJames Stuart Mackenzie, Esq;
ˣThomas Harley, Esq;

James

James Grenville, Esq;
Sir Joseph Yorke, K. B.
Hon. Seymour Conway, Esq
Welbore Ellis, Esq;
Humphry Morice, Esq;
Richard Rigby, Esq;
Sir Thomas Sewell
Sir John Eardley Wilmot
Isaac Barré, Esq;
Sir John Shelley, Bart.
Thomas Townshend
Henry Fr. Carteret
Sir Laurence Dundas, Bart.
Sir Thomas Parker, Knt.
Charles Jenkinson, Esq;
Sir William Lynch, K. B.
Sir John Goodricke, Bart.
Sir William Meredith, Bart.

Henry Flood, Esq;
Charles Townshend, Esq;

Clerks of the Council in Ordinary.
Hon. Robert Walpole,
Stephen Cottrell,
George Chetwynd, William
  Fawkner, Esqrs.
Clerks Extraordinary,
Richard Gilebar,
Robert Tarrant, Esqrs.
Hon. Richard Chetwynd
Thomas Gilbert, jun. Esq;
Keeper of the Council Records,
Stephen Cottrell, Esq;
Keepers of the Council Chamber,
T. Dring, Wm Booker, Gents.
Fire-keeper, V. Litchfield
Necessary-woman, E. Litchfield

Lord CHAMBERLAIN *of the King's Houshold, and the Officers and Servants under his Direction. (Stable-Yard, St. James's.)*

Lord Chamberlain,
EARL of Hertford,
  Wages 100l a Year
Board Wages 1100l a Year
Vice Chamberlain,
Lord Hinchingbrook,
Wages 600l a Year
Board Wages 559l 8s 4d a Year
Secretary to Lord Chamberlain,
Whitshed Keene, Esq;
Francis Price, Esq; *Deputy*
James Ely, Esq; *First Clerk*
Samuel Betty, *Second Clerk*
John Legarde, *Chamber-keeper*
Lords of the King's Bedchamber
Earl of Ashburnham, Groom
  of the Stole, 2000l
Lord Robert Bertie
Duke of Queensberry
Earl of Orford
  Oxford
Lord Willoughby de Broke
Earl of Denbigh

Duke of Roxburgh
Earl Fauconberg
  Winchelsea
  Aylesford
Lord Onslow
  Boston
Salary 1000l a Year each
Grooms of the Bedchamber,
Sir James Peachy, Bart.
Sir James Wright, Bart.
Sir John Mordaunt, Bart.
Sir Cha. Thompson, Bt. K. B.
Hon. Col. William Harcourt
Hon. Henry Vernon
Sir George Osborne, Bart.
Hon. Major-Gen. Henry St.
  John
Sir Philip Hales, Bart.
Hon. William Gordon
Charles Herbert, Esq;
Col. Lascelles, Sal. 500l. a Year
Gentlemen of the Privy Chamber,
Solomon Dayrolle, FRS.
               Timo-

[71]

Timothy Earle, Efq; J. Short, J. Leman, W. D. Grimes, Efqrs. Sir F. Charleton, Bart. Selwood Hewett, W. Baynes, C. Stuart, T. Barker, C. Churchill, Ja. Theobalds, Ja. Brydges, H. Shubrooke, Wm Bafford, Efqrs. Sir J. Caldwell, Bart. Sir J. Stanley, Bart. Tho. Edwards Freeman, Hugh Powell, J. Beale Bonnell, T. Lowfield, Th. Lockyer, J. Tomlinfon, C. Anderfon, Jervoife Clarke, Donatius Obrien, Efqrs. Sir P. Soame, Bart. Rich. Croft, T. Hotchkin, Pereg. Bertie, Lee Steere, Rob. Bird, Rob. Bromley, Ph. Glover, Cary Elwes, T. King, Tho. Gryffin, Dodington Egerton, Rd. Willis, Efqs. Sir NevilleHickman, Bt. T. Strong, John Hart Cotton, J. Mytton, C. Selwin, C. Hale, Efqrs. Sir F. L. Rogers, Bt. P. Furye, Efq; Sir Rowland Wynne, Bart.

Mafter of the Ceremonies,
Sir Clement Cotterel Dormer, Knt. Salary 300l a Year
Affiftant, Stephen Cotterel, Efq; 6s 8d a Day
Marfhal, Stephen Cotterel, Efq; 100l a Year
Cup-bearers, 33l 6s 8d
Gould Clarges, W. Hetling, P. Mathews, W. Clarke, Efqrs.
Carvers, 33l 6s 8d
John Fowle, J. Grove, Wm. Edwards, Wm. Fordyce, Efqrs
Gentlemen Sewers, 33l 6s 8d
Edw. Whitehoufe,
Thomas Wilfon,
Benjamin Panniot,

Charles Puickzeke, Efqrs.
Gentleman Ufhers of the Privy Chamber, 200l each
William Hudfon, Efq;
Arthur Gregory, Efq;
Capt. Thomas Tutteridge
Major Johnfon
GentlemenUfhers, DailyWaiters,
Sir Francis Molineux, Knt. *Black Rod.*
Lindley Simfon, Edw. Sneyd, Wm Fitzherbert, Efqrs. 150l
Affiftant Gentleman Ufher,
George Ann Cooke, Efq; 66l 13s 4d a Year
Grooms of the Privy Chamber,
Edward Capel, Samuel Pegge, Tho. Colins,
Wm. Fordyce, Efqrs. 73l
Gentlemen Ufhers, Quarter Waiters in Ordinary,
J. Freemantle, Fred. Chapman, Ed. Mainwaring, Wm Plaxton, Edward Whitehoufe, Henry Baynes, John Welfh, Edm. Armftrong, Efqrs.
Chamber keeper, Rt. Spike, 20l
Sewers of the Great Chamber,
Tho. Woollam, Wm Harrifon, John Cowen, Ifaac Mark, James Johnfon, Jof. Afhford, Morris Byrne, 38l 15s 7d
Pages of the Prefence,
Fr. Shaw, J. Eldred, JohnLegard, Dav. Clarkfon, 25l
Grooms of the Great Chamber,
Henry Gomond, N. Hammond, Fra. Barker, Wm Hull, John Milliet, Wm Snigg, John Webb, John Gerken, Tho. Storey,
W. Everard, 40l

G 2 *Coffer*

Coffer Bearers, 27l 7s 6d
T. Thorpe, John King
Pages of the Back Stairs, 80l
F. Pavonarius, Pen. Hawkins,
Wm Reynolds, William Ramus,
Geo. Erneſt, T. Stillingfleet,
F. Palman, Eſqrs
Antiquarian, Keeper of th
Medals, Drawings, &c.
Rich. Dalton, Eſq;
Librarian, Fred. Barnard, Eſq
Clerk in the Library,
William Graham
Porter, Joſeph Gerrard
Princ. Barber T. Vincent, 170l
Hair-dreſſer, Frederick Albert
Pages of the Bed-chamber.
John Little, John Hannington,
Edw. Dawlrn, W. Ramus,
Iſaac Walton, Eſqrs. 80l
REMOVING-WARDROBE.
Yeoman, J. Calthorpe, Eſq; 230l
Grooms, T. Panton, jun. Eſq;
Charles Lynn, Eſq; 136l
Pages, R Evans, Will. Brine,
Will. Whiſſel, Eſqrs. 100l each
M. M'Donnell, *Aſſiſtant.*
Stephen Noſt, } *Servants*;
John Noſt, }
Standing Wardrobe Keepers.
At ST. JAMES's,
Thomas Williams, Eſq; 110l
At WINDSOR-CASTLE,
Joſeph Hewitt, Eſq; 160l
At HAMPTON-COURT, *ana*
Keeper of the private Lodge,
Hon. Mrs. Eliz. Moſtyn, 200l
At KENSINGTON,
Mrs. Rachael Lloyd, 100l
Wardrobe Keeper, and Keeper
of the Royal Apartments at
Somerſet Houſe.
100l
MASTER *of the* ROBES,
Lord Brudenell, 500l

Yeoman, James Madan, Eſq;
Page, Henry Hope
Grooms, Alexander Charles,
John Malliet, Francis Minet,
Bruſher, John Yvounet,
Meſſ. to the Robes, John Biſhop
Furrier of the Robes,
Tobias Kleinert, 20l
Waiters, John Teede,
Thomas Taylor,
Clerk, John Malliet
Taylor, Thomas Darwell
Meſſenger, John Biſhop
Laundreſs of the Body Linen,
Mrs. Mary Hicks
Sempſtreſs and Starcher,
Mrs. Jemima Gregory, 400l
Neceſſary Woman,
Mrs. A. Brandenburg, 127l
Neceſſ. Woman at Kenſington,
Mrs. Jane Hunter

JEWEL-OFFICE, 1597.
Maſter, Earl of Darlington
Patent Fees, 450l a Year
Yeo. C. Hope, Eſq; 106l 15s
William Egerton, Eſq; 50l
Groom,
John Paddey, Eſq; 105l 8s 4d
Clk. W. Egerton, Eſq; 13l 6s 8d
Goldſmith, T. Heming, Eſq;
Serjeants at Arms, 100l
Joſeph Smith, J. A. Stainſby
N. Kenderley, Alex. Barker,
G. B. Kennet, C. Simpſon,
W. Bibbins, J. Probert, Cavin
Delane, Eſqrs.
Serjeant at Arms attending the
Lord Treaſurer,
Henry Brougham, jun. Eſq;
5s 6d a Day
Serjeant at Arms attending the
Lord Chancellor,
Rich. Jephſon, Eſq; 3s a Day
Ser-

Serjeant at Arms attending the
House of Commons,
Edward Colman, Efq; 100l
Serjeant at Arms attending the
City of London,
R. Berisford, Efq; 6s 8d a Day.
Groom Porter, 550l a Year,
George Powlett, Efq;
Mafter of the Revels,
Solomon Dayrolle, Efq; 100l
His Yeoman, 46l 11s 8d
John Underwood, Efq;
Hiftoriographer,
Richard Stonhewer, Efq; 200l
Knight Harbinger,
Richard Stonhewer, Efq;
Mafter of Mechanics. Anth.
Shepherd, D.D. F.R.S. 2col
Examiner of all Plays, &c.
John Larpent, jun. Efq; 400l
Deputy, Ed. Capell, Efq; 200l
Poet Laureat,
Wm. Whitehead, Efq; 100l
Receiver of the Civil Lift De-
ductions from all Salaries ex-
ceeding 50l Th. Aftle, Efq;
Deputy, 6cl
Embellifher of Letters to the
Eaftern Princes, J. Holland, 6ol.

Monnot, J. Padmore, Wm.
North, J. Edwards, Hanbury
Potter, J. Child, Tho. Creff-
well, John Smith, S. Leo-
nard, Ralph Heflop, W. C.
Ranfpach, H. Gladwell, R.
Wilfon, Tho. Ellis, Ja. Dickins,
M. Slater, John Painter, Wm.
Major. Tho. Maclean, Wm.
Garlick, Wm. Flint, John
Gurnell

Clerks of the Cheque, 99l 15s
Thomas Chetham,
Thomas Dring, Efqrs.
Meffengers to the Chancellor of
the Exchequer,
Edw. Harland, Tho. Alderton
Meffenger of the G. Wardrobe,
Mr. Edward Henney
Meffenger to Lord Chancellor,
Mr. Harry Harmood
Meff. to the Printing-Prefs,
Edward Bibbins, jun.

Band of Mufick, 24. — 40l.
Mafter, J. Stanley, B M 20cl
Conductor, C. Weideman, 10cl
T. Vincent, G. Peat, J. Ahing-
ton, Edw. Gibbs, John Jones,

Forty Meffengers in Ordinary,
at 45l *a Year, and daily Pay*
when employed. viz.
Wm. Dick, George Collins,
Jof. Sharp, M. Roworth, Edward Mann, William King,
Andrew Staley, Daniel Ar-
douin, George Long, William
Cock, Thomas Ruffel, Jo-
feph Hind, F. Dav. Lauzun,
Geo. Coates, William Needham, William Pearfon, Roder.
Ogg, Wm Booth, Stephen

T. Jones, Wm. Howard, J.
Perkins, J. Gordon, Roufe
Compton, Ch. Scola, Stephen
Jone:, Benj. Chriftian, Tho.
Atwood, Robert Rawlins, P.
Saifon, Charles Burney, A.
Webber, Luff. Atterbury, A.
Robertfon, Sq. Laud, Tho.
Thackray, —— Simpfon, R.
Hay, J. Crofdill
Ser. Trum. J. Probart, Efq; 100
Vocal Performer in Ordinary,
John Beard, Efq; 10cl

[74]

Instrument-keeper,
Henry Ann Mouchett, 40l
Instrument-maker, Tho. Smith
Organ-builder, John Byfield
Physicians in Ordinary, 300l.
Sir Edw. Wilmott, Bart. FRS.
Sir Cl. Wintringham, Bt. FRS.
Dr Richard Warren, FRS.
Sir Noah Thomas, Knt. FRS.
Physicians extra to his Majesty,
Sir Richard Jebb, Bart. F R S.
Sir John Pringle, Bart. F. R S.
Dr. Lucas Pepys
Oculist, Baron de Wenzell
Physician to the Houshold,
Dr Tho. Gisborne, F R S. 200l
Apothecaries to the Person,
John Devaynes, Esq; 320l
Tho. Wainwright, Esq; 160l
Apothecaries to the Houshold,
Rt Halifax, E Holdich, Esqs 160l
Chemist, Dr. John Amyatt, 100l
Serjeant Surgeons,
Sir Cæsar Hawkins, Bart.
Da. Middleton, Esq;
Pen. Hawkins, Esq; 396l 13s 4d
Surgeons extra to the Person,
John Gunning, Esq;
John Hunter, Esq;
Surgeon to the Houshold,
Geo. Edw. Hawkins, Esq; 280l
Anatomist, John Andrews, Esq;
Aurist Operator, —Maule, Esq;
Operators for the Teeth,
T. Berdmore, J. Spence.
All in Gift of Lord Chamberl.

HOUSEKEEPERS,
At Newmarket,
200l
At Windsor-Castle,
Lady Mary Churchill, 320l
At Kensington,
Mrs. Rachael Lloyd
At Westminster,
Mrs Ann Blackerby, 6s. 8d. a day

Under House-keep. at St James's,
Lady Hart, 100l
Hampton-Court,
Mary Anderson, 320l
At Somerset-House,
Mrs Greville, 200l
Under Housekeeper,
100l
At Whitehall,
John Manners, Esq; 650l
At the Queen's Palace,
Mrs Elizabeth Stainforth
At Richmond-Lodge,
Mrs Tunstall
N. B. The following have no Salaries unless inserted after their Names :
Master of the Tennis Court,
Richard Beresford, Esq; 132l
Locksmiths, J. Fenwick, Ed. Gascoigne, Wm Rogers, G. Fairbone, J. Davis
Card-maker, Charles Gibson
Druggist, John Anstrobus
Optician, Mr Peter Dollond
Gunsmith, James Whissell
Printers, Charles Eyre, and ✕William Strahan, Esqrs.
Statuary, Jos. Wilton, Esq;
Harpsichord maker,
James Handcock
Geographer, Thomas Jefferys
Topograph. Mr. Hamilton Leslie
Hydrographers, Mr T. Kitchen, sen. and Mr T. Kitchen, jun.
Shipwright and Barge-builder,
George Searle
Sword-cutler, John Bland
Hatters, G. Wagner, Esq; & Son
Math. Instr. Maker, Jere. Sisson
Furrier and Skinner, Sam. West
Mole Taker, Fra. Dyer, 81 1s 8d
Turners, B. Crompton,
T. Ayliffe

Per-

[75]

Perfumer,
Watch-maker,
Thomas Mudge, Efq; 15ol
Clock maker,
Ben. Vulliamy, 15ol
Surveyor of the Pictures,
Richard Dalton, Efq; 2ool
Principal Portrait Painter,
A. Ramfay, Efq; 2ool
Painter in Enam. and Miniat.
Jeremiah Meyer, Efq;
Mezzotinto Engraver,
Valentine Green, F.A.S.
Seal Engraver,
Thomas Major
Bookfeller and Stationer by Patent, Mrs. K. Caftle
Stat. in Ord. Mr. F. J. Knight
Bookfeller, Geo. Nicoll.
Bookbinder, W. Shropfhire
Rat-killer,
F. Schomberg, 48l 3s 4d Year
Herb-ftrewer,
Honor Battifcombe, 24l
Mafter of the Barges,
William Sawyer, 10ol a Year
Watermen, 48. With Badges, Coats, Shirts, Stockings, &c. and 12 penfionary, 3l 2s 6d a Year each
Diftiller, Charles Bedell
Diftiller of Milk-water,
Pin-maker, Tho. Trott
Comb-maker,
Spatterdafh-makers,
Aaron Eaton, fen. and jun.
Fifhhook-maker, Mrs S. Ford

RANGERS, KEEPERS, &c.
Windfor Foreft and Great Park,
Duke of Cumberland

Out Ranger, ×G. Onflow, Efq;
Windfor Little Park,
Earl of Pomfret
Cranbourn-Chace & Hampton-Court-Park, D. of Glocefter
Richmond, Earl of Bute
Dep. Ranger, Ph. Medows, Efq;
North of Trent,
×RtHon. C. W. Cornewall, Efq
S. of Trent. ×Right Hon. Sir Fletcher Norton, Knt.
St. James's Park, E. of Orford
Dep. ×Lord William Gordon
New Foreft, Warden & Keeper,
Duke of Glocefter
Sherwood Foreft, D. Newcaftle
Greenwich Park,
Epping Foreft, Earl Tylney
Bufhy Park, Lady North
Salcey Foreft, F. Montagu, Efq;
Mafter of Game, D. of Grafton
Wichwood Foreft, Oxfordfhire,
Duke of Marlborough
Dartmore Foreft, Devon, Sir Francis Henry Drake, Bart.
St. Briavel's Caftle in the Foreft of Deane, Earl of Berkeley
Whittlebury Foreft, Northampt.
Duke of Grafton
Waltham Foreft, Lincolnfhire,
Rickmond Foreft, Yorkfhire,

Rockingham Foreft, ×Earl of Upper Offory
Surveyor General of his Majefty's Woods and Parks,
John Pitt, Efq;
Surveyor Gen. of the Crown Lands, &c.
×Hon. John St. John
Deputy,
Clerks, W. Harrifon, John M'Gachen

Mafter

[76]

Master of the Harriers, Earl of Denbigh, 2000l a Year
Master of the Buck-Hounds, *Visc. Bateman, 2341l
Master of the Stag-Hounds, Earl of Essex, 800l
12 Huntsmen at 60l. *each, &* 6 *for the Master of the Buck-Hounds*
Master Huntsman and his Horses, William Kennedy, 100l
Master-Falconer, Duke of St. Alban's, 21cl
Water-Bailiffs of the Thames above Staines. John Scott, and G. Brumell, Esq;

GREAT WARDROBE. 1485
In Park-street, Westminster.
Keeper, Lord Pelham, 200cl
Dep. W. Ashburnham, Esf. 150l
Assistant, J. Fallowfield, Esf. 50l
Comp. *Th. Gilbert, Esq; 300l
Patent Clerk. Sir Geo. Mont. Metham, 300l
Under Clerks, Wm Chamberlayne, J. Fallowfield, Esqrs.
Cl. of the Robes and Wardrobes, EdwardWhitehouse, Esq; 196l
Deputy,
    Serjeant Skinner,
J. Fallowfield, Esq; 13l 6s 8d
Yeoman Arras Worker, Thomas Cosham, 2s per day.
Arras Taylor, Tho. Cosham, .. 1s 8d per day
Messenger, Edw. Henney, 2cl
Running Porter, Ditto, 3cl
Und. Porter, John Wilson, 2cl
Housemaid, Eliza. Walton, 20l
Packers, T. Burfoot, and N. Pearfe
Woollen-draper, G. Chapman
Mercers, John Bigge, William Barlow

Gold Lacemen, F. Plumer, and Percival Bentley
Embroiderers, Rd. Harrison, and Mary Ingall
Upholsterer, John Gilroy
Cabinet-makers. Will. Gates, and B. Parran
Silk Laceman, Edward Parker
Taylors, Henry Humfrays, and John White
Joiner and Chairmaker, John Russell
Coffer-maker, Edward Smith
Bookseller, George Nicol
Linen-drapers, John Harrison, and Thomas Roe
Sempstress, Maria Lloyd
Glover,
Herald Painters, Josiah Sarney, and Robert Morris
Belt-maker, and Sword Cutler, John Bland.
Feather-dresser, W. Gwillim;
Hatter and Hosier, Rd. Tayler
Cap and Bonnet-maker, Richard Harrison
Paper-hanging-makers, Messrs. Bromwich, Isherwood, and Bradley
Stationer, Francis Knight.

ROYAL CHAPELS, &c.
Lord High Almoner,
The Archbishop of York
Sub Almoner,
Rev. Richard Kaye, LL. D. 97l 11s 8d
Dean of the Chapel,
Bishop of London, 20cl
Sub-dean,
Anselm Bayly, LL.D. 91l 5s
Confessor of the Houshold,
Dr Dav. Wm Morgan, 36l 10s
Clerk of the King's Closet,
Bp of Winchester, 6l 18s

Deputy

Deputy Clerks,
Rev. Newton Ogle, D. D Dean of Winchester. Rev. Cha. Poyntz, D. D. Rev. Wm Buller, M.A Canon of Windsor
Closet-Keep. Mr. Pa , 4 1 l
To ditto for washing the Chaplains Surplices, and other Necessaries for the Closet, 5 0 l

CHAPLAINS in ORDINARY.
January,
Dr. WmParker, F. R. S Rector of St. James's, Westminster.
Dr. Rich. Kaye, F.R.S. Sub-Almoner to his Majesty, Archdeacon of Nottingham, a Preb. of York, Durham, and Southwell, Rector of Kirkby, in Nottinghamsh. and Brother to Sir John Lyster Kaye, Bart.
Dr. Samuel Glasse, F R. S Rector of Hanwell, Middlesex
Dr. Anth. Hamilton, Archdeacon of Colchester, Rector of Great and Little Hadham, Her s, Vicar of St. Martin's in the Fields, and Præcentor of St. Paul's, F. R. S.
February,] Dr. John Dechair, Rector of Little Rising ton, n. Glocestershire, and Vicar of Horley and Hornton, Oxon
Dr. Wm. Hayward Roberts
Wm. Arnald, B. D. Pracentor of Litchfield, and Canon of Windsor
Mr. Sturges, Pr. of Winchester
March,
Dr. Christopher Wilson, Canon Residentiary of St. Paul's
Dr. Hen. Barton, Warden of Merton College, Oxford

Dr. H. Matt. Schutz, Rector of March Gibbons, Bucks
Mr Edward Beadon, Rector of North Stoneham, Hants
April,
Dr. Edward Barnard, Provost of Eton Col. & Canon of Windfor
Dr. Spencer Madan, Prebendary of Peterborough, Rector of West Halton, and Vicar of Haxay, Lincolnshire
Dr. H. R. Courtenay, Rector of St. George's, Hanover-sq. & of Leigh, in Kent
D. Fred. Wollaston, Prebendary of Peterborough, & F. R. S.
May,
Dr. R. Fawcett, Vicar of Newe.
Mr. John Longe, Rector of Spixworth, Norfolk
Mr. Samuel Nott, Prebendary of Winchester, Rector of Houghton, Hants, and V. of Blandford-Forum, Dorsetsh.
Dr. William Vincent
Jun.,] Dr. Hen. Stebbing, Preacher at Gray's Inn
Dr. H. JeromeDe Salis, Rector of the United Parishes of St. Anthony and St. J. Baptist, in the City of London, Vicar of Wing, in Bucks, & FRS
Dr. T. Hollingbery, Archdeacon of Chichester, Rector of Rottingdean, Suffex, and Chaplain to the Lord Warden, to the Cinque Ports, and Dover Castle
Dr. Robert Markham, Rector of Whitechapel
July,
Mr. George Taylor, Rector of Church Eyton, Staffordshire
Mr. J. Scott, Rector of St Lawrence & St John, Southampt.

Dr. George Horne, President of
Magdalen College, Oxford.
August.
Mr. Alex. Jacob, Rect. of Eadcombe, Somersetsh. and Lect.
of St. Dunstan in the East.
Dr. John Strachey, Rector of
Erpingham, Norfolk
Dr. Richard Scrope, Rector of
Castle Combe, Wilts; also
Rector of Aston-Tirrold and
of Tubney, Berks
Mr. Wm Collier, Hebrew Professor, and Fellow of Trinity
College, Cambridge

September,
Mr. Thomas Barnard, Rector
of Newmarket and Wethersfield, Suffolk
Mr. William Morice, Rect.
of Allhallows, Bread-street
Mr. Thomas Taylor, Rector of
Wootton, in Surry
Dr. Nicoll
October.] Mr. Tho. Wright,
Rector of Birkin, Yorkshire
Mr James Smith
Mr. Lewis Boisdaune, Vicar
of East Meon, Hants, and
Rector of Treford, Sussex
Mr. James Strode, Vicar of
Cheshunt, in Hertfordshire

November,
Dr. John Douglas, Canon-Residentiary of St. Paul's, and
Rector of St. Austin, London
Dr. Tho. Marriot, Prebend of
Westminster, Rector of St.
Michael Bassishaw, London.
Mr. Wm. Holwell, Vicar of
Thornbury, Glocestershire
Mr. T. Fountaine, Preb. of Wor.
Vicar of Old Windsor, and
Rect. of N. Tidsworth, Wilt

D'ce
Ian Dr. Nich
Broker to L
Preb. of W
of St. Burien,
Dr. Thomas F
of Brasted,
Dr. Za. Brook
of Divinity
Dr. Samuel I
Professor of
versity of C
of Warsop, l
Ten Priests
Rev. Anselm
Henry Evan
William Fit
Moses Wig
Dr. Da. W.
John Gibbo
Henry War
William Cl
William H
John Horne
Sixteen Gentle
jesty's Chap
Rich. Ladd,
Rob. Denham
. Hudson,
Ed. Ayrton,
. Hayes, M.
ohn Dyne,
David Wood,
Organists a
Dr. James Nar
Dupuis. 14
Violist, Mr. J
Lutenist, Mr. E
N. B. Five
3 Gentlemen w
Serjeant o
William Dick
Serjeant; so
plices, &c. 6
hall, 49l 2s

[79]

Yeoman of the Vestry, | Mr. Thompson
Thomas Foster, 54l 15s | GERMAN CHAPEL.
Groom of the Vestry, | Preachers,
William Horn, 51l 12s 6d | Rev. Mr. Schroder,
Organ blower, Th. Leach, 20l | 284l a Year
Bell-ringer, Wm. Seamer, 15l | Rev. Mr. Mithoff, 2431 a Year
Tuner of the Regalls, | Reader, Rev. Mr F. Pafche, 62l
John Gordon, 56l | Clerk, Dan. Kannmaker, 60l
Edm. Ayrton, *for keeping and* | Porter, 60l
maintaining ten Children of | For Neceſſaries, Ann Steidel, 16l
the Chapel Royal, at 24l *a* | DUTCH CHAPEL.
Year each, 240l *and ſo* | Preachers,
teaching them, 80l | Rev. Godfrey Woide, 160l
WHITEHALL CHAPEL, | Rev. Philip van Swinden,
Reading Chaplains, | M. A. F. R. S. 16cl
Rev. Mr. Elte, | Reader, Rev. Godfrey Woide
Rev. R. J. Evans, M A. 8cl each | FRENCH CHAPEL *in the* Friary,
Cloſet-keeper, T. Richardſon, 50l | *at* 11, *and* 4 *Afternoon.*
Chapel-keeper, Benja. Cham- | Preachers,
  berlain, 50l | Rev. Sam. Mauzy, M.A. 160l
  SOMERSET HOUSE. | Rev. John Perny, M. A. 160l
Chaplain | Rev. — Giffardiere, M.A. 16ol
  HAMPTON COURT. | Reader, Rev. Mr. Bangis, 40l
Chaplain, Reader, and Preacher | *Sexton and Porter,*
Dr. Lillington. | Gabriel Verdier, 15l
  KENSINGTON. | Dutch *in the ſame Chapel at* 9,
Houſhold Chaplain, | *and at* 2 *in the Afternoon.*

LEVEE DAYS.
His Majeſty's, every Wedneſday and Friday; and during the ſitting of Parliament, every Monday.
Queen's Drawing-room, every Thurſday.
The Princeſs Amelia's, on the third Tueſday in the Month.

Preachers at his Majeſty's Chapel, Whitehall,
30l. *per Annum.*

From OXFORD. | From CAMBRIDGE.
Jan. T. Stinton, A M *Exeter* 2 | Wm. Pearce, B M *St. John's* 1
Feb. Edw. Edwards, D D *Jeſus* 1 | Wm. Cooke, A.M. *King's* 2
Mar. J. White, A M *Wadham,* 1 | William Bond, A M *Caius* 1
Apr. Rich. Hele, A M *Trinity* 1 | Tho. Kipling, BD *St. John's* 2
May James Chelſum, D D *Ch. C* 1 | M. A. Stephenſon, A M *Clar. b.* 2
June C. Mortimer, A M *Linc.* 2 | Ed. Walſby, A M *Benet* 2
July T. Nicholſon, B D *Queen's* 1 | —— Hayter, A M *King's* 2
Aug. Geo. Turner, A M *Merton* 1 | J. Cranke, A M *Trinity.* 2
Sep. Cha. Campbell, B D *Worc.* 2 | G. Borlaſe, B D *Pet. Col.* 2

[80]

From OXFORD.	From CAMBRIDGE.
Oɴ. H.Randolf, AM Magd 1	E. Mapletoft, AM Christ's Coll. 2
Nov. Fra. Tutte, AM Chriſt Ch 1	Cha. Norris, AM Trinity 2
Dec. J. Burrough, DD Magd 2	Sam. Blackhall, BD Eman 1

N. B. The Figure after each Name ſhews whether the Preacher's Turn is for the 1ſt or 2d Part of the Month.

His MAJESTY's HOUSHOLD.

Lord Steward,
WILLIAM, Earl Talbot, 146cl. a year
Treaſurer of the Houſhold,
Earl of Saliſbury, 1200l
Comptroller,
✻ Right Hon. Sir Richard Worſley, Bart. 1200l
Cofferer,
✻Viſ. Beauchamp, 500l.
Deputy Cofferer,
✻H. S. Conway, Eſq;
Clerks, P. Nicol, H. Hunter, George Nicol
Clerk of Veniſon Warrants,
Peter Nicol, Eſq;
Maſter of the Houſhold,
✻Sir Francis Henry Drake, Bt.
Clerks of the Green Cloth,
✻ G. Bridges Brudenell, Eſq.
✻Richard Vernon, Eſq;
✻Sir Ralph Payne, K. B.
Clerks Comptrollers,
✻Sir W. Auguſt. Cunynghame, Bart. ✻Sir William Gordon, K. B. ✻Lovel Stanhope, Eſq; 1018l each.

Aſſiſt. Clerks,
John Fanſhaw, Wm Blenman, Henry Boulton, Joſeph Stephenſon, William Bray.
Meſſenger to the Board of Green Cloth, Alex. Law, 76l
Porter to ditto, Wm Fuller, 48l

Chamber Keepers,
T. Hammond, Jane Stephenſon

Neceſſary Woman to ditto,
Ann Spencer, 35l
ACCOMPTING HOUSE,
Yeoman, G. Secker, Eſq; 100l
Edward Salter, 80l
Grooms,
John Staples, John Webſter, 58l
Chamber-keepers,
T. Hammond, Mary Edwards 40l
PANTRY:
Gentleman, Iſaac Clarke, 200l
Groom, Samuel Daller, 60l
Porter, George Robſon, 50l
BUTTERY:
Gentleman, Robt Butcher, 200l
Yeoman, Hugh Hughes, 100l
Groom, Abraham Holles, 90l
Aſſiſtant, James Taylor
WINE CELLAR:
Gentleman, T. Stillingfleet, 300l
Yeoman, John Davidſon, 120l
Groom, John Mackie, 100l
Aſſiſtant, Richard Hall
Porter, John Tucker, 50l
Keeper of the Store-cellar,
Robert Drake, 100l
Coffee-room, Mary Hornby
EWRY:
Gentleman, H. N. Willis, 280l
Yeoman, David Evans, 100l
Aſſiſtant, Alex. Roſs, 40l
Sole Houſhold Laundreſs,
Henrietta Willis
SPICERY:
Clerk, Joſeph Ramus, Eſq; 200l
Aſſiſtant Clerk, J. Wall, 100l
Porter, Th. Molineux, 30l

Woob-

[81]

COAL-YARD:
Clerk, John Gale, 17ol
Yeoman, Jeremiah Fox, 12ol
Coal Porters, George Worley,
Rob. Henderson, Th. Deane, Wm Milner, Wm Chisholm, Wm Frye, 40l each
CONFECTIONRY:
Yeoman, Thomas Street, Frederick Kuhff, 50l each
Groom, Rich. Robinson, 40l
PASTRY:
Yeoman, William Roberts, 50l
Groom, John Pot, 40l
Furner, Tho. Doughty, 30l
SILVER SCULLERY:
Yeoman, Edward Williams, 70l
Groom, Nath. Wilson, 60l
Assistants, Wm Davidson, Wm Wakefield, Rowland Hopkins, 30l
Whitener, Jane Lewis, 30l
Pan-keepers, 30l. each,
Rich. Warren, William Temple
PewterScowerer, Jane Edge, 30l
Assistants, Dorothy Stamford, Walt. Gibons, Dan. Warford
BUTTER and EGG OFFICE.
Keeper, Eliz. Dyer, 60l
Deliverer of Greens,
John Hook, 60l
HARBINGERS:
Gentleman, T. Willis, Esq; 60l
Yeomen, Rob. Parsons, Tho. Stone, Hen. Bright, Jn Basset, Archib. Sinclair, Rob. Elliot, 50l each
Keeper of Ice-Houses,
Frances Talbot, 100l
ALMONRY,
Yeoman, Rev. William Charles Dyer, 50l
Groom, William Lewis, 40l
Serjeant Porter,
W. Gardner, Esq; 120l

Yeomen Porters, 60l
Th. Morgan, Hugh Watts,
Adam Younger
Grooms, 50l
William Lewis, David Rice, John Randall
Porters at Somerset-house,
William Stevenson, 50l
Basil Rogers, John Gercken
Porter at the Gate of the Queen's House,
Philip Cross, 60l
1st Assistant Porter, and Sweeper of the Courts at ditto,
David Trehern, 30l
2d Ditto, George Harlow, 25l
Watchman at ditto,
Humphry Wheelwright
Car-takers,
Yeoman, John Stephenson, 50l
Groom, Joseph Johnson, 40l
MARSHALSEA.
Knight Marshal,
Sir Sydney Meadows, Knt.
Marshal's Men, 20l
Robert Lee, Wm Simmons, R. Franklin, Thomas King, Rob. Smith, Wm Shipman
Coroner of the Verge,
Henry Norton Willis, 30l
Clerk of the Verge,
William Bray, Esq; 30l
Cock and Crier, John Barrett
Debenture Office,
1st Clerk, Geo. Talbot, Esq;
2d Clerk, Cha. Talbot, jun.
Watchman at St. James's,
Charles Parrott, 45l 7s 6d
Bell-ringer, Ann Loman, 25l
Water Engine-turner,
Benj. Drawbridge, 25l
Cistern-cleaner,
William Martin, 55l 13s 6d
Sweeper of the Courts at St. James's, Mary Rickley

H

[82]

Wine Porters, J. Earl, G. Birch
Keeper of the Fire Buckets,
Margaret Barker, 30l
Keeper of Parkgate, Kenfington,
John Elly, 27l
Table Decker to the Maids of Honour & Bed-ChamberWomen,
James Eaton, 50l
Table Decker to the Chaplains,
John Lewis, 50l
  KITCHEN,
Clerk Comptroller,
John Secker, Esq; 50 ol
Clerk, Ch. Ramus, Efq; 250l
1ſt Clerk, H. Wheelwright, 150l
Junior Clerks, Peter Baron, John Byde, 58l
Porters, 30l Jn Love, Jn Good
Firſt Maſter Cook,
John Dixon, Efq; 237l 10s
Second Maſter Cook,
W. Weybrow, 217l 10s
Yeoman of the Mouth,
G. Harris, 140l
Yeomen of the Kitchen,
Nath. Gardiner, Peter Donaldson, 130l
Grooms, 100l.
Th. Winfield, W. Smailes, Wm. Cope, Geo. Rowlinson
Children,
Cha. Smith, Alex. Kennedy, Roger Beare, J. Pye, 90l. each
Maſter Scowerers,
Joshua Evans, John Luke, 80l
Aſſiſtant Scowerers, 30l. each.
Dan. Stratford, Tho. Alden, John Painter, William George, Richard Miles, Tho. Pindirll

6 *Turn-broches,* 2 *Door-keepers,* 2 *Soil-carriers,* 25l. each
  PURVEYORS,
Of Bread, Thomas Angelie, John Dyer, 50l
Baker, James Sheridine
Wine, John Carbonell, Rich. Stainforth, Arch. Paxton
Fiſh, Mary Fordham, Joſ. Arnold, Eliz. Ziletto.
Poulterers, William Hutton, John Bickerton, Tho. Wood
Linen-draper, Marg. Stewart
Grocers, Thomas Wells, Eliz. Fleming, John Clarke.
Oilmen, Rd Warner, Rt Frisby
Purveyor of Muſtard and Vinegar, John Clarke
Butchers, Eliz. Knutton, Tho. Sears, J. Eldridge, Caleb Smith
Fiſhmonger, Eliz. Maiſhfield
Purveyor of Bacon, Butter and Cheeſe, Louis Ramus
Braziers and Ironmongers, Norris, Hart, and Hopkins
Pewterer, James Miſt
Tallow-chandlers, Handcock, Netherſole, and Rainforth
Waxchandlers, Iſ. & Jn. Barrett
Oyſters, Thomas Wilton
Cutler, Drew Drury
Glaſs-man, John Thompson
China-man, John Cooper
Turner, Jonathan Ordway
Brewer, T. Bentley
Tea-man, Robert Sanxay
Cork-cutter, Richard Gimbert
Fruit, Savage Bear
Lemons & Oranges, J. Wiſeman

The Officers of Yeomen of the Guards to his Majeſty, inſtituted by Henry VII, anno 1486.—*At firſt there were only* 50 *Yeomen, but afterwards* 100: *Of which* 8 *are called Uſhers, who have each* 10l. *per ann. more than the other Yesmen.*

HUGH Viſcount Falmouth, *Captain,* 1000l a Year
 Nathan Garrick, Eſq; *Lieutenant,* 500l

            Enſign,

[83]

Enfign, J. Benjafield, Efq; 300l
Clerk of the Cheque,
Thomas Gregg, Efq; 150l.
Exons, William Trent, Nath.
Caufton, Samuel Warburton,
Francis Barker, Efqrs. 150l.
Secr. James Crane, Efq;
Eight Ufhers, 49l 11s 3d
Wm. Johnfon, Peter Campbell, John Broughton, William Jones, John Bull, Samuel Brown, Wm. Perkins, Ifrael Jones
100 *Yeomen at* 39l 11s 3d
4 *Superannuated, at* 25l
6 *Yeomen Hangers and* 2 *Yeomen Bed-goers, at* 10l *each.*
Meffengers, Wm Whitehead, Thomas Panton

The Honourable Band of GENTLEMEN PENSIONERS,
Eftablifhed 1590.

GEORGE, Lord Edgcumbe, *Captain,* 1000l a Year
Villers William Lewis, Efq; *Lieutenant,* 500l
John Lee Warner, Efq; *Standard bearer,* 310l
Thomas Hayward, Efq; *Clerk of the Cheque,* 120l

Gentlemen Penfioners who wait | *Gentlemen of the Band who*
in the New Year *and* Mid- | *wait in the* Lady Day *and*
fummer *Quarters,* | Michaelmas *Quarters,*

1 William Sands,   1 Samuel Aveline,
2 Thomas Poultney,   2 John Moone,
3 Richard Bridger,   3 John Paddey,
4 James Parker,   4 John Bennerman,
5 Fletcher Main,   5 Edward Weft,
6 William Spencer,   6 Charles Whiftons,
7 John Bicknall,   7 John Ingram,
8 Abraham Ewings,   8 Frank Capell,
9 Samuel Spalding,   9 Joseph Manwaring,
10 John Wild,   10 John Burton,
11 Andrew Thacker,   11 John Taylor,
12 John Phipps,   12 Triftram Maries Madox,
13 Thomas Powfey,   13 Lewis Gafchlin,
14 Samuel Atkins,   14 Martin Wright,
15 Stephen Artand,   15 Thomas Hughes,
16 Geering Lane,   16 Aaron Kendall,
17 Andrew Alpine,   17 Tradway Odber,
18 Robert Pitt,   18 Harry Hooley
19 John Rice   19 Thomas Panton Carr
20 Thomas Sandford, Efqrs.   20 Thomas Benfon, Efqrs.
100l. a Year each   100l a Year each

Philip Cade, Efq; *Pay-mafter.*   Cha. Friday, Gent. *Harbinger.*
Mr. James Walker, *Axe-keeper and Meffenger.*

A LIST of *Officers and Servants* under the MASTER of HORSE.

Master of the Horse,
Duke of Montagu, K G
1266l 13s 4d a Year
Auditor and Clerk Martial,
Benj. Carpenter, Esq; 260l a Y.
Equerries, 300l a Year each,
Benjamin Carpenter, Esq;
Sir William Hamilton, K. B.
T. Bishop, J. Johnston,
Frecheville Ramsden, Esq;
Edward Mathew, Esq;
Phil. Goldsworthy, Esq;
Pages of Honour, 26cl
Geo. Bristow, Will. Paul Cerjat, Hen. Lev. Hall, Sol. Hen. Durell, Esqrs.
Equer. of the Crown Stable,
James St. Amour, Esq; 200l
Gentleman of the Horse,
Richard Berenger, Esq; 256l
C. of Sta. W Stephens, Esq; 224l
Under Clerk, D. Parker, 10cl
Clerk of the Avery,
Charles Palmer, Esq; 125l
Store-keeper, R. Drake, jun. 93l
Riding Pur. Rt Drake, Esq; 200l
Surveyor of Highways,
John Smith, Esq; 82l a Year
Purveyors and Graniters,
Capt. George Swiney,
Henry Reveley, Esq; 94l
Serjeant of the Carriages,
Mr. Charleton, 86l
Yeoman of the Carriages,
John Greenberry, 36l a Year
Yeomen Riders,
Mr. James Montagu, 186l
Mr. Thomas Smith, 130l
Assistant, Wm. Parnham, 40l
Riding Surv. Ralph Bell, Esq; 30l

Serj. Farrier, Geo. Shaw, 98l
Marsh. Farr. Edw. Snape, 50l
Yeo. Far. Grif. Howell, 36l 10s
Esq; *Sadler,* R. Harrison, 58l
Yeoman Sadler, J. Hardisty, 36l
Coachmaker, John Barnard, 36l
Harness Maker, W. Ringsted
Bitt-maker, William Kerr
Sedar Chair-maker to their Majesties, Samuel Vaughan
Mews-keeper, Edw. Lloyd, 36l
Stable-keepers, 36l a Year each.
Kensington, Fred. Countze
Hampton-court, John Cook,
Windsor, Geo. Woods, 27l 6s
Newmarket, Match. Tims, 25l
Twelve Footmen, at 53l. each.
Four ditto for the Master of the Horse, 53l each
Six Coachmen, and one for the Master of the Horse, 65l
King's Coachman,
—— Williams, 73l a Year
King's Postchaise-man,
Thomas Frere, 40l a year
Chaiseman, Richard Gray, 40l
Eight Postilions, 30l a Year
Seven Helpers, 30l a Year
Four Chairmen, 42l a Year
12 *Hunting Grooms, and Six for the Master of the Horse,* 60l
Bot. Groom, Jn Wilkinson, 82l
Gent. Armourer, Jo. Griffin, 3.1l
Page of Back Stairs, D Parker, 31l
Porter, John Holland, 18l
Porter at Upper Gate, E Gale, 25l
Messenger, Ch. M'Grigor, 25l
For keeping six Running Horses at Newmarket,
Tho. Panton, Esq; 600l. a Year
Hampton

Hampton Court Stud.
Stud-keeper, Th. Parnham, 40l
Stud Farrier, John Spencer, 20l
1st Stud Groom, Th. Parnham
Groom, James Fishwick, 36l
4 Helpers, Robert Shepherd,
Wm Oakes, Tho. Ringham,
John Johnson, 30l *each*
Heater of Water for the Horses

Sarah Peat, 25l
Watchman, Rich. Scott, 26l
Pumper at the Mews,
William Ruston, 23l 8s
Milliner, Jane Mott, 10l 10s
2 *Door-keepers to the great Stables*, at 23l 8s *each*
Office-keeper, E. M'Grigor, 15l

His Majesty's Board of Works, &c. (Scotland Yard.)

Surveyor General,
× **W**Hitshed Keene, Esq;
Comptroller,
Sir W. Chambers, Knt.
Surv. of the Private Roads,
×Hon. Henry Fane
Master Mason and Deputy Surveyor,
Master Carpenter,
Robert Taylor, Esq; 200l
Architects, 300l *each*,
James Adam, Esq; F. R. S.
Thomas Sandby, Esq;
Paymaster of the Works,
×Geo. Aug. Selwyn, Esq; 500l
Deputy, Gabriel Mathias
Secretary, Clerk to the Board, and Clerk Itinerant,
Kenton Couse, Esq; 200l
Surv. of Gardens and Waters,
William Varey, Esq; 500l
Chief Clerk and Clerk Engrosser,
Richard Ripley, Esq;
Other Clerks of the Works,
At St. James's, Whitehall, and Westminster, John Woolfe
At Richm. & Kew, Th. Fülling
At Hampton-court, Wm. Rice
Clerk at Newmarket and New Park Lodge, James Payne
At the Tower, S. Pepys Cockerell
At Kensington, John Smith
At Windsor Castle, and Queen's Lodge, T. Tildesley
The Mews, Hen. Holland, jun.
The Queen's Palace and Carle-

ton-House, Kenton Couse
Greenwich Palace, Wm Leach
Labourers in Trust,
Cl' of the King's Private Roads,
Samuel Warren
Clerk to Comptroller, Th. Fülling
Office Clerks, John Yenn,
Geo. Horsley,
Edw. Crocker,
ARTIFICERS *by Patent.*
Master Carver, Sam. Norman
Master Glaziers,
At Whitehall, Westminster, Tower, and Somerset-House,
St. James's, Hampton-Court, Kensington, and Greenwich,
Richard and John Cobbett
Master Joiners, Mess. Kelsey and West
Serjeant Painter, James Stuart
Master Plaisterer, Tho. Clarke
Wire Worker, Sarah Bacon
Bricklayer at the Tower, and Kensington, Mr. Henry Holland
Ditto, at the Queen's Palace, King's Mews, Whitehall, and Westminster; John Groves
Ditto, at St. James's, Ed. Gray
Ditto, at Richmond, Sol. Brown
Ditto, at Windsor, Tho. Reeve
Ditto, at Hampton-court, &c.
Salter Field
Carpenter at the Tower, and Mews, William Miles
At St. James's, Westminster, & Greenwich, —— Colt

[86]

At Kensington, and Whitehall, James Filewood
At Hampton-court, G. Shakespeare
At Windsor, Henry Emblin
At Newmarket, John May
Smith *at Kensington*, Ja. Palmer
Clock-maker, *and Smith at Windsor*, John Davis
Engine-maker *to the Palaces*, Eph. Brookes
Engine Keeper *at Whitehall*, Leonard Phillips
Engine Keeper *at St. James's*, Thomas Blakely
Glazier *at Richmond, and Kew*, R. Cobbet
At Windsor, Rowland Davis
Joiner *at St. James's, and Hampton-Court*, W. Greenell
At Windsor, Thomas Jenner
At the Mews, Wm Clarke
Whitehall, Westminster, Richmond, and Kew, James Arrow
Ironmonger, Fra. Barron
Mat-layer *&* Turner, J. Gerard
Mason, John Devall
At Windsor, J. Slingsby
At Richmond and Hampton-court, Edward Anderson
At Kew Palace, T. Hardwick
Painter, Elizabeth Betts
Painter *at Kensington*, W. Evans
Pavier, William Meredith
Plaisterer, Thomas Clark
At New Park Lodge, John Engleheart
Plumbers *at Windsor*, Mary and Wm Henry Cutler
Pump-maker, John Wright
Blacksmiths, Mary Hartley, Wm Palmer, & Dan. Cooper
later, John Westcot
Tin-man, Gideon Dare

Master Gardener,
At St. James's, and Kensington, Thomas Robinson
At Richmond, John Haverfield
At Hampton Court, L. Brown
At Windsor, Adam Younger
Office Keeper, John Spence
Messenger, John Banks.

Officers of the Duchy of CORNWALL.
Lord Warden of the Stannaries, and Steward of the Duchy of Cornwall,
Rt Hon. Hum. Morice, 450l
Vice Warden,
×Henry Rosewarne, Esq; 400l
Surveyor General,
Sir Edw. Bayntun, Bt. 466l
Auditor of the Duchy,
×John Buller, Esq; 220l
Dep. Auditors, Rd. Gray, and Richard Gray, Jun. Esqrs.
Steward of the Hundreds,
Nich. Donnithorne Arthur, Esq;
Stewards of the Stannary Court,
Martin Davis, John Lawry, John Thomas, Fra. Polkinghorne, Esqrs.
Assay-Master of Tin,
John Luxmore, Esq; 200l
Receiver General,
×Edw. Elliot, Esq; 77l a Year
Comptroller of the Stannaries,
John Luxmore, Esq; 50l a Year
Supervisors of the Tin in Cornwall and Devon,
John White, George Johns, John Peters, Jos. Taunton, 80l a Year

TREASURER *of the* CHAMBER'S *Office, Cleveland-row*
×Rt. Hon. Lord Cha. Spencer, 469l 8s a Year
Deputy, ×Hugh Owen, Esq;
Comptroller of the Chamber,
Tho. Jones, Esq; 150l
Clerk, William Webb
Office-keeper, James Eaton

The Establishment of his Royal Highness, GEORGE AUGUSTUS
FREDERIC, *Prince of* WALES.

- *Groom of the Stole,*
Lord Southampton
Gentlemen of the Bed-chamber,
⁕Earl of Courtown
⁕Lord John Clinton
⁕Lord Viscount Parker
Treasurer and Secretary,
Lt. Col. Hotham
Master of th' Robes and Privy Purse,
Henry Lyte, Esq;
Grooms of the Bed-chamber,
Hon. Mr. Legge, Hon. Step. Digby, John Johnson, Esq;

First Equerry and Commissioner of the Stables,
Lt. Col. Lake
Equerries, Lt. Col. Hulse, Lt. Col. Sir John Dyer, Bart,
Lt. Col. Stevens
Pages of the Back Stairs,
Tho. Robinson, John Lockley
Jn Christian Santhague, Esqrs
Pages Man, John Sharp
Clerk of Stables, J. Montagu.
Sempstress, Mrs. Marg. Scott
Housekeeper, Mrs. Nowel

The Establishment of Her MAJESTY's HOUSHOLD.

Lord Chamberlain, 120ol
Earl of Aylesbury
Vice Chamberlain, 50ol
(Vacant.)
Mistress of the Robes, 50ol
Duchess Dow. of Ancaster
Ladies of the Bed-chamber, 50ol
Duchess of Argyll
Countess Dow. of Effingham
Countess Dow. of Egremont
Countess of Hertford
Countess Dow. of Holdernesse
Viscountess.Weymouth.
Maids of Honour ⁕, 3col
Miss Diana Beauclerk
Miss Mary Tryon ⁕
Miss Ann Boscawen
Miss Caroline Vernon
Miss Elizabeth Jefferyes
Miss Charlotte Gunning
Bed-chamber Women, 30ol
Hon. Mrs. Frances Tracy
Hon. Mrs. Anne Brudenell
Mrs. Mary Boughton
Mrs. Margaret Bloodworth.

Mrs. Sophia Fielding
Keepers of Robes, Mrs. Schwellenbergen, Mrs. Hagerdorn
Assistants, Mrs. Laverocke, Mrs. Pascall
Sempstress and Laundress,
Mrs. Deborah Chetwynd
Gentlemen Ushers of the Private Chamber, 20ol
Edwin Fran. Stanhope, Esq;
Maj. Gen. Wynyard,
John Jenkinson, Esq;
Gentlemen Ushers Daily Waiters,
William Allen, Esq;
Col. Gust. Guydickens, Esq;
John Cowslade, Esq; 150l
Gent. Ushers Quarterly Waiters,
Hen. Revely, Tho. Fauquier, John Smith, Esqrs. 100l
Pages of the Presence,
Mr. Henry Sutherland
Mr. Joseph Cooper
Physicians, 200l
Sir John Pringle, Bart. F R S;
Sir George Baker, Bart. FRS.

⁕ All the Maids of Honour are stiled Hon. and rank as
Barons Daughters.

Physician Extraordinary,
Dr. W. Hunter, F R S. 200l
Physician to the Houshold,
Dr. John Turton, F R S.
Surgeon, 150l
Pennell Hawkins, Esq;
Surgeon to the Houshold, 150l
William Bromfield, Esq;
Apothecary,
Mr. Aug. Hermann Brande
Apothecary to the Houshold,
Mr. John Devaynes
Pages of the Back Stairs, 80l
Mess. F. Nicolay, Fred. Albert,
Lewis Albert, H. Compton,
Assist. Tho. Davenport
Hair Dresser, Edward Evans
Mantuamaker, Mary M'Kenzie
Necessary Woman to the Private Apartmts, Mrs Jane More, 56l
Necessary Woman to the Public Apartments, Mrs. A. White, 34l
Treasurer, the Earl of Guilford
Treas. Cl' Vinc. Mathias, Esq;
Secretary and Comptroller,
×Hon. Geo. Aug. North, Esq;
Attorney-General,
250l
Sollicitor-General,
×Charles Ambler, Esq; 180l
Mess. to attend the Treasurer,
Geo. Hawkins, Philip Maule
Master of the Horse, 800l
Earl Waldegrave
Equerries, 220l *each,*
J. Schutz, Esq; Col. J. Crawford, Hon. John West
Pages of Honour, 150l *each,*
George Hotham, Esq;
John Spencer Smith, Esq;
Clerk of the Stables,
William Cowden, Esq; 150l
Bottleman, L. Matthey, 50l
Five Coachmen, 45l each
Eight Footmen, and 3 for the

Master of Horse, 41l 1s each
Two Grooms, 55l 10s each
Four Chairmen, 39l 17s 6d
Five Postillions, 20l 10s each
Five Helpers, 20l 10s each.
Queen's Band of Musick,
Mr. Hay, 1st Violin
————, Organist
Mr. Brown, 2d Violin
Mr. Rawlings, 3d Violin
Mr. Murray, 4th Violin
Mr. Vincent, 1st Hautboy
Mr. Simpson, 2d Hautboy
Mr. Gordon, Violoncello
Mr. Bennet, Tenor
Mr. Zuckert, Double-bass
Queen's Chamber Band,
Signor Bach, Signor Abel, Mr. Simpson, Mr. F. Nicolai

The Establishment of Prince WILLIAM *and Prince* EDWARD.
Governors, Gen. Budé, J. Bruyeres, Esq;
Preceptors, Rev. J. Majendie, Rev. A. Humphry.
Pages, C. Magnollay, H. Miller
Pages Man, John Hand
Porters, F. Winkworth, and W. Tuckfield
Housekeepers, Mrs. Whitehouse, Mrs. Fraser
Five Maid Servants.
Dancing Master, Phil. Denoyer
Writing Master, Mr. Roberts
Watchman, Solomon White

The Establishment of the ROYAL NURSERY.
Governess,
Lady Charlotte Finch, 600l
Sub-Governess,
Miss M. C. Goldsworthy, 300l
Assist. Sub-Governess,
Miss Hamilton
French

[89]

French Teacher,
Mad. Moula, 300l
English ditto, Miss Planta 100l
Wet Nurse to the Pr. of Wales,
Mrs. Margaret Scott, 200l
Wet Nurse to Prince Frederick,
Mrs. Mary Griffith, 200l
Wet Nurse to Prince William,
Mrs. Sarah Tuting, 200l
Wet Nurse to the Princess Royal,
Mrs. Frances Muttlebury, 200l
Wet Nurse to Prince Edward,
Mrs. Anne Percy, 200l
Ditto to Princess Aug. Sophia,
Mrs. Dorothy Thursby, 200l
Ditto to Princess Elizabeth,
Mrs. Spinluff, 200l
Ditto to Pr. Ernest Augustus,
Mrs. Cheveley, 200l
Ditto to Prince Augustus Frederick, Mrs. Prescot
Ditto to Pr. Adolphus, Mrs. Hopkins
Do to Prs. Mary, Mrs. Adams
Do to Prs. Sophia, Mrs. Willis
Do to Pr. Octavius, Mrs. Harris
Pages to the younger Princes and Princesses, C. Powell, —— Braund
Dress't to Princesses, Miss Niven
Assistant, Miss Sorrell,
Dry Nurse to the Princes,
Mrs. Martha Baulk
Necessary Woman to the Nursery,
Rockers, Mrs. C. E. Rhelingen, and Mrs. Mary Randal
Nursery Maid, Georgiana Long
Workwoman to the Princes,
Miss Elizabeth Chapman
Ditto to the Princesses,
Miss Griffiths.

The Establishment of his Royal Highness the Duke of GLOUCESTER.

Treasurer, Ed. Le Grand, Esq;
Gentleman of the Horse,
Grooms of the Bedchamber,
Maj. Gen. Amherst, Col. Cox,
Lieut. Col. Heywood
Equerries, Hon. Capt. Bennet,
Mr. Miller, Col. Lowther
Secretary, Rev. Dr. Duval, F. R. S.
Page of the Back Stairs, Mr. Alex. Stiell
Pages of the Presence, Mr. John Alcock, Mr. Robert Bryant, John Knight
Housekeeper, Mrs. Han. Wood
Butler, Mr. Alex. Lockhart
Cook, Frederick Plinke
Gent. Porter, Mr. John Shield
Clk. of Stables, Mr. Alex. Stiell
Musical Establishment,
Signor Felice Giardini,
Signor G. Cirri
An under Butler, two Coachmen, Six Footmen, Two Postillions, two Helpers, four House Maids, Two Kitchen Maids, a Page's Man, Two Runners, Six Grooms

The Establishment of his Royal Highness the Duke of CUMBERLAND.

Treasurer, Ed. Le Grand, Esq;
Grooms of the Bedchamber,
Lieut. Gen. Craig, Colonel Deaken, Capt. Jennings
Equerries, Lieut. Col. Sir Tho. Fowke, Col. Garth, T. B. Parkyns, Esq;
Secretary, Rev. Dr. Duval, FRS
Pages, Mr. Miller, Mr. Jackson, and Mr. Broadhurst
Pages of the Presence,
Mr. Waterhouse, and Mr. Jackson, jun.

House Steward and Clerk of
  the Kitchen,
Mr. James Galloway
  Keeper of the Wardrobe,
Mr. Jackson, jun.
Butler, Mr. Flower
Cook, Mr. Card
Porter, Mr. Smith
Housekeeper, Mrs. Flower
Clerk of the Stables, Mr. Stiell
  Band of Musick,
Signor Felice Giardini
Mr. Redmond Simpson
Mr. William Waterhouse
  Clerk of the Musick,
Mr. Redmond Simpson
Three Housemaids, Five Footmen, Two Coachmen, Four Grooms, Two Postillions, and Helpers

The Princess AMELIA's *Establishment.*
Ladies of the Bedchamber,
Lady Harriott Vernon,
Lady Anne Howard,
Lady Mary Fitz Gerald, 400l

Gentlemen Ushers,
Lt. Col. Rolt, Lt. Col. Stephens, and Capt. Wadman, 100l
Page of Honour,
Edward Stephens, Esq; 100l
Bedchamber Women,
Mrs. Middleton, Miss Howard, and Miss Russell, 100l
Housekeeper, Mrs. Godin
Wardrobe Women,
Mrs. Judd, & Mrs. Mavor, 30l
Pri. Purse, and HouseSteward,
John Turner, Esq; 400l
Pages of the Back Stairs,
Philip Hughs, Edw. Smith, Edward Powell, Esqrs. 100l
Porter of the Back Stairs,
George Watts, 60l
Clerk of the Stables,
J. Stillingfleet, 60l
Coachman, Wm Kingston, 40l
Under Butlers, William Watts, and Aaron Boyce, 40l
Four Footmen, 41l 1s each
Two Chairmen, 30l each
Two Postillions, 25l each
Two Helpers, 20l each

HERALDS COLLEGE. 1340. (*St. Bennet's Hill.*)

Earl Marshal and Hereditary Marshal of England,
THE Duke of Norfolk
Dep. E. of Effingham
3 KINGS.
Garter Princip. King of Arms,
Ralph Bigland, Esq;
Clarenceux King of Arms,
Isaac Heard, Esq;
Norroy King of Arms,
Peter Dore, Esq;
6 HERALDS.
Chester, Jn Martin Leake, Esq;
York, George Fletcher, Esq;
Lancaster, Tho. Lock, Esq;
Windsor, Geo. Harrison, Esq;

Somerset, J. C. Brooke, F.S.A.
Richmond, Ra. Bigland, jun. Esq
4 PURSUIVANTS.
Blue Mantle, Ch. Townley, Esq.
Rouge Croix, Fr. Townsend, Gt
Portcullis, J. Doddington Forsh, Gent.
Rouge Dragon, B. Pingo, Gent.
Earl Marshal's Secretary,
Isaac Heard, Esq;
Registrar. Ralph Bigland, Esq;

Heralds Extraordinary.
Norfolk, Ste. Mart. Leake, Esq;
Mowbray, J. Edmondson, Esq;
Nottingham, Edm. Kelly, Esq;

KNIGHTS *of the Most Noble Order of the* **GARTER,**
Instituted January 19, 1350.

1 The SOVEREIGN	2 The Prince of Wales
3 Duke of Gloucester	4 Landgrave of Hesse Cassel
5 Prince Ferdinand	6 Prince of Orange
7 Duke of Cumberland	8 Bishop of Osnabrug
9 Duke of Mecklen. Strelitz	10 Prince of Brunswick
11 Duke of Leeds	12 Duke of Newcastle
13 Duke of Montagu	14 Duke of Northumberland
15 Earl of Hertford	16 Marquis of Rockingham
17 Earl of Bute	18 Duke of Marlborough
19 Duke of Grafton	20 Earl Gower
21 × Lord North	22 Earl of Rochford
23 Visc. Weymouth	24
25	26

Dr. John Thomas, Bishop of Winchester, *Prelate of the Order.*
Dr. John Hume, Bishop of Salisbury, *Chancellor.*
Rev. and Hon. John Harley, D. D. *Registrar.*
Ralph Bigland, Esq; *Garter Principal King of Arms.*
Sir Francis Molyneux, Knt. *Usher of the Black Rod.*

KNIGHTS COMPANIONS *of the Most Honourable Order of the* BATH. *Instituted* 1399, *and revived* 1725.

1760 The SOVEREIGN.	1767 His R. H. Bp of Osnabrug
1725 Earl of Breadalbane	1744 Sir Henry Calthorpe
1747 Lord Hawke	1753 Lord Beaulieu
1753 Rt Hon. Sir Edw. Walpole	1761 Sir George Pococke
1761 Rt Hon. Sir Jos. Yorke	1761 ×Sir John Griffin Griffin
1761 Lord Amherst	1761 ×Sir George Warren
1761 ×Sir Charles Frederick	1763 Earl of Bellamont
1764 Sir William Draper	1768 Sir Horace Mann, Bt.
1770 Sir John Lindsay	1771 ×Sir Ralph Payne
1771 Sir Eyre Coote	1771 Sir Cha. Thompson, Bt.
1771 Rt. Hon Sir Wil. Lynch	1772 Sir Rob. Murray Keith
1772 Sir William Hamilton	1772 ×Lord Macartney
1774 Sir Rt Gunning, Bart.	1774 ×Sir Geo. Howard
1774 Rt Hon. Sir J. Blaquiere	1775 ×Sir William Gordon
1775 ×Sir John Irwin	1776 Sir Guy Carleton
1776 Sir William Howe	1777 ×Sir Henry Clinton
1778 Sir Edward Hughes	1779 ×Sir James Harris
1779 Earl of Antrim	1779 ×Sir Hector Monro
1780 Sir Tho. Wroughton	1780 Sir Richard Pierson

1780 ×Sir George Brydges Rodney, Bart.
Dr. John Thomas, Bishop of Rochester, *Dean of the Order.*
Thomas Gery Cullum, Esq; BATH *King of Arms.*
John Suffield Brown, Esq; *Genealogist, & Blanc Coursier Herald.*

William

William Whitehead, Esq; *Registrar and Secretary*.
Isaac Heard, Esq; *Gentleman Usher of the Scarlet Rod, and Brunswic Herald*.
William Rowland Tryon, Gent. *Messenger*.

KNIGHTS *of the Most Antient Order of the* THISTLE.
Instituted 1540, *revived* 1703.
The SOVEREIGN.

1 Earl of Portmore
2 His R. H. Prince Wm Henry
3 Duke of Queensberry
4 Earl of Carlisle
5 Duke of Buccleugh
6 Viscount Stormont
7 Duke of Roxburgh
8 Earl of Northington
9 Earl of Roseberry
10 Earl of Galloway
11 Duke of Gordon
12 Marquis of Lothian

Dr. Rt Hamilton, *Dean of the Order*. × Geo. Dempster, Esq; *Sec*.
Campbell Hooke, Esq; *Lion King of Arms*.
Robert Quarme, Esq; *Gentleman Usher of the Green Rod*.

FOREIGN MINISTERS *from the Northern Provinces*:

Germany and Hungary,
Envoy Extra and Min. Plen.
Count de Belgioso, *Portman-square*
Sec. Baron de Raigersfeldt
Russia,
Envoy Ext. and Min. Plen. M. de Simolin, *Grosvenor-square*
Cons. M. Lisakewitz
Sec. M. Dourasioff
Sweden,
Env. Ex. B. de Nolken, *Soho-sq*.
Sec. M. Asp
Consul, M. Grill
Denmark,
Env. Ex. Monf. de Dreyer, *Bulstrode-street*
Consuls, Nich. Fursman, Peter Ancker
Poland,] *Min. Res*. M. Bukaty
Prussia,
Minister Plenipotentiary, Comte

de Maltzan, *Corke-str*.
Secretary,
M. Jeanneret de Dunilac
Hanover,
Minister, Baron de Alvensleben, *Dover-street*
Bavaria,
Envoy Extra, *and Minister Plenipo*. Count de Haslang, *Golden-square*. Minister also for the Elector Palatine
Hesse Cassel,
Min. Res. Baron Kutzleben
Saxony,
Env. Ex. Co. Bruhl, *Dover-st*,
Secretary, Mr. Ernest
Holland,
Hans Towns,
P. Amsinck, Esq; *Ag. & Cons.*
Steel-yard, *Thames-street*

His Majesty's MINISTERS in the *Northern Provinces.*

Vienna,
Env. Extra and Plenipo. ×Sir
Robt Murray Keith, K. B.
Brussels,
Resident, Alleyne Fitzherbert, Esf
Russia,
Envoy Extra and Plenipo.
×Sir James Harris, K. B.
Sweden,
Env. Ex. Sir T. Wroughton, K. B.
Copenhagen,
Env. Ex. Morton Eden, Esq;
Poland,
Min. Plen.
Commissary at the Republic of Dantzig, Alex. Gibsone, Esq;
Prussia,
Envoy Ex. Hugh Elliot, Esq;

Saxony,
Env. Ext. ×Sir Jn Stepney, Bt.
Min. Plenipo. to the Elector Palatine, and *Minister* to the Diet of Ratisbon,
Alex. Gibsone, Esq;
Electors of Cologne, Mentz, Triers, & Circle of Westphalia,
Min. Plen.
Holland,

Rotterdam,
Agent,
Agent at the Brill for his Britannic Majesty's Packet,
Resident with the Hans Towns, Emanuel Mathias, Esq;

FOREIGN MINISTERS *from the Southern Provinces.*

France,

Spain,

Two Sicilies,
Env. Extra, Prince Caramanico
Lower Brook street
Secretary, M. Phlijger
Portugal,
Envoy Extra, and Min. Plen.
Chev. de Pinto, *South Aud. str.*

In his Absence, Chev. de Sousa and Holstein
Secretary, M. de Freire
Sardinia,
Env. Extra, Marquis de Cordon, *Lincoln's-Inn-fields*
Venice,
Resident, Count de Cavally
Republic of Genoa,
Minister, M. d'Ageno

His Majesty's MINISTERS *to the Southern Provinces.*

France,

Spain,

Portugal,
Envoy Extra and Plenipo.
Hon. Robert Walpole.
Constantinople,
Ambass. Sir Rob. Ainslie, Knt.
Sardinia,
Envoy Extra and Plenipo.
Lord Mountstuart.

Naples,
Envoy Extra and Plenipo.
Hon. Sir Wm Hamilton, K. B.
Florence,
Envoy Extra,
Sir Horace Mann, Bt. K. B.
Venice,
Resident, John Strange, Esq;
Swiss Cantons,
Minister, Wm Norton, Esq;

I

His Majesty's CONSULS *Abroad, for the Protection of Trade.*

Portugal,
Lisbon, Sir John Hort, Bart. Conful General
Oporto, John Whitehead, Esq;
Faro, John Lempriere, Esq;
Madeira, Cha. Murray, Esq;

Spain,
Conf. Gen.
Alicant,
Barcelona,
Cadiz,
Canaries,
Carthagena,
Corunna,
Malaga,
Seville and *St. Lucar,*

Italy,
Cagliari, Clem. Richardson Esq;
Genoa, John Collet, Esq;
Leghorn, John Udney, Esq;
Naples, James Douglas, Esq;
Nice, John Birkbeck, Esq;
Sicily and Malta, Daniel Boomeester, Esq;
Venice, Robert Richie, Esq;
Zante, Peter Sargint, Esq;

Morocco,
Cha. Logie, Esq; *Conful General.*

Barbary,
Algiers, Agent and Conful General, Natha. Davison, Esq;
Tripoli, George Cooke, Esq;
Tunis, James Trail, Esq;
Pruffia, Memel, Rt Byres, Esq;
Ruffia, Walter Shairp, Esq;

Denmark,
Elfineur, Nich. Fenwick, Esq;

Norway,
Bergen, John Wallace, Esq;
Drontheim, Alex. Brown, Esq;

Sweden,
Gothenburg, &c. T. Erskine, Esq
Oflend, Nieuport, and Bruges, John Peter, Esq;
Trieste, Fiume, &c.
Nathaniel Green, Esq;

Confuls appointed by the **Turkey Company,**
Aleppo, John Abbott, Esq;
Smyrna, Anthony Hayes, Esq;
Cyprus, John Baldwin, Esq;
Tripoly in Syria, Thomas Phillips Vernon, Esq;
Latichea, John Murrat, Esq;
Salonica, John Olifer, Esq;
Patras, Daniel Paul, Esq;

Officers of the TREASURY. *(Whitehall.)*

Lords *Commiſſioners.* (5)
×LORD North, KG 4000l
×Lord Weſtcote,
×Lord Viscount Palmerſton
×Sir Richard Sutton, Bart.
×John Buller, sen. Esq; 1600l. a Year each

Joint Secretaries,
×Sir Grey Cooper, Bart. ×John Robinson, Esq;

Private Sec. to the Firſt Lord.
William Brummell, Esq;
Chief Clerks, Milw. Rowe, Esq, Sir Ferdinando Poole, Bart.

Tho. Pratt, Fr. Reynolds, Esqrs.
Other Clerks on the Eſtabliſhment,
T. Tomkins, J. Royer W. Speer,
W. Beldam, Francis Dancer, Edward Bisſhopp, Tho. Cotton,
Geo. Herbert, Hen. Fowler,
E. Chamberlayne, J. Ma. Leake,
W. Mitford, T. Dyer, Sir Edw.
Boughton, Bart. G. Ed. Ramus,
W. Brummell, Geo. Trenchard
Goodenough, Bryan Broughton,
Dean Poyntz, Wm Edw. Smith,
Hen. Webſter, Wm Pembroke.
Clerks

Clerks of the Revenues,
William Speer, 400l
George Herbert, Hen. Fowler,
Fr. Dancer, J. Royer, Sir Edw.
Loughton, Bart. 200l W. Ed.
Smith, W. Pembroke, 100l
Thomas Pratt, Esq; *for taking Care of the Papers,* 40cl
Office Keeper,
Benedict Schaller, 300l a year, *and to find Coals and Candles for the Office.*
Sollicitors, 500l
Hugh Valence Jones, Esq;

Wm. Chamberlayne, Esq;
Messengers of the Exchequer,
John Walker, Tho. Harrison,
Wm Refs, Tho. Gibbons
Messengers of the Chamber,
Samuel Darnley, and Samuel Darnley, jun. 6s 8d a day
Housekeeper to the Levee Room,
Elizabeth Shaw
Necess. Woman, Mrs. Appleby
Bagbearer and Ranger of Books,
William Watson
Door-keeper, Hanbury Potter

Officers of the RECEIPT *of his Majesty's* EXCHEQUER.

Chancellor and Treasurer,
R T. Hon. Lord North, 1800l
Auditor, Duke of Newcastle
Chief Clk. Edw. Wilford, Esq;
Clerk of the Debentures,
John Hughson, Esq;
Clerk of the Registers and Issues,
Robert Jennings, Esq;
Clerk of the Cash-book,
H. Pynyot, Esq;
Assist. Clerks, James Fisher, David Moreau
For making out Excheq. Bills,
Ch. Cl. Wm Cracroft, Esq;
Ab. Acworth, J. Fisher, Esqrs.
Mess. to the Auditor's Office,
John Jackson
His Deputy, James Pilfold

In the Offices for ANNUITIES *under the* AUDITOR.
Ch. Clk. Nich. Paxton, Esq;
Other Clerks, William Moone, Ellis Wrench, David Moreau, Alex. Hayworths, Esqrs.
Chief Clerk. K. Tynes
Other Clks. M Cock, J. Paddy, W. Hucks, R. Edmonds, Esq.
Messenger, Tho. Littlefoot

Examiners of Tellers Vouchers,
John Hays, Henry Saxby, John Meheux, Esqrs.
Clerk of the Pells,
Rt Hon. Sir Ed. Walpole, K.P.
Dep. and 1st Cl. E. Roberts, Esq
Clk. of Exitus, C. Roberts Esq
Cl. of Declarat. W. Kingsman
Cl. of Patents, Aug. Baron
Assistant Clerk, Jos. Cotton
Ingrossing Clerk, Wm. Blake
Assist. Edward Kinsman

OLD ANNUITY PELLS OFFICE.
Chief Clerk, Wm. Blake, Esq;
Other Clerks. Wm. Oram, Jn Mills, Brackley Kennett, John Kingsman

NEW ANNUITY PELLS OFFICE.
Chief Clerk, L. Theobald, Esq;
Other Clerks, J. Touchett, Ham. Clement, J. Holmes

Four TELLERS *of the* RECEIPT, &c.
1 Earl of Hardwicke
Dep. and 1st Cl. D. Wray, Esq;
W. Wright, J. Langton,

T. Wing, Efqrs.
2 Earl of Northington
Dep. & 1ft Clerk, W. Price, Efq;
John Price, Hen. Sealey, Rob.
Fran. Suft, Efqrs.
3 Earl Temple
His Dep. & 1ft Cl. J. Wells, Efq
T. Smith, P. Cade, R. Woodward, Efqrs.
4 *Hon. J. J. Pratt
His Deputy and 1ft Clerk,
Charles Townfhend, Efq;
T. Jones, T. Penyng, G. Harris
Money Porters, Fra. Williams,
Fra. Petit, Tem. Au. Goodman
Porter to the Exch. J. Jackfon
Superintend. of Exch. Watch.
J. Jackfon, and Th. Littlefoot,
36l 10s each
Eight eftablifhed Watchmen,
at 36l 10s per ann.

TALLY-COURT.
Chamberlain,
Hon. Fred. North
Montagu Burgoyne, Efq;
Deputies, Abraham Farley,
Ja. Galloway, Wm Hammond,
Geo. Rofe, Efqrs.
Tally-writer for the Auditor,
Abraham Ackworth, Efq;
Clks. W. Jones, & P. Mowbray
Clerk of the Introitus,
(Vacant.)
Tally-cutter, Th. Lambe, Efq;
His Dep Cha. Alexander
Ufher of the Exchequer,
Hon. Horace Walpole, Efq,
His Dep. Charles Bedford, Efq;
His Clerk, William Harris
Yeoman Ufher, Wm. Harris
Paymafter of Exchequer Bills,
Edm. Bott, George Ritzo
Nat. Barwell, Efq;
Comptroller of Exchequer Bills,
John Thornton, Efq;

Accomptant, Wm Jones, Efq;
Clerks, W. Cook, F. Wanion,
Rich. Ripley
Houfekeeper, Mrs. Appleby
Meffenger, James Piffold

TAX OFFICE.
Commiffioners, 500l each.
Chrift. Rigby, J. Trenchard,
Daniel Bull, Geo. Blount,
Ch. Deering, J. Eames, G.
Heathcote, Efqrs.
Sec. George Rofe, Efq; 90l
Affift. Sec. Ed. Naifh, Efq; 60l
Solic. Hen. Wilmot, Efq; 100l
Clerks. Chriftopher Fowler, 60l
Chriftopher Fowler, jun. 50l
John Henry, 50l G. Burfey,
T. Brent, 40l
Chamber-keeper and Meffenger,
Jacob Knockey, 60l
Neceff. Wo. Mrs. Creffwell, 20l
Ten general Surveyors, 100l
Samuel Lea, Ant. Oldfield,
J. Palmer, Wm. White,
P. Maurice, Fra. Coulfon,
Wm. Smith, Tho. Jones,
Jof. Faikney
173 *Surveyors of Count.* 50l. a
Year in Eng. 40l in Wales.

IMPREST OFFICE,
Scotland-yard.
Auditor, *Wm Aiflabie, Efq;
Deputy, John Bray, Efq;
Clerks, Charles Harris,
Edw. Beckwith, J. Beckwith,
B. Cobbe, G. Harris, T. Taylor
Office-keeper, Mrs. Harris

IMPREST OFFICE,
Lincoln's-Inn.
Auditor, Lord Sondes
Deputy, John Lloyd, Efq;
Clerks, T. Dobfon, J. Hughes,
Brid. T. Hooke, John Walker,
Ja. Davids
Office-keeper, Thompfon Tuttle

[97]

Auditors of the Land Revenue, Land Tax, and Window Tax, viz. for the Counties of Lincoln Nottingham, Chester and Derby.—Palace-yard.
H. Shelly, Fr. Warden, Michael Sergifon, Eſqrs.
Dep. Aud. Rd. Gray, Eſq;
Clerk, Rd. Gray, jun.
Auditor for all the other Counties in England,
James Weſt, Eſq; for Life

Deputy, Beriah Hills, Eſq;
1ſt Clerk, James Rowlands
2d, Richard Gray
For the Principality of Wales,
Lord Newborough
1ſt Clerk, Owen Davies
2d Clerk, John Fenwick

Paymaſter of Penſions,
Right Hon. Lord Gage
Deputy, Tho. Hopkins, Eſq;

High Court of CHANCERY.
(*Office in Chancery-lane.*)

Lord High Chancellor of Great Britain,
EDWARD Lord Thurlow
Maſter or Keeper of the Rolls,
Rt. Hon. Sir Tho. Sewell, Kt.
Maſters in Chancery, 100l
Rt. Hon. Sir T. Sewell, Knt.
P. Holford, Eſq; *Sym. Inn,* FRS
Thomas Anguiſh, Eſq; *Sym. Inn*
✶Wm Graves, Eſq; *Sym. Inn*
Samuel Pechell, Eſq; *Sym. Inn*
John Eames, Eſq; *Sym. Inn*
Edw. Montagu, Eſq; *Sym. Inn*
Edw. Leeds, Eſq; *Lincoln's Inn*
Wm Weller Pepys, Eſq; *Sym. Inn*
John Hett, Eſq; *Sym. Inn*
✶Jn Ord, Eſq; No. 25, *Lincoln's Inn Old Buildings*
· C. Bicknel, Eſq. *Chancery-lane*
Accomptant General,
Tho. Anguiſh, Eſq; *Linc. Inn*
Clerks, T. Cracroft, J. Warren,
E. Smith, J. Parkinſon
Clerk of Crown, ✶Hon. J. Yorke
Deputy Clerk of the Crown,
Charles Frewen, Eſq;
Clerks, T. Rugeley, JnPenſam
Prothonotary, Rev. Ch. Willes,
Robert Wilmot, Eſq;
Deputy, John Adams
Six Clerks,
Samuel Reynardſon, F R S.

W. Mitford, Chriſt. Zincke, Neh. Winter, William Sewell, Eſqrs.
Deputies, Meſſrs. Dalton, Trollop, Nicholls, Wainwright, Briſtow, Vanheythuyſen
Sixty Sworn Clerks,
In Mr. Reynardſon's Diviſion,
John Colman, Fr. Douce,
Fr. Dalton, S. Thoyts, John Seaman, Wm Maton, Ch. Owen Cambridge, R Preſton, J Silveſte
In Mr. Mitford's Diviſion,
Joſ. Nicholls, Solomon Fell, Geo. Bowles, John Cottrell, Th. Handley, Darcy Tancred, John Rittſon
In Mr. Zincke's Diviſion,
Robert Cheſter, Tho. William Baynard, R. Smith, Robert Wainwright, Tho. Sheppard, Ch. Frewen, Peter Confett
In Mr. Woodford's Diviſion,
Fr. Ja. Scrope, William Meares, Henry Gale, Elb. Woodcock, R. Briſtow, Th. Marriot, C. Heblethwayte
In Mr. Winter's Diviſion,
John Radcliffe, Tho. Metcalfe, J. Greenhill, E. Boutflower, Herbert Croft, George Birch, G. L Van Heythuyſen, J Wilday

[93]

In Mr. Sewell's Division,
Rd. Palmer, Joseph Hill,
Henry Barker, W. Mic. Lally,
W. Trollope, A. Hilton, W.
Hobbs, J. Cheveley, Esquires.
Record-keeper, J. H. Bateman
Princ. Regist. D. of St. Alban's
   Lord Chancellor's Registers,
Ben. Green, J. Dickins, Esqrs.
Master of the Rolls Registers,
Stephen Martin Leake, Esq;
Peter Wright, Esq;
Ck of Exceptions, John Paulson
  Bag-bearer to the Registers,
Thomas Phillipson
    Entering Registers,
Francis Dickens, Esq;
His Clerk, William Edwards
James Weldon, Esq;
His Clerk, John Forster
Cl. of Reports, Tho. Elde, Esq;
His Clerks, J. Vicary, G. Kimber
  Register of the Affidavits,
Edw. Woodcock, Esq;
Deputy,
    HANAPER *Office.*
  Master of the Hanaper,
Earl of Northington
Deputy, John Church, Esq;
Clerk, Henry Edw. Church
   DISPENSATION *Office.*
Clerk, Hon. Apsley Bathurst
Dep. Charles Talbot, Esq;
His Clerk, Will. Tayleure, Esq;
Ward. of the Fleet, J. Eyles, Esq;
Keep. of Records in the Tower,
Rt. Hon. Sir Jn Shelley, Bt.
Ch. Clk. Tho. Astle, Esq; 2001
  Records, down to 1483, are
  kept in the Tower, and since
  that time in the Rolls Chapel.
Clerk of the Records in the
  Rolls Chapel, Jn Kipling, Esq;
  EXAMINER'S OFFICE.
Henry Flitcroft, Esq; *Examiner.*
His Deputies, Alex. Williams,

J. Bateman, James Dancer
Copying Cks under Mr. Flitcroft,
W. Langley, Jonath. Langley,
W. Dance, W. Butcher
John Spooner, Esq; *Examiner*
His Deputies, E. Edmonds, ——
Morgan, John Smith
Copying Cks under Mr. Spooner,
John Morgan, John Wills,
James Heatley, J. Smith
  Clerks of the Petty Bag,
Henry Thomas, Charles Deave,
Thomas Mendham, Esqrs.
Deputy, J. Love
Patentee of the Subpœna Office,
Wm. Courtenay, jun. Esq;
Their Clerk, G. Hardisty
Rec. of the Sixpenny Writ Office,
D. Minet, Esq;
Deputy, Peter Sykes
Chafe Wax, A. Cowper, Esq;
Dep. Rob. Appleyard
Sealer, Rev. Wm. Lloyd
Deputy, Mr. John Dowse
  Clerk of the Letters Patent,
Valentine Hen. Wilmot, Esq;
Deputy, James Seton
Exam. of the Letters Patent,
And. Huddlestone
  Clerk of the Presentations,
    (Vacant.)
Deputy, —— Welsh.

Commissioners of BANKRUPTS
    First List.

Thomas Nugent, Esq; *Queen*
  square, Holborn
John Gascoyne Fanshaw, Esq
  Bedford-row, or No. 7, Lin
  coln's-inn Old-buildings
John Scott, Esq; *No. 8, Hol*
  born-court, Gray's-inn
John Acton, Gent. *Swithin's*
  lane
Sam. Denison, Gent. *Feather*
  stone-buildings
               Seco

Newman-street, Oxford-road
Joseph Eyre, Gent. Town-ditch, Christ's Hospital
Third List.
Wm. Bumpsted, Esq; No. 4, Holborn-court, Gray's-inn.
Henry Hunter, Esq; Holborn-row, Lincoln's inn-fields
Henry Russell, Esq; No. 25, Lincoln's-inn Old-buildings
Henry Cowper, Esq; No. 11, Paper-buildings, Temple
Richard Hargrave, Gent. Cheshunt, Hertfordshire, or at Grigsby's Coffee-house.
Fourth List.
John Cookson, Esq; Great Queen-st. Lincoln's-inn-fields
John Crofts, Esq; No. 4, Bedford-row
Lancelot Brown, Esq; No. 8, Lincoln's-inn New-square
Edward King, Esq; Cook's-court, Carey-street
David Rees, Gent. Featherstone-buildings
Fifth List.
Fowler Walker, Esq; No. 6, Lincoln's-inn New-square
Francis Talbot Scott, Esq; No. 15, Lincoln's-inn Old-sq.
John Thomas Batt, Esq; No. 1, Lincoln's-inn New-square
J. Reeve, Esq. Pump-C. Temple
Francis Russell, Gent. Red-lion-square, Holborn
Sixth List.
×Charles Robinson, Esq; No. 5, Lincoln's inn Old-buildings
John Nares, Esq; No. 3, Fig-tree-court, Temple
Sylvester Douglas, Esq; Lin-

Edward Wilmot, Esq; ditto
H. Stebbing, Esq; No. 1, Pump-court, Temple
John Elderton, Gent. No. 10, Lincoln's-inn New-square
Robert Fry, Gent. Feather-stone-buildings
Eighth List.
Thomas Burrell, Esq; No. 9, Lincoln's-inn New-square
Richard Calvert, Esq; No. 7, Lincoln's-inn Old-buildings.
William Boscawen, Esq; Cloysters, in the Temple
Charles Bragge, Esq; Elm-court, Temple
Robert Hassell, Gent. No. 5, Lincoln's-inn Old-buildings
Ninth List.
Henry Boult Cay, Esq; Cursitors street
John Bicknell, Esq; No. 3, Lincoln's-inn Old-buildings
T. Erskine, Esq; Serjeant's-inn, Fleet-street
Anthony Pye, Esq; Feather-stone-buildings
John Lancaster, Gent. Holborn
Tenth List.
Cha. Nalson Cole, Esq; Carey-st
George Hardinge, Esq; Adelphi Buildings
Robert Peers, Esq; New Ormond-street
John Blake, Gent. Essex-street, Strand
Walter Pye, Gent. Lincoln's-inn
Eleventh List.
Nathaniel Jones, Esq; No. 1, Church-yard-court, Temple
An

Andrew Hudleston, Efq; No. 5, *Concy-court, Gray's-inn*
John Lloyd, Efq; *Hendon, Middlefex*
William Morgan, Gent. No. 31, *Orchard ftreet*
John Willington, Gent. *Church-yard-court, Temple*
Twelfth Lift.
Robert Comyn, Efq; No. 11, *Lincoln's-inn Old fquare*
Thomas Mulfo, Efq; *Rathbone-Place*
Randle Ford, Efq; No. 7, *Lincoln's inn Old fquare*
James Templer, jun. Efq; *Bedford-fquare*
Aug. Pechell, Efq *Lincoln's-inn*
Thirteenth Lift.
Michael Dodfon, Efq; *Bofwell-court, Carey-ftreet*
J. B. Burges, Efq; *Lincoln's-inn*
William Jones, Efq; *Lamb's-buildings, Temple*
James Martin, Gent. *Effex-court, Temp'e*
(One Vacant.)

A Lift of the Meffengers to the Commiffioners of Bankruptcy.
Geo. Surridge, *Symond's-inn*
David Caddell, *Goldfmith-ftreet*
Tho. Vaughan, *Chancery-lane*
James Down, *Chancery-lane*
James Paris, *Chancery-lane*
Thomas Powell, *Symond's-inn*
Jo. Wells, *Fetter-lane*
James Willfon, *New-inn*
Patentee for making out Commiffions of Bankruptcy,
Hon. John Yorke
Dep. John Heaton
Clerk, Edmund Hodgfon
Sealers, Robert Appleyard, James Dowfe
Clerk of the Briefs,
William Philipps, Efq;

Dep. Rob. Tay. Raynes, Efq;
Clerks of the Inrolments,
The fix Clerks in Chancery, and three Clerks of the Petty Bag
Sworn Clerks, John Mitford, Thomas Brigftock
Clerk of Inrollments of Proceedings under Commiffions of Bankrupt, Harry Harmood, Efq;
Clerk of the Cuftodies of Ideots and Lunaticks,
Cha. Hen. Talbot, Efq;
Chief Clerk, —— Taleure
Corporation of Curfitors,
Principal, Tho. Gataker, Efq;
His Affiftants, J. Walker, Efq;
Curfitors,
Hugh Valence Jones, Thomas Lamb, Thomas Stephens, Charles Frewen, J. Hingefton, Elb. Woodcock, Law. Cottam, Henry Peele, Thomas Lloyd, R. Appleyard, Jeg. Wellard, R. Nuthall, Aug. Greenland, Tho. Hammond, George Hill, Ralph Aldus, Jern. Chevely, John Holt, John Vernon, jun. and Craven Ord, Efqrs.
Bag-bearer, Wm. Warren.

LORD CHANCELLOR'S OFFICERS.

Purfe-bearer, John Holt, Efq;
Principal Secretary,
Henry Wilmot, Efq;
Secretary of Bankrupts,
George Hill, Efq;
Clerk, James Turner
Secretary to the Prefentations,
Robert Talbot, Efq;
Sec. of the Comm. of Peace
Charles Bragge, Efq;
Secretary of Lunaticks,
Joseph Hill, Efq;

Com-

Commissioners of Lunaticks,
J. S. Colepeper, Cha. Cotton,
Aug. Greenland, Esqrs. Leon.
Martin, Cha. Owen, Gents.
  Receiver of the Fines,
John Fanshaw, Esq;
  Secretary of Decrees, Injunctions, and Appeals,
Randle Ford, Esq;
  Secretary of the Briefs,
(Vacant)
  Serjeant at Arms,
Richard Jephson, Esq;
  Deputy Serjeant at Arms,
Francis Mackljy, Esq;
  Messenger or Pursuivant,
Harry Harmood, Esq;
  Deputy, Mr. James Smith
  Gentlemen of the Chamber,
Mr. Gower and Mr. Brooks

Usher of the Hall,
Mr. Robert Aldus
  Cryer of the Court of Chancery,
Samuel Scholey
  Court Keeper, Robert Bloame
  Tipstaff, Mr. Groves
  Hall-keeper,
Walter Williams.
OFFICERS TO THE MASTER of the ROLLS.
  Chief Secretary,
Charles Deaves, Esq;
  Under Secretary,
Thomas Mendham, Esq;
  Train-bearer,
(Vacant.)
  Usher of the Court,
Samuel Seddon, Esq;
  Deputy, Mr. John Turner
  Tipstaff, Robert Appleyard.

N. B. *The figures prefixed shew the Rank of the twelve Judges.*

Court of KING's BENCH.

Lord Chief Justice and Judges,

1 **E**ARL of Mansfield, 5500l.
5 Edward Willes, Esq;
6 Sir W. H. Ashurst, Knt.
11 Francis Buller, Esq;
  Salary, 2400l. *a Year each.*
Master of the Crown office,
Sir James Burrow, Kt. F.R.S.
Marshal, Benj. Thomas, Esq;
Secondary, Fran. Barlow, Esq;
Cl. of the Rules S. Midgley, Esq;
  Clerks in Court,
F. Barlow, S. Midgley, R. Belt,
G. Lepipre, David Poole,
J. F. Abbot, J.O. Jones, Henry
Dealtry, Esqrs.
  Chief Clerks on Pleas Side,
Lord Viscount Stormont, and
  John Way, Esq.
Secondary, Ed. Benton, Esq;

Assistant, Rob. Forster, jun. Esq;
  Cl. of the Rules, T. Cowper, Esq
  Cl. of the Papers, Rob. Austen
  Clerk of the Day Rules,
John Way, Esq;
  Clerk of the Dockets,
Deputy, John Stride
  Clerk of the Declarations,
Deputy, J. Maddacks
Clk. of Bails, Posteas, & Estreats,
Richard Walter
  Signer of the Writs, J. Heberden
  Signer of the Bills for Middsx.
William Marshall
  Custodes Brevium,
Sir David Lindsay, Bart. F.R.S.
John Way, Esq;
  Clerk of the Upper Treasury,
Mr. Thomas White,
  Clerk of the Outer Treasury,
James Walker, Esq;
                    Filazer,

[102]

Filazer, Exigenter, and Clerk of the Outlawries, (Office in the Inner-Temple.)
Mr. Patience, Tho. Adams
Cl. of the Errors, J. Way, Esq;
Chief Cryer, John Cronkton
Cryers, Mr. Lloyd, M. Player
Ushers, Ca. Creed, D. Hewett
Deputy-Marshal, —— Jorden
Tipstaff to Lord Chief Justice,

To the other Judges,
Sherf. Holloway, Nath. Hill
Marsh. and Assoc. to Ch. Just. John Way, Esq;
Train-bearer, John Douse
Clerk of Nisi Prius in London and Middlesex, Mr. T. Lowten
Cryer at Nisi Prius in London and Middlesex, H. Woodgate

Receiver-General of the Profits of the Seals in the King's-Bench and Common Pleas,
Duke of Grafton
Seals, —— Rogers
Clerks of the Assize,
Home, Jerome Knap, Esq;
Associate, Mr. Wm Pope
Midland, John Blencowe, Esq;
Associate, Mr. Adams
Norfolk, Gerrard Dutton Fleetwood, Esq;
Associate, Mr. Bury
Northern, John Rigge, Esq;
Associate, Mr. Wharter
Oxford, Meredith Price, Esq;
Associate, Mr. Benj. Price
Western, John Follet, Esq;
Associate, Mr. John Clarke

Court of COMMON PLEAS, (1215.)

Chief Justice and Judges,
2 **R**T. Hon. Lord Loughborough, 4500l
4 Sir Henry Gould, Knt.
7 Sir G. Nares, Knt.
12 John Heath, Esq; 2400l
Office of Custos Brevium,
John Browning, Esq; Sir Rob. Eden, Bart. Fred. Young, and Edw. Gore, Esqrs.
Deputy, John Walton, Esq;
Prothonotaries,
Wm Mainwaring, Henry Earle, Anth. Dickins, Esqrs.
Secondaries, Hen. Fothergill, Alex. Gerrard, Wm. Skinn
Cl' of the Judgm. and Reversals, Rowland Lickbarrow
Cl' of Dockets & Declarations, Samuel Underwood
Clerk of the Recoveries, G. Byard

Assistant Clerk, Tho. Sherwood
Clerk of the Warrants Inrollments, and Estreats,
Keene Fitzgerald, Esq;
Deputy, Richard Lee
Chirographer,
Sir George Colebrooke, Bart.
Secondary, James Garth, Esq;
Reg. Geo. Keightley, Esq;
Clerk of the Treasury,
Thomas Jeffereys, Esq;
Treasury-keep. G. Stubbs, Esq;
Marshal to Chief Justice, (Vacant.)
Associate, (Vacant.)
Cryer, (Vacant.)
Trainbearer, (Vacant.)
Clerk of the Juries,
Mr. Bever
Deputy, Mr. Harrison
Exigenter, J. Meddowcroft, Esq;
Cl'

Cl' of the E.[T]oins, Mr. Wright
Deputy, Mr. Bolton
Cl' of the King's Silver Office
William Daw, Esq;
Deputy, Tho. Sam. Lemage
Clerk of the Errors, S. Hough

Clerk of the Outlawries,
John Way, Esq;
Clerk of the Jurats,
Michael Doriet, Esq;
Hereditary Chief Proclamator,
John Walker, Esq;

A LIST of the FILAZERS of the Court of COMMON PLEAS.

Counties.	Principals.	Execut. by	Counties.	Principals.	Execut by
Bedford			Sussex		Roberts, No. 7, Clifford's Inn
Berks		Roberts, No. 7, Clifford's Inn	Surry	Peyton	
Bucks	Jones		Kent		
Oxford			Essex	King	
Cornwall			Hertf		
Gloucester			Bristol		Clarke, King's-Bench-Office
Hereford			Dorset	Clarke	
Worcester			Poole		
London	Willes	Same	Somerset		
Middlesex			Suffolk	Lenton	Same
Hants	Lawes	Same	Cambridge	Ward	Ward, No. 8, Staple's Inn
Wilts			Huntingd.		
			Derby	Keepe	Rider, No. 115, Fetter-Lane
Cumberl.	Dawson	Same	Leicester		
Northum.			Notting.		
Westmor.			Warwick		
Newcastle			Devon	Batten	Batten, No. 4, Hare-co.
Norfolk	Roberts	Same	Kingston upon Hull	Lee	Lee, No. 8, Staple's Inn
Stafford			York		
Northam.			Yorkshire		
Salop					
Rutland			Lincoln	Sibthorp	Kelham & Johnson, No. 92, Hatton-st.
Monmouth					

The Court of EXCHEQUER.

× **R**IGHT Hon. Ld North
  Chancellor.
 Lord Chief Baron,
5 Sir John Skynner, Knt. 3500l

Three Barons, 2400l each,
8 Sir James Eyre, Knt.
9 Sir Beaumont Hotham, Kt.
10 Sir Richard Perryn, Knt.
      Cursitor

Curſitor Baron,
Francis Maseres, Eſq; F.R.S.
Secretary to the Chancellor,
Hon. G. A. North
Aſſiſtant Secretary,
James Best, Eſq;
King's Remembrance Office.
Remembrancer,
Lionel Felton Hervey, Eſq;
Deputy, Francis Ingram, Eſq;
1ſt *Secondary,* Charles Eyre, Eſq;
2d *Secondary,* R. Wood, Eſq;
Sworn Clerks,
Adam Martin, Ed. Taylor, Da. Burt. Fowler, Alex. Bennet, Will. Land
L. Treaſurer's Remembrancer,
Rt.H. Sir Richard Heron, Bart.
Dep. T. Chapman, Eſq; F.S.A.
Firſt Secondary,
John Perrot, Eſq;
Second Secondary,
Thomas Chapman, Eſq;
Sworn Clerks,
William-Seabrooke Wells
Jn Kipling, J. A. Grimwood
Filazer,
William-Seabrooke Wells
Clerk of the Errors in the Exchequer Chamber,
Philip Fonnereau, Eſq;

Deputy, William Cecil
Hereditary Chief Uſher,
John Walker, Eſq;
Deputy, Devereux Davies
Marſhal of the Court of Exchequer,
Maſter, Edmund Walker, Eſq;
Deputy,
Foreign Oppoſer,
John Duffell, Eſq;
Dep. Allatſon Burgh, Eſq;
Clerk of the Eſtreats,
Hon. H. Walpole
Deputy, Mr. Wm. Harris
Surveyor of the Green Wax,
George Roſe, Eſq;
Clerk of the Nichills,
Robert Forſter, junior, Eſq;
OFFICE *of* PLEAS,
Lincoln's-inn.
Maſter, Sir Edward Walpole
Dep. Tho. Collingwood, Eſq;
Attorneys,
Elias White, Edw. Kinaſton,
Rogers Jortin, Joſhua Peart
REGISTER *of* DEEDS *in the County of Middleſex.*
Office in Bell-yard.
Lionel Felton Hervey, Eſq;
Edw. Penton, Eſq;
Keene Fitzgerald, Eſq;

The PIPE-OFFICE, *Gray's-Inn.*

Clerk of the Pipe,
R T. H. Sir J. Shelley, Bt
Deputy, Edward Woodcock, Eſq;
Firſt Secondary,
Henry Cranmer, Eſq;
2d *Sec.* Robert Winter, Eſq;
Six Sworn Attorneys,
James Farrer, Ja. Cranmer,

P. Sykes, Allatſon Burgh,
Dan. Crofts, Jn Heaton, Eſqs
Board-End Clerks,
James Paine, Joſ. Hornby
Bag-bearer, Joſ. Porter
Comptroller of the Pipe,
Hon. Horace Walpole
Deputy Comp. John Smith
Clerk, William Harris

(105)

First-Fruits Office, in the Temple.
Remembrancer, George Barker Devon, efq;
Dep. Remembrancer, and Senior Clerk, Jn. Bacon, Efq. F.S.A.
Jun. Cl. William Shrigley
Receiver, Edw. Mulfo, efq;
Deputy, John Bacon
Comptroller of Firſt-Fruits and Tenths, ×Hon. Tho. DeGrey, efq
Deputy, John Bacon

Queen Anne's Bounty Office. (Dean's-Yard, Weſtmſter.)
Treaſurer, Vinc. Matthias, eſq;
Secretary, Rob. Chester, efq;
Solicitor,

Juſtices of the Grand Seſſions for the Counties in Wales.
Chester, Montgomery, Flint, and Denbigh Shires.
Ch. Juſ. ×Lloyd Kenyon, eſq;
Hon. Daines Barrington, eſq;
Brecon, Glamorgan, and Radnor Shires.

Tenths Office. (Temple.)
Receiver, Robert Chester, efq;
His Clerks, George Kipling, and Thomas Trufhit

John Williams, efq;
× Abel Moyſey, eſq.
Cardigan, Pembroke, and Carmarthen Shires.
W Beard, ×A. Macdonald, eſqrs

Augmentation-Office for Accounts of Abbey-Lands.
(New-Palace-Yard.)
Keeper of Records, H. Brooker

Angleſey, Carnarvon, and Merioneth Shires.
James Hayes, efq;
Thomas Potter, efq.

Serjeants at Law and **King's Counsel.**
Att.-Gen. ×James Wallace, efq;
Solic-Gen. ×Ja. Mansfield, efq;
King's Serjeant.
George Hill, efq.
King's Counſel.
×Charles Ambler, efq;
×Richard Jackson, efq;
Gryffyd Price, ×Fra. Cockayne Cuſt, Geo. Lewis Newnham, Ed. Bearcroft, John Madocks, Hon. Daines Barrington, J.

Froſt Widmore, Fran. Burton, ×Arch. Macdonald, Will Selwyn, ×Lloyd Kenyon, Jn. Lee, R. P. Arden, Hen. Howarth, and Tho. Cowper, efqrs.
Serjeants.
Anthony Keck, Joſeph Sayer, John Aſpinall, Wm. Kempe, Tho. Walker, Harley Vaughan, Naſh Groſe, James Adair, James Clayton Bolton, efqrs.

Duchy Court of Lancaster. (Gray's-Inn.)
Chancellor, Tho. E. of Clarendon
Attor.-Gen. × John Orde, efq;
Rec.-Gen. ×Thomas Orde, eſq;
Auditor of the South Parts, Sir W. H. Aſhhurſt, knt.
Audit. of North, S. Pechell, efq;
Clerk of the Council, Reg. and Sec.
× W. Maſterman, efq;

King's Serj. ×Jas. Wallace, efq;
King's Counſ. ×Sir Grey Cooper, Bart. Jn Tho. Batt. efq;
Surv. of Lands & Woods South of Trent, Fra. Ruſſell, eſq;
Surv. of Lands North of Trent, John Crowder, eſq;

K

(106)

Surv. of Woods North of Trent, Leicestersh. and Northamptonsh.
Will. Meiteman, esq; Jonath. Forster, esq; Leiceste
Swo.. Attorney in Court for the Derbysh. Mr. John Goodwin,
Crown, Francis Russell, esq; Ashborn
The other Sw. Att. T. Lloyd, esq; Staffordsh. Mr. Tho. Hinckley,
Ufs. & Mes. Chr. Saverland, gent Litchfield
  Receivers of the Rents. Monmouthshire, Richard Lucas,
Lancashire, P. Mottram, esq; esq; Magna Hock
Stockport Essex, Middlesex, and Hertford,
Yorksh. & Nottinghamsh. Fra. Mr. Tho. Aincon, Temple
  Russell, esq; Red-lion-square All other Count. South of Trent,
Lincolnsh. Geo. Denshire, jun. & Wales, Mr Jn. Thomas,
  esq; Stamford Pell-Office, Westminster-Hall

Officers of the County Palatine of LANCASTER.

Chancellor, Tho. E. of Clarendon | Cursitor, Mr. Thomas Bolton
Secretary, Francis Russel, esq; | Seal-Keeper, Mr. John Nabb
Vice Chancellor, Wm. Swinner- | Prothonotary,
  ton, esq; | Deputy, Mr. John Cross
Attorney-General and Serjeant, | Clerk of the Crown, Rt. Hon
  *James Wallace, esq; | Lord Ducie
Register, Examiner, and First | Deputy, Mr. Tho. Hankinson
  Clerk, *Tho. Orde, esq; | Cl. of the Peace, Geo. Kenyon,
Clerks of the Chancery, Mr. Ja. | esq;
  Mahon, Mr. Wm. Shawe | Deputy, Mr. James Taylor
  Mr. Jn. Grimshaw, Mr. Jn. | Messenger, Wm. Webb
  Nabb, Mr. Tho Wilson

Marshalsea Court, Southwark, and the Court of his Majesty's
  Palace at Westminster. Sittings every Friday.

Judges. | Four Counsels.
Lord Steward of the Houshold, | J. Chetwood, H. Boult Cay,
  Earl Talbot | J. M. Ellis, J. Brown, esqrs.
Knight-Marshal, Sir Sidney | Six Attornies.
  Medows | W. Monk, Rd. Kelsall, Christo-
Steward of the Court, Levett | pher Hobson, Ra. Hodgson,
  Blackbourne, esq; | R. Heighway, Jn. Woolrich
Deputy, Danby Pickering, esq; | Six Marshalmen.
Prothonotary, Rich. Bulstrode, | Rob. Lee, H. Mackender, R.
  esq; | Franklin, Tho. King, Rob.
Deputy, Mr. Robt Stainbank | Smith, Wm. Marshalman

(107)

The College of DOCTORS of LAW, exercent in the Ecclesiastical and Admiralty Courts, incorporated June 22, 1768. (Doctors-Commons.)

Rt. Worshipful Peter Calvert, LL. D. *Official Principal of the Arches Court of Canterbury, Master-Keeper or Commissary of the Prerogative Court of* Canterbury

Sir James Marriott, knt. *Judge of the High Court of Admiralty of* England, *and Master of Trinity-Hall,* Cambridge

Dr. William Wynne, *his Majesty's Advoc. - Gen. Vicar-Gen. to the Archbp. of* Canterbury, *Chancellor of the Diocese of* London, *Commissary to the Dean and Chapter of* St. Paul's, *and Commissary of* Bedford.

Dr. Andrew Coltee Ducarel, *Commissary of the City and Diocese of* Canterbury, *of the Royal Peculiar of* St. Catherine's, *of the Sub-Deaneries of* South-Malling, Pagham, *and* Terring, *in* Sussex, *and* F.R.A.S.S.

Dr. Geo. Harris, *his Majesty's Advoc. in his Office of Admiralty, Chancellor of the Dioceses of* Durham, Hereford, Landaff, *and* Winchester, *and Commissary of* Essex, Hertfordshire, *and* Surry

Dr. William Macham

Dr. Francis Simpson, *Chancellor of the Diocese of* Lincoln, *Official to the Archdeacons of* London, Canterbury, Middlesex, *and* Rochester

Dr. Thomas Bever, *Commiss. to the Archd. of* Huntingdon, *Judge of the* Cinque-

Ports, *Chancellor of* Bangor, *Comm:iss. to the Dean and Chapter of* Westminster, *and Official to the Archdeacon of* Oxford

Dr. Wm. Compton, *of Caius College,* Cambridge, *Chancellor of the Diocese of* Ely

Dr. William Scott, *Camden Professor in the University of* Oxford.

Dr. David Stephenson

REGISTERS, and other Officers.

Master of the Faculties, Dr. S. Hallifax, *Regius Profess. of Civil Law at* Cambridge.

Registers of the Arches Court.
Mr. John Grene
Godf. Lee Farrant, esq; *Princip. Regist. of the High Court of Admiralty of* England, *of the High Court of Delegates, and of the High Court of Appeals for Prizes, and one of the Clks. in the Prerogative-Office.*

Mr. Nath. Bishop, *Dep. Reg. of the Admiralty and Delegates, and Court of App. for Prizes*

Rev. Geo. Jubb, D. D. *Principal Register of the Prerogative Court of* Canterbury.

Deputy Registers, as also of the Faculty Office.
Mr. Henry Stevens
Mr. Geo. Gostling, jun.
Mr. John Grene.

Principal Registers of the Province of Canterbury.
Thomas Frost, esq; and
The Rev. E. Gibson

K 2

(198)

Register of the Faculty-Office.
George Goſtling, Eſq;
Proctors.
Ph. Champion Creſpigny, eſq; King's Proctor
Godf. Lee Forrant, eſq;
Mr. Hen. Major,
Mr. George Goſtling, *Dep.- Regiſt. of the Royal Peculiar of* St. Catherine's
Mr. Tho. Adderley, *Dep.-Reg. to the Commiſſ. of* Surry
Mr. Nath. Biſhop
Mr. Roger Altham, *Regiſter of the Archdeaconry of* Middleſex, *Regiſter to the Dean and Chapter of* Weſtminſter, *and Dep.-Reg. of the Dioceſe and Archdeac. of* Rocheſter.
Mr. Wright Bateman
Mr. Rob. Longden, *Dep.-Reg. to the Archdeacon of* Surry
Mr. Mark Holman, *Deputy-Regiſter of the Dioceſe, and to the Archdeac. of* London
Mr. John Grene
Meſſrs. Ed. Cheſlyn, Jn. Stevens, Wm. Geering, Mic. Fountain, G. Faulkner, J. Clarke, Ch. Al. Crickitt, Wm. Fuller

Mr. John Terriano, *one of the Clerks in the Prerogat.-Office*
Mr. Robert Jenner, *Deputy-Regiſter of the Dean and Chapter of* St. Paul's
Meſſ. G. Goſtling, jun. *(Proctor to the Admiralty,)* Ste. Luſhington, Edward Cooper, J. Heſeltine, J. Townley, Rob. Nath. Bogg, W. Abbot, Roger Longden, Hen. Blake, Chas. Biſhop, George Bellas, H. Goſtling, W. Wells, Geo. Marſh, *(one of the Clerks of the Prerogative Office,)* R. Slade, Ric. Cheſlyn Creſwell, T. Teſt, G. Bogg, T. Adderley. jun. J. Walker, M. Swabey, T. M. Morton, John Beard, Rob. Dodwell, John Shepheard, John Beard, John Bartholomew Bicknell, John Webb.
Apparator-Gen. of the Province of. Canterbury. Geo. Marſhal *Marſhal and Serjeant at Mace of the High Court of Admiralty of* England.
William Brough, eſq;
His Deputy, John Crickett

PRIVY-SEAL.

Lord Privy-Seal.
Earl of Dartmouth
Clerks to Privy-Seal.
Richard Grenville, eſq;
Richard Potenger, eſq;
Peter Cuchet Jouvencel, eſq;

Jacob Reynardſon, eſq;
Deputies.
Joſeph Belſon, eſq;
John Larpent, jun. eſq;
Secr. Ralph Heſlop, eſq;
Office-keeper, Mr. J. Routledge

SIGNET-OFFICE.

Chief Clerks.
William Blair, James Rivers, Joſ. Copley, and Montagu Wilkinſon, eſqrs.

Deputies
Rd. Shadwell, Ch. Brietzcke, John Jones, eſqrs.
Office-Keep. Mr. J. Routledge

TENANTS, &c. in England and Wales.

rl of Upper	Suffolk, Duke of Grafton
	Surry, Lord Onslow
f St. Alban's	Suffex, Duke of Richmond
Defpencer	Warwick, Earl of Hertford
of Hardwicke	Weftmorland, *Sir James Lowther
Cholmondeley	
Edgcumbe	Wilts, Earl of Aylefbury
ir James Low-	Worcefter, Earl of Coventry
	Yorkfhire, Eaft Riding,
eorge Caven-	Earl of Carlifle
	Lieut. and u4. Rot.
ulett	Yorkfhire, Weft Riding,
gby	Marquis of Rockingham
of Darlington,	Yorkfhire, North Riding,
	Earl Fauconberg, Lord Lieutenant
1am, Cuft. Rot.	
tochford	Marquis of Rockingham, Cuftos Rotulorum
of Berkeley	
ount Bateman	Tower Hamlets, Earl Cornwallis
of Salifbury	
ike of Man-	**WALES.**
	Anglefey, Sir Nicholas Bayly, Bart.
Dorfet	
l of Derby	Brecon, *Charles Morgan efq;
of Rutland	Cardiganfhire, *E. of Lifbutne
of Ancafter	Caermarthen, J Vaughan, efq;
e of Northum-	Caernarvon, Ld Newborough
	Derbigh, * Richard Myddelton, efq;
te of Beaufort	
f Orford	Flint.
arl of North-	*Sir Roger Moftyn, Bart. Cuft. Rot.
, Duke of Nor-	Owen Salufbury Brereton, Efq; Conftable of the Caftle
uke of New-	Glamorgan, Earl of Plymouth
of Marlbo-	Merioneth, *Sir Watkin Williams Wynn, Bart
f Winchelfea	Montgomery, Earl of Powis
live	Pembroke, *Hugh Owen, Efq;
d North	Haverfordweft, Lord Milford
ord Rivers	
lower	Radnor, Earl of Oxford

K 3

SECRETARY of STATE's OFFICE. *(St. James's.)*

NORTHERN DEPARTM.
Secretary of State.
Vifcount Stormont, K. T.
Under Secretaries.
B Langlois, W. Frafer, efqrs.
Chief Clerk, Jere. Sneyd, efq;
Sen. Clerks, Bryan Broughton, and G. Auft, efqrs.
Clerks, T. Bidwell, R. Carter, J. W. Jenkins, W. Money, and J. Manby, gents.
Chamber-Keepers, Rich. Turner, W. Milburn
Deputy, Thomas Ancell
Necef. Woman, Mrs. Southcott

SOUTHERN DEPARTM.
Secretary of State.
Earl of Hillfborough
Under Secretaries.
Robert Bell, efq;
Sir Stanier Porten, Knt.
Chief Clerk, Rd. Shadwell, efq;
Sen. Clerks, William Duck, Ch. Brietzcke, John Morin, efq&
Clerks, G. Randall, W. Henry, Higden, G. W. Carrington, T. Daw, J. Naffau Colleton, Hon. R. Chetwynd, gents.
Chamber-Keepers, Wm. Kirby, John Doudiet
Necef. Woman, Mrs. Emmitt

Gazette-Writer, Wm. Frafer, efq; 300l.
Deputy, George Auft, efq;
Secretary of Latin Language, Tho. Ramfden, efq; 200l.
Keeper of State Papers, Sir Stanier Porten, Knt.
Deputies, Sir Jofeph Ayloffe, Bart. Dr. Ducarel, and Tho, Aftle, efqrs.
Collect. and Tranfmitter of State Papers, Tho. Ramfden, efq;
Embellifher, T. Holland, efq;
Decypherer of Letters, Edw. Willes, efq; 500l. a year

AMERICAN DEPARTMENT. *(Whitehall.)*

Secretary of State.
× Lord George Germain
Under Secretary.
William Knox, efq.
Benjamin Thompfon, efq;
Chief Clerk, Wm. Pollock, efq;
Senior Clerks, John Larpent, Wm. Sawer, efqrs.

Clerks, Cha. Hanb. Williams, Wm. Allen, Eardley Wilmot, Charles Peace, Geo. Lew. Palman, Gents
Chamb.-Keep. Jn. Phil. Muley
Deputy ditto, Nath. Crowder
Neceffary-Woman, Mrs. Muly

Commiffioners of Trade and Plantations. (Whitehall.) 1660.

Lords Commiffioners.
Ld. Chancellor, Firft Commiff. of the Treaf. Ld. Pref. of the Council, Firft Commiff. of the Admiralty, Princip. Sec. of State, Chanc. of Excheq. Bp. of London, and Surv. and Aud. Gen. of all his

Majesty's Revenues in America, for the time being, together with Lord Granham, ˟ Lord Rob. Spencer, ˟W. Eden, ˟Hon. Thomas De Grey, ˟And. Stuart, Edward Gibbon, Hans Sloane, Benjamin Langlois, esqrs. 100l. each
*Sec.*ᴿ d. Cumberland,esq.750l.
*Dep.Sec.*Sil.Bradbury,esq.300l

Joint Sol. and Clerks of the Reports, Grey Elliot and John Goddard, esqrs.
Clerks, W. Berkley, W. Roberts, L. Dole Nelme, J. Powell, W.Lloyd, Jn. Goddard, F. R. Clark, W. Hughes
Counſ.toBoard,˟R.Jackſon,eſq;
Chamb.-Keep. Wm. Bonnick
Meſſ.& Door-Keep. Edw.Searle
Neceſſary Woman, Mary Searle

The Staff of the Army in America.

COMMANDERS in Chief, Gen. Frederick Haldimand, and Gen. ˟ Sir Hen. Clinton, K. B.
Adjutant-General,
Deputy-Adjutant-General, Major Richard St. George
Quarter-Maſter-General in New York, Col. Wm. Dalrymple.
Dep.-Quar.-Maſt.-Gen. at New York,
Aſſiſtant Deputy Quarter-Maſter-Gen. Lieut And. Durnford,
Muſter-Maſter-General, Lieut. Col. John Burgoyne
Maj. of Brigade, Jn.Small, A.Ph.Skeen,Th. Moncrieffe,eſqrs.
Barrack-Maſter-General, Major William Crofbie
Judge-Advocate, H. T. Cramahé, esq;
Aſſiſt. to Quarter-Maſt.-Gen.
Commiſſary-General of the Muſters, James Pitcher
Two Deputies to Ditto, Wm. Porter, James Webb
Commiſſ.-Gen. of Stores and Proviſions, Daniel Weir, esq.
Provoſt-Marſhall, Mr. Cunningham

Hospitals in North-America.

Superintend. Gen. of all the Hoſpitals, John Mervin Nooth
Phyſicians, M. Morris, R. Veal, C. Blagden, R Knox, H. Kennedy, W. Bruce, R. Roberts, J. M. Hayes.
Purveyor, and Phyſician Extra, J Mallet and W. Barr
Surgeons, A. Grant, J. Field, T. Forſter, P. Cole, J. Hayes, J. Weir, R. Hope, J. Mallet, J. Stuart, H. Beaumont, R. Knowles, J. Auchinlech, J. Marſhall, A Potto, B. Mace, J. Jefferies, R. Smith
Apothecaries, M. Croker, G. Browne, W. Payne, R. Mon-

ington, V. Wood, D. Mandeville, R. Proctor, P.
Bernard, A. Edwards, R. Bishop.

GOVERNMENTS IN AMERICA.

QUEBEC.
Gov. Lt. Gen. Fred. Haldimand
Lt.-Gov. Maj Gen. Tho. Clarke
Tn.-Maj. of Queb. Wm. Dunbar
Sec. George Pownall, esq;
Surveyor-Gen. of Canada, Sam. Holland, Esq. 36s.4.
Superintendant of Indians, Lt-Col. John Campbell
Clerk of the Crown, Wm Gordon, esq;
Ch.-Juft. Hon. P. Livius, FRS.
Judges, John Frazer, Edw. Southoufe, esqrs.
Rec.-Gen. Sir Th. Mills, Knt.
Provoft-Marfh.
Attorn.-Gen. James Monk, esq;
Judge of Adm. J. Potts, esq;
Collect. Thomas Ainflie
Compt. Colin Drummond
Agent, Rich. Cumberland, esq;
Provinc. Agent, T. Walker, esq;
Surveyor of Woods in Canada, 10s. per diem, and 40l. per ann.
Inspecter of Lands, Adolphus Benzell, esq; 300l.
Storekeeper at Quebec, Thomas Peckham, 8s. per diem
Clerk of the Survey, Kenelon Chandler, 5s. per diem

ST. JOHN's, in the Gulph of St. Lawrence.
Gov. Walter Paterson, esq;
Lt.-Gov. Tho. Desbrisay, esq;
Ch.-Juft. Peter Stuart, esq;
At.-Gen. Phillips Calbeck, esq;
Sec. and Reg. Tho. Desbrisay, esq;
Prov.-Marfh. and Rec. and Coll. of the King's Quit-Rents, Wm. Falton, esq;

Cl. of Courts, John Budd, esq;
Cl. of the Council, W. Nesbitt, esq;
Nav. Officer, Jav. Higgins, esq;
Commiffary of Stores and Prov. John Wepfter
Gov. Chap. Rev. Rich. Grant
Agent for the Ifland, Samuel Smith, esq.

NEWFOUNDLAND.
Gov. Richard Edwards, Esq;
Lt.-Gov. at St. John's, Lt. Gen. William Amherst
Ditto at Placentia, Lt.-Col. Jof. Gorham
Collect. Alex. Dunn, esq;
Compt. J. Hays
Nav. Officer,

NOVA SCOTIA, CAPE BRETON, &c.
Gov. Francis Legge, esq;
Lt-Gov. Sir An. Snape Hamond
Ch.-Juft. B. Finucane
Affift.-Judges, Ch. Morris, and Ifaac Deschamps, esq;
Attorn.-Gen. W. Nesbitt, esq;
Sol.-Gen. Rich. Gibbons, esq;
Prov.-Marfh. Jn. Fenton, esq;
Cl. of Crown, Geatt. Monk, esq;
Sec. Rd. Bulkeley, esq;
Treaf. Ben. Green, jun. esq;
Regifter, Arthur Goold, esq;
Chief Surveyor of Lands, Chr. Morris, esq;
Clerk to the Council, Richard Bulkeley, esq;
Nav. Offic. Winkw. Tonge, esq;
Collect. of the Customs, Henry Newton, esq;
Compt. Wil. Falcon, esq;
Surveyor and Searcher, John Newton, esq;

Judge of the V.-Adm. Court of Hen. Preston, esq.
Appeals, Jonath. Sewall, esq; *Commiss.* Geo. Baillie, esq;
Judge of the V.-Adm. Court, Nav. Off. Steph. Haven, esq;
Richard Bulkeley, esq; *Provin.Agent*, Grey Elliott, esq;
Judge of the Court of Escheats, *Port of Savannoh.*
Richard Bulkeley, esq; *Collect.* Alex. Thomson, esq;
Rec. of the King's Quit-Rents, Compt.&Search. W. Brown, esq;
Jos. Woodinass, esq; *Port of Sunbury.*
Dep.Aud. Mr. Laugh. Campbell *Collect.* James Kitching, esq;
Agent, Rich. Cumberland, esq; *Compt.&Sear.* If. Antrobus, esq;

NEW YORK.
Gov. Major-Gen. Ja Robertson
Lt.-Gov. Andrew Elliott, esq;
Ch. Just.
Att.-Gen. J. Tabor Kempe, esq;
Sec. to the Prov. Wm. Knox, esq;
Collect. and Rec.-Gen. of the Quit-Rents, Andrew Elliot, esq;
Compt. Lamb. Moore, esq;
Control. of Ordn. Th. Furnis, esq;
Storekeeper, F. Stephens, esq;
J. of V.-Adm. R. Morris, esq;
Register, Rich. Nichols, esq;
Nav. Officer, Sam. Kemble
Surv.-Gen. Edw. Fanning

SOUTH CAROLINA.
Gov.
Lt.-Gov. Wm. Bull, esq;
Sec. Tho. Skottowe

NORTH CAROLINA.
Gov. Josiah Martin, esq;
Lt.-Gov. Geo. Mercer, esq;

GEORGIA.
Gov. Sir Ja. Wright, Bart.
Lieut. Gov. Jn. Graham, esq.
Ch.-Just. Ant. Stokes, esq;
Attor.-Gen. Cha. Pryce, esq;
Sec. B. Thompson, esq; F.R.S.
Prov.-Marsh. James Ford, esq;
Treas. Noble Jones, esq;
King's Ag. J. B. West
Rec.Gen.QuitRts. Sir P. Houston
Sur.Gen.of Land, P. Yonge, esq;
Dep.-Audit. Grey Elliot, esq;
Clerk of the Crown and Pleas,

EAST FLORIDA.
Gov. Col. Patrick Tonyn
Lt.-Gov. John Moultree, esq;
Ch.-Just. James Hume, esq;
Attor.-Gen. J. Gordon, esq;

CIV. ORDN. in E. FLORIDA.
Storekeeper and Paymaster.
—— Hall, esq; 8s. *per diem*
Cl. of Survey and Cheque, John Penn, 5s. *per diem*

St. AUGUSTINE.
Coll. of the Customs, Sir John Burdett, Bart.
Deputy, John Holmes, esq;
Compt. and Nav. Officer, Alex. Skinner, esq;
Cl. of the Common Pleas, &c.
John H lmes, esq;

WEST FLORIDA.
Gov. Peter Chester, esq;
Lt.-Gov. Elias Durnford, esq;
Ch.-Justice, Wm. Clifton, esq;
Attor.-Gen. Edm. Rush Wegg
Cl. of Council, Sec. and Reg. Ja. Macpherson, esq;
Prov.-Marsh. Sam. Hannay
Vend. Mast. & Nav. Off. Alex. Ross

CIV. ORDN. in W. FLORIDA.
Storekeeper and Paymaster, Arthur Neil, esq; 8s. *per diem*
Clerk of Survey, Joseph Smith, 5s. *per diem*
Clerk of Cheque, Ben. Gowar, 5s. *per diem*

(114)

Barrack-Maſt. John Browne, Eſq; 5s. *per diem*
Surg. Jn. Lorimer, 6s. *per diem*

TOBAGO.

Lt. Gov. Peter Campbell, eſq;
Sec. and Reg. A. Wood, eſq;
Pro. Marſh. Hen. Ellis, eſq;
Naval Off. Ed. Sedgewick, eſq;
Agent, Alex. Campbell, eſq;
Ch.-Juſt. Walt. Robertſon, eſq;
Collect. & Receiv Gen. Peter Franklin, eſq;
Compt. Ja. Gordon, eſq;
Sole Searcher, J. Fowler, eſq;
Sec. Reg. and Cl. of Council, Commiſſary and Storekeeper of all Stores ſent to the Iſland, Alex. Wood, eſq;
Nav. Off. Edw. Sedgewick, eſq;
Prov.-Marſh. Henry Ellis
Surv.-Gen. of Cuſt. for all the W. India iſlands, except Jamaica, Wm. Senhouſe, eſq;
Adjuſter of Diff. in the Ceded Iſlands, Wm. Hewitt, eſq;
Storekeeper of the Ordnance, —— Taylor, eſq;

JAMAICA.

Gov. Maj. Gen. John Dalling
Lt.-Gov. Brig. Gen. Campbell
Sec. Cha. Wm. Wyndhım, eſq;
Prov.-Marſh. Nev. Aldworth
Nav. Officer, Ja. Irvine, eſq;
Rec.-Gen. T. W. Partington, eſq;
Reg. in Ch. P. C. Wyndham, eſq;
Clerk of Court, T. Farley
Att.-Gen. Rob. Sewell, eſq;
Agent, Steph. Fuller, eſq;
FortCharles, Gov. E. Smith, eſq;
Dep. Gov.
Lieut. Sam. Betts, eſq;

BARBADOES.

Gov. Maj. Ge. Ja. Cunningham
Prov.-Mar. Fra. Reynolds, eſq
Nav. Officer, Robert Butcher
Sec. and Cl. of Courts, Percy

Charles Wyndham, eſq;
Att.-Gen. Wm. Moore, eſq;
Reg. in Chan. G. Aug. Selwyn
Dep. and Clerk of the Crown, George Errington, eſq;
Collect. of Bridge-Town, Joſeph Keeling, eſq;
Compt. Henry Falkingham, eſq;
Agent, Samuel Eſtwick, LL.D.

LEEWARD ISLANDS.

Gen.-Gov. and Vice-Admiral, Will. Matthew Burt, eſq;
Lt.-Gen. Rd. Haw. Loſack, eſq;
Sec. and Clerk of the Crown, Ja. Townſhend Oſwald, eſq;
Attorney-Gen
Sol.-Gen. John Stanley, eſq;
Prov. Marſh. Gen. J. Pownall, eſq
Vendue-Maſt. Dan. Bull, eſq;

ST. CHRISTOPHER'S.

Lt.-Gov. James Poole, eſq;
Ch.-Juſt. W. Payne Georges, eſq

ANTIGUA.

Lt.-Gov. James Prevoſt, eſq;
Ch.-Juſt. Steph. Blizard, eſq;

MONTSERRAT.

Lt.-Gov. Lt.-Gen. Carpenter
Ch.-Juſt. Henry Dyer, eſq;

NEVIS.

Lt.-Gov. Lt.-Gen. Ja. Johnſton
Ch.-Juſt. John Daſent, eſq;
Nav. Off. T. Seabright
Ag. to Leew. Iſl. H. Wilmot, eſq;

BERMUDAS.

Gov. William Browne, eſq;
Lt.-Gov. Capt. George Bruere
Sec. and Prov.-Marſh.-Gen. William O'Brien, eſq;
Att.-Gen. J. Grove Palmer, eſq;

BAHAMA ISLANDS.

Gov. Robert Maxwell, eſq;
Lt.-Gov. John Gambier, eſq;
Ch.-Juſt. Tho. Atwood, eſq;
Att.-Gen. and Vendue-Maſter, Robert Sterling
Judge of Admiralty, William Hutchinſon, eſq;

TURK's ISLAND.
Agent, And. Symmer

AFRICA.
SENI-GAMBIA.
Gov. (vacant)
Lt.-Gov. Joseph Wall, esq.
Superintendant of Trade, Joseph Wall, esq.
Ch.-Just. Edw. Morse, esq;
Sec. & Clerk of Council, J. P. Demerain, esq;
Chapl. Rev. D. Morgan, D.D
Agent, Robert Browne, esq;

ORDNANCE.
Storekeeper, Dav. Buffington, esq; 8s. per diem
Clerk of the Cheque, Gilbert Stanton, 5s. per diem
Surg. Dan. Bullivant, 6s. per diem
Barrack-Mast. —— Morgan, 5s. per diem
Surg.-Gen. to the Hospital, Wm Bishopp, esq;
4 Mates to ditto, at 5s. each.
Sec. for Moorish Affairs, Benj. Roberts, esq; 100l. per ann

ISLANDS, &c. in EUROPE.
MINORCA.
Gov. Gen. Ja. Murray, 730l.
Sec. to the Gov. Henry Saver.

esq; 182l. 10s.
Chapl. to the Gov. Rev. Wm. Ralfe, 12 1l. 13s. 4d.
Lt.-Gov. Sir Wm. Draper, K.B. 730l.
Commiss.-Gen. of Stores, Capt. W. Courtenay, 730l.
Com. of Must. and Dep. J. Adv. Lt. Joseph Collins, 1821. 10s.
Lt.-Gov. of Fort St. Philip, Lt.-Gen. John Thomas, 730l.
Fort-Maj. Lt. A. Hamilton, 73l.
Fort-Adj. 73l.
Capt. of the Ports of Fort St. Philip, Ro. Frampton, esq; 9 1l. 5s.
Ch. Engineer,

GIBRALTAR.
Gov. Lt.-Gen. Eliott, 730l.
Lt. Gov. Lt. Gen. R. Boyd, 730 l.
Com. Stores, Daines Barrington, esq; 547l. 10s.
Chap. to the Gov. J. Chalmers, 12 1l. 13s. 4d.
Sec. to the Gov. John Raleigh, esq; 1821. 10s.
Dep. Jud. Adv. and Com. Must. Duncan Fraser, esq; 365l.
Tn. Maj. Capt Horsburgh, 9 1l 5s
Town-Adj. Wm. Kenyon
Surgeon Major. Arth. Baine.

WAR-OFFICE. (Whitehall.)
Secretary at War.
× R T. H. Ch Jenkinson, esq;
Dep. Sec. and 1st Clerk, Matth. Lewis, esq;
Other Clerks,
Harman Leece, Cha. Marsh, W. Smith, Leonard Morse, F. R. S. John Davis, Seb. E. Channing. Andrew Clinton, Thomas Hume Bowles, Z. R. Taylor, William

Clements, James Weir, Ch. Plenderleath
Paymaster of Widows Pensions, Hon. Henry Fox
Deputy, John Powell, esq;
Examiner of Army Accounts, Wm. Smith, esq;
Assistant, Z. R Taylor
Messenger, Wm. Stacey
Office-keeper, Mrs. Ann Fannen
Necessary Woman, Eliz. Green

Office of Paymaster-General of his Majesty's Forces. Whitehall
Pay-master General.
× R T. Honble. Richard Rigby

Dep. T. Caswall, esq;
Cashier, John Powell, esq;
Accompt. Cha. Bembridge, esq;

Ledger Keeper,
John Adam Fred. Hesse, esq;
Computer of Off-reckouings,
Thomas Bangham, esq.
Cashier of Half-pay,
Robt. Randoll, esq;
1st *Clerk*, R. Moleworth, esq;
Clerks, P. G. Craufurd, FRS.
G. C. Hesse, Da. Thomas, KeeneStables, Da.Palairet, Peter Burrell, R. H. Bradshaw, J. Stephenson.
Keeper of the Stores, P.Burrell

Office-keeper and Messenger,
Wm. Tomlinson
Dep. Mess. James Barker
House-keeper, MarthaSeymour
PAY-MASTERS,
Gibraltar, Wm. Sloper, esq;
Nova Scotia, G. J Williams, esq
Quebec, CharlesBembridge, esq
Montreal, Th, Boone, esq;
Minorca, Rob. Digby, esq;
Louisbourg, Peter Elwin, esq;
New York, DeanePoyntz, esq;
*Dep. Paymast. to Forces in the West.-In.*R.H.Bradshaw,esq

COMMISSIONERS and OFFICERS of the CUSTOMS.

Commissioners.
Edward Hooper, esq. F. R. S.
Henry Pelham, esq.
Sir John Frederick, Bt. F.R.S.
Sir William Musgrave, Bart.
James Jeffreys, esq.
Tho. Boone, esq.
Welb. Ellis Agar, esq;
W. Hey, esq.
Tho. Allan, esq; 1000l. each.
Sec. Ed. Stanley, esq; F. R. S. LL.D. 710l. for himself and clerks
Clerk of the Western Ports, John Lowe, esq. 285l.
Cl. of the Northern Ports, Jos. Spilsbury, esq. 180l.
Ch. Cl. J. Williams, esq; 80l.
Plantation-Cl Jas. Powell, 170l.
Clerk of the Minutes, John Gale, 100l.
Cl. of the Bond-Office, Thomas Shaw, 80l.
Cl. of the Petitions, Walt. Adams
Rec.-Gen. William Mellish, esq. 1000l.
Assistant, T. Jones, esq. 100l.
Ch. Teller, Vinc. Matthias, esq;
Compt.-Gen. H. V. Jones, esq. 1350l. a year for himself, 2 assistants, and 4 clerks
Collect. inwards, Duke of New-

castle, 663l. 13s. 4d.
Dep. Wm. Suckling, esq.
Rec. of grand Receipts, J. Deacon
Ditto of Plontation Receipts, Lancelot Dunn
Ditto Wine-Duties, W. Mucklow
Cl. of the Ships Entries, Martin Chalice
Cl. of the Rates, Wm. Simms
Cl. of the Certificates, Charles Rogers, F. R. S.
Collect. outwards, Duke of Manchester
Dep. J. Meller, esq.
Dep. for foreign Business, Wm. Bates, esq.
Receiver, J. Dodson
Coast Dep. Benj. Green
Compt. Duke of Newcastle
Dep. James Hume, esq.
Surv.-Gen. Lord Pelham
Dep. Tho. Fanshaw, esq.
Surv. Lord Stawel!
Dep. G. T. Brathwayte, esq.
Collect. of petty Cust. Thomas Meggs, esq; 62l. 6s. 8d.
Deputy, Pere. Sims
Customer of Cloth and petty Cust. Perry Player, esq.
Compt. of ditto, Lancelot Harrison, esq.
Dep.-Compt. Wm. Read

Customer of great Customs, and Collect. of Wool and Leather, F. A. Barnard, esq. 50l.
Deputy, John Seymour
Compt. of great Customs, Dr. Richard Williams
Deputy, Perry Player
Collect. of the Coal-Duties, Rob. Weston, esq.
Compt. of ditto, H. Bishopp, esq;
Regist. of Certificate-Cockets and Debentures, Wm. Clarke, esq.
Copying Cl. A. Greenwood
Examiner of dry Goods, Wm. Moreton, 60l.
Examiner of Wine-Duties, Jn. Goldham, 80l.
Assist. Cl. of Ships Entries, Wm. Read, 60l.
Register of Warrants, William Saxby, 40l.
Clerk of the Coast Business, Wm. May, 50l.
Solicitors.
London and Western Ports, Geo. Medcalfe, esq. 300l.
North. Ports, J. Tyton, esq. 250l.
Bonds and Criminal Prosecutions, Geo. Litchfield, esq. 250l.
For Coast-Bonds, Wm. Cooper, esq. 50l.
Auditor of Solicitor's Accounts, Dan. Flowerden, esq.
Accountant of petty Receipts, John Cope Freeman, esq; 135l. for himself and two clerks
Compt. of the Issues and Payments of the Rec.-Gen. Hen. Ellison, esq. 580l. for himself and three clerks
Deputy, John Lowe
Inspect. of the Out-Port Collectors Accounts, Wm. Edington, esq. 60l. for himself and four clerks
Inspect.-Gen. of the Exports and Imports, J. Pelham, esq. 780l. for himself and 5 clerks

Assist. John Tomkyns, 120l.
Reg.-Gen. of all trading Ships belonging to Great Britain, Peter Shaw, esq. 060l. for himself and five clerks
Deputy, John Dalley
Surv. of the Out-Ports, Rob. Thompson, esq. 365l.
Inspector of Prosecutions, Wm. Poyntz, esq. He has 1s. i the Pound of what is pai into the Exchequer.
Examiners of the Out-Port Books, Wm. Moreton, esq. Dr. St. Demainbray, Fra. Blackstone G. Huddesford, esq. 100l. each
Examiner of the Sufficiency of Officers Securities, Mordecai Cutts, esq. 150l.
Surv. Gen. resident in London, Mich. Collinson, Ar. Hammond, and T. Monday, esqrs. 400l. each
Surv.-Gen. of the Riding Officers for the Coast of Kent, E Milward, esq. 35l.
Two clerks, 50l.
Surv.-Gen. for Sussex, Hen. Norton, esq. 35l.
Two clerks, 50l.
Surv.-Gen. of Riding Officers and Supervisors in Essex, Tho. Clamtree, esq. 250l.
Ditto in *Suffolk,* R. Norton esq. 250l.
Examiner of Tobacco, John Easton, esq. 200l.
Tobacco-Officers.
Regist.-Gen. Hen. Halcombe, esq. 300l.
1st Cl. E. Clutterbuck, 150l.
Cls. Wm. Smith, Sol. Sam. Laurence, 50l. Peter Graham H. Sampson Fry, 40l. each
Tobacco-Cl. under the Collect. inwards, Cha. Thredder, 80l.
Dep. Dudson Filip, 40l.

L

(118)

Under the Comptr. W. Fletcher, 8ol. Edward Lacy, 40l.
Computer,
Inspect. — Burton, 50l.
Jerquers, Messrs. W. Armstrong, Ja. Burne, J. Tombs Kenneth M'Pherson, each 100l.
Inspect. of Sloops and Boats, Sam. Brown and Clks, 275l.
Land-Surveyors, 200l.
Messrs. B. Batley, Win. Serjeant, Edmd. Horrex, Cha. Bromfield, Robt. Coker, Ja. Keill, Tho. Brown, T. Cheatham, Walter Thomas, Rich. Foster, Esqrs.
Cl. to the Land-Surv. J Greenail
Surv of Paper, S. Squire, 100l.
Surv. of the Keys, F. Ford, 100l.
Sur. of Bagga. T. Wiggens, 150l.
Inspect. of the River, Rob. Weskett, A. Sabery, J. Kelly, 100l. each
Addit. Inf. Nich. Ridley, 100l.
19 Pat. King's Waiters, 52l. each
19 Deputies without Salary
31 Land-Waiters, 80l. each
6 Addit. Land-Waiters, 60l.
Exam. of Out-Pt. Officers Four. Western Ports, John Lowe,
North. Pts. Ja. Powell, 25l. each
Inspect. of the Exchequer-Books in the Out-Ports. Heneage Legge, esq. 300l.
Deputy, Charles May
Husband for the 4½ per Cent. Duty.
Edm. Armstrong, esq. 160l.
Assist. John Hyatt, 20l.
Compt. or Husb. P. Gregson, 100l.
Examiner of their Accounts, Edward Stanley, esq. 250l.
Rec. of Fines and Forfeitures, John Dering, esq. 400l.
Comot. on ditto, *R. Shafto, esq. who has 1½d. in the Pound

on all Money remitted to the Receiver
Register of his Majesty's Warrants, Heneage Legge, esq;
Deputy, Charles May
Gaugers, Ed. Fenton, —Richardson, T. Walmesley, 80l. each
Ch. Searcher, Hon. Will. Legge
Dep. George Bye
Five Under Searchers.
Ten Deputies, W. Hankin, sen. R. Devins, W. Hankin, jun. E. Robbins, J. Miller, J. Wood, O. Arrowsmith, T. Fitter, T. Waterhouse, H. Reed.
D puted Searchers, Jn. Goodeve, Tho. Hale, Rob. Weston, R. Hereford, Rd. Seddon, H. Fielder, R. Hodgson, G. Robinson, D. M'Andrew, esqrs.
Surv. of Land-Carriage Officers, Isaac Philips, 60l.
Surv. of Buildings, W. Rice, 40l
Surv. of Coast Waiters, Edw. Whitehouse, 60l.
Paym. of Incid. Tho. Beet, 70l.
Examin. of inferior Officers Bills, (Vacant,)
KING'S WAREHOUSE.
Surv. J. Hetherington, esq. 200l
Assist. Hen. Shepherd, 80l.
J. Pritchard, 50l.
Warehouse-keep. for the Crown J. Walker, 60l.
For the Collect. Ja. Needham
Surv. of East India Warehouse, Dr. S. Demainbray, 150l.
For Clerks, 100l.
Jerquer of unrated East-India Goods, D. Macleane
Warehousekp. of India Goods, S Bowerman, J. Seddon, 100l. ea
Comptrollers to ditto, F. Coke J. Brunsdon.
Computer of the 15 per Cent

Duties, P. White, 100l.
Compt. of the Pepper Warehouse, Jere. Simmonds, 50l.
Collect. of ditto, Joseph Barnes
Computer of the Duties on unrat. E. India Gds. Wm. Suckling
Appraisers, Tho. Pearce, Tho. Alderton, 30l. each
Sur. of Naviga. J. Jarratt, 100l.
For two Watermen, 60l.
Usher of the Customhouse, Wm. Varey, esq. 6l.
Deputy, C. Causton

Housekeeper, Bridget Kelley, 38 5l. for herself and servts.
Doorkeepers to the Commissioners, W Davidson, Isaac Grigg, 60l. ea
Engine-maker, S. Hadley
Smith, Daniel Cooper
Carpenter, Wm. Miller
Ironmonger, —— Basire
Tallow-chandler, Sarah Cheney
Scale-maker, Sam. Freeman
Armourer, Sarah Collumbell
Instrument-maker, —— Gilbert
Stationer, Mrs. Katherine Castle

EXCISE-OFFICE, Broad-Street. 1643.

Commissioners, 1000l. each.
D, Papillon, Ant. Lucas, Wm. Lowndes, W. Burrell, LL.D. Stamp Brooksbank, John Pownall, Heneage Legge, Charles Garth, esqrs.
Secretary, 725l.
Richard Gamon, esq;
1st Cl. Jos. Stevens, esq; 100l.
2d Cl. Will. Jackson, 60l.
3d Cl. Jonathan Lawton, 40l.
General Accomptants.
Goul. Bruere, *Excise*, 260l.
Rich. Paton, *ditto*, 250l.
Sam. Marriott, *Malt*, 250l.
Jn. Morris, *Hides*, &c. 226l.
Edw. Mulso, *Soap*, &c. 200l.
James Webb, *Coaches*, 200l.
Fr. Hooker, *Auctions*, 200l.
Accomptant for Fines.
J. Phillipson, 170l.
Accompts. London Brewery.
Benj. Da Costa, Thomas Rix, 120l. each
Clerk of the Bills of Exchange.
John Jenner, 100l.
Chief Examiners.
1st. Will. Lush, 160l.
2d. John Bromley, 126l.
3d. John Priestley, 110l.
Corresp. Barth. Sykes, 180l.
Dep. John Collins, 120l.
Assist. Tho. Burton, 90l.

1st Clerk, John Bishop, 90l.
Cl. of the Diaries. B. Bottle, 100l.
5 General Surveyors.
Jn. Dewick, T. Cooper, Jn. Betts, Ch. Barnes, and Isaac Cooper, 145l. each.
General Surveyors of Distillery and Brandy, 100l. each.
Mat. Finley, Henry Denton, Henry Cocksedge, Silvanus Chirm, Tho. Moss,
Examiners of the Distillery.
J. Oulfnam, 90l. W. Calvert, W. Church, & J. Wetherall, 60l. each.
Examiners of the Brewery.
J. Adams, 90l. J. Ferry, W. Taylor, D. Cahusar, R. Goldsborough, & J. Pierce
Examiners of Soap & Candles.
J. Collimore, 90l. F. Neale, J. Nicolson, H. Smith, 60l. ea.
J. Oulfnam, A. Thwaites, R. Harefceugh, 50l. each.
Surv. of Glass, J. Jackson, 140l.
Su. of Coaches, W. Lawson, 90l.
Plate-Licen. R. Forrest, 90l.
Inspect. of Spir. Liquors Licen es and Coaches, E. A. Rix, 100l.
Clerk of the Securities.
Joseph Toller, esq;
1st Clerk, Wm. Hird
Storekp. W. Williams, esq; 120l.

L 2

(120)

Rec.-Gen. G. J. Williams, esq; for himself and Clerks, 2500l.
1st Clerk, Edward Littleton
Comptroller of Cash.
Sir Richard Temple, bart. for himself and 2 Clerks, 80cl.
Insp.-Gen. of Coffee, Tea, &c.
Montagu Burgoyne, esq; 500l.
Insp.-Gen. of Brewery thro' England and Wales.
J. Leese, esq; 200l. and 10s. per day, when on duty.
Register to the Commissioners.
Thomas Rider, esq; 450l.
1st Clerk, Rob. Pritchard, 80l.
John Overall, 50l.
Solicitor, Spencer Schutz, esq; for himself and 2 Clerks, 610l
Auditor of Excise.
Rd. Stonhewer, esq; for himself, Dep. and 5 Clerks, 1240l.
Auditor of Hides, &c.
Tho. Rumsey, esq; for himself and 2 Clerks, 400l.
Comptroller of Accompts.
John Butler, esq; for himself, Dep. and Clerks, 1425l.
Dep. Tho. Conway, esq; 400l.
First Clerk, Ja. Brown, 120l.
Clerk of the Distribution, 50l.
Commissioners for Appeals.
Robert Coney, J. Cowslade, G. Chad, Dan. Bull, esqrs. 200l. each
Register to the Court of Appeals. William Milton, esq; 100l.
Clerk of Incidents, J. Purdue
Housek. Mrs. Cavendish, 200l.
Deputy, Sarah Thesiger, 120l.
Door-keepers, Edw. Cock, Jn. Doratt, and Rd. Weaver
COLLECTORS of the EXCISE
Barnstaple, Jos. Hurd
Bath, Thomas Ball
Bedford, Geo. Rowley
Bristol, Benj. Fidoe.
Bucks, Simon Verlander

Cambridge, Daniel Ritson
Canterbury, Simon Esdale
Chester, Thomas Richardson
Cornwall, Tho. Topping
Coventry, John Bonning
Cumberland, Marmad. Clarke
Derby, William Cowper
Don after, Thomas Jeffres
Dorset, John Warwick
Durham, B. Willis
Essex, John Hutchinson
Exon, Miles Rogers
Gloucester, Cook Watson
Grantham, Bartw. Davison
Hants, Thomas Collis
Hereford, William Symons
Hertford, Rd. Richardson
Isle of Wight, Geo. Barton
Lancaster, Jn. Belsey
Leeds, John Crofts
Litchfield, Will. Green
Lincoln, J. Hutchinson
Liverpool, R. Fawcett
Lynn, Wm. Birdsworth
Manchester, Cayley Johnson
Marlborough, Henry Dent
Northampton, Joseph Deane
Northumberland, Proct. Coulter
Norwich, John Snelgrove
Oxon, Thomas Young
Reading, Wm Pearce
Richmond, John Shaw
Rochester,
Salisbury, William Boyd
Salop, William Alexander
Sheffield, John Sturgels
Suffolk, Rich. Powell
Surry, Thomas Burston
Sussex, Richard Lampert
Taunton, Jam. Hawkesley
Tiverton, Samuel Hall
Wales, East, Philip Davis
Wales, Middle, John Weeks
Wales, North, Simon Pedley
Wales, West, Thomas Jones
Wolverhampton, J. Barrett
Worcester, Thomas Sockett
York, Isaac Pleifance

The VICTUALLING-OFFICE, (Tower-Hill.)

Seven Commiſſioners.

JOAH Bates, Eſq; Comp. of Treaſ. Accompts.
J. Hanway, Eſq; Cooperage.
A. Chorley, Eſq; Bake-houſe
John Slade, Eſq; Brew-houſe
James Kirk, Eſq; Accounts
Wm. Lance, Eſq; Cutting-houſe
Sir Mont. Burgoyne, Bart. Hoy-taker
400l. year each
Secretary, J. Watts, Eſq; 200l
Clerks to ditto.
T. Wilkens, chief, 100l
F. Tench, T. Pilkerton, 50l
Extra Clerks.
Jn. Brady, R. Southerton, W. Goſling, J. Goſling, 50l each
Caſh Accomptant.
Denham Briggs, 120l
Clerks to ditto.
Thomas Neville, chief, 60l
Ex.Cl. Step. Sayer, J. A. Smith, D. Berry, 50l each
Extra Clerks, 50l each.
Edw. Green, John Watts, jun.
Richard Searle, D Baron, Mag. Faulk, 50l each.
Chief Clerk for examining and ſtating impreſt Accounts.
Wm. Sayer, 80l
Joſ Hughes, clerk to ditto, 50l
Extra. Edw. Terry, 50l
Clerk for keeping a Charge on the Treaſurer.
John Smith 80l
J. Drummond, clerk to dit. 10l
Ext. G. Deſborough, J. Prime, 50l.
Accomptant for Stores.
Richard Henſhaw, 120l
Clerks to ditto.
Benj. Jennings, chief, 60l
Richard Holt, 50l
John Bryan, 50l
James Jones, 50l

Extra. J. Rickords, H. Heſlip, W. Tyler, J. W. Tonkins, J. Smith, T.S. Smith, 50l ea.
Clerk to bring up accounts of ſtores in arrears, James Hutchins, 80l.
Rob. Smith, his Chief Cl. 50l
Extra. H. E. Williams, W. Kingdom, 50l. each
Chief Clerk keeping a charge on Purſers, and adjuſting accounts with Tranſport Maſters
Ralph Collier, 80l.
His Clerk, John Williams, 50l
Ext. W. Bryan, R. Foot, 50l ea.
Clk. of the Iſſues, J. Hume, 80l
Clerk to do. S. Peace, 50l
Cl. for ſtating Purſers accounts,
R. S. Moody, 100l,
Rich. Birt, his cl rk, 50l.
Extra. Tho. Collier, 50l
Maſt. Cooper, Jam. Young, 80l
Clerks to do. F. Sherwood, 50l
R. Adcock, 50l
Extra to do. P. Barnes, 50l
Clerk of the Cutting-houſe
James Morriſon, 80l. John Hughes, his clerk, 50l
Clerk of the dry Stores
Richard Hatley, 80l
Clerk to ditto. T. Shore, 50l
Extra. Tho. Pitt, 50l.
Clerk of the Brewhouſe.
Charles Frankland, 60l
H s Clk. John Hume, 50l
Extra Cl. to do. C. Burton, 50l
Petty War. Lab. J. Apley, 20l
Victualling Officer at Deptford
Benj. Collier, 200l
Cl. Tho. Butcher, 50l
Extra. cl. T. Simpſon, 50l
Boatſwain of Wharf at ditto.
James Fuize, 40l
Clerk of the Mills at Rother-

L 3

Birbe. William Painter, 80l
His *clerk*, W. De Leftre, 50l
Clerk of the Cheque, and Muf-
ter-mafter of the Workmen,
&c *at London.*
Tho. Wheeler, 80l. His *Cls.*
 R Bagnold, J. Bright, fen.
 W. Whitewood, W. Ouch-
 terlony, 50l each
 Short Allowance Clerk.
William Henlock, 50l
His Cl. Henry Lay, 5cl
Surveyor. James Arrow, 60l
His Cl. William Co-ing, 50l
Hoytaker, Jn. St. Barbe, 60l
Jonathan Holt, *cl.* 50l
Ext.do J. Lovet-, S. -ilver, 50l
 Clerks at Tower Wharf.
Jof. Stocks, 50l
Boatfwain, J. Maxey, 50l
Maft.butcher. W.Harwood, 40l
Meff.and Porter, Rt.Perry, 20l
 AGENT VICTUALLERS,

&c. at the Out-Ports.
Agent at PORTSMOUTH.
John Thomas, 200l
Storekeeper, Fred. Fofter, 80l
Cl. Cheque, Jof.Littlefield, 8cl
Maft Cooper, John Reeks, 60l
Agent at PLYMOUTH.
Dig. Tinkin, 200l.
Storekeeper, Wm. Crees, 80l
Cl. Cheq. Alex. Gordon, 80l
Maft. Coop. Sam. Hunn, 60l
Agent at CHATHAM.
Tho. Moore Slade, 200l
Storekeeper, Jn. Burton, 50l
Agent at DOVER.
Michael Ruffel, 200l
Storekeeper. Tho. King, 50l
Cl. Cheque, J. Wellard, 40l
Maft.Coop. B. Worthington 50l
Agent at GIBRALTER.
Wm. Davies, 250l
Clerk, Edward Dallin, 90l
Storekeeper, W. Vaughan, 75l

SALT-OFFICE. (York-Buildings.) March 25, 1094.)

Commiffioners.
Henry Talbot, efq; Sir John
 Grefham, bart. Oliver Til-
 fon, Milward Rowe, John
 Hillerfdon, efqrs. 500l. each.
 Comptroller and Clerks.
George Hall, efq; 350l.
Deputy, Nath. Gibfon
Clks. S. Ardron, W. Greenwood
Treafurer, Wm. Inglis, efq; for
 himfelf and Clerks, 430l.
Dep. Alex. Rennald, efq;
Clerk, John Hull
Billman, Apfley Brett
Sec. Fra. Toplady, efq; 200l.
Affift. Sec. John Elliott, 60l.
 Accomptant-General.
Tho. Ryder, efq; 200l.
His Clerk, 40l.
Clerk to the Affiftant-Secretary.
Tho. Batfon Wills, 60l.
Sol. and *Cl.* J. Follett, efq; 150l.
Correfpond. John Elliot, 100l.

Clk.to Corrcfp. Rich.Dalley, 80l.
Chief Acct. and *Clk.of Securities*
Tho. Matthews, 180l.
 Accomptants.
W. Bacon, W Barf. King. 80l.ea
Affift. Cls. Rt.Gale Handley, 70l
 (Vacant.) 50l.
Houfekpr. Sarah Baker, 100l.
Storekeeper and *Clerk of the*
 Charity and Diaries.
Richard Beauchamp, 80l.
Door-keeper, R. Lumley, 50l.
Meffenger, William Watt, 50l.
 Collector of London *Port.*
Samuel Warren, 70l.
 Affiftant Searcher.
Samuel Sumpter, 70l.
 Surveyors, 60l. each.
Francis Bill, Charles Burnett
Boatmen, Jof.Lock, Jn.Hill, 30l.
Porter, John Hardy, 30l.
 Watchmen, 25l.
Wm.Hughfon, James Taylor

GENERAL POST-OFFICE,

Erected by Act of Parliament, 27 Dec. 1660. Lombard-ſtreet.

Poſtmaſters Gen ral, 2000l. Yarmouth, Henry Potts, 60l.
Rt Hon. Francis Baron Le *Aſſiſt.* C. Coltion, 60l.
·Deſpencer Kent, E. Barnes, 60l.
Rt. Hon. H. F. Carteret *Aſſiſt.* Will. Ogilvy, 50l.
Sec. Anthony Todd, eſq; 2000l. *Clk. Bye Nights*, J. Wildman, 60l.
Clerk to th- Poſtmaſter General. Sorters, Edw. Tho. Witcomb,
Daniel Braithwaite, eſq; 100l. C. Evans, J. Irwin, J. Bapt.
Clerks to the Secretary. Auſtin, Henry Deſborough,
Thomas Todd, eſq; 100l. Joſeph Ruddick, Edmund
Hum. Walcot, 100l. O. Godby, Butk. Overall, T. Kempe,
 90l. T. Ault, Sel. H. Wil l- Jo. Hutton, Daniel Stow,
 ams, 70l. Robert Wall, 60l. Freder. Smith, J. Hallott,
Tho. Pryce, 50l. J. Haylock, Samuel Brown,
Rec. Gen. Rt. Trevor, eſq; 300l. Fr. Delavaux, J. Barber, W.
Clerks to the Receiver General. Addiſon, J. Ho. Briggs, J.
J. Maddiſon, 150l. Jn. Bow- Phœnix, T. Hird, G. Wikle,
 den, 100l. Matt. Slater, J. R. Ball, W.
Accomptant-General. Williams, W. Baldy, J. Car-
W. Fauquier, eſq; 300l. ter, W. Watts, and W. Ri-
Deputy, i ho. Church, eſq; 90l. chardſon, T. H ldſworth, P.
Clerks to the Accompt. General Heddon, F. J Pippard, F.
C. Walcott, 80l. Tho. Campbell Haigh. J. Marr, 50l. each
 70l. F. Edwards, 60l. Rich. 2 *Facers*, C. J. Creſwell, J.
 Fancourt, 50l. Pa mer 40l. each.
Inſpectors of the miſ-ſent and Window-Man and Alphabet-
dead Letters. *Keeper on the General Days,*
T. Todd, H. Walcot, eſqrs. Henry Piers, 60l.
Solicitor to the Poſt-Office. *Window-Man on the Bye-Days,*
Sam. Palmer, eſq; 200l. S. Arcron, 50l.
Reſident Surveyor. *Inſp. of Franks*, Wm. Rowe, 5 l.
Nathan Draper, eſq; 300l. *Inſpector of Franks on the Bye-*
Comptr. of the Inland Office. *Days,* Charles Coultſon
Samuel Potts, eſq; 200l. *Inſpector of the Letter-Carriers,*
Dep. Compt. John Watts, 100l. Cha. Poynter, 60l.
Comptr of th Bye Nights. 81 *Lett.-Carr.* at 11s. a week
Wm. Boulton, eſq; 16 *Supernumerary ditto*, at 5s.
Clerks of the Roads. *Door-Keep. to the Poſt-M.-Gen.*
Cheſter, Jacob Shann, 100l. John Commins
Aſſiſt. J. Ridley, 60l. *Court-Poſt,* Henry Penton, eſq.
North, William Boulton, 2l. a day
Aſſiſt. Wm. Rowe, 60l. *Deliverer of the Letters to the*
Weſt, John Briggs, 60l. *Houſe of Commons,* Charles
Aſſiſt. T. J. Burton. 50l. Coultſon, 6s. 8d. a day
Briſtol, T. Bayley, 60l. *Mail-Maker,* Tho. Foſter
Aſſiſt. Iſaac Cabane, 60l. *Inſpect. of the Curriers, Coachm.*

and Waterm. Rd. Hargrave, Ch. Saverland, W. Cox, and Jn. Williams, 52l.
Eight Meſſeng. at 12s. a week Watchman, John Whale
Houſe-Kp. Ann Oſborne, 40l.

BYE-LETTER-OFFICE.
Compt. and Reſid. Surv. Philip Allen, eſq. 500l.
Acrompt. T. Hyett, eſq. 200l.
Collect. Wm. Ward, eſq; 200l.
Cls. John Weaver, 100l. John Wyldbore, Sol. Ja. Brown, 70l. Rob. Dillon, 60l.
Inſpect. of the dead and miſ-ſent Letters, John Watts, 80l.
Store-Keeper, Tho. Bavin, 50l.
Riding Surv. Rd. Arbuthnot, Geo. Hodgſon, Johnſon Wilkinſon, eſqs.

Cls. J. Starr, 90l. R. Bigge, 80l. G. An ell, 70l. John Rowning, 60l. J Braithwaite, 50l. T. S. Starkes, 40l.
Sec. Ant. Todd, eſq. 50l.
Meſſenger, Wm. Rainſley 10 Lett.-Carr. at 11s. a week
1 Supernumerary ditto.
Manager of the Packet-Boats at the Brill, C. Saverland, eſq. 120l
Agents, John Walcot, eſq. at Dover, 150l.
C. Cox, eſq. at Harwich, 15l
St. Bell, eſq. at Falmouth, 12:l.
Wm. Hudſon, eſq. at Liſbon
John Foxcroft, and H. Finlay, eſqrs. Deputy Poſt-Maſters-Gen. and F. Daſhwood, eſq Sec. at New-York
G. Roupell, eſq; Deputy Poſtmaſter Gen. for the Southern Diſtrict of Charles Town, South Carolina.

FOREIGN OFFICE.
Compt. Cha. Jackſon, eſq. 150l.
Dep.-Compt. Geo. Langton, 100l.

A daily Poſt is eſtabliſhed (Sunday excepted) to and from this Office, and the following Poſt Towns, and Places in their reſpective Diſtricts.

Abingdon, Alresford, Amerſham, Amprhill, Annan, Appleby, Aſhburton, Attleborough.
Banbury, Barnard's-Caſtle, Barnet, Barnſley, Bath, Bawtry, Beccles, Beconsfield, Bedford, Bewdley, Biggleſwade, Birmingham, Bicester, Blackburn, Bradford Yorkſhire, Braintree, Bridgewater, Brighthelmſton (from Midſumm. to Michaelmas), Briſtol, Bromley, Bromyard, Brough, Burnwood, Burrowbridge, Bury St. Edmund's, Burton upon Trent, Bungay.
Calne, Cambridge, Canterbury, Carliſle, Caxton, Chatham, Chelmsford, Cheſterfield,

Cheſter, Chicheſter, Chippenham, Chipping-Norton, Cirenceſter, Cobham, Cockermouth, Colcheſter, Colnbrook, Colſterworth, Congleton, Coventry, Croydon. Darking, Darlington, Dartford, Daventry, Deal, Derby, Dereham, Donaghadee, Doncaſter, Dover, Dumfries, Dunſtable, Durham.
Eaſt Grinſted, Enſtone, Epſom, Eſher, Exeter, Eye. Fairford, Fakenham, Fareham, Farringdon, Ferrybridge, Feverſham, Foot's-Cray, Frome.
Gainſborough, Gateſhead, Gerrard's-Croſs, Glouceſter, Godalmin, Goſport, Grantham, Graveſend, Guildford

Halifax, Halsted, Harwich, Haslemere, Hatfield, Havant, Henley, Hertford, Hereford, Hitchin, Holm's-Chapel, Holt, Holyhead, Hounslow, Hull, Hungerford, Huntingdon, Huthersfield. Ingatestone, Ipswich, Ireland (by Holyhead and Port Patrick), Isleworth. Kelvedon, Kendal, Kidderminster, Kington, Knutsford. Lancaster, Leachlade, Leatherhead, Ledbury, Leeds, Leicester, Lewes, Lincoln, Litchfield, Liverpool, Loughborough, Lowestoff, Luton, Lynn. Macclesfield, Maidenhead, Maidston, Manchester, Manningtree, Mansfield, Margate, Marlborough, Middlewich, Midhurst, Monmouth. Namptwich, Nettlebed, Newark, Newbury, Newcastle upon Tyne, Newcastle under Line, Newmarket, Newport-Pagnel, Northallerton, Northampton, Nottingham, Norwich. Oxford. Penrith, Petersfield, Plymouth, Pool, Portsmouth, Preston. Queenborough. Ramsbury, Reading, Retford, Ringwood, Ripley, Rochdale, Rochester, Rofs, Royston, Rumford, Rumsey, Ryegate. Salisbury, Sandwich, Saxmundham, Sevenoaks, St Alban's, Sheffield, Shields North and South, Shipston upon Stower, Shifnall, Shrewsbury, Sittingbourn, Southall, Southampton, Stafford, Stamford, Staines, Stevenage, Stilton, Stockport, Stoke Norfolk, Stone, Stourbridge, Stratford on Avon, Stroud Gloucestershire, Sudbury, Sunderland, Swaffham. Tadcaster, Taunton, Tetfworth, Thame, Thetford Tiverton, Tunbridge, Tuxford. Uxbridge. Wakefield, Wallingford, Waltham-crofs, Ware, Warrington, Warwick, Watford, Wells Somersetshire, Wells Norfolk, Wellington in Somerset, Welwyn, Wetherby, Whitehaven, Wigan, Wight Isle of, Winborn, Winchester, Windham Norfolk, Windsor, Wingham Kent, Witham Essex, Wolverhampton, Worcester, Workfop, Wellington, Woburn, Woodstock, Wycombe High, Yarmouth Norfolk, York.

A mail is dispatched from London to Edinburgh, and from Edinburgh to London, every Day, Wednesday and Sunday excepted; as also to and from Morpeth, Alnwick, Belford, and Berwick and a Post established, six Times a Week, between Edinburgh and Aberdeen, Glasgow, Greenock, and the intermediate Towns.

Letters are sent from hence on Mondays, Tuesdays, Thursdays, and Saturdays, for Arundel, Brighthelmston, Horncastle, Folkstone, Hythe, Lymington, Witney, Uttoxeter, Stockton, Yarm, Petworth, Steyning, Shoreham, Wisbich, Grays, Newport in Shropshire, Peterborough, Spalding, Boston, and Louth; and return hither on Mondays, Wednesdays, Thursdays, and Saturdays. Likewise to the Devizes, Melksham, Trowbridge, Saffron Walden, and Brecknock, every Day, Friday and Sunday excepted; and return on Mondays, Wednesdays, Thursdays, and Saturdays.

To Somerton, Ilminster, Chard, and Axminster, every day, except Sunday and Monday; and back every day. To Blandford, on Tuesday, Wednesday, Thursday, and Saturday.

FOREIGN LETTERS.

Letters from London to any Part of Holland, France, or Flanders (or to the Town of Geneva in Switzerland through France), pay no foreign Postage.

Postage of a single Letter in British Pence.

From any Part of Holland, France, or Flanders, to London	10
Between London and any Part of Spain, Portugal, thro' France, or by Lisbon	18
Between London and any Part of Italy, Sicily, Turkey, Switzerland, and Minorca, through France, except to Geneva)	15
Between London and any Part of Italy, Sicily, Turkey, Germany, Switzerland, Denmark, Sweden, Russia, and all Parts of the North, through Holland or Flanders	12

Letters and Packets from any Part of Great Britain, Ireland, or America, for any of the Places before-mentioned beyond the Seas, not in his Majesty's Dominions, are, besides the said Foreign Rates they may be chargeable with, to pay, at the Office at which they are put in, the full Port to London, without which they cannot be forwarded.

All Double, Treble, and other Letters and Packets whatever (except by the Penny-Post), pay in Proportion to the respective Rates of Single Letters before specified; Packets chargeable by Weight pay after the Rate of four Single Letters for every Ounce Weight and upwards.

PENNY-POST.

For the Port of every Letter or Packet, paffing or re-paffing within the Cities of London or Weftminfter, the Borough of Southwark, and their Suburbs (which Letter or Packet is not to exceed the Weight of four Ounces, unlefs coming from, or paffing to, the General-Poft), One Penny upon putting in the fame, as alfo a Penny upon the Delivery of fuch as are directed to any Place beyond the faid Cities, Borough, or Suburbs, and within the Diftrict of the Penny-Poft Delivery.

A New and Correct Lift of the Penny-Poft, (Erected 1683.) *Comptroller*, Sir Fr. Charlton, Bart. 200l. *His Clerk*, James Thoms, 30l. *Collector*, Ralph Cauldwell, 70l. *His Deputy*, John Painter. *Accomptant*, Herb. Thomas, 70l.

Five Sorters, one at each Office, at 15s. per Week, and Houfes, Fire, &c. *Eleven Sub-Sorters*, at 12s. per Week, and near feventy *Meffengers*, at 8s. per Week.

A Lift of the Five Principal Offices, *fhewing where they are kept, and the Hours in which Letters and Parcels are conveyed to the following and adjacent Places.*

Chief PENNY-POST-OFFICE is kept in *Throgmorton-ftreet*, oppofite *Bartholomew-Lane*.

Hours f. a.	f. a.		f. a.	
- 1	Alderfbrook	9 3	Edmonton	- 1	Maryland Point
- 1	Averyhatch	7 -	Frog-lane	7 3	Mile End *and*
- 1	Barking	— -	Green Man	9 -	Green
7 1	Ball's-pond	9 -	Garries	7 3	Mount-Mill
	Newington	7 3	Green-ftreet	7 1	Newington-
- 1	Bee-hive	7 3	Hackney		Stock
7 3	Bethnal-Green	— 1	Haggerfton	7 1	Newington-Gr.
9 3	Blackm. Hole	7 1	Ham-Eaft	7 -	Oldford
9 3	Boarded-River	- -	Ham-Weft	- 1	Palmers-Green
7 1	Bow	10 4	Hoghill	7 1	Plaftow *in* Effex
7 —	Bew's Farm	9 3	Hoxton	9 -	Ripple-fide
7 1	Bromley *in* Mid.	9 -	Holloway Up.	7 3	Ruckolds
7 -	Bufh-Hill		Holloway Downs, Effex	7 -	Sir J. Oldcaftle
7 3	Cambridge-hea	- 3	Holloway Low.	7 -	Southgate
7 3	Can'bury-houfe	- 1	Jenkins	- 3	Standford-Hill
7 -	Chigwell *and*	9 1	Ilford	7 -	Stepney
	Row	7 3	Iflington	7 -	Salter's Build.
7 -	Chingford	7 1	Kingfland & Gr	7 1	Snarfbrook
9 3	Copenhagen	7 -	Laytonftone	9 -	Stratford
- 1	Cranbrook by Ilford	7 -	Loughton-Hall		Tanner's-End *near* Edmon.
7 3	Dalfton	7 -	Lowlayton	7 3	Torrington lane
		7 -	Loxford	7 -	Tottenham

(128)

Hours	f. a.	f. a.
f. a.	7 - Walthamstow	9 3 Woods-Close
- Tottenham-	7 - Wanstead	7 - Woodford
high-crofs	7 - Winchmore-	7 - Woodford Row
- 1 Valentine & H	Hill	and Bridge
1 Upton		

Westminster Penny-Post-Office is kept in Coventry-Street, near Piccadilly.

Hours	f. a.	a. f.
f. a.	7 - Drivers-Hill	- Kenfal Gr. and
7 5 Abery Farm	7 - Dollers-Hill	7 Common
7 - Acton E. & W.	7 - Dolfton-Hill	7 2 Kenfington
7 2 Acton Wells	7 2 Ealing Great	2 Kenfington
7 4 Bafewatering	and Little	7 Gore
7 2 Blacklands	7 2 Ealing-Lane	7 2 Kenfington
7 2 Bloodybridge	7 2 Earls-Court	7 Gravel-pits
7 2 Bofton-Heufe	7 - Fortune-Gate	7 2 Knightfbridge
7 2 Brentford Old	7 2 Foards-Hook	7 - Kingfberry and
and New	7 - Frog-Lane	Green
7 2 Brentford-End	7 - Frayers Place	7 - Laurence-ftreet
7 - Brents Cow-H.	7 2 Fulham & Fiel.	near Hendon
7 - Brent-ftreet	7 2 Gagglegoofe Gr.	7 4 Leafing-Green
7 2 Brook-Green	7 2 Great and Lit-	7 2 Lime-Kilns
7 2 Broom-Houfes	tle Holland-	7 2 London-Stile
7 2 Brompt. park	Houfe	7 1 3 Marybone
7 2 Bline-lane-H.	7 - Grove-Houfe	and Park
7 - Burrows	7 - The Green-Man	7 - Mafha Maps
7 - Caftlebear	Uxb. Road	7 and Mafh-
7 - Childs-Hill	7 - Goulders Green	Brands
7 2 Corney's-Houfe	7 - Gunfbery	- Mill-Hill
7 - Cow H. Farm	7 - Gutters Hedge	7 - Neefdon
7 - Chalk-Hill	7 2 Hammerfmith	7 5 Neat-Houfes
7 2 Chelfea Great	7 - Handwell and	7 2 Normans-Land
and Little	Heath	7 2 North-End
7 2 Chelfea College	- - Hanger-Lane	7 - North-High-
and Common	and Hill	7 way
and Fields	7 - The Haven	2 Notting-Hill
7 2 Chifwick	7 - Hendon	- - Old Oak Com.
7 2 Crichlewood	7 - The Hide	7 - Oxgate
7 - Collings Deep	7 - Holders-Hill	7 4 Paddington and
7 - Counters Bridge	7 - Hog-Lane	7 Green
7 - Crabtree-Houfe	7 - Holdfon-Green	2 Paddingwick-
7 - Dole-ftreet	7 - Heywood-Hill	7 Green
7 - Dewell-Lane	7 2 Harlicon-Fields	5 Pimlico
7 - Dollis	7 2 Hocome-Field	7 2 Purfers Crofs
7 - Drayton-Green	7 - Hullingham Gr.	7 - Pages-ftreet
7 2 Daws-Lane	7 - Kilburn	7 near Hendon

(129)

Hours					
f. a.	7	2 Sion-House	7	2	Turnham- Green
7 2 Parsons-Green	7	2 Sion-Lane			
7 - Park-Hill	7	- St. John's Wood	7	1 5	Tyburn Road
7 - Parsons-Street	7	2 Stanford-Brook	7	2	Walam-Green
7 2 Sandy-End	7	2 Starch-Green	7	-	Uxendon
7 - Scollop-Green	7	2 Strand on the Green	7	-	Wemly and Green
7 2 Shepherds-bush					
7 - Sherrick-Green near Wilsdon	7	2 Sutton-Court and Little Sutton	7	4	Westburn- Green
7 - Shoot-up-Hill			7	-	West-End
7 - Silk Bridge	7	1 5 Tatnam Ct. and Road	7	-	Wilsdon-Green
7 2 Sion-Hill			7	2	Windmill-Lane

Hermitage Penny-Post-Office *is kept in* Queen-Street, Little Tower-Hill.

Hours				
f. a.	7	2 K. David's Fort	7	2 Poplar
7 2 Blackwall	7	2 Limehouse and Hole	7	2 Ratcliff
7 2 Isle of Dogs.			7	2 Step. *and* Cause.

Southwark Penny-Post-Office *is kept in St. Saviour's Church-yard, in the Borough, and, on Account of the Distance of the following Places, Letters and Parcels must be at this Office by Ten o'Clock the preceding Evening, to be forwarded by the first Delivery.*

Hours		
f. a.	f. a.	f. a.
5 - Balam	5 2 Cole-Harbour	5 3 Lamb. & Marsh
5 2 Barns T. & El.	5 2 Deptford Upper and Lower	5 2 Lambeth (Sou-
5 2 Barns Common	5 - Dulw. & Com.	5 - Lee *and* Green
5 2 Batterf. & Ryes	5 - Eltham & Sou	5 - Lewisham *and* Southend
5 - Beckingham	5 - Gammon-Hill	5 2 Lime Kilns
5 - Bedington Cor.	5 2 Garrets-Green	5 2 Long Barn
5 2 Biggin	5 2 Greenwich	5 2 Long Hedge
5 - Blackheath	5 3 Grange-Road	5 2 Lougber House
5 2 Bleaks-Hall	5 2 Grove-Street	5 - Martin Abbey and Mill
5 2 Brif. Causeway	5 Hatcham House	
5 - Brockley Upper and Lower Burnt Ash	5 - Ireland-Green	5 - Marsh Gate
	5 2 Kensington and Washway and Common	5 2 Mitcham
5 2 Camberwell		5 2 Mortlake
5 - Charlton	5 - Kew-Green	5 - Morden College
5 2 Claph. & Com.	5 - Kidbrook	5 - Morden
5 - Clayhill	5 - Knights-Hill	5 - Millpond Brid.
5 - Crooms-Hill	5 2 Lark-Hall	5 . Mottingham
		5 2 Newington Butts

M

Hours.	t. a.	f. a.
f. a.	5 2 Red Houfe	5 2 Stretham
5 2 New Crofs	5 - Ricklemarfh	5 - Stump Hill
5 2 Nine Elms	5 - Roehampton	5 - Tooting Upper
5 - Norwood	7 3 Rotherhith	and Lower
5 2 Peckham T.	5 - Roufa Green	5 2 Vauxhall
Lane and Rey	5 2 Sheen Eaft	5 2 Wallworth
5 2 Pigs Marfh	5 - Sidnam	5 2 Wandf.&Com.
5 - Plumftead	5 - Shooter's Hill	5 - Wellhall
5 - Penze Common	5 3 Stangate	5 - Wimbleton
5 2 Putney&Heath	5 2 Stockwell	5 - Woolwich
and Bowl. Gr.	5 - South End	5 . Weftham
5 2 Ravenfburg	5 - Stone Farm	

St. Clement's, in Blackmore-Street. On *Account of the Dif-*
tance of the following Places, Letters and Parcels muft be at
this Office by Ten o'Clock the preceding Evening, to be for-
warded by the firft Delivery.

f. a.	5 - Finchley	5 2 North End,
5 2 Battle Bridge	5 - Frog Lane	Hampftead
5 - Bone Gate	5 - Golders Hill	5 2 Pancrafs
5 2 Brill	5 2 Hampftead	5 2 Pinder of Wak
5 2 Canewood	5 2 High-Gate	5 - South Green
5 - Chalk Farm.	5 - Hornfey	5 - Totteridge
5 - Cole Harbour	5 - Haverftock Hill	5 - Whetfton
5 - Coney-Hatch	5 2 Kentifh Town	5 - Wood Green
5 - Eaft Barnet	5 - Muffel Hill	5 - Windmill Hill

The 31 ELDER BRETHREN *of the* TRINITY-HOUSE,
(*Water-lane, Tower-ftreet.*)

SIR John Major, Bart.
John, Earl of Sandwich, Mafter.
Capt. John Barker
Capt. Charles Pigot
1734 Capt. John Jolly
1757 Sir Piercy Brett, Knt.
1761 Edw. Lord Hawke, K.B.
1765 Capt. Gilbert Slater
1766 Sir Geo. Pocock, K. B.
1767 Capt. John Pickett
×Hon. Aug. Keppel
1768 His Grace George, Duke of Marlborough, K.G.
1769 ×Sir Wm James, Bt, FRS. *Deputy Mafter.*

1770 Ld Vifc. Weymouth, KG
×Sir Hugh Pallifer, Bart.
1771 ×Rt Hon. Ld North, KG
W.H.E. Rochford, KG
1774 Capt. Jofhua Mauger
Capt. Michael James
×Capt. Anthony Bacon
1775 ×Capt. John Durand
Capt. John Travers
1776 Capt. John Barth. Lanty
Capt. Timothy Mangles
1778 Capt. John Adddifon
Capt. John Dickinfon
Capt. George Burton
×Rt. Hon. Ld. Mulgrave
1779 Capt. Anthony Calvert
1780 Capt. Thomas. Brown
(One vacant.)

Mr. Charles Wildbore, *Secret.* | Dav. Court, Joſh. Savage, Tho
Jon. Thompſon, Eſq; *Solicitor.* | Althrop, Edward Smith
                                         Clerks.

TRUSTEES of Sir *John Morden's* COLLEGE *at Blackheath, for Decayed Merchants. Meet at Batſon's Coffee-houſe.* -

WILLIAM Clarke, Eſq;
Samuel Smith, Eſq;
× William Ewer, Eſq;
James Lee, Eſq;
Samuel Boſanquet, Eſq:

John Free, Eſq;
Richard Willis, Eſq;
Treaſurer, John Bennet, Eſq
     Chaplain,
Rev. Mr. Moſes Browne.

The SHERIFFS of the ſeveral Counties for the Year 1781.

Berkſhire,   EDw. Loveden Loveden, of Buſcot, Eſq;
Bedfordſhire,   John Harvey, of Northill, Eſq;
Bucks,   Joſeph Bullock, of Caversfield, Eſq;
Cumberland,   Thomas Storey, of Mirehouſe, Eſq;
Cheſhire,   William Davenport, of Bramhall, Eſq;
Camb' and Hunt', John Johnſon, of Leverington, Eſq:
Cornwall,   Sir John St. Aubin, of Clowance, Bart.
Devon,   John B. Cholwich, of Farringdon, Eſq;
Dorſetſhire,   Lewis Dymock Groſvenor Tregonnell, of
                         Dorcheſter, Eſq:
Derbyſhire,   Samuel Frith, of Bank-Hall, Eſq:
Eſſex,   Richard Wyatt, of Hornchurch, Eſq;
Glouceſterſhire,   John Morris, of Shephouſe, Eſq:
Hertfordſhire,   Tho. Clutterbuck, jun. of Watford, Eſq;
Herefordſhire,   Edmund Patteſhall, of Allenſmoor, Eſq;
Kent,   John Cator, of Beckenham. Eſq;
Leiceſterſhire,   Edm. Craddock Hartopp, of Newbold, Eſq;
Lincolnſhire,   Edward Nelthorpe, of Scawby, Eſq;
Monmouthſhire,   William Jones, of Naſh, Eſq.
Northumberland, Charles Brandling, of Goſforth Houſe. Eſq;
Northamptonſhire, Nicholls Raynsford, of Brixworth, Eſq;
Norfolk,   Robert Lee Doughty, of Hanworth, Eſq;
Nottinghamſhire, Lancelot Rolleſton, of Watnall, Eſq;
Oxon.   Richard Paul Joddrell, of Lewknor, Eſq;
Rutlandſhire,   Thomas Saunders, of Mercott. Eſq;
Shropſhire,   Edw. Ch. Windſor, of Harnage Grange, Eſq;
Somerſetſhire,   John Ford, of Hadſpen, Eſq;
Staffordſhire,   Philip Keay, of Abbots Bromley, Eſq:
Suffolk,   Chs. Kent, of Fornham St. Genoveve, Eſq;
Southampton,   Benjamin Smith, of Lys, Eſq;
Surry,   William Northey, of Epſom, Eſq;
Suſſex,   William Peachey, of Kidford, Eſq;

(132)

Warwickshire,	John Webb, of Sherbourne, Esq;
Worcestershire,	John Darke, of Bredon, Esq;
Wiltshire,	William Hayter, of Newton Toney, Esq;
Yorkshire,	Humphrey Osbaldeston, of Hunmanby, Esq;

SOUTH-WALES.

Brecon,	Lewis Williams, of Pentwyn, Esq;
Carmarthen,	Sir William Mansell, of Iscoed, Bart.
Cardigan,	David Lloyd, of Altyroden, Esq;
Glamorgan,	Charles Bowen, of Merthyrmawr, Esq;
Pembroke,	Henry Scourfield, of Robeston-Hall, Esq;
Radnor,	Jonathan Bowen, of Knighton, Esq;

NORTH-WALES.

Anglesey,	Jonath. Bodyckan Sparrow, of Redhill, Esq;
Caernarvon,	Edward Carreg, of Carreg, Esq;
Denbigh,	Hon. Tho. Fitzmaurice, of Leweny. Esq;
Flint,	Henry Thrale, of Bachegrig, Esq;
Merioneth,	Edward Lloyd, of Maesmore, Esq;
Montgomery,	Hugh Mears, of Finnant, Esq;

STAMP DUTIES, 1694. (Stamp-Office, Lincoln's-Inn.)

Commissioners.
James Bindley, Wm. Baillie, Wm. Waller, Martin Whit ̅ , esqrs. 50l. (One vacant.)
Sec. John Brettell, esq; 30cl.
Receiver-General
Jn. Rofs Mackye, esq; 6col.
Comptroller.
Patrick Brydone, esq; 40cl.
Secretary's Clerks.
Ch. Edwards Beresford, 13cl.
William Gregson, 7cl.
Humphry Haydon, 6cl.
Thomas Brown, 6cl.
William Kappen, 50l.
Receiver-General's Clerks.
James Dugdale, 14cl. Francis Fludyer, 6ol. Geo. Thring, 6ol. John Tilby, 6ol. Will. Hall Baillie, 6ol. Peter Hart, 5cl. and as *Clerk of Apprentices Indentures,* 1cl.
Comptroller's Clerks.
John Lloyd, 1col.
George Longcroft, 6ol.

Robert Thompson, 6ol.
Jn. Beck, 6cl. R. Wheeler, 50l.
orresp. Richard Hale, 100l.
Accomptant Clerk.
Ben. Radcliffe, 10cl.
Assistant, Wm. Griffin, 50l.
Teller of Stamps.
William Wright, 100l.
Assistant, 50l.
Solicitor, Gibbs Crawfurd, esq; 10cl.
Clerk of the Securities.
James Royer, 100l.
Register of Warrants.
E. Chamberlayne, esq; 14cl.
Assistant, Peter Glossop, 5cl.
Warehouse-Keeper of unstamped Goods. Tho. Clarson, 70l.
Assistant, John Hunt, 50l.
Wareh.-Keep. of stamped Goods, Geo. Whatley, esq; 200l.
Assistant, Geo. Brooke, 100l.
Packer, Tho. Burch, 50l.
Inspectors of Courts and Corporations in the Country.

Tho. London, Alex. Emerson, Samp. Mosman, 100l. each
Inspector of ditto in Town.
Samuel Roycroft, 100l.
Assistant, Will. Rob. Duill, 50l.
Housekeeper, 70l.
Distributor for London.
Francis Blackstone, 50l.
Supervisor of the Stampers.
William Allen, 100l.
Assist. to ditto, Geo. Harris, 10l.
Ditto as a Stamper, 50l.
39 *Stampers,* 50l. each
3 *Rolling-press Printers,* 55l.
7 *Layers of Paper,* and
2 *Wetters of ditto,* 50l. each
Rolling-Press Office, Charles Smelt, 50l.
Billman, W. Gaywood, 50l.
Chamber-Keeper, R. King, 50l.
Porter, Francis Mollison, 40l.
Messenger, David Wilson, 30l.
Two Watchmen, at 30l. each.

Entering Clk. of Cards and Dice, Samuel Pritchard, 50l.
7 *Surveyors to ditto,* 45l. each
One ditto, at 60l.
Marker of Dice and Engraver
Thomas Major, 50l.
Register of Pamphlets.
Robert Harris, 50l.
Assistant, H. Claridge, 20l.
3 *Inspectors of gaming-houses,* at 20l. each.
WINE-LICENCE Branch.
Solicitor, Alex. Baillie, 60l.
Register, Rich. Turner, 100l.
Cl. of Licences, W. Bennet, 100l.
Assist. Cl. Wm. R. Duill, 50l.
Four Inspectors, 50l. each.
Daniel Cass, Thomas Howse, John Gill, John Jacques
Register and Comptroller of the Apprent. Duty. J. Bennet, 150l.
His Clerk, Henry Alleyne, 50l.
Entering Clerk, D. Wilson, 30l.

HAWKERS and PEDLARS Office. (Gray's-Inn.)
Commissioners, (3.)
James Turner, Humbo Rigby, P. Beaumont, esqrs. 100l. ea.
Comptr. W. Brummell, esq; 100l.
Cashier, Fr. Steward, esq; 100l.
Solicitor, James Best, esq; 50l.
Chief Clerk, Sam. Warren, 50l.
Second Clerk, Will. Smith. 50l.
Riding Surveyors, 100l. each.
John Hewit, Wm Smith, Jn.

Fenwick, William Gwillim, G. W. Grove, Rob. Alnwick, Ja. A. Buchanan, Rt. Robertson, Cs. Herbert, Rd. Bint. Supernum. Rd. Wetherelt, 100l.
Surveyors in London, and ten Miles adjacent, 50l. each
Richard Ham, J. Woodman, Griffin Blackwall, P. Smith
Housekeeper, Sarah Lucas, 30s.

Office for Hackney Coaches and Chairs. (Great-Queen-Street, Lincoln's-Inn-Fields.)

Commissioners. (5.)
Jn. Cookson, Jn. Soley, R. Capper, W. Morton Pleydell, Jac. Reynardson, esqrs. 200l. ea.
Receiv. Edw. Moore, esq; 100l.
Register, Edw. Moore, esq; 100l.

Solicitor, Matt. Cheffall, 50l.
Housekeeper, So. Johnson, 50l.
Messengers, Rob. Williams, G. Edmunds, Jos. Hillier, 47l. ea.
Street-keepers, 42l. each, John Walker, and Jos. Marshall

By Act Geo. III. the Commissioners are impowered to licence 1000 Hackney-Coachmen, and every Proprietor to pay the weekly Sum of 5s. to the Receiver at the Office every Month.

(134)

His MAJESTY's MINT, (Tower.) 1066.

Warden.
Sir Robert Pigot, Bart. for himself and a Clerk, 45ol.
Master and Worker.
Rt. Hon. Lord. Cadogan, for himself and 3 Clerks, 650l.
Comptroller, John Buller, efq; for himself and Clerk, 350l.
King's Affay-mafter.
Joseph Lucas, efq; for himself and Clerk, 225.
Chief Engraver.
Lewis Pingo, efq; 200l.
2d Engraver, Ral. Ocks, 80l.
Affiftant Engraver.
John Pingo, 80l.
Surveyor of the Meltings, and Clerk of the Irons.
✕ Geo. Selwyn, efq; for himself and Clerk, 132l. 10s.
Deputy, John Jones
Smith Affift. to the Engraver.
Ruben Fletcher, 40l.
Surveyor of the Money Preffes.

John Chambers, 40l.
Surveyor, John Vardy
Two Auditors, 20l. each
Weigher and Teller.
Maurice Morgan, for himfelf and Clerk, 142l. 10s.
Deputy, Afher Jones
King's Clk. and *Clk. of the Paper*
Wm. Dick, 100l.
Solicit. John Vernon, efq; 60l.
Provoft to the Comp. of Moneyers acting as Engi. D. Kemp, 100
The Company, 40l. each
Warden's Dep. Edw. Lucas, efq;
Mafter's Dep. W. Gregory, efq;
Comptroller's Deputy and Clerk.
James Morrifon
Dep. to King's Clk. ———Norris.
Clk. to Warden, Jn. Twells, 100l.
Clk. to the Mafter, Tho. Day
Porter, John Kempe, 45l.
The Mafter's Affay-mafter:
Mr. Stanefby Alchorne
Office-keeper, S. Godfrey, 25l.

ADMIRALTY-OFFICE. (Charing-Crofs.)

Lords Commiffioners, (7.)
John, Earl of Sandwich, *Firft Lord.* Salary, 3000l. a year
✕Earl Lifburne, ✕Hen. Penton, efq; ✕Ld. Mulgrave, ✕Ba. Gafcoyne, efq; ✕Ch. Francis Greville, efq; ✕George Darby, efq; 1000l. each.
Sec. ✕Ph. Stephens, efq; 800l.
Dep. Sec. G. Jackfon, efq; 500l.
Clerks on the Eftablifhment.
Jn. Ibbetfon, 200l. H. Parker, 150l. T. Fearne, 120l. Wm. Bryer, 100l. Charles Wright, 80l. Joseph Belfon, 70l. Simon Devert Barkham, 60l.
Other Clerks on the Eftablifhment.
Rob. Robinfon, Wm. Gimber, Tho Kite, W. Gafcoigne, J. Frefhfield, T. Brifbane, W.

Pearce, M. Hollinworth, R. Maxwell, E. Banes, 50l. ea.
French Tranflator.
John Bindley, 100l.
MARINE DEPARTMENT.
Sec. ✕Ph. Stephens, efq; 300l.
1ft Clk. G. Jackfon, efq; 200l.
2d Clk. Jam. Madden, 100l.
3d Clerk, John Bindley, 70l.
Ext. Cls. H. Parker, G. Coombe
Paymafter of Marines, Gabriel Stewart, efq; *Office in Great Newport-ftreet.*
Agent, Griff. Williams, efq; *Office in Bartlet's-Buildings.*
Secretary to Commiffioners of the Longitude; John Ibbetfon, 80l.
Meffenger, Wm. Cook 50l.
Affiftants to ditto, Wm. Downing, 40l. John Mann, 30l.

(135)

Porter, Rich. Hutchinson, 30l. | *Counsel to Admiralty and Navy*,
Housekeeper, Eliz. Bell, 40l. | ✶Fr. Cockayne Cuſt, eſq; 100l.
3 *Watchmen*, 20l. a year each | *Solicitor to Admiralty and Navy*.
Necef. Wom. Eliz. Butler, 30l. | James Dyſon, eſq; 400l.
Gardener, John Tucker, 30l. | *Kg's Proft*✶P. C. Creſpigny, eſq
Inspector of Repairs. | *Admir. ditto*, G. Goſtling, eſq;
James Arrow, 30l. | *Regiſter of the Admiralty Court*,
ADMIRALTY-COURT. | Godfrey Lee Farrant
Judge of the Admiralty. | *Deputy to ditto*, Nat. Biſhop
Sir J. Marriott, 800l. a year | *Marſhal*, Wm. Brough
Kg's Adv. Gen. Dr. Wm. Wynne | *Deputy to ditto*, John Crickitt
Admiralty ditto, Dr. G. Harris, | *Judge-Advocate to the Fleet*.
13l. 6s. 8d. in Time of Peace, | Geo. Jackſon, eſq; 10s. per Day,
and 20ol. additional in Time | *Deputy to ditto*, Tho. Binſteed.
of War | 8s. per Day

PAY-OFFICE of the NAVY. (Broad-Street.)

Treaſurer of the Navy, 2000l. | field, jun. John Slade, jun*
✶Rt. Hon. Welbore Ellis, Eſq | Chriſt. Cooke.
Paymaſter and Accomptant. | *Clerk for paying Navy Bills*.
Andrew Douglas, eſq; 500l. | John Slade, 80l.
Clerks for Payment of Wages. | *Ditto for writing Ledgers*.
In Broad-ſtreet, Adam Jellicoe, | Fr. Cooke, Wm. Smyth, 80l. E.
80l. Robert Radcliffe, 40l. | Clarke, J. Creſſent, 50l.
At Portſmouth, Wm. Taylor, | *Extr. Clerk*, G. Fennell, 50l.
John Swaffield, 40l. each | *Caſhier of the Victualling*.
At Plymouth, Jas. Lynch, 80l. | G. Swaffield, eſq; 150l.
Wm. Hill, 40l. | *Clerks to ditto*, J. Fennell, 70l.
At Chatham and Sheerneſs, Ja. | C. W. Dilke, Rob. Walker,
Malpas, 80l. T. Parr, 40l. | John Davies, 50l. each
Extra Clerks, at 50l. | *Meſſ*. Wm. Ward, 1s. 8d. per Day
Ja. Slade, W. Hulme, Tho. Far- | *Porter*, Wm Goſling, 18l. 5s.
row, Arch. Douglas, Joſeph | *Doorkeeper*, Cha. Tweedie, 20l.
Swaffield, Samuel Jellicoe, | *Houſekeeper*, Cha. Inglis, 40l.
Alex. Trotter, John Swaf- | *Bargemaſter*, Wm. Maſſam, 6l.

NAVY-OFFICE. (Crutched-Fryars.)

11. Principal Officers and Commiſſioners of his Majeſty's
Navy, with their Clerks, &c. viz.

1. *Comptroller of the Navy*. | ſon, J. Moyringh, Thomas
Charles Middleton, eſq; 8ol. | Coulſon, 60, William Foſ-
Clerks to ditto in his Office for | ter, Thomas Evans, Ch.
Accompts. | Wright, George White,
Tho. Davies *Chief Clerk*, 180l. | John Nelſon, 50l. each.
Richard Preſtwood, 110l. W. | *For Foreign Accounts*.
Peyton 70l. Maurice Nel- | Geo. Hartwell, *Chief Clk*. 100l.

(136)

Tho. Soame, G. Rainier, Will. Caffell, 5ol.
Clerks to ditto in his Office for Seamens Wages.
Chief Clerk, Benj. Holl, 200l.
E. Falkingham, B. Hartwell.
Ph. Thomas, Barber Fennell.
Benj. Robertfon, Ste. Haven, Fr. Wilfon, J. Davidfon, B. Spurrell, J. Dickens, G. Hicks, P. E. Ottey, 50l.
Attendant on do. J. Barrett, 20l.

2. *Surveyor of the Navy.*
Sir Jn. Williams, knt. and Ed. Hunt, efq, 800l. each.
1ft Affift. T. Mitchell, efq; 300l. more for Houfe Rent, 50l.
2d Affift. Jn. Linmer, efq; 200l. more for Houfe Rent, 30l.

Clerks to the Surveyor.
R. Bromley, Ch. Clerk, 100l.
W. Mills, 70l. H. Terry, 60l. T. Flint, W. Smith, Cha. Derrick, Tho. Gwillim, John Cook, Cha. Eye, 50l. each.

3. *Clerk of the Acts.*
Geo. Marfh, efq; 800l.
Affiftant to ditto.
Jofhua Thomas, efq; 460l. more for Houfe Rent, 50l.

Clerks to the Clerk of the Acts.
Rob. Gregfon, Ch. Clerk, 180l. John Kent, J. Margetfon, 80l. John Andrews, Charles Fofter, Major Woolhead, T. Berkenhead, 60l, R. A. Nelfon, 6ol. Will. Walker, G. Balfton, J. Walker, 50l.
Ext. Cls. W. Rufhton, W. K. Welch, John Bates, 50l.
Clerk of the Petition Office.
John Harris, 50l.
Clerk of the Remittance Bills.
Charles Holloway, 50l.

4. *Compt. of Treafurer's Accts.*
Timothy Brett, efq; 800l.

Clerks to dit o.
O. Standert, Chief Clerk, 150l. Jonat. Dodd, 95l. H. Mattocks, jun. 75l. James Roberts 60l. Benj. Stow, 50l.
Ticket Office under his Infpection.
W. Paynter, Ch. Clk, 200l. W. Player, 2d do. 200l. W. King, 80l. J. Hunter, G. Arnold, P. E. Ottey, J. Campbell, P. Hyatt, C. Wade, W. Wiggett, 50l. each. *Ext. Clks,* 50l. each.
L. Bond, T. Mudge, W. Sterling, F. Delacombe, T. Edwards, G. Player, G Dayfh, W Hodgfon J. Mafterton, H. H. Williams, J. Allen, 50l.
Doorkeeper, T. Errington, 20l.

5. *Compt. of Victualling Accts.*
Wm. Palmer, efq; 800l.
Clerks to ditto.
Jof. Poole, Ch. Clerk, 100l.
Tho. Herne, H. Bennet, 50l.

6. *Compt. of the Storek.'s Accts,*
Hon. Wm. Bateman, 800l.
Cls. to ditto, Jn. Holden, Ch. Cl. 100l. Ben. Wakefield, Jn. Pigott, Tho. Fowden, W. Coleman, Ja. Bailey, G. Jackfon, R. L. Davis, 50l. each.

Extra. Commiff. of the Navy,
7. Sir Rd. Temple, bart. Edw. Le Cras, efq; 800l. each
Cls. to Sir R. Temple, E. Pucell, S. Nicholfon, 50l. each
Cls. to E. Le Cras, J. N. Salt, 50l. P. Facey, 30l.

Marine Department.
W. Paynter, *Ticket Office,* 100l.
T. Davies, *Compt's Office,* 60l.
Rd. Preftwood, *ditto,* 30l.
Hewling Lufon, *extra,* 50l.
Meffengers, &c. to the Navy Off.
Meffenger, Ja. Hayfom, 50l.
Affift. Wm. Benge, 30l. Edw. Widen, 20l.

*Lab. & Attend.*W. Phillips, 20l.
Porter, Dan. Baynes, 25l. more
for House Rent, 10l.
Tho. King, *attends the Back Gate* at 1s. a day
Housekeeper, Isab. Barkley, 40l.
more for Servants, 40l.
Thomas Sabe *takes Care of* 14 *Lamps,* at 50s. each
4 *Watchmen,* at 12l. a year each
Ratcatcher, Edm. Jenkins, 4l.
Bargemaster, Jacob Adams

DEPTFORD YARD.
Under the immediate Inspection of the Navy Board.
Officers of the Yard.
Cl. of Checque, Ja. Butler Morn, 200l. and 5l. for stationary
Storekeep. W. Matthews, 200l. and 10l. for ditto
Mast. Shipw. Adam Hayes, 200l. and 4l. for ditto
Mast. Shipwright's Assist. John Puckey, 1 col.
2d Ditto and Mast. Caulker, 100l.
Cl. of Surv. Peter Butt, 200l. and 6l. for stationary
Mast. Attend. Rog Gastril, 20cl and 1l. for ditto
Boatswain, Math. Brasnel, 8cl
Purveyor, Benjamin Slade, 60l.
Surgeon, Wm. Troward, 100l besides his two-pences
Porter, John Lynn, 30l.
Messenger, Edmund Jenkins

WOOLWICH YARD,
Under the immediate Inspection of the Navy Board.
Officers of the Yard.
Cl. of Checque, Phil. Soley, 150l.
Storkeep. 150l.
Mast. Shipw. J. Jenner, 150l.
Assistant, John Nelson, 80l.
2d Ditto and Master Caulker, —— Tippet, 80l.
Cl. of Surv. R. Hunter, 150l.

Mast Attend. Benj. Hunter, 150l
Cl. of Rope Yd. J. Houusom, 100l.
Mast Ropemk. Rd. Ackland, 100l.
Boatswain, Joseph Smith, 70l.
Purveyor, John Cross, 60l.
Surgeon, Edward Wood, 100l.
besides his two-pences
Porter, Tho. Butler, 25l.
Messenger, John Russel

CHATHAM YARD.
8. *Commissioner Resident,*
Charles Proby, esq; 500l.
more for Paper and Firing 12l.
Cls. to ditto, W. Sugden, 50l.
Mic. Lock, 50l. G. Davis, 40l.
Officers of the Yard.
Cl. of Checque, W. Campbell, 200l.
Storekp. J. Weatherall, 200l.
Mast. Shipw. Ni Phillips, 200l.
Cl. of Surv. J. Hamilton, 200l.
Mast. Attend. Magnus Falconer, W. Hammond, 200l. each
MSt.ipw. Assist. E Mackie, 100l
2d *Ditto,* Wm. Payne, 10cl.
Mast. Caulk. W. Peake, 100l.
Cl. of Rope Yd. F. Forest, 100l.
Mast. Ropem. J. Jenner, 100l.
Boatswain, John Frazier, 80l.
Purveyor, Wm. Kettle, 50l.
Surg. Hugh Mackleraith, 100l.
besides his two-pences
Porter, John Adamson, 30l.

SHEERNESS YARD.
Under the Inspection of the Commissioner at Chatham.
Cl. of Checque, J. Williams, 150l.
Storekeeper, James Clyde, 150l.
Mast. Shipw. H. Peake, 150l.
Cl. of Surv. S. Hodgson, 150l.
Mast. Attend. J. Westcott, 150l.
Mast. Shipw.'s Assist. and Mast. Caulk. 80l.
Boatswain, John Pack, 70l.
Surgeon, Robert Bellas, 100l.
besides his two-pences
Porter, Nicholas Silver, 25l.

(138)

PORTSMOUTH YARD.
9. *Commissioner Resident,*
Henry Martin, esq; 500l.
for Paper and Firing, 12l.
Cls. John Jeffery, 50l. James Beezley, 40l. *Extra.* John Mackrell Poulden, 50l.
Officers of the Yard.
Cl. of Checque, Tho: Snell, 200l.
Storekp. John Greenway, 200l.
Must. Shipw. G. White, 200l.
C. of Surv. Jn. Sowers, 200l.
Mast. Attendant, W. Nicholson,
Jos Gilbert, 200l. each
Mast. Shipw. Assist. F Pollard, W. Rule, 100l. each
Mast: Caulker, 100l.
Cl. of Rope Yd. Ja. Russel, 100l.
Mast. Ropemk. Pet. Martin, 100l.
Boatswain, And. Jefferies, 80l.
Purveyor, Joseph Hollis, 80l.
Chapl. Rich. Walter, M. A.
Surgeon, David Ramsey Kerr, 100l. besides his two-pences
Porter, T. Butler, 3cl.
ROYAL ACADEMY.
Gov. Henry Martin, esq; 100l.
1st Mast. Geo. Witchell, 150l.
Usher, John Bradley, 100l.
French Mast. P. Hemmery, 100l.
Drawing Mast. J. Jeffery, 100l.
Surg. Dav. Ramsey Kerr, 20.

PLYMOUTH YARD.
10. *Commissioner Resident,*
Pa. H. Ourry, S. Walis, esqrs, 500l. for Paper and Firing, 12l.
Clerks, John Johns, 50l. J. Delacomb, 40l.
Extra, Rob. Ellery, 50l.
Officers of the Yard.
Cl. of Checque, John Lloyd, 200l.
Storekeep. Phil. Justice, 200l.
Mast. Shipw. Jn. Henslow, 200l.
Cl. of Surv. Ralph Payne, 200l.
Joint Masters Attendant, Benj. Hall, P. Robinson, 200l. each

Cl. of Rope Yd. Jas. Young, 100l.
Mast. Ropemk. Jn. Linzee, 100l.
1st M. Shipw. Ass. M. Ware, 100l.
2d Ditto, J. Tovery
Mr. Caulk. Sam. Mansfield, 100l.
Boatswain, Rich. Dutton, 70l.
Purveyor, Wm. Andrews, 50l.
Mast. Boatbuilder, W. Collins
Mast. Mastmaker, H. Williams
Mast. Sailmaker, J. Rawlings
Mast Smith, Wm. Lemyn
Chapl. Robert Hughes, M. A.
Surgeon, Rob. Mowbray, 100l.
besides his twopences
Porter, Rich. Wharton, 30l.

DEAL.
Cl. of Checque, and Storekeeper, Geo. Lawrance, 200l. for sending the Downs List, 12l.
Cls. to Do. J. Sayer, W. Hodgman

HARWICH.
Cl. of Cheque and Storekeeper, Richard Russell, 100l. for stationary, 5l.
Cl. to Ditto, John Russell, 30l.

KINSALE.
Nav. Off. T. Foxworthy, 95l. house rent 1l. stationary 5l.
Cl. to Ditto, John Heard, 3cl.

GIBRALTAR.
Nav. Off. J. A Pownoll, 200l.
Cl. Henry Jenkins, 50l.

MAHON.
Muster Master and Storekeeper, Christ. Hill Harris, 200l.
Cl. to Ditto, Alex. Lopdell, 50l.

ANTIGUA.
Storekeep. and Nav. Off. Ant. Munton, 200l.
Cls. A. Dow, 70l. W. Seaman, 50l.
M. Shipw. Alex Innis, 200l.

HALIFAX, Nova Scotia.
Commis. Sir And. Snape Hamond 500l. more to him for extra charges, 500l.

lerks to Ditto, L. Horner, 50l.
ext.charges, 50l. F. Hutchin-
fon, 40l. extra charges. 40l.
torekeep. and Nav. Off. G.
Thomas, 2col. houfe rt. 30l.
ls. to Ditto, Jacob Hurd, 80l.
R. Burns, 50l.
M. Shipw. John Loader, 2c3l. *falary and fictionary ware.*
Clerk to ditto, John Millar, 50l.
Maſt Attend. Rd. Prowſe, 200l.

NEW-YORK.
Naval Officer and Muſter Maſt.
Wm. Fowler, 200l.

JAMAICA.
Muſt.-Maſt. & Storekp.

200l. houſe rent, 50l.
Cls. T Sutton, 8cl, LR. Allen, 70
Maſt. Shipw. John North, 200l.
houſe rent 30l.
Cl. to Ditto, And. Clarke, 60l.
Maſt. Attend. at Jam. W Fotfar.

Surv. Gen. of all his Majeſty's Woods in America, John Wentvorth, eſq; 800l
Surv. of is Mai.'s Woods in Canada, Sam. Mackay, eſq; 10s. a day, and 40l. a year
Add.it. Surv. Gen. in Canada, Ch. de la Naudiere, eſq; 300l.
Inſp. & Surv. of Woods in Quebec, Philip Skene, eſq; 300l.

THE ROYAL HOSPITAL AT GREENWICH.

GOVERNORS.—The Great Officers of State, and Perſons in high Poſts under the King, &c. &c.

24 COMMISSIONERS.
Sir H. Palliſer, Bart. Capt. J Mapleſden, Alex. Hood, eſq;
*W. Eden eſq; Sir Jn. Major.
bt. T. Bret, eſq; Ja. Stuart, eſq;
Sir Pier. Brett, kt. *Jn. Cleveland, eſq; Per. Cuſt, eſq; J. T. Savary, eſq; T. Hicks, eſq; J. Barker, eſq; G. Marſh, eſq; W. Wells, eſq; *Sir W James, bt. Rev J. Cooke, J. Campbell, eſq; Joah Bates, eſq; Sir Rd. Bickerton, bt. C. Reynolds, eſq; J. Durand, eſq. W. Allen, eſq; J. Hardy, eſq; *M. Fonnereau, eſq;

OFFICERS.
Maſt. *Sir H. Palliſer, Bt 1000l.
His Cl. George Hartwell, 50l.
Lt. Gov. Jer. Mapleſden, 400l.
Treaſ. Alex. Hood, eſq; 200l.
His Cls Ed Boxley, 50l. P Burrell
Captains (4), 230l. each.
J. T. Allwright, 2. F. Lynn, 3. Ja. Chads, 4. G. R. Walters.
Lieutenants (8), 115l. each.
A. Gordon, H. Moyle, C. Beſ-

ſon. Rob. Kerr, H. Smith, W. Anſell, A. Fortye, G. Spearing
Sec. J. Ibbetſon, eſq; FRS 160l.
His Cl. Francis Cook, 60l.
Auditor, *Wm. Eden, eſq; 100l.
His Cl. Wm. Ferguſon, 50l.
Surv. Ja Stuart, eſq; FRS. 200l
Cl of Wks. Rob. Mylne, eſq; F. R. S. 5s. per day.
Phyſ. Dr. Jas. Hoffack, 10s. p.d.
Surgeon, Mr. Wm. Taylor, 150l.
His Serv. , 30l.
His Aſſiſtants, Dav. Story, Tho. Carnarvon, 50l. each
Diſpenſer, John Pocock, 50l.
His Aſſiſt. Wm. Wheatley, 30l.
Chaplains, Rev. Jn. Cooke, Jn. Maule, 130l. each
Steward Mr. Jn. Godby, 160l.
His Cls. D. Ball, 60l. M. Mallahat, 40l. J. Samworth, 40l. W. Ball, 40l.
Cl of Chec. Mr. S. J Maule, 100l.
His Cls. Theo. Court, 60l. Geo. Smith, 40l. John Elder, 40l.
E. Smith, 40l.

(140)

Matrons, M. Burt, Sar. Smith, Eleanor Power, 40l. each
Maſt. Brew. S.C.Hickman, 60l.
Butler, William Saword, 25l.
Mates, P.Lewis, J.Skeen, 15lea.
Schoolmaſter, Th.Furbor, 150l.
Organiſt, Lufton Relfe, 60l.
Meſſenger, Wm. Coxe, 30l.
Cook of Eaſt Kitch. S. Troke, 30l. *His Mates*, J.Matthews, 20l. N. Joyce, 15l.
Cook of Weſt Kitch. A. Moore, 30l. *His Mates*, R. Hunt, 20l. J. Kendreck, 15l.
Sculleryman, Nich. Livitt, 20l. *His Mates*, Rt. Ruſſel, Wm. Garner, 15l. each
Port. J. Webb, J.Scott, 15l. ea
Barber, John Mackanefs, 12l.
2300 Penſioners, Nurſes 140, Boys 150, their Nurſes 5.

RECEIVER'S OFFICE, on Tower-Hill, for Greenwich Hoſpital, where 6d. a Month is paid by all Seamen in the Merchants Service.
Three Commiſſioners.
Commiſſ. and Receiver, Tho. Hicks, eſq; 300l.
His Cls. J.Bryan, 50l. W Gray, 40l

Commiſſ. and Accomptant, ×J. Clevland, eſq; 200l.
Cl. to ditto, H. Mattocks, 50l.
Commiſſ. and Comptroller, John Beverley, eſq; 100l.
Cl. to ditto, Cha. Eve, jun. 40l.
Cl. at Cuſtom-Houſe, to take an account of the daily arrival of ſhips, Jn. Dalley, 50l.
Solicitor, Samuel Smith, eſq;
Houſekeeper, Marg. Silver, 20l.
Meſſenger Wm. Newnum, 20l.

Commiſſioners for ſick and hurt Seamen. Office Tower-Hill.
Commiſſ. W. Farquharſon, eſq; 465l. V.Corbett, eſq; and R. Lulman, eſq;
Sec. Rich. Waite Cox, 200l.
1ſt Cl. Nathan Crow, 100l.
2d Cl. Sam. Parſons, 100l.
Ext. Cls. Jo.Hefford, R.Lloyd, P.Nettle, J.Smith, H.Buſſel, Sa. Knight, J. Hunter, N. Huber, W. Harriſon, R. W. Cox, jun. J. Stewart, J. Spicer, J.Collier, T.Binches, B. Phillips, 50l. each.
Meſſenger, John Walker, 30l.
Houſekeeper, Mrs. Walker

Royal Hoſpital at HASLAR, near PORTSMOUTH, for ſick and hurt Seamen and Marines.

Phyſicians, Ja. Lind, M. D. John Lind, M. D. 200l.
Surgeon, Edw. Young, 150l.
Steward, John Merritt, 100l.
Agent, Thomas Holden, 10ol.
Diſpenſer, Wm. Shadbolt, 100l.
Chapl. Rev. R. Hudſon, 50l.
Steward's Cl. Wm.Hewett, 50l.
Agent's Cl. Dan.Shoveler, 50l
Aſſiſt. Diſpenſ. N. Taylor,
Matron, Martha Hewett, 25l.
Porter, J.Arundell, 30l. *Ferryman*, W.Loney, 20l. *Butler*, Nicholls, 20l *Barber*, J.Motley, 20l. *Cook*, Ma.Nicholls, 12
Pumpg. Wat. J.Caſtleman, 45

Royal Hoſpital at PLYMOUTH.
Phyſician, Wm. Farr, M.D.200l.
Surgeon, Francis Geach, 150l.
Steward, Abra. Jeffery, 100l.
Cl. to Ditto, Geo. Cleather, 50l.
Agent, Samuel Day, 100l.
Cl. to Ditto, Fr. Keys, 50l.
Diſpenſ. John Raggett, 100l.
Aſſiſtant, W. Richardſon, 50
Chapl. Rev. Joſias Foote, 50
Matron, Mary Parker, 25l.
Butler, Joſeph Netten, 20l.
Porters, John Baylis, 30l. J King, 20l.
Barber Richard Hutchins,

A New and Correct LIST *of the* ROYAL NAVY *of Great-Britain, containing the Names of all the Ships either in or out of Commission.*

List of King's Ships not in Commission.

60	Achilles	32	Niger
32	Apollo	50	Preston
40	Artois	74	Prince of Wales
74	Arrogant	32	Providence
90	Blenheim	64	Revenge
70	Boyne	84	Royal William
50	Centurion	64	Raisonable
60	Dreadnought	50	Salisbury
64	Essex	36	Santa Margareta
60	Firme	20	Sphynx
74	Hercules	64	St. Anne
74	Kent	74	Temeraire
44	Launceston	74	Tiger
28	Milford	28	Virginia
64	Modeste	32	Winchelsea
98	Neptune		

List of King's Ships now in Commission.

First Rate.
100 Britannia, *Vice Ad. Darby,* 1st *Capt. Rear Adm. Kempenfelt,* 2d *Capt. J. Brady.*
100 Royal George, *Capt. J. Bourmaster*
100 Victory, *Admiral Drake, Capt. S. W. Clayton.*

Second Rates.
98 Barfleur, *Rear Adm. Hood, Capt. J. Inglefield.*
98 Duke, *Sir C. Douglas*
98 Formidable, *J. Cleland*
98 London, *Rear Adm. Graves, Capt. D. Graves*
90 Namur, *H. Sawyer*
98 Ocean *G. Ourry.*
98 Prince George, *Admiral Digby, Capt. Williams*
98 Princess Royal, *Adm. Rowley, Capt. J. T. Duckworth*
98 Sandwich, *Ad. Sir G. B. Rodney, Capt. W. Young.*
90 Union, *J. Dalrymple*

Third Rates.
98 Queen
74 Ajax, *J. Symons*
74 Albion, *G. Bowyer*
74 Alcide, *C. Thompson*
74 Alexander, *Lord Longford*
74 Alfred, *W. Bayne*
64 America, *S. Thompson*
64 Asia, *G. Vandeput*
74 Bedford, *E. Affleck*
64 Belleisle, *R. Barber*
64 Belliqueux, *T. Fitzherbert*
74 Bellona, *R. Onslow*
74 Berwick, *Hon. K. Stewart*
64 Bienfaisant, *R. Braithwaite*
60 Buffalo, *R. Calder*
70 Burford, *P. Rainier.*

80 Cambridge [*Guard Ship*] B. *Hartwell*
74 Canada, *Sir G. Collier*
74 Centaur, *J. N. P. Nott*
74 Conqueror, *W. Dickson*
74 Courageux, *Lord Mulgrave*
74 Culloden, *G. Balfour*
74 Cumberland, *J. Peyton, sen.*
74 Dragon, *J. Ferguson*
74 Dublin, *S. Uvedale*
74 Defence, *James Cranston*
70 Diligence, *Adm. Sir Thos. Pye, Capt. A. Hunt*
64 Eagle, *A. Reddall*
74 Edgar, *J. Elliott*
74 Egmont, *R. Fanshaw*
74 Elizabeth, *Hon. F. Maitland*
64 Europe, *W. Swiney*
64 Exeter, *R. King*
74 Fame, *J. Butchart*
74 Fortitude, *Sir R. Bickerton*
80 Foudroyant, *J. Jervis*
80 Gibraltar, *W. Sterling*
74 Grafton, *W. Affleck*
74 Hector, *Sir J. Hamilton*
74 Hero, *J. Hawkes*
64 Inflexible, *R. Cotton*
64 Intrepid, *J. Ferguson*
74 Invincible, *C. Saxton*
74 Lenox, *W. Bennett*
64 Lion, *Hon. W. Cornwallis*
64 Magnanime, *C. Wolseley*
74 Mars [*a Prison Ship*] *Lieut. T. Cox*
74 Magnificent, *J. Elphinston*
74 Marlborough, *T. Penry*
70 Monarca, *J. Gell*
74 Monarch, *F. Reynolds*
64 Monmouth, *J. Alms*
74 Montagu, *J. Houlton*
64 Nonsuch, *Sir J. Wallace*
70 Orford, (*Hosp. Ship*) *Lieut. Vavasor*
80 Princess Amelia, *J. Matartney*
70 Princessa, *Sir T. Rich*

64 Prince William, *S. Douglas*
64 Prudent, *T. Burnett*
64 Prothee, *H. F. Evans*
74 Ramillies, *J. Moutray*
64 Repulse, *Sir D. Dent*
74 Resolution, *Rear Ad. Sir C. Ogle, Capt. Lord R. Manners*
74 Robuste, *P. Cosby*
74 Royal Oak, *Vice Adm. Arbuthnot*
64 Ruby, *Vice Adm. Parker, Capt. J. Couling*
74 Russell, *Rear Ad. F. S. Drake*
74 Shrewsbury, *M. Robinson*
64 St. Alban's, *C. Inglis*
64 Sterling-Castle, *R. Carkett*
74 Suffolk, *A. Crespin*
74 Sultan, *A. Gardner*
74 Superb, *Rear Adm. Sir E. Hughes, Capt. R. Simonton*
74 Terrible
74 Thunderer, *Hon. R. B. Walsingham*
74 Torbay, *J. L. Gidoin*
64 Trident, *A. P. Molloy*
74 Triumph, *P. Affleck*
74 Vengeance, *Com. Hotham, Capt. J. Holloway*
74 Valiant, *S. C. Goodall*
64 Vigilant, *Sir G. Home*
64 Worcester, *G. Talbot*
74 Warspite, *W. Grant*
64 Yarmouth, *S. Lutwidge*

Fourth Rates.

50 Adamant, *G d. Johnstone*
50 Antelope
50 Assistance, *J. Worth*
50 Bristol, *T. Caulfield*
50 Chatham, *J. Ord*
60 Conquestadore, *Vice Adm. Roddam, Capt. J. Orrock*
60 Dunkirk, *Rear Adm. H. Parker, Capt J. Milligen*
50 Hannibal, *B. Caldwell*
60 Jersey, (*Hosp. Ship*)
50 Isis, *E. Sutton*

50 Jupiter, *T. Pafley*
50 Leander, *T. Shirley*
60 Medway, *H. Harmood*
60 Panther, *J. Hervey*
50 Portland, *Rear Admiral Edwards, Capt. T. Lloyd*
50 Renown, *J. Henry*
60 Rippon, *Adm. Sir E. Vernon, Capt. J. Blankett*
50 Romney, *Com. G. Johnstone, Capt. R. Home*
50 Warwick, *H.GK: Elphinstone*

Fifth Rates.

32 Active, *T. Mackenzie*
42 Assurance, *J. Cumming*
32 Æolus, *G. Keppel*
44 Acteon, *F. Parry*
32 Alarm, *Sir Rich. Pearson*
32 Amazon, *Hon. W. C. Finch*
32 Ambuscade, *H. R.S. Conway*
32 Amphion, *J. Bazeley*
32 Blonde, *A. Barclay*
36 La Blanche, *S. Uppleby*
36 La Belle Poule
32 Boston, *W. Dudingston*
32 Brune, *F. J. Hartwell*
32 Cerberus, *R. Mann*
44 Charon, *T. Symonds*
32 Cleopatra, *G. Murray*
32 Convert, *H. Harvey*
32 Danae, *S. Graves*
32 Diamond, *C. Parker*
32 Diana, *Sir W. C. Burnaby*
32 Dædalus, *T. Pringle*
32 Emerald, *S. Marshall*
44 Endymion, *P. Carteret*
42 La Fortune, *H. C. Christian*
36 Flora, *W. P. Williams*
32 Fox, *Hon. T. Windsor*
32 Huffar, *C. M. Pole*
44 Janus, *W. H. K. O'Hara*
32 Jason, *J. Piggott*
32 Juno, *J. Montagu*
32 Iris, *G. Dawson*
32 Iphigenia, *C. Hope*
32 Licorne, *Hon. T. Cadogan*

32 Lowestoffe, *C. E. Nugent*
36 La Prudente, *W. Waldgrave*
36 La Nymphe, *J. Ford*
38 Minerva, *C. Fielding*
36 Monsieur, —— *Watts*
32 Oifeau, *H. Lloyd*
32 Orpheus, *J. Colpoy*
36 Pallas, *T. Spry*
32 Pearl, *G. Montagu*
32 Raleigh, *J. Gambier*
32 Richmond, *C. Hudson*
44 Roebuck, *A. S. Douglas*
44 Romulus, *G. Gayton*
36 Santa Monica, *J. Lindsey*
32 Sartine, *A. M'Coy*
32 Southampton, *W. Garnier*
32 Stag, *R. P. Cooper*
32 Thames, *T. Howe*
32 Thetis, *R. Lindzee*
36 Venus, *J. Douglas* [2]
44 Ulysses, *T. Dumaresq*

Sixth Rates.

20 Albemarle, *T. Taylor*
28 Alcimena, *J. Brine*
24 Amphitrite, *R. Biggs*
20 Ariadne, *M. Squire*
28 Aurora, *H. Collins*
28 Boreas
28 Brilliant, *R. Curtis*
24 Camel, *J. Pakenham*
20 Camilla, *J. Collins*
28 Carysfort, *W. Peacock*
24 Champion, *T. West*
28 Charles Town, *H. F. Evans*
28 Coventry
28 Crescent, *Hon. T. Pakenham*
28 Cyclops, *J. Robinson*
20 Daphne, *Lord Harvey*
24 Deal Castle, *J. Hawkins*
28 Delawar, *C. Mason*
30 Dromedary, *Rear Ad. Evans Capt. W. Denne*
28 Enterprize, *P. Leflie*
28 La Ellis
24 Fowey
28 Guadaloupe, *H. Robinson*

20 Galatea, *J. Reed*	12 Badger, *C. Walker*
24 Garland, *C. Chamberlain*	14 Barbadoes, *R. Milbank*
28 Greyhound, *W. Fookes*	14 Beaumont, *T. M. Ruffel*
28 Hinchinbrook	14 Beaver, *J. Peyton, jun.*
24 Hinde, *W. Young*	14 Bonetta, *R. Dundas*
24 Hyena, *E. Dodd*	14 Cabot, *H. Cromwell*
24 Hydra, *E. Garner*	14 Camelion, *R. Johnstone*
28 L'Esperance	12 Childers, *H.J.W.Chetwynd*
* 28 Lizard, *E. Dodd*	14 Cormorant, *R. M'Evoy*
28 Maidstone, *W. Parker*	18 Cygnet, *P. Baskerville*
20 Mentor, *R. Deane*	14 Delight, *J. Ingils* (1)
28 Medea, *H. Duncan*	14 Drake, *W. Browne*
28 Mercury, *J. Prescott*	10 Endeavour, *F. Wooldridge*
08 Nemesis, *R. R. Bligh*	18 Echo, *J. Manly*
24 Pandora, *A. Parrey*	14 Fairy, *J. Browne*
28 Pegasus, *J. Stanhope*	16 St. Firmin, *J. Faulkner*
24 Pelican, *T. Haynes*	10 Florida, *C. Osborn*
20 Perseus, *J. Dacres*	14 Fly, *B. Douglas*
28 Pomona, *G. Collingwood*	14 Fortune, *J. Breton*
24 Porcupine, *Sir C.H.Knowles*	16 Fury, *A. Agnew*
28 Proserpine, *G. A. Byron*	14 Guay Trouin, *G. Stoney*
30 Ranger, *H. Bakie*	16 Hawke, *R. Murray*
28 Resource, *P. Fotheringham*	14 Helena, *F. Roberts*
20 Scarborough	14 Hazard, *J. Pellew*
20 Seaford, *B. Christian*	18 Halifax, *E. Bowers*
20 Seahorse, *A. Panton*	14 Hornet, *Hon. T. Pitt*
28 Shark, *H. Lloyd*	14 Hound, *J. M'Namara*
28 Solebay, *T. Everett*	16 Jamaica, *C. Dixon*
20 Squirrel, *T. Piercy*	12 Kite, *H. Trollope*
28 Surprise, *S. Reeve*	12 Lively, *W. Coxlyon*
28 Sybil, *Lord C. Fitzgerald*	16 Lynx, *J. Norman*
28 Tartar, *A. Graeme*	14 Loyalist, *J. P. Ardefoif*
24 Terrmegant, *A. Kempe*	14 Martin, *H. Wyborn*
28 Triton, *J. M'Laurin*	18 Merlin, *Hon. J. Luttrell*
28 Vestal, *Hon. G. Berkley*	14 Nymph
	16 Ostrich, *Sir J. Wheate*
Sloops.	14 Otter, *R. Creyk*
14 Albany, *H. Mowatt*	14 Pacahunta, *J. Rodney*
10 Ardrney, *J. L. Nasmith*	14 Pelican, *J. Hardy*
12 Alert, *J. Vashon*	16 Porcupine, *S. Hulke*
14 Alligator, *A. Frodham*	12 Port Antonio, *J. Reid*
14 Antigua, *F. Pender*	18 Port Royal
14 Allegiance	16 Porto, *Hon. T. Lumley*
14 Atalanta, *S. Edwards*	12 Rattlesnake, *W. Clements*
14 Avenger, *G. Sterling*	14 Savage, *J. Graves*
	16 Shark, *R. M'Douall*

14	Star, *J. Ingram*		Cruiser, *A. Hayne*
14	Stork, *F. L. Montais*		Expedition, *R. Noble*,
16	Surprife, *G. Day*		Ferret, *G. Mowbray*
14	Swallow		Fly, *M. Ponfonby*
14	Scout, *J. Ellis*		Flying Fifh, *J. Mac Dougal*
16	Scourge, *C. Knatchbull*		Griffin, *J. Cook*
14	St. Vincent, *G. Wilkinfon*		Hope, *J. P. Rochfort*
14	Swift, *J. Applin*		Liberty, *V. C. Berkley*
16	Sylph, *G. A. Pulteney*		Lark, *P. D'Auvergne*
14	Trepaffey, *J. Smith*		Meredith, *J. Alexander*
14	Tobago, *C. Hotchkeys*		Monkey, *J. Glosford*
14	Victor, *G. M'Kenzie.*		Mutine, *S. Cox*
10	Viper, *J. Dickenfon*		Nimble, *W. Furnival*
14	Volcano, *T. Marfhall*		Pheafant, *G. Matthews*
14	Vulture, *A. Sutherland*		Rambler, *J. George*
8	Wolf, *M. Cole*		Refolution, *J. Douglas*
16	Zebra, *Bourchier*		Ranger, *A. Hood*
14	Zephyr, *J. Inglis* (2)		Repulfe, *E. Byam*

Armed Ships.

20	Alfred, *D. Collins*		Sprightly, *W. Snow*
20	Britannia, *E. Thomborough*		Speedwell, *J. Gibfon*
20	Canceaux, *J. Schankz*		Sultana *L. Fabian*
20	Charlotte, *J. Nunn*		True Briton, *C. Cobb*

Bombs.

10	Flying Fifh		Carcafs, *E. Edwards*
20	Greenwich, *W. Daniel*		Ætna, *Gardiner*
10	Germain, *F. T. Drake*		Terror, *C. Wood*
20	Heart of Oak, *W. Redman*		Thunder, *J. Wallace*
20	Leithe, *P. Roche*		Vefuvius
20	London, *S. Rains*		

Fire-Ships.

20	Lord Amherft, *J. Kinneer*		Blaft, *G. Bowen*
20	Mackworth, *J. Dickenfon*		Explofion
20	Merchant, *Sir H. Heron*		Firebrand, *G. Robertfon*
20	Manilla, *S. Robinfon*		Furnace, *J. Wright*
20	Molly *W. Long*		Harpy, *P. Walfh*
10	Port Morant		Incendiary, *W. A. Merrick*
20	Queen, *J. Brenton*		Lightening *G. Campbell*
20	Sandwich, *W. Bett*		Pluto, *T. Geary*
20	Satisfaction, *J. Sawher*		Salamander, *J. Finch*
20	Three Brothers, *T. Hawker*		Sulphur, *T. Bofton*
22	Vigilant, *Goldfborough*		Vulcan, *A. Edgar*
20	William, *T. Rowe*		

Cutters commanded by Lieutenants.

Royal Yachts.

Active, *W. Quaeme*		Dorfet, *Sir A. Schomberg*
Advice, *J. B. Rofs*		Fubbs, *P. T. Percival*
Bufy, *J. Cotes*		Medina
		Princefs Augufta, *C. Fortefcue*

(146)

Ships building at different Places.

90 Atlas	44 Dolphin	20 Narciſſus
64 A.rica	64 Director	90 Prince
64 Anſon	32 Druid	74 Powerful
64 Agamemnon	50 Europa	64 Polyphemys
64 Ardent	44 Experiment	38 Phaeton
44 Argo	24 Euridice	36 Perſeverance
38 Arethuſa	98 Glo:y	14 Pigmy *Cutter*
32 Andromache	74 Goliah	32 Quebec
32 Aſtrea	74 Ganges	100 Royal Sovereign
16 Ariel, [*Sloop*]	50 Grampus	44 Regulus
8 Alecto [*Fireſhip*]	44 Gladiator	44 Reſiſtance
74 Bulwark	44 Guardian	98 St. George
74 Bombay Caſtle	32 Hermione	64 Sampſon
8 Baſiliſk, *Fireſhip*	90 Impregnable	64 Standard
74 Cæſar	64 Indefatigable	64 Sceptre
74 Carnatic	74 Irreſiſtible	64 Scipio
64 Crown	16 Inſpector [*Sloop*]	64 Stately
50 Cato	74 Leviathan	44 Serapis
32 Ceres	50 Leopard	32 Succeſs
24 Crocodile	38 Latona	50 Truſty
44 Cockatrice *Cutter*	50 Meduſa	8 Tiſiphone, *Fireſhip*
74 Defiance	44 Mediator	74 Vanguard
64 Dictator	32 Mermaid	64 Veteran
64 Diadem	22 Mirmidon	74 Warrior
44 Diomed		

ADMIRALS of the ROYAL NAVY.

Admiral of the Fleet
ord Hawke, K. B. Vice-Admiral of England

Admirals of the White.
Hon. John Forbes, General of Marines
Sir Thomas Frankland, Bart.
Duke of Bolton
Earl of Northeſk
Sir Thomas Pye, Knt.
Francis Geary, Eſq.
×Sir Geo. Brydges Rodney, Bt.
Rear Admiral of Great-Britain
James Young, Eſq;

Admirals of the Blue.
Sir Piercy Brett Kt.

Sir James Douglas, Knt.
Lord Edgcumbe
Samuel Graves, Eſq.
× Hon. Auguſtus Keppel
His R. H. D. of Cumberland
Matthew Buckle, Eſq.
Robert Mann, Eſq.

Vice Admirals of the Red.
Clark Gayton
John Montagu, Eſq.
Sir Robert Harland, Bart.
×Richard Viſcount Howe
×Hugh Pigot, Eſq.
× Lord Shuldham
John Vaughan, Eſq.
Robert Duff, Eſq.

Vice Admirals of the White.
John Reynolds, Esq
Sir Hugh Palliser, Bart.
Hon. John Byron
Matthew Barton, Esq.
Sir Peter Parker, Knt.
Hon. Samuel Barrington
Marriott Arbuthnot, Esq.
Robert Roddam, Esq.
×George Darby, Esq.
John Campbell, Esq

Vice Admirals of the Blue.
James Gambier, Esq.
William Lloyd, Esq.
Francis William Drake, Esq.
Sir Ed. Hughes, K. B.
Hyde Parker, Esq.
John Evans, Esq.
Mark Milbanke, Esq.

Rear Admirals of the Red
Nicholas Vincent, Esq.
John Storr, Esq.

Sir Edw. Vernon, Knt.
Joshua Rowley, Esq.
Richard Edwards, Esq.
Thomas Graves, Esq.
Robert Digby, Esq.
Sir John Lockhart Ross, Bart.

Rear Admirals of the White.
Cha. Webber, Esq.
William Langdon, Esq.
Benjamin Marlow, Esq.
Alexander Hood, Esq.
Alexander Innes, Esq.

Rear Admirals of the Blue.
Sir Chaloner Ogle Kt.
Sir Samuel Hood, Bart.
Stephen Moore, Esq.
Sir Richard Hughes, Bart.
Francis Samuel Drake, Esq.
Richard Kempenfelt, Esq.

Rt. Hon. Lord Hawke, K. B. Vice Admiral of England, and Lieutenant of the Admiralty thereof, 20s. per day, and 10s. per month for 16 servants.
Sir George Brydges Rodney, Bart. K. B. Rear Admiral of England, 16s. per day, and 10s. per month for twelve servants.
John Earl of Breadalbane, Vice Admiral of Scotland, and Judge of the Admiralty, &c. there, 1000l.

Rear Admirals, superannuated, upon half-pay, 17s. 6d. a Day.

Hon. G. Murray,	Edw. Falkingham,	Richard Knight,
Thorpe Fowke,	W. Bladwell,	J. Galbraith,
Robert Robinson,	Cha. Knowler,	John Harrison,
George Elliot,	Henry Rosewell,	M. Whitwell,
John Hardy,	T. Knowler,	Esqrs.
	John Hale,	

Superannuated Commissioner of the Navy, 500l. a year.
Sir Richard Hughes, Bart.

The CAPTAINS, *&c. with the Dates of their First Commissions, from which they take Post.*

1741.	1743.	1744.
JOHN BRETT, Mar. 25	F. Cornwall Feb. 11	C. Norbury Nov. 17
		Hon A. Stuart Feb. 20

1746.	William Brereton 25	Wm. Baine July 1
Jn. Douglas, April. 0	Charles Middleton	Hon. Philip Tufton
Cha. Proby, Sept. 17	May 2	Perceval 21
1748.	Sir Digby Dent, Bt.	M. Robinson Aug 12
Day. Brodie, Mar. 9	July 7	Cha. Fielding Aug 27
James Kirke June 23	John Lafory 29	John Jervis Oct. 13
1755.	George Balfour 26	Samuel Thompson
Edw. Lecras Feb. 4	Thomas Owen 28	Nov. 5
1756.	Rob. Kirk Oct. 1.	John Hughes 21
Jervis Maplesden	James Smith 18	M. Graham 21
May 21	John Dalrymple 18	1761.
1757.	Brod. Hartwell 18	A. Duncan Feb. 21
P. H. Ourry Feb.	G. Nightingale 18	Sir C. Douglas. Bart.
Tho. Cornewall 7	Herbert Sawyer	Mar. 13.
Tho. Taylor Mar. 2	Dec. 26	Rich. Brathwaite
Edm. Affleck 23	John Mourtray 28	April 6
And. Wilkinson 2	1759.	Rob. Keeler May 19
Tho. Baillie 30	Walter Sterling	Philips Cosby do
Arch Kennedy Apr 5	Jan. 10.	John Wilson July 3
Tho. Knackston 5	Richard King 29	Joseph Mead 7
John Elliot 5	John Elphinston	T. Fitzherbert 10
Sir A. Schomberg,	Feb. 1	Sam. Cornish 24
Knight 5	Robert J celyn 9	John Neal Pleydell
Sam. Wallis 8	H. F. Maitland Mar 9	Nott Sept. 24
Tho. Burnett May 5	Welton Varlo	John Brisbane 24
Sam. Spencer June	May 12	John Houlton Nov 5
X Hon. Rob. B. Wal	John Cleland 15	Charles Wolsely 9
singham June 15	R. Norbury June 4	John Peighin Dec. 1
Wm Hotham Aug 17	Rob. Barbor 4	Charles Inglis 15
Sir Jn. Lindsay, K. B.	J. Faulknor July 9	1762.
Sept. 29	Ph. Affleck Aug. 20	S. Cranston Goodall
Mich. Clements 29	Sr Rich. Bickelton,	Jan. 13
Tay. Penny Nov.	Bart. 21	Cha. Saxton 28
Jos. Peyton Dec. 2	J. Fortescue Sept. 4	J. Bover Mar. 12
Joshua Loring 19	Fran. Burslem Oct. 4	Chal. Ogle 29
Henry Martin 19	Rob. Hathorn 27	J. Botterel Apr. 7
1758.	Hon T Shirley No. 19	James Cranston 7
Max. Jacobs Jan. 4	Jos. Fraine Dec. 11	X Hon. K Stewart 15
John Bray 9	1760.	Wm. Hay 12
John Clark 19	S. Uvedale Feb. 18	Fran. Reynolds 12
John Stukely Somer-	Rob. Lambert Fel.	Rich. Onslow 14
set Mar. 2	18	Cha. Ellys May 10
John Stanton 4	Wm. Bennet Mar. 5	Tho. Halum 24
Rob. Carket 12	Hon. John Leveson	Rob. Kingsmill 26
John Carter Allen 21	Gower June 30	Stair Douglas May 29

(149)

Lin. Holmes *July* 2
SirG. CollierKt. 12
✕ G Johnſt.ne*Aug* 1
Hon. C. Napier 15
✕ Hon. J. Luttrel 25
JohnBrooks *Sept.* 24
Patrick Drummond
    Oct. 22
George Bowyer 28
Rich. Smith *Nov.* 1
✕ Hon. Per. Bertie 6
George Ourry 10
    1763.
J. Ferguſon *June* 6
Joſ. Norwood 7
SirH.Parker*July* 18
    1764.
Rowl. Cotton *May* 7
    1765.
Ben.Caldwell*Apr.* 1.
Hon. W. Cornwallis
    April 20
Patrick Mouat 28
J. O'Hara *June* 20
M. Henry Paſcal 20
James Alms 20
William Allen 20
John M'Bride 20
Charles Hudſon 20
✕ Rt.H.L. Mulgrave
    June 20
Geo. Vandeput 20
F. G. Gordon *July* 3
John Leary *July* 13
M. Pattiſon *Aug* 21
    1766.
C. Buckner *Feb.* 17
John Geil *Mar.* 4
J. Chadds *April* 2
W. Dickſon *May* 2
Allan Gardner 19
Ld. Longford 21
Sir Wm. Abdy, Bart
    June 24
J. Macartney *Sept.* 4

1768.
R b Fanſhaw*May* 25
Wm. Greenwood 26
Tho. Biſhop do
Jn. Lewis Gidoin do
George Gatoyn do
John Milligen do
George Talbot do
John Urry do
James Hawker do
Sir John Hamilton,
  Bart do
Wm. Locker do
George Murry do
W. Garnier *Aug.* 3
    1770.
Alexander Barkley
    May 30
Rob. Linzee *Oct.* 3
Sir An. Snape Hammond, Knt. *Dec.* 7
    1771.
Alexander Lvine
    Jun. 10
W. Hamilton do
SirJ.Wallace,Kt. do
Henry Bellew do
Philip Carteret 10
Anthony Hunt do
William Malthy do
Edward Medows do
Wm.PeereWilliams
    ditto
Evelyn Sutton do
ThomasSymonds 18
Tho. Paſley *Jan.* 21
Samuel Marſhall 24
John Symons 28
Sir Tho. Rich, Bt.
    Feb. 14
Hen.Lloyd,*Mar.*23
    1772.
Cornthwaite Omaney *Feb.* 22
C. Thompſon*Mar.* 7
E. Thompſon *Ap.* 7

GidJohnſtone*June* 2
James Cumming
    July 30
Chri. Atkins *Sept.* 18
Ja. Worth *Nov.* 2
    1773.
St. John Chinnery,
    June 25
Sir Richard Pearſon,
  Bart. do
John Ford do
JohnColpoys*Aug.*25
G.RobinſonWalters
    Sept. 2
Pat. Fotheringham,
    Oct. 9
Skeff. Lutwidge do
    1774.
JohnRobinſon*Ap*26
Arch. Dickſon 31
G.Montagu,*Apr.*15
W. Affleck, *June* 4
Wm. Judd, *Sept.* 7
    1775.
Tyringham Howe
    Jan. 13
T. Dumareſq. 21
HonKGElphinſton,
    May 11
Tobias Furneaux
    Aug. 10
Ja.Montagu *Nov.*14
    1776.
H. Duncan, *Feb.* 7
Ja. Piggott 22
Ell. Salter, *Mar.* 21
Sa. Uppleby,*April* 8
Alex. Scott 25
Hon. W. Waldegrave *May* 30
ThomasMackenzie,
    June 12
James Reid *July* 5
Toby Caulfield. 6
e Hon C. Phipps
    Auguſt 1
Tho.Pringle,*Nov*25

(150)

1777.	Tho. Sp‑y 5	Sir George Home,
Sir W. C. Burnaby,	Tho. Gaborian 13	Bart. 21
Bt. Jan. 16	Farmery Epworth 13	Thomas Newnham
Hon. W. C. Finch	John Orde 19	30
March 18	R. Simonton July 9	Charles Cotton,
John Linzee Feb. 16	John Chapman 13	Aug. 10
Roger Curtis, Ap. 30	Wm. Young Sept. 23	Robert Sutton 10
H. Robinson May 8	Js. Gambier, Oct. 9	David Graves Sept. 9
Henry Harvey 9	Harry Harmood 17	Edward Garner Oct. 1
Robert Man 30	C. Chamberlayne 28	Walter Young do
J.A Panton June 26	Peter Rainer 29	Will. Lockhart 7
James Jones Aug. 2	Tho. Lloyd 30	William Denire 20
William Parker 28	John Kendall	Matthew Squire
Sam. Warren Sept. 5	Nov. 24	Nov. 6
C. H. Everitt 7	Hugh Cloberry Chris-	Roddam Home 6
George Dawson 9	tian Dec. 8	William Knell 22
John Bourmaster 9	Wm. Truscott 14	F. J. Hartwell Dec.
Samuel Graves 15	1779.	19
John Harvey 16	Tho.Haynes Jan. 30	James Brine 30
W. Duddingston 19	Hon. Hugh Seymour	1780.
Geo. Young Nov. 7.	Conway Feb. 8	Brabazon Christian
John Henry 22	Adex. M'Coy 10	Jan. 1
Char. Hope 29	Ambrose Reddall 20	John Pakenham 1
R. Rod. Bligh Dec. 6	Will. Cumming 27	Erasmus Gower 9
1778.	J. Stanhope. Mar. 5	John Cowling 13
Alex. Græme Jan. 24	Henry Collins 20	Abraham Crespin 17
R. P. Cooper 26	Philip Patton 22	John Holloway 17
George Keppel 26	Ch. Morris Pole 22	Lord R. Manners 17
Benj. Hill 28	John Brown 25	Henry Ball 25
J. Collins Feb. 1	G. A. Byron April 3	Patrick Leslie 26
Samuel Reeve 1	John Douglas 5	William Peacock 27
Hon. T. Winsor 7	Robert Boyle Nicho-	George Wilson
Hon. T. Cadogan 20	las 19	Feb. 1
Rob. Biggs Mar. 18	William Swiney	Sir C. H. Knowles 2
Francis Parry Ap. 7	May 2	W. H. K. O'Hara
Isaac Prescott 8	Ch. Ed. Nugent 2	15
Anthony James Pye	James Orrok 5	William Fox 15
Molloy 11	William Fooks 14	Hugh Bakie 19
John Bazely 15	Charles Powell Ha-	Hon. T Pakenham
William Blair 18	milton 18	March 2
Christ. Mason 22	Edmund Dod do	Robert Deans 9
Sam. Wittewronge	Horatio Nelson	Lord Hervey 15
Clayton 23	June 11	Thomas Piercy
Hugh Bromedge 29	John Butchart 15	April 19
H. F. Evans 29	Thomas Lenox Fre-	Arthur Kempe May
Ant. Parry May 2	derick July 14	30

(151)

Smith Child 15,	J. Knowles July 1	James King 3
Howell Lloyd do	John Wil. Payne 8	John Inglefield 11
Thomas Tonken do	Jas. Bradby Aug. 26	Thomas Weft 19
An. Sn. Douglas do	Robert Calder 27	Chichefter Fortefcue
Right Hon. Lord C.	J. R. Decres S pt 13	Nov. 2
Fitzgerald 23	Hon. G. Berkeley 15	Ifaac Vaillant 23
Thos. Allen June 7	John Gore Oct. 2	

MASTERS and COMMANDERS.

1744.	W. Brograve Oct. 31	John Boyle do
JOHN Loving,	1761.	1777.
Jan. 12	Wm. Kite Mar. 4	John Howorth Feb. 1
1745.	John Hay May 4	F. L'Montais May 3
Hon. Rich. Barry	John Bowerbank 19	John Graves June 2
Apr. 11	Ja. Feattus July 7	J. Brenton Aug. 23
1747.	Tho. Prefcott 22	William Carlyon 28
George Blyke Nov. 3	W. F. Bourk 24	J. Ferguffon Sept. 5
G. Hudfon, Feb. 16	Fran. Lynn Oct. 26	John Brudenell 15
1755.	S. Hammock 30	J. Bourchier Oct. 8
W. Younge, Aug. 5	J. Cunningham,	William Grant 24
1756.	Nov. 19	Chrifto. Rigby 25
David Haye Nov. 10	1762.	William Owen
1757.	R. Hafwell Mar. 26	Nov. 7
James Mackenzie,	J. Bagfter May 14	Hercules Wyborn 19
Ap. 4	John Carey June 14	Alexan. Agnew 20
John Moore May 2	J. Thorp, Aug. 17	James Watt 23
Hen. Rich. Dubois 2	1765.	Jofeph Brown Dec. 1
John Hatch June 14	Thomas Pemble	Sir H. Heron, Bart. 1
R. Higgs July 20	June 20	Peter Foulkes 15
1758.	1768.	1778.
Dav. Pryce Jan. 11	James Robertfon	Richard Murray
Reg. Cocks Mar. 12	May 26	Jan. 26
Jof. Cave Aug. 10	Jam. How Jones do	John Becher Feb. 1
Fra. Richards Sep. 27	Robert Dring, Aug. 3	Lewis Robertfon 9
1759.	1771.	Thomas Totty 17
Sam. Taylor Mar. 2	Ja. Ayfcough Jan. 10	H. Pemberton Ap. 1
M. Kearny Aug. 20	Cuthbert-Baines 21	St. Alban Roy 11
R. Taylor Sept. 21	1773.	John Inglis (1) 11
Th. Allwright 21	Roger Wills June 25	Edw. Edwards 22
B. Fielding Nov. 19	Jof. Tathwell do	Peter Aplin 23
1760.	1774.	John Breton 29
W. Ofborn Mar. 1	Edw. Thornbrough	James Lyfs 29
Rich. Teale 5	April 15	T. Marfhall May 5
E. V. Yates June 2	1776.	T. B. Mainwaring 13
Peter Forbes 2	Jof. Nunn June 12	Martin Cole do

(152)

W. G. Fairfax	do	John Manley 16	Will. Bett 30
Thomas Hicks	do	Henry Cromwell 18	George Day 31
John Reynolds	14	Peter Rothe do	William Strudwich
David Collins	15	John Wallace do	1780 31
Richard Trotten	16	John Inglis (2) *June* 1	Peter Clements
Philip Walſh	18	John Cowling 3	*Jan.* 23
David Laird	18	Charles Wood 4	T. Gouldelbrough
Billy Douglas *July* 18		Charles Hotchkys 15	25
Alexander Edgar		James Dickinſon 19	Hon. J. W. Chetwynd 27
Aug. 27		William Daniel	
James Douglas	9	*July* 14	Jam. Samber, *Feb.* 1
William Yeo *Oct.* 1		Thomas Hawker 14	Francis Roberts 4
John Wainwright	16	John Thomas	S. H. Walker *March*
Richard Cryek	17	Duckworth 21	22
Thos. Durell	28	John Frodſham 30	William Chambers
George Robertſon		Thomas Boſton do	*April* 7
Nov. 4		James Vaſhon	John Schank 8
James Kinneer	19	*Aug.* 5	John Hope Bowers
George Stoney	do	*Sir John Borlaſe	*May* 15
James Ellis	do	Warren, Bart. do	William Heath 15
Joſ. Peyton *Dec.* 14		H. E. Stanhope 6	Fr. Tho. Drake 15
Samp. Edwards	26	Ch. Knatchbull 11	Charles Stirling 15
1779.		E. J. Moiarty 11	John Wright 30
Benj. Runwa *Jan.* 13		Stephen Rains 12	Alb. Bertie *June* 3
Will James	13	Arthur Walter 25	James Williams 7
John Blankett	30	Jemes Norman 27	Edw. Pellew *July* 1
Geo. Ar. Pulteney		Walter Long 30	Robert M'Evoy 8
Feb. 1		Arthur Philip	John Buchanan 17
J. L. Naſmith	27	*Sept.* 2	William White 17
Francis Tinley		Thomas Rawe 9	Hon. T. Lumley 25
Mar. 1		William Auguſtus	Jam. Clark *Aug.* 2
Thomas Drury	do	Merrick 13	Thomas Geary 26
Thos. Graves	15	Henry Chads 18	Geo. Campbell 27
Rich. Bickerton	do	Hon. Seymour	Edw. Thornbrough
William Browne	do	Finch do	jun. *Sept.* 14
Wm. Wardlaw	do	Charles George	James Smyth 16
Ralph Dundas		Heywood *Oct.* 8	James Burney *Oct.* 2
April 3		Will. Redmon 16	John Williamſon 3
Tho. Farnham	do	Peter Baſkerville 24	Hon. J. Luttrell 27
John Thomas	9	Sir J. Wheate, Bt.	Robert M'Dowall
Henry Trollope	16	*Nov.* 15	*Nov.* 23
Samuel Oſborn	29	J. P. Ardeſoif.	And. Sutherland 27
Benj. Bechinoe	30	Bart. 15	
David Phipps *May* 1		George Bowen 19	

[153]

The LIEUTENANTS *of his Majesty's* FLEET, *with the Dates of their first Commissions.*

1741.	Griffith Meare 14	Wm. Allen *July* 10
A L. Gordon	George Matthews 18	J. Puckinghorn *Au.* 2
Feb. 25	Isaac Covell *June* 3	Rob. Walter *Nov.* 4
1744.	John Skinner 10	D. Campbell *Dec.* 2
Anth. Fortye *June* 6	Henry Baker *July* 15	1756.
W. Runsiman *July* 7	Ja. Croucher *Aug.* 4	Daniel Burr *Feb.* 19
Mich. Hinde *Aug.* 11	Rich. Williams 15	Tho. Montague 19
John Treherne 17	Edw. Waud *Nov.* 9	Horatio Ripley 26
Isaac Hoy *Oct.* 6	1747.	Edward Hill *Mar.* 5
James Furneaux 15	Isaac Crouch *Feb.* 5	John Mann 20
John Walsh *Nov.* 23	Robert Hay *Ap.* 24	Edw. Reddish *Ap.* 14
John Neale *Feb.* 15	R. Edgcombe *May* 18	Wm Parsons Hoe *J* 14
John Hallam 26	Sam. Spendlove 28	Charles Cæsar 16
Wm. Ansell 26	W. Robinson (1st)	Joseph Hanby *Ma* 14
Rt Gordon *March* 1	*July* 18	Sam. Walton 18
Simon Turner 1	Geo. Ellery *Sept.* 18	Hugh Roch *June* 20
Robert Gideon 7	John O'Bryen 28	G Collingwood *July* 4
1745.	Pat. Calder *Nov.* 6	Paul Brustis 13
John Bernard 29	Samuel Short 21	Christ. Raper *Sept.* 13
J. Puddicombe *Ap.* 15	James Combes 23	Rd. Thomas *Oct.* 1
James Kyd *May* 3	P. VanCourt *Dec.* 25	T Hollingworth *Nov* 5
Ja. Lawson *June* 3	Th. Pigott 31	Robert Curry 8
James Munro *July* 8	Rob. Kerr *Jan.* 9	Henry Brome 9
Ja. Watson 13	Alex. Brown (1) 29	Lewis Gellie 9
Jos. Salmon 13	Thomas Moody 29	Thomas Bradshaw 9
John Ball 20	Samuel Swinton 29	James Baron 9
T. Williams *Aug.* 10	1748	John Oakley 13
John Brock *Sept.* 22	John Cope *Ap.* 16	Henry H. Hart 13
Hon. J. Wemyss 26	Alex. Keith *May* 24	Edward Lower 15
John Thane *Oct.* 1	Ric. Vis. Boyne *June* 2	Wm. Dickens 16
Henry Moyle 23	1750.	Richard Beale 26
John Hall *Nov.* 26	John Willes *Mar.* 1	Henry Townsend 30
Ric. Vavasor *Jan.* 30	Tho. Hudson *Oct.* 29	Wm Haswell *Dec.* 1
H. Costobadie *Feb.* 12	1753.	Edward Kerswell 7
Tho. Cobby *Mar.* 4	D. Shuckforth *June* 7	1757.
1746.	Matt. Kirby *Oct.* 31	Wm Hansford *Jan.* 6
Lewis Davies *Ap.* 2	1754.	W. Williams *Feb.* 10
David Boog 3	Hen. Collins *Ap.* 6	Bar. Fenwick 23
R. Mortimer 4	John Harris *July* 3	Richard Pinfold 23
Henry Parkin 17	1755.	A. Clark 23
William Hall 21	John Carteret *Feb.* 27	D. Butler *March* 3
J. Woodward *Ap.* 25	J. Brown (1st) *May* 2	J. Gauntlett 10
Geo. Newton *May* 9	Edw. Howorth 21	Tho. Arthur Ley 21

O Nich.

Nich. Rooke *Mar.* 23	Wm. Crosbe *Mar.* 20	Hen Jackson. *Dec.* 28
W. Martin (2d) *Ap.* 2	James Carteret 28	1759.
Edw. Colmbine 2	Henry Lewis *Apr.* 1	M. Wilkinson *Jan.* 2
John Purcell 4	James Hilgrove 5	Ja. de Haviland 12
Wm. Haygarth 6	Robert Wilson 6	Edward Roberts 18
Wm. Bensley 6	John James *May* 12	Tho. Rayment 22
Isaac Charley 6	Francis Exton 12	Henry Mouat 22
John Richardson 6	G. Mackenzie (1) 18	Robert Mayne 26
John Brown (2d) 6	David Kinloch 22	W. Meldrum 29
J. Arrowsmith *May* 6	Henry Dodd 22	Joseph Shank 29
John Doherty 10	S. Barnesley *June* 13	Rd. Stevens *Feb.* 12
William Stevens 11	Hyde Curtis 20	Charles Logie 13
If. Stephenson *Jun* 15	Christ. Ord *July* 14	John May 21
Ja. Sutherland 15	Henry Savage 20	Tho. Herbert 21
Rd. Phi. Shewen 17	Cha. Dobson 30	Ja. Gordon (2d) 22
John Cowe 17	Mat. Legeyt *Aug.* 1	Tho. Allen (1st) 22
Trevor Cuckow 21	William Don 2	Robert Parry . 22
T. P. Braithwaite,	John Robson 21	J. Tr. Colingwood 22
July 10	Par. Stuart 25	James Gaborian 27
John Shairp 22	Jn. Cowling *Sept.* 8	James Hill *March* 1
Charles Prince 25	John Galbraith 21	Thomas Townsend 7
Nath. Vincent 28	T. Underdown 30	Caleb Colton 9
John Baird *Aug.* 12	Ja. Glasford *Oct.* 1	Edmund Elliston 30
John Shadforth 24	Wm. Shammon 5	A. Cunningham *Ap* 7
Thomas Townley 25	John Read 6	Alex. Fr. Baillie 24
James Disher 31	Alex. Todd . 6	Charles Clarke 30
Geo. Spearing *Sept.* 8	Wm. Palmer 8	Sam. Burford *May* 2
John Ides Short 21	Lamb Brabazon 10	Edw. Atkinson 12
Joseph Jackson 24	David Arthur 11	John Mathews 14
John Hammett 29	Sam. Steward 18	W. Henderson 22
Wm. Bacon *Oct.* 27	John Luce 18	Ant. Gibbes *June* 2
Lord Rutherford	Walter Coltheart 26	Ar. Edwards 12
Nov. 12	Edward Palmer 27	Gilbert Fairlie 18
Arthur Hayne 22	Henry Lambert 27	James Nicholas 25
Fr La Powlett *Dec.* 1	Peter Tait 27	T. Lawrie *July* 10
H. Ashington 14	James Preston 27	Francis Ford 16
1758.	James Boyd 27	Reynell Michell 19
W. Smith (1) *Ja.* 17	Charles Besson 27	Joseph Lash 20
Rob. Tomlinson 19	Wm. Burstall 27	Thomas Cock 20
J. Gordon (1st) 24	Pearson Boys 27	Wm. Babb *Aug.* 2
J. Screech 25	H. Newton *Dec.* 2	John Forth 5
S. Puddicombe *Feb.* 2	John Marriot 16	Nic. Clifford 6
Essex Bowen 28	John Reid 21	John Wadman 6
Dav Chandler *Mar* 20	David Lockwood 21	Richard Kemp 6

Jn.

[155]

Jn. Littlefield *Aug.* 6	J. Alexander *Mar.* 17	Chrift. Major *Feb.* 1
Bernard Weftlake 10	James Neale 20	Timothy Bird 2
W. Elletfon 20	George Moubray 29	John Payne 4
George Lindfay 20	James Cook *Ap.* 1	John Weyman 27
J. Annington 22	John Burdall 2	Steph. Harris *Mar.* 16
George Bourn 23	John Lowder 2	Wm. Quarme 19
John Orde (1) 23	William Brooke 4	Charles Ofborne 23
Wm. Lurcock 23	Jofeph Breedon 4	Tho. Mackie 23
Wm. Reynolds 24	Rob. Gillingham 4	Al. Fordyce 30
J. Phœdra Chubb 28	Richard Lang 11	Thomas Liell *Apr.* 1
Thomas Tilly 29	Bravel Friend 21	Hon. Da. Stuart 15
John Jarvis *Sept.* 3	David Jefferfon 25	R. Boger (1) *May* 8
Ro. M'Dowall 7	Ezekiel Nafh *June* 2	John Norris 8
Charles Marfhal 10	Tho. Geary 12	Tho. Morrice 8
John Bligh 11	Tim. Hopkins *Sept* 19	Jof. Harrington 12
Tho. Edwards 19	Ja. Grierfon 19	John Weft 21
Fran. Broughton 20	John Whifton 19	Nath. Philips *June* 5
Philip Hue 22	Ja Hamilton,(2) 25	Edward Iggulden 7
Tho. Dyfon 24	Ja. Hull *July* 3	George Noble 19
D. Pryce Cumbye 24	Walter Watts 5	G. Younghufband 17
John Tyrwhitt 24	Hugh Lloyd 4	Jofeph Garrow 19
Thomas Dewey 27	Sir Edward Bindlofs,	Henry Mafter 23
Wm Ofborne *Oct.* 10	Bart. *Aug.* 27	Andrew Godfrey 24
Wm. Hemmings 10	James Warden 27	James George 24
Rich. Saunders 16	Rob. Carter 27	James M'Namara 25
Wm. Gafcey 18	Henry Smith 27	Anth. Jones *July* 1
George Menat 19	Robert Young 28	Charles Hunter 6
T. Laugharn *Nov.* 7	Robert Milne *Sept.* 6	William Scott 10
Cha. Kelly 15	William Bell 6	Geo. Barlow 17
Nath. Gooding 23	Walter Gwennap 6	J. Kempthorne *Aug* 6
John Girling 30	Henry Baynes *Oct.* 4	John Gaydon, 7
T. Lefingham *Dec.* 7	Daniel Difney 11	Wm. Smithett 7
Geo. Mennell 8	Tho. Hill . *Nov.* 8	James Cafe 7
1760.	Richard Douglas 27	John Brooks 7
Ja. Clarke (1) *Jan.* 5	W. Roxburgh *Dec.* 1	Francis Nott 7
George Wilkinfon 9	Robert Potts 9	William Oakley 13
Jay Bracey 9	John Newton 10	Jof. Hooley 18
F. Woolridge 24	Samuel John 10	S. Hayter 28
William Hunter 24	J. Langford 10	Jonathan Dove 31
John Okes *Feb.* 7	J. Gibfon 10	G. Stainforth *Sept.* 11
Francis Keir 26	T. Richardfon 23	Lucius Obrien 19
John Veyfey 28	1761.	Edm. Paddefon *Oct.* 3
Cut. Adamfon *Mar.* 4	John Webb *Jan.* 18	Samuel Scott 5
W. Robertfon 12	John Yetts 19	Edward Down 12
Rich. Shordiche 17	John St. Barbe 21	Step. Metcalf 14

[156]

Edm. Bower *Oct.* 16	H. Maton *Aug.* 25	Wm. Robinson (2)
Stephen Norris 22	John Young *Sept.* 2	*June* 26.
M. Hindman 27	John Cartwright 15	Jac. Waller *Sept.* 4
John Forster 30	Rich. Fowler 29	1767.
T. Appleby *Nov.* 12	Christ. Day *Oct.* 7	George Teer *Apr* 18
Thomas Lewes 20	James Godwin 8	Abr. Guyot *Aug.* 31
Cha. Emery *Dec.* 3	Wm. Davidson 16	1768.
C. C. Crocke 4	Edward Eyam 26	John Hills *May* 26
Henry Tuite 15	Richard Iago *Nov.* 6	John SaltWynell 26
Ed. Winnie: 15	Thomas Hayward 6	Christmas Paul 26
George Dumaresq 17	Hugh Lawson 6	W. H. Atkinson 26
George Truslel 22	Wm. Dickson 15	GRobertson2*Dec.* 15
1762.	T. Saund. Grove 21	1769.
Archibald Dow *Ja*26	William Ward 21	Wm Senhouse *Jan.* 2
Wm Thomas *Feb.* 2	John Bowen 24	SirD. Murray *Feb.* 19
Samuel Greig 4	Da. M'Killop *Dec.* 16	Rupert Geo. *Ap.* 25
Dan. Bradby, *Mar.* 8	Martin Waghorn 16	R. Curgenven *June* 7
Geo. Surtees 17	Wm. Smith (2d) 31	J. Maude 20
William Grieve 18		Geo. Hume *Sept.* 13
Fiske Manistre *Ap.* 9	1763.	1770.
John Starr *May* 5	C. Cartwright. *Feb.* 1	W. Grosvenor *Feb.* 2
George Pollard 7	Charles Kendall 1	J. Knight *May* 25
Michael Jackson 24	Jerem. Bigg *Mar.* 15	M. Richards *Aug.* 13
John Burrows 24	John Turner 15	George Bayne *Oct.* 3
John Kent 31	Rt Shipman *Ap.* 27	1771.
William Cunning-	Jn. Stoddart *July* 30	C L. Carne *Jan.* 10
ham *June* 5	John Piddle *Oct.* 2	George Philips 10
Stephen Stephens 20	J. Shortland *Dec.* 12	Oliver Delancy 18
Richard Smith 25	1764.	Green Despard 19
Chr. Roberts *July* 5	Wm. Stewart *Feb.* 7	Pat. Sinclair. 29
Andrew Nixon 7	Stephen Parker 13	Tho. Scott *Feb.* 6
William Abbs 7	Rob. Cowan *Ap.* 29	H. Crawford *Mar.* 1
John Halfum 7	W.P.Burnaby *May* 2	T. Newton *May* 12
John Scott 9	1765.	Lewis Fabian *July* 17
John Graves 13	Al. Brown (2) *Apr.* 1	John Forbes 19
Timothy Kelly 17	Wm Crosby *June* 20	A. Saunders *Aug.* 20
J. C. Plowden 19	Robert Taynton 20	CapelBaynes *Sept.* 28
Ellis Troughton 25	Hon. P. Stopford 20	Wm. Bristow *Oct.* 2
Alex. Kirkwood 26	Charles Colvill 20	J. Robert Mosse 4
John Moore 26	H. Thomas *July* 13	Jos. Haynes 8
Wm. Cayley 26	T. Cunningham 13	1772.
W. A. Brandreth 26	ArthurClark *Nov.* 21	John Peyton *Feb.* 10
Wm. Stedman 30	1766.	Whitlock Nichol 12
John Dilkes 31	J. E. Sewell *Feb.* 24	FrancisPender *June* 7
WmBudworth *Aug* 9	Tho. Wetenhall 28	R. Calcott *July* 23
Stephen Sandys 21	John Trigg *May* 28	J.

J. McDougall July 30	Rd. Graves Dec. 24	rett rr
John Polkinghorne	Guftavus Logie 30	Ld Cranftoun 19
Aug. 1	John Prime Iron	Richard Hawford 26
Job Hanmer Dec. 8	Rochfort 30	Wm Waddell 11
1773.	1776.	William Scott (2) 12
Ch. Sandys Jan. 7	Geo. Oakes Jan. 6	Hen. D'Efterre Darby
Goodwin Colquitt 9	Paget Bayly 21	13
John Hutt April 10	John Rickman Feb. 8	Ralph Milbanke 14
N Charrington June 6	Samuel Abfon 22	Wm. Newton. 15
E. Collingwood 25	Edward Bowater 26	Ja. Dundas 15
Thomas Byard 25	W. Charfley Mar. 10	Donald Sutherland 16
John Douglas(2) 25	Rd. Boger (2) 23	William Nowell 19
Gabriel Bray 25	Charles Loggie 29	Wm. Tahourdin 20
David Ramfay 25	John Cook Ap. 20	Hon. M. DeCourcy 20
George Dunn 25	H. Reynolds May 7	John Sam. Silly 22
A. Stanhope July 21	David Knox 10	John Auchinlick 26
Rob. Wynch 30	Hon. C. Carpenter 10	John Gold 26
Wm Albany Otway,	Dunbar Maclellan 11	John Wilby 26
Aug. 25	George Scott 12	Richard Grindall 29
Ric. Bridges Sept. 11	W. H. Kelley 16	James Lys 30
Walt. Griffith Nov. 1	Hen. Ch. Bridges 23	John Luck 31
V. C. Berkeley Dec. 5	William Edge 26	S. Tatham Dec. 6
1774.	Thomas Macnamara	George Tripp 6
Cha. Cobb, Feb. 3	Ruffell June 2	J. Maitland 9
Walter Harris, 23	Fr. Th. Drake 6	John Stone 12
John Winter Ap. 19	Robert Barton 6	Walter Jewell 14
G. Turnbull, May 13	George Burdon 7	Robert Leaver 16
Geo. Countefs July 8	Robert Sutton 7	Thomas Walbeoff 17
B. Prideaux Aug. 3	Thomas Butler 12	Thomas Forwood 20
W. Lechmere Dec. 20	John Starke 22	Wm Springthorpe 20
1775.	John Langhorne 25	Martin Digby 23
G. Ball, Jan. 4	E. J. Moriarty 29	1777.
W. Fulk Greville 11	Jofiah Clofton July 3	Th. Walton Jan. 9
J. Dela Touche May 6	New Hill Eaftwood 5	John Thompfon 9
J. Sum. Browne 10	Sylverius Moriarty 6	Tho. Parr 20
C. Collingwood Ja 17	James Cornwallis 9	William Titcher 21
Charles Egan 23	James Cotes 10	Robert Devereux
Gerald Gibbons 26	John Elphinfton 11	Fancourt 29
James Drew July 29	John Phelips 13	Henry Blaxfton 29
Jn Davall Burr Aug. 10	Geo. Lumfdain 11	Tho. Hurd 30
Ifaac Smith 19	Ch. Lyndon Aug. 1	C. W. Paterfon Feb. 3
Hon. M. Fortefcue	Samuel Thompfon 2	Robert Parker 3
Sept. 3	Alexander Allen 11	Thomas Lee 7
Alex. Chriftie Oct. 17	Jas Sawmarez Sept. 7	M. Hollinberry 19
G. Saunders Nov. 29	Mark Robinfon Oct. 5	John Ofborn 22
George Atkins 29	Cheney Hugh Gar-	Milham Ponfonby 25

[158]

R. C. Reynolds *Feb* 26	Tho. Parke *July* 4	J. Stevenson *Sept.* 23
William Eslington 28	Cha. Bartholomew 4	Jn. P. Robinson 23
Sir J. Barclay, Bt. 30	Humphry West 10	Jacob Adams 26
G. Edwards *Mar.* 1	George Brisac 10	Edward Fudger 27
Benjamin Archer 15	James Lecky 14	Wm. Meares *Oct.* 1
Morgan Laugharne 17	Warwick Oben 14	John Steph. Hall 2
Robert Chafe 19	Edward Roe 14	George Rice 2
Tho. Hardy 20	Alexander Hood 18	Philip Mansfield 8
David Mackay 21	Edw. Pakenham 18	Henry Parke 8
Maurice Delgarno 24	Alex. Frafer 18	T. Manley Hulke 9
John Hinckley 28	Thomas Lewis 18	Anthony Donadieu 9
And. Lockart *Ap.* 7	James Alms 26	W. Barker Peppen 10
Goodwin Keats 7	William Luke *Aug.* 1	John O'Bryen 13
Ch. Seymour Lynn 11	George Blagdon	And. Mitchell 11
David Allen 18	Westcott 6	Ro. Parry Young 18
Charles Bawden 24	William Alfray 20	John Rawlings 22
Samuel Edwards 29	Isaac Schomberg 21	John Witherston 24
Henry Thorp *May* 3	Thomas Pewtrifs 23	Edmund Nagle 25
Samuel Symes 3	J. Aylmer 25	Peter Rivett 26
Step. Peter Mouat 6	John Dewson 28	Michael Lane 27
John Deeble 7	Hon. Patrick Napier	Henry Deacon 28
J. G. Manley 7	*Sept.* 5	Thomas Wolley 31
Th. Revell Shivers 9	George Mackenzie	Rob. Browne, *Nov.* 1
Adrian Renou 9	(2d) 5	G. A. M'Cleverty 5
George Gregory 10	Robert Hibbs 5	John Cannon 5
John Hardy 10	Charles Henry Lane 6	Scory Barker 6
Bowles Mitchell 18	Manley Dixon 7	Charles Hughes 7
Lauchlan Hunter 21	John Gardiner 8	Charles Boyles 10
Thomas Floyd 21	Joseph Price 11	T. Sal. Richards 12
Safry Hills 30	John Melcombe 15	George Maxwell 19
Francis Fayerman 30	Edward Marsh 15	John Monkton 19
W. B. Rush 30	George Burlton 15	Griffith Jones 20
Joseph Lind 31	W. Samwell 19	Rich. Bruere 23
P. D'Auvergne *June* 2	T. Hooper 19	H. Tonken 24
Andrew Congulon 4	John Drew 19	Henry Gunter 25
Rd Rudsdell 6	George Morris 19	Thomas Spry *Dec* 1
Samuel Blow 20	Wm. Cockburne 19	John Salisbury 3
John Langley 20	J. Keith Shepherd 19	Norris Thompson 5
Jonathan Faulknor 24	Nathan Brunton 19	J. E. F. Wright 6
Joseph Eastwood 26	Archibald Groat 19	Edward Webb 6
William Burchell 28	Ker. Thompson 19	Hon. W. Carnegie 7
Rich. Wimbleton 28	Tho. Arch. Orrok 19	Richard Tilledge 8
Alex. Douglas 28	Thomas Peyton 19	Charles Lane 8
Thom. Tireman 28	Fra. Collingwood 20	Henry Festing 8
W. Newton (2) *July* 3	R. Taylor Appleby 20	Walter Anderson 9

J. Worlock *Dec.* 13	G. Aug. Atkinſon	Edw. Crawley *May* 7
John Trokes 15	James Ward 5	Robert Harriſon 9
John Ferrier 16	Joſeph. Turner 5	George Hart 9
Francis Pickmore 18	Hugh Fraſer 10	Winter Cuming 10
John Lawford 23	Ralph Milbanke(2d)	Samuel Ball 13
Peter Hill 27	11	Peter Kelley 13
William Domett 27	William Miller 18	Henry Pullen 13
Wm Granvill Lobb 27	Charles Burt 18	C. Papps Price 13
1778.	Wm Robert Davis 18	John Watherſton 13
S. Horſenail *Jan.* 1	Carew Reynell 18	Richard Thomas 13
George Irwin 1	Francis Phipps 18	Joſeph Bird 13
Ambroſe Crofton 1	Robert Nicholl 19	Paul Parry 13
Comer Brand 3	David Seton *April* 1	James Bengaugh 13
Robert Noble 6	Henry Spencer 6	Francis Randall 16
W. Hopſon Player 7	Edw. Shepherd 7	C. Spencer Parry 16
Ambroſe Warham 9	William Skipfey 7	Geo. Balderſton 16
J. Shapcote 12	Robert Drane 8	H. Edmonſton 16
John Clark 15	A. Schuyler 10	James Malcolm 16
Robert Love 20	Henry Stevenſon 10	Hon. Al. Cochrane 19
Chriſt. Halliday 23	Peircy Brett 10	John Sutton 21
Tho. Dickenſon 25	John Spriggs 10	Thomas Hoar 21
Martin Lindſay 25	Edward O'Bryen 11	Matthew Davis 22
Michael Stanhope 25	George Pattiſon 11	Edward Pringle 22
James Linde 25	Gerrard D'Arcy 11	Francis Biſhop 25
Will. Ruſſel 27	John Nunn 14	Walter Hughes 25
Tho. Woodyear 30	Joſ. Henry Laſh 17	Thomas Foley 25
John Larkhan *Feb.* 4	G. H. Stevens 17	T. Butler (2d) 26
Tho. Willis, 11	T. Philip Durell 17	Rich. Incledon 26
J. Child Purvis 11	Wilfred Colling-	William Dalby 26
Lewis Vickers 14	wood 18	Ed. Tyrrel Smith 27
Thomas Wood 14	J. A. Atkinſon 18	John Lowe 28
W. Alnwick 17	George Loſack 18	William Clark 28
J. Biſlett 17	David Miller 20	Robert Fitzhugh
Leonard Moſey 17	Tho. Stephenſon 21	, Haſſard 30
Michael Ogilvie 18	Chriſt. Kele 22	Tobias Love 30
Wm. Robinſon 18	George Palmer 23	John Willes 30
Hon. Ja. C. Pitt 18	Hen. Lidgbird Ball 23	Ed. Haddock *June* 4
John Hance 20	Alex. Curling 29	Richard Gomm 6
James Kirkland 23	F Edilbury Davies 29	Hugh Congalton 6
Jonathan Upton 23	Benjamin Hulke 29	J. F. Fortescue 11
Alex. Day. Brough-	Tho. Hamilton 29	Wm. Wolſeley 11
ton 24	Daniel Folliott 30	Roger Trounce 16
Robert Williams 25	Alexander Scott 30	Francis Loveday 16
Callis Hawford 28	Samuel Johnſon 30	Rob. Twycroſs 26
Rich. Rawe, *Mar.* 5	Charles Baker *May* 5	Chriſt. Hudſon *July* 1
Alexander Roſs 5	Terence M'Donald 6	Thomas Floyd (2d) 2

Tho. Taylor *July* 9	John Cadman *Oct.* 9	Rich. Lucas *Nov.* 19
William Wall (1) 9	John Gwatkin 9	Edw. Woodnott 22
O. Roberts 12	Wm Dan. Wandby 9	James Hill *Nov.* 23
Robert Willson 17	Rob. Caufzar 11	Robert Watson 24
Richard Oakley 20	Obadiah Newell 16	John Dolling 24
Rowley Bulteel 22	Wm. Smith (3d) 16	James King (2) 24
Wm. Crofbe, jun. 23	Charles Dixon 16	John Wichey 25
James May 23	Thomas Sowerby 18	David Crawford 25
James Preston 24	James Wood 18	C. J. M. Mansfield 25
John Deacon 24	Josiah Rogers 19	Philip King 26
Samuel Cox 25	Will. Charleton 19	Charles Elder 26
PeterDeppyAbbot 25	Ch. Fr. Hampton 21	Miles Lowley 27
James Jack 25	Richard Willis 23	Humphry Stokes 27
Joseph Ellison 30	D. G. Watson 23	John Covey 27
John Tayleure 30	Richard Fisher 24	W. O'Bryen Drury 28
Will. Furnivall 31	T. W. Fitzherbert 24	Richard Leggatt 30
C. F. Kellaway *Aug.* 5	Will. Simpson 24	Dan. Shiels 30
S. Michell 5	Edw. Yelland 27	Rob. Basden *Dec.* 3
John West 5	J. Dickons Inglis 27	John Davids 7
John Sam. Smith 7	James Pasmore 28	Charles Vaughan 7
Alex. John Ball 7	William Fry 28	Andrew Waid 7
Richard Hill 13	Alex. Auld 28	Tho. Crawley 7
Duncan Campbell 13	James Hewett 29	Andrew Wemyss 8
Isaac Coffin 18	John Hay 31	O. Edwards 8
Wm Carthew 18	n M'Killop *Nov.* 4	Rich. Raggett 15
Grof. Winkworth 21	J. L. Walker 4	Henry Gideon 21
Daniel Dobrée 23	S. Mackenzie 5	Tho. Edward 24
J. Hawkins *Sept.* 4	Wm. Fox (2d) 6	John Mackenzie 24
Rd. Littlewort 9	Sa. W. Elphinston 6	William Marsh 26
Solomon Ferris 9	Edw. Gl. Osborne 6	Rich. Rutherfurd 31
David Moyes 10	John Parrey 6	George Murray 31
Joseph Jordan 16	Thomas Hand 6	Thomas Dalby 31
David Stow 16	Robert Barlow 6	Charles Craven 31
Ponsonby Cox 17	George Keppel 6	1779.
John Meares 18	William Read 6	W. Pemberton *Jan.* 9
Theo. Jones 18	Wm. Chantrell 7	Monta. Blackwell 10
Robert Mostyn 23	Thomas Robinson 7	Wm. Roberts 11
R. H. Hichens 28	H. Holland Searle 9	Wm. Wall (2) 16
Wm Hen. Douglas 28	Wm. Browell 10	Tho. Russell 16
J. Douglas (2d) *Oct.* 1	Sam. Featherstone 10	Rich. Nash 16
Edward Longcroft 2	Wm. Bell 12	Francis Waters 20
Rowland Philipps 2	Jos. Brown Bunce 12	Tho. Jeynens 21
Cha. Eastley 5	Joshua Mulock 14	John Cooke (2) 21
William Dalton 5	Andrew Christie 17	Pulling Brown 23
Wm. C. Hughes 5	Wm Williams (2) 17	Will. Champion 23
John Pietie 9	James Palmer 18	Will. Leggatt 23
Edward Dalton 9	James Hardy 19	Henry Marsh *Feb.* 1

Henry Carew Feb.	1	Chap. Jacobs Apr.	6	Ant. Jepfon July	30
Hugh Sandry	1	Rich. d Willand	6	Clement Johnfon	30
R. Rofe Bradley	9	W. Cerocold	11	Ia. Higginfon Aug.	5
John Atkinfon	10	G. Hire	12	Murd. Mackenzie	5
Wil. M'Guire	10	James Black	12	Philip Jones	6
Will. Harvey	13	Jeremiah Beale	15	Hugh Norris	6
Jof. Royal Loring	17	John M'Laurin	16	Edw. Williams	9
James Colnett	22	Jof. Murray	26	Azariah Uzu'd	13
Tho. Larcom	25	John Brown (3)	26	Richard Coller	17
Eliab Harvey	26	George Hill	28	Charles Vinicombe	
John Prowfe Mar.	1	M. Lucul. Ryall	30	Penrofe	17
W. Delap	3	Francis Cole	30	John Irwin	20
Philip Hancorne	3	E. E. Watmough		B. Swann	20
A. Brown	5	May	3	Savage Gardener	20
Rd. Shuckburgh	8	Barth. James	6	Purfer Dowers	21
George Dundas	8	Davidge Gould	7	Robert Varden	21
Jofeph Sall	13	Thomas Wilfon	10	Will. Lanyon	23
John Webber	15	John Ellis	14	Matt. Gerrard	26
George Doyel	15	John Symon	17	Vm Wilfon	27
Wm. Ormond	15	Tho. Linthorne	19	David Hotchkis	27
John Reid	22	Rich. Dorrill	20	Richard Piercy	28
Lewis Lane	23	James Kellie	27	Francis Rofs	28
Gain Davifon	30	Martin Hinton	28	George Keith	30
Richard Morrice	31	John Howe	29	a. Golench Sept.	3
James Deacon	31	Wm Tucker June		ohn Whitly	3
Cha. Mill	31	John Smith	5	James Rogers	5
John Blucett April	1	Tho. Surridge	6	Wm. Turner	6
Ifrael Pillew	1	John Stevens	10	Tho. Prefland	6
John Lefly	1	John Hewett	11	Richard Retaiick	6
Sam. Mackenzie	1	Rich. Purvis	12	Hugh Cuppage	6
J DouglasBrifbane	1	Rich. Roufe	12	Benjamin Butler	11
Jn. Jof. Faunton	1	John Mortimer	12	Thomas Beves	13
Tho. Tonkin	2	W. J. Stephens	12	Ralph Grey	16
John Crimes	2	Rich. Sainthill	16	William Newfon	16
Matthew Brown	3	Wm. Simpfon	17	Fran. Mefiervy	16
John Bover	3	Sam. Cheetham	19	John Moneur	20
John Lee	3	Wm Somerville	2	J. Tulloh	20
John Power	3	Rob. Beatfon	30	ohn Elliot	20
William Snow	5	Ja. Turner July	19	Edw. Herbert	21
Sir R. J. Strachan	5	Tho. Crawfurd	21	J. Harris Nicholas	23
Charles Tyler	5	John Wells	22	John Rule	25
James Brimer	5	Hen. M'Cullagh	22	James Smith Oct.	2
Robert Montagu	5	John Drummond	26	Abraham Bardon	2
George Long	5	Wm Hawford	26	ohn Trantum	7
Andrew Douglas	6	Thomas Miles	26	Ch. Dudley Pater	8
John Fife	6	James Seward	30	Herbert Browell	8

[162]

John Bonnar *Oct.* 8	Tho. Wells *Jan.* 14	Geo. Garner *Apr.* 10
Nathaniel Shields 8	G. W. Maxwell 14	James Horn 17
Joseph Clapp 8	R. R. Bowyer 17	Alex. M'Gregor 21
Noah Webb 8	T. R. Jackson 17	John Burley 21
Jonas Rose 9	Will. Cowan 17	John Douglas (3) 21
Stephen Rains 14	Rich. Nairne 26	Charles Lock 21
Richard Storey 15	Tho. Harrison 26	George Satey 21
Samuel Goodion 16	W. A. Brice *Feb.* 2	W. Williamson 24
Rich. Thoresby 16	Will. Page 3	John Luke 24
Thomas Wills 20	George Dancer 4	Shuldam Peard 26
Paul Minchin 20	John Wren 5	Joseph Crouch 26
Wm. Burgess 22	Hen. Hicks 5	Robert Larkan 28
George Dyer 25	Sam. Magoch 6	S. Wickham *May* 5
Will. Moore 28	And. Wood 11	Fred. Lapenotiere 6
Parker Jn. Harrison	Charles Wilson 15	J. J. Webber 6
Nov. 18	Charles Patton 17	Joseph Lawson 8
Thomas Ozard 18	LenoxThompson 19	Henry Nicholls 20
Robert Corner 20	John Norris 19	George Davey 25
Jn. Rd. Falener 20	Rich. Hoare 25	Thomas Ireland 25
Farq. Mackintosh 26	MarkWentworth 28	Henry Wray *June* 5
John Mitchell 26	F. R. Mowatt *Mar.* 1	Thomas Smith 5
Wm Wright 2	Steph. E'ery 2	David Conway 10
Ch. OliverWorth 30	James Bullock 3	John Baker 12
John Loring *Dec.* 3	Tho. Brown 17	Henry Inman 14
H.YoungDaracott 3	James Bignall 17	Caleb Hill 21
John Smith 4	Edward Clether 17	John M'Key *July* 1
Wm. Chappell 4	Alex. Douglas (2) 17	Edw. Sterling Dick-
Matthew Smith 4	Philip Helyman 17	son 9
Wm. Milner 7	Robert Hughes	Joseph Blake 9
Wm Cuming 7	17	Jermyn John Sy-
Tho.Williams (2) 8	John Marsh 17	monds 15
Charles Miller 17	G. Langley 18	Patrick Carnegy 17
John Fenton 17	WilsonRathborne 18	Edw. Seymour Bai-
James Somerville 23	Rich. Filkin 24	ley 17
John Fitzgerald 23	James Vaughan 25	RichardFaulknor 18
J.HallumMounier 23	John Draper 26	Val. Edwards 18
John Boyle 24	Adam Littlejohn 31	Daniel Burgess 21
William Ross 24	Sam. Vans *Apr.* 1	J. Pengelly *Aug.* 24
G. Moorhead 24	Bar. Mansfield 1	Edw. JekyllCanes 24
John Tindall 29	J. C. Rothery 4	William Stagg 24
1780.	Ralph Wilson 5	James Symons 26
Ed. Crouch *Jan.* 5	And. Mouncher 6	James Atkins 28
Wm. Ogilvy 8	Robert Stupart 8	L. Dundas Bruce 28
James Addison 14	George Scott 10	Lionel Hill *Sept.* 1
Tho. Richbell 14	G. F. Alms 10	John Spencer 5

Nat. Portlock	14	J Clarke Searle	9	Henry How	6
Edw. Marsh (2 d)	14	Clem. Richardson	28	Robert Baley	14
J. Nicholl Morris	14	William Taylor	28	G. Freder. Ryves	18
T. Tivitoe Bishop	14	Henry Roberts	28	J. Ides Short, jun	27
Wm. Dodderidge	19	James Trevenen	28	G. Vancouver	Dec. 9
Richard Brewer	26	Edward Riou	28	Henry Martin	11
Hen. Vaughan Oct.	3	J J, O'Brien Nov.	1	Robert Gill	15
Alex. Menzies	6	Alexander Mouat	1	Alexander Home	18
John Vowells	7	Robert Mackie	1	Richard Hergest	22
Henry Barwell	9	W. Smith Bradshaw	4	Aug. Markett	22

The Pay of the Officers of the Royal Navy in each Rate, FLAG OFFICERS, *and the* CAPTAINS *to Fl·gs per Day.*

Admiral and Commanders in Chief of the Fleet   £ 5 0 0
An Admiral   —   —   —   3 10 0
Vice Admiral   —   —   —   2 10 0
Rear Admiral   —   —   —   1 15 0
First Captain to the Commanders in Chief   —   1 15 0

OFFICERS.	First.	Second	Third	Fourth	Fifth	6th.
	l. s. d.	*l. s. d.*	*l. s. d.*	*l. s. d.*	*l. s. d.*	*l. s.*
Capt. per day	1 0 0	0 16 0	0 13 6	0 10 0	0 8 0	0 8
Lieut. per day	0 5 0	0 5 0	0 4 0	0 4 0	0 4 0	0 4
Mast. per mon.	9 2 0	8 8 0	7 6 0	6 12 0	6 2 8	5 0

2d Master & Pilots of yachts, each 3*l* 10s

List of the Officers belonging to the TOWER *of* LONDON.
Constable and Chief Gov. Lieut. Gen. Ch. E. Cornwallis, 1000l
Lieut. Gov. Lieut. Gen. Charles Vernon, 700l
Dep. Lieut. John Gore, Esq; 365l
Major, Lieut. Col. John Parr, 182l 10s
Chapl. Rev. T. Cowper, 121l 13s 4d. *Phyf.* Dr. Robert Petrie, 182l. 10s. *Gent. Porter,* S. Madan, 84l 6s 8d. *Gent. Goaler,* Mr. D. Kinghorne, 70l. *Surg.* Mr. Lewis Davis, 45l 12s 6d *Gov. of St. Catharine's, near the Tower,* Edw. Waller, Esq; 400l.

Civil Branch of the Office of Ordnance, Tower of London.

Master-General,	*Lieutenant-General,*
Right Hon. Geo. Viscount Townshend, 1500l	Rt Hon. Jeffery Lord Amherst, K.B. Sal. 1100l a year

Sur—

[164]

Surveyor-General,
✗Sir C. Frederick, K.B. F.R.S. Sal. 700l a year
Clerk of the Ordnance,
✗Sir Cha. Cocks, Bart. ſalary 500l a year, and 100l for Cheque on the Store-keeper.
Storekeeper. ✗H Strachey Eſq; 400l
Clerk of the Deliveries,
✗John Kenrick, Eſq;
Treaſurer and Paymaſter,
✗William Adam, Eſq; 500l
Secretary to the Maſter General,
✗John Courtney, Eſq; 220l
Under Sec. to Maſter General, James Johnſton, Eſq; 180l
Secretary to the Board,
John Boddington, Eſq; 200l
Extra. Clerk to Ditto,
Rob. Crew, 50l
Clerk under the Maſter General, Henry Symonds, 80l
Supernumerary Clerk to ditto,
David Jones, 50l
Clerks in Ord. under Lieut. Gen. Anthony Wheelock, 180l
Nicholas Witwer, 80l
Extra Cl. to dit. Fra. Davis, 50l
Clks in Ord. under the Surv. Gen. John Vidgen, 180l
J. Wooler, R. Forman,
T. W. Clarke, J. Okes, 80l
Extra Clerks under ditto,
John Davis, Steph. M'Lean,
Val. James Lloyd, 50l each.
Supernum. R. Forman, jun.
Joſ Wheeler, Sam. Eagles,
John Angel, 50l each
Clks in Ord. under Clk Ordnance, John Boddington, 210l
Edward Short, 180l
J. Humphrey, Joſ. Sparrow, Jn. Pariſh, Wm. Adams, Oliff Adams, S. Wakefield, 80l each.
Extra Clerks under ditto,
W. Nettleſhip, 60l L. Mumford,

G. Giles, P. Saunders, Rob. Maples, C. S. Smith, 50l each
Supernum G. Clay, J. Bainouin, Cha. Cordery, Rt. Gray, John Brookſbank, S. Rayner, 50l ea.
Clerks in Ord. under Store keep. Johnſon Robinſon, 180l
Wm Gregory, John Wilkinſon, Thomas Day, 80l a Year each
Extra Clerks under Store-keep.
Richard Dickinſon, R. Steel, Edward Miles, 50l each
Supern. John Thomas, Tho. Hoſkins Cutbuſh, 50l. each
Aſſiſtant, Wm. Bentley, 50l
Clerks in Ordinary under the Clerks of the Deliveries,
W. Weaver, 180l P. Veitch, 80l
Clerks Extraordinary under the Clerk of the Deliveries,
Walt. Yonge, J. Hardwick, Supernum. Joachim Dolge, Richard Welbank
Aſſiſtants, Edward Eaſtland, James Slater, Wm. Spencer
Sup. T. Cutbuch, J. Dolge, 50l
Clerks in Ord. under the Treaſ. Cuth. Fiſher, Eſq; Dep. Treaſ. 180l. F. Hanrott, Clark Durnford, 80l each
Extra. to Ditto,
Anthony Frith, James Wright, Wm. Payne, 50l each
Supernum. Tho. Haberfield, Wm. Mackie, Wm. Ruddick
Aſſiſtant, Edward Coleman
Cl. to Chief Eng. Wm Teſt, 70l
Proof-maſters,
T. Hartwell, R. Forman, 20l
Clerk of the Works,
Thomas Hartwell, 120l
Clk of the Cheque in the Tower, Clement Horton, 80l
Clerk in the Small Gun Office,
M. E. Wilks, 60l
Purv. for Land, E. Sutton 100l

[165]

Superintendant of Transports,
John Dickinson, Esq; 6s per D.
Purv. for Sea, R. Webb, 40l
Assistant Recorders,
Jn Boddington, Jn Humfrey, 20l
Council to the Ordnance,
Sir Richard Sutton, Bart. 300l
Architect,
Edw. Bol. Frederick, Esq; 120l
Armourer, Jn Cooper, 45l 12s 6d
Mast. Furbisher, (vacant) 80l
Furbishers at Windsor, W. Carpenter, John Miller, 20l each
Furbisher at Hampton Court, and at St. James's,
Joseph Deely, 60l
Messenger, Jn Dan. Lauzun, 80l
Tower Bar. Master, J. Jones, 40l
Storek. of Saltpetre, E. Short, 60l
Astronomical Observator, Rev. N. Maskelyne, DD FRS 100l
Modeller, Th. Butler, Esq; 100l
Assistant Modellers, W. Eaton, 73l. Cha. Gilbert, 54l 15s
OFFICERS at OUT-PORTS and GARRISONS.

PORTSMOUTH.
Store-keep. Richard Veal, 180l
Clerk of Survey, J. Blake, 73l
Ck of Cheq. F. Matthews, 54l 15s
Ext. Clerks, B. Bullock, F. Sadler, John Peck, 36l 10s
Barrack Contract. T. Matthews
Overseers of Works, Henry Gillett, 9 1l 5s G. Feldtner, 73l

WOOLWICH.
Store-k. John Cockburn, 160l
Ck of Surv. N. Campbell, 54l 15s
Ck of Cheque, W Sansom, 54l 15s
Clerk of the Foundery, James Delestang, 54l 15s
Extra. Cks, A. Genet, Miles Sansom, W. Chambers 36l 10s each
Clerk of the Works,
Tho. Powrey, Esq; 6s per Day
Overseer of the new Barracks,
W. Latimer, Esq; 10s per D.

Inspector of ditto,
John Bruyeres, Esq; 10s per D.
Inspect. of Royal Brass Foundry,
David Moreau, Esq; 10s per D.
Mess. T. Edwards, 5s per Diem.
GRAVESEND & TILBURY FORT,
John Harrison, 100l
Cl. Cheq. T. Masterson, 3s a day.
CHATHAM.
Store-keeper, John Parr, 140l
Clerk of the Survey, Wm Saltonstall, 54l 15s
Ck of Cheque, W. Akid, 54l 15s
Extra. Clerks. 36l 10s
Wm. Dav. Irwin, John Howe
Barrack Master, C. Vanderlaan, 6s per Day.

PLYMOUTH.
Store-keep. Wm Redston, 120l
Cl. of Survey, Rt Atkinson, 73l
Ck of Cheque, W. Smith, 54l 15s
Ex. Clerks, 36l 10s S. Forman, Tho. Parkins and J. Cleader

SHEERNESS.
Store-k. John Dixon, 100l
Cl. of Survey, W Sumpter 54l 15s
Ck of Cheque, A. Long, 54l 15s
Ext. Cl. John Hare, 36l 10s

UPNOR-CASTLE.
Store-k. Tho. Hodgson, 80l
Cl. of Cheq. J. Richards, 36l 10s

FEVERSHAM.
Store-keeper, Ed. Wilkes, 100l
Clerk, W. Sumpter, 54l 15s
Extra. R. Wilkes, 36l 10s
Master worker, Rd Hall, 90l

PURFLEET.
Store-keep. Wm. James, 7s a da.
Cl. of Surv. J. Clowdesly, 54l 15s
Cl. of Cheq. R. Coleman, 54l 15s
Extra. Cl's. Wm Bates, Geo Cowell, 36l 10s
Store-Keeper at Edinburgh, Benj. Bartlet, 9 1l 5s a year
Stirling, Rob. Alexander, 40l
Berwick, J. Barrow, 40l

Hull, Wm Sherman, 50l
Chester, W. Lawrence, 40l
Scarb. Cast. Rd. Sollitt, 5s 6d a day, and 20l a year ho. rent
Guernsey, C. Baldock, 40l
Jersey, T. Pipon, 100l
Pendennis, Rd. Pearce, 40l
Fort William, W. Cleaver, 40l
Carlisle, Geo. Blamire, 30l
Dover, Thomas Biggs, Storekeeper, 5s 6d a day
Overseer, Tho. Biggs, 5s perD.
Labourers at the Tower.
Thirteen, at 26l. each
STORE-KEEPERS Abroad.
Gibraltar, J.T. Savary, Esq; 10s
Cl. of Survey, J. Ward, 4s a day
Clerk of Cheque, J. Stones, 4s a day
Clerk of the Works, Sam. Cockcroft, 4s a day
Extra Clerk, Arthur Gilmour, John Bolton, 2s 6d a day each
Barrack Mast. J.T. Savary, 40l
Minorca, W. Alcock, 10s a day
Ditto *Bar. Master*, 120l a year
Cks of Survey, James Brinkhurst
Cheque, Jn Bullock, 4s a day
Works, John Tinling, 4s a day
Extra. W. Forbes, W. Littlefoot
Surgeon, Alex. Small, 6s a day
Jamaica, Rob. Benton, 10s
Annapolis, Tho. Williams, 5s
Placentia, And. Lemercier, 6s
St. John's, Newfoundland, Edward White, 6s a day
Antigua, Peter Alsop, 7s 6d a day
Pensacola, John Brown, Barrack-master, 5s a day

Milit. Branch of the Ordnance.
Chief Engineer & Colonel,

803l

Dir. & Lieut. Colonels, Ja. Bramham, William Green, 365 l
Sub Dir. & Majors at 15s a day
Matthew Dixon, John Archer,

H. Gordon, John Brewse,
Engineers in Ord. & Captains at 10s a day, Lt. Cols. H. Debbieg, R. Dawson, Col. Wm Roy, J. Phipps, Wm. Spry, Tho. Bassett, Rob. Morse, A. D'Aubant, Fre. G. Mulcaster, E. Durnford, Alexander Mercer, And. Fraser

Engineers extra. & Captains & Lieutenants at 6s a day.
J. Marr, G. Townshend, A. Robertson, R. Pringle, J. Moncrief, J. Camble, T. Hartcup, Goth. Mann, William Twiss, J. Wade, John Evelegh, Mat. Pitts

Sub-engineers, and Lieuts. at 4s 8d a day.
Wm Parker, Tho. Hyde Page, H. Rudyard, W. Campbell Skinner, A. Durnford, A. Sutherland, Desm. Durnford, B. Fisher, C. Shipley, H. Haldane, Th. Nepean, J. Caddy, W. Booth, W. Fyers

Practitioner Engineers & Ensigns, at 3s 8d a day.
J. Chilcot, T. Skinner, J. R. Douglas, John James Roberton, Ja. Stratton, W. Johnston, W. Kesteman, J. Johnson, Cha. Holloway, T. Wheldale, J. Humfrey, J. Fiddes, R. Hockings, R. Beatson, R. D'Arcy, B. Slack, J. Lees, G. Bridges, L. Hay, W. Birch, J. Glenie, W. Malton, G. Phipps, T. Smart

Royal Military Academy at Woolwich.
Governor, G. Visc. Townshend Lieut.

*Lieut.Gov.*Col. Bramham, 25ol
Infpector, Capt. G. Smith, 23ol
Profeffor of Fortifica. and Artill.
J. Landmann, F.R.S. 20ol
Profeffor of the Mathematics,
Charles Hutton, LL.D.F.R.S. 20ol
Claffic, Arithmetic and Writing Maft. Rev. W Green, M.A. 15ol
Drawing Mafters, Paul Sandby, 15ol Gamaliel Maffiot, 10ol
French Maft. F. Huguenine, 10ol
Fencing Maft. Mr Mollard, 10ol
Dancing Mafter, Geo. Ware
Clerk to the Academy, Capt. Chapman, 45l 12s 6d
Modellers, Tho. Powrie, 2s 6d *per day*
Geo. Short, 4s *ditto*

Laboratory at Woolwich.
Comptroller,
× Sir C. Frederick, K.B. 26ol.
Chief Fire Mafter,
Capt. Bloomfield, 15ol
Fire-Mafter's Mate,
Capt. Sam. Tovey, 8ol
Clerk, George Ayres, 52l
Artificers, William Piper
William Pitcher, 54l 15s
Thomas Walton, Wm Turnbull, 45l 12s 6d
Labourers, Rob. Polton, Matth. Peddler, 27l 7s 6d
Looking after the Clock,
Ainsworth Thwaites, 6l 6s
Mafter of the Montague,
William Waterer, 27ol
Mafter of the Marlborough,
Abraham Faffet, 1ool
Shallop, (*vacant.*)
Ma. Found. J. and P. Verbrugen
Repairing the Houfhold Waggons
James Dettilin, 8ol

Superintendant of the Foundery, 50ol
J. Bullock, *Bookbind.* 3s 6d a day
Fra. Hanrot, *coach-hire,* 4ol
J. Wright, *Officer - keeper to the Treafurer,* 26l
Geo. Gilpin, *Lab. to the Obfervatory at Greenwich,* 26l
Eleanor Johnfon, *Houfe-k. to the Office in the Tower,* 50l
Jef. & Eliz. Okes, *Houfe-k. to the Office in St. Margaret's-ftreet, Weftminfter,* 50l

Drawing Room in the Tower.
Mathemat. Maft. R. Burrows, 10ol *per ann.*
Chief Draftm. G. Haines, 10ol
Affift. Draft. S. Fane, 5s *per day*
Draw. Maft. H. Gilder, 5s *per d.*
Under ditto, T. Chamberlaine, W. Teft, J. Potter, F. Gould, 5s *per day*
T. Sandby, J. Chamberlain, J. Evans, J. Read, T. Cubit, Geo. Beck, 3s 6d *per day*
W. Wooley, T. Peckham, N. Coltman, R. Dickinfon, 3s *per day*
Hen. Caftleman, J. Wilfon, J. Gould, H. Johnfton, 2s 6d *per day*
S. Penfon, W. Paine, F. Lauzun, F. Groves, Ifaac Swan, G. Tinling, A. Spicer, J. Dixon, C. Edridge, J. Byres, E. White, W. Allen, C. Meachum, W. Bartlett, W. Hulme, H. Poole, C. Tabor, V. Munbee, T. Franklin, 2s. *per day*

Commissioners and Officers of the Royal Hospital at Chelsea.

Commissioners.
THE President of the Council
First Lord of the Treasury
Two Secretaries of State
Paymaster-Gen. of Land Forces
Secretary at War
Two Comptrollers of Army Accounts
The Gov. and Lieut. Governor

Military Officers.
✕ Gen. Sir Geo. Howard, K.B. *Gov.* 500l
Lt. Gen. B. Hale, *Lt.-gov.* 400l
Capt. William Bulkeley, *maj.* 150l
Lewis Grant, *adj.* 100l
Rev. Wm Jennings, Rev. John Jago, *chaplains*, 100l
Dr. Mounsey, F.R.S. *phys.* 100l
Rob. Adair, Esq; *surgeon*, 100l
Surgeon's-mates,
Alexander Reid, Wm. North
Apoth. Rich. Rob. Graham, Esq;
Truss-maker, Alexander Reid
Treas. Paym. Gen. of the Land Forces for the Time being.
Deputy, Hon. Frederick Vane
Clerk, Charles Harris
Sec. and Reg. Jn. Powell, Esq;
Clerks, John Hussey, Jos. Lynn
Agent and paymaster to the out Pensioners, Wm. Drummell, Esq;

Clerks, S. Hawksworth, Thomas Hammond
Cha. Cooper, Esq; *comptroller*
Percival Beaumont, Esq; *steward*
Fr. Dav. Pittonet, *register*
Peter Gauthey, *wardrobe keeper*
Emanuel Burnet, *master cook*
Geo. Horsington, *second cook*
Hugh Faulconer, James Dove John Morris, *under cooks*
Benj. Jones, *master butler*
James Capp, *second butler*
Mr. Campion, *master baker*
Rt. Adam, F.R.S. *clerk of wks*
Edw. Anderson, *master mason*
John Davis, *master smith*
Mr. Woodward, *painter*
Mr. Devall, *plumber*
John Davis, *engine-keeper*
Mr. Fitter, *clock-keeper*
Thomas Broadhurst, *gardener*
Fra. Gander, *master lamp lighter*
Geo Church, *comptr. of coal yard*
Mrs. Susanna Powell, *matron*
George Church, *porter*
John Lucas, *master barber*
James Hopson, *scullery man*
Henry Medley, *sexton*
Rich. Dobbinson, *ush. of the ball*
W. Brett, *canal keep. & turnco.*
R. Barnes, *Cellarman*
John Higgins and And. Grant, *Sweepers*

CINQUE PORTS.
Lord Warden, and Constable of Dover Castle,
✕Lord North, K.G.
Lieutenant, Tho. Best, Esq;
Dep. Lieut. Thomas Bateman Lane, Esq;

Captain of Deal Castle,
Marquis of Carmarthen
Captain of Walmer Castle,
William Scot, Esq;

Captain of Sandgate Castle,
✕William Evelyn, Esq;
Captain of Arckliffe Fort,
James Hammond, Esq;
Capt. Moats Bulwark,
John Latham, Esq;
Register of Dover Castle,
Mr. Tho. Bateman Lane
Chaplain, Rev. Dr. Hollingberry
Sec. James Wright, Esq;

General

General and Staff-Officers in Great-Britain.

Adjutant-General,
Lt. Gen. Wm. Amherst.
Dep Adjutant-General,
Lt. Col. Adam Williamson.
Quarter-Master General,
Maj. Gen. George Morrison.
Dep. Quarter-Master General,
Col. Roy
Pay-Master General,
×Rt. Hon. Richard Rigby
Commiss. General of Musters,
Thomas Bowlby, Esq;
Deputy Commissary-General,
Welbore Ellis Agar, Esq;
Six Deputy Commissaries.
Clerk, John A. F. Hesse
Judge Advocate General,
×Sir Charles Gould, Knt.
Deputy Judge Adv. General,

Physician General,
Sir Edward Wilmot, Bart.
Surg. Gen. D. Middleton, Esq;

Apothecary Gen. Geo. Garnier
DrumMaj Gen. C. Stuart, Esq;
NORTH BRITAIN,
Commander in Chief, Lt. Gen.
Alexander Mackay
Adjut. Gen. × Major General
Skene
Dept. Adj. Gen. Lieut. Col.
John Gunning
Barrack-Master Gen. × Sir
Hector Monro, K. B.
Judge Adv. Sir J. Dunbar, Bt.
BaggageMaster, Maj. G. Skene
Comptrollers of Army Accounts,
Henry Bunbury, and Christ.
D'Oyley, Esqrs. 750l. each
Secretary, Tho. Fauquier, 300l
Clerks, Robert Quarme, David Crowe, John Paradise,
Sam. Hays, William White
Office Keeper, Charles Hoare
Messenger, Richard Harris
NecessaryWom. Mary Browne.

List of AGENTS; *and their Habitations.*
Adair and Bullock, *Whitehall*
Armstrong, Capt. *Percy-street*
Bellingham, Allan, *Dublin*
Bishopp and Brummell, *Vine-str. Piccadilly*
Brown, Rob. *Abingdon-build.*
Cox and Mair, *Craig's-court*
Cuthbertson, Bennet, *Dublin*
Fitter, Ja. *Great Pulteney-str.*
Hanfard, H. J. *Gerrard-st. Soho*
Lamb, John, *Golden-square*
Meyricks, *Parliament-street*
Montgomery, Sir Wm. *Dublin*
Nixon, John, *Dublin*
Powell and Cooke, *facing the Admiralty*

Richardson, John, *Crown-court, Westminster*
Russell, Ja. *Craven-str. Strand*
Roberts and Sons, *Castle-street, Leicester-fields*
Ross and Gray, *Conduit-street*
Waring, Maj. Holt, *Dublin*
Wilkinson, Montagu, *Conduit-street*
Williams, Capt. Griffith, *Bartlett's Buildings*
Willis, Thomas, *Wardour-str.*
Wood, Adam, *Great Titchfield-street, Cavendish-square*
Wybrants, Stephen, *Dublin*

Daily

[170]

Daily Pay of each Rank in his Majesty's Land Forces on the *British* Establishment.

Rank	Royal Reg. of Horse-Guards F. Pay	Subsist.	Dragoons F. Pay	Subsist.	Foot-Guards F. Pay	Subsist.	Foot F. Pay	Subsist.
Colonel and Captain	2 1	1 11	1 15	1 6 6	1 19	1 10	1 4	18
Lieutenant Colonel and Captain	1 9 6	1 2 6	1 4 6	18 6	1 8	1 1	17	13 6
Major and Captain	1 7	1 1 6	1 1	15 6	1 4	18	15	11 6
Captain	1 6	16	6	11 6	16	12 6	10	7 6
Captain Lieutenant or Lieutenant	15	11 6		7	6		4 8	3 6
Cornet h.-gds & dr. Enf. f.-g. Enf. or 2d Lt. f	14 8	11	8	6	5 10	4 5	3 8	3
Chaplain	6 8	5	6 6	5	6 8	3	6 8	3
Adjutant (Solicitor in foot-guards the same)	5	4 6	5	4	4	3	4	3
Quarter-Master	8	6 6	5 6	4 4	4	3	4	3
Surgeon	6	4 6	6	4	4	3	4	3
Surgeon's-Mate					3	3	3	3
Drum-Major					1	1	1	1
Deputy Marshal					1 10	1	1 6	1
Serjeant	3	2 6	2 9	2 3	1 2	1	1	8
Corporal (Kettle-drum in horse-gds the same)	3	2 6	2 3	1 9	2	1	1	8
Drummer	2 8	2	2 3	1 9				
Trumpeter	2 6	2				10	8	6
Private Man	2 6	2	1 9	1 5	1 7¼	6¾	1 6	6
Allowance on the Establishment to — Colonel	4	4	2 4	2 4	1 1½	1 ½	1	1
Ditto for Hautbois per troop or Captain company	4 2	2	2 4	2	6¼	6¾	1 6	
Agent			1 2	1 2	6¼	6¼		

A LIST of the ARMY.

The GENERAL and FIELD OFFICERS of his Majesty's Forces, with the Regiments they severally belong to.

N. B. f g stands for Foot Guards; h g for Horse Guards; g g for Grenadier Guards; d g for Dragoon Guards; f for Foot, &c. § Upon Half-pay.

GENERALS. 1765.

J A. Oglethorpe, § *Feb.* 22
1770.
Lord J. Murray, 42 f 30
Earl of Loudoun, 3 f g 30
×Earl Panmure, 2 d 30

1772.
Cuthbert-Ellison,
Viscount Falmouth *May* 25
Earl of Sandwich 25
×Rt H. Hen. Seymour Conway,
  Royal Reg. Horse Guards 25
Ja. Abercromby, 44 f 25
×Lord Rob. Manners, 3 d g 25
Earl Waldegrave, 2 f g 25
His R. H. the Duke of Gloucester, 1 f g 25

1777.
×Sir G. Howard, K.B. 1 dg. Gov.
  of Chelsea Hospital *Aug.* 29
Rt H. Sir J. Yorke, K.B. 5 d 29
×Lord Rob. Bertie, 2 h g 29
×Philip Honywood, 4 h 29

1778.
Duke of Argyll, 1 f *Mar.* 24
Hon. John Fitzwilliam, 2 h 24
Wm. A'Court Ashe, 11 f 24
Lord Amherst, 3, and 60 f 24
× Sir J. Griffin Griffin, 1
  t h g g 14

Studholm Hodgson, 4 f *Ap.* 14
George Aug. Elliott, 15 d 14

LIEUTENANT GENERALS.

1770.
×Hon. Rob. Monkton, 17 f.
  Governor of Portsmouth, 30
Edward Sandford, 10 f 30
Theodore Dury, Marines 30
×John Lambton, 68 f 30
John Parslow, 30 f 30
Thomas Gage, 22 f 30
Visc. Townshend, 2 d g 30
Lord Fred. Cavendish, 34 f 30
Duke of Richmond 30
Earl of Pembroke, 1 d 30
John Severn, 8 d 30
Sir John Sebright, 18 f 30
Hon. George Cary, 43 f 30

1772.
Hon. J. Murray, 13 f *May* 25
Geo. Williamson, Artillery 25
Cyrus Trapaud, 52 f 25
Sir Wm. Boothby, Bar:. 6 f 25
×Hon. W. Keppel, 12 d 25
Sir Rich. Peirson, 1; d 25
Benj. Carpenter, 4 d 25
Bigoe Armstrong, 8 25
Earl of Shelburne 25
Wm. Haviland, 4. 25

✕ Rt Hon. Sir Jn Irwin, K. B. Commander in Chief in Ireland, 3 h g May 25
C. Vernon, Lt of the Tower 25
David Græme, 19 f 25

1777.
Rob. Melvill, W. Ind. *Aug.* 29
M. Frederick, 54 f 29
John Thomas, Lieut. Gov. of Fort St. Philip 29
Horn Elphinston, 53 f 29
Wm. Evelyn, 29 f 29
James Johnston, 6 d 29
James Johnston, 11 d 29
Hon. Philip Sherrard, 69 f 29
Hon. G. L. Parker, 20 f 29
Earl of Drogheda, 18 d 29
Francis Grant, 63 f 29
Hon. Alex. Mackay, 21 f 29
Wm Augustus Pitt, 10 d 29
✕ Lord Adam Gordon, 26 f 29
Fred. Haldimand, 60 f Governor of Quebec 29
Wm Alex. Sorel, 48 f 29
Hon. Alex. Maitland, 49 f 29
Rt. Hon. Jn Pomeroy, 64 f 29
Earl of Eglington, 51 f 29
✕ Simon Fraser, 71 f 29
Hunt Walsh, 56 f 29
George Preston, 17 d 29
Sir Guy Carleton, K. B. 47 f 29
Sir C. Thompson, Bart. K. B. 29
Robert Clerk 29
Sir William Draper, K. B. Lt. Gov. of Minorca 29
R. Cunninghame, 14 f 29
Hon. Sir Wm Howe, K. B. 23 f 29
✕ Lord George Lennox, 25 f 29
H. Fletcher Campbell, 35 f 29
Jn Hale, Gov. of Londonderry 29
R. Boyd, 39 L. Gov. Gibralt. 29
✕ Sir H. Clinton, KB 12 f 29
Lord Southampton, 3 d 29

Bernard Hale, Lt. Governor of Chelsea Hospital *Aug.* 29
✕ John Burgoyne, 29
Sir R. Hamilton, Bart. 40 f 29
Robert Robinson, Governor of Pendennis 29
Francis Craig, 1 f g 29
Earl Ligonier, 9 f 29
Earl Percy, 5 f 29
William Tayler, 24 f 29
Sir Eyre Coote, K. B. 37 f 29
Earl Cornwallis, 33 f 29

1779.
Wm Amherst, 32 f *Feb.* 27
Robert Watson, Lieut. Gov. of Portsmouth, 27
Daniel Jones, 2 f 27
John Mackenzie, Marines, 27
John Bell, Marines 27
Jorden Wren, 41 f 27
Lanc. Baugh, 58 f 27
Sir D. Lindsay, Bart. 59 f 27
Henry Smith, Marines, 27

MAJOR-GENERALS.
1770.
John Salter, *April* 30
Nevill Tatton, 30

1777.
Hezekiah Fleming, § 29
Edward Maxwell, 67 f 29
William-Style, 3 f g 29
Henry Lister, 2 f g 29
Ja. Robertson, 16 f 29
Eyre Massey, 27 f 29
William Tryon, 70 f 29
George Warde, 1 h 29
James Cunningham, Governor of Barbadoes. 29
✕ Rob. Skene, Adjutant Gen. North Britain, 29
Flower Mocher, 9 d 29
Joseph Gabbet, 66 f 29
Robert Sloper, 14 d 29
✕ Staates Long Morris, 61 f 29
✕ Hon. John Vaughan, 46 f 29

, 65 f *Aug.* 29, of Dominica,   *Aug.* 29
ofs, §   29 Patrick Tonyn, Governor of
, Bart. 38 f 29   Eaſt Florida,   29
ʃov. of Jamai- Arthur Preſton, 9 d   29
              29 Gabriel Chriſtie, 60 f   29
, 19 d g   29 Patrick Mackellar, Engin. 29
79 f   29 James Bramham, ditto,   29
·tillery   29 Charles Roſs, 39 f   29
:ith, K.B. §   29 Will. Green, Engin.   29
5 f   29 George Scott, 83 f   29
;, Artillery   29 Charles O'Hara, 2 f g   29
t, 15 f g   29 Robert Sandford,   29
n, 1 h g   29 John Roberts, 90 f   29
, 7 f   29 Lof. Ant. Tottenham,   29
g   29 Ant. St. Leger, 86 f   29
ı, Bart. 50 f 29 William Rowley, §   29
on, Quarter-   Francis Maclean, 82 f   29
ral, 75 f   29 Henry Trelawney, 2 f g 29
, 31 f   29 Arch. M'Nab, 41 f   29
v. of *Cheſter* 29 Peter Bathurſt   29
79.   Wm. Roy, Dep. Q. M. G. 29
, Lieut. Gov. Hon. Wm. Gordon, 81 f   29
1   *Feb.* 27 John Maunſell, §   29
:d, 3 f g   27 John Godwin, Artil.   29
62 f   27 Stewart Douglas, §   29
Philipſon, *Ditto* Robert Preſcott, 28 f 29
               27 J. Patterſon, 63 f   29
10 f.   27 Henry Gladwin   -   29
t, 60 f   27 Paſton Gould, 30 f   29
  Artil.   27 Hon. W. Harcourt, 16 d 29
l. g.   27 John Burgoyne, 14 d   29
, 64 f.   27 *Hon. H. L. Luttrell, 1 h 29
ınd, Artil.   27 Wm. Dalrymple, Quart. Maſt.
  John, 36 f 27   Gen. in America   29
, 1 f g   27 Wm. Picton, 12 f   29
  3 f g   27 *Sir Hector Munro, K.B. 29
, Knt. 80 f.   27 Hon. E. Stopford, 66 f 29
, Bt. 3 f g   27 David Ogilvie, 13 f   29
  57 f.   27 Hon. Wm. Hervey, §   29
. 1762.   Weſt Hyde, 1 f g   29
l, § *Feb.* 19 Thomas Twiſleton, 3 f g   29
                  John Fletcher, 32 f *Aug.* 29
              19 Humphry Stevens, 3 f g   29
ley, Governor Francis Laſcelles, 3 d   29
                                         John

John Deaken, 1 f g	29	Allan Campbell, 36 f 25
J. Murray, 77 f. *Dec.*	18	Barry St. Leger, 34 f 25
J. Lord Macleod, 73 f	19	James Rooke, 14 f 25
S. Townfend, *Aid de Camp to*		Sir Alex. Purves, Bart. 18 f 25
the King,	19	Sam. Birch, 17 d 25
Wm. Meadows, *ditto,*	19	Charles Crofbie, 67 f 25
T. O. Mordaunt, *ditto,*	19	Martin Tucker, 2 h 25
1779.		Winter Blathwayt, Blues 25
Arthur G. Martin, 2 f g *Feb.* 27		John Howard, 1 f g 25
Benj. Gordon, 48 f	27	Hon. Col. Gordon, 3 f g 25
Lawr. Reynolds, 68 f	27	Ralph Abercrombie, 3 h 25
Sir Henry Calder, Bt. 49 f	27	Lord Robert Ker, 6 d 25
Hon. T. Bruce, *Aid de Camp*		John Anftruther, 52 f 25
to the King,	27	William Schutz, 2 f g 25
George Ainflie, *ditto,*	27	James Webfter, 33 f 25
✕James Adeane, *ditto,*	27	Chapel Norton, 2 f g 25
Henry Pringle, 51 f	27	Thomas Bisfhop, 2 f g 25
Edward Smith, 2 h g g	27	Alexander Rigby, 25 f 25
✕Sir J. Wrottefley, Bt. 1 f g	27	Thomas Frafer, 1 f 25
James D'Auvergne, 1 h g.	27	**LIEUTENANT COLONELS.**
T. James, Artil.	27	1760.
Tho. Bland, 7 d	27	Edward Windus, § *Jan.* 17
Felix Bulkeley, 2 h g	27	John Rutter, *Feb.* 8
C. Wilfon Lyon, 18 d	27	1761.
Ar. Tuker Collins, do	27	Sir Hugh Williams, § *Feb.* 11
Walter Caruthers, do	27	Thomas Bate, § *Oct.* 2
Philip Skene, 69 f	27	Wm. Blacket, Lieut. Gov. of
Thomas Marriott, Marines	27	Plymouth 5
Hen. Watfon Powell, 53 f	27	P. Chefter, Gov. of W Flor. *Oct.* 6
T. Stirling, *Aid de Camp to*		John Tullikens, § 10
the King,	27	1762.
Philip Roberts, §	27	John Tufton Mafon § *Jan.* 5.
Tho. Cox, 1 f g	27	James Seton, 10
George Garth, *Aid de Camp to*		Paul Emil. Irving, Lieutenant
the King, *Feb.* 27		Gov. of Guernfey 15
Richard Grenville, *ditto,*	27	Paul Pechell, 20
1780.] His R. H. Pr. Frede-		Jofeph Widdens, § 23
rick, Bp. of Ofnaburg, *Nov.* 1.		Robert Campbell, *Feb.* 2
John Campbell, 74 f	25	John Reid, 95 f 3
John Leland, 1 t g	25	James Money, § 5
Enoch Markham, 46 f	25	Frecheville Ramfden, Lieut.
James Hamilton, 21 f	25	Gov. of Carlifle, 5
Allen M'Lean, 84 f	25	James Stuart, § 20
John Stratton, Artillery	25	John Cofnan, § 24

Wm.

[175]

Wm. Miles	April 19	Geo. Hotham,	8
Thomas Hay	May 21	John Hill, 9 f	11
1764.		James Coates, 19 f	11
Alex. Johnstone,	Nov. 23	Sir Philip Ainslie,	11
1765.		David Dundas, 12 d	11
Robert Raitt, §	Mar. 21	Ralph Dundas, 11 d Sept.	11
1767.		Adam Williamson, 18 f	12
1772.] Wm Piers, §	May 25	George Etherington, 60 f	19
J. Goreham, Lieut. Governor		Lewis Val. Fuser, 60 f	20
of Placentia	25	Richard Whyte, 96 f	20
Robert Preston, §	25	Alured Clarke, 7 f	20
Rob. E. Fell, §	25	William Stiell, 60 f	21
Nat. Heywood, §	25	*Hon.R.S.Conway,1fg Oct.18	
Charles Chapman, §	25	John Brown, Marines, Nov. 15	
Sir James Johnstone, Bart.	25	Archibald Campbell, 71 f	23
Francis Allesieu, §	25	Rob. Abercromby, 37 f	30
Thomas Ogle, §	25	James Hugonin, 4 d Dec. 22	
Richard Ridley, §	25	Geo. Hastings, 3 f g	29
J. Walkinshaw Crawford, §	25	1776.	
Richard Sherlock, §	25	John Lind, 20 f	Jan. 6
James Murray,	25	Alexander Dickson, 16 f	6
Sir Allen M'Lean, §	25	Gerard Lake, 1 f g	11
Samuel Zobell, §	25	William Sherriffe, 47 f	20
Richard Parker, §	25	LdSpencerHamilton,2 f g Feb.1	
William Morris,	25	John Woodford, 1 f g	2
William Hunter, §	25	William Grinfield, 3 f g	3
Sir Ja. Langham, Bt.	25	Sir Thomas Fowke, 3 f g	4
C. Egerton, §	25	John Gordon, 50 f	19
Charles Long, §	25	Samuel Hulse, 1 f g	20
John Martin, Marines	July 21	Albemarle Bertie, ditto Ap.	1
1773.		Henry Shaw, 11 f	12
Wm. Egerton, Lt. Gov. of		Cha.Vallency, Engineer	25
Scilly,	28	Michael Cox, 1 f g	26
1775.		Tho.Pigot,Ch.Eng.Ireland,	26
J. Gunning, 82 f	Jan. 23	H. J.T.DeBurgh, 1fg June	15
James Bruce, 70 f	Feb. 9	James Stewart, 13 d July	15
Gustavus Guydickens, 3 f g	22	Thomas Carleton, 29 f	31
James Stewart, 1 f g	Apr. 4	1777.	
Earl of Lincoln, 1 f g	5	W.Cavend.Lyster, 3 f g Jan.16	
John Mansell, 3 d g	27	Tho. Musgrave, 40 f	28
Fra. Hall, 3 f g	May 3	James Marsh, 43 f	28
Geo. Morgan, 2 f g	26	James Cockburne, 35 f	28
Alex. Stewart, 3 f	July 7	Charles Leigh, 3 f g April	12
James Craufurd, 73 f	26	Andrew Bruce, 54 f July	13

James

James Ogilvie, 4 f	22	Henry Hope, 44 f	Oct. 5
Mason Bolton, 8 f	22	Edw. Mitchell, 27 f	7
Thomas Carlton, 29 f	22	Earl of Balcarras, 24 f	18
Nic. Sutherland, 47 f	29	Hon. Ch. Stuart, 26 f	26
Gavin Cochrane, 58 f July	29	Cornel. Cuyler, 55 f Nov.	16
William Roberts, 41 f Aug.	26	John Swin Dyer, 1 f g	21
Robert Kingston, 86 f	29	Geo. Gledstanes, 72 f Dec.	16
William Ogle, 52 f	29	Thomas Dundas, 80 f	27
Hon. Mark Napier, §	29	Earl of Seaforth, 78 f	29
Matthew Dixon, Engineer,	29	1778.	
Charles Farrington, Artil.	29	E. of Harrington, 85 f Jan.	16
Abraham Tovey, ditto,	29	Hon. R. Fitzpatrick, 1 f g	23
×Sir Rob Laurie, Bt. 16 d	29	Nesbitt Balfour, 23 f	31
John Tupper, Marines,	29	Wm. Dalrymple, 2 f Mar.	26
Wm. Kellet, 39 f	29	Edm. Stevens, 1 f g May	15
Wm. Hamilton, 2 f	29	Visc. Chewton, 87 f	16
Hugh Powell, 15 f	29	Thomas Trigge, 12 f June	6
James Mark Prevost, 60 f	29	Lord Rawdon	15
John M'Donell, 76 f	29	Peter Craig, 56 f	18
John Innes, Artillery,	29	William Gardiner, 45 f	29
William Martin, ditto,	29	Geo. Mackenzie, 73 f Sept.	24
John Archer, Engineer,	29	Charles Gordon, 77 f	24
Harry Gordon, ditto,	29	Henry Johnson, 17 f Oct.	5
William Edmestone, 48 f	29	Turner Straubenzee, 52 f	5
Thomas Adams, 12 f	29	John Yorke, 22 f	11
Anthony Haslam, 5 f	29	H. E. Fox, 38 f	12
Forbes M'Bean, Artillery	29	Duncan M'Pherson, 3 f g Nov.	6
Sir F. J. Buchanan, ditto	29	Robert Farquhar, 81 f	9
David Hay, ditto	29	J. W. T. Watson, 3 f g	20
Jos. Winter, ditto	29	James Lumsdaine, 1 f Dec.	10
David Home, 2 d	29	Charles Home, 6 f	10
John Brewse, Engineer	29	Lowther Pennington, 2 f g	14
Hugh Debbeig, ditto	29	Patrick Bellew, 1 f g	10
Richard Dawson, ditto	29	John Byde, 2 f g Dec.	30
And. Edhouse, 13 f Aug.	29	R. S. Jones, 1 f g	30
Ant. Lovibond, 1 d g	29	1779.] C. Grey, 59 f Jan.	22
A. Fotheringh. Ogilvie, 83 f	29	Tho. Sloughter, 2 f g Feb.	22
Normand Lamont, 55 f	29	John Duroure, 2 f g Mar.	15
Duncan M'Pherson, 42 f	29	Charles Eustace, Dep. Quart.	
Charles Tuffnell, r r h g	29	Mast. Gen. in Ireland	18
Mont. Agnew, 1 d g	29	R. H. Pye, 1 f g April	23
Stephen Kemble, 60 f	29	Phil. de la Motte, 21 d	27
Hon. J. Stopford, 15 f	29	Philip Goldsworthy, 1 d	28
James Stuart, 5 d	29	Philip Crompton, 4 h May	2
Dan. Danvers Rich, 5 f g Sept.	1	F. R. Humphreys, 79 f	1
Jeremiah French, 31 f	13	F. E. Gwynne, 20 d	5

[177]

Andrew Lyon, 8 d   May 8
Rich. Timms, 2 h g   29
Sir W. Innes, Bt. 2 d g Aug. 12
John Hughes, Marines,   12
William Souter, ditto   23
Alexander Trotter, ditto   24
Harrie Innes, ditto   25
Wm. Faucitt, 3 f g   Sept. 18
Lord Sheffield, 22 d   Oct. 11
John Shee, 75 f   13
Fran. Aug. Eliott, 19 d   20
Alexander M'Donald, 71 f   25
James Hamilton, 2 f g   28
Earl De Lawarr, 2 f g Nov. 20
James Balfour, 99 f   29
William Mackintosh, 97 f   30
Rich. Boycott, 91 f   Dec. 1
Fred. Thomas, 1 f g   26
Hon. James Stuart, 92 f   27
    1780.
Fr. J. Perkins, Marines Jan. 17
Earl of Winchelsea, 87 f   17
James Holwell, 93 f   Feb. 7
John Acloin, 61 f   March 8
Alex. Campbell, 95 f April 7
Francis D'Oyly, 1 f g   27
Samuel Archer, 3 f g   29
Robert Lovelace, 2 f g May 5
Tho. Dufour Eaton, 1 h g   13
Hon. R. F. Greville, 1 f g   18
William Fullarton, 98 f   29
John Sutton, 2 f g   June 7
Sir James Duffe, 1 f g July 18
James Moncrief, Engin. Oct. 7
Sir James Murray, 94 f   7
J. Sawbridge, 1 h g g Nov. 20
S. H. Mangin, 5 d   25
Edw. Hicks, 70 f   25
Grice Blakeney, 14 d   25
Paulus Æmilius Irving, 47 f 25
John Small, 84 f   25
James Cousseau, 37 f   25
Beamsley Glazier, 60 f   25
Thomas Pringle, 67 f   25
Edmund Eyre, 54 f   25
Theodore Hultaine, 66 f   25
Henry Harnage, 62 f   25
Henry Nooth, 4 d   25

Joseph Ferguson, 64 f Dec. 25
    MAJORS.   1745.
Sir C. Leighton §   May 1
Robert Mitford §   4
Matt. Swiney   Oct. 4
Scot Floyer §   4
    1751.
H. Hart, Lt. G. Sheerness Mar. 3
1754.] Cha. Craven § Sept. 24
1759.] Ja. Johnston, § Dec. 11
1760.] Pet. Labiliere, § Jan. 17
Wm. Walters §   25
Bar. Corneille §   Aug. 2
1761. Cha. Veaitch § Feb. 18
Henry Boisragon §   28
T. Whitwick Knightly June 16
1762.] Nevinson Poole, Lieut.
    Gov. of Pendennis   Feb. 3
Robert Acland   3
George Carr   12
Francis Drake   24
Sir Jn. Whitefoord, Bt. §   26
Donald Campbell   Mar. 2
John Tucker   3
Robert Gordon   May 7
Francis Gore, Lieut. Gov. of
    the Caribbee Islands   8
Charles Webb §   9
Thomas Cole §   Nov. 26
Rich. Hawkins,   § 26
1767.] Thomas Bell § Jan. 7
1768] B. Bromhead § May 9
1770.] Philip Baggs § Sept. 13
    1772.
John Watson, Invalids July 23
Thomas Smelt   23
1776.] A. Dundas, 54 f Jan. 6
Valentine Gardiner, 16 f   11
William Hatsell, 19 f   11
Griffith Williams, Artill. Feb. 17
Alexander Nesbit, 31 f Mar. 4
Thomas Baskerville, 50 f   12
Rd Bettesworth, Irish Artil. 15
Tho. Dawson, 3 f   Apr. 20
Chr. Maxwell, 30 f   June 7
Philip Walsh, 12 d   July 15
Nich. Loftus, 1 h   15
    Q   Rob.

[178]

Rob. M'Leroth, 64 f	28	James Dawson, 58 f	29
Bulleine Fancourt, 56 f	*Oct.* 3	John Hallowes, 56 f	29
Joseph Ferguson, 46 f	10	William Cowley, 22 f	29
George Fonter, 21 f	*Nov.* 5	William Gauntlett, 61 f	29
Geo. Forbes, 9 f	11	Richard Temple, 23 f	29
1777.] A. Gordon, 26 f	*Mar.* 25	Francis Marsh, 65 f	29
A. S. de Peister, 8 f	*May* 6	Peter Damboon, 2 f	29
Abraham Nixon, 1 f	12	Archibald Campbell, 1 f	29
William Yorke, 69 f	*June* 24	James Abercromby, 3 f	29
Hen. Bruen 15 f	*July* 12	William Handfield, 38 f	29
William Agnew, 24 f	14	George Sinclair, 65 f	29
Rob. Douglas, Marines	*Aug.* 29	George Lewis, Artil.	29
Tho. Heathcote, Ma.	29	William Lewis, Marines	29
Maurice Wemys, ditto	29	Mordeca Abbott, ditto	29
William Rotheram, ditto	29	Miles Sandys, ditto	29
Duncan Urquhart, 50 f	29	Thomas Woollocombe, 2 f	29
John Bowater, ditto	29	John Hedges, 43 f	29
Tho. Averne, ditto	29	Christ. Middleton, Marines	29
George Thompson 43 f	29	Henry Fletcher, ditto	29
David, Lord Colvill, 51 f	29	John Barclay, ditto	29
Colin Graham, 16 f	29	John Graham, ditto	29
Alexander Ross, 81 f	29	W. Mad. Richardson, 3 f	29
Geo. Anderson, Artillery	29	Charles Lyons, 69 f	29
James Fraser, 71 f	29	John Breese, 54 f	29
John Nairne, 51 f	29	J. Augustus Ivers, 30 f	29
Tho. Duval, Marines	29	Tho. Groves, Marines,	29
James Campbell, 51 f	29	William Brown, 59 f	29
Edward Jenkins, 79 f	29	Will. M'Carmick, 93 f	29
Robert Hoyes, 34 f	29	Philip Fall	29
Hon. Arch. Erskine, 11 f	29	Hon. J. Leslie, 3 f	29
Edward Eyre, 40 f	29	Robert Mason Lewis, 10 d	29
Geo. Reynolds 49 f	29	John Hardy, 56 f	29
Arch. M'Arthur, 71 f	29	John Freke, 39 f	29
H. A. Powlet, 45 f	29	James Gordon, 80 f	29
Edmund Strachan, 32 f	29	John Johnston, Marines	29
William Robertson, 36 f	29	John Carter, Artillery	29
John Major banks, 19 f	29	Joseph Walton, ditto	29
Benj. Steholin, Artl.	29	Christ. Carleton, 29 f	*Sept.* 13
Duncan Drummond, ditto	29	George Harris, 5 f	*Oct.* 7
James Barker, 56 f	29	Will. Hughes, 53 f	8
John Campbell, Marines	29	David Ferguson, 43 f	26
George Preston, ditto	29	Cha. Lenox Smyth, 2 h	*Nov.* 4
John Forbes, 29 f	29	Richard Vyse, 18 d	4
Charles Stewart, 63 f	29	Charles Burton, 2 h gg	*Dec.* 12
Alex. Baillie, Fort Major of		Christ. Horstall, 72 f	16
Fort George	29	Sir H. Dalrymple, Kt. 77 f	17
William Cawthorne, 44 f	29	James Stuart, 78 f	18
C. Tarrant, Engin. in Irel.	29	Alex. Donaldson, 76 f	19

Hon. M. Ramsay, 83 f	21	Lord Cathcart, 38 f	*April* 13
James Hen. Craig, 82 f	22	Charles Lumm, 44 f	14
John Whyte, 83 f	23	Thomas Mecan, 23 f	14
Sir R. Stuart, Bt. 77 f	25	Thomas Warburton, 7 d	26
Alex. Campbell, 74 f	26	Richard Broohe, 3 d g	27
John Elphinston, 73 f	27	Alexander Hart, 6 d	28
John Macdonald, 81 f	28	Basil Heron, 2 d	30
Lord Barriedale, 76 f	29	Thomas Staples, 4 h	*May* 1
John Campbell, 74 f	30	Henry Haslard, 1 d	1
Alexander Robertson, 82 f	31	James Telfer, 15 d	2
1778.		Richard Grant, 19 d	4
Hon. R. H. Southwell, 8 d *Jan.* 7		John Floyd, 21 d	5
Sir E. T. Bannerman, Bt. 36 f	26	William Price, 3 d	7
James Holwell, 2 f *March* 26		Cha. Henchman, 16 d *June* 10	
William King, 58 f	31	John Farnaby, 2 h g	29
Richard Downes, 1 d g *Ap.* 2		Tho. Mallock, 2 d g *Aug.* 12	
Fred. Spiesmacher, 60 f *May* 14		James Ferrier, Eng. in Irel. 12	
Henry Knight, 45 f	21	B. C. Payne, 99 f	21
Will. Maxwell, 10 f	23	A. K. Gordon, 90 f	22
Robert Douglas, 47 f	29	Joseph Duffaux, 97 f	23
Hugh Lord, 75 f	30	Colin Mackenzie, 92 f	24
Oliver De Lancy, 17 d *June* 3		Peter Hunter, 92 f	25
William Barlow, 12 f	6	Hon. H. F. Stanhope, 86 f	26
Andrew Cathcart, 10 f	29	*J. W. Egerton, 22 d	27
Will. Calderwood, 1 hg *Aug.* 5		J. S. Patton, 93 f	28
James Weymyss, 63 f	10	Hon. C. Cathcart, 98 f	29
Charles Graham, 42 f	25	Hon. H. Phipps, 85 f	30
William Crosbie, 7 f *Sept.* 20		Richard Crewe, 85 f	31
James Mackenzie, 73 f	24	Thomas Lister,	*Sept.* 4
Ham. Maxwell, 73 f	24	Charles Brownlow, 57 f	18
Norman Macleod, 73 f	24	Hon. G. Damer, 87 f *Oct.* 5	
Tho. Armstrong, 17 f *Oct.* 5		John Campbell, 96 f	10
Tho. Coare, 28 f	6	Alexander Mair, 88 f	12
Will. Browne, 49 f	12	George Leathes, 20 d	20
Will. Dancy, 33 f	14	J. H. Harris, 84 d	22
Simon Fraser, 71 f	14	John Lloyd, 60 f	22
Edward Drew, 35 f	28	Patrick Ferguson, 71 f	25
James Stuart, 68 f *Nov.* 12		John St. Leger, 90 f *Nov.* 26	
Hon. S. D. Strangways, 20 f · c		M. H. Ballie, 94 f	27
Arch. Erskine, 22 f *Dec.* 6		John Joiner Ellis, 89 f	29
James Flint, 25 f	10	Hon. C. G. Legge, 96 f	30
John Stanton, 14 f	16	Dudley Ackland, 91 f *Dec.* 1	
1779] G. Vaughan, 2 h g *Jan.* 9		William Cotton, 27 f	4
Nar. Huson, 59 f	22	Anthony Lefroy, 13 d	24
Arthur Pomeroy, 0 d *Feb.* 14		James Moncrieff, Engineer, 25	
T. Humberston, 78 f *Mar.* 22		Q 2	1780

1780.			
W. Montgomery, 40 f	*March* 6	John Money, 9 f	25
William Owen, 61 f	*May* 3	Samuel Moore, 56 f	25
Francis Minshall, 1 h g	13	Thomas Walmceley, 18 d	25
F. J. Scott, 6 f	*July* 14	T. Coppinger Moyle, 28 f	25
Barn. Tarleton, 70 f	*Aug.* 22	George Morley, 62 f	25
Arch. Robertson, Engineer,	22	Richard England, 47 f	25
J. G. Simcoe, 40 f	22	John Kay, 12 f	25
Alexander Rofs, 45	*Nov.* 14	Trevor Hull, 36 f	25
John Jaques, 51 f	14	Henry Bathurst, Blues	25
Richard Baugh, 49 f	14	Matthew Johnson, 46 f	25
James Stevenson 6c f	14	Richard Fleming, 36 f	25
Charles Crawford, 13 f	14	James Horsburg, 39 f	25
John Dickson, 58 f	14	Richard St. George	*Dec.* 12

GENERAL OFFICERS
having Local Rank.

GENERALS *in America.*

F REDERICK Haldimand, *Jan.* 1, 1776

Sam. Wildey Robarts, 13 f	14
John Mercier, 39 f	14
Frederick Dilney, 21 f	14
Henry Hamilton, 56 f	14
Gilbert King, 5 d	11
Timothy Newmarsh, 7 f	14
Anothy Cliffe, 4 h	14
David Gardyne, 66 f	14
Miles Staveley, Blues	14
Rich. Ber Lernoult, 8 f	14
John Mackay, 65 f	14
John Vignoles, 39 f	25
Stephen Bromfield, 54 f	25
Ralph Ramsay, 6 f	25
John Gillan, 55 f	25
Samuel Haynes, 1 h g g	25
John Sinner, 70 f	25
John Glover, 72 f	25
William Chester, 69 f	25
Thomas Boyd, 16 f	25
Francis Hutchinson, 60 f	25
Samuel Knolles, 51 f	25
Wetwang Marsh, 32 f	25
Daniel Vaughan, 39 f	25
Abdy Mawe, 32 f	25
John Mac Gill, 29 f	25
Archibald Campbell, 29 f	25
William Monsell, 29 f	25
John Bridges Shaw, 68 f	25
Henry Ogilvie, 50 f	25
Hugh Maginnis, 38 f	25

Sir Guy Carlton, K. B. 1
Hon. Sir W. Howe, K. B. 1
Sir H. Clinton, K. B. 1

LIEUTENANT GENERALS *in America.*

Earl Percy, 1776, *Jan.* 1
Earl Cornwallis 1
Robert Melvill, 1777, *Aug.* 29
West-Indies

MAJOR GENERALS *in America.*

James Robertson 1776, *Jan.* 1
Eyre Massey 1
Hon. John Vaughan 1
Sir R. Pigot, Bt. 1
James Grant 1
William Phillips 1
Richard Prescott 1
William Tryon 1
Thomas Clarke 1
Charles Grey, 1777, *Mar.* 4
Sir T. S. Wilson, Bt. *Apr.* 30
× Sir H. Monro, K. B. *May* 9
East-Indies

BRIGADIERS *in E. Indies,*
John Caillaud, 1763, *July* 8
John Carnac, 1764, *May* 12

[181]

A LIST of his Majesty's LAND FORCES, with their Agents, and Stations. G stands for Gen. L for Lt. Gen. M for Major Gen. C for Colonel, and LC for Lieut. Col.

COLONELS. Rank Raised. Lieut. Cols. Majors. Agents. Stations.

Two Troops of HORSE GUARDS raised in 1660.

1 Lothian, Marquis of	M	1660	1 D'Auvergne, James	1 Calderwood, Will.	Adair and Co. London and Westminster
			2 Eaton, Tho. Duff.	2 Minshul, Francis	
2 ×Lord R. Bertie	G	1660	1 Buckley, Felix	1 Vaughan, George	Ross and Grey Westminster
			2 Tinims, Richard	2 Farnaby, John	

Two Troops of HORSE GRENADIER GUARDS.

1 ×Griffin Sir J. G.	G	1693	×Adeane, James	Sawbridge, Jacob	Cox and Mair London and Westminster
2 Lord Amherst	G	1702	Smith, Edward	Burton, Charles	Ross and Grey

One Royal Regiment of HORSE GUARDS.

×Conway, H. S.	G	1661	Blathwayt, Winter	Tuffnell, Charles I. C	Wilkinson GreatBritain

Four Regiments of HORSE.

1 Ward, George	M	1685	×Luttrell, Hon. H.L.	Loftus, Nicholas	Montgomery Ireland
2 Fitzwilliam, John	G	1685	Tucker, Martin	Smyth, Ch. Len.	Wybrants&Co. Do
3 Irvin, Sir John	L	1685	Abercrombie, Ralph	Annesley, Hon. Marc.	Montgomery Do
4 ×Honeywood, Ph.	G	1688	Vyse, Richard	Staples, Thomas	Waring Do

Three Regiments of DRAGOON GUARDS.

1 ×Howard, Sir Geo.	G	1685	Lovibond, Anth.	Downes, Richard	Ross and Grey GreatBritain
2 Townshend, Visc.	L	1685	Innes, Sir Will. Bart.	Mallack, Thomas	Cox and Mair Do
3 ×Manners, Ld Rob.	G	1685	Mansell, John	Brooke, Richard	Fitter Do

Twenty-two Regiments of DRAGOONS.

1 Pembroke, Visc.	L	1683	Goldsworthy, Philip	Hafford, Henry	Lambe GreatBritain
2 ×Panmure, Earl of	G	1681	Home, David	Heron, Basil	Cox and Mair Do
3 Southampton, Lord	G	1685	Lascelles, Francis	Price, William	Willis Do

[182]

4	Carpenter, Benj.	L	1685	Hugonin, James	Nooth, Henry	Lamb	Do
5	Yorke, Sir Joseph	G	1688	Stewart, James	Mangin, Sam. Hen.	Wybrants	Ireland
6	Johnston, James	L	1689	Kerr, Lord Robert	Hart, Alexander	Lamb	GreatBritain
7	×Clinton, Sir Henry	G	1690	Bland, Thomas	Warburton, Thomas	Cox and Mair	Do
8	Severne, John	L	1693	Lyon, Andrew	Southwell, Henry	Wybrants	Ireland
9	Mocher, Flower	M	1713	Prefton, Arthur	Pomeroy, Arthur	Montgomery	Do
10	Pitt, Wm. Aug.	L	1715	Mordaunt, T. Ofbert	Lewis, Rob. Niafon	Cox and Mair	GreatBritain
11	Johnfton, James	L	1715	Dundas, Ralph	Grant, Richard	Rofs and Grey	Do
12	×Keppell, Hon. Wm	L	1715	Dundas, David	Walfh, Philip	Montgomery	Ireland
13	Pierfon, Rich.	L	1715	Stewart, James	Lefroy, Anthony		Do
14	Sloper, Robert	M	1715	Burgoyne, John	Blakeney, Grice		Do
15	Eliott, Geo. Aug.	G	1759	Ainflie, George	Telfer, James	Cox and Mair	GreatBritain
16	Harcourt, Hon. W. C	1759	Laurie, Sir Robert	Hinchman, Charles	Cowden	America
17	Prefton, George	L	1759	Birch, Samuel	De Lancy, Oliver	Cox and Mair	Do
18	Drogheda, E. of	L	1759	Lyon, Cha. Wilfon		Montgomery	Ireland
19	Manners, Ruff.	M	1779	Eliott, Fra. Auguftus	Lambert, Benjamin	Bifhop and Co.	GreatBritain
20	×Phillipfon, R. B.	M	1779	Gwyn, F. E.	Leathes, George	Lamb	Do
21	Douglas, John	M	1779	De la Motte, P.	Floyd, John	Cox and Mair	Do
22			1780	Sheffield, Lord	Egerton, J. W.	Adair and Bullock	GreatBritain

Three Regiments of FOOT-GUARDS.

[183]

Regiments of FOOT.

#	Colonel		Year	Lt. Colonel	Major	Agent	Location
1	Argyll, Duke of	G	1633	Frafer, Thomas	Nickfon, Abrah.	Rofs and Grey	GreatBritain
2	Jones, Daniel	M	1661	Lumfdaine, James	Campbell, Alex.	Ditto	Do
3	Style, William	M	1665	Dalrymple, William	Darnboon, Peter	Meyricks	Do
4	Hodgfon, Studh.	G	1680	Stewart, Alexander	Dawfon, Tho.	Hockett	Ireland
5	Percy, Earl	L	1674	Ogilvie, James	Tomlinfon, Thomas	Adair	N. America
6	Boothby, Sir Wm	L	1673	Harris, George	Battier, J. G.	Bifhopp	Do
7	Prefcott, Richard	M	1685	Home, Charles	Balfour, James	Cox and Mair	Do
8	Armftrong, Bigoe	L	1685	Clarke, Alured	Crofbie, William	Rofs and Grey	Do
9	Ligonier, Earl	L	1685	Bolton, Muf.	De Peifter, A. S.	Armftrong	Do
10	Sandford, Edward	L	1685	Hill, John	Forbes, Gordon	Cox and Mair	Do
11	Afhe, A'Court, W.G		1685	Smith, Francis	C Cathcart, Andrew	Do	Do
12	Picton, William		1685	Shawe, Henry	Efkine, Hon. Arch	Wybrants	Ireland
13	Murray, Ja.	L	1685	Trigge, Thomas	Barlow, William	Meyricks	Gibraltar
14	Cunninghame, Rt	L	1685	Ogilvy, David	C Edhoufe, Awarew LC	Rofs and Grey	GreatBritain
15	Faucitt, Will.	M	1685	Rooke, James	Stanton, John	Do	America
16	Robertfon, James	M	1688	Stopford, Jofeph LC	Bruen, Henry	Do	Do
17	x Monckton, Rob.	L	1688	Dickfon, Alexander	Gardiner, Valentine	Meyricks	Do
18	Sebright, SirJohn	L	1688	Johnfon, Henry	Armftrong, Thomas	Hanford	Do
19	Graeme, David	F.	1688	Williamfon, Adam	Purves, Sir Alexander	Cox and Mair	GreatBritain
20	Parker, G. Lane	L	1688	Coates, James	Majoribanks, John	Montgomery	Ireland
21	Mackay, Hon. A.	L	1678	Lind, John	Strangeways, S. D.	Cox and Mair	America
22	Gage, Hon Thomas	L	1639	Hamilton, James	Fortfcr, George	Rofs and Grey	Do
23	Howe, Hon.SirW.	L	1689	York, John	Erfkine, Archibald	Cox and Mair	Do
24	Taylar, William	L	1685	Balfour, Nefbit	Mecan, Thomas	Do	Do
				Balcarras, Earl of	C Agnew, William	Roberts	

No.	Name	Rank	Year	Name	Name	Agent	Location
25	×Lenox, Ld George	L	1689	Rigby, Alexander	Flint, James	Adair and Bullock	Great Britain
26	×Gordon, Lord Adam	M	1689	Stuart, Charles	Gordon, Andrew	Meyricks	America
27	Massey, Eyre	M	1689	Mitchell, Edward, M	Cotton, William	Roberts	Do
28	Grey, Charles	M	1694		Coore, Thomas	Meyricks	Do
29	Evelyn, William	L	1702	Carleton, Thomas	Carleton, Christoph. C	Cowden	Do
30	Parflow, John	L	1702	Gould, Pafton	Maxwell, Christoph.	Wybrants	Ireland
31	Clarke, Thomas	M	1702	French, Jeremiah C	Nesbit, Alexander	Meyricks	America
32	Amherst, William, M	L	1702	Fletcher, John	Strachan, Edmund C	Heath	Ireland
33	Cornwallis, Earl	L	1702	Webster, James	Dansey, William	Meyricks	America
34	Cavendish, Ld Fred.	L	1702	St. Leger, Barry	Dundas, Alex.	Cox and Mair	Do
35	Campbell, H. F.	L	1701	Cockburne, James	Drew, Edward	Grey and Ogilvie	Do
36	×St. John, Henry	L	1702	Campbell, Allan	Knox, John	Montgomery	Ireland
37	Coote, Sir Eyre	L	1702	Abercromby, Robert	Couſteau, James	Hesle and Son	America
38	Pigot, Robert	M	1702	Fox, Hen. Edward	Cathcart, Lord	Roberts	Do
39	Boyd, Robert	L	1702		Kellett, William LC	Cox and Mair	Gibraltar
40	Hamilton, Sir Rob.	L	1717	Musgrave, Thomas	Montgomery, Wm. LC	Do	America
41	Wren, Jorden	M	1719	McNab, Archibald C	Roberts, Wm. LC	Powell and Cooke	Great Britain
42	Murray, Lord John	G	1739	Stirling, Thomas	Graham, Charles	Anderſon and Co.	America
43	Cary, George	L	1741	Marsh, James	Fergufon, David	Cox and Mair	Do
44	Abercromby, Ja.	G	1741	Hope, Henry	Lumm, Charles	Do	Do
45	Haviland, William	L	1741	Gardiner, William	Knight, Henry	Hanfard	Do
46	×Vaughan, Hon. J.	M	1741	Markham, Enoch C	Fergufon, Joſeph	Meyricks	Do
47	Carleton, Sir Guy	L	1741	Sutherland, N.	Irving, P. Æmilius	Adair and Bullock	Do
48	Sorell, William	L	1741	Gordon, Benjamin	Hedges, John	Meyricks	Weſt Indies
49	Maitland, Alex.	L	1743	Calder, Sir Henry	Browne, William	Roſs and Grey	Do
50	×Wilſon, Sir T. S.	M	1755	Gordon, John	Baſkerville, Tho.	Meyricks	Great Britain

No.	Colonel		Year	Lt. Colonel	Major	Agent
52	Trapaud, Cyrus			Strabenzie, Turner	Ogle, William	Meyricks
53	Elphinston, R.D.H.	L	1755	Powell, HenryWatson	Hughes, William	Ross and Grey
54	Frederick Marisco	L	1755	Bruce, Andrew	Eyre, Edmund	Do
55	Grant, James	M	1755	Cuyler, Cornelius	Lamont, Norm. LC	Cox and Mair
56	Walsh, Hunt	L	1755	Craig, Peter	Fancourt, Bulleine	Meyricks
57	*Irwin, Sir John	L	1755	Campbell, John	C Blownlow, Charles	Cox and Mair
58	Baugh, Lancelot	M	1755	Cochran, Gavin	King, Wm.	Do
59	Lindsay, Sir David	M	1755	Gray, George	Huton, Narcissus	Ross and Grey
60	Amherst,LordGCinCh				Prevost, J. M. LC	⎫
	Haldimand, Fred.	G		Kemble, Stephen	Spiesmacher, Fred.	⎬ Do
	Christie, Gabriel	C		Etherington, George	Lloyd, John	⎭
	Dalling, John	M		Stiell, Wm	Glazier, Beamsley	
	Prevost, Augustine	C		Fuser, Lewis Valen.	Owen, William	
61	*Morris, S. L.	M	1758	Acklom, John	Harnage, Henry	Cox and Mair
62	Mathew, Edward	M	1758	Anstruther, John	C Wemyss, James	Bishopp
63	Grant, Francis	L	1758	Patterson, James	C M'Leroth, Robert	Cox and Mair
64	Pomeroy, John	L	1758	Leslie, Alexander	Marth, Francis	Meyricks
65	Calcroft, Thomas	M	1758	Bruce, Thomas	C Roper Henry	Cox and Mair
66	Gabbett, Joseph	M	1758	Stopford, Edward	Pringle, Thomas	Montgomery
67	Maxwell, Edward	M	1758	Crosbie, Charles	Stewart, James	Cane
68	*Lambton, John	L	1758	Reynolds, Lawrence	York, William	Montgomery
69	Sherrard,Hon.Phil.	L	1758	Skene, Philip	Hicks, Edward	Fitter
70	Tryon, Will.	M	1758	Bruce, James		Elwin
71	*Fraser, Simon	L		M'Donald, Alexand.	Fraser, S. M'Donald	Ross and Grey
			1778	Campbell, Arch.	M'Arthur, Arch.	
72	Ross, Charles			Gledstone, Geo.	Horsall, Christ.	Lamb

* The Number of each Battalion of Infantry in the foregoing List, serving in Great Britain, is 670, in North America 804, in Ireland 474.

73	Macleod, John Lord	1778	Crauford, James	Elphinston J. Mackenzie, J.	} Bishopp
			Mackenzie, Geo.	Maxwell, H. Macleod, N.	
74	Campbell, John	1778	Campbell, John	Campbell, Alex. Campbell, John	} Ross and Grey
75	Morison, George M	1778	Shee, John	Lord, Hugh	} Hesse
76		1778	M'Donnel, John	Donaldson, Al. Caithness, Earl	} Bishopp
77	×Murray, James	1778	Gordon, Charles	Dalymple, Sir Hugh Stuart, Sir R.	} Montgomery
78	Hall, Tho.	1778	Seaforth, Earl of	Stuart, J. Pumberston, T.	Meyricks
79	Humphreys, F. R.	1778		Cribb, Richard	Cox and Mair
80	Erskine, Sir Will.	1778	Dundas, Tho.	Gordon, J. Maxwell, W.	Do
81	Gordon, Hon. W.	1778	Farquhar, Robert	Ross, Alex. Macdonald, J.	} Montgomery
82	M'Lean, Fran.	1778	Gunning, John	Craig, J. H Robertson, A.	} Cox and Mair
83	Scott, George	1778	Ogilvy, A. F.	Ramsey, Hon Malcombe. Whyte, John	} Do
84	Clinton, Sir Henry M	1778	M'Lean, Allan	Harris, John Adolp. Small, John	} Do
85		1779	Harrington, Earl of	Phipps, Henry Crewe, Richard	} Do.
86	St. Leger, Anth.	1779	Kingston, Rob.	Stanhope, H. F.	Meyricks
87		1779	Chewton, Viscount	Winchelsea, Earl Damer, Hon. George	Ross and Gray
88	Keating, Thomas	1779	Leith, Sir Alex.	Mair, Alexander	Cox and Mair
89	Carey, Hon. L.	1779		Ellis, John Jolner	Meyricks

90	Tottenham, L. A.	1780	Gordon, Arch. Kin. Leger, St. John	} Hanfard	Great-Britain
91	Ackland, Dudley	1780	Boycott, Rich. Ackland, Dudley	Fitter	Do
92		1780	Stuart, Hon. James Mackenzie, Colin Hunter, Peter	} Gray	Do
93	M'Carmick, William	1780	Holwell, James Patton, J. S.	Clare	Do
94	Prefcott, Robert	1780	Murray, Sir James Baillie, Mac. Hugh	Rofs and Gray	Do
95	Reid, John	1780	Campbell, Alex. Pierfon, Francis	Cox and Mair	Do
96	White, Richard	1780	Campbell, John Legge, Hon. C. G.	} Willis	Do
97	Stanton, Samuel	1780	Maclintofh William Duflaux, Joseph	Vellegin	Do
98		1780	Fullarton, William Cathcart, Hon. Charles	Bifhop	Do
99	Rainsford, Charles	1780	Balfour, James Payne, Benj. Charles	Hefse.	Do
100		1780	Humberfton, T. F. M. Montrofor, Robert		Do

Twenty-six independent Companies of INVALIDS to do Duty in the Garrisons of Great Britain and Scilly Islands.

The FIELD OFFICERS of the 70 Companies of MARINES.
Gen. Hon. John Forbes. Lieut. Gen.

Colonels.	Cols. Commandant.	Lieut. Colonels.	Majors.	Agent.
Elliot, John	Mackenzie, J. L	Marriott, T. Martin, J.	Heathcote, T. Wemis, M.	
×Wallingham,Hon.R. B.	Bell, John L	Brown, J. Tupper, J.	Rotheram, W. Bowater, J.	Williams
	Smith, Henry L	Napier, F. Hughes, J.	Averne, T. Duvall, T.	
Hotham, William	Collins, A T.	Souter, W. Trotter, A.	Campbell, J. Preston, G.	
	Carruthers, Wal.	Innes, H. Perkins, J. F.	Lewis, W. Abbott, M.	

Royal Regiment of ARTILLERY, Four BATTALIONS, viz.

Colonels.	Lieut. Colonels.	Majors.	Paymasters.	Station.
1 James, Thomas	1	1 Phillips, William	Messrs.	Great Britain
2 Williamson, Geo. L.	2 Cleveland, Sam.	2 Martin, William	Cox and	Gibraltar and Minorca
3 Godwin, John	3 Brome, Jos.	3 Macbean, Forbes	Mair	Great Britain
4 Pattison, James	4 Tovey, Abraham	4		America

The Governors, Lieutenant Governors, and Agents, of the Garrisons in Great Britain.

Garrisons.	Governors.	per Ann	Lieut. Governors.	per Ann	Agents.
Fort Augustus, near Inv. George,	Hodgson, Studholm, L.	500 0 0	Trapaud, Alexander	300 0 0	Adair
Berwick and Holy Island	×Vaughan Hon. John M	600 0 0	Campbell, John C.	300 0 0	Do
Blackness	Weir, Hon. Ch. Hope	300 0 0	Hill, William	182 10 0	Meyricks
Calshot	Burrard, Sir H.	45 12 6	Stuart, John	73 0 0	Hesse
Carlisle	Darlington, Earl of	182 10 0	None		
Chester	Rainsford, Charles M	182 10 0	Ramsden, Frech.	182 10 0	Cox and Mair
Cinque Ports, Warden	×North, Lord		Fraser, Thomas	182 10 0	
		500 0 0	Best, Thomas	182 10 0	

(189)

Place	Name					Agent
Jersey	×Conway, R.H.H.S.G.		365	0	0	Wilkinson
Languard Fort	Mackay, Hon. Alex.	L.	109	10	0	Cox and Mair
St. Maws	Pigot, Sir Robert,	M.	300	00	6	Meyricks
Perdennis	Robinson, Robert,	M.				
Plymouth	Waldegrave, Earl,	G.	1229	02	6	Rofs and Grey
Portland	Traver, John		91	05	0	Madden
Portsmouth	Monckton, Robert					
R	×Pallifer, Sir Hugh	L.	700	00	0	Meyricks
Scarborough	Godolphin, Lord		16	00	0	
Scilly	Craig, Francis	L.	300	00	0	Meyricks
Sheerness						
South-sea Castle						Cox and Mair
Stirling	Campbell, Sir James	G.	300	00	0	Rofs and Gray
Tower	Cornwallis, E. Conftable	L.	1000	00	0	
Tynmouth	×Gordon, Lord Adam,	L.	300	00	0	Do
Upnor	Browne, William	C.	132	10	0	Cox and Mair
Wight, Isle of	×Worfley, Sir Richard		500	00	0	Kirkey
William, Fort	×Murray, Hon. J.	M.	1182	11	0	Cox and Mair
Windfor	Montagu, Duke of					
Yarmouth, North	Arbuthnot, Capt. John,	M.	182	10	0	Cox and Mair
St. James's Park	Non					
	Majr. Gunner, Brome, Jol.		36	10	0	Do

An Alphabetical LIST of the prefent BARONETS of ENGLAND, their moſt uſual Places of Abode, with the Time when they, or their Anceſtors, were ſo honoured.

The Dates are according to the prefent Method of beginning the Year the firſt of January.

N. B. Where we have not been able to come at the Chriſtian Name of the preſent BARONET, we have put that of the laſt deceaſed.

ABDY, William, a Captain in the Navy, Chobham-Place, Surry, July 7, 1641.
Acland, T. Dyke, Columpton, Devonſh. June 24, 1644.
Acton, Richard, Aldenham, Shropſhire, Jan. 7, 1644.
Alleyne, John Gay, Barbadoes, March 20, 1769.
Allin, ———, Somerly Town, Suffolk, Dec. 14, 1699.
Alſton, Rowland, Odell, Bedfordſhire, June 13, 1642.
Alſton, Evelyn, Mile-end, Middleſex, Jan. 20, 1682.
Anderſon, Reverend William, Rector of Lea, Lincolnſhire Dec. 11, 1660.
Andrews, William, Norton, Norfolk, Dec. 11, 1641.
Andrews, Joſeph, Shaw-Place, Berks, July 21, 1766.
Armytage, George, Kirklees, Yorkſhire, July 4, 1738.
Aſgill, Charles, London, April 7, 1761.
Aſhburnham, William, (Biſhop of Chicheſter) Bromham, Suſfex, and Chicheſter-Palace, May 15, 1661.
✗Aſtley, Edward, Melton-Conſtable, Norfolk, June 25, 1660.
Aſton, Willoughby, Wadley, Berkſhire, July 25, 1628.
Aubrey, Tho. Llantrithyd, Glamorganſh. July 23, 1660.
Ayloffe, Joſeph, F. R. S. Framfield, Suſſex, Nov. 25, 1612.
Bacon, Edmond, Premier of England, Raveningham, in Norfolk, May 22, 1611.
Baker, George, M. D. F. R. S. Auguſt 24, 1776.
✗Bampfylde, Charles Warwick, Poltimore, Devonſhire July 24, 1641.
Barker, Wm. March 29, 1676.
Barrington, Fitzwilliam, Lilley, Herts, and Swaynſton, Iſle of Wight, July 29, 1611.
✗Baſſett, Francis, Tehidy, Cornwall, Oct. 19, 1779.
Baſtard, William, Ketley, Devonſhire, Sept. 4, 1779.
Bayntun, Edward, Spye-Park, Wiltſhire, July 9, 1762.
Beaumont, George, Dunmow, Eſſex, Feb. 21, 1661.
Beckwith, Jonathan, Virginia, April 15, 1681.
Bedingfield, Richard, Oxborough, Norfolk, Jan. 2, 1661.

Bindloſs, Edward, Weſtminſter, Aug. 16, 1641.
×Biſhopp, Cecil, Parham, Suſſex, July 24, 1620.
Blackett, Edward, Matfen, Northumbl. Dec. 12, 1673.
Blackwell, Lambert, Sproufton-Hall, Norfolk, July 16, 1718.
×Blake, Patrick, F. R. S. Langham, Suffolk, Sept. 19, 1772.
Blake, Francis, Twiſel-Caſtle, Durham, May 3, 1774.
Blakiſton, Matthew, London, April 22, 1763.
Blois, John, Cockfield-Hall, Suffolk, April 15, 1686.
Blount, Walter, Morley, Shropſhire, Oct. 5, 1642.
Blount, Charles William, Odiham, Hants, June 17, 1720.
Booth, Rev. Geo. Aſhton-Under-Line, Lancaſhire, May 22, 1611.
Boothby, William, Broadlow-Aſh, Derbyſh. July 13, 1660.
Boughton, Edward, Lawford-hall, Warwickſhire, and Poſton, Herefordſhire, Aug. 4, 1641.
Bowyer, Wm. Denham-court, Buckinghamſh. June 25, 1660.
Boyd, John, Danſon, Kent, May 20, 1775.
Boynton, Griffith, Burton-Agnes, Yorkſh. May 25, 1618.
Bradſhaigh, Roger, Haigh, Lancaſhire, Nov. 17, 1679.
Bridges, Brooke, Goodneſtone, Kent, April 19, 1718.
×Bridgman, H. Lever, Lancaſhire, and Weſton, Salop, June 7, 1660.
Bridgman, Francis, Ridley, Cheſhire, Nov. 12, 1673.
Brigges, John, Blackbrooke, Monmouthſhire, Aug. 12, 1644.
Bromley, Geo. of Eaſt-Stoke, Nottingh. Oct. 29, 1757.
Brooke, Rd. Norton, Cheſhire, Dec. 12, 1662.
Broughton, T. Dodington, Cheſhire, and Broughton, Staf. Mar. 10, 1661.
Browne, John, Sunning, Berks, May 10, 1665.
Browne, James, Weſtminſter, March 11, 1732.
Buck, Charles, Hamby-Grange, Lincolnſh. Dec. 22, 1660.
Buckworth, Everard, Sheen, Surry, April 1, 1697.
×Bunbury, Tho. Charles, Milden-Hall, Suff. June 29, 1681.
Burdet, Robert, Foremark, Derbyſhire, Feb. 25, 1619.
Burdett, Charles, Acomb, near York, June 10, 1666.
Burnaby, Wil. Chal. Broughton-Hall, Oxon, October 31, 1767.
Burgoyne, Montagu, Sutton, Bedfordſhire, July 15, 1641.
Burrard, Harry, Walhampton, Hants, March 20, 1769.
×Burrell, Mer. Weſt-Grinſted, Suſſex, July 12, 1766.
Burton, Charles, Stockerton, Leiceſterſhire, July 22, 1622.
Carew, Thomas, Haccomb, Devonſh. Aug. 2, 1661.
Caſtleton, William, Hingham, Norf. Aug. 9, 1641.

Cave, Thomas, F. R. S. Stanford upon Avon, Northampton-
shire, June 30, 1641.
Cavendish, Henry, Doveridge, Derbysh. May 7, 1755.
Cayley, George, Brompton, Yorkshire, April 26, 1661.
Champneys, Tho. Orchardley, Somersetshire, Jan. 26, 1767.
Chapman, John, Barkway, Herts, June 27, 1720.
Charlton, Francis, Ludford, Herefordsh. May 12, 1686.
Chernock, Villiers, Holeot, Bedfordshire, June 27, 1720.
Cheere, Henry, Westminster, July 18, 1766.
Chetwode, John, F. R. S. Oakley, Staffordshire, April 6, 17c0.
Chichester, John, Raleigh, Devonshire, Aug. 1, 1641.
Child, Cæsar, Woodford, Essex, Feb. 4, 1685.
✕Clarges, Thomas, Aston, Hertfordsh. Oct. 30, 1674.
Clarke, John, Enfield, Middlesex, July 25, 1698.
✕Clavering, Thomas, Axwell, Durham, June 1661.
✕Clayton, Robert, Marden, Surry, Jan. 13, 1732.
Clayton, Richard, Adlington, Lancashire, May 3, 1774.
Cleike, Francis Carr, July 11, 1660.
✕Clerke, Phillip Jennings, Duddleston-hall, Salop, October 26, 1774.
Clifton, Gervas, Clifton, Nottinghamshire, May 22, 1611.
✕Cocks, Charles, Dumbledon, Gloucestersh. Sept. 19, 1772.
✕Codrington, Wm. Dodington, Gloucestersh. Apr. 21, 1721.
Coghill, John, Coghill-Hall, Yorkshire, July 25, 1778.
Colebrooke, George, Boulogne, Oct. 12, 1759.
Colleton, John, Exeter, Devonsh. Feb. 18, 1661.
Colt, John Dutton, Leominster, Herefordsh. Mar. 2, 1693.
Compton, Walter, Hartbury, Gloucestershire, May 6, 1686.
Conyers, Blaxton, Chester-le-street, Durham, July 14, 1628.
Cooke, George, Wheatley, Yorkshire, May 10, 1661.
Cope, Rev. Richard, D. D. Hampshire, June 29, 1611.
Cope, Charles, Ranton-Abby, Staffordshire, March 1, 1714.
Copley, Joseph, Sprotbrough, Yorkshire, July 5, 1778
✕Cornewall, Geo. Moccas-court, near Hereford, Aug. 4, 1764.
Cotton, John Hynde, Madingley, Cambridgesh. July 14, 1641.
✕Cotton, Robert Salusbury, Cumbermere-Abbey, Cheshire, Mar. 29, 1677.
Croft, Archer, Kensington, Middlesex, Nov. 18, 1671.
Cullum, Rev. John, Hardwick, Suffolk, June 18, 1660.
Cunliffe, Foster, Chester, March 24, 1759.
Daeth, Narborough, Knowlton, Kent, July 16, 1716.
Dalston, John, Capt. Lieut. of Marines, Feb. 15, 1641.
Danvers, John, Swithland, Leicestershire, July 4, 1746.
Dashwood, Henry-Watkin, Kirtlington, Oxen. Sept. 16, 1634.
✕Davers, Charles, Rushbrook, Suffolk, May 12, 1682.
Davie, John, Creedy, Devonshire, Sept. 9, 1641.
✕Delaval, John Hussey, Fordcastle, Northumberl. July 1, 1761.

D'Oyley, William, Little Milton, Oxfordshire, July 7, 1700.
D'Oyly, John, July 29, 1663, at Bengal, in the East Indies.
Drake, Francis Henry, Buckland, Devonshire, Aug. 2, 1622.
Dryden, John, Canons-Asby, Northamptonsh. Nov. 16, 1619.
Dukenfield, Nathaniel, Dukenfield, Cheshire, June 16, 1665.
×Dundas, Rt. Hon. Law. Aske-Hall, Yorksh. Nov. 23, 1762.
×Duntze, John, Rockbere-House, near Exeter, Oct. 29, 1774.
Dyer, John, St. James's-street, July 6, 1678.
Dyke, John Dixon, Lullingstone, Kent, March 3, 1677.
East, William, Hall-Place, Berks, June 3, 1766.
×Eden, John, Windleston, Durham, November 13, 1672.
Eden, Robert, Gov. of Maryland, America, Sept. 10, 1776.
×Edmonstone, Arch. Duntreath, Stirlingshire, May 3, 1774.
Edwards, Thomas, Grete, Shropshire, Feb. 12, 1645.
×Egerton, Thomas, Heaton, Lancashire, April 5, 1617.
Eliot, John, M D Peembee. and Cecil-str. London, July 25, 1778.
Elton, Abraham, Bristol, Somersetshire, October 3, 1717.
Elwes, Henry, Brentford End, Middlesex, June 20, 1660.
Englefield, Henry, White Nigh's, Berkshire, Nov. 25, 1612.
Evelyn, Frederick, Wotton, Surry, Aug. 6, 1713.
Etherington, Hen. Kingston upon Hull, Yorksh. Nov. 11, 1775.
Everard, Hugh, Bromfield Green, Essex, Jan. 29, 1629.
Every, John, Eggington, Derbyshire, May 26, 1641.
Eversfield, Charles, Grove, Sussex, May 4, 1725.
Eyles-Styles, John, December 1, 1714.
Fagg, William, Mystole, Kent, December 11, 1660.
Farmer, George, (eldest Son of the late Capt. Farmer of the Quebec Frigate) Mount-Pleasant, Sussex, Oct. 26, 1779.
×Farnaby, Cha. Kippington, near Sevenoaks, Kent, July 21, 1726.
Fetherstonhaugh, Harry, Fetherston-Castle, Northumberland, Jan. 3, 1747.
Filmer, John, East Sutton, Kent, December 24, 1674.
×Fleming, Michael Le, Rydal, Westmoreland, Oct. 4, 1705.
Fletewood, Thomas, Martin-Sands, Cheshire, June 29, 1611.
Fludyer, Samuel, Leigh, Kent, Nov. 13, 1759.
Foley, Robert Ralph, Thorp-Lee, Surry, June 27, 1767.
′ Folkes, Martin, F. R. S. Hillington-Hall, Norf. May 3, 1774.
′ Foulis, William, Ingleby-Manor. Yorkshire, Feb. 6, 1620.
Frankland, Tho. Stockeld-Park, Yorkshire, Dec. 24, 1660.
Frederick, John, Burwood-Park, Surry, June 10, 1723.
Freke, John, resides in Ireland, June 4, 1713.
Gage, Tho. Coldham-Hall, near Bury, Suffolk, July 15, 1660.

Gerrard, Thomas, Brynn, Lancashire, May 22, 1611
Gibbes, Philip, Springhead, Barbadoes, May 30, 1774
Gibbons, William, Stanwell-Place, Middlesex, Apr. 21, 1750
×Gideon, Sampson, Abington-Hall, Cambridgeshire, May 19, 1759.
Glyn, George, Ewell, Surrey, Sept. 25, 1759.
Gooch, Thomas, Benacre-Hall, Suffolk, and Birmingham, Warwickshire, Nov. 4, 1746.
Goodricke, John, Ribston-Hall and Bramham Park, Yorkshire, Aug. 14, 1641.
Gordon, Samuel, Newark, Nottinghamshire, August 21, 1764.
Goring, Henry, Highden, Sussex, July 29, 1627.
×Gough, Henry, Edgbaston, Warwickshire, March 29, 1728.
Graham, Bellingham, Norton-Conyers, Yorksh. Nov. 17, 1662.
Gresley, Nigel, Knypersley, Shropshire, June 29, 1611.
Gresham, John, Titsey, near Limpsfield, Surry, July 31, 1660.
Grey, Henry, Howick, Northumberland, Jan. 11, 1746.
×Guise, Wm. Rendcombe, Gloucestershire, July 10, 1661.
Gunning, Robert, K. B. Eltham, Kent, Oct. 27, 1778.
Haggerstone, Thomas, Haggerstone, Durham, Aug. 15, 1643.
Hales, Edward, St. Stephen's, near Canterbury, Kent, June 29, 1611.
Hales, Philip, July 12, 1660.
Hales, John, Lincoln, August 28, 1660.
Halford, Charles, Wistow, Leicestershire, Dec. 18, 1641.
Halton, William, Hertford, near Huntingdon, Sept. 12, 1642.
Hamilton, John, Marlborough-House, Portsmouth, July 6, 1776.
Hanham, William Tho. Winbourn, Dorsetsh. May 24, 1667.
Hanmer, Walden, Hanmer, Flintshire, May 3, 1774.
×Harbord, Harbord, Gunton, Norf. March 22, 1746.
Harland, Robert, Spreughton, Suffolk, March 19, 1771.
Harpur, Harry, Caulk-Hall, Derbyshire, Sept. 8, 1626.
Harrington, James, Bourton, Gloucester, June 29, 1611.
Hatton, Thomas, Long-Stanton, Cambridgesh. July 5, 1641.
Hawkins, Cæsar, Kelston, Somerset, July 25, 1778.
Head, Edmund, June 9, 1676.
Heathcote, Gilbert, Normanton, Rutlandsh. Jan. 19, 1733.
Heathcote, Thomas, F. R. S. Hursley, Hants, Aug. 19, 1733.
Heron, Thomas, Bowlby, Yorkshire, Nov. 28, 1662.
Heron, Rt. Hon. Richard, Newark, Nottingham. July 25, 1778.
Hesketh, Robert, Rufford, Lancashire, May 6, 1761.
Hesilrigge, Robert, Noseley-Hall, Leicestershire, July 21, 1619.
Hewet, Thomas, Potton, Bedfordshire, Oct. 11, 1621.
Heyman, Peter, Lancashire, Aug. 12, 1641.
Hickman, Nevil Geo. Thonock, Lincolnsh. Nov. 16, 1643.
Hicks, John Baptist, Hertfordshire, July 21, 1619.
Hildyard, Robert, Winestead, Yorkshire, June 25, 1660.

Hill, Rowland, Hawkestone, Shropshire, Jan. 20, 1727.
✗Hoghton Henry, F.R.S. Hoghton, Lancashire, May 22, 1611.
Holte, Charles, Erdington-Hall, Warwicksh. Nov. 25, 1612.
Honywood, John, Evington, Kent, July 19, 1660.
Hood, Samuel, Catherington, Hants, May 19, 1778.
Hort, John, late of Castle-strange, Middlesex, Aug. 29, 1767.
Horton, Watts, Chadderton, Lancashire, Jan. 21, 1764.
Hoskyns, Hungerford, Harwood, Herefordshire, Dec. 18, 1676.
Hudson, Charles, Eltham, Kent, July 3, 1660.
Hughes, Richard, Southampton, July 17, 1773.
Hulse, Edward, Bremer, Hants, Feb. 7, 1739.
Hume, Abraham, Wormlybury, Herts, April 4, 1769.
Hunlocke, Henry, Wingerworth, Derbysh. Feb. 28, 1643.
Jacob, Hildebrand, Yew Hall, Oxfordsh. Jan. 11, 1665.
✗James, William, F. R. S. Eltham, Kent, July 25, 1778.
Ibberson, James, Denton, Yorkshire, June 2, 1748.
Jebb, Rich. M.D. F. A.S. Trent Place, Barnet, Mid. July 25, 1778.
Jenkinson, Banks, Oxford, May 18, 1661.
Jerningham, William, Coffey-Hall, Norfolk, Oct. 16, 1621.
Johnson, John, New-York, America, Nov. 27, 1755.
Jones, William, Ramsbury, Wilts, May 3, 1774.
Isham, Justinian, Lamport, Northamptonsh. May 30, 1627.
Kaye, John Lyster, Grainge, Yorksh. Feb. 4, 1642.
Kemp, William, Norwich, Norfolk, March 14, 1642.
Keyt, Tho. Char. Ebrington, Gloucestersh. Dec. 22, 1660.
Knatchbull, Ed. Mersham Hatch, Kent, Aug. 4, 1641.
Knollys, Francis, Thame, Oxfordshire, April 1, 1754.
Knowles, Charles-Henry, Oct. 31, 1765.
Lade, John, Warbleton, Sussex, March 14, 1758.
Lake, James-Winter, Edmonton, Middlesex, Oct. 17, 1711.
Lambert, John, Paris, Feb. 5, 1711.
Langham, James, Cottesbroke, Northamp. June 7, 1660.
Langley, Haldanby, Higham-Gobion, Bedfordsh. May 26, 1641.
Laroche, James, Over, Gloucestershire, Aug. 24, 1776.
✗Lawley, Robert, Cavewell, Staffordshire, Aug. 16, 1641.
Lawson, Hen. Brough-Hall, Yorkshire, July 6, 1665.
Lawson, Gilfred, Brayton-Hall, Cumberl. Mar. 31, 1688.
Lee, Wm. Hartwell, Buckinghamsh. Aug. 16, 1660.
Legard, John, Ganton, Yorkshire, Dec. 29, 1660.
Leicester, John Fleming, Tabley, Cheshire, Aug. 10, 1660.
Leigh, Egerton, Manchester, Lancashire, May 15, 1773.
✗Leighton, Charlton, Watlesborough, Shropsh. Mar. 2, 1693.
Leith, Alexander, Burgh St. Peter, Norfolk, Nov. 11, 1775.
‹Lemon, William, Carelew, Cornwall, May 3, 1774.
‹Lippincot, Henry, Stoke-Bishop, Gloucestersh. July 25, 1778.
Littleton, Edw. Pillaton-Hall, Staffordsh. June 21, 1627.

Lloyd, Edward, Pengwern, Flintſhire, July 25, 1778.
XLong, Ja. Tylney, Draycot-Cerne, Wilts, Sept. 1, 1662.
Loraine, Wm. Kirk-Harle, Northumberland, Sept. 26, 1664,
XLowther, James, Lowther-hall, Weſtmoreland, June 11, 1642.
Lowther, Rev. Wm. Swillington, Yorkſhire, Aug. 22, 1764.
Lyde, Lionel, Ayot St. Lawrence, Herts, Sept. 19, 1772.
Mackworth, Henry, Lynn Regis, Norfolk, June 4, 1619.
XMackworth, Herbert, F. R. S. of the Gnoll, Glamorgan-
  ſhire, Aug. 24, 1776.
Mainwaring, Henry, Pever, Cheſhire, Nov. 22, 1660.
Mann, Horatio, Envoy Extraord. at Florence, March 3, 1755,
Major, John, Worlingworth, Suffolk, July 15, 1765.
Mannock, Thomas, Gifford's-Hall, Suffolk, June 1, 1627.
Manſell, Ed. Vaughan, Trinſaran, Carmarthenſh. Feb. 22, 1697.
Manſell, Wm. Iſchoed, Carmarthenſh. Jan. 14, 1622.
Markham, Ja. John, Sedgebroke, Lincolnſh. Aug. 15, 1642.
Martin, Mordaunt, Long-Melford, Suffolk, Mar. 28, 1667.
XMawbey, Joſeph, Botleys, Surry, July 30, 1765.
XMiddleton, Wm. Belſay-Caſtle, Northumb. Oct. 14, 1664.
Mill, Rev. Charles, Biſham-Abbey, Bucks, Dec. 31, 1619.
Millbank, Ralph, Halnaby, Yorkſhire, Aug. 7, 1661.
Miller, Thomas, Chicheſter, Suſſex, Oct. 29, 1705.
Milner, Wm. Nun-Appleton, Yorkſhire, Feb. 26, 1717.
Mitchell, Andrew, Weſt-ſhore, Shetland, June 19, 1724.
Moleſworth, William, Pencarrow, Cornwall, July 19, 1689,
Molineux, William, Wellow, Nottinghamſh. June 29, 1611.
Monnoux, Philip, Sandy, Bedfordſh. Dec. 4, 1660.
Montgomery, Wm. Macbiehill, Tweedaleſhire, North Britain,
  March 28, 1774.
Moore, John, Fawley, Berkſh. May 21, 1627.
Moore, John, K. B. Vice-Admiral of White, Mar. 4, 1766.
Mordaunt, John, Walton, Warwickſhire, June 29, 1611.
More, William, More-Hall, Lancaſhire, Nov. 22, 1675.
XMoſtyn, Roger, Moſtyn, Flintſh. Aug. 3, 1660.
Moſtyn, Pyers, Talacre, Flintſh. Apr. 28, 1670.
Muſgrave, Philip, F. R. S. Eden-Hall, Cumb. June 29, 1611.
Naper, Cha. Sowdley-houſe, Buckinghamſh. Feb. 25, 1682.
Nelthrop, John, Barton, Lincolnſhire, May 10, 1666.
Newdigate, Roger, Arbury, Warwickſh. July 24, 1677.
Northcote, Stafford, Hayne, Devonſh. July 16, 1641.
O'Carrol, John, Dalton, Yorkſhire, Feb. 18, 1742.
Oglander, William, Nunwell, Iſle of Wight, Dec. 12, 1665.
O'Neil, Randal, Upper Clanaboys, Ireland, Nov. 13, 1643.
Oſborne, George, Chickſands, Bedfordſh. Feb. 11, 1661.
Owen, Wm. Orielton, Pembrokeſh. Aug. 11, 1641.
Oxenden, Henry, Broome, Kent, May 8, 1678.

Packington, Herb. Perrot, Weftwood, Worcefterfhire, June 22, 1620.
✗Pallifer, Hugh, the Vatch, Bucks, June 25, 1773.
Palmer, Charles-Harcourt, Dorney-Court, Buckinghamfhire, June 29, 1621.
Palmer, John, Carleton, Northamptonfh. June 7, 1660.
Parker, Rev. Henry, D.D. Rector of Glympton, and Rother-field Gray, Oxfordfhire, July 1, 1681.
Parkyns, Tho. Bunny, Nottinghamfh. May 18, 1681.
Parfons, Mark, Epfom, Surry, Apr. 9, 1661.
Paul, Onefiphorus, Woodchefter, Gloucefterfh. Sept. 3. 1762.
Payne, Gillies, Tempsford-Hall, Bedfordfh. Oct. 31, 1737.
Peachy, James, Weft-dean, Suffex, March 21, 1737.
Pennington, Jof. Muncafter, Cumberl. June 21, 1676.
✗Pennyman, James, Beverley, Yorkfhire, Feb. 22, 1663.
Pepperell, Wm. Bofton, New-England, Oct. 29, 1774.
Perrot, Richard, Richmond, Surry, July 1, 1716.
Pefhall, John, near Halefowen, Salop, Nov. 25, 1612.
Peyton, Yelverton, Southampton, May 22, 1611.
Peyton, Henry, Doddington, Ifle of Ely, Auguft 24, 1776.
Pile, Seymour, Axford, Wiltfhire, September 12, 1628.
Playters, John, Sotterly, Suffolk, Auguft 13, 1623.
Pole, John, Shute, Devonfhire, Sept. 12, 1628.
Poole, Ferdinando, Lewes, Suffex, Oct. 25, 1677.
Preftwich, Elias, Holme, Lancafhire, April 25, 1644.
Price, Charles, of Rofe-Hall, Jamaica, Jan. 16, 1768.
Prideaux, John, Netherton, Devonfhire, July 17, 1622.
Pringle, John, M.D. F.R.S. Pall-Mall, June 3, 1766.
Proctor, Thomas Beauchamp, Langley Park, Norfolk, Feb. 20, 1745.
Pryce, Edw. Manly, New-Town-Hall, Montgomeryfh. Aug. 15, 1628.
✗Ramfden, John, Byrom, Yorkfhire, Nov. 30, 1689.
Raymond, Cha. Valentine Houfe, Effex, May 3, 1774.
Read, John, Shipton, Oxfordfhire, March 14, 1641.
Rich, Thomas, Sunning, Berkfhire, March 20, 1641.
Rich, Robert, Stondon, Effex, Jan. 24, 1676.
Richards, Philip, in Spain, Feb. 22, 1684.
Riddell, James, LL.D. Sunart, Argylefh. July 25, 1778.
✗Ridley, Matthew White, Blagden, Northumb. May 6, 1756.
Rivers-Gay, Rev. Peter, Woolwich, Kent, July 19, 1621.
Robinfon, George, Cranford, Northamptonfh. June 22, 1660.
Robinfon, Norton, Newby, Yorkfhire, Feb. 13, 1690.
Robinfon, William, Edgeley, Yorkfhire, March 10, 1731.
✗Rodney, Geo. Bridges, Gr. Alresfrd, Hants, Jan. 21, 1764.
✗Rogers, Fred. Blachford, Devonfhire, Feb. 21, 1699.
✗Rous, John, Henham-Hall, Suffolk, Aug. 17, 1660.

xRumbold, Thomas, Woodhall, He ts, March, 27, 1779.
xRuſhout, John, Northwick, Worceſterſhire, June 17, 1661.
Ruſſell, John, Checkers, Bucks, Jan. 19, 1629.
St. Aubin, John, Clowance, Cornwall, Dec. 11, 1671.
St. John, Henry Paulet, Farley, Hants, Sept. 19, 1772.
St. Quintin, William, Scamſton, Yorkſhire, March 8, 1642.
Samwell, Thomas, Upton, Northamptonſhire, Dec. 22, 1675.
xSavile, George, F. R. S. Ruſford, Nottingh. June 29, 1611.
Scot, Wm. Mezangere in Normandy, Auguſt o, 1653.
Sebright, John, Beachwood, Herefordſhire, Dec. 20, 1626.
Shaw, John, Eltham, Kent, April 15, 1665.
Sheffield, John, Normanby, Lincolnſhire, March 1, 1755.
Shelly, Rt. Hon. John, Michael-Grove, Suſſex, May 22, 1611.
xShuckburgh, Geo. F.R.S. Shuckburgh, Warw. June 26, 1660.
Skipwith, Peyton, Preſtwood in Virginia, Dec. 20, 1622.
Skipwith, Tho. George, Newbold-Hall, Warw. Oct. 25, 1670.
Smith, Jarrit, Briſtol, Somerſetſhire, Jan. 27, 1763.
Smith, John, F.R.S. Sydling St. Nicholas, Dorſet. May 3, 1774.
Smyth, ———, Hill-Hall, Eſſex, Nov. 28, 1661.
xSmyth, Robert, Beer-Church-Hall, Eſſex, March 30, 1665.
Smyth, Robert, Farnham, Suffolk, Dec. 2, 1714.
Smythe, Edward, Acton-Purnell, Shropſhire, Feb. 23, 1660.
Soame, Peter, Haydon, Eſſex, Feb. 5, 1685.
Standiſh, Frank, Duxbury, Lancaſhire, Feb. 8, 1677.
Stanley, John-Thomas, Alderly, Cheſhire, June 25, 1660.
Stanley, William, Hooton, Cheſhire, June 17, 1661.
Stapleton, Tho. Greys Ct. near Henley, Oxfordſh. Dec. 20, 1679.
Stapylton, John, Myton, Yorkſhire, June 22, 1660.
xStepney, John, Llanelly, Carmarthenſh. Nov. 24, 1621.
Stonehouſe, Rev. James Radley, Berkſhire, May 7, 1628.
Strickland, George, Boynton, Yorkſhire, July 30, 1641.
Style, Charles Wateringbury, Kent, April 21, 1627.
xSutton, Richard, Norwood-Park, Notts, Sept. 25, 1772.
Swynburne, Edw. Chapheaton, Northumberland, Sept. 26, 1660.
xSymons, Rich. the Meend, Herefordſhire, May 3, 1774.
Tancred, Thomas, Brampton, Yorkſhire, Nov. 17, 1662.
Taylor, John, F.R.S. of Liſſon-hall, Jamaica, July 25, 1778.
Tempeſt, Henry, Tong, Yorkſhire, May 25, 1664.
Temple, Richard, Commiſſioner of the Navy, Nov. 25, 1612.
Thomas, Edmund, Wenvoe, Glamorganſh. Dec. 24, 1694.
Thomas, George, Yapton-Place, Suſſex, Sept. 6, 1766.
Thompſon, Charles, K. B. Chiſelhurſt, Kent, Jan. 4, 1622.
xThorold, John, Syſton Park, Lincolnſhire, Aug. 24, 1642.
Throckmorton, Rob. Bucknall, Berks, Sept. 1, 1642.
Tichborne, Henry, Tichborne, Hampſhire, March 8, 1621.
Trelawney, Rev. Harry, Trelawney, Cornwall, July 1, 1628.

✕ Trevelyan, John. Nettlecombe, Somersetshire, Jan. 24, 1662.
Trollope, Thomas. Casewick, Lincolnshire, Feb. 5, 1642.
Turner, John, Workham, Norfolk, April 27, 1727.
• Turner, Gregory-Page, Blackheath, Kent, Aug. 24, 1733.
Twysden, Wm. East Peewham, Kent, June 29, 1611.
Twysden, John Papillon, Bradbourne, Kent, June 13, 1666.
| Tynte, Charles Kemeys, Hanewell, Somersetsh. Jan. 7, 1674.
Vandeput, George, Lamptea., Middlesex, Nov. 7, 1723.
✕ Van-Neck, G. W. Heveningham, Suffolk, Dec. 10, 1751.
Vavasor, Walter, Haslewood, Yorkshire, Oct. 24, 1628.
Vincent, Francis, Stoke-Dabernon, Surry, July 26, 1620.
Vyvyan, Richard. Trelowarren, Cornwall, Feb. 12, 1645.
✕ Wake, Wm. Courteen-Hall, Northamptonsh. Dec. 5, 1621.
Warburton, Peter, Arley, Cheshire, June 27, 1660.
✕ Warren, John Borlase, Little Marlow, Bucks, May 20, 1775.
Warrender, Patrick, Lockhead, Scotland, June 2, 1715.
Watson, Charles, Fel. of All Souls Col. Oxford, Mar. 22, 1760.
Webb, John, F. R. S. April 2, 1644.
Webster, Godfrey, Battle-Abby, Sussex, May 21, 1703.
Welcome, Anthony, ———, March 19, 1700.
Wheate, Jacob, Leachlade, Gloucestershire, May 2, 1696.
Wheeler, Wm. Lemington Hastings, Warwicksh. Aug. 11, 1660.
Whichcote, Christopher, Aswarby, Lincolnshire, Apr. 2, 1660.
Williams, David, Sarrat, in Hertfordshire, May 4, 1664.
Williams, Hugh, Nant, Carnarvonshire, June 17, 1661.
Williams, Edward, Langoed-Castle, Brecknocksh. Nov. 2, 1774.
✕ Williams-Wynne, Watkin, Winstay, Denbighsh. July 6, 1688.
Williams, Booth, Clapton, Northamptonsh. April 6, 1746.
Williamson, Hedw. Monkweremouth, Durham, June 3, 1642.
Willis, William, London, Dec. 15, 1641.
Wilmot, Edw. M. D. Chaddedon, Derbysh. Feb. 17, 1759.
Wilmot, Robert, Osmalton, near Derby, Sept. 19, 1772.
Wilson, Thomas Spencer, East-Bourne, Sussex, Mar. 4, 1661.
Winn, George Allanson, Little Warley, Essex; Branehamâ€”
Biggin, Yorkshire, Aug. 24, 1776.
Winnington, Edw. Stantford-c. Worcestersh. Feb. 28, 1755.
Wintringham, Clifton, F. R. S. Physi. to the King, Oct. 29, 1774.
Wodehouse, John, Kemberley, Norfolk, June 29, 1611.
Wolsely, Wm. Wolsely, Staffordshire, Nov. 24, 1628
Wolstenholme, Fran. (late of Enfield, Middlesex) Jan. 10, 1665.
Wombwell, George, Wombwell, Yorksh. July 25, 1778.
Woolaston, Isaac Lawrence, Lowesby, Leicestersh. Jan. 17, 1749.
Woolf, Jacob, Penton, Lincolnshire, Oct. 18, 1766.
✕ Worsley, Rd. F. R. S. Appledurcombe, I. of Wight, June 29, 1611.
Wray, Cecil, Summer Castle, Lincolnshire, Nov. 25, 1617.
Wrey, Bourchier, Tawstock, Devonshire, June 30, 1618.
Wright, James, Woodford, Essex, Oct. 12, 1772.

Wright, James, Gov. of Georgia, Dec. 8, 1772.
×Wrottelley, John, Wrottefley, Staffordſh. Aug. 30, 1642.
Wyche, Cyril, Duchy of Holſtein, Dec. 20, 1729.
Wynne, John, Lees-Wood, Flintſhire, Auguſt 9, 1731.
Wynne, Rowland, Noſtell, Yorkſhire, Dec. 3, 1660.
Wyvill, Marm. Conſtable-Burton, Yorkſhire, Nov. 25, 1612.
Yeo, William, Pyrland, Somerſetſhire, June 16, 1759.
Yeomans, Rev. Robert, Vicar of Pittleworth, Hants, Jan. 12, 1665.
×Yonge, G. Eſtcott, Devon. F.R.S. Sept. 26, 1661.
Young, William, Delaford, near Iver, Bucks, Mar. 20, 1769.

BARONETS of NOVA SCOTIA, reſident in England.
Carr, Robert, Bath, July 31, 1637.
×Gaſcoigne, Thomas, Parlington, Yorkſhire, 1622.
Longueville, Thomas, Preſtatin, Flintſhire, —, 1638.
Meredith, Wm. Henbury, Cheſhire, Jan. 2, 1640.
Muſgrave, Wm. Hayton-Caſtle, Cumberland, Oct. 20, 1628.
Pickering, Edward, in Ireland.
Pilkington, Michael, Chevet, Yorkſhire, June 29, 1635.
Slingſby, Tho. Turner, Scriven-Park, Yorkſhire, Oct. 23, 1638.

Beſides the above, there are ſeveral to whom the Dignity of Baronet has been granted, but neither they nor their Succeſſors have taken out their Patents, as Sir Robert Cornwall, (who was created in Hanover by K. George II.) and Sir James Bunce, &c.

The Rev. the DEANS, &c. in England and Wales. [In the King's Gift, except thoſe in Wales, which are in the Gift of the Biſhops.]

PROVINCE of Canterbury.

HON. Ja. Cornwallis, LL D
Briſt. John Hallam, A M
Chicheſter, C. Harward, D D
Ely, William Cooke, D D
Exeter, Jeremiah Mills, D D
Glouc. Joſiah Tucker, D D
Hereford, Nat. Wetherell, D D
Lichf. Baptiſt Proby, D D
Lincoln, the Bp of Glouceſter

London, St. Paul's, the Biſhop of Briſtol.
Weſtminſt. the Bp of Rocheſter
Windſor, Hon. John Harley, D I
Norwich, Philip Lloyd, D D
Oxford, Chriſt-Church, Lewi
Bagot, L L D
Peterb. Charle Tarrant, D D
Rocheſt. Richard Cuſt, D D
Saliſbury, Rowney Noel, D D
Wells, Ld. Francis Seymour.
Wincheſt. Newton Ogle, D
Guernſey, Elias Criſpien.
Jerſey, Fra. Le Breton, A M
Worc. Robert Foley, D D

(201)

St. Asaph, Wm Davies Shipley, M A
Bangor, Tho. Lloyd, D D
  Precentor of St. Davids.
Francis Wollaston, LL B
  Archdeacon of Llandaff,
William Adams, D D
  Precentor of Llandaff.
Robert Price, A M
  PROVINCE *of* YORK.
John Fountayne, D D
Carlisle, Thomas Percy, D D
Chester, Wm Smith, D D
Durham, Hon. and Rev. W. Digby, LL D

The Worshipful the CHANCELLORS *of the several Dioceses.*
PROVINCE *of* Canterbury.
Peter Calvert, LL D
  Dean of the Arches.
William Wynne, L L D.
  Vicar General.
Andrew Coltee Ducarrell, L L D *Commissary.*
Bristol, Ja. Backhouse, B D
Chich. Drake Hollingbery A M
Ely, Wm. Compton, L L D
Exeter, Jam. Carrington, L L B
Glouc. Jam. Benson, L L D
Hereford, Geo. Harris, L L D
Litchfield & Coventry, R. Smallbroke, LL D
Lincoln, Francis Simpson, LLD
London Wm Wynne, L L D
Norwich, Geo. Sandby, D D
Oxford, Benj. Wheeler, D D
Peterb. Thomas Crofts, LL D
Rochester, W. Burrell, L L D
Salisbury, ×Sir Cha. Gould, Knt. L L B
Winchest. Geo. Harris, L L D
Wells, Edward Willes, L L B
Worcester, W. Burrell, L L D
St. Asaph, Wm Shipley, A M
Bangor, Geo. Harris, L L D
St. Davids, Rd. Beadon, B D
Landaff, Wm. Thomas, A M

PROVINCE *of* YORK,
York, Joseph Banks, LL B
Carlisle, Rd. Burn, L L D
Coester, S. Peploe, L L D
Durham, Geo. Harris, LL D
Richmond, ×Wm Eden, A M

The ARCHDEACONS *in the several Dioceses.*
[*All appointed by the Bishops of those Dioceses to which they belong.*]
Province of CANTERBURY.
REV. Wm Backhouse, D D
  BATH and WELLS 3.
Wells, William Willes, M A
Taunton, Tho. Camplin, L L D
Bath, John Chapman, D D
  BRISTOL 1.
Dorset, Geo. Watson Hand, A M
  CHICHESTER 2.
Chichester, T. Hollingbery, D D
Lewes, John Courtail, A M
  ELY 1.
Richard Watson, D D. F.R.S
  EXETER 4.
Exeter, Bishop of Exeter.
Cornwall, J. Sleech, A M
Totnefs, Ralph Barnes, A M
Barnstaple, W. Hole, B D
  GLOUCESTER 1.
James Webster, M A
  HEREFORD 2.
Hereford, Hon. J. Harley, D D
Salop, Robert Clive, A M
  LITCHFIELD and Cov. 4
Salop, Egerton Leigh, A M
Derby, Hen. Egerton, A M
Staff. John Carver, L L B
Covent. N. Fotheringham, A M
  LINCOLN 6.
Bedford, Hadley Coxe, A M
Bucks, Luke Heslop, B D
Hunting. Mich. Tyson, A M
Lincoln, John Gordon, D D
Leicest. James Bickham, D D
Stow, John Towne, B D

S

LONDON 5.
London, Richard Beadon, D D
Essex, James Waller, D D
Middlesex, John Hotham, D.D.
Colchest. Ant. Hamilton, D D
St. Albans, Ja. Ibbetson, D D
    NORWICH 4.
Norwich, J. Berney, D D
Norfolk, Tho. Warburton, M A
Suffolk, Hen. Goodall, D D
Sudbury, J. Chapman, D D
    OXFORD 1.
Tho. Randolph, D D
    NORTHAMPTON 1.
William Browne, D D
    ROCHESTER 1.
John Law, D D
    SALISBURY 3.
Berks, Wm Dodwell, D D
Sarum, Wm Whitworth A M
Wilts, Arthur Coham, A M
    WINCHESTER 2.
Winchester, Th. Balguy, D D
Surry, Bishop of Oxford
    WORCESTER 1.
John Warren, LL D
    ST. DAVIDS 4.
St. Davids, Cha. Moss, A M
Carmar. Geo. Holcombe, A M
Cardigan, T. Vincent, A M
Brecon, Edw. Edwards, A M
    ST. ASAPH 1.
Bishop of *St. Asaph*.
    BANGOR 3.
Anglesea, Bishop of *Bangor*.
Bangor, Bishop of *Bangor*.
Merioneth, John Ellis, A M
    LANDAFF.
William Adams, D D
    PROVINCE of YORK 4.
Cleveland, F. Blackburn, A M
E. Rid. Rob. Oliver, A M
Nottingh. Richard Kaye, D D
York, Will. Cooper, DD FRS
Carlisle, John Law, A M
    CHESTER 2.
Chester, Abel Ward, A. M.
Richmond, S. Peploe, D D

DURHAM 2.
Durham, Sam. Dickens, D D
Northumb. John Sharp, D D

PREBENDS, &c. *in his Ma-*
jesty's Gift.
    LONDON. ST. PAUL'S.
    Canons Residentiary (4.)
THE Bishop of Bristol,
    Dean.
Christopher Wilson, D D
John Douglas, D D FRS
John Jeffreys, D D
    WESTMINSTER *Prebends*.
Thomas Wilson, D D
John Taylor, L L D
Sir Rd. Cope, Bt. DD, *Sub-Dean*
John Blair, L L D FRS
Joseph Hoare, D D F R S
William Bell, D D
William Stockwood, A M
Charles Wake, L L D.
Thomas Marriot, D D
Nathan Wetherell, D D
Hon. N. Boscawen, D D
Robert Clive, M A
    WINDSOR *Canons*.
John Bostocke, D D
John Lockman, D D
Edward Barnard, D D
Thomas Hurdis, D D
Philip Du Val, D D FRS
William Buller, A M
John James Majendie, DD FRS
John Hallam, A M
Thomas Bray, D D
Anthony Shepherd, D D FRS
Bishop of Landaff
William Arnald, B D
    CANTERBURY *Prebends*.
*Thomas Tanner, D D
William Tatton, D D
Richard Sutton, D D
Lynford Caryl, D D
Heneage Dering, D D
*John Benson, D D

*George Berkeley, L L D
Bennet Storer, D D
Richard Palmer, D D
William Barford, D D
Richard Lucas, D D
Everard Buckworth, LL D
*In the Archbishop's Gift.
WORCESTER Prebends.
William Jennings, B D
Thomas Evans, D D
†Thomas Randolph, D D
John Young, D D
Gregory Parry, A M
Ja. Stillingfleet, A M

Tho. Fountaine, A M
Matthew Lamb, D D
Ja. Torkington, LL D
John Carver, LL D
OXFORD.
Canons of Christchurch.
Benj. Kennicott, D D F R S
Edward Smallwell, D D
Henry Bathurst, LL D
§Benjamin. Wheeler, D D
William Flemington, D D
Cyril Jackson, B D. F R S
Arthur Onslow, B D
‡ George Jubb, D D

†Annexed to the Margaret Professorship, in Oxford, by Act of Parl. ‡ As King's Heb. Prof. § As King's Profes. of Div.

The Lord Mayor, Aldermen, &c. of the City of London, with the Time of their Election, the Wards over which they preside and their Places of Residence.

THE Rt. H. Sir WATKIN LEWES, Knt. Lord Mayor, elected Ald. of Lime-Street Ward in 1772; Mansion House.

Bridge without	45	Robert Alsop, Esq; *Father of the City.* Great Marlborough Street.
Portsoken	61	×‡Rt. Hon. Tho. Harley, *Aldersgate-Str.*
Bread street	65	Brass Crosby, Esq; *Chatham - Square, Black-Friars-Bridge.*
Bishopsgate	69	James Townsend, Esq; *Bruce-Castle*
Queenhithe	72	×Fred. Bull, Esq; *Leadenhall-Street.*
Farringdon without	69	×John Wilkes, Esq; *Princes co. Westm.*
Langborn	69	×John Sawbridge, Esq; *N. Burlington st.*
Aldersgate	66	*Sir Tho. Hallifax, Knt. *Birchin-Lane*
Cripplegate	67	‡Sir James Esdaile, Knt. *Bunhill-Row*
Castle-Baynard	67	‡Samuel Plumbe, Esq; *Foster-Lane.*
Cornhill	67	‡Brackley Kennett, Esq; *Pall-Mall*
Recorder, 1779	}	James Adair, Esq; *Queen-Squre, Bloomsbury.* Salary 600l. per Ann.
Bassishaw	72	†Wm. Plomer, Esq; *George st. Minories*
Walbrook	73	†‡Nathaniel Thomas, Esq; *Bridge-street Black-Fryars*
Coleman-Street	73	†Robert Peckham, Esq; *Austin Friars*
Cordwainer	74	†×G. Hayley, Esq; *Ayliff st. Goodman's fi.*
Vintry	74	×†Nath. Newnham, Esq; *Paper-Buildings, Temple*
Bread-Street	76	††‡RichardClark, Esq; *New Broad-Street*
Bridge within	76	T. Wooldridge, Esq; *Portland-street*

Cheap 80 William Crichton, Efq; *Philpot lane*
N. B. *All before the Recorder have paſſed the chair;—thoſe marked thus* † *have ſerved the office of Sheriff,—and thus* ‡ *are Colonels of the city Militia.*
SHERIFFS, T. Sainſbury and Will. Crichton, Eſqrs; Ald.
CHAMBERLAIN. ✕ John Wilkes, Eſq;
Common Serjeant, Th. Nugent, Eſq; *Town Clerk,* Wm Rix, Eſq;
Judges of the Sheriffs Court, Walter Long, Fr. Maſeres, Eſqs; 100l.
Four common Pleaders,
John Wm Roſe, John Silveſter, Alex. Luders, Jn Ahmuty, Eſqrs.
Comptroller of the chamber, Dutton Seaman, Eſq;
Collector of the City Dues at the Cuſtom-Houſe, Charles Sommers
Secondary of the Poultry compter, William Bolton, Eſq;
——— *of Wood-ſtreet ditto,* John Raincock, Eſq;
Remembrancer, Peter Roberts, Eſq; *Solic.* Mr James Roberts
Four Eſquires of the Lord Mayor's houſhold.
Sword-bearer, Heron Powney, Eſq; *Common Cryer,* W. Biſhop, Eſq;
Common Hunt, Ja. Chamneſs, Eſq; *Water bailiff,* Wm Dawſon, Eſq;
CHAMBERLAIN'S OFFICE.
Inner Office. William Montague, *principal Clerk.*
Cha. Mead, Richard Keys, *Aſſiſtants.*
Outer Office. Henry Parker, *Clerk of the Chamber.*
John Davis, *Yeoman of the chamb.* H. Groome, *Hall-keeper*

An Accurate Liſt of the Deputies and Common Council-men of the City of London, elected December 21, 1780.
This mark * *denotes the new members,* Dec. 21, 1780.

Alderſgate 8.
Jeremiah Percy, *Plumber, Dep.*
Charles Aldridge, *Goldſmith*
John Bailey, *Joiner*
Benj. Maud, *Goldſmith*
Ja. Brogden, *Goldſmith Dep.*
Nath. Wright, *Carpenter*
John Mott, *Innholder*
Thomas Iſherwood, *Stationer*
Aldgate 6.
Joſ. Partridge, *Clothworker, Dep.*
S. Thorp, *Tin-plate-worker*
Cha. Lincoln *Fletcher*
John Bellett, *Upholder*

Tho. Holdſworth, *Vintner*
Gab. Heath, *Tyler & Bricklayer*
Baſſiſhaw 4.
Gab. Leckey, *Skinner, Dep.*
Sam. Knight, *Clothworker*
John Firth, *Glover*
*Solomon Wadd, *Muſician*
Billingſgate 10.
Charles Eaſton, *Maſon, Dep.*
John Kittermaſter, *Fiſhmonger*
Wm Deane, *Merch-Taylor*
R. Barnevelt, *Merch-Taylor*
Joſiah Dornford, *Cooper*
Tho. Gorſt, *ditto*
Samuel Hanlon, *Joiner*
Thomas Dunnage, *Cutler*

Tho. Wm Preſton, *Wheelwri*.
Thomas Edgley, *Fiſhmonger*
 Biſhopſgate 14.
Edward Wix, *Tyler and Bricklayer, Dep*.
Richard Blackall, *Muſician*
Mich. Eaton, *Merch-Taylor*
John Ward, *Clothworker*
John Merry, *Draper*
Henry George, *Weaver*
John Faſſon, *Pewterer*
Wm Cooke, *Blackſmith*
Richard Draper, *Glover*
John Pinhorn, *Waxchandler*
Wm Judd, *Joiner, Dep.*
Sam. Provey, *Clothworker*
R. Bullcock, *Tin-plate-worker*
Samuel Nelme, *Vintner*
 Breadſtreet 12.
W. Saxby, *Painter-ſtainer, Dep.*
John Walker, *Ironmonger*
John Hemans, *Glover*
Wm. Bedford, *Draper*
Peter Ja. Bennett, *Goldſmith*
John James, *Dyer*
Wm Hallier, *Tin-plate-worker*
James Chapman, *Girdler*
Thomas Wright, *Innholder*
John Payne, *Goldſmith*
C. Hammerton, *Tyler & Bric.*
* Arthur Sheer Lofty, *Salter*
 Bridge 15.
Geo. Cooper, *Goldſmith, Dep.*
Sam. Baughan, *Dyer*
Jacob Wrench, *Draper*.
Marm. Thompſon, *Fiſhmonger*
Wm Rowlatt, *Glover*
Joſeph Jewſon, *Turner*
W. Anderſon, *Merch-Taylor*
C. Corderoy, *Haberdaſher*
John Cobb, *Barber*
Coles Child, *Weaver*
John Rowlatt, *Glover*
John Dowley, *Blackſmith*
Joſeph Brown, *Wheelwright*
* John Gray, *Fiſhmonger*
* Edward Smith, *Skinner*

 Broad-ſtreet 10.
J. Ellis, *Scrivener, Dep.*
Geo. Sharp, *Girdler*
James Evans, *Skinner*
Wm Acton, *Painter-ſtainer*
Pet. Nich. Friſquett, *Haberd.*
John Gibſon, *Painter-ſtainer*
Dav. Stuart, *Spectacle-maker*
John Sealy, *Grocer*
James Harris, *Painter-ſtainer*
Tho. Williams, *Wheelwright*
 Candlewick 8.
Edw. Watſon, *Founder, Dep.*
Cha. Raſhfield, *Cooper*
Robert Ward, *Goldſmith*
Peter Perchard, *Goldſmith*.
William Gill, *Stationer*
Thomas Davies, *Feltmaker*
Mathias Palling, *Joiner*
John Hotham, *Mer. h. Tayl.*
 Caſtlebaynard 10
John Hopkins, *Grocer, Dep.*
Hen. Major, Eſq; *Haberdaſher.*
R. Harris, *Tin-plate-worker*
T. Harriſon, *Stationer*
R. Manning, *Draper*
Mid. Young, *Tin-plate-worker.*
Wm Hurford, *Barber*
Tipping Rigby, *Draper*.
William Box, *Apothecary*
Will. Sharpe, *Painter-ſtainer*.
 Cheap 12.
John Smith, *Ironmonger, Dep.*
John Boydell, *Stationer*
Jn. Withers, *Tyler & Brick.*
Tho. Vezey, *Glover*
John Marlar, Eſq; *Haberdaſher.*
N. Forſter, *Merchant-Taylor*
Rich. Briſtow, *Goldſmith*
Robert Holden, *Mercer*
Rob. Mackey, Eſq; *Joine*
Edw. Pearſon, *Goldſmith*
Joſhua Wilkinſon, *Goldſm.*
* John Cowley, *Clothworker*.
 Coleman-Street 6
R. Winbolt, *Goldſmith, Dep.*
Henry Cothery, *Innholder.*

Tho. Ruffel, *Carpenter*
Wm Lewis, *ditto*
John Jacob, *Joiner*
* Wm. Chapman, *Arm. & Br.*
 Cordwainer 8.
Lake Young, *Glazier, Dep.*
Edward Beynon, *Glover*
John Barnes, *Goldsmith*
Sam. Hanning, *Carpenter*
John Chapman, *Glover*
Thomas Tilfon, *Glover*
Edward Kemble, *Salter*
* William Rowe, *Skinner*
 Cornhill 6.
Henry Parker, *Stationer*, Deputy
Wm Bythefea, *Salter*
Wm Shenton, *Merch-Taylor*
Henry Wright, *Draper*
James Bate, *Stationer*
* Wm. Nicholfon, *Needlemaker*
 Cripplegate within 8.
Henry White, *Fifhmonger, Dep.*
Edw. Dowling, *Cutler*
Wm Gifford, *Leather-feller*
Richard Mathew, *Cooper*
Ifaac Mather, *Plumber*
James Simpfon, *Glazier*
Tho. Vallance, *Stationer*
James Birt, *Upholder*
 Cripplegate without 4.
J. Banner, *Plumber*
Rob. French, *Tallow-chandl.*
Henry Banner, *Joiner*
John Hale, *Brewer*
 Dowgate 8.
Francis Hilton, *Dyer, Dep.*
Wm. Clemmons, *Barber*
Jn. Packman, *Tallow-chan.*
R. Holder, *Mufician*
William Gates, *Mafon*
Jof. Stevenfon, *Cooper*
Geo. Smirthwaite, *Innholder*
John Salter, *Plumber*
 Farringdon within 17.
John Clements, *Pewterer, Dep.*
Thomas Vanhagen, *Joiner*

Thomas Caflon, *Stationer*
Stanley, Crowder, *Stationer*
* Tho. Lidiard, *Clockmaker*
Cha. Maynard, *Upholder*
Gedaliah Gatfield, *Mufician*
Sylvanus Hall, *Currier*
John Cooke, *Mufician*
Edward Parifh, *Wheelwright*
Thomas Patrick, *Tinplate-w.*
* John Pearkes, *Fifhmonger*
W. Carter, *Merchant-Taylor*
* George Heming, *Goldfmith*
Wm. Powell, *Painterftainer*
Benj. Hamnett, *Bafket-maker*
Daniel Pinder, *Dyer*
 Farringdon without 16.
 North fide.
Rowland Atkinfon, *Wheelwright, Dep.*
Rich. Brewer, *Joiner*
Tho. Goodwin, *Painterftainer*
John Champion, *Carpenter*
William Sharpe, *Weaver*
James Branfcombe, *Dyer*
William Newman, *Currier*
* Guy Warwick, *Merchant-Taylor*
 South fide.
Thomas Thorp, *Vintner, Dept.*
Ezekiel Delight, *Vintner*
Geo. Wyatt, *Draper*
Wm Wright, *Innholder*
William Stiles, *Cock*
Tho. Burnell, *Mafon*
John Lucas, *Butcher*
William Miller, *Mafon.*
 Langborn 10.
T. Witherby, *Cooper, Dep.*
John Newman, *Joiner*
Ingham Fofter, *Ironmonger*
Geo. Maynard, *Vintner*
Chriftopher Corrall, *Goldfmith*
Peter Pope, *Haberdafher*
Thomas Burrow, *Vintner*
Edward Tutet, *Clockmaker*
George Bodley, *Fifhmonger*
Thomas Hudfon, *Carpenter*

Lime street 4.
Samuel Browne, *Draper, Dep.*
J. W. Benson, *Apothecary*,
James Sharp, *Draper*
John Hardy, *Musician*
  Portsoken 5.
Robert Harding, *Salter, Dep.*
Wm Wilson, *Gunmaker*
Joseph Wife, *Draper*
Ant. Facer Kemp, *Distiller*
* Benj Bunn, *Loriner*
  Queenhithe 6.
Wm Hur.frys, *Cooper, Dep.*
Wm Beswick, *Pavior*
Benjamin Shaw, *Cooper*
Richard Clarke, *Musician*
Robert Exam, *Leatherseller*
* Wm. Champion, *Carpenter*
  Tower 12
Cha. Wilkins, *Salter, Dep.*
William Worth, *Butcher*
Anderton Poole, *Coachmaker*
Humphry Jefferis, *Fletcher*
John Close, *Wheelwright*
James Antell, *Cooper*

Wm Bagster, *Apothecary*
Ben. Robertson, Esq; *Glover*
William Shone, *Glass-seller*
Tho. Rogers, *Spectacle-maker*
* Wm. Broadhurst, *Ironmonger*
* Wm. Surman, *Musician*
  Vintry 9.
Godfrey Wilson, *Farrier, Dep.*
Thomas Furnell, *Goldsmith*
Robert Evered, *Glover*
John Walford, *Apothecary*
Wm Wryghte, *Glover*
Lau. Holker, *Ironmonger*
G. M. Macauley, *Bowyer*
John Elmes, *Tyler & Brickl.*
James Haslam, *Fruiterer*
  Walbrook 8.
Richard Dixon, *Cooper, Dep.*
Rich. Alsager, *Clothworker*
Jona. Turner, *Leather-seller*
Tho. Axford, *Musician*
Christopher Parker, *Glover*
Robert Wyatt, *Skinner*
James Rutherford, *Baker*
John Lewis, *Clothworker*

Receiver General of the Land-Tax for City of London & Middlesex, Richard Bagot, Esq;
Deputy Receiver, Tho. Rumsey, Esq;—*The Office at the Excise Office in Broad-Street.*
Receiver General of Window-Light Tax for London and Middlesex, Robert Wilson, Esq;—*The Office in Lombard-Street.*
Receivers General of the Duties on inhabited Houses for London and Middlesex, William Brummell and Bryan Broughton, Esqrs; – *The Office, Charing-Cross.*

His Majesty's Commissioners *of the* Lieutenancy *for the* City *of* London.

The LORD MAYOR, Aldermen and Recorder for the time being: See a List *of the present*, in p. 203.

Sir Gilbert Heathcote, Bart. | Sir George Colebroke, Bart.

George Aufrere	Samuel Beachcroft	John Calvert
John Apthorpe	Jonathan Barnard	Peter Calvert
James Adams	Lyde Brown	Felix Calvert
John Boyd	XPeregrine Cust	Sir Robert Carr, Bart.

Richard Lomax Clay	Daniel Lafcelles	Thomas Selwin
Edward Davis	×Edward Lewis	John Skey
George Dealtry	Beefton Long	Thomas Smith
Thomas Dinely	Samuel Marſh	Samuel Smith
Thomas Thomas	Nathaniel Martin	William Smith
William Fauquier	James Matthias	Richard Speed
Richard Fuller	Joſeph Melliſh	Laurence Sullivan
Stephen Peter Godin	Richard Neave	John Thornton
Robert Gofling	John Nightingale	James Tierney
Thomas Hankey	Peter Nouaille	Stracy Till
Charles Harris	Edward Payne	Jn Albretch Vaſſiner
John Harriſon	James Pell	Samuel Vaughan
George Hayter	John Pott	×Hon. Tho. Walpole
Henry Hoare	George Prefcott	×Hon. Ric. Walpole
Richard Hoare	Arthur Radcliffe	Joſeph Watkins
Matthew Kenrick	Henry Raper	Thomas Wilkinſon
Ralph Knox	John Rivington	John Wilſon, Eſqrs.
×Robert Ladbroke	John Sargent	

The above Gentlemen are Eſquires by Virtue of the King's Commiſ.

Samuel Smith, Eſq. *Clerk and Treaſurer.*

Tho. Smith, Eſq; *Muſter-Maſter.* John Crocker, *Meſſenger.*

FIELD OFFICERS *and* COMMANDERS *of the Six Regiments of the City Militia.*

Firſt, Yellow Regiment, Rt. Hon. THO. HARLEY, Col.

Lieut. Col. John Favell,
Major, Philip Oriell,
1 Capt. John Lind,
2 Capt. John Crocker,
3 Capt. Tho. Thorp,
4 Capt. Peter Longes,
5 Capt. P. Oriel, *jun.*
Capt. Lieut. Char. Pickever.

Second, Red Regiment, SAMUEL PLUMBE, Eſq; Col.

Lieut. Col. William Wyatt,
Major, Edward Stone,
1 Capt. John Bayley,
2 Capt. John Willoughby
3 Capt. Wm. Surridge,
4 Capt. Wm. Ruſſel,
5 Capt. Matth. Heſſe,
Capt. Lieut. John Forfur.

Third, Orange Regiment, BRACKLEY KENNET, Eſq; Col.

Lieut. Col. Thomas Kennett,
Major, John Fuller,
1 Capt. Edward York,
2 Capt. John Difford,
3 Capt. Peter Sufflee,
4 Capt. John Bennet,
5 Capt. Nich. Simmonds.
Capt. Lieut. Tho. Latham.

Fourth, Green Regiment, Sir JAMES ESDAILE, Col.
Lieut. Col. William Howes, 3 Capt. Joseph Crich
Major, Benjamin Cole, 4 Capt. John Keene,
1 Capt. Robt. Downes, 5 Capt. James Simpson,
2 Capt. Wm Champante, Capt. Lt. Rd. Whitecombe.
Fifth, Blue Regiment, NATHANIEL THOMAS, Esq; Col.
Lieut. Col. James Harriott, 3 Capt. Charles Lincoln,
Major, Peter Sharp, 4 Capt. Robert Horne,
1 Capt. Thomas Gates, 5 Capt. Nicholas Simmons,
2 Capt. Stephen Clarke, Capt. Lieut. J. Richardson.
Sixth, White Regiment, RICHARD CLARK, Col.
Lieut. Col. James Oates, 3 Capt. John Downes,
Major, Robert Holden, 4 Capt. Thomas Davis,
1 Capt. William White, 5 Capt. Tho. Will. Preston,
2 Capt. William Lane, Capt. Lieut. John Abbot.

N. B. *The above Gentlemen are Esquires by virtue of their Commissions.*

The Honourable ARTILLERY Company.

H. is Royal Highness GEORGE, PRINCE of WALES, *Capt. Gen.*
Brass Crosby, Esq; Alderman, President.
Rt. Hon. Sir Watkin Lewes, Knt. Ld Mayor, Vice Presi.
William Plomer, Esq; Alderman, Treasurer.
The Rev. Mr. Jos. Cookson, Chaplain.
Mr. William Withy, Surgeon.
Capt. Steph. Clarke, Adjutant.
Capt. John Keen, Engineer.
Thomas Mead, Armourer.
Capt. Peter Longes, Clerk.
Mr. John Roake, Messenger.

MEMBERS of the COURT of WESTMINTER.
The Dean, the Bp of Rochester.
High Steward, The Duke of Newcastle.
Dep. Steward, Ja. Sayer, Esq;
High-Bailiff, Th. Corbett, Esq;
Dep. Bailiff, Francis Grojan. Esq;

St. Margaret's, and St. John's.
Burgesses. Nic. Spencer, Esq; Mr. J. Bacchus, Mr. R. Pearce, Mr. Tho. Wilson, Mr. R. Lewis, Mr. J. Phillips, Mr. Godfric.
Assistants. Mr Marsault, Mr. Eves, Mr. Wiggins, Mr. Price, Mr. Simpson, Mr. Snow, Mr. Wood.

St. Martin's.
Burgesses. Capt. Chr. Pinchbeck, Mr. Henry Jaffray.
Assistants. Cha. Marsh, Esq; Mr. Adams.

St. Ann's.
Burgesses. Mr. Sam. Potts, Mr. Tho. Chamberlain.
Assistants. Mr. Tho. Dobson.

St. James's.
Burgesses. Brack. Kennett, Esq; × Rob. Mackreth, Esq;
Assistants. Mr. Watlington, and Mr. Taylor.

St. George's.
Burgess. Mr. G. Shakespeare.
Assistant. Mr. Wm. Evans.

(210)

St. Paul's, Covent Garden.
Mr. George Leigh.
Affiftant. Mr. John Lucas.
  St. Clements.
Burgefs. Mr Sampf. Rainsforth
Affiftant. Mr. Ralph Williams.

High Conftable, Mr. W. Snell.
Town Clerk, Mr. John Jackfon.
Court Keeper, Mr. William Jackfon.
Cryer and Mace-Bearer, Griffith Rowland.

COMMITTEE OF CITY LANDS.

ALDERMEN.

Brafs Crofby, Efq; *Chatham-Square.*
John Sawbridge, Efq; *New Burlington ftreet*
Sir T. Hallifax, Kt. *Birchin-lane*
Samuel Plumbe, Efq; *Fofter-lane*
Brackley Kennett, Efq; *Pall-mall*
Wm. Plomer, Efq; *Aldgate*
Robert Peckham, Efq; *Auftin-Friars*
Richard Clark, Efq; *New Broad-Street*
John Burnell, Efq; *Green-Street, Leicefter-Fields.*
John Hart, Efq; *Thames-ftreet*
Evan Pugh, Efq; *Bifhopf-gate-ftreet*
Thomas Sainfbury, Efq; *Sheriff, Ludgate-Hill*

COMMONERS.

Mr. Nath. Wright, *Alderfgate*
Mr Charles Lincoln, *Aldgate*

Mr *Dep.* G. Leckey, *Baffifhaw*
Mr J Kittermafter, *Billingfg.*
Mr J. Merry, *Bifhopfgate*
Mr John Hemans, *Bread-ftr.*
Mr Clement Corderoy, *Bridge*
Mr John Sealy, *Broad-ftreet*
Mr *Dep.* Edw. Watfon, *Candlewick*
Mr *Dep.* J. Hopkins, *Caftlebayn.*
Mr Nath. Forlter, *Cheapfide*
Mr John Jacob, *Coleman-ftr.*
Mr John Chapman, *Cordwainer*
Mr Henry Wright, *Cornhill*
Mr *Dep.* H. White, *Cripplegate*
Mr William Gates, *Dowgate*
Mr Geo. Gatfield, *Farringdon-within*
Mr *Dep.* Rowland Atkinfon, *Farringdon without*
Mr Tho. Burrow, *Langhorn*
Mr *Dep.* Rob. Harding, *Portfoken*
Mr Wm. Befwick, *Queenhithe*
Mr *Dep.* Ch. Wilkins, *Tower*
Mr *Dep.* Godf. Wilfon, *Vintry*
Mr Richard Alfager, *Walbrook*

COMMISSIONERS *of* SEWERS, LAMPS, *and* PAVEMENTS.

The LORD MAYOR
All the Aldermen and their Deputies
Alderf. within, Mr. C. Aldridge
Alderf. without, Mr. John Mott
Aldgate, Mr. Sam. Thorp
Baffifhaw, Mr. Tho. Swanfon
Billingfgate, Mr. Tho. Gorft
Bifhopfgate within, Mr. Henry

Bifhopfg. without, Mr. Robert Bulicock
Bread-ftreet, Mr. Jn. Hemans,
Bridge, Mr. William Rowlatt
Broad-ftr. Mr. P. N. Frifqueit
Candlewick, Mr. William Gill
Caftlebaynard, Mr. W. Hurford
Cheap, Mr. Nicholas Forfter
Coleman-ftreet, Mr. T. Ruffell
Cordwainer, Mr. S. Hanning

Cripplegate within, Mr Wm Gifford.
Cripplegate without, Mr John Banner, Mr. Robert French
Dowgate, Mr. Jof. Stevenfon
Farringd. within, Mr B Hamnet
Farringdon without, Mr Rich. Brewer, Mr. Tho. Thorp
Langborn, Mr Peter Pope
Lime-ftreet, Mr James Sharp
Portfoken, Mr Cha. Parnell
Queenhith, Mr Rich. Clarke
Tower, Mr James Anfell
Vintry, Mr Lau. Holker
Walbrook, Mr Thomas Axford
C ief Clerk, Mr Henry Hall.
Affift. Cl. Mr. W. Bond, Mr. J. White.

DIRECTORS of the EAST INDIA COMPANY.

The Bufinefs is under the Management of 24 Directors, including the Chairman and Deputy Chairman, elected the firft Week in April:—They have a Salary of 150 l. per Ann. each, the Chairman and Deputy Chairman 200 l.

The Figures before each Name denote the Number of Years each Gentleman is to remain in the Direction, and the Letters after each Name the Committees they are upon. The Chairman and Deputy Chairman are upon all Committees.

a denotes Accounts, b Buying, c Correfpondence, h Houfe, l Lawfuits, m Military Fund, p Private Trade, g Prevent the Growth of Private Trade, s Shipping, t Treafury, w Warehoufe.

1 William Devaynes, Efq; *Chairman. Spring Gardens.*
2 Lawrence Sullivan, Efq; *Dep. Chairman, Bloomfbury-fquare.*
3 Francis Baring, Efq; *Mincing-lane,* a b h g l m
1 Charles Boddam, Efq; *Gracechurch-ftreet,* b g s w
4 Benjamin Booth, Efq; *Lincoln's-inn Square,* a c t
4 Thomas Cheap, Efq; a b l m g
3 George Cuming, Efq; *New London-ftreet,* c s t
4 Lionel Darell, Efq; jun. *Dean-Street, Soho,* a b h g
1 ×Henry Fletcher, Efq; *Southampton-row,* b h m p g s w
2 William George Freeman, Efq; *Lamb's Conduit-ftr.* a b l g w
4×Robert Gregory, Efq; *Berners-ftreet,* a l p s w.
3 John Harrifon, Efq; *Charterhoufe-fquare,* c t
2×Sir William James, Bart. *Gerard-ftreet, Soho* c s t
3 John Manfhip, Efq; *Queen's-fquare, Ormond-ftreet,* c t w
1 John Michie, Efq; *Spring-gardens,* b h l m p s w
2 William Mills, jun. Efq; a b h m p g
3 James Moffatt, Efq; *Charlton, Kent,* l p s w
4 John Roberts, Efq; *Pall-mall.*
1 John Purling, Efq; *Portland-place,* c t
3 Henry Savage, Efq; *Arundel-ftreet,* c t.
2 John Stables, Efq; *Bedford-ftreet,* b h m p s w
1 Nathaniel Smith, Efq; *Bloomfbury-fquare,* a l m p s
  John Woodhoufe, Efq; *New Bridge-ftreet,* c l m p t

OTHER OFFICERS.
Secretary, Peter Michell, Esq;
Deputy, Richard Holt.
Examiner of India Correspondence, Samuel Wilks.
Accomptant, Samuel Nicoll.
Deputy, Wm. Richardson.
Treasurer, William Harris.
Deputy, Warwick Roades.
Paym. fail. voyages, Ynyr Burges
Cl. to Com. of Ship. C.T. Coggan
Cl. to Com. of pr. Trade Ri. Cole
Priv. Trade outw. John Haffey
Transfer Office for Stock and Annuities.
Tr. Accomptant. Ja. Donaldson
Freight Office.
Richard Cole, Wm. Settle.
Auditor's Office.
Auditor, John Annis.
Writer and Compiler of India Correspond. John Hoole.
Cl. to Committee of Law-Suits, Samuel Way.
Cl. to Com. of Buying, H. Playford.
Assistant, John Burford.
Cl. to Com. of Warehouses, Wm. Settle.
Cl. to Com. of the Military Fund, Mr. Jona. Howkins Barnard.
Assistant, Will. Forsteen.
Warehouse-Keepers.
At Boto'ph Wharf, R. Twifs.

Deputy, Joseph Jennion.
Of Teas, &c. Sim. Holbrook.
Deputy, Jn Stiles Mordaunt.
Of Bengal Goods, Peter Corbett.
Assistant, Geo. Sibley.
To Pri. Trade, Nath. Basnett.
Assistant, Charles Pearse.
Coast & Surat, Geo. Mordaunt.
Assistant, Henry Dickinson.
Pepper, Philip Cray.
Mister Attendant of Shipping, Capt. John Oliver.
Deputy, Thomas Warner.
Surv. of Ship. Gabr. Snodgrass
Standing Council, Ge. Rous, Esq;
Sollicitor, John Smith, Esq;
Surv. of Build. Ric. Jupp, jun.
Door-keepers, Ed. Stillard & Is. Pizey.
Governors of the Company's Settlements.
Bengal, Warren Hastings, Esq;
Bombay, Wm Hornby, Esq;
F. St. Geo. Lord Macartney
Fort Marlboro', Wm Broff, Esq;
St. Helena, Jn Skottowe, Esq;
SUPREME COURT OF JUDICATURE AT FORT WILLIAM IN BENGAL.
Sir Elij. Impey, Kt. Ch. Justice.
Sir Rt. Chambers, Jn. Hyde, Esqrs. Puisne Judges.
Advocate Gen. Sir J. Day, Knt.

·The SOUTH-SEA COMPANY.
The Business is managed by a Governor, Sub-Governor, Deputy Governor, and 21 Directors, chosen triennially before Feb. 6.
The King's Most Excellent Majesty, Governor.

Tho. Coventry, Esq; Sub-Gov.
×Samuel Salt, Esq; Dep. Gov.
Richard Neal Badcock, Esq;
Henry Berners, Esq;
Endmund Boehm, jun. Esq;
Barrington Buggin, Esq;
Robert Darell, Esq;
Wm Fauquier, Esq;
Thomas Hawys, Esq;
Edward Hippisley, Esq;
John Shadwell Horton, Esq;

James Neave, Esq;
Peter Pierson, Esq;
Richard Puller, Esq;
John Raymond, Esq;
Henry Revely, Esq;
Robert Thornton, Esq;
    Elected Feb. 2, 1781.
Joseph Berens, Esq;
John Bond, Esq;
Andrew Giraldot, jun. Esq;
Joseph Paice, Esq;

(213)

Richard Sheldon, Efq;
Gregory Lewis Way, Efq;
Cashier, Peter Burrel.
Dep. Cash. Wm Richardfon.
Secretary, Claud. Crefpigny.
Accomptant, John Robins.
Dep. Acc. John Tipp.

Chief Clerk of the Stock and New Annuities, Edw. Mountency.
Chief Cl. of the Old Annuities and 3 per ct. 1751, Val. Lawford
Council, x Rich. Jackfon, Efq;
Housekeeper, Martha Way, 70l.

Committee of the Company of Merchants trading to AFRICA.
(*Office*, Scotch-yard, Bufh-lane, Cannon-ftreet.)

For London.
John Shoolbred, Efq;
James Bogle French, Efq;
Charles Cleland, Efq;
For Briftol.
Jonh Taylor Vaughan, Efq;
Thomas Farr, Efq;
John Pedder, Efq;

For Liverpool.
John Manefby, Efq;
Robert Bollefton, Efq;
Henry Blundell, Efq;

Thomas Rutherfoord, Efq; *Sec*
Benj. Potts, *Messenger*.

The LEVANT *or* TURKEY *Company*.
(*Meet at* Salters-Hall.)

x Rt. Hon. Lord North, *Gov.*
Rich. Willis, Efq; *Dep. Gov.*
x Wm Ewer, Efq; *Treasurer*.

Mr. Tho. Furley Forfter, *Sec*
Accomptant and Collector

The Governor, Consuls, &c. of the RUSSIA *Company*.
Edmund Boehm, Efq; *Gov.*
Jn. Thornton, J. Cornwall, J.
A. Ricker, E. Forfter, Efqrs.
Consuls.
Assistants, Robert Dingley,
Henry Norris, Efq; Sir John
Major, Bart. George Prefcott,
John Brogden, Ja. Mathias,
Wm. Thornton Aftele, Geo.
Peters, Tho. Raikes, Robert

Thornton, Hugh Atkins, Hen.
Handley Norris, Wm Raikes,
Godfrey Thornton, Ch. Beft,
Edw. Greathead, Roger Boehm,
John Wm Anderfon, John Paris, S. Thornton, Alex. Sharp,
Tho. Furly Forfter, Edmund
Boehm, jun.
M. Sierra, *Secretary*, No. 3,
Staining-lane.

The Committee of the HUDSON's BAY *Company*.
Bibye Lake, Efq; *Gov.*
Samuel Wegg, Efq; *Dep. Gov.*
Sir James Winter Lake, Bart.
Hermanus Berens, Efq;
Wm Baker, Efq;

Richard Hulfe, Efq;
Jofeph Berens, Efq;
Nich. Cæfar Corfellis, Efq;
Captain James Buggin.
Mr. Wm Redknap, *Secretary*.

Directors of the MILLION BANK.
Sir J. Burrow, R. Burrow, B. Boddington, Barrington Buggin, Hermanus
Berens, Edward Forfter,
Bibye Lake, Efqrs. Sir Ja.
Winter Lake, Bart. James
Martin, Robert Macky, Jof.
John Harrifon

Paice, Tho. Page, Cha. Palmer, Tho. Page, jun. Wm Raper, T. Rogers, Lee Steere, T.
Sikes, If. Solly, R. Stone,
G. Woodward Vane, Mark
Weyland, Francis Willes,
John Yerbury, Efqrs.
Secretary

BANK of ENGLAND.

Directors.
Booth, Daniel, Efq; *Gov.*
Ewer, William, Efq; *Dep. Gov.*
Beachcroft, Samuel, Efq;
Drehm, Roger, Efq;
Bofanquet, Samuel, Efq;
Clay, Richard, Efq;
Cooke, William, Efq;
Darell, Edward, Efq;
Dea, Thomas, Efq;
Drake, George, Efq;
Fonnereau, Martyn, Efq;
Gauffen, Peter, Efq;
Hake, Chriftopher, Efq;
Halhed, William, Efq;
Hayter, George, Efq;
Jackfon, Thomas Scott, Efq;
Mee, Benjamin, jun. Efq;
Neave, Richard, Efq;
Payne, Edward, Efq;
Puller, Chriftopher, Efq;
Raikes, Thomas, Efq;
Snell, William, Efq;
Thomas, Thomas, Efq;
Thornton, Godfrey, Efq;
Thornton, Samuel, Efq;
Weyland, Mark, Efq;

Other **OFFICERS.**
Secretary, Robert Lewin, Efq;
Deputy, Mr. Martin.

Accomptant-Gen John Payne, Efq;
Deputy, Mr. William Edwards.
1/t Cl. of the Specie, Mr. Tho. Pollard
1ft Cl. of 4 per cent. Jofeph Poole.
1ft Cl. of 3 ½ per cent. Mr Rogers
1ft Cl. of 3 per cent. Confol. Mr. Miller.
1ft Cl. of 3 per cent. Reduced, Mr. Kimin.
1ft Cl. of Bank Stock, Mr. Millington
1ft Cl. of Cheque Offi. Mr. Bailey
Principal Cafhier, Abraham Newland, Efq.
Cafhiers, Thomas Thompfon, Sewallis Larchin, W. Gardner, Wm Jackfon, Jn. Boult, John Warren, John Nixon, Owen Gething, Thomas Ormes, William Lander.
Firft Teller, Mr. Greenway.
1ft Cl. of Difc. Office, Mr. Rogers
1ft Cl. of Draw. Accompt Office under Cafhiers, Mr. Clifford.
1ft Cl. of Bill Office in the Hall, Mr. Church.
1ft Clerk of Bullion Office, Mr. Etheridge.

Lift of the **BANKERS** *in* **LONDON.**

Afgill (Sir Charles) John and William Nightingale No. 70, Lombard-ftreet

Barclay, Bevan, and Bening, No. 56, Lombard-ftreet

Batfon, Stephenfon and Hoggart, No. 69, Lombard-ftreet

Biddulph, Cocks, Elliot and Praed, Charing-crofs

Bland, Barnet and Hoare, No. 62, Lombard-ftreet

Boldero, Barnfton, Carter, Snaith and Barnfton, No. 5, Manfion-houfe-ftreet

Boldero, Kendall, Adey, E. G. Boldero, and Brafier, No. 77, Lombard-ftreet

Browns, Collinfon and Tritton, No. 58, Lombard-ftreet

Caftel, Whately and Powell, No. 66, Lombard-ftreet

Chambers, Hercy and Birch, New Bond-ftreet

Child (Robert) and Co. No. 1, Fleet-street
Coutts (Thomas) and Co. near Durham-yard, Strand
Croft, Backwell, Roberts and Croft, Pall-mall
Currie, Lefevre, James, Yallowley, and Co. No. 29, Cornhill
Denne, William and Cornelius, Robert Snow, and William Sandby, without Temple-bar
Dorrien, Rucker, Dorrien and Martin, No. 22, Finch-lane
Drummond (Robert and Henry) and Co. Charing-cross
Esdaile, Sir James, and Son, Hammitt and Esdaile, Birchin-lane
Exchange Banking Company, St. James's-street
Fuller (William) and Son, No. 24, Lombard-street
Fuller, Son, Halford and Vaughan, No. 84, Cornhill
Gines and Atkinson, No. 50, Lombard-street
Gosling, Robert and Francis, No. 19, Fleet-street
Hallidays, Duntze, Praed and Co. No. 3, Freeman's c. Cornh.
Halifax (Sir Thomas) Mills, Glyn, Mills and Mitten, No. 18, Birchin-lane
Hanbury, Taylor, Lloyd and Bowman, No. 60, Lombard-street
Hankey (Joseph-Chaplin) Thomas Hankey, and Steph. Hall, No. 7, Fenchurch-street
Hoare, Henry, Rich. and Henry, No. 37, Fleet-street
Hodsoll and Michell, near Catherine-street, Strand
Ladbroke, Rawlinson and Porker, Bank-buildings
Langston, Polhill, Towgood and Amory, No. 29, Clement's lane
Lee, Ayton, Brassey and Satterthwaite, No. 71, Lombard-str.
Lemon (Sir William) Buller, Furly, Lubbock and Co. No. 11, Mansionhouse-street
Lowe, Vere, and Williams, No. 20, Birchin-lane
Marlar, Pell and Down, No. 1, Bartholomew-lane
Martin, Stone, Blackwell and Foote, No. 68, Lombard-street
Mayne and Graham, Jermyn-street, St. James's
Mildred and Walker, No. 2, Whitehart-court, Gracechurch-st.
Prescotts, Grotes, Culverden and Hollingworth, No. 62, Threadneedle-street
Pybus, Byde, Dorsett and Cockell, No. 148, New Bond-street
Raymond (Sir Charles) Harley and Cameron, George-street, by the Mansion-house
Reade, Moorhouse and Co. No. 76, Lombard-street
Smith, Payne and Smith, George-street, by the Mansion-house
Smith (Samuel) and Son, No. 12, Aldermanbury
Smith, Wright and Gray, No. 21, Lombard-street
Staples, Baron T. Dimsdale, Son and Co. No. 50, Cornhill
Walpole, Clark, Bourne and Pott, No. 28, Lombard-street
Welch, Rogers and Co. No. 80, Cornhill
Wickenden, Moffatt, Kensington and Boler, No. 20, Lombard st.
Wright (Anthony) and Son, Henrietta-street, Covent-garden

Directors of the Amicable Society for a perpetual Assurance.
(Office in Serjeant's-Inn, Fleet-street.)

Old Directors.
William Barrett, Esq;
William Boulton, Esq;
Thomas Brookbank Esq;
Mr. Thomas Ellis.
John Rivington, Esq;
Mr. Alexander Whitchurch.
Rev. Moses Wight, A. M.
New Dir. elected May, 1789.
Rev. Thomas Ball, A. M.
Mr. Francis Crooke,

Mr. Samuel Marriott,
George Stubbs, Esq;
Register, Mr. Jof. Baldwin
Assistant Register, Mr. Charles Brand
Auditors, Mr. Ja. Bottomley
Mr. Francis Ruddle,
Mr. Robert Browne,
Mr. Francis Walkingame,
Mr. Thomas Cranage,
Messenger, John Orlton.

OFFICES of INSURANCE for Houses and Goods.

Royal Exchange, Cornhill, and Conduit-street, Hanover-square.
Ja. Henckell, Esq; Gov.
Beeston Long, Esq; Sub. Gov.
James Tierney, Esq; Dep. Gov.
Directors.
Mr. Lewis Agassiz
Mr. John Wm Anderson
Alex. Baxter, Esq;
Mr. John Bell
Mr. John Peter Blaquiere
Mr. Thomas Boddington
Mr. William Bosanquet
Mr. Stratford Canning
Mr. John Henry Cazenove
Francis Degen, Esq;
Mr. William Devisme
Mr. Edward Forster
Capt. Leslie Grove
Mr. Richard Lee
Mr. Charles Lindegren
Mr. John Dan. Lucadou
William Manning, Esq;
Mr. Abraham Roberts
Mr. Hen. Handley Norris
Mr. William Raikes
Capt. Henry Hinde Pelly
Mr. William Robinson
Capt. Nicholas Skottowe
Mr. Arthur Stert
John Ekins, Treasurer

Wm Kekewich, Secretary
Geo. Clift. Accomptant

SUN FIRE-OFFICE, Cornhill, and Craig's Court, Charing-Cross.
John Harrison, Esq; Chairman
Tho. Watts, Esq; Secretary
Lillie Ainscombe, Esq;
John Barwick, Esq;
Calverly Bewicke, Esq;
Henry Boulton, Esq;
Wm Burrell, Esq; LLD
John Chalie, Esq;
Robert Darell, Esq;
Thomas Dea, Esq;
Mr. Charles Foulis
William Godfrey, Esq;
Joseph Grove, Esq;
Mr. W. Hamilton
Ja. Haughton Langstone, Esq.
Geo. Mason, Esq;
Mr. John Moffat
David Pitcairn, MD
Nicholas Pearse, Esq;
Frederick Pigou, Esq;
Henry Plant, Esq;
Samuel Pole, Esq;
Will. Thornton, Astell, Esq;
Hugh Watts, Esq;

London Assurance, *(Birchin-lane)* for Houses and Goods.
John Barker, Esq; *Gov.*
Alex. Aubert, Esq; *Sub-Gov.*
Silvan. Grove, Esq; *Dep. Gov.*
Mr. Matthew Arbouin
Mr. William Arnold
Mr. Anthony Aubert
Mr. John Lucie Blackman
Mr. John Brogden
Mr. Mark Cramer
Mr. John Free
Mr. Samuel Gardiner, jun.
John Henniker, Esq;
Mr. Thomas Lane
Mr. Peter Laprimaudaye
Mr. James Lee
Mr. Charles Madockes
Mr. James Mathias
Mr. Arnold Mello
Hughes Minet, Esq;
Mr. John Paris
Mr. Thomas Porteus
Mr. Matthew Purling
Mr. Daniel Henry Rucker
Mr. Richard Shubrick
Capt. Gilbert Slater
Mr. Yvon Thomas
Mr. Samuel Turner, *Directors*
Accomptat, George Hall
Secretary, Edward Austen

HAND-IN-HAND FIRE-OFFICE, against *Sepulchre's* Church. Insures Houses only.
Directors elected Nov. 11, 1780.
Mr. Thomas Baskerfield, Mr. William Beaumont, Joseph Brockhurst, Esq; Mr. P. Bunnell, Rt. Butler, Esq; Mr. Tho. Collins, Mr. Bicknell Coney, Mr. James Dixon, Mr. John Dowson, Mr. Thomas Eld, Sir James Esdaile, Knt. Geo. Evans, Esq; Mr. Joseph Flight,

Mr. James Bogle French, Henry Hurt, Esq; Mr. Caleb Jeacocke, Mr. John Muggeridge, Mr. James Inglish, Thomas Scott, Esq; Mr. John Sweet, Mr. Thomas Smith, Mr. John Wellford, Mr. Thomas Wellings, Mr. George Wright.
Secretary, Benjamin Rouse.

UNION FIRE-OFFICE, *Maiden-lane, Cheapside,* for Goods only, on much the same terms as the *Hand-in-Hand* Office does Houses only.

Directors, elec. Sep. 13, 1780.
Edward Jeffries, Esq; Mr. Thomas Jordan, Mr. William Loveday, × Nathaniel Pollhill, Esq; John Rivington, Esq; Mr. Henry Rutt, Mr. Thomas Shrimpton, Mr. Joseph Stonard

The Sixteen following are to be continued according to th Deed of Settlement.

For one Year.
George Brough, Esq; Mr. William Caldwall, Mr. Francis Hamilton, Mr. Samuel Lawrence, Thomas Lucas, Esquire, Mr. John Relph, Mr. Sandeforth Streatfeild, Mr. John Towers.

For two Years.
Mr. Cornelius Denne, Mr. Thomas Dunn, Thomas Edwards, Esq; Mr. Robert Maitland, Thomas Page, Esq; Mr. John Warren, Mr. John Wells, Mr. Joseph Wells.
Clerk, Charles Hartley.

T 3

(218

WESTMINSTER *Fire-Office, for insuring Houses, Bedford-street, Covent-Garden.*

Elected Oct. 1, 1779.
Edward Gray, Esq; John Pratt, Esq; Simon Lesage, Esq; Thomas Broosbank, Esq; John Groves, Esq; Mr. Henry Page, Mr. Benjamin Wood, Mr. Thomas Gayfere, Mr. William Barlow.

Elected Oct. 21, 1780.
George Mercer, Esq; Richard Filewood, Esq; Tho. Chamberlayne, Esq; Geo. Shakespeare, Esq; Mr. John Henry Rigg, Mr. William Ince, Mr. John Gregory, jun. Mr. John White, Mr. George Lockitt. George Browne, *Secretary*. Geo. Browne, jun. } *Cl.*
Robert Byfield }

Office for Equitable Assurance on Lives and Survivorships, in Bride-Street, *near* Blackfriars Bridge.

President.
* Sir Charles Gould, Knt.
Vice-Presidents.
* Sir William James Bart.
Mr. Deputy John Smith.
Trustees.
Geo. Adey, Esq; * Sir C. Gould, Knt. Alderman Sainsbury, John Saxon, Esq; Mr. Dep. J. Smith.

Directors. G. Adey, Esq; S. T. Adey, W. Bray, Esq; Rev. Robert Bromley, Rev. R. Lewis, Mr. J. Pond, J Ragsdale, Alderman Sainsbury, Esq; Mr. Jn Saxon, Rev. Dr. Anthony Webster, Dr. H. Smith, Jn Woodhouse, Esq.
Actuary, Mr. Wm Morgan.
Assistant, Mr. Tho. Cooper.

☞ *A Weekly Meeting of the Directors is held every Wednesday, and Attendance given daily from Nine to Three a' Clock.*

SOCIETY *for the Encouragement of Arts, Manufactures and Commerce. Instituted* 1753.
(*Office, in the* Adelphi.)

President.
Lord Romney, LLD FRS
Vice-Presidents.
Duke of Richmond, FRS
D. of Northumberland, FRS
Earl of Radnor
Earl Percy
✗ Hon. Charles Marsham
✗ Sir Geo. Savile, Bart. FRS
Edward Hooper, Esq; FRS
Owen Salusbury Brereton, Esq; FRS
Keane Fitz-Gerald, Esq; FRS
Joshua Steel, Esq;

Chairm. of the Com. of Accounts.
Mr. Ashburner
Mr. Oforio
Of the Comm. of Correspondence.
Val. Green, Esq; FAS
Mr. Peter Chavany
Of the Committee of Polite Arts.
M. Duane, Esq; FRS
Edward Bridgen, Esq; ASS
Of Agriculture.
Nathaniel Jarmin, Esq,
Mr. James Hebert.
Of Manufactures.
Michael Lovell, Esq;
Mr. Peter Chavany

Of Mechanics.
Mr. Joseph Hodgkinson,
Joseph Hurlock, Esq;
Of Chemistry.
Mr. J. Wingfield
Mr. J. Butts.
Of Colonies and Trade.
James Clarke, Esq

G. Whitfoord, Esq;
Principal Secretary.
Mr Sam. More, 15cl.
Assistant Secretary, Mr. R. Samuel
Register, G. Cockings, 50l.
Collector, Mr. John Haywood.
Messenger, Mr. Ja. Haywood.

SOCIETY of ARTISTS of *Great Britain.*
Instituted by Charter the 26th of January, 1765.
Geo. Robertson, Esq; *President*
Sam. Turner, Esq. *VicePres.*
J. Smith, Esq; *Treasurer*
Mr. Isaac Taylor, *Secretary.*
Directors.
Painters. Messrs. T. Beach, R. Carver, S. Gilpin, A. Greffe, H. Hodgins, J. Jennings, W. Marlow, W. Miller, F. Parsons, J.

Smart, C. Stuart, P. J. Taffaert, F. X. Vispre
Sculptors. Messrs. T. Allwood, J. Paine, jun.
Architects. F. Rogers, J. Paine, *sen.*
Engravers. W. Byrne, J. Miller, J. Hearne.
Elected Oct. 18, 1780.

ROYAL ACADEMY of ARTS, *instituted Dec.* 10, 1768.
The KING, *Patron.*
Sir J. Reynolds, Knt. *President.*
Sir W. Chambers, Knt. *Treas.*
G. Mich. Moser, Esq; *Keeper.*
F. M. Newton, Esq; *Secretary.*
E. Penny, Esq; *Prof. of Painting.*
T. Sandby, Esq; *Prof. of Arch.*
S. Wale, Esq; *Prof. Perspective.*
Dr Hunter, *Prof. of Anatomy.*
Rich. Wilson, Esq; *Librarian.*
Council. Geo. Barret, F. Bartolozzi, Mason Chamberlin, Nath. Hone, G. M. Moser, Tho. Sandby, Dom. Serres, Johan Zoffany, Esqrs.
Visitors. F. Bartolozzi, A. Carni, Ch. Catton, Rich. Cosway, Na. Dance, Jos. Nollekins, Ben. West, Jos. Wilton, Johan Zoffany Esqis.
F. M. Newton, *Clerk.*
[*Elected Dec.* 12, 1780.]

WELSH CHARITY, *Gray's-Inn-Lane.*
His Royal Highness the Prince of WALES, *Patron.*
Lord Grosvenor. *President.*
Duke of Beaufort, Duke of Rutland, Sir W. W. Wynne, Bart. T Powell, Esq; Lord Paget, Earl of Plymouth, Lord Bulkeley, Lord Cardiff, Earl of Powis, Earl of Surrey.

Lord Clive, *Vice-Presiden.*
Rt. Hon. Sir Watkin Lewes, Knt. Lord Mayer, *Treasurer*
Mr. Rich. Jones, *Vice-Treas.*
Rev. Evan Evans, *Chaplain.*
Dr. Henry Haskey, *Physician.*
Mr. Robinson, and Mr. Valentine Jones, *Surgeons.*
Mr. Ja. Farmer, *Apothecary.*

The Royal College of PHYSICIANS, *Warwick-Lane*, established 1523.

Those marked § are Fellows of the Royal Society, and those marked * are Commissioners for granting Licences to Persons for keeping Houses for the Reception of Lunatics. Elected Sept. 30, 1780.

PRESIDENT.
§* Dr. William Pitcairn, *Warwick-court, Warwick-lane.*

FELLOWS.
Sir Edward Wilmot, Bart. *Physician to the King, Harringstone, Dorsetshire.*
Dr Ambrose Dawson, *Liverpool, Lancashire.*
Dr Russel Plumptre, *King's Prof. of Physic, Cambridge.*
Dr Matth. Morley, *Vauxhall*
Dr Tho. Addams, *Reading.*
Dr T. Lawrence, El. *Essex-str.*
Dr Edm. Crynes, *Kenilworth, Warwickshire.*
§ Dr Will. Heberden, Elect. *Pall-Mall.*
Dr Wm M. shet, *Grantham, Lincolnshire.*
Dr John Monro, Elect. *Bedford-square.*
§ Dr Tho. Wilbraham, Elect. *Queen-street, Westminster.*
Dr Tho. Wharton, *Durham.*
Dr. Anthony Addington, *Reading, Berks.*
§ Dr Rich. Brocklesby, Elect. *Norfolk-street.*
Dr John Clerke, *Epsom.*
§ Sir George Baker, Bt. Elect. *Censor, Physician to the Queen, Jermyn-street.*
§ Sir Noah Thomas, Knt. *Physician to the King, Albemarle-street.*
Dr Wm Cadogan, *George-street, Hanover-square.*
§ Dr Tho. Gisborne, *Censor, Physician to the King's House-*
hold, Gifford street, Burlington gardens.
§ Dr Tho. Healde, *St. Mary Axe*
* Dr Richard Tyson, *Register, Queen-square.*
§ Dr Rich. Warren, *Physician to the King, Sackville-str.*
Dr Robert Glynn Clobery, *Cambridge.*
§ Sir Clifton Wintringham, Bt. *Phys. to the King, Dover-str.*
§ Sir John Pringle, Bt. *Phys. Extr. to the King, and Phys. to the Queen, Pall-Mall.*
Dr Swithin Adee, *Oxford.*
Dr Thomas Brooke, *Charles-street, St. James's-square.*
Dr. Robert Thomlinson, *Treasury, Aldermary Churchyard, Bow-lane.*
§ Dr John Lewis Petit, *Great Marlborough street.*
§* Dr John Turton, *Phys. to the Queen's Household, Adam-street, Adelphi build.*
§ Sir Richard Jebb, Bart. *Physician Extraordinary to the King, Great George-street.*
§ Dr Donald Monro, *Jermyn-street*
* Dr Henry Revell Reynolds, *Red-lion-street.*
§* Dr Richard Wright, *Park-place, St. James's street.*
Dr John Parsons, *Oxford.*
Dr Lucas Pepys, *Physician Extraor. to the King, Wimpole-street, Cavendish-square.*
Dr John Burges, *Censor, Mortimer-street.*
Dr Jn Rawlinson, *Watling-str.*

Dr Rich. Budd, *Censor, Chatham-square.*
§Dr Fr. Milman, *Censor, Lower Brook-street, Grosvenor-sq.*
Dr If. Pehnington, *Cambridge.*
Dr Cha. Elsden Bagge, *Lym-Regis, Norfolk.*

LICENTIATES.

Dr John Andree, *Hatton-street.*
§Dr Peter Canvane, *Bath.*
Dr Moses Griffith, *Colchester.*
§ Dr Charles Morton, *British Museum.*
§Sir John Baptist Silvester, Knt. *Bath, Somersetshire.*
Dr Geo. Lamont, *Gloucester-court, St. James's-street.*
Dr Philip de la Cour, *Bath.*
§Mr James Dargent, *Great Marlborough-street.*
§Dr Dan. Pet. Layard, *Lower Brook-street, Grosvenor-sq.*
Dr Edw. Archer, *Gray's-inn.*
§ Dr Wm Hunter, *Physician Extraordinary to the Queen, Windmill-str. Hay-market.*
Dr Samuel Wathen, *Dorking, Surry.*
Dr Chris. Kelly, *Knightsbridge.*
Dr Wm. Watson, *Lincoln's-inn-fields.*
Dr Tho. Milner, *Maidstone.*
§ Dr Mich. Morris.
Sir John Eliot, Bart. *Cecil-str.*
Dr Tho. Dawson, *Hackney.*
Dr Hugh Smith, *Bride-street, Black-friars.*
Dr Will. Grant, *Lime-street.*
Dr James Ford, *Albemarle-str.*
§ Dr Max. Garthshore, *St. Martin's-lane, Westminster.*
§Dr Thomas Dickson, *New Broad-street Buildings.*

§Dr Jn Morgan, *Philadelphia.*
Dr Rob. Knox, *George-street, Hanover-square.*
§Dr. Rd Saunders, *Spring Gard.*
Dr Sam. Chapman, *Sudbury.*
Dr Dd. Orme, *Gr. St. Helens.*
Dr Tho. Menningham, *Bath.*
Dr John Hill, *St. Mary Axe.*
Dr Hugh Alexander Kennedy.
Dr John Napier, *Rathbone-place, Oxford-street.*
§Dr George Fordyce, *Essex-str.*
Dr William Baylies.
Dr John Ford, *Old Jewry.*
Dr Joseph Allen, *Dulwich.*
Dr James Walker.
Dr Fr. de Valangin, *Fore-st.*
Dr. Will. Vaughan, *Union-court, Old Broad-street.*
Dr John Leake, *Craven-street.*
§Dr R. Bromfield, *Gerrard-st.*
Dr Rowland Jackson.
Dr P. Swinton, *Salisbury-court*
Dr Alex. Hay, *Jermyn-str.*
§Dr John Caverhill.
Dr William Saunders, *Jeffries-square, St. Mary Axe.*
Dr James Maddocks, *Capel-court, near the Royal-Exchange.*
Dr George Hicks, *Stable-yard, St. James's*
§Dr J. C. Lettsom, *Gr. Eastcheap*
Dr Gilbert Thompson, *Size-lane, Watling-str. et.*
Dr J. Carmichael Smyth, *Charlotte-str. near Great Russel-str.*
Dr Isaac Henriques Sequeira, *Mark-lane*
Dr N. Hulme, *Chartre-house-sq.*
Dr Richard William Stack.
Dr Hen. Krohn, *Southampton-street, Covent-garden.*
Dr Michael Teighe, *Rathbone Place, Oxford-street.*

(222)

Dr Robert Robertson, *Howard-street, Strand.*	§ Dr. S. F. Simmons, *Air-str. Picadilly*
Dr. And. Douglas, *Bedford-street, Bedford-square.*	Dr. Seguin Henry Jackson, *Compton-street, Soho.*
Dr John Hunter, *Leicester-fields*	Dr. John Sims, *Paternoster-row*
Dr John Jebb, *Craven-street.*	Dr. Anthony Fothergill, *Northampton.*
Dr. John Lee, *Bath.*	
Dr James Sims, *Bartholomew-lane.*	Dr Ja. Ford, *junior, Jermyn-st.*
	Dr. Stephen Pellett, *Reading.*

The ROYAL SOCIETY (Incorporated 1663.)
[No. 7, *Crane-court, Fleet-street.*]

Patron. The KING.

President.
Joseph Banks, Esq;

Council elect. Nov. 30, 1780.

Sir Ja. Burrow, Knt. *Vice-Pres.*	Samuel Harper, M. A.
Sir George Baker, Bart.	Thomas, Earl of Macclesfield
Charles Blagden, M D	Nevil Maskelyne, D D
John Campbell, Esq;	Const. John Lord Mulgrave
Anthony Hamilton, D D	Sir William Musgrave, Bart.
R. B. Hodgkinson, Esq;	Sir Geo. Shuckburgh, Bart.
George Hinton, D D	George Stevens, Esq;
George Keate, Esq;	Benjamin Way, Esq;
	Richard Warren, M. D.
	Sam. Wegg, Esq; *Treasurer*
	Joseph Planta, Esq; } *Secr.*
	Pa. Hen. Maty, M A }

GRESHAM COLLEGE, founded by Sir Thomas Gresham, 1581, for Lectures to be read during Term Time. These Lectures are now read in the Gresham Lecture-room, over the Royal Exchange, and in the following order, viz.

Professors £10 *per Ann. each.*

Monday — Divinity, Benjamin Hallifax, D. D.
Tuesday — Civil Law, Joseph Jefferies, LL. D.
Wednesday - Astronomy, William Cockayne, LL. D.
Thursday — Geometry, Samuel Kettilby, D. D.
Friday — Rhetoric, Joseph Whately, LL. B.
Saturday { Physic, Thomas Healde, M.D. F.R.S.
{ Music, Mr. Theodore Aylward.

SION COLLEGE, London-wall, founded by the Will of Thomas White, S. T. P. Anno 1603, incorporated 3d July, 1630, by Letters Patent, and confirmed by King Charles II. the 20th June, 1664.

President.	*Assistants.*
James Waller, D. D.	Peter Whalley, M. A.
Deans.	Will. Romaine, M. A.
Stephen Eaton, M. A.	Thomas Weales, D. D.
Robert Wright, M. A.	Samuel Carr, M. A.

Fellows, who are the whole body of Rectors or Vicars within the City. To the name of each living is added the sum it is charged in the King's books, and after the incumbent's name is set the annual value, as fixed by act of parliament in 1671, of those livings (51 in number) where their churches were rebuilt.

This ‡ denotes the Archbishop of Canterbury's peculiars, r. rector, and v. vicar.

St Alban's, Wood-street, r.	£23	16	10	H.&R. Mr Aylmer	170
Allhallows, Barking, v.	36	13	1	Dr Stinion, F R S	
Allhallows, Bread-st. ‡ r.	33	13	4	Mr Morice	140
Allhallows, Thames-st. r.	41	18	1	Dr Vincent	200
Allhallows, Lombard-st. ‡ r.	22	6	8	Dr Barford	110
Allhallows, Staining, r. not in charge.				Mr Ellis	
Allhallows, London-wall, r.	8	16	8	Mr Mence	
St Alphage, r.	8	0	0	Mr Wynne	
St Andrew Undershaft, r.	30	11	3	Mr Carr	
St Anne, Black-Friars, r.	17	10	0	Mr Romaine	160
St Anne, Aldersgate, r.	19	2	1	Mr. Snowe	140
St Antholin, r.	36	1	5	Dr De Salis, FRS	120
St Austin, r.	43	13	1	Dr Douglas, FRS	172
St Bartho. Exchange, r.	18	1	8	Mr Dicey	100
St Bennet Finck, v. not in charge.				Mr Bostock	100
St Bennet, Gracechurch, ‡ r.	43	11	3	Mr. Elsley	140
St Bennet, Paul's wharf,	23	3	6	Mr Gibson	100
Christ-church, v.	53	6	8	Dr Bell	200
St Christopher, r.	14	0	0	Mr Willis	120
St Clement, Eastcheap, r.	32	18	4	Mr Kerrich	140
St Dionis Backchurch, ‡ r.	25	0	0	Dr Tatton	
St Dunstan, East, ‡ r.	60	7	11	Mr Winstanley	200
St Edmund the King, r.	34	14	2	Dr Milles, F R S	200
St Ethelburga, r.	11	12	6	Mr Gilbank	
St George, Botolph-lane, r.	31	16	0	Mr Hand	200
St Helen's, r. not in charge.				Mr Naish	
St James's, Duke's place, not in charge.				Mr Moore	
St James's, Garlickhythe, r.	17	14	7	Mr Onslow	100
St Katherine Coleman, r.	5	6	8	Mr Andrews	
St Katherine, Creechur. v. not in charge				Dr Parker, F R S	
St Lawrence, Jewry, v.	37	17	11	Mr Hutton	120
St Magnus, London-br. r.	100	17	1	Mr Gibson	170
St Margaret, Lothbury, r.	13	6	8	Dr Whitfield	100
St Marg. Patten, Rood-l. r.	22	0	0	Mr Whalley	120
St Martin, Ludgate, r.	33	17	8	Dr Waller	160
St Martin, Outwith, r.	13	9	9	Mr Fayting	

Parish	£	s.	d.	Minister	£
St Mary, Abchurch, r.	20	0	0	Mr. Underwood	120
St Mary, Aldermanbury, r. not in charge				Mr Lawrence	150
St Mary Aldermary, ✝ r.	53	0	0	Dr Wollaston, FRS	150
St Mary Le Bow, ✝ r.	66	2	3	Dr Apthorp	200
St Mary Hill, r.	52	13	4	Dr Griffith	200
St Mary Magd. Old Fish-st. r.	19	5	0	Dr Fitzherbert	120
St Mary Somerset, r.	17	0	1	Dr Jones	110
St Mary Woolnoth,	43	13	0	Mr. Newton	160
St Matthew, Friday-st. r.	47	14	4	Dr Lort, FRS	150
St Michael, Bassishaw, r.	14	0	9	Dr Marriott	132
St Michael, Cornhill, r.	35	1	0	Dr Finch	140
St Michael, Crooked-l. ✝ r.	26	1	8	Mr Lane	100
St Michael, Queenhythe, r.	24	7	4	Mr Trebeck	160
St Mich. Royal, College-hill, ✝ r.	25	13	6	Mr Fenton	140
St Michael, Wood-street, r.	24	0	4	Dr Woodcock	100
St Mildred, Bread-street, r.	26	11	0	Mr Crowther	130
St Mildred, Poultry, r.	18	13	0	Mr Bromley	170
St Nicholas, Coleabby, r.	26	12	4	Dr Jeffreys	130
St Olave, Hart-street, r.	41	1	1	Dr Owen, FRS	
St Olave, Jewry, v.	23	6	8	Mr Altham	120
St Peter, Cornhill, r.	39	5	0	Dr Thomas	110
St Peter le Poor, Broad-st. r.	5	16	7	Mr Heslop	
St Stephen, Coleman-st. v.	11	0	8	Dr Webster	110
St Stephen, Walbroke, r.	26	7	0	Dr Wilson	100
St Swithin, Lond. stone, ✝ r.	26	7	11	Dr Palmer	140
Trinity, in the Minories, not in charge.				Mr Fly	
St Vedast, Foster-lane, ✝ r.	44	16	3	Mr Wollaston FRS	160
St Andrew, Holborn, r.	18	0	0	Mr Barton	
St Barth. the Gr. Smithfield, r.	8	0	0	Mr Edwardes	
St Bartholomew the Less, r.	13	6	8	Dr Kettilby	
St Botolph, Aldersgate, r. not in charge.				Mr Garden	
St Botolph, Bishopsgate, r.	20	0	0	Dr Conybeare	
St Botolph, Aldgate, not in charge.				Mr Wright	
St Bride's, v.	16	0	0		120
Christ-ch. Spitalfields, not in charge.				Mr Pritchard	
St Dunstan in the West, v.	26	4	9	Mr Williamson	
St Geo. the Mart. Qu. sq. r. not in charge				Mr Eton	
St Giles, Cripplegate, v.	32	5	0	Mr Hand	
St James, Clerkenwell, r. not in charge				Mr Sellon	
St John, Clerkenwell, not in charge				Mr Whitaker	
St Leonard, Shoreditch, v.	17	0	0	Mr. Blake	
St Luke, Middlesex, r.				Mr Waring	
St Mary, Whitechapel, r.	31	17	3	Dr Markham	
St Sepulchre's, v.	29	0	0	Dr Weales	200

W. Clements, M. A. *Librarian.* Mr. Simpson, *Secretary.*

(225)

A List of the Court of Assistants elected by the Governors of the Charity for the Relief of the poor WIDOWS and CHILDREN of CLERGYMEN, on the 9th of Nov. 1780.

President.
The Most Rev. His Grace Frederick, Lord Archbishop of Canterbury

Vice-President.
Sir John Skynner, Knt. Lord Chief Baron of his Majesty's Court of Exchequer.

Treasurers.
Stephen Lushington, Esq;
Joseph Banks, Esq;
James Sharpe, Esq.

Court of Assistants.
Roger Altham, Esq;
Sir George Baker, Bart.
Thomas Bromwich, Esq;
Kempe Brydges, Esq;
James Calvert, Esq;
The Lord Bishop of Chester
Bicknell Coney, Esq;
Mr. Stafford Crane
*Sir William Dolben, Bart.
Mr. Isaac Dudley
The Lord Bishop of Ely
Mr. Baron Eyre
James Ford, M. D.
Thomas Gisborne, M.D.
George Harris, LL.D.
George Hayter, Esq;

Rev. John Jeffreys, D.D.
Robert Jenner, Esq;
Rev. Richard Kaye, LL. D.
Rev. Samuel Kettilby, D. D.
Mr. Thomas Kilner
Thomas Kynaston, Esq;
The Lord Bishop of Lincoln
Rev. John Lloyd, D. D.
Mr. Edward Loxham
Rev. John Jas. Majendie, D.D.
Rev. Herbert Mayo, D.D.
Rev. Richard Neate, LL.B.
The Lord Bishop of Oxford
John Perrott, Esq;
Sir George Pocock, K.B.
Sir Joshua Reynolds, Knt.
*Samuel Salt, Esq;
William Sandby, Esq;
Hon. and Rev. G. Talbot, D.D.
Mr. John Townsend
Mr. Archdeacon Waller
Richard Warren, M. D.
Joseph Wilcox, Esq;
The Lord Bishop of Worcester
The Lord Bp. of Winchester
Thomas Wyld, Esq;
Register, Mr. T. Wall, (No. 13.)
Paper-Buildings, Temple
Messenger, Jn. Orlton,

LAUDABLE SOCIETY for the BENEFIT of WIDOWS.

Directors.

Mr. Stan. Crowder
Mr. Jn Biggerstaff
Mr. Sa. Lawrence
Mr. Lake Young
Mr. John Priestly
Mr. Hen. Watkins
Mr. Wm. Cutlove
Mr. John Denyer
Mr. Martin Long

Mr. T. Sanderson
Mr. Jos. Holden
Mr. James Noakes
Mr. Tho. Cranage
Mr. G. Fleming
Mr. Walt. Adams
Mr. Joseph Faikney
Mr. Job Marks
Mr. Rob. Furnass

Mr. Dan. Fossick
Mr. John Hough,
Mr. Giles Lane
Nath. Hayward, esq.
Mr. Gilbert Fisher
Mr. Tho. Davis
Sec. Mr. Mic. Fisher,
Wych-street
Messeng. J. Orlton

ANTIQUARY SOCIETY, Chancery-Lane.
Incorporated November 2, 1751.—His MAJESTY, Patron.
The COUNCIL, elected April 21, 1780.

Rev. Jeremiah Milles, D D. Dean of Exeter, F.R.S. *Préfident.*
Thomas Astle, efq. F.R.S.
Sir Jo. Ayloffe, Bt. F.R.S. *V.P.*
Hon. D. Barrington, FRS. *VP.*
Frederick Lord Bo⸺on
⨯ O. Sal. Brereton, efq. FRS. *VP*
Edward Bridgen, e:q. F.R.S. *Treafurer.*
Sir Wm. Chambers, Kt. FRS.
Mathew Duane, efq. F.R.S.
R. Gough, efq; F.R.S. *Director.*
Ant. Hamilton, D.D. F.R.S.
Tho. Brand Hollis. efq. F.R.S.
Sir R. Jebb, Bart. M D. F.R.S.
Edward King, efq. F.R S.
Mich. Lort, B. D. F. S. *V. P*
Tho. Morell, D.D. F.R.S *Sec.*
Rev. Wm. Norris, A. M. *Sec.*
William Earl of Radnor
Henry Stebbing, D.D. F.R.S.
Ralph Willet, efq. F.R.S.
Daniel Wray, Efq. F. R. S.

BRITISH MUSEUM, Montague-Houfe, 1753.
Forty-two Truftees;—21 By virtue of their offices—6 Reprefenting the Sloane, Cotton, and Oxford families, marked S. C. O.—and 15 chofen by the former 27.

21 *Truftees by Office.*
Archbifhop of Canterbury
The Lord-Chancellor
Lord-Prefident of Council
Firft Lord of the Treafury
Lord-Privy-Seal
Firft Lord of the Admiralty
Lord-Steward
Lord-Chamberlain
Three Secretaries of State.
Bifhop of London
Speaker of Houfe of Commons
Chancellor of the Exchequer
Ld.-Ch.-Juftice King's-Bench
Mafter of the Rolls
Ld.-Ch.-Juftice Com.-Pleas
Attorney-General
Solicitor-General
Prefident of Royal Society
Prefident of Col. of Phyficians
6 *Family Truftees.*
C. john Bofworth, D. D.
S.⨯Francis Annefley, Efq;
S. Earl of Oxford
O. Duke of Portland, F. R. S.
C. S. Lord Cadogan.
Right Hon. Welbore Ellis

15 *Truftees Elected.*
Earl of Belborough
Guftavus Brander, Efq; F.R.S.
Earl of Bute
Lord Cha. Cavendifh, F.R.S.
Matthew Duane, Efq; F. R. S.
Charles Gray, Efq; F.R.S.
Earl of Hardwicke, F.R.S.
Rev. R. Kaye, LL.D. F.R.S.
D. of Northumberland, F.R.S.
Lord Sandys
⨯ Hans Sloane, Efq; F. R. S.
Wm. Watfon, M. D. F.R.S.
Daniel Wray, Efq; F. R. S.
Hon. Hen. Cavendifh, F.R.S.
Principal Librarian.
Charles Morton, M.D.F.R.S.
Under Librarians.
Jof. Planta, efq; (Sec. of the R. S.) has the care of the MSS. and Medals
And. Gifford, D. D. F. S. A. his Affiftant
Dan. Ch. Solander, M.D. LL.D. F. R. S. has the care of Natural Hiftory

Edward Gray, M. D. F. R. S. | Rev. P. H. Maty, M. A. Secret.
Affist. | of the Royal Soc. his Affiftant.
Rev. S. Harper, M. A. F. R. S. | *Keeper of the Reading-Room.*
care of the printed Books. | Rev. Mr. Penneck, B.D. F.R.S.

SOCIETY for promoting Chriftian Knowledge, 1699,
Meet every Tuefday in Bartlet's Buildings, Holborn.
They are Overfeers of all the Charity-Schools, diftribute Religious Books and Tracts, and fupport the Proteftant Miffion in the Eaft-Indies, jointly with the King of Denmark.

Treafurers. | *Secretary.*
Rev. Rob. Poole Finch, D.D. | Rev. Mr. Michael Hallings
Henry Hoare, Efq; | *Bookf.* Rivington and Sons.
Robert Gofling, Efq; | *Clerk.* John Robinfon.

SOCIETY for propagating the Gofpel in Foreign Parts
Incorporated by Charter, 1701,
Meet at Q. Anne's Bounty-Office, Dean's-Yard, Weftminfter.
The Archbifhop of Canterbury, *Prefident.*
Jn. Bacon, Efq; F. S. A. *Treaf.* Rev. Mr. Boucher, *Affift. Sec.*
Rev. Wm. Morrice, D. D. *Sec.* Samuel Norcott, *Meffenger*
They are Truftees for Codrington-College, in Barbadoes,
fupported by Plantations in that Ifland.
Legacies, Benefactions, and Subfcriptions, are received by John
Bacon, Efq; at the Firft-Fruits-Office, Temple.

The COMPANY for propagating the Gofpel in New-England
and Parts adjacent in America, incorporated by K. Charles
II. Feb. 7, 1661, in the fourteenth Year of his Reign.
Governor.
Alex. Champion, Efq; *Treafurer.* William Lane, *Clerk.*

CHARTER-HOUSE, Founded by Tho. Sutton, Efq; in 1611.
Governors. | Rev. Sam. Berdmore, D. D.
The KING, The QUEEN, | *Under Schoolmafter.*
Archbifhop of Canterbury, | Rev. William Bird, M. A.
Lord-Chancellor, E. Bathurft | *Affift.* Rev. E. Wollafton, M. A.
Duke of Grafton, Duke of | *Reader,* Edm. L. Baines, LL.B.
Marlborough, Mar. of Rock- | *Writing-maft.* Mr. King
ingham, Earl Gower, E. of | *Phyf.* Dr. Nathaniel Hulme
Sandwich, E. of Rochford, | *Surgeon,* Mr. Godman
E. of Bute, Bp. of London, | *Apoth.* Mr. John Devaynes
E. of Mansfield, Vifc. Wey- | *Organift,* Mr. John Jones
mouth, L. Camden & L. North | *Steward of the Courts.*
Mafter, Rev. W. Ramfden, DD | Edw. Bearcroft, Efq; F. R. S.
Preacher, Tho. Sainfbury, D.D
Receiv. Herbert Croftes, Efq; | St. Bartholomew's Hofpital,
Auditor, Tho. Melmoth, Efq; | Founded by Hen. VIII. 1539.
Regifter, Henry Sayer, Efq. | × Rt. H. Th. Harley, *Prefident*
Upper Schoolmafter. | × John Darker, Efq; *Treafurer*

(228)

Rev. Sam. Kettilby, D.D *Vicar*
Rd. Tyson, M D. David Pitcairne, M.D. Rich. Budd, M.D. F.R.S. *Physicians*
Wm. Robinson, *Apothecary*
Mr. Percival Pott, F. R. S.
Mr. Stafford Crane, Mr. Robt. Young, *Surgeons*
Mr. E. Pitt, Mr. J. Earle, Mr. Charles Blicke, *Assist. Surgeons*
Mr. Thomas Wall, *Clerk*
Mr. Tho. Cole, *Steward*
Mr. John Banning, *Renter*
Mrs. Sandiford, *Matron*
John Dale, *Porter*

Christ's Hospital,
Founded by Edw. VI. 1552.
Robert Alsop, Esq; *President*
Tho. Burfoot, Esq; *Treasurer*
Dr. Wm. Pitcairne, *Physician*
Mr. Dale Ingram, *Surgeon*
Mr. Jo. Roberts, *Apothecary*
Mr. Joseph Eyre, *Chief Clerk*
Mr. Tho. Smith, *Clerk and Rec.*
Mr. Robt. Court, *Wardrobe Keeper and Assist. Clerk*
Rev. James Boyer, M. A. *Grammar-Master*
Rev. Matthew Field, M. A. *Under Grammar-Master*
Rev. Nicholas Layton, M. A. *Master of the Reading-School*
Mr. William Wales, F.R.S *Master of the Mathematics.*
Mr. J. Attwood, *Writing-Mast.*
Mr. B. Green, *Drawing-Mast.*
Mr. Rob. Hudson, *Music-Mast.*
Mr. John Perry, *Steward*
Mrs. Lois Gibson, *Matron at Hertford.*
Mr. Wm. Green, *Schoolmaster*
Mr. J. Frost, *Surg. and Apoth.*
Mrs. Durcombe, *Girls Sch Mist.*
Sus. Richardson, *under ditto.*

Bridewell and Bethlem,
Founded by Edw. VI. 1553.
Brackley Kennert, esq; & Ald·

President of both Hospitals
Mr. Ald. Thomas, *Treas.* to both
Henry Cranke, Esq; *Auditor Gen.* to both
Rev. Moses Wight, M. A. *Preacher* to Bridewell
Rev T. Bowen, M A. *Read.* to do.
John Monro, M. D. *Physician* to both Hospitals
Mr. Rich. Crowther, *Surgeon* to both
Mr. Jn. Gozna, *Apoth.* to both
Jn. Woodhouse, Esq; *Cl.* to both
Mr. John Griffiths, *Steward* to Bridewell
Mrs. Lyon, *Matron* to ditto
Mr. Henry White, *Steward* to Bethlem
Mrs. Mary Spencer, *Matron* to Bethlem.

St. Thomas's Hospital,
Founded by Edw. VI. 1553.
Samuel Plumbe, Esq; Alderman *President*
Edw. Jefferies Esq; *Treasurer*
Rev. T. Green, M. A. *Hospitaller*
Dr. Geo. Fordyce, F R S. Dr. J. Rawlinson, Dr. H. B. Reynolds, *Physicians*
Mr. T. Smith, Mr. G. Martin, Mr. Waring. *Surgeons*
Mr. Geo. Whitfield, *Apoth.*
Mr. Oliver Cromwell, *Clerk*
Mr. Ant. Wingfield, *Receiver*
Mr. Richard Leeson, *Steward*
Mr. John Beard, *Butler*
Mrs. Wright, *Matron*
Mr. Richard Hooper, *Brewer*
Mr. John Cross, *Baker*

Laudable Society of Annuitants, Bartholomew-Lane.
Mr. Geo. Fleming, *President.*
Mr. E. Gibbs, Mr. J. Triquet, Mr. J. Davidson, *Vice-Pres.*
D. Ormond, *Secretary.*

Hospital for French Protestants and their Descendants, incor-

porated 1718, 200 Beds, besides 42 for Lunatics in an adjoining House.
John Buissiere, Esq; *Governor*
Jacob Allbert, Esq; *Sub.-Gov.*
Peter Gaussen, Esq; *Treasurer.*
Fran. Duroure, Esq; *Secretary*
Rev. J. Carles, M. A. *Chapl.*
James Dargent, M.D. F.R.S. *Physician*
Mr. Peter Girod, *Surg. & Apct.*
Mr. Peter Hervé, *Steward*
Mrs. Hervé, *Matron*

Guy's Hospital, founded by Tho. Guy, Esq; in 1722.
*Tho. Lucas, Esq; *President*
Geo. Brough, Esq; *Treasurer*
Dr. Wm. Saunders, Dr. James Hervey, *Physicians*
Mr J.Warner,FRS.Mr J.Frank, Mr. W. Lucas, *Surgeons*
Rev. R. P. Finch, D.D. *Chapl.*
Mr. John Harrison, *Clerk*
Mr. Ben. Stead, *Apothecary*
James Simpson, *Assist. Apoth.*
Tho. Callaway, *Steward*
Will. Richardson, *Accomptant*
Sarah Wallis, *Matron*
Susannah Durant, *Cook*
Mark Haddock, *Butler*
Sim. Whayman, *Surgery-man*
Tho. Cox, *Porter*
John Keen, *Beadle*
Wm. Clark, *Keeper of the Lunatic Men*
Jane Page, *Keeper of the Lunatic Women*

Humane Society instituted for the Recovery of drowned Persons, 1774.
Mr. Alderman Bull, *President*
James Horsfall, esq; *Treasurer*
Mr. Davis, *Receiver*
Dr. Cogan and Dr. Hawes, *Institutors*

Medical Assistants, 137.

Westminster Infirmary, instituted by Subscription, 1719.
Duke of Newcastle, *President*
Earl of Lincoln, Hugh Earl Percy, Bp. of Rochester, Ld. Sandys, *Sir G.Savile, Bart. * Sir W.W.Wynne, Bart. Sir Henry Cheere, Bart. C. Lowndes, Esq; *Vice Pres.*
John Merest, Esq; *Treasurer*
Dr. Mich. Morris, F. R. S. Dr. J. Dargent, F.R.S. Dr. Geo. Hicks, *Physicians*
Mr. Jn. Pyle, Mr. H. Watson, F. R. S. Mr. Jn. Ob. Justamond, F. R. S. *Surgeons*
Mr. Jabez Ward, *Apoth.*
Rev. T. Champnes, *Chaplain*
Mr. W. Watson, *Sec.* and *Rec.*
Mrs. Mary Turner, *Matron*
Mr. John Turner, *Messenger*

St. George's Hospital, instituted by Subscription, 1733.
The KING, *President*
His Grace Fred. Lord Archbp. of Canterbury, Earl of Hertford, E. of Guildford, *V.-Pres.*
J. Ad. Fred. Hesse, Ch. Carter, Esq. *Treasurers*
Dr.T.Gisborne,FRS. Dr.Don. Monro,FRS. Lr.R.Wright, FRS. Dr. J. Burges, *Physicians*
Jn. Gunning, J. Hunter, FRS. Cha. Hawkins, Geo. Hawkins, Esqrs. *Surgeons*
Ch Bromfield, Esq; *Assist. Sur.*
Matt. Yatman, Jos. Partridge, R. Halifax, J. Devaynes, Esqrs. *Visiting Apoth.*
Rev. Mr. Clarke, *Chaplain*
Mr.Wm.Dampier,*House Apoth.*
Rev. Mr. Clarke, *Secretary*
J. Attwell, *Matron*

(230)

The Foundling Hospital, in Lambs Conduit Fields, incorporated in 1739.
The KING, *Patron*
※ Rt.Hon.Ld. North, *President*
E. of Abercorn, E. of Dartmouth, Ld. Le Despencer, Jon. Hanway,esq; T. Nugent, esq; Alex. Scott, esq; *Vice-Presidents.*
G. Whatley, Esq; *Treas.*
Rev. Mr. Harper, *Chaplain*
Rev. Mr. Jackson, *Morning Preacher*
T. Collingwood, *Secretary*
Mr. John Dagge, *Solicitor*
Dr. C. Morton, F.R.S. Dr. W. Watson, F.R.S. *Physicians*
Mr. Tho. Patch, *Surgeon*
Mr. R. M'Clellan, *Apothecary*
Mr. Charles Biggs, *Steward*
Mr. R. Atchison, *Schoolmaster*
Mr. J. Archer, *Treasurer's Clerk*
Jemima Jones, *Matron.*

London Hospital, instituted 1740. Incorporated Dec. 9, 1758. Whitechapel-Road.
His R.H. D. of Glocester, *Pres.*
Duke of Rutland, John Dorrien, Esq; ※ Jos. Mellish, Esq; *Vice-Presidents*
John Spiller, Esq; *Treasurer*
Rev. Mr. Audley, *Chaplain*
Dr. Tho. Dickson, F.R.S. Dr. Tho. Healde, F. R.S. Dr. J. Maddocks, *Physicians*
Mr. Rich. Grindall, F. R. S. Mr. G. Neale, Mr. William Blizard, *Surgeons*
Mr. Dan. Eldridge, *Apothecary*
Mr. Jn. Cole, *Secretary* and *Rec.*
Mr. Gabriel Bowler, *Steward*
E. Patterson, M. Stainbank *Mat.*

Middlesex Hospital for Sick and Lame, and Lying-in married Women, in Mary le Bone Fields, instituted by Subscription, 1745.
D. of Northumberland, *Presid.*
Duke of Rutland, E. Gower, ※ Ld. Algernon Percy, Ld. Grosvenor, Lord Scarsdale, ※ Sir Robt. Clayton, Bart. *Vice-Presidents*
J. Machin, Esq; Will. Wright, esq; *Treas.*
Dr. H. A. Kennedy, Dr. Knox, Dr. J. C. Smyth, Dr. Fran. Milman, F.R.S. *Physicians*
Dr. Khron and Dr. Denman, *Men-Midwives*
Mr. Samuel Howard, F.R.S. Mr. J. Chafy, J. Wyatt, F.R.S
Mr. Daniel Minors, *Sur.*
Mr. J. Tufon, *House-Surg.*
Rev. Mr. Ja. Clark, *Chaplain*
Mr. G. Plagaven, *Secretary*
Mr. T. Cuff, *Coll.*
Mr. Joseph Roper, *Apothecary*
Mrs. Eliz. Brittridge, *Matron and Midwife*
Mrs. Eliz. Whincop, 2d *ditto*

Small-Pox Hospital, in Cold-Bath Fields, and Hospital for Inoculation, at Pancras, instituted in 1746.
The KING, *Patron*
Duke of Grafton, *President*
Du. of Northumberland, Marquis of Caermarthen, Tho. Lucas, Esq; Mr. Alderman Clark, *Vice Presidents.*
Charles Maverly, Esq; *Treas.*
Lamb's-Conduit-Street
Dr. Edw. Archer, *Physician*
Mr. R. Reynolds, Castle-Yard, Holborn. *Sec.* and *Rec.*
Mr. Rich. Squirrel, *Apothecary* and *Stew.* Cold-Bath-Fields
Mrs. S. Runnington, *Mat. ditto*
Mr. Matthew Enderup, *Apoth.* at Pancras
Mrs. Susan. Lay, *Matron ditto*

(231)

Lock Hospital, near Hyde-Park-Corner, 1746.
Duke of Ancaster, *President*
Duke of Manchester, Duke of Rutland, Marquis of Rockingham, Earl of Dartmouth, Lord Sondes, ✕ Lord G. Sutton, *Vice-Presidents*
John Way, and Edw. Webster, Esqrs. *Treasurers*
Sir N. Thomas, MD.F R S. *Phys.*
Rev. Mr. Madan, *Chaplain*
Mr. Tho. Williams, C. Bromfeild, Esq; *Surgeons*
James Bromfeild, Esq; Mr. T. Evans, *Visiting Apothecaries*
Mr. Tho. Green, *House-Surg.*
Mr. Jabez Fisher, *Secretary*
Mr. John Walker, *Collector*
Mrs. A. Morgan, *Matron*

Corporation for sick and maimed Seamen in the Merchants Service, incorporated 24th June, 1747. Office in the Royal Exchange.
Richard Becher, Esq; *Presid.*
COMMITTEE.
Isaac Akerman, Benjamin Bewicke, Wm. Blacke, Wm. Bowden, Geo Brough, Rd. Cooke, John Cornwall, Jn. Dorrien, Pet. Gaussen, Ja. Henckell, George Hooper, James Matthias, Henry-Handley Norris, Ja. Norman, David Powell, *junior*, Wm. Raikes, Tho. Raikes, Wm. Reynolds, Wm. Scullard, Sam. Thornton, Sam. Waterman. Esqrs.
W. Oddy, *Rec. & Sec.*
Mr. John Waring, *Surgeon.*

The British Lying-In-Hospital for Married Women in Brownlow-Str. Long-Acre, instituted Nov. 1749.
Duke of Portland, *President.*

Lord Grosvenor, Rt. Hon. Earl Spencer, Sir John Chapman, Bart.
Dr. Daniel Peter Layard, F.R.S. *Vice-Presidents*
Henry Bottero, Esq; *Treas.*
Dr. Hunter and Dr. Kelly, *Consulting Physicians.*
Dr. Rob. Bromfield, Dr. Maxwell Garthshore, *Physicians.*
Mr. W. Graves, and Mr. Mitch. Underwood, *Surgeons*
Mr. M. P. Julliott, *Apothecary.*
Rev. Mr Steph. Degnahon, *Chap.*
Mr. Thomas Yewd, *Sec.*
Mrs. H. Dennis, *Matr. & Midw.*
Six Nurses, 62 Beds.

City of London Lying-In-Hospital, instituted March 30, 1750, City Road.
✕ George Hayley, Esq; *Pres.*
Henry Shiffner, Rich. Hoare, Wm. Gordon, Wm. Pocock, Esqrs. *Vice-Pres.*
John Paterson, Esq; *Treas.*
Dr. Nathaniel Hulme, *Physician in Ordinary.*
Dr. Rob. Mac Laurin, *Man-Midwife in Ordinary.*
Dr. David Orme, *Man-Midwife Extraordinary.*
Dr. Sa. Wathen, *Man-Midwife Extraordinary.*
Dr. Moses Griffith, *Physician and Man-Midwife Extraord.*
Mr. Wm. Lucas, *Surg. in Ord.*
Mr. Rich. Ball, *Surg. Extra.*
Mr. William Ball, *Apoth.*
Rev. Joseph Cookson, *Chap.*
Mr. Philip Constables, *Sec.*
Mrs. A. Newby, *Matr. and Mid.*

St. Luke's Hospital for Lunatics, Moorfields, 1751.
Duke of Montagu, *President.*
James Sperling, Edw. Payne, John Elliott, Ste. Peter Godin, Esqrs. *Vice-Pres.*

Mr. Wm. Prowting. *Treaf.*
Dr. Tho. Brooke, *Phyfician.*
Mr. John Waring, *Surgeon.*
Mr. J. Meadows, *Refid. Apoth.*
Mr. Tho. Webfter, *Sec.*

MARINE SOCIETY'S OF-
FICE, in Bifhopfgate-ftreet,
inftituted 1756, incorpora-
ted June 1772.
Prefident, Robert Lord Romney
Vice-Prefidents.
SirW.Dolben, Bt. SirH.Mack-
worth, Bt. G.Pococke, K.B.
Beefton Long, Efq; Tho.
Walker, Efq; Jn. Frere, Efq.
Treaf. John Thornton, Efq;
Vice.-Treaf. JonasHanway, Efq;
Clerk, Mr. Weatherhead
Meffenger, Robert Ruffell.

General Medical Afylum,
Welbeck - Street, Mary-
bone, inftituted 1776.
His Grace the Duke of Port-
land, *Prefident.*
Ld. Le Defpencer, ×Vifc. Pal-
merftone,×Vifc. Beauchamp,
×Ld. G.H.F. Cavendifh,×Ld.
R. Spencer, Bp. of Landaff,
Hon. Mr. Bouverie, Tho. Se-
win, efq; Ch. Selwin, efq;
Vice-Prefidents.
John Sheldon, efq; *Treafurer.*
Dr. Wilfon, Dr. Hafkey, Dr.
Wallis, *Phyficians.*
Dr. Lowder, *Manmidwife.*
Mr. J. Sheldon, jun. Mr. W.
Smart, Mr. J. Brookes, jun.
Surgeons.
Mr. John Lewis, *Apothecary.*
Mr. James Roffe, *Sec.* and *Rec.*
Mrs. Eliz. Harris, *Houfekeeper*

The Afylum, or Houfe of Re-
fuge for Orphan Girls, near
Weftminfter - Bridge, infti-
tuted 1758.
×Rt. Hon. Lord North, *Prefident*
Rt. Hon. Lord Vere,

Rt. Hon. and Rt. Rev. James
Lord Bifhop of Hereford,
Sir. Arch. Croft, Bart.
Sir Cha. Kemeys Tynte, Bart.
Sir H.W. Dafhwood, Bart.
×AfshetonCurzon, Efq; *V.-Prs.*
Rev. F. Kelly Maxwell, M.A.
Chaplain, Treaf. and *Sec.*
Sir R. febb, Bt. F.R.S. *Phyf.*
Samuel Howard, F. R. S.
Carfan, *Surgeons.*
Mr. Mofes Paul Julliot, *Apoth.*

Magdalen-Houfe, St. George's
Fields, inftituted 1758.
The QUEEN, *Patronefs.*
Earl of Hertford, *Prefident.*
Lord Romney, Earl Percy,
Rob. Dingley, Nath. Caftle-
ton, Rich. Becher, John
Barker, Efqrs, *Vice-Prs.*
Michael James, Efq; *Treaf.*
Abra. Winterbottom, *Sec.*
Dr. Wm. Saunders, *Phyfician.*
W. Blizard, John Andree, *Surg*
And. Johnfton, J. Harris, *Apoth.*
Rev. Mr. Dobey, *Chapl.*
Richard Du Horty, *Steward.*
Eliz. Butler, *Matron.*
Charlotte Smith, *Affift. Mat.*
Robert Faucitt, *Meffenger*,

Weftminfter New Lying-In
Hofpital, near Weftminfter-
Bridge, on the Surry fide,
inftituted by Subfcript.1765.
Lord Grofvenor *Prefident.*
× Sir Harbord Harbord, Bart.
×Sir Jofeph Mawbey, Bart.
Lieut.-Gen. G. Williamfon
Lt. - Gen. Boyd, × Crifp
Molineux, Efqrs, *Vice-Prs.*
Rev. Mr. Stainfby, *Chaplain.*
Dr. John Leake, *Phyfician* and
Man-Midwife.
Dr. James Ford, *Phyfician* and
Man-Midwife Extraord.
Mr. Sherfon, Mr. Grant, *Su-
perintendant Apothecaries.*

(233)

Dr. Rd. Saunders, *Consult. Phyf.* Mr. Lewis Poignand, *Surgeon.* Mr. John West, *Sec.* Mr. Wm. Davis, *Receiver.* Mrs. Mary Claverley, *Matron and Midwife.*

Difpenfary for Relief of the INFANT POOR, Soho-fquare, inftituted 1769. *Prefident,* Earl of Winchelfea *Vice-Prefidents.* The Rt. Hon. Earl Percy × Sir Watk. Will. Wynne, Bart. ✗ Sir Sampfon Gideon, Bart. Sir George Colebrooke, Bart. ✗ Sir George Cornewall, Bart. James Coutts, Efq; *Treaf.* John Townfon, Efq; *Phyf. in ord.* Dr. Geo. Armftrong *Confulting Phyficians.* Sir John Pringle, Bart. Dr. Brocklefby, Dr. Warren, Dr. Turton, Dr. Hunter, Dr. Watfon, Dr. Saunders, Dr. James Ford, Dr. Garthfhore. *Sec.* Mr. Jofeph Kemp *Receiver.* Mr. William Davis.

General Difpenfary for Relief of the Poor, Alderfgate-ftreet, inftituted 1770. Earl of Dartmouth, *Prefident.* Sir Lionel Lyde, Bart. ✗ Right Hon. Tho. Harley, Alderman Saintfbury, Daniel Mildred, Efq; *Vice-Prefidents.* James Johnfon, Efq; *Treafurer.* Nathaniel Hulme, M. D. Jas. Sims, M. D. Adair Crawford, M. D. *Phyficians* .C. Lettfom, M.D. F R S. *Phyf. Ext.* Sr. Geo. Vaux, Mr. William Norris, *Surgeons.* Mr. William Slater, *Apoth.* Mr. Midford Young, *Secretary.*

MEDICAL SOCIETY of London, Crane-Court, Fleet-ftreet, inftituted 1773. The Counc. elected Jan. 18, 178 *Prefident,* Sam. Foart Simmons, M. D. F. R. S. *Treafurer,* Mr. Philip Hurlock *Librarian,* Nath. Hulme, M.D. *Phyficians,* J. C. Lettfom, M.D. F. R. S. George Edwards, M. D. John Rogers, M. D. *Surgs.* Mr. Jo. Hooper, Mr. W. French, Mr. A. Blackwell *Apothecaries,* Mr Cuth. Potts, Mr. S. Price, Mr. Ja. Birkit *Secretaries.* Loftus Wood, M.D. Mr. Ed Ford *Meffenger,* Jacob Rayer.

WESTMINSTER GENERAL DISPENSARY, Gerard-Street, Soho. Inftituted June 6, 1774. *Prefident,* His Grace the Duke of Northumberland *Vice-Prefidents.* Earl of Rochford, ✗ Lord Vifc. Beauchamp, ✗ Earl of Lincoln, ✗ Sir Watk. Williams Wynn, Bart. ✗ Sir Mic. Le Fleming, Bart. John Lind, Efq; FRS. Maurice Lloyd, Efq. William Porter Gillies, Efq; *Treafurers* J. Hunter, M. D. H. Seguin Jackfon, M. D. S. F. Simmons, M. D. FRS. *Phyficians* James Ford, M. D. *Confuling Phyfician and Man-Midwife* Rob. Bland, M. D. *Man-Mid.* Mr. Edward Ford, *Surgeon* Mr. John Barron, *Apothec.* Mr. John Gray, *Sec. & Receiv.* Rob. Collins, *Meffenger* Elizabeth Collins, *Houfekeeper.*

The MISERICORDIA, or Hofpital for the Cure and Relief of indigent Perfons afflicted with the Venereal Difeafe, in Great-Ayliffe-street, Goodman's - Fields, instituted in 1774.

Mr. Wm. Jackson, *Apothecary*
Mrs. Ruth Merrett,-*Matron*.

✘ Sir Geo. Yonge, Bart. *Prefi.*
✘Fred. Bull, Esq; Ald. Wm. Plomer, Esq; Ald. And. Thomson, Beeston Long, Esq; *Vice-Presidents*
Jonas Hanway, Esq; *Treasurer*
Rev. Herbert Jones, *Chaplain*
Dr. Wm. Grant, *Physician*
Mr. Wm. Blizard, Mr. Alex. Maxwell, *Surgeons*
Mr. Robert Smith, *Secretary*
Mr. Wm. Burke, *Clerk*

Scots Hospital and Corporation, of the foundation of K. Charles II. re-incorporated by his present Majesty Hall, Water-la. Black-Friars. Duke of B ccleugh, *President* Dukes of Queesbury and Argyle, Earls of Findlater and Seafield, Hon. Sir Law. Dundas, Sir James Cockburn, bart. Arch. Douglas, of Douglas, esq: *Vice-Presidents*. Arthur Edie, esq; *Treasurer*.

UNIVERSITY of OXFORD.

Colleges.	Founded.	Heads of Colleges.	Elected.
University	872	Nath. Wetherell, D. D. *Master*	1764
Baliol	1262	Theo. Leigh, D. D. *Master*	1726
Merton	1274	Henry Barton, D. D. *Warden*	1759
Exeter	1316	Thomas Bray, D. D. *Rector*	1772
Oriel	1337	John Clark, D. D. *Provost*	1768
Queen's	1340	Tho. Fothergill, D. D. *Provost*	1767
New College	1375	John Oglander, D. D. *Warden*	1768
Lincoln	1427	Richard Hutchins, D. D. *Rector*	1755
All Souls	1437	Hon. John Tracy, D. D. *Warden*	1767
Magdalen	1449	Geo. Horne, D. D. *President*	1768
Brasenose	1511	Tho. Barker, D. D. *Principal*	1777
Corpus Christi	1516	Tho. Randolph, D. D. *President*	1748
Christ Church	1532	Lewis Bagot, L L. D. *Dean*	1777
Trinity	1555	Jos. Chapman, D. D. *President*	1776
St. John's	1557	Samuel Dennis, D. D. *President*	1772
Jesus	1571	Joseph Hoare, D. D. *Principal*	1768
Wadham	1613	James Gerard, D. D. *Warden*	1777
Pembroke	1620	William Adams, D. D. *Master*	1775
Worcester	1713	Wm Sheffield, D. D. *Provost*	1777
Hertford	1740	Bein. Hodgson, LL.D. *Principal*	1775
Alban Hall		. Francis Randolph, D.D. *Principal*	1759
Edmund Hall		George Dixon, D. D. *Principal*	1760
St. Mary Hall		Tho. Nowell, D. D. *Principal*	1764
New-Inn Hall		Rob. Chambers, LL.D. *Principal*	1767
Magdalen Hall		Wm. Denison, D. D. *Principal*	1755

✘ Right Hon. Lord North, K. G. *Chancellor*, elected in 1772.
Lord Leigh, *High Steward*, appointed in 1767.
Samuel Dennis, D. D. President of St. John's, *Vice-Chancellor*, 1780.

PRO-VICE-CHANCELLORS.

Thomas Fothergill, D.D. Provoſt of Queen's College
Nathan Wetherell, D.D. Maſter of Univerſity College
George Horne, D D. Preſident of Magdalen College
Joſeph Chapman, D.D. Preſident of Trinity College.

PROCTORS.

Waſhbourne Cooke, A.M. New College.
Alexander Litchfield, A.M. Wadham College.

PROFESSORS.	Appointed or elected.	
Regius Profeſſor of Divinity	Benj. Wheeler, D. D.	1776
Ditto Civil Law	Robert Vanſittart, LL.D.	1767
Ditto Phyſic	William Vivian, M. D.	1772
Ditto Hebrew	George Jubb, D. D.	1780
Ditto Greek	William Sharp, D. D.	1763
Ditto Modern Hiſtory	Thomas Nowell, D. D.	1771
Margaret Prof. of Divinity	Tho. Randolph, D. D.	1768
Savil. Profeſſor in Aſtronomy	Thomas Hornſby, M. A.	1762
Ditto Geometry	John Smith, M. D.	1766
Profeſſor of Nat. Philoſophy	Benjamin Wheeler, D.D.	1767
Ditto of Moral Philoſophy	Ch. Tyr. Morgan, A.M.	1776
Camden Profeſſor of Hiſtory	William Scott, LL. D.	1773
Abp. Laud's Prof. of Arabic	Joſeph White, B.D.	1774
Ld. Almoner's Prof. of Arabic	Henry Ford,	1780
Reader in Chemiſtry and Anat.	John Parſons, M. D.	1769
Vinerian Profeſſor of the Laws of England	Rd Wooddeſon, D.C.L.	1777
Univerſity Orator	James Bandinel, D. D.	1776
Keeper of Bodleian Library	John Price, B. D.	1768
Keeper of the Archives	Benj. Buckler, D. D.	1777
Keeper of Aſhmolean Muſeum	William Sheffield, D.D.	1772
———— Radcliffe Library	B. Kennicott, D.D.F.R.S.	1767
Clinical Lecturer	John Parſons, M.D.	1780
Profeſſor of Botany	Hum. Sibthorpe, M. D.	1747
———— Poetry	John Randolph, M. A.	1776
———— Muſic	Philip Hayes, D. Muſ.	1777

UNIVERSITY OFFICERS.

Univerſity Regiſtrar   Rev. Samuel Forſter, LL. D.
Eſquire Beadles
- Rob. Eyton, M. A. of Phyſic and Arts
- James Matthews, M. A. of Divinity
- Robert Paget, LL.D. of Law

Yeoman Beadles
- Mr. Ja. Reynolds, of Phyſic and Arts
- Mr. James Arnold, of Divinity
- Mr. Charles Cox, of Law

Clerk   Iohn Green
Virger   William Mathews

OXFORD Terms in 1781.

Lent	begins	Jan. 15	ends	April 7
Easter	———	May 2	———	May 31
Act	———	June 15	———	July 4
Michaelmas	———	Oct. 10	———	Dec. 17

Oxford Act, July 8.

UNIVERSITY of CAMBRIDGE.

Duke of Grafton, *Chancellor* 1768
Earl of Hardwicke, *High Steward* 1764
And. Pemberton, M.A. *Commissary* 1779

Coll. and Halls.	Founded.	Heads of Colleges.		Elected.
Peter-House	1257	Bp. of Carlisle, D. D.	*Master*	1754
Clare-Hall	1326	Pet. Ste. Goddard, D.D.	*Master*	1762
Pembroke-Hall	1343	James Browne, D. D.	*Master*	1771
Corpus Christi or Bene't Coll.	1351	Wm. Colman, D.D.	*Master*	1778
Trinity-Hall	1350	Sir Jas. Marriott, LL.D.	*Master*	1764
Gonvil and Caius	1348	John Smith, D. D.	*Master*	1764
King's	1441	Wm. Cooke, D. D.	*Provost*	1772
Queen's	1448	Rob. Plumptre, D.D.	*President*	1760
Catherine-Hall	1475	Lowther Yates, D.D.	*Master*	1779
Jesus-College	1496	Lyndford Caryl, D.D.	*Master*	1758
Christ's	1505	John Barker, D.D.	*Master*	1780
St. John's	1509	J. Chevallier, D. D.	*Master,*	1775
Magdalen	1519	Hon. Bart. Wallop, M.A.	*Mast.*	1774
Trinity	1546	Bp. of Peterborough,	*Master*	1768
Emanuel	1584	Richard Farmer, D.D.	*Master*	1775
Sidney	1598	Wm. Elliston, D. D.	*Master*	1760

● CAPUT { John Barker, D.D. Christ's Coll. *V.-Chan.*
William Colman, D.D. Bene't Coll. *Div.*
Joseph Jowett, LL.D. Trinity Hall, *Law.*
I. Pennington, M.D. St. John's Coll. *Physic.*
E. Mapletoft, M.A. Christ's Col. *Sen. Non. Reg.*
Josh. Waterhouse, M.A. Cath. Hall, *Sen. Reg.*

Proctors { John Wilson, M.A. Trinity College
William Wyatt, M.A. Pembroke Hall

Moderators { Thomas Cautley, M.A. Trinity College
George Pretyman, M.A. Pembroke Hall

Taxors { Francis Barnes, M.A. King's College
Job Wallace, M.A. Bene't College.

Scrutators { Adam Wall, M.A. Christ's College
John Torkington, B.D. Clare Hall

1502	Margaret Prof. of Div.	Zachary Brooke, D. D.	1765
1540	Regius Prof. of Divin.	Rich. Watson, DD. FRS.	1771
1540	——— of Law	Sam. Hallifax, D. D.	1770
1540	——— of Physic	Russel Plumptre, M. D.	1741
	Casuistical Professor	Rob. Plumptre, D. D.	1769

1540	Hebrew Profeffor	William Collier, M. A. 1771
1511	Greek Profeffor	William Cooke, M. A. 1780
1663	Mathematical Profeffor	Ed. Waring, M.D. F.R.S. 1760
1632	Arabic Profeffor	William Craven, B. D. 1770
1704	Profeffor of Aftronomy	Ant. Shepherd, DD. FRS. 1760
1749	Aftronomy, Lowndes's	John Smith, D.D. F.R.S. 1771
1707	Anatomy	C Collignon, M.D.FRS. 1753
1724	Modern Hiftory	John Symonds, LL. D. 1771
1705	Chemiftry	Ifaac Pennington, M.D. 1774
	Botany	Tho. Martyn, B. D. 1761
1727	Woodwardian Lecturer	Thomas Green, M.A. 1778
1504	Ly. Margaret's Preacher	Richard Farmer, D. D. 1774
1684	Mufic	John Randall, D. Muf. 1756
1511	Public Orator	William Pearce, B. D. 1778
	Principal Librarian	Richard Farmer, D.D. 1778
	Librarian	Stephen Whiffon, B. D. 1751
	Regifter	George Borlafe, A.M 1778

Efquire Beadles, Francis Dawes, M. A. John Beverley, M. A. and William Matthew, LL. B.

* Every *Univerfity Grace* muft pafs the CAPUT, before it can be introduced into the SENATE.

CAMBRIDGE Terms in 1781.

Lent	begins	Jan. 13	ends	April	6
Eafter	——	April 25	——	July	6
Michaelmas	——	Oct. 10	——	Dec.	16

Commencement, Tuefday, July 3.

A LIST of the PEERS of SCOTLAND.

The Sixteen Peers marked thus * are elected to reprefent the Scots Peerage in the Houfe of Lords. † Englifh Peers. § Irifh Peers. ‖ Minors. ‡ Roman Catholics. Sons ‡ are Members of the Houfe of Commons. *b* are Baronets.

DUKES of the BLOOD ROYAL 3.

Rothfay ‖† Geo. Auguftus, Prince of Wales, Earl o Carrick
1764 Edinburgh † William Henry, Duke of Gloucefter
1766 Strathern † Henry Frederick, Duke of Cumberland

DUKES 9.

Creat.	Title.	Names.	Eldeft Sons.
1643	Hamilton	†Douglas Hamilton	Marq. of Clydfdale
1673	Buccleugh	†Henry Scot	Earl of Dalkeith
1675	Lennox	†Charles Lennox	Earl of Darnly
1684	Gordon	*Alexander Gordon	Marq. of Huntly
1684	Queenfberry	×James Douglas	E. of Drumlanrig
1703	Argyll	+John Campbell	Marquis of Lorn
1703	Athol	*John Murray	M. of Tullibardin
1707	Montrofe	†William Graham	×M. of Graham
1707	Roxburgh	†John Kerr	M. of Beaumon

(238)

MARQUISSES 3.

1694 Tweedale	George Hay	Earl of Gifford
1701 Lothian	*William John Kerr	Earl of Ancram
1701 Annandale	G. V. Bem. Johnstone	Earl of Hartfield

EARLS 45.

1275 Sutherland (Ctfs. of)	‖Eliz. Sutherland		Lord Strathnaver
1399 Crawfurd	George Crawfurd		Visc. Garnock
1452 Errol	George Hay		Lord Hay
1457 Rothes(Ctfs.of)	Jane Eliz. Leslie		Lord Leslie
1457 Morton	‖Geo. Douglas		Lord Aberdour
1469 Buchan	StewartErskine,LL.D.		Lord Cardross
1488 Glencairn	*James Cunningham		Lord Kilmaurs
1503 Egington	*Arch. Montgomery		LordMontgomery
1509 Cassilis	*David Kennedy		Lord Kennedy
1581 Moray	Francis Stewart		Lord Down
1604 Home	Alexander Home *b*		Lord Dunglass
1605 Wigtoun	Ham. Fleming		Lord Fleming
1606 Strathmore	‖John Bowes Lyon		Lord Glamis
1606 Abercorn	*§James Hamilton		Lord Paisley
1619 Haddington	Tho. Hamilton		Lord Binning
1619 Kelly	Alexander Erskine		Viscount Fenton
1623 Galloway	*John Stewart		Lord Garlies
1624 Lauderdale	James Maitland		Visc. Maitland
1633 Loudoun	*John Campbell, FRS.		Lord Mauchlane
1633 Kinnoul	†Thomas Hay		Viscount Dupplin
1633 Dumfries	Patrick M'Dowal		Lord Crighton
1633 Dalhousie	*George Ramsay		Lord Ramsay
1633 Elgin and Kincardin	Thomas Bruce		Lord Bruce
1633 Traquair	‡Charles Stewart		Lord Linton
1637 Findlater & Seafield	James Ogilvy		Lord Deskford
1641 Leven and Melvill	David Leslie		Lord Balgony
1646 Dysert	Lionel Tollemache		Lord Huntingtour
1646 Selkirk	Dunbar Douglas		Lord Dare
1647 Northesk	George Carnegy		Lord Rosehill
1651 Balcarras	Alex. Lindsay		LordCummerland
1660 Newburgh	‡—— Ratcliffe		Lord Kennard
1651 Aboyn	Charles Gordon		Lord Strathaven
1660 Dundonald	Archibald Cochran		Lord Cochran
1677 Kintore	David Falconer		Lord Halkertoun
1678 Breadalbane	John Campbell *b*		Lord Glenorchy
1682 Aberdeen	*George Gordon *b*		Lord Haddo
1686 Dunmore	*John Murray		Lord Fincastle

1505 Orkney, Ctfs.	Mary Obrien	Lord Kirkwall
1697 Marchmont	*H. Campbell, F.R.S. *b*	†Lord Polwarth
1701 Hyndford	John Carmichael *b*	Lord Carmichael
1703 Stair *b*	John Dalrymple *b*	Visc. Dalrymple
1703 Roseberry *b*	*Niel Primrose *b*	Lord Dalmeny
1703 Glasgow	‖George Boyle	Lord Boyle
1703 Bute	John Stuart *b*	†Ld. Mountstuart
1703 Hopetoun	John Hope, F. R. S.	Lord Hope
1703 Portmore	Charles Collier	Visc. Milsington
1706 Deloraine	Henry Scot	Visc. Hermitage

VISCOUNTS 5.

1620 Falkland	Lucius Carey	
1623 Stormont	*David Murray	
1641 Arbuthnot	John Arbuthnot	
1662 Dumblain	†Thomas Osborne	

BARONS 28.

1424 Somerville	James Somerville	
1440 Forbes	James Forbes, Lt.-Gov. of Ft.-William	
1442 Cathcart	William Schaw Cathcart	
1445 Saltoun	George Fraser	
1445 Gray	John Gray	
1489 Sempill	John Sempill	
1509 Elphinstone	Charles Elphinstone	
1563 Torphichen	James Sandilands	
1600 Lindores	John Leslie	
1606 Blantyre	Alexander Stewart	
1609 Cranstoun	William Cranstoun	
1609 Colvill, of Culrofs,	John Colvill	
1627 Napier	‖William Napier *b*	
1627 Fairfax	Henry Fairfax	
1628 Reay	Hugh Mackay *b*	
1628 Aston	Walter Aston	
1633 Kircudbright	John Maclellan	
1640 Mordington	Mary Weaver	
1642 Bamff	William Ogilvy *b*	
1643 Elibank	George Murray *b*	
1648 Belhaven	—— Hamilton	
1650 Forrester	Cecilia Forrester	
1651 Rollo	John Rollo	
1651 Ruthven	James Ruthven	
1651 Colvill of Ochiltree	} David Colvill	
1660 Newark	David Leslie	
1661 Bellenden	John Bellenden	
1682 Kinnaird	George Kinnaird	

(240)

Authentic List of the Baronets of Scotland.
Those marked * are Peers.

1625 Gordon of Gordonston
Strachan of Thornſn
*Wemyſs of Wemyſs
*Campbell of Glenurchy
Innes of Innes
*Livingſton of Dunipace
Douglas of Glenbervie
*M'Donald of Slate
*Murray of Cockpool
Colquhoun of Luſs
Gordon of Cluny
Leſlie of Wardis
Gordon of Leſsmore
Ramſay of Balmain
*Forreſter of Corſtorphine
Graham of Braco
1626 Forbes of Monymuſk
Johnſton of Caſkieben
Burnet of Leys
Moncrieff of Moncriefi
Ogilvie of Carnouſie
*Gordon of Lochinvar
Murray of Clermonth
Fla kader of Tulliallan
Ogilvie of Innerquharity
1627 *M'Kay of Strathnaver
Maxwell of Calderwood
*Sir James Stewart
*Napier of Marchieſton
Livingſton of Kinnaird
Cuningham of Cuninghamhead
*Carmichael, Weſterraw
M'Gill, Cranſton Riddle
*Ogilvie of Bamſſ
Johnſton of Elphinſton
Cockburn of Langtour
Campbell of Lundie
1628 *Aitchiſon of Clancairny
Montgomery, Skelmorly
1628 Campbell of Auchinbreck
Campbell of Ardnamurchan
Hope of Craighall
Preſton of Airdrie

Riddell of Riddell
Murray of Blackbarony
*Murray of Elibank
*M'Kenzie of Tarbet
*Elphinſtone of Elphinſtone
*Forbes of Caſtleforbes
Hamilton of Killoch
Slingſby of Scriven
1629 Bruce of Stanhouſe
Nicolſon of Laſwade
Arnot of Arnot
Oliphant of Newton
Agnew of Lochnaw
Keith of Ludquhairn
1630 Hannay of Mochrum
Forbes of Craigievar
Murray of Dunnerne
Croſbie of Croſbie Park
Sibbald of Rankeillor
Richardſon of Pencaitland
Cuningham of Robertland
1631 Wardlaw of Pittrevie
Sinclair of Cainſby
Gordon of Embo
M'Lean of Morvaren
1633 Balfour of Denmill
Cuningham of Auchinhervie
1634 Munro of Foulis
Foulis of Colinton
*Bingham of Caſtewar
Vernate of Carleton
1635 Hamilton of Broomhill
Gaſcoigne of Barnebow
Norton of Chetton
Pilkington of Stainlie
1635 Hay of Smithfield
Widdrington of Cartington
Bolles of Aſburton
Raney of Rotham
1636 Fortescue of Salden
Thomſon of Dudingſton

ongford	Barclay of Pearston
Stevenston	Cuninghame Capringt)n
Kedleston	Nisbet of Dean
the Neale	1670 Bennet of Grubbett
Lochend	Wallace of Craigie
)f Carnock	1671 Cockburn of that ilk
Valleyfield	Home of Blackadder
ireenhead	Halket of Pitfirran
raid	Scot of Ancrum
HaytonCastle	1672 Hope of Carse
Ratlingcourt	Jardin of Applegirth
)f Jordanhill	1673 Murray of Auchtertyre
Gogar	Murray of Balmanno
Silvertonhill	1677 Dick of Prestonfield
f Farm	Lockhart of Carstairs
Barras	1678 Gilmour of Craigmillar
f Pitarrow	1679 Campbell of Ardkinlas
rk	Dalmahoy of that ilk
'owburn	Clerk of Pennycuick
f Orchardton	Cochran of OchiltreeP.
bercorn	1680 Baird of Newbyth
of Fordell	Maitland P.
Stanhope	1681 Maxwell of Monreith
of Stair P.	1682 Bannerman of Elsick
)f Cults	Kennedy of Culean P.
Garleton	Maxwell Netherpollock
ongformacus	1683 Pringle of Stitchel
Inglison	Seton of Pitmedden
Gartmore	Stewart of Blair
f Lochore	Maxwell of Springkell
that ilk	Sharp of Scotscraig
'urveshall	1685 Dalziel of Binns
Whitehill	Grierson of Lag
:obs	Kilpatrick of Closeburn
Alva	Lawrie of Maxwelton
Cambo	1686 Brown of Coalston
Glenae P.	Calder of Muirton
Evelick	Kinloch of Gilmerton
Banff	Miln of Barntoun
Glorat	Paterson of Bannockburn
rleston B.	1687 Hall of Dunglass
onington	Inglis of Cramond
Ardoch	Stewart of Allanbank
vton	Threipland of Fingask
plum	Paterson of Eccles
Kelhead	1688 Bruce of Balkasky
	Houston of that ilk

Lander of Idington 1701 Elphinston of Logie
1685 Livingston of W. quarter Whiteford of Whiteford
1690 Lauder of Fountainhall 1702 Gibson of Addsefton
1692 Hamilton of Barnton Suttle of Balgone
1694 Dunbar of Mochrum Cunninghame of Miln-
1695 Baird of Sauchton-hall craig
Cumming of Culter 1703 Fergufon of Kilkerran
Dickfon of Carberry H. M'Dougal, Alderston
169- Hope of Kirkliston M'Kenzie of Skatewell
Home of Manderston Pollock of that ilk
1698 Dalrymple of Cranston Hamilton of Rofehall
Dalrymple, N. Berwick 1704 Gordon of Dalpholly
Dunbar of Durn Murray of Melgum P.
Hume of Renton Mackenzie of Royston
Stewart of Cultnefs Grant of Grant
1700 Dalrymple of Newhails Nairn of Dunfinnan
Elliot of Minto Rochead of Innerleith
Dunbar of Thunderton Wedderburn, Blacknefs
Forbes of Foveran 1705 Grant of Cullen
Belfches Wifhart, Tofts Stewart of Goodtrees
Johnfton of Wefterhall Holburn of Menftrie
Nicolfon of Kemnay Naefmith of Davick

Officers of State in Scotland.

Earl of Marchmont, *Keeper of the Great Seal*, 3000l. a-year
Rt. Hn. Ja. Stewart Mackenzie. *Ld. Privy Seal* for life, 3000l
X Rt. Hon. Ld. Fred. Campbell, *Lord Regifter*, 2000l.
Earl of Breadalbane, *Vice-Admiral*, 1000l.
Vifc. Stormont, *Lord Juftice-General*, 2600l.
R. Durdas, efq; *Ld. Pref* 1300l.
Ja. Montgomery, Efq, *Ld. Ch. Baron of Exchequer*, 2000l.
XH. Dundas, efq; *Ld. Ad.* 1000l.
Th. Millar, efq; *Lord Juf. Clerk*.
Earl of Marchmont, *Keeper of the Great Seal*.
Earl of Errol, *L. High Conftable*.
Earl of Lauderdale, *Heretable Royal Standard Bearer*.
James Erfkine, Efq; *Knight Marefchal*, 40cl.
Duke of Argyle, *Heretable Keeper of the King's Houfhold*.
Sir Jn. Anftruther, *Heret. Carv.*
X Sir Jam. Cockburn, Bt. *Heret. Ufher of the White Rod*, 300l.
Mr. Seton, of Touch, *Heretable Armour-Bearer*.
Dr. Hume and Dr. Cullen, *Phy*.
Dr. Hope, *Botanift*.
Gilbert Laurie, Efq; *Apothec*.
Dr. Robertfon, *Hiftoriographer for Scotland*, 200l.
Ja. and Tho. Abercrombie, Efqrs, *Limners*.
Ja. Maxwell, Efq; *Falconer*
Mark & Charles Kers, Efqrs. *Printers and Stat.*
D. Rofs, efq; *Maft. of the Revels*.
Sir Pa. Crawford, *Confervator of Scots Privileges at Campvere*.
Duke of Hamilton, *Keeper of Holyrood-Houfe*.
Du. of Athol, *Keep. of Falkland*.
Vifc. Stormont, *Keeper of Scoon*.
Marquis of Annandale, *Keeper of Lochmaben*.

Duke of Argyle, *Keeper of Dunstaffnage and Carrick.*

Duke of Hamilton, *Keeper of Linlithgow.*

Rd. Wardrope *Keeper of the Wardrobe,* 55l. 11s. 4d.

Tho. Frafer, *Under-Keeper,* 40l.

James Pringle, Efq; *Master of the Works,* 400l.

G. Sandy, *Clerk of the Stores,* 30l.

OFFICERS of the CHAPEL-ROYAL.

Rev. Alex. Carlifle, *Almoner;* 4l. 13s. 4d.

John Lawfe, *his Deputy.*

Drs. Alex. Webfter, G. Wifhart, and John Dryfdale, *Deans of the Chapel-Royal,* 60l. each.

Dr. Wm. Robertfon, Alex. Bryce, Dr. A. Geard, *Chaplains,* 50l. each.

COURT of SESSION.

Robert Dundas of Arnifton, Efq; *Lord Prefident,* 1300l.

Lords of Seffion, 700l. each.

Th. Millar, Efq; *Ld. Juf. Clerk,*

Henry Home, of Kaimes,

Alex. Bofwell, of Auchinleck,

James Erfkine, of Alva,

James Veitch, of Elliock,

John Campbell, of Stonefield,

Francis Garden, of Gardenfton,

Robert Bruce, of Kennet,

Sir David Dalrymple, Bart. of New Hailes,

James Burnet, of Mountbodo,

Alex. Lockhart, of Covington

Da. Rofs, of Ankerville,

Rob. Macqueen, of Braxfield,

Dav. Dalrymple of Wefthall.

PRINCIPAL CLERKS of the SESSION.

Meffrs. Al. Tait, A Campbell, A. Robertfon, A. Orme, A. Menzies, J. Colquhoune.

Meffrs. A. Rofs, T. Bruce, G. Kirkpatrick, J. Callender, A.

Stevenfon, K. Dunbar, *Dep. Clerks.*

Tho. Gibfon, *King's Clerk.*

Alex. Rofs, *Deputy ditto.*

Ch. Anderfon, *Extractor to ditto.*

Sir Rob. Anftruther, Rob. Waddell, *Princ. Clerks to the Bills.*

Charles Inglis, Laur. Inglis, & W. Finlayfon, *Deputy Clerks.*

The Hon. Baron Maule, *Clerk to the Regifter of Safines.*

Alex. Robertfon, *his Clerk.*

John Flockhart, *Clerk to the Regift. of Hornings.*

Jof. Williamfon, fen. and Jof. Williamfon, jun. *Clerks to the Commiffion of Teinds.*

Th. Alves, *Dep. Clerk of Teinds.*

Mr. J. Robertfon Barclay, *Clerk to the Admiffion of Notaries.*

R. Ruffel, *his Deputy.*

Alexander Gordon, *Keeper the Minute-Book.*

COURT of JUSTICIARY.

David Vifc. Stormont, *Lord Juftice-General,* 2000l.

Th. Millar, *Ld Juf. Clerk,* 500l.

Commiffioners, 200l. each.

Henry Home, of Kaimes,

Robert Bruce, of Kennet.

Fr. Garden, of Gardenfton,

Sir Dav. Dalrymple, bart.

Rob. Macqueen, of Branfie'd

Hen. Dundas, Efq; *His Majefty's Advocate,* 1000l.

Mr. Wm. Nairn, Mr. Robert Blair, and Mr. John Pringle, *Dep. Adv.* 100l. each

Alex. Murray, Efq; *Sol. Gen.* 400l

George Muir, *Principal Clerk.*

Alex. Hart, *Second Clerk.*

Robert Auld, Wm. Campbell, and Alex Hart, *Cir. Cls.*

COURT of EXCHEQUER.

Ja. Montgomery, Efq; *Lord Chief Baron,* 2000l.

(244)

Jn. Maule, Fletcher Norton, Esqrs. Sir J. Dalrymple, and Cosmo Gordon, Esq; *Barons.*
A. Stuart, Esq; and Sir P. Warrender, Bt. *King's Remembrancers,* 250l. each.
David Moncrieffe, Esq; *Deputy* ditto and *Solicitor,* 190l.
G. C. Maxwell, and W. Anderson, *Lord Treasurer's Rememb.* 200l.
James Townsend Oswald, Esq. *Principal Auditor,* 120ol.
Fr. Anderson, *Dep.-Aud.* 200l.
Thomas Dundas, Esq; *Clerk of the Pipe,* 200l.
Thomas and Robert Melsches, *Presenters of Signatures*
Ld. Bellenden, *Heret. Ush.* 271l.
Thomas Tod, *Dep. Ush.* 50l.
G. Inglis, H. Mackenzie, D. Taylor, R. Turner, W. Walker, J. Sommers, *Attornies*
John Fordyce, Esq; *Rec.-Gen. of Land-Rents,* 650l.
John Anstruther, Esq; *Rec.-Gen. of Bishops Rents,* 400l.
Tho. Tod, *Examiner,* 50l.
W. Burnet, *Cl to Port-Bonds,* 40l.
John Maughan, *Register of Resignations,* 40l.
J. Montgomery, *Mursh. of Court.*
[His Majesty gives a bounty of 2000l. per annum, to be distributed by the Barons to such poor persons as they judge proper.]

PRIVY-SEAL OFFICE.
Rt. Hon. Jas. Stuart M'Kenzie, for life, 3000l.
Alex. Menzies, Esq; *Deputy.*
David Kinlock, of Gilmerton, Esq; *Writer to the Privy Seal.*
Fra. Anderson, Esq; *Deputy.*

SIGNET.
✕ Henry Dundas, Esq. *Keep.*

Geo. Sandy, *Und.-Keep.* and *Clk.*
Alex. Alison, *Assistant-Clerk.*

COURT of ADMIRALTY.
Jn. Earl of Breadalbane, *Lord Vice-Admiral,* 1000l.
James Philp, Esq; *Judge-Adm.*
Ban. Wm. M'Leod, Esq; *J.-Dep.*
John Munro, *Procurator-Fiscal*
Wm. Campbell, Esq; *Clerk.*

COMMISSARY-COURT.
Jn. Mackenzie, Andr. Balfour Rob. Craig, and Geo. Ferguson, Esqrs. *Commissaries.*
Wm. Nairn, *Principal Clerk.*
Alex. Duncan, *Deputy.*
James Balfour, *Fisc.*

GREAT-SEAL OFFICE.
Hugh Earl of Marchmont, *Lord Keeper,* 3000l.
Mr. T. Cockburne, *his Deputy.*
Usher and *Appender.*
Robt. Meikle, *his Deputy.*

Establishment of POLICE
Pres. D. of Queensberry, 2000l.
Lords, 800l. each.
Earls of Lauderdale, Leven, Galloway, and Dalhousie.
Gentlemen, 400l. each.
Sir Rob. Menzies, Alex. Fraser, Esq; Tho. Dundas, Esq;
Sec. Sir Arch. Hope, Bt. 300l.
Cashier, Ja. M'Douall, Esq. 100l.
Solicit. Hon. R. Sandilands, 100l.

WINDOW and HOUSE TAX OFFICE.
Sir R. Laurie, and Ja. Durham, Esq; *Surveyors-General.*
Geo. Innes, *Assistant to the Surveyors-General.*

OFFICERS of the MINT.
Jn. Elliot, Esq; *General,* 300l.
G. Mackay, Esq; *Master,* 200l
James Hay, Esq. *Warden,* 150l.

(245)

James Gartſhore, Counter-Warden, 60l.
Alexander Gardner, *Aſſay-Maſter*, 100l.
Tho. Simpſon, *Engraver*, 50l.
Jo. Flochart, *Clerk*, 40l.
David Robertſon, *Smith*, 33l.

POST-OFFICE.

Rob. Oliphant, of Roſſie, Eſq; *Poſt-Maſter-General*.
David Roſs, *Secretary*.
James Beveridge, *Solicitor*.
John Buchan, *Accountant*.
Mr. David Bennet, *Prin. Clk.*
William Ker, *Inſpector of Eye-Letters*.
James Ewan, *his Aſſiſtant*.
Sam. French, Thomas Matthew, and Martin Mowbray, *Clerks*.
Jo. Swanſton, *Cl. to foreign Let.*

LYON-OFFICE.

John Hook Campbell, Eſq; *Lord Lyon*, for life, 30cl.
Robert Boſwell, Eſq; *Lyon Deputy*, and *Prin. Clerk*.
James Cumming, Eſq; *Keeper of the Lyon Records*.
Rob. Ranken, *Lyon-Clerk-Dep*.
Heralds, 25l. each.
John Douglas, *Albany*,
George Brodie, *Rothſay*,
Thomas Huſband, *Roſs*,
Geo Douglas, *Marchmont*.
Ken. M'Kenzie, *Snowdown*,
Wm. Robertſon, *Iſlay*,
Purſuivants, 16l. 13s. 4d. each.
William Douglas, *Unicorn*,
Arch. Campbell, *Bute*,
Malcolm Grant, *Carrick*,
Thomas Nicolſon, *Kintyre*,
Patrick Begbie, *Ormond*,
James Mitchell, *Dingwall*,
John Cuming, *Fiſcal*.
Macer of Court, R. Thomſon.

Solicitors before the Lyon-Court,
William Richardſon,
William Walker,
Samuel Watſon,
William Scott.

LIST of Commiſſioners and Truſtees for Fiſheries, Manufactures, and Improvements in Scotland.

Duke of Buccleugh, H. C. Hope Weir, Lord Preſident, Lord Chief Baron, Lord Preſident, Lord Juſtice-Clerk, Lord Stonefield, Lord Kames Lord Advocate, Baron Maule Lord Gardenſtone, David Kinloch, George Cierl, Robert Oliphant, Lord Ankerville, Walter Scot, Thom. Dundas, Lord Elliock, Col. Rob. Campbell, Baron Gorden, Solliciter Gen. Rob. Arburthnot.
Secretary, James Guthrie.

LORD-REGISTER's Office.

Lord Fred. Campbell, *Lord-Regiſter*. 2000l. per ann.
Alex. Tait, Archibald Campbell, Alex. Robertſon, Alex. Orme, Alex. Menzies, James Colquhoun, *Deputies*.
James Ker, Alex. Robertſon, *Deputy-Keepers of Records*.

CHANCERY.

David Scott, Eſq; *Director*
Alex. Watſon, *Deputy-Director*
John Irvine, *Principal Clerk*

LIST of the Royal College of Phyſicians in Edinburgh.
N. B. Thoſe mark'd thus † are Profeſſors in the Univerſity.
†Dr. Monro, *Preſident*, Sir A. Dick, Bt. Sir J. Pringle, Bart. Dr. Baird, Dr. Threipland, *Elect*. Dr. Lind, at Haſlar, Dr. Drummond

Brift. †Dr. Home, *Elect.*
Dr. Cumming at *Dorchester,*
Dr. Stevenson at *Glasgow,*
Dr. Cullen, *Elect.* Dr. Grant,
Vice-Pref. and Elect. Dr.
Baylies at *Dref.* Dr. Gen.
Dr. Gardiner, *Elect.* and *Librarian,* †Dr. Hope, *Elect.*
†Dr. Young, Dr. Butter at *Derby,* Dr. Walker at *Jamaica,* Dr. Livingston at *Aberdeen,* Dr. Petrie at *Lincoln,* Dr. Garthshore at *London* Dr. Wilson at *Newcast.* Dr. Morgan at *Pensyl.* Dr. Steedman *Cenf.*
Dr. Hay *Treas.* †Dr. Black *Censor,* Dr. M'Kittrick at *Andov.* Dr. Shippen at *Phila.*
Dr. M'Farlane, Dr. Spence at *Guildford,* Dr. Ja Lind.
Dr. Duncan, Dr. Hamilton,
Dr. Buchan, Dr. Hamilton
L. Reg. Dr. Sprey, Dr. Spens, Dr. Hunter *Fiscal,*
Dr. Langlands, Dr. Rutherford *Secretary,* Dr. Gregory,
Dr. Beerenbrock, D. Powell,
Dr. Dunbar, Dr. Gillespie

Honorary Fellows.

Henry Duke of Buccleugh
John, Earl of Bute
Count Carbury, Primarius Professor of Medicine in the University of Turin
Dr. Gaubius, Prof. of Medicine and Chymistry in the University of Leyden.
Hon. ex. off. Dr. Ja. Flint, Prof. of Med. in the Univ. of St. Andrews.
Dr. Stork, First Physician to the Emperor and Empress of Germany.

Licenciate in Medicine.
Dr. Spence

Clerk. Robert Boswell.

Governors, &c. of the Bank of Scotland.
Earl of Marchmont, *Governor*
Right Hon. Henry Dundas, *Deputy-Governor.*
Ordinary Directors.
Oliver Coult, Sir Hugh Crawford, Geo. Falconer, J. Gordon, Rog. Hog, Alex. Houstoun, Alex. Keith, jun. John M Laurin, Patrick Miller, Alex. Robertson, Alex. Wallace.
Extraordinary Directors.
D. of Buccleugh, D. of Montrose, E. of Lauderdale, E. of Hopetoun, E. of Panmure, William Binning, George Fairholme, William Hay, Geo. Ramsay, Col. Jam. St Clair, Patrick Warrander, Robert Whyte.
Treasurer, James Spence

Governors, &c. of the Royal Bank of Scotland.
Duke of Buccleugh, *Governor*
Lord Elliock, *Dep. Gov.*
Ordinary Directors.
Dav. Anderson, W. Fullarton, John Russel, Sir Rd. Hope, John Davidson, George Brown, Jas. Stirling, Gilb. Laurie, William Miller.
Extraordinary Directors.
Duke of Montrose, Ld Alva, Ld. Braxfield, Robert Campbell, John Pringle, Dr. Stewart. Moncrief, Lt Gen. Campbell, James Hunter-Blair, J. Campbell.
Cashier.
William Simpson.

EXCISE-OFFICE.
Alex. Udny, Geo. Brown, Gil-

John Thompson, Esq; *Secret.* for himself and Clerks, 440l.
John Caw, *Dep-Sec.* 100l.
Wm. Campbell, Esq; *Auditor,* for self and Clerks, 510l.
Dav. Geddes, *Deputy-Auditor*
Wal. Scott, Esq; *Cashier,* for self and Clerks, 550l.
Alex. Alison, *Deputy-Cashier*
Ja. Balmain, *Solicitor,* for self and Clerks, 180l.
Jo. Bonar, *Deputy-Solicitor*
Ja. Bonar, *Assist.-Sol.* 80l.
Mil. Rowe, *Agent* at Lond. 50l.

General Accomptants.
R. Chalmers, and J. Ramsay, *Accomptants.*
Robert Laurie
John Hepburn
Alexander Thomson
Edward Broughton
James Lowndes
Walter Morton
John Blackader
Allan Begg
James Bruce
Assist.-Accompt. &c. W. Taylor
John Caw, *Storekeeper*
J. Maitland, *Gen. Examiner,* &c. 140l.
Alex. Fraser, *his Assist.* 40l.
C. Campbell, *Permit-Examiner*
Laurence and Ann Dundas, *Joint Housekeepers,* 60l.

STAMP-OFFICE.

Alex. Menzies, Esq; *Head-Distributor* and *Collecter*
T. Blair, A. Clark, *Clerks*
Mr. Geo. Duncan, *Comptroller*

Officers of his Majesty's Revenues of Customs, Salt-Duty, and Seizures.

G. Clerk Maxwell, Basil Cochran, Wm. Nelthrop, Ad. Smith, James Buchanan, Esqrs. *Commissioners,* 500l.
Rich. Elliston Philips, *Secretary,* for self and Clerks, 530l.
Shadrach Moyse, 1*st Clerk,* 160l.
Rob. Campbell, Esq; *Rec.-Gen.* for self and Clerks, 380l.
James Ogilvie, *First Clerk, or Deputy to the Rec. Gen.* 150l.
Geo. Burges, Esq; *Compt.-Gen.* for self and Clerks, 430l.
Rich. Gardner, *Assistant,* 100l.
Samuel Charteris, *Solicitor,* for self and Clerks, 300l.
Jn. Macgowan, and Jn. Davidson, *Assistant-Solicitors*
John Lord Colvil, and David Reid, Esq; *Inspectors-General of Out-Ports,* 130l. each
J. Wightman, Esq; *Inspector of Imports and Exports,* 100l.
John Mackenzie, *Examiner of Customs,* 100l.
Cathcart Boyd, *Examiner of Salt,* 120l.
Cha. Douglas, *Supervisor-General of the Salt Duty,* 130l.
Robt. Cairns, *Assistant-Register-General of Tobacco,* 150l.
Fra. Anderson, *Inspect. of Seiz.*
Kenneth M'Kenzie, *Register of Seizures,* 50
Alexander Menzies, *Inspector of Securities,* 70l.
James Garety, *Register of Shipping,* 50l.
Isabel Rowley, *Housekeeper*

UNIVERSITIES in SCOTLAND.

St. ANDREW's.
Earl of Kinnoul, *Chancellor*
Robert Watson, *Principal*
Professors.
John Flint, M. D. Medicine
Geo. Forest, Nat. Philosophy
John Cook, Mor. Philosophy
N. Vilant, Mathemat.
George Hill, Greek
John Hunter, Humanity
William Baron, Logic
Hugh Cleghorn, Civil History

New-College.
James Morrison, *Principal*
Professors.
———, Divinity
Wm. Brown, Church Hist.
———, Hebrew

GLASGOW.
Duke of Montrose, *Chancellor*
Earl of Lauderdale, *Ld. Rector*
W. Leichman, D.D. *Principal*
Professors.
William Wright, Divinity
John Young, LL. D. Greek
Jn. Millar, Civil and Scots Law
Tho. Reid, D.D. and A. M'Arthur, Mor. Philos.
Ja. Williamson, Mathemat.
Js. Clow, and Jos. Garden, Logic
Jn. Anderson, F.R.S. Nat. Phil.
Will. Richardson, Humanity
Alex. Stevenson, Medicine
T Hamilton, Anatomy & Botany
Patrick Cuming, Orient. Lang.
Alex. Wilson, Pract. Astr.
Hugh Macleod, History

EDINBURGH.
Lord Provost, Magistrates, and Council, of Edin. *Patrons.*
W. Robertson, D.D. *Principal*
Professors.
Dr. Robert Hamilton, and A. Hunter, Divinity
Dr. James Robertson, Hebrew
Rob. Cumming, Eccles. Hist.
John Bruce, Logic
Andrew Dalzel, Greek
G. Stuart, LL.D. and J. Hill, Humanity
Matt. Stewart, Mathematics
Adam Ferguson, Mor. Phil.
John Robison, Nat. Phil.
Alex. Tytler, Civil History
Wm. Wallace, Scotch Law
Robert Dick, Civil Law
Allan M'Conochie, Law of Nature and Nations
Hugh Blair, D.D. Rhetoric
John Hope, M. D. Botany
Francis Home, Mat. Med.
Wm. Cullen, M.D. Pract. Med.
J. Gregory, M.D. Phys. & Med.
Jos. Black, M. D. Chymistry
A. Monro, M.D. Anatomy
Tho. Young, M. D. Midwifry
John Walker, Nat. Hist.

ABERDEEN.

King's-College.
John Chalmers *Principal*
Rod. Macleod, *Sub-Principal*
Professors.
Alex. Gerard, Divinity
Wm. Thom, Civil Law
Sir Alex. Gordon, Medicine
Wm. Ogilvy, Humanity
John Leslie, Greek
Tho. Gordon, and James Dunbar, Philosophy
John Ross, Orient. Lang.

Marischal-College.
Earl of Bute, *Chancellor*
G. Cambell, D. D. *Principal*
Professors:
Rob. Hamilton, Orient. Lang.
Alex. Donaldson, Medicine
William Kennedy, Greek
J. Beattie, Moral Philosophy
Francis Skene, Nat. Philo.
George Skene, Nat. History
Patrick Copland, Mathemat.

(249)

Lord Lieut. Gen. and Gen. Governor of Ireland, his Excellency FREDERICK, Earl of CARLISLE, K. T.

His Majefty's Moft Honourable Privy Council.

Lord Primate	Earl of Briftol	Sir R. Heron, Bart.
Lord Chancellor	—— Clermont	Sir E. Walpole, K.B.
Archbp. of Dublin	—— Inchiquin	Sir J. Blaquire, K.B.
—— Cafhell	—— Conyngham	Sir J. Irwine, K.B.
—— Tuam	Vifc. Valentia	Thomas Conolly
Duke of Leinfter	—— Beauchamp	William Brownlow
Earl of Weftmeath	Lord F. Campbell	Owen Wynne
—— Donnegall	Bifhop of Meath	Theo. Jones
—— Montrath	Baron Milton	Henry King
—— Drogheda	—— Annaly	James Forefcue
—— Befsborough	—— Macartney	Edward Cary
—— Tyrone	—— Gosford	Silver Oliver
—— Hillfborough	—— Clonmore	Geo. Aug. Eliott
—— Shannon	—— Tracton	Henry Flood
—— Clanbraffil	—— Mufkerry	Charles Dillon
—— Mornington	E. S. Pery	Ag. Vefey
—— Arran	John Ponfonby	Jofhua Cooper
—— Courtown	John Beresford	Richard Jackfon
—— Miltown	J. H. Hutchinfon	John Pomeroy
—— Howth	W. G. Hamilton	Wm. Burton
—— Bellamont	Rd. Rigby	H. Theo. Clements
—— Roden	Marcus Patterfon	John Scott
—— Ely	H. S. Conway	W. H. Burgh
—— Nugent	Sir W. Ofborne, Bt.	John Forfter
—— Glandore	Sir C. Molyneux, Bt.	W. Eden
—— Abercorn	Sir A. Brooke, Bt.	John O'Neil
—— Hertford	Sir H. Cavendifh, Bt.	Luke Gardiner

The Lords of Parliament, and Peers of Ireland.
Abbreviations, E. D. Engl. Duke; E. M. Engl. Marquis; E. E. Engl. Earl; S. E. Scots Earl; E. V. Engl. Vifcount; E. B. Engl. Baron; K. B. Knight of the Bath K. G. Knight of the Garter; ‡ A Commoner of Great Britain; § A Baronet; || A Minor; * A Papift.

Name.	Title.	Creation.
HIS R. H. Wm. Henry	E. of Conaught, E. D.	1764
His R. H. Henry Frederick	E. of Dublin, E. D.	1766
Lord Chancellor Right Hon. James Hewitt, Lord Lifford		1763

ARCHBISHOPS. Promotion.

DR. Richard Robinfon	Armagh, prim. of all Irel.	1765
Dr. Robert Fowler	Dublin, prim. of Irel.	1779
Dr. Charles Agar,	Cafhel, pr. of Munfter	1779
Dr. Jemmet Browne Y	Tuam, pr. of Conaught	1775

(250)

DUKE.		Creations.	Eldest Sons.
William Fitz-Gerald	Leinster, E. V.	1766	M. of Kildare
EARLS.		LORDS.	
John Smyth de Burgh	Clanricarde	1543	Dunkellyn
Edmund Boyle	Cork & Orrery } E. B. {	1620 1660	Dungarvan
Wm. R. M'Donnel	Antrim K. B.	1620	Dunluce
Thomas Nugent	Westmeath	1621	Delvin
Basil Fielding	Desmond, E. E.	1622	Fielding
Anthony Brabazon	Meath	1627	Brabazon
Richard Barry	Barrymore	1627	Buttevant
Arthur Chichester	Don-gall	1647	Chichester
Richard Lambart	Cavan	1647	Vis.Kilcoursie
Morough O'Bryen	Inchiquin,	1654	O'Bryen
Charles Hen. Coote	Mountrath	1660	Castle-Coote
Charles Moore	Drogheda	1661	Moore
George Talbot	Wat. & Wex. E. E.	1661	Talbot
George Forbes	Granard	1684	Forbes
Fr. Christ. Rynhart	Athlone	1691	Aghrim
Will. Fitz-William	Fitz-William, E E.	1716	M'ltown
Fr. Tho. Fitz-Maurice	Kerry	1722	Clan-Maurice
John Bligh	Darnley, E. B.	1725	Clifton
John Child Tylney	Tylney	1731	Castlemaine
John James Perceval	Egmont, E. B.	1733	Perceval
William Ponsonby	Bessborough, E. B.	1739	Duncannon
Ralph Verney	Verney	1742	Fermanagh
William Maule	Panmure	1743	Maule
G. de le Poer Beresford	Tyrone	1746	Le Poer
Henry Thomas Butler	Carrick	1748	Ikerrin
Chas. W. Wentworth	Malton, E M. K G.	1750	Malton
Wills Hill	Hillsborough, E. E.	1751	Kilwarlin
John Fitzpatrick	Upper Ossory	1751	Gowran
William Petty	Shelburne, E. B.	1753	Fitz-Maurice
Richard Boyle	Shannon	1756	Boyle
Clotwor. Skeffington	Massareene	1756	Loughneagh
Robert Herbert Butler	Lanesborough	1756	Newtown
James Hamilton	Clanbrassil	1756	Limerick
George Rochfort	Belvedere	1756	Bellfield
John Wandesford	Wandesford	1758	Castlecomer
Thomas Birmingham	Louth	1759	Athenry
James Duff	Fife	1759	Macduff
Garret Wesley, Mus. D.	Mornington	1760	Wellesley
Peter Ludlow	Ludlow	1760	Preston
George Carpenter	Tyrconnel	1761	Carlingford
John Rawdon	Moira	1762	Rawdon
Arthur Saund. Gore	Arran	1762	Sudley
James Stopford	Courtown	1762	Stopford

Joseph Leeson	Miltown	1763	Rusborough
James Caulfield	Charlemount	1763	Caulfield
‖ John Savile	Mexborough	1766	Pollington
Edw. Turnour	Winterton	1766	Turnour
§ Thomas Taylor	Bective	1766	Headfort
Thomas St. Lawrence	Howth	1767	St. Lawrence
§ Charles Coote	Bellamont, K. B.	1767	Collonny
§ Edward King	Kingston	1768	Kingsborough
Cha. Wm. Molyneux	Sefton	1771	Molyneux
Robert Jocelyn	Roden	1771	Jocelyn
Henry Loftus	Ely	1771	Loftus
Keneth Mackenzie	Seaforth	1771	Fortrose
John Browne	Altamont	1771	Westport
§ Ralph Gore	Ross	1772	Gore
‡ Wilmot Vaughan	Lisburne	1776	Vaughan
Edward Ligonier	Ligonier	1776	Clonmel
§ John Meade	Clanwilliam	1776	Gillford
‡ Rob. Nugent Craggs	Nugent	1776	Clare
William Crosbie	Glandore	1776	Crosbie
Francis Vernon	Shipbrooke	1777	Orwell
Edward Stratford	Aldborough	1777	Amiens
Wm. Henry Fortescue	Clermont	1777	Fortescue
Henry Conyngham	Conyngham	1780	Conyngham
Stephen Moore	Mount Cashel	1780	MountCashel

VISCOUNTS.

EDMUND Butler	Mountgarret	1550
§ Arthur Annesley	Valentia	1621
John Netterville	Netterville	1622
John Needham	Kilmory	1625
Richd. Lumley Saunderson	Lumley, E. E.	1628
Rev. Philip Smythe	Strangford	1628
§ ‡ Philip Wenman	Wenman	1628
* Francis Taaffe	Taaffe	1628
Charles Jones	Ranelagh	1628
Richard Fitz-William	Fitz-William	1629
Charles Cockaine	Cullen	1642
Thomas Charles Tracy	Tracy	1642
‡ Tho. James Bulkeley	Bulkeley	1643
George Barnwall	Kingsland	1646
§ George James Cholmondeley	Cholmondeley, E. E.	1661
§ John-Christopher Dawney	Downe	1680
§ ‡ Richard Howe	Howe	1701
§ James Hamilton	Strabane, S. E.	1701
Richard Nassau Molesworth	Molesworth	1716
William Chetwynd	Chetwynd	1717
‡ George Brodrick	Midleton	1717
Richard Hamilton	Boyne Y 2	1717

(252)

Joshua Allen	Allen	1717
§ James Bucknall Grimston	Grimston	1719
‡ W. Wildman Barrington	Barrington	1720
§ Wm. Hall Gage, E. B.	Gage	1720
‡ Henry Temple	Palmerston	1722
‡ John Bateman	Bateman	1725
Robert Monckton Arundel	Galway	1727
Richard Wingfield	Powerscourt	1743
William Flower	Ashbrook	1751
Harvey Morres	Mount Morres	1763
Arthur Trevor	Dungannon	1766
Francis Charles Annesley	Glerawly	1766
§ Thomas Geo. Southwell	Southwell	1776
§ Thomas Vesey	De Vesci	1776
Wm. Willoughby Cole	Enniskillen	1776
John Dawson	Carlow	1776
James Hewitt	Lifford	1780
Otway Cuffe	Desart	1780
John Creighton	Erne	1780
Berry Barey	Farnham	1780
Simon Luttrell	Carhampton	1780
Bernard Ward	Bangor	1780
‡§ Penyston Lamb	Melbourne	1780
James Agar	Clifden	1780
John Bourke	Naas	1780

BISHOPS.   Promotions.

HON. Dr. Henry Maxwell	Meath	1766
Dr. Charles Jackson	Kildare	1772
Dr. John Garnet	Clogher	1758
Dr. William Gore	Lim. Ardfert and Aghadoe	1772
Dr. Charles Dodgson, F. R. S.	Elphin	1775
Dr. James Trail	Down and Connor	1765
Dr. William Newcome	Waterford and Lismore	1779
Rt. Hon. F. Hervey, D.D. and E. E.	Derry	1768
Dr. Isaac Mann	Corke and Ross	1772
Dr. Walter Cope	Clonf. & Kilmacduagh	1772
Dr. Jos. Deane Bourke	Leighlin and Fernes	1772
Dr. George Lewis Jones	Kilmore	1774
Dr. James Hawkins	Raphoe	1780
Dr. John Hotham	Ossory	1779
Dr. Thomas Barnard	Killaloe and Kilfenora	1780
Dr. William Breresford	Dromore	1780
Dr. Richard Woodward	Cloyne	1781
Dr. William Cecil Pery	Killala and Achoney	1781

BARONS.

Name.	Title.	Creation
JOHN de Courcy	Kinsale	1374

* James Butler	Cahier	1583
Andrew Tho. Stewart	Caftle Stewart	1619
Henry Digby	Digby, E. B.	1620
Cadwallader Davis Blaney	Blayney	1621
Rev. Robert Sherrard	Sherrard, E. E.	1627
Francis Seymour Conway	Conway E. E. K. G.	1712
George Evans	Carbery	1718
§ Henry Aylmer	Aylmer	1713
John Jofhua Proby	Carysfort	1753
Jofeph Damer	Milton, E. B.	1753
Edward Mich. Pakenham	Longford	1758
John Lyfaght	Lifle	1752
John Hanger	Col:raine	1762
‡ Edward Clive	Clive	1762
Drigue Billers Olmius	Waltham	1766
John Gore	Annaly	1766
‡ § Conftantine John Phipps	Mulgrave	1768
John Eyre	Eyre	1768
Thomas Dawfon	Dartrey	1770
‡ George Macartney	Macartney, K. B.	1776
Archibald Achefon	Gosford	1776
Ralph Howard	Clonmore	1776
§ Richard Philipps	Milford	1776
§ Thomas Wynn	Newborough	1776
§ Charles Bingham	Lucan	1776
§ Alexander Macdonald	Macdonald	1776
‡ § William Mayne	Newhaven	1776
‡ William Edwardes	Kenfington	1776
§ ‡ William Henry Lyttelton	Weftcote	1776
Robert Henley Ongley	Ongley	1776
‡ Molyneux Shuldham	Shuldham	1776
Sentleger Sentleger	Doneraile	1776
Clotworthy Upton	Templetown	1776
Hugh Maffey	Maffey	1776
MoftRev. Rich. Robinfon, D.D.	Rokeby	1777
James Dennis	Tracton	1780
Robert Tilfon Deane	Mufkerry	1780
Armar Lowry Corry	Belmore	1780
Thomas Knox	Welier	1780
John Barker Holroyd	Sheffield	1780

PEERESSES.

Ellis Agar	Countefs of Brandon	1758
Elizabeth Mafon	Countefs of Grandifon	1767
Elizabeth Ormfby Rowley	Vifcountefs Langford	1766
Catherine Perceval	Baronefs Arden	1770

List of the new COMMONS of IRELAND, (No. 300) corrected (from Authority) to Dec. 16, 1779. With an Alphabet of their Surnames, referring to the several places they represent. The Figures included ( ) are the Numbers sent by the County; and the Names of the Counties in Capitals. Those marked thus ‡ are Commoners of Great-Britain.

1. ANTRIM (10).
‡ Hon. H. S. Conway
James Wilson, Esq;
 2. Borough of Antrim
Hon. Wm. John Skeffington
Hon. Chi. Skeffington
 3. Borough of Belfast
Hon. Henry Skeffington
Alexander Crookshank, Esq;
 4. Borough of Lisburne
Fitzherbert Richards, Esq;
Rt. Hon. Richard Heron, Esq;
 5. Borough of Randalstown.
Rt. Hon. John O'Neill, Esq;

6. ARMAGH (6)
Rt. Hon. Wm. Brownlow
Thomas Dawson, Esq;
 7. Borough of Armagh
Henry Meredyth, Esq;
George Rawson, Esq;
 8. Borough of Charlemount
Sir Annesley Stewart, Bart.
Henry Gratton, Esq;
 9. CARRICFERGUS,
 and Town (2)
Conway Rd. Dobbs, Esq;
Barry Yelverton, Esq,
 10. CATHERLOGH (6)
William Burton, Esq;
Beauch. Bagenal, Esq.
 11. Borough of Catherlogh
John Prendergast, Esq;
Arthur Dawson, Esq;
 12. Borough of Old Leighlin
R. Hon. Sir J. Blaquiere, K.B.
Robert Jephson, Esq;
 13. CAVAN (6)
George Montgomery, Esq;
Hon. J. J. B. Maxwell

14. Borough of Belturbet
Robert Birch, Esq;
Ch. Fr. Sheridan, Esq;
 15. Borough of Cavan
Thomas Nesbit, Esq;
John Clements, Esq;
 16. CLARE (4)
Edw. Fitzgerald, Esq;
Sir Lucius O'Brien, Bart.
 17. Borough of Ennis
Rt. Hon. William Burton
Francis Bernard, jun. Esq.
 18. CORK (26)
Richard Townsend, Esq;
 19. Borough of Baltimore
Jocelyn Deane, Esq;
William Evans, Esq;
 20. Town of Bandon-bridge
Wm. Brab. Ponsonby, Esq;
Lodge Morres, Esq;
 21. Borough of Castlemartyr
Hon. James Lysaght
Riggs Falkiner, Esq;
 22. Borough of Charleville
Richard Cox, Esq;
Thomas Warren, Esq;
 23. Borough of Clognikelty.
Thomas Adderly, Esq;
Attiwell Wood, Esq;
 24. City of Cork
Richard Longfield, Esq;
Rt. Hon. Jn. Hely Hutchinson
 25. Borough of Doneraile
Hon. Hayes Sentleger
Hon. Richard Sentleger
 26. Borough of Kinsale
Rt. Hon. Agmondisham Vesey,
James Kearney, Esq;

27. Borough of Mallow
Denham Jephson, sen. Esq;
Denham Jephson, jun. Esq;
28. Borough of Midleton
Hon. Tho. Broderick
Hon. Henry Broderick
29. Borough of Rathcormuck
William Tonson, Esq;
Fra. Ber. Beamish, Esq;
30. Town of Youghal.
James Uniacke, Esq;
Robert Uniacke, Esq;
31. DONEGAL. (12)
Robert Clements, Esq;
Alexander Montgomery, Esq;
32. Borough of Ballyshannon
John Staples, Esq;
Sir Michael Cromie, Kt.
33. Borough of Donegal
H. V. Brooke, Esq;
Henry Cope, Esq.
34. Borough of Killybegs
Sir Henry Hamilton, Bt.
John Knox, Esq;
35. Borough of Lifford
Hon. Abraham Creighton.
Sir Nicholas Lawless, Bart.
36. Borough of St. Johnstown
Hugh Howard, Esq;
Robert Howard, Esq;
37. DOWN (14)
Hon. Arthur Hill
Robert Stewart, Esq;
38. Borough of Bangor
Edward Hunt, Esq.
Hon. Edward Ward
39. Borough of Downpatrick
Clotworthy Rowley, Esq;
Hon. Rob. Henry Southwell
40. Borough of Hillsborough
Wm. Montgomery, Esq;
James Bailie, Esq ;
41. Borough of Killyleagh
Sir John Blackwood, Bt.
Robert Blackwood, Esq;

42. Borough of Newry
Robert Ross, Esq;
Isaac Corry, jun. Esq;
43. Borough of Newtown
Sir John Browne, Bart.
James Somerville, Esq;
44. DROGHEDA.
and Town (2)
William Meade Ogle, Esq;
Sydenham Singleton, Esq;
45 DUBLIN (10)
Luke Gardiner, Esq;
Sir Edward Newenham, Kt.
46. City of Dublin
W. Clement, M. D.
Sir Samuel Bradstreet, Bt.
47. University of Dublin
Rt. Hon. Walter Burgh,
J. Fitzgibbon, jun. Esq.
48. Borough of Newcastle
Hon. John Butler
Robert Gamble, Esq,
49. Borough of Swords
J. Cobbe, Esq;
Charles King, Esq;
50. FERMANAGH (4)
Rt. Hon. Sir Arthur Brooke, Bt.
Mervyn Archdall, Esq;
51. Borough of Inniskillen
John Leigh, Esq;
Rt. Hon. Henry Flood
52. GALWAY (8)
Dennis Daly, Esq;
W. P. K. Trench, Esq;
53. Town of Athenry
J. Blakeney, of Ashfield, Esq;
J. Blakeney, of Abbot, Esq;
54. Town of Galway
Anthony Daly, Esq;
Dennis Bowes Daly, Esq;
55. Borough of Tuam
Hon. James Browne
Sir Henry Lynche Blosse
56. KERRY (8)
Arth. Blennerhasset, Esq;
Rowland Bateman, Esq;

(256)

57. Borough of Ardfert
Lord Visc. Crosbie
Maurice Copinger, Esq;
58. Borough of Dingle-Icouch
Robert Fitz Gerald, Esq;
Robert Alexander, Esq;
59. Borough of Tralee
John Toler, Esq;
Thomas Lloyd, jun. Esq;
60. KILDARE (10)
Rt. Hon. Ld. Ch. Fitzgerald
Arthur Pomeroy, Esq;
61. Borough of Athy
T. Burgh, of Chapelizod, Esq;
Tho. Burgh, of Oldtown, Esq;
62. Borough of Harristown
Hon. Richard Allen
Michael Keating, Esq;
63. Borough of Kildare
Sir Fitzgerald Aylmer, Bart.
Simon Digby, Esq;
64. Borough of Naas
Hon. John Bourke,
Thomas Allan, Esq;
65. KILKENNY (16)
Rt. Hon. John Ponsonby
Joseph Deane, Esq.
66. Borough of Callen
Hon. Pierce Butler
George Agar, Esq;
67. Borough of St. Cannice
alias Irishtown
John Monck Mason, Esq;
John Hamilton, Esq;
68. Borough of Ennisteage
John Flood, Esq;
John Parnell, Esq;
69. Borough of Gowran
John Butler, Esq;
Sir Boyle Roche, Kt.
70. City of Kilkenny
Eland Mossom, Esq;
G. P. Bushe, Esq.
71. Borough of Knoctopher
Sir Hercules Langrishe, Bart.
Andrew Caldwell, Esq;

72. Borough of Thomastown
Robert Ford, Esq.
Edw. Bellingham Swan, Esq.
73. KING's (6)
Sir William Parsons, Bart.
John Lloyd, Esq.
74. Borough of Bannagher
Peter Holmes, Esq.
James Cavendish, Esq.
75. Borough of Philipstown
John Handcock, Esq;
Hugh Carleton, Esq;
76. LEITRIM (6)
Rt. Hon. Hen. Theo. Clements
Rt. Hon. Theoph. Jones
77. Borough of Carrick
Edward Sneyd, Esq;
Robert Tighe, Esq;
78. Borough of Jamestown
Hon. John Brown, jun.
Richard Martin, Esq.
79. LIMERICK (8)
Rt. Hon. Silver Oliver
Sir Henry Harstonge, Bt.
80. Borough of Askeyton
Joseph Hoare, Esq.
Hon. Hugh Massy
81. Borough of Kilmallock
William Christmas, Esq;
John Finlay, Esq;
82. City of Limerick.
Rt. Hon. Edmund Sexton Pery
Thomas Smyth, Esq.
83. LONDONDERRY (8)
Rt. Hon. Tho. Conolly
Rt. Hon. Edward Cary
84. Borough of Coleraine
Rt. Hon. Richard Jackson
Hon. Richard Annesley
85. City of Londonderry
Hugh Hill, Esq.
James Alexander, Esq.
86. Bor. of Newt. Limavady
Alexander Murray, Esq.
William Colvill, Esq,

87. LONGFORD (10)
Henry Gore, Esq.
Lau. Harman Harman, Esq.
88. Borough of Granard
Thomas Maunsell, jun. Esq.
William Long Kinsman, Esq.
89. Bor. of Lanesborough
Robert Dillon, Esq.
John Hely Hutchinson, Esq.
90. Borough of Longford
David Latouche, jun. Esq.
John Tunnadine, Esq.
91. Bor. of St. Johnstown
‡ Hon. John Vaughan
Sackville Hamilton, Esq.
92. LOUTH (10)
Rt. Hon. James Fortescue,
John Foster, Esq.
93. Borough of Atherdee
Francis M'Namara, Esq.
Peter Metge, Esq.
94. Borough of Carlingford
Thomas Knox, jun. Esq.
Theophilus Blakeney, Esq.
95. Borough of Dundalk
William Cunyngham, Esq.

96. Borough of Dunleer
John Thomas Foster, Esq.
William Tho. Monsel, Esq.
97. MAYO (4)
James Cuffe, Esq.
Hon. George Browne
98. Borough of Castlebar
Stephen Popham, Esq.
Thomas Coghlan, Esq.
99. MEATH (14)
Here. Langford Rowley, Esq.
George Lowther, Esq.
100. Borough of Athboy
Edward Tighe, Esq.
William Chapman, Esq.
101. Borough of Duleek
Andrew Ram, Esq.
Hon. Col. Edward Stopford

102. Borough of Kells
Hon. Thomas Taylor
Thomas Moore, Esq.
103. Borough of Navan
John Preston, Esq.
Joseph Preston, Esq.
104. Borough of Ratoath
John Forbes, Esq.
George Putlands, Esq.
105. Borough of Trim
Rt. Hon. John Pomeroy, Esq.
Hon. R. Wesley
106. MONAGHAN (4)
Alexander Montgomery, Esq.
Thomas Tennison, Esq.
107. Borough of Monaghan
Robert Dobson, Esq;
Lt. Gen. Rob. Cuninghame
108. QUEEN's (8)
Charles Henry Coote, Esq.
John Warburton, Esq.
109. Borough of Ballynakill
Sir Wil. Montgomery, Bt.
John Moore, Esq;
110. Borough of Maryborough
Sir John Parnell, Bart.
John Tydd, Esq.
111. Borough of Portarlington
Hon. Joseph Dawson
Sir Roger Palmer, Bart.
112. ROSCOMMON (8)
Thomas Mahon, Esq.
Edward Crofton, Esq.
113. Borough of Boyle
Rt. Hon. Henry King
L rd Vis. Kingsborough
114. Borough of Roscommon
Robert Sandford Esq;
Henry Sandford, jun. Esq.
115. Borough of Tulsk
William Caulfield, Esq.
Ja. Carigue Ponsonby, Esq.
116. SLIGO (4)
Right Hon. Owen Wynne
Rt. Hon. Joshua Cooper

117. Borough of Sligo
Rt. Hon. Owen Wynne
R. H. Hutchinson, Esq.
118. TIPPERARY (8)
Henry Prittie, Esq.
Francis Mathew, Esq.
119. City of Cashel
Wm. Pennefather, Esq.
Richard Pennefather, Esq.
120. Borough of Clonmell
Stephen Moore, Esq.
Guy Moore Coote, Esq.
121. Borough of Fethard
Corn. O'Callaghan, Esq.
David Walsh, Esq.
122. TYRONE (10)
James Stewart, Esq.
123. Borough of Augher
George Hamilton, Esq.
William Fostick, Esq.
124. Bor. or City of Clogher
Rt Hon Sir Capel Molyneux, Bart
Thomas St. George, Esq.
125. Borough of Dungannon
Thomas Knox, Esq.
Charles O'Hara, Esq.
126. Borough of Strabane
Sir John Stuart Hamilton, Bart.
Henry Pomeroy, Esq.
127. WATERFORD (10)
Rt. Hon. John Beresford
Sir James May, Bart.
128. City of Waterford
Rt. Hon. Sir W. Osborne, Bart.
Godfrey Greene, Esq.
129. Borough of Dungarvan
Sir Henry Cavendish, Bart.
Richard Musgrave, Esq.
130. Borough of Lismore.
Nicholas Lysaght, Esq.
Lt. Col. Hugh Cane
131. Borough of Tallagh
Corn. Bolton. jun. Esq;
Rob. Shap. Carew Esq.

132. WESTMEATH (10)
Hon. Robert Rochford
Ben. Chapman, Esq.
133. Borough of Athlone
Sir Richard St. George, Bart.
William Hancock, Esq.
134. Borough of Fore
James Fitzgerald, Esq.
Hon. G. F. Nugent
135. Borough of Kilbeggan
Charles Lambart, Esq.
Sir Richard Johnston, Bart.
136. Manor of Mullingar
Rt. Hon. John Scott,
Sir Skef. Smyth, Bart.
137. WEXFORD (18)
Geo. Ogle, Esq.
Vesey Colclough, Esq.
138. Borough of Bannow
Henry Loftus, Esq.
Nich. Loftus Tottenham, Esq.
139. Borough of Clomines
Arthur Loftus, Esq.
Charles Tottenham, of New-Ross, Esq.
140. Bor. of Enniscorthy
Fred. Flood, Esq.
Mountesford Longfield, Esq.
141. Borough of Fethard
Charles Tottenham, Esq.
Ponsonby Tottenham Esq:
142. Borough of Newborough,
alias Gorey
Hump. Ram, Esq.
Stephen Ram, Esq.
143. Town of New-Ross.
Charles Tottenham, of Balley-currey, Esq.
Robert Leigh, Esq.
144. Borough of Taghmon
Lt. Col. Thomas Bigott
William Alex. English, Esq.
145. Town of Wexford
Richard Nevill, Esq.
Richard Le Hunte, Esq.

(259)

146. WICKLOW (10)
Hon. William Brabazon
Hon. John Stratford
  147. Borough of Ballinglas
Hon. Benj. Oneal Stratford
John Godley, Esq;
  148. Borough of Bleſinton
John Dillon, Esq.
John Reilly, Esq.

149. Borough of Carysfort
† Thomas Oſborne, Eſq.
Warden Flood, Eſq.
  150. Borough of Wicklow
Hon. Robert Ward
George Ponſonby, Eſq.

A L P H A B E T.

*** *The figures annexed to each Name, refer to the county or town the Gentleman repreſents.*

Adderly, 23
Agar, 66
Alexander, 58, 85
Allan, 64
Allen, 62
Anneſley, 84
Archdall, 50
Aylmer, 63
Bagenal, 10
Bailie, 40
Barry, 13
Bateman, 56
Beamiſh, 29
Beresford, 127
Bernard, 17
Birch, 14
Blackwood, 41, ib.
Blakeney, 53, ib. 94
Blaquiere, 12
Blennerhaſſet, 56
Bloſſe, 55
Bolton, 131
Bourke, 64
Brabazon, 146
Bradſtreet, 46
Brodrick, 28, ib.
Brooke, 33 50
Browne 43, 55, 78, 97
Brownlow, 6
Burgh, 47, 61, ib.
Burton, 10, 17
Buſhe, 70
Butler, 48, 66, 69.

Caldwell, 71
Cane, 130
Carew, 131
Carleton, 75
Cary, 83
Cavendiſh, 74, 129
Caulfield, 115
Chapman, 100, 132
Chriſtmas 81,
Clement, 46
Clements, 15, 31, 76
Cobbe, 49
Coghlan, 98
Colclough, 137
Colvill, 86
Conolly, 83
Conway, 1
Conyngham, 95
Cooper, 116
Coote, 108, 120
Cope, 33
Copinger, 57
Corry, 42
Cox, 22
Creighton, 35
Crofton, 112
Cromie, 32
Crookſhank, 3
Croſbie, 57
Cuffe, 97
Cuninghame, 95, 107
Daly, 52, 54
Dawſon, 6, 11, 108, 111
Deane, 19, 65

Digby, 63
Dillon, 89, 148
Dobbs, 97
Dobſon, 107
Engliſh 141
Evans, 19
Falkiner, 21
Finlay, 81
Fitz-Gerald, 16, 58
  60, 134
Fitzgibbon, 47
Flood, 51, 66, 140,
  149
Forbes, 104
Forde, 72
Foſter, 92, 96
Fortescue, 92
Fortick, 123
Gamble, 48
Gardiner, 45
Godley, 147
Gore 87
Gratton, 8
Greene, 128
Hamilton, 34, 64, 91,
  123, 126
Handcock, 75, 133
Harman, 87
Hartſtonge, 79
Headfort, 102
Heron, 4
Hill, 37, 85
Hoare, 80
Holmes, 74
Howard, 36

(260)

Hunt, 38	Montgomery, 13,	Rowley, 39, 99
Hutchinson, 24, 89,	31, 40, 106, 109	Sandford, 114, ib.
117	Moore, 102, 109, 120	Scott, 136
Jackson, 4, 84	Morres, 20,	Sheridan, 14
Jephson, 12, 27, ib.	Murray, 86	Singleton, 44
Johnston, 135	Musgrave, 129	Skeffington, 2, ib. 3
Jones, 76	Nesbit, 14	Smyth, 82, 136
Kearney, 26	Nevill, 145	Sneyd, 77
Keating, 62	Newenham, 45	Somervill, 43
Kilwarling, 37	Nugent, 134	Southwell, 39
King, 49, 113	O'Brien, 16	Staples, 32
Kingsborough 37, 113	O'Callaghan, 121	Stewart, 8, 37, 122
Kingsman, 88	Ogle, 44, 137	Stopford, 101
Knox, 34, 94, 125	O'Hara, 125	St. George, 124, 133
Lambart, 135	Oliver, 79	Stratford, 146, 147
Langrishe, 71	O'Neil, 5	Swan, 72
Latouche, 90	Osborne, 128, 149	Tennison, 106
Lawless, 35	Palmer, 111	Tighe, 77, 100
Le Hunte, 145	Parnell, 68, 110	Toler, 59
Leigh, 51, 143	Parsons, 73	Tonson, 29
Lloyd, 59, 73	Pennefather, 119, ib.	Tottenham, 138, 139,
Loftus, 138, 139	Pery, 82	141, 143
Longfield, 24, 140	Piggott, 144	Townsend, 18
Lowther, 99	Pomeroy, 60, 105,	Trench, 52
Lysaght, 21, 130	126	Tunnadine, 90
Mahon, 112	Ponsonby, 20, 65,	Tydd, 110
Martin, 78	115, 150	Vaughan, 91
Mason, 67	Popham, 98	Vesey, 26
Massey, 80	Prendergast, 11	Uniacke 30, ib.
Matthew, 118	Preston, 103, ib.	Warburton, 108
Maunsell, 88	Prittie, 118	Walshe, 121
Maxwell, 13	Putland, 104	Ward, 38, 150
May, 127	Ram, 101, 142	Warren, 22
Meredyth, 7	Rawson, 4	Wesley, 105
Metge, 93	Reilley, 148	Wilson, 1
Molyneux, 124	Richard, 4	Wood, 23
M'Namara, 93	Rochfort, 132	Wynne, 116
Monsel, 96	Ross, 42	Yelverton, 9

COURT of CHANCERY.

Thus ‡ marked in the Four Courts, and all the King's Council, are Benchers of the Hon. Society of King's Inn. And thus † marked, Commissioners to hear and determine Causes in Chancery, in the absence of the Lord Chancellor; a Judge to be always one.

(26)

‡ Ld. CHANCELLOR, Rt. Hon. Jas. Hewit, Visc. Lifford
‡† Master of the Rolls, Rt. Hon. Rich. Rigby.
Dep. Clerks and Keepers of the Rolls, Marcus Patterson, and Francis Perry, Esqrs.
Masters in Chancery, 4.
‡† C. Walker, Esq;
‡† John Tunnadine, Esq;
‡† F. Vesey, Esq;
‡† T. Borroughs, Esq;
Six Clerks.
W. Deane, Esq;
Denis Kelly, Esq;
Geo. Drew, Esq;
H. Cope, Esq;
Henry Palmer, Esq.
Richard Fleming, Esq;
‡ Clerk of the Crown and Hanaper, Hon. Hen. S. Conway, Dep. Clerk of the Crown & Hanaper, Con. Heatley, Esq;
‡ Registers, Wills Earl of Hillsborough, and Geo. Roth, Esq; Dep. Const. Cullen.
Cursitor, Cha. F. Scudamore, Esq; Dep. Ste. Wybrants, Esq;
Reg. and Cl. of the Faculties, D. Magill, Esq;
Clerk of the Recognizances, W. Deane, Esq;
Sec. to the Ld. Chancellor, Pat. Halpenny, Esq;
Purse-bearer, J. Hewitt, Esq;
Chief Exam. W. Ryves, Esq;
2d. Exam. John Godley, Esq;
Dep. Exam. Tho. Tench, and Wm. Patrickson, Esqrs.
Usher and Accountant Gen.
‡ Rich. Power, L. L. D.
Deputy, Geo. Roth,
Clerk of the Records, William Hogar, Esq;
Z

Twenty Commissioners of Bankrupts appointed by the Lord-Chancellor.
Amb. Smith, Tho. Kingsbury, Ste. Dickson, James Johnston, Robert Paul, Rob. French, J. O'Connor, Brett Norton, Sam. Forth, James Dunkin, Samuel Spencer, Ed. Nowlan, George Cartland, James O'Hara, Fr. Dobbs, Anthony King, Jos. Husband, Henry Doyel, Dennis George, and Ed. Ransford, Esqrs.
Secretary of Bankrupts.
John Hewitt, Esq;
Messengers, Wm. M'Kay, and Gawen Lane, Gents.
Pursuivant, Hugh Reilly, Esq;

COURT OF KING'S BENCH, Office, Kennedy's Lane.
‡† LORD CHIEF JUSTICE Rt. Hon. Ld. Annaly.
‡† 2d. Just. Chrift. Robinson Esq; ‡† 3d. Just. W. Henn, Esq
‡ Clerk of the Crown, Prothon. Keeper of the Writs, Philizer, Cl. of the Entries, and Cl. of the Errors, Henry B. Carter, Esq; for Life, 500l. per an.
Dep. Cl. of the Crown, Tho. Tisdall, Esq;
Dep. Prothon. Keeper of the Writs, Cl. of the Entries, & Cl. of the Errors, Ja. Hamilton, Esq;
Cl. to Ld. Ch. Just. Annaly Patrick Corbett, Esq;
Cl. to Mr. Just. Robinson, J. Ford, Esq;
Cl. to Mr. Just. Henn, Wm. Harrison, Esq;
Dep. Philizer. Tho. Church,
Seal-keeper Robert Moore

COURT of COMMON PLEAS, Office, Wine-Tavern-street.
‡† LORD CHIEF JUSTICE, Rt. Hon. Marcus Patterson.
‡† 2d Justice, Godf. Lill, Esq.
‡† 3d Just. Robert Hellen, Esq.
‡ Keepers of the Writs, Tho. Acton, Mathias Scott, Esqrs.
‡ Prothonotary, Visc. Farnham
Secondary, Hector Graham, Esq. Common-Pleas-Office.
Cl. of the King's Silver,
Philizer, Tho. Dulhunty, Esq.
Exigenter, Tho. Dulhunty, Esf.
Cl. of the Warrants, R. Fenner, Esq. Common-Pleas-Office
Clerk of the Entries, Isaac Bomford, Gent. Fishamble-str.
Cl. of the Essoins, Cl. of the Errors, and Cl. of the Juries, Joshua Carter, Gent. Common Pleas-Office
Clerk of the Outlawries, T. Tisdall, Esq. Ken Lane
Examiners, Hector Graham, John Carroll, Wm. Lyster, and Crof. Malone, Esqrs.
Cl. to Ld. Ch. Just. Paterson, Thomas Tisdall, Esq.
Cl. to Mr. Just. Lill, John Boland, Esq.
Cl. to Mr. Just. Hellen, John Carroll, Esq.

COURT OF EXCHEQUER. Treasury Office, Dublin-Castle.
LORD High Treasurer, Duke of Devonshire
Joint Vice-Treasurers, Rt. Hon. Earl Nugent, Rt. Hon. H. Flood, Rt Hon Ch Townshend, Esq.
Deputy Vice-Treasurer Rt. Hon. H. T. Clements,
Clerks in the Treasury, viz. John Cooper, J. Michell, R. Ashworth, J. Walker, Austin Cooper, J. Cooper, jun. and J. Kelly, Esqrs.
Ledger-Keeper, John Mitchell, Esq.
Cashier, or Teller of the Exchequer, Rt. Hon. Wm. Burton, His Clerks, viz. Cash-keeper. Tho. Higinbotham, Esq.
Examiner of his Vouchers and Keeper of the Ledger, Robert Wade, Esq.
Assist. Ro. Wade, Gent.
Keeper of the House for Receipt, James Murray.
‡ Chancellor of the Exchequer, Rt. Hon. W. Hamilton
‡† Ld. Ch. Baron, Rt. Hon. Lord Trafton
‡† Second Baron, Richard Power, Esq.
‡† Third Baron, Geo. Hamilton, Esq. Auditor-General, Rt. H. E. of Roden, and Rob. Ld. Jocelyn. Dep. Ro. Waller, Esq.
Clerks, Sam. Fenner, William Bower, & Tho. Bond, Gents.
Commissioners of Treasury Accounts, Ld. Chancellor, Cha. of the Exchequer, Ld. Ch. Baron and Barons of the Exchequer
Alnager of Ireland, Rt. Hon. Sir John Blaquiere, K. B.
Surveyor Gen. of Lands, Supervisor and Valuer of his Majesty's Honours, &c. Hon. Rt. Rochford, Dep. M. Handcock, Esq. Exch. Office, Kennedy-lane
Chief Remem. ‡ James, Earl of Clanbrassil, Dep. J Macartney Esq. Filacer, Henry Doyel, Esq.

(263)

Aud. of Accounts, Sam. Heatly, Efq. Reg. John Browne.
Treafurers or Second Remembrancer, Richard Morgan and Rich. Hely Hutchinfon, Efq. Dep. And. Carmichael, Efq.
Secondaries, Dan. Beere, Rd. Beere, and Z. D. Williams.
Clerk of the Pleas of the Exchequer, Fran. Plumptre, Efq. Dep. Cha. Farran, and Peter King, Efqrs.
Clerk of the Pipe, Hon. Jn. Butler.
Dep. Tho. Cade, Gent.
Chief Chamb. Sir Rog. Palmer, Bart. and Wm. Hen. Palmer, Efq.
Second Chamberlain, Edw. Cooke, Efq.
Comptroller of the Pipe, Edward Tighe, Efq.
Usher of the Exchequer, P. Higginfon, Efq.
Tranfcriptor and Foreign Appofer, Edm. Burroughs, Gent.
Summonifter and Clerk of the Eftreats, Nich. Morifon, Efq.
Marfhals of the Four Courts, Ja. Dexter, Efq. & Wm. his Son
Clerk of the Pells, Rt. Hon. Cha. Jenkinfon
Deputy, H. Standifh, Efq.
Rememb. Cl. and Receiver of the Firft Fruits, Ja. Glafscock and Nich. Kempfton, Efqrs.
Cryer of the Exchequer, Randal M'Alifter, Efq.
Purfuivant, Wm. Hamilton, Efq.
Aud. of Foreign Accounts and Imprefts, Wm. Montgomery, and Hen. Thompfon, Efqrs.
Clerk to Lord Chief Baron Dennis, D. Hugan, Efq;

Clerk to Baron Power, Richard Evans, Efq.
Clerk to Baron Hamilton, Robert Hamilton, Efq.
Keeper of the Seals, Earber Hendley, Efq.
Cl. of the Rules of the Com. Law, Peter King, Efq.
Clerk and Signer of Writs, Jofeph Farran, Gent.
Examinator, Dom. M'Caufland, Efq.

KING's COUNCIL.
‡ Prime Serjt. Hon. James Browne.
‡ Att. Gen. Rt. Hon. J. Scott
‡ Sollicitor General, Hugh Carleton, Efq.
‡ Second Serjeant, Attirvill Wood, Efq.
‡ Third Serjeant, James Fitzgerald, Efq.
‡ Hon. Jn. Hely Hutchinfon
‡ T. Kelly, Efq.
‡ Geo. Hart, Efq.
‡ Ja. Shiell, Efq.
‡ Rt. Barry, Efq.
‡ Rob. Sibthorpe, Efq.
‡ Fred. Flood, Efq.
‡ Bar. Yelverton, Efq, Ely Pl.
‡ John M'Mullen, Efq.
‡ Maurice Copinger, Efq;
‡ Arthur Wolfe, Efq.
‡ Hugh Wilfon, Efq.
‡ Henry Duquery, Efq.
‡ William Doyle, Efq.
Cl. to the Prime Serj.
Edward Bell, Efq.
Clks. to the Attorney Gen. Tho. Tifdall, Efq. and John Bradfhaw, Efq.
Clk. to the Solicitor Gen. John Carleton, Efq.
Clk. to Mr. Serj. Wood, James Pied, Gent.
Clerk to Mr. Serj. Fitzgerald, (vacant)

Treasurer to the Hon. Society of King's Inns, Rt. Hon. Lord Chancellor; Steward, John Rohinson, Gent.

STATE OFFICERS.

Lord Almoner, the Primate

Prin. Sec. of State, Rt. Hon. John Hely Hutchinson.

Chief Sec. to the Lord Lieut. Rt. Hon. William Eden.

Under Sec. Sackville Hamilton, Esq.

Cl. of the Council, Ld. G. Germain, Dept. W. Greene, H. Upton, and J. Patrickson, Esqrs.

State Physician, Robt. Emmett, M. D. F. R. S.

State Surgeon, Arch. Richardson, Esq;

Compiler of the Dublin Gazette, Hon. Mr. Hewitt.

Ulster King of Arms, Wm. Hawkins, Esq; Deputy, Wm. Bryan, Esq;

Athlone, Pursuivant at Arms, Geo. Winstanley, Esq; Deputy T. M. Winstanley, Gent.

Solicitor in Criminal Causes, Nich. Morrison, Esq;

Mast. of the Ce em. and Gent. Usher to the Ld. Lt. J. Lees, Esq.

Chief Serj. at Arms, Dixie Coddington, Esq;

Second Serjeant at Arms, Hump. Minchin, Esq; Dep. Jol. Griffiths, Esq.

Usher and Keeper of the Counc. Cham. Rd. Moore, Esq.

Constable of Dublin Castle, Hon. H. S. Conway, Dep. Rt. Hon. H. T. Clements

Chaplain Rev. Alex. Staples

Chapl. of his Maj. Rl. Chapel of St. Matthew, near Ringsend, Rev. Dean John Brocas

Housekeeper a keeper of Dubli Lucy Waite

Master of his M ing-house in Dub Broom, Gent.

Ranger of the and Master of th Clements, Esq; d that of the Rt. Clements.

Keepers of the Ld Geo. Germair ner, and Rob. G Dep. Ranger, Ranger of th Kildare, Wm. S Director and St State Music, Sam Mas. of Revels,

CLERKS of the House of Lords, Gayer, L. L. D Gayer, Esq.

Clerks of the I Commons, Henr Shapland Carew,

Chaplain to th of Commons, Rev

King's Printer the late Mr. Bou Corrector and St Majesty's Print n Meredyth, Esq. C. Woodward.

PREROGATIV JUDGE, S. Rad Registers, the R Friend, and John Marshal, Mat. Metropolitical magh, Vicar Ger Radcliffe, J. U. I Register, Henr Dep. Ja. Maculla, Consistory Cour Judge, Ste. Rad

Reg. Alexander Maclaine, Efq.

COURT OF ADMIRALTY.
JUDGE, Warden, Flood, Efq. J. U. D.
Lords of the Admiralty's Advocate, Ja. Shield, L. L. L.
Regifter, T. Tifdall, Efq.
Proctor, W. Robinet, Efq.
Marfhal, Hugh O'Neile, Efq.
Vice Admiral of Munfter, Wm. Earl of Befborough.
——— of Leinfter, Vifc Fitzwilliam
——— of Ulfter, Rt. Hon. Will. Burton.
——— of Connaught. Cha. Wm. Earl of Sefton

COURT of DELEGATES.
Regifter of Appeals and Provocations Spiritual, Thomas Acton, Efq.

GENERAL OFFICERS.
Commander in Chief, Rt. Hon. Lieut.Gen.Sir John Irwin, K B
Lieut. Gen. Robert Cunningham, Maj. Gen. Laun. Baugh, Maj. Gen. Ed. Maxwell, Maj. Gen. F. Mocher Major Gen. J. Gabbet, Maj. Gen. E. Maffey, Maj. Gen. Earl of Rofs.
Sec. to the Board of General Officers, F. Palmer, Efq.
Aides de Camp to the Lord Lieut. Hon. Capt. North, Rt. Hon. Lord Strathaven, Sir James Erfkine, Bart.
Mufter-mafter-general, Rich. E. of Shannon, Dep. Matthew Handcock, Efq.
Commiffioners, Geo. Ball, Gideon Tabuteau, Step. Wybrants, David Winftanley, Robert Mullock Jofeph Smith, and Rob. Wybrants.

Adjutant Gen. Lieut. Col. H L. Luttrell
Dep. AdjGen.Capt HBowyer
Quart. Maft. Gen. Lt. Col. D. Dundas
Deputy Quarter Mafter Gen. Charles Euftace, Efq.
Phyfician Gen. Sir Nathaniel Barry, Bart. M. D.
Advocate General and Judge Martial, Walt. Hore, Efq.
Surgeon General, William Ruxton, Efq.
Provoft Marfhal Gen. John Clarke, jun. Efq.

ARTILLERY REGIMENT.
Colonel in Chief, Lieut. Gen. Charles Earl of Drogheda
Colonel (er. fec.) Lieut. Gen. Bernard Hale
Lt. Col. Commandant, John Stratton
Maj. R. Betterworth.

ORDNANCE.
Office, Lower Caftle-yard.
Civil Branch, Mafter General, Major Gen. Cha. Earl of Drogheda, 1500l.
Lt. Gen. Bern. Hale, Efq. 600l
Surv. Gen. R. Ward, Efq. 450l
Clerk of the Ordnance, Jof. Keene, Efq. 300l
Principal Storekeeper, Tho. Coghlan, Efq. 200l
Clerk of the Deliveries, Rob. Tighe, Efq
Treafurer, Thomas Burgh, Efq, 200l
Sec. to the Mafter Gen. Hen. Meredyth, Efq. 182l 10s
Proof-Mafters, Tho. Trulock, Wm. Stokes

Clerk of the Works, Wm. Stokes.

LABORATORY, Comptroller, Ralph Ward, Esq. 150l.
Fire-Master, David Robinson, Esq. 100l
Engineers, Chief Engineer, Lt. Col. Thomas Pigott, Esq. as Lt. Col.
Director, Lt. Col. Char. Vallancy as Major.
Engineers in Ordinary, Tho. Jarrat and Charles Tarrant

Company of Battle-Axe-Guards Lorenz. More, Esq; Col. as Capt.
T. Hungerford Townsend, Capt. as Lieutenant
Tho. Smith, Esq. Capt. as Lieut.

Commissioners, &c. of all his Majesty's Barracks.
Rt Hon. Sir Jn. Irwine, Hon. Ponsonby Moore, Thomas St. George, Tho. Tisdall, James Cavendish, Wm. Handcock, Ralph Ward, and Fitzherbert Richards, Esqrs.
Supervisor of Accounts, Tho. St. George, Esq.
Secretary to the Commissioners, Richard Thwaites, Esq.

Governors of Counties.
Antrim, Earl of Antrim
Armagh, Earl of Charlemont
Carlow, William Burton, Beauchamp Bagnal, Clement Wolseley, and John Rochfor, Esqrs.
Cavan, Earl of Bellamont
Clare, Earl of Inchiquin
Cork, Earl of Shannon
Donegal, Earl of Ross and Earl Cunningham
Down, Earl of Hillsborough
Dublin, Earl of Howth, Luke Gardiner, and Richard Talbot, Esqrs.
Fermanagh, Earl of Ely, Viscount Enniskillen, Viscount Erne, Right Hon. Sir Ar. Brooke, Bart. Sir James Callwell, Bt. Moryn Archall, Esq.
Galway, John Baron Eyre, W. P. K. Trench, and D. Daly, Esqrs.
Kerry, Earl of Kerry
Kildare, Duke of Leinster
Kilkenny, Earl of Besborough
King's County, E. of Drogheda
Leitrim, Right Hon. Owen Wynne, Rob. Clements, Esq.
Limerick, Lord Muskerry
Londonderry County and City, and Town of Coleraine, Earl Cunningham and Rt. Hon. Thomas Conolly
Longford, Earl of Granard
Louth, Earl of Clanbrassil
Mayo, Charles Baron Lucan, Sir Roger Palmer, Bart.
Earl of Altamont, Earl of Arran, James Cuffe, Esq.
Monaghan, Earl of Clermont
Meath, Earl of Drogheda
Queen's County, Visc. Carlow, Earl of Drogheda, William Pole, Esq.
Roscommon, Earl of Kingston, Thomas Mahon, Esq.
Sligo, Earl of Kingston, Right Hon. Owen Wynne, Esq. Rt. Hon. Joshua Cooper, Esq.
Tipperary, Visc. Mountcashel, Sir Corn. Maude, Bt. Henry Prittie, Francis Mathew, Corn. O'Callaghan, and Richard Penefather, Esqrs.
Tyrone, Lord Weller.
Waterford City and County, Earl of Tyrone
Westmeath, Earl of Westmeath, Earl Belvidere

Wexford, Earl of Arran, Earl of Ely, Vifc. Valentia, and Geo. Ogle, Efq.
Wicklow, Earl of Aldborough, Earl of Milltown, Hon. Benj. Oneal Stratford, Sir Skeffington Smith, Bart. and Samuel Hayes, Efq.

Governors of Forts and Garrifons, &c.

Londonderry and Culmore Fort, Gov. Lieut. General John Hale, 1l. per diem
Cork, Gov. Nicholas Lyfaght, Efq. 1l per diem
Lt. Gov. John Leland, Efq.
Limerick, Gov. Lieut. Gen. Sir Henry Clinton, K. B. 1l. per diem
Kinfale, Gov. Lieut. Gen. R. Cunninghame, 1l per diem.
Duncannon, Governor, Ld. Robert Bertie, 1l. per diem
Rofs Caftle, Gov. Sir Fran. Lumm, Bart. 10s. per diem
Charlemont, Gov. Sir Guy Carleton, K. B. 1l. per diem
Galway, Gov. Lieut. Col. Rob. Sandford, 11s. per diem
Carrickfergus. Gov. Nehemiah Donnellan, Efq. Conftable, Hon. Col. A Brown
Maryborough, Conftable Charles Earl of Drogheda
Athlone, &c. Conft. Charles Lord Vifcount Ranelagh
Caftlemain, Conftable, Tho. Halcott, Efq.

Commiffioners of Cuftoms. Rt. Hon. John Beresford, J. Monck Mafon, Rich. Townfend, Lord Clifden, Sir Her. Langrifhe, Bart. Rob. Rofs, John Parnell.

For the Inland Department.
Secr. Vaughan Montgomery
Firft Clerk, Rob Lovett, Efq

Clerks of the Minutes, Geo. Waller, and John Healy, Efq
For the Port Bufinefs.
Secr. Sackv. Hamilton, Efq. Second Secretary

Chief Cl. in the Secretary's Office, Wm. Molefworth, Efq.
Clerk of the Minutes, Wm. Morgan, Efq.
Council, M. Copinger, Efq.
Solicitor, G. E. Howard, Efq
Solicitor in England, Sir Robert W fton, Bart
Clerk of the Quit-Rents, Richard Vernon, Efq
Regifter of the Forfeitures, Henry Sandford, Efq.
Clerk in the Forfeiture Office, Hon. Richard Bourke, Efq.
Solicitor for the King's Rents, &c. John Bradfhaw, Efq.
Clerk of the Informations in Dublin Port, Rob. Stafford, Gt.
Examiner and Comptroller of the Collectors Accounts of Incidents, John Armitt, Efq.
Paymafter of Corn Premiums, Sir Roger Palmer, Bart.
Examiners of Corn Premiums P. Lebas, and W. Wetherall, Efqs
Clerk, Wool Accounts, John Wetherall, Gent.
Clerk, Ship Entries, Edw. Sedgwick, Efq
Clerk, Land Permits, John Cooper, Gent
Clerk, Coaft Permits, Jof. Lefanu, Gent
Clerk of the Commiffioners Cheque Book, A. Worthington
Examinator of the Cuftoms, Henry Gore, Efq
Examinator of the Excife, John Swan, Efq.
Examinator of Diaries, Edward Hamilton, Efq

(268)

Examinator of the Hearth-money, John Hewit, Efq
Store-keeper, St. Wright, Efq Dep. J. Standifh, Efq. Cheque on ditto, James Stables, Gent.
Dublin Port, Collector, Rt Hon. Theophilus Jones
Surveyors on the Cuftom-Houfe Quay, Hen. Duquery, and Charles Dawfon, Efqrs.
Surveyor & Comptroller in the Store, Matthias Scott, Efq;
Surv. & Gauger on the Cuftom Houfe Quay, Love Hiat, Efq
Jerquer, Conolly Norman, Efq
Surv. Afton's Quay, Toby Purcell, Gent
Surveyor, Rogerfon's Quay, Benjamin Span, Gent
Surveyors of Land-Carriage Officers, William Owen, and James Grove, Gents.
Tide Surv. Jervis Quay Monf. Mercer, Gt Surv. of the North Wall, Bryan Conner, Gent.
Surveyors Ringfend, John White, Bingham Burke, J. Mac Dermot, J. Reid, and G. Eeles, Gents
Infpector of the Revenue Boats and Examinator of the Tide Surveyors Diaries, Tho. Caufar, Gent

PATENTEE OFFICERS.

Comptr. and Accompt. Rt. Hon. Agmond. Vefey, Dep. Wm. Wetheral. Surv. Gen. of the Cuftoms in Ireland, L. Gardiner, Efq. Dep. Rob. Gardiner, Efq. -
Cuftomer and Collector of the Port of Dublin, John Fofter, Efq. Deputies, John Sheppey, and R. Eaton, Efqrs.

Comptroller, Robert Tighe, Efq; Deputy, W. Large, Gt.
Craner and Wharfinger, Hen. Tilfon, Efq; Deputy, Wilcow Hincks
Tafters of Wines, Rt Hon. John Beresford, and Marcus Beresford, Efqrs
Searcher, Packer, and Gauger Thomas Clements, Efq.
Stamper of Cards and Dice in the Port of Dublin, Robert Lovett, Elq.
Affay Mafter and Receiver of the Duties on Plate, Thomas Nuttall, Efq
Maker of Weights, James Warren, Goldfmith, Cork-hill
Surveyors Gen. Theo. Blakeney, for Connaught; T. Morris, for Ulfter; James Blaquiere, for Leinfter, Rob. Gordon, for Munfter, Efqrs
Commiffioners of the Impreft Office, and for managing the Stamp Duties.
Henry Loftus, Edw. Tighe, Rich. Hely Hutchinfon, Ed. Bellingham Swan, Efqrs. and Sir Fred. Flood, Bart.
Secretary, Hon. J. Dawfon.
Rec. Gen. Hon. J. Bourke
His Clerks, Wm. Hutton, Wm. Daniel
Sec. Ralph Ward, Efq.
His Clerks, Cha. Efte, Rob. Smith, Henry Kendall
Comptrol. Pet. Holmes, Efq.
His Clerks, Geo. L'Eftrange, Wm. Kelly. and Thomas Irwin
Solicitor, Rich. Waller, Efq
Clerk of the Securities, Warehoufe Keeper of Stampt Goods, and Diftributor for Dublin, Meredyth Workman

Teller of Stamps, Sir Geo. Maffy, Knt.
Teller in, Thomas Finney
Warehouse Keeper of Unftampt Goods, William Leflie Badham
Packer of Country Goods, John Shehey
Inspector of the Courts, Tim. O'Brien
House-keeper, Mary Hutton
Register of Pamphlets, Tho. L'Eftrange
Supervifor of the Stampers, Jonathan Fisher
Infpector of Dies and Plates, John Debenham
Chamber-keeper, T. Clarke
Meffenger and Door-keeper, Mich. Sheridan.

Commiffioners of Appeals. Rob. Barry, Rich. Malone, Cl. Rowley, John Tunnadine, and John Tydd, Efqrs. Their Secretary, Hen. Coddington, Gent.

Bankers of Dublin.
Mr. William Gleadowe and Company, Mary's Abbey
Meffrs. David Latouche and Sons, Caftle-ftreet
John Finlay, Efq. and Co. Upper Ormond's Kay
John Dawfon Cotes, Thomas-ftreet

Bankers of Cork.
Meff. Falkiner, Rogers, and Co. near the Cuftom-Houfe.
M. Warren, Bernard, Tonfon, Jefferys, and Cuthbert, in Paulftreet. Eben. and Sam. Pike, John Pim, and Hon. William Williams, Hewit, and Co. South Mall.

Bankers of Waterford.
Alderman Simon Newport Henry Herbert, and B. Rivers
Bankers of Clonmell.
Wm. and Phineas Ryall.

General Poft-Office, Dublin.
Right Hon. William Henry Earl Clermont, Poft-Mafter General, and Treafurer
John Lee, Efq. Secretary and Comptroller
Wm. Fortrefcue Accomptant
Robert Shaw, Clerk to the Poft-Mafter General
Wm. Maturin, Clerk of the Munfter-Road
Tho. Jones, Clerk of Connaught Road
Richard Boulger, Clerk of the North Road.

Trinity College, near Dublin.
Chancellor, His Royal Highnefs the Duke of Glouceffer.
Vice Chancellor, His Grace the Lord Primate.
Vifitors, the Chancellor, Vice Chancellor, and Arch-Bifhop of Dublin
Provoft, Right Hon. John Hely Hutchinfon, L L. D.
Senior Fellows.
Vice Provoft and Auditor, W. Clement, M. D.
Sen. Lectur. Dr. J. Forfayeth
Burfar, Dr. J. Douglas.
Regifter and Sen. Dean, Rev. Dr. Rich. Murray
Librarian, Rev. Dr. Tho. Leland
Catechift, and Sen. Proctor, Rev. Dr. R. Murray
Profeffors of the Univerfity King's Profeffors.
Divinity, Rev. Dr. Br. Difney
Com. Law, Dr. Pat. Duigenan

(270)

Civil Law, Rev. Hen Dabzac, D. D.
Phyſic, W. Clement, M. D.
Greek, Rev. Dr. H. Dubzac
Greek, Rev. J. Drought
Ital. and Span. Mr. A. Vieyra
Aſſiſtants, Mr. Kearney and Mr. Fitzgerald
Eraſmus Smith's Profeſſors.
Mathematicks, Dr. Murray.
Aſſiſtants, Mr. Fitzgerald and Mr. Waller
Oriental Tongues, Dr. Forſayeth. Aſſiſtants, Mr. Hales and Mr. Day.
Oratory, Dr. Leland. Aſſiſtant, Mr. Kearney
Hiſtory, Dr. Leland. Aſſiſtant, Mr. Kearney.
Nat. Philoſ. Dr. Wilſon.
Profeſſor of Muſick.
E. of Mornington, Muſ. D.
Lecturers.
Divinity, H. Dabzac, D. D.
Anat. G. Cleghorn, M. D.
Chymiſtry, James Thornton, M. D.
Botany, Edw. Hill, M. D.
Chemiſt. Pat. Haſtings
Law Agent, William Lyſter

The College of Phyſicians.
PRESIDENT.
Fran. Hutcheſon M. D.
VICE-PRESIDENT.
Edward Hill, M. D.
FELLOWS.
Conſtantine Barbor, M. D.
Sir Nat. Barry, Bt. M. D.
Henry Quin, Truſt.
Sam. Cloſſy, M. D.
Ar. Saunders, M. D.
James Thornton, M.D. Cenſor
W. Harvey, M. D.
Francis Hopkins, M.D. Cenſor

HONORARY FELLOW.
Patrick Hewetſon, M. D.
Licentiates in Phyſick.
George Fletcher, M. D.
Robert Emmet, M. D.
Jn. Purcell, M. D.
Garret Huſſey, M. D.
Daniel Cooke, M. D.
John Michael Daley, M. D.
Licentiates in Midwifry
Mat. Carter, M. D.
Sir Field. Ould, Knt. M. D.
The King's Profeſſors, according to the Will of the late Sir Patrick Dun, Knt. M. D. Dr Henry Quin, Theory and Practice—Dr. Nat. Barry, Chirurgery and Midwifry—Dr. Conſt. Barbor, Pharmacy and the Materia Medica

Rev DEANS of Ireland
Th. Webb, A. M. Kilmore
Rd. Marlay, A. M. Ferns
James King, D. D. Raphoe
Rich. Dobbs, A. M. Connor
John Brocas, A. M. Kilala
Arthur Champagne, A. M. Clonmacnoiſe
John Erſkine, M. A. Cork
Ch. Coote, D. D. Kilfenora
Ralp. Walſh, A. M. Dromore
Wm. Craddock, M. A. St. Patrick's Dublin
Wm. Digby, A. M. Clonfort
Ja. Dickſon, A. M. Down
Robert Bligh, Elphin
Rich. Stewart, D.D. Leighlin
E. Ledwich, L L.D. Kildare
John Hewitt, A. M. Cloyne
H. Hamilton, D.D. Armagh
R. Hancock, A. M. Achonry
Cutts Harman, A. M. Waterford

Edward Bayly, D. D. Ardfert
Rt Rev. Dr. Char. Jackson Lord Bishop of Kildare, Christ Church, Dublin
John Lewis, A. M. Ossory
Hon. and Rev. MauriceCrofbie, D. D. Limerick
Robert Gorges, LL. B. Kilmacdaugh
John Jebb, D. D. Cashel
J. Ryder, LL. D. Lismore

Wensley Bond, M. A. Rosse
W. French, A. M. Ardagh
Rt. Rev. Dr. R. Woodward, (Lord Bishop of Cloyne) Clogher
Robert Clarke, D. D. Tuam
Rich. Moor, A. M. Emly
Rt. Rev. Dr. W. Cecil Pery, (Lord Bishop of Killala) Derry
Sam. Rustall, M. A. Kildaloe

A Correct List of the Baronets of Ireland, with the Dates of their Creations, from the first Institution of that Order in Ireland (by the Letters Patent of King JAMES I. Dated Sept. 30, 1619) to the present time. Thus marked † by PrivySeal.

1621 Fitzgerald Aylmer, of Donedea, Co. Kildare, Jan. 25
1622 Henry Lynch Blosse, of Galway, June 8
1622 George Tuite, of the Sonnagh, Co. Westmeath, June 6
1622 Valentine Blake, of Galway, July 10
1622 Patrick Barnewall, of Crickstown, Co. Westmeath, Feb. 24
1623 Robert Newcomen, of Kenaugh, Co. Longford, Dec. 30
1627 Alexander MacDonnel, of Moye, Co. Antrim, Nov. 30
1628 Robert Staples, of Lysson, Co. Tyrone, July 18
1628 Ulick Bourke, of Grimsk, Co. Roscommon, Aug. 2
1628 † Tho. Butler, of Cloughgrennan, Co. Carlow, Aug. 16
1628 Thomas Esmond, of Clonegall, Co. Wexford, Jan. 28
1629 William Osborne, of Ballintaylor, Co. Tipperary, Oct. 15
1651 John Morres, of Knockagh, Co. Tipperary, March 28
1645 Kildare Burrowes, of Giltown, Co. Kildare, Feb. 11
1660 Will. Pigot Piers, of Tristenagh, Co. Westmeath, Feb. 18
1660 Thomas Giffard, of Castlejordan, Co. Meath, March 4
1662 Thomas Dancer, of Waterford, Aug. 12
1665 Richard Gething, of Moyallow, Co. Cork, Aug. 1
1665 † Henry O'Neile, Feb. 23
1671 Gregory Byrne, of Tymoge, Queen's Co. May 17
1677 William Parsons, of Parson's Town, King's Co. Dec. 15
1678 Richard Reynell, Aug. 2
1681 Harry Hartstonge, April 20
1681 Emanuel Moore, of Rosscarbury, Co. Cork, June 29
1683 Jam. Caldwell, of Wellsborough, Co. Fermanagh, June 23
1686 Lucius O'Brien, of Dromolen, Co. Clare, Nov. 9
1688 Patrick Bellew, of Barmeath, Co. Lowth, Dec. 11
1704 Rd. Levinge, Oct. 26
1706 Richard Cox, of Dunmanway, Co. Cork, Nov. 21
1709 Robert Deane, of Dromore, Co. Cork March 10
1271 Henry Echlin, Knt. Oct. 17

(272)

1723 Tho. Burdet, of Dunmore, Co. Carlow, remainder to the Issue Male of his only Sister Anne, Wife to Walter Weldon, of Rahern, Queen's Co. July 11
1730 Capel Molyneux, of Castle Dillon, Armagh Co. July 4
1730 Nicholas Baily, of Placenuyd, Co. Anglesea, July 4
1744 John Coulthurst, jun. of Ardrum Co. Cork, Aug. 3
1744 Richard Wolfely, of Mount Arran, Co. Carlow, Jan. 19
1748 James Somerville, June 14
1758 Wm. Evans Morres, of the Co. Kilkenny, April 24
1758 Mar. Lowth. Crofton, Mote, Co. Roscommon, June 12
1758 Charles Burton, October 2
1759 Samuel Bradstreet, of Dublin, July 14
1760 George Ribton, of Stillorgan, Co. Dublin, April 21
1760 Booth Gore, of Artarmon, Co. Sligo, Aug. 30
1761 Wm. Yorke, April 13
1763 James May, of Mayfield, Co. Waterford, June 30
1763 Robert Blackwood, of Battyliddy, Co. Down, July 1
1763 James Cotter, of Rochfoirest, Co. Cork, Aug. 11
1764 Arthur Brooke, of Colebrooke, Co. Fermanagh, Jan. 3
1766 John Blunden, of Kilkenny, March 12
1766 Rich St. George, of Athlow, Co. Westmeath, Mar. 12
1766 John Parnell, of Rathleague, Queen's Co.
1768 Richard Steefe
1768 James Nugent, of Donore, Co. Westmeath, June 21
1768 Edw. Loftus, of Mount Loftus. Co. Kilkenny, June 21
1768 John Freke, of Castle-Freke, Co. Corke, June 21
1772 Richard Johnfon, of Gilford, Co. Down, July 2
1774 Henry Hamilton, Manor Cuningham, Donegal, Nov. 22
1774 John Allen Jonston, Co. Dublin, Nov. 22
1774 Francis Lumm, of Lumville, King's County, Nov. 12
1775 Edward Barry, M. D. of the City of Dublin, July 8
1776 Michael Cromie, of Stacumine, Co. Kildare, July 2
1776 Ralph Fetherstone, of Ardagh, Co. Longford, July 2
1776 Skeffington Smith, of Tinny Park, Co. Wiclow, July 2
1776 Nicholas Lawlefs, of Abingdon, Co. Limerick, July 2
1777 Hercules Langrishe, of Knocktopher, Kilkenny, Jan. 28
1777 Roger Palmer, of Castle-Lachin, Co. of Mayo, May 3.
1778 James Strat. Tynte, of Dunlavan, Co. Wicklow, July 7
1778 John Miller, of Ballicafey, Co. of Clare, July 7.
1778 Riggs Falkiner, of Ann-Mount, Co. of Corke, July 7.
1779 Charles French, of Clogha, Co. of Galway, July 6.
1779 Hugh Hill, of Londonderry, July 6.
1780 Fred. Flood, of Newton Ormound, Kilkenny, May 9
1780 Robert Waller, of Newport, Tipperary, May 10
1780 J. Stuart Hamilton of Dunnamana, Co. Tyrone, Dec. 2.
1780 John Tottenham, Tottenham Green, Co. Wexford, Dec. 2.
1780 Neal O'Donnell, of Newport, Co. of Mayo, Dec. 2

F I N I S.

Corrected to February 8, 1781.

A
COMPANION
TO THE
ROYAL KALENDAR,
For the YEAR 1781:

Being a LIST of all the

CHANGES IN ADMINISTRATION,

From the Accession of the present King

In OCTOBER, 1760,

To the present Time.

TO WHICH IS PREFIXED,

A List of the late and present House of Commons,

SHEWING

The Changes made in the Members of Parliament, by the General Election in SEPTEMBER, 1780;

With the Names of the Candidates where the Elections were contested, the Numbers polled, and the Decisions since made by the Select Committees.

Also the Dates when each City and Borough first sent Representatives to Parliament, the Right of Election in each Place, and the supposed Number of Voters.

THE TWENTY NINTH EDITION.

With an APPENDIX, containing the CASES of the controverted Elections in the Years 1774 and 1775; with the Determinations of the several Committees upon the same.

LONDON:

Printed for J. ALMON and J. DEBRETT, opposite Burlington-House, Piccadilly. 1781.

[Price One Shilling.]

ADVERTISEMENT.

THIS Edition contains a Lift of the late and prefent Houfe of Commons, fhewing the Changes made in the Members of Parliament by the General Election in 1780. And it is further improved with the Additions of the Date when each City and Borough firft fent Reprefentatives to Parliament, the Right of Election in each Place, and the fuppofed Number of Electors. Where the Right of Election has been afcertained by a Refolution of the Houfe of Commons, the Date of that Refolution is given. Where there is no Date to the Right of Election, there has been no Refolution of the Houfe upon it, and the Cuftom, which is given, is ftill adhered to. The fuppofed Number of Electors follow.

EXPLANATION.

Abingdon firft fent Reprefentatives to Parliament in the 4th Year of the Reign of Philip and Mary. The Right of Election is in the Inhabitants not receiving Alms, or any Charity, by a Refolution of the Houfe of Commons of the 18th of January, 1708. The fuppofed Number of Voters are 600.

Refpecting the Lifts of Changes in all the great Offices, the Rule laid down and purfued in this little Book, is, in each office firft giving the Perfon or Perfons who held that Department at the Acceffion of the prefent King, and then the Changes, or Alterations, which have been fince made, follow with their Dates.

No Pains have been fpared to be as accurate as poffible: But Notice of any Errors will, at all Times be thankfully received by the Publifher; together with any Hints for Improvement.

A LIST of the late and present Members of Parliament.

₊ The names in Roman characters are the gentlemen elected at the General Election in 1774, and the names in *Italic* characters, are the gentlemen elected afterwards.

₊ The names in Roman characters are the gentlemen elected at the General Election in 1780, and the names in *Italic* characters are the gentlemen who were candidates. The figures shew the numbers who voted for each person.

Abington, Berks.

JOHN Mayor, esq.

4 Phil. and Mary.

RE-elected 137
Thomas Wooldridge 55

In the inhabitants paying scot and lot, and not receiving alms or any charity. 18 Jan. 1708.—600.

Agmondesham, Bucks. 28 Edw. I. 21 Ja. I.
William Drake, esq. re-elected
William Drake, jun. esq. re-elected
In the inhabitants paying scot and lot only. 1 Dec.1705. —130.

St. Albans, Herts. 35 Edw. I. 7 Edw. VI.
Sir Richard Sutton, bart. William Charles Sloper, esq.
John Radcliffe, esq. re-elected
In the mayor, aldermen, and freemen, and such householders only as pay scot and lot. 27 April, 1714.—1000.

Aldborough, Suffolk. 3 Eliz.
Richard Combe, esq. P. Champion Crespigny, esq.
T. Fonnereau, esq. died in 1779
Martin Fonnereau, esq. re-elected
Resolved by the committee not to be in the bailiffs, burgesses, and freemen, receiving alms; but in the bailiffs and burgesses, resident within the borough, not receiving alms. 23 Dec. 1709. To which the house disagreed. In the inhabitants paying scot and lot. *Custom.*—So.

A 2 *Ald-*

Aldborough, Yorkshire. Ult. Phil. and Mary.
Abel Smith, esq. vacated in   Sir Rich. Sutton, bart. made
    1778   his election for Sandwich
Hon. Wm. Hanger   Hon. Edw. Onslow
C. Wilkinson, esq. vacat. 1777   Charles Mellish, esq.
W. Baker, esq.

Not in the select number of burgesses, holding by burgage-tenure ; but all the inhabitants paying scot and lot have a right to vote. 17 May, 1690.—57.

Andover, Hants. 23 Edw. I.
Sir Jn. Griffin Griffin, K.B.   re-elected
Benj. Lethieullier, esq.   re-elected

In the bailiff and select number of burgesses only. 28 Jan. 1702. 2 April, 1689.

Anglesea.
Lord Visc. Bulkeley   re-elected

Appleby, Westmoreland. 23 Edw. I.
Phil. Honeywood, esq.   re-elected
George Johnstone, esq.   William Lowther, esq made
                               his election for Carlisle
                               Hon. W. Pitt

Burgage tenure.—120.

Arundel, Sussex. 23 Edw. I.
Thomas Brand, esq.   Sir P. Crawford, knt.   167
G. Lew. Newnham, esq.   Thomas Fitzherbert, esq. 131
                             Hon. Percy Windham   69

Only in the inhabitants of the said borough, paying scot and lot. 22 Feb. 1693.—100.

Ashburton, Devon. 26 Edw. I.
Charles Boone, esq.   re-elected
Robert Palk, esq.   re-elected

In the freeholders having lands or tenements holden of the said borough only ; and the freeholders of lands and tenements called Halshanger and Hallwell-lands, lying within the borough, and subject to pay borough-rent, have a right to vote. 20 Feb. 1707.—200.

Aylesbury, Bucks. 1 Mary.
Anthony Bacon, esq.   re-elected   433
Jn. Aubrey, esq.   Thomas Ord, esq.   374
                          J. Smith   135

In all the householders of the said borough, not receiving alms : persons receiving alms, pursuant to the will of Mr Bedford, disabled from voting. 28 Jan. 1695. 7 Feb. 1698. —450.

Banbury, Oxfordshire 1 Mary.
Lord North   re-elected; vacated in 1778, and re-elected, as also in 1780

In the mayor, aldermen, and capital burgesses of Banbury only. 29 Dec. 1691.—19.

Barnstable, Devon. 23 Edw. I.
John Cleveland, esq.   re-elected
W. Devaynes, esq.   Francis Basset, esq.
                        William Devaynes, esq.

In the corporation and burgesses.—326.

Bath, Somersetshire. 23 Edw. I.
John Smith, esq. died in 1775   Hon J. Jefferies Pratt
Sir John Sebright, bart.
Abel Moyfey, esq.   19   re-elected

In the mayor, aldermen, and common council only. 27 Jan. 1706.—30.

Beaumaris, Anglesea.
Sir Hugh Williams, bart.   Sir G. Warren, K. B.

In the mayor and capital burgesses of the said borough. 3 March, 1725.—24.

Bedfordshire.
Earl of Upper Ossory   re-elected
Sir Thomas Hampden   Hon. St. Andrew St. John

Bedford Town. 23 Edw. I.
Sir W. Wake, bart.   re-elected   421
Sam. Whitbread, esq.   re elected   673
                      J. Kenrick   304

In the burgesses, freemen, and inhabitants, being householders of Bedford, not receiving alms. 22 April, 1690.—1000.

Bedwin, Wilts. 23 Edw. I.
Paul Methuin, esq.   re-elected
Earl of Courtown vacat. 1774   Sir Merrick Burrell, bart.
Lord Cranburn

In the freeholders and inhabitants of ancient burgage-messuages. 26 March 1729.——80.

Beeralston, Devon. 27 Eliz.
Sir F. Hen. Drake, bart.   Lord Algernon Percy made
Hon. Geo. Hobart.   his elect. for Northumb.
                       Lord Visc. Fielding
                       Lord Macartney

In the freehold tenants of the said borough, holding by burgage-tenure, and paying 3d. per annum, or more, ancient bur—

burgage-rent, to the lord of the said borough, and in them only. 6 June, 1721.—70.

Berkshire.

Chris. Griffith, esq. died 1776
W. H. Hartley, esq.   re-elected
John Elwes, esq.   re-elected

Berwick, Northumberland. Hen. VIII.

Hon. John Vaughan   re-elected.
J. Wilkinson, esq.   Sir J. Huss. Delaval, bart.

Stated in the report to be in the freemen of Berwick. 9 March, 1695.—500.

Beverley, Yorkshire. 23 Edw. I. 5 Eliz.

Sir J. Pennyman, bart.   re-elected
G. F. Tufnel, Esq.   Evelyn Anderson, Esq.

In the burgage-holders—1000.

Bewdley, Worcestershire. James I.

Lord Westcote   re-elected

In the bailiff and twelve capital burgesses, who elect other burgesses to vote with them.—In the bailiff and burgesses, appointed by the charter 3° Jac. Primi, exclusive to all others. 28 April, 1662.—Not in all the inhabitants of the said borough. 27 May, 1679.

Bishop's-Castle, Shropshire. 17 Eliz.

Henry Strachey, esq. vacated   Henry Strachey, esq.
  in 1778
Alex. Wedderburne, esq. created a peer in 1780
Wm. Clive, esq.   re-elected

Agreed to be in the bailiff and all the burgesses within the borough. 3 Feb. 1699.—100.

Blechingley, Surry. 23 Edw. I.

Sir Robert Clayton, bart.   re-elected
Frederick Standart, esq.   John Kenrick, esq.

Resolved to be in the borough-holders, and that the bailiff had nothing to do with the election. 22 March, 1723.—90.

Bodmyn, Cornwall. 23 Edw. I.

Geo. Hunt, esq.   re-elected
Sir James Laroche, bart.   William Masterman, esq.
                                   Sir James Laroche

In the mayor, aldermen, and common council.—36.

Boroughbridge, Yorkshire. 1 Mary.

Anthony Eyre, esq.   re-elected
William Philips, esq.   Charles Ambler, esq.

In the burgage-holders.—65.

Bossiney, Cornwall. 7 Edw. VI.
Lord Mount Stuart, called to
 the House of Peers in 1776
Hon. *Charles Stuart* re-elected
Hon. H. L. Luttrell re-elected
 In the freemen in the borough.—20.
Boston, Lincolnshire. Edw. VI.
Lord Robert Bertie re-elected
Charles Amcotts, esq. died in
 1777
Humphrey Sibthorpe, esq. re-elected
 Sir Christopher Whichcot
 In the commonalty, and not in the mayor, aldermen, and common council. 8 May, 1628.——Only in the mayor, aldermen, common council, and freemen of the said borough, resident within the said borough, and paying scot and lot. 20 March, 1711.——Only in the mayor, aldermen, common council, and freemen of the said borough, resident in the said borough, paying scot and lot, and claiming their freedom by birth or servitude. 2 March, 1719.—200.
Brackley, Northamptonshire. 1 Edw. VI.
Wm. Egerton, esq. John. Wm. Egerton, esq.
Timothy Caswall, esq. re-elected
 In the mayor, aldermen, and burgesses of the said borough. 20 April, 1714.——33.
Bramber, Sussex. 23 Edw. I.
Thomas Thornton, esq. re-elected
Sir Henry Gough, bart. re-elected
 Agreed to be in the persons inhabiting ancient houses, or in houses built on ancient foundations, paying scot and lot. 18 Jan. 10 Mar. 1703. 1 June, 1715.——20.
Brecon County.
Charles Morgan, esq. re-elected
 Brecon Town.
Charles Van, esq. died 1778
Charles Gould, esq. re-elected
 In the corporation and free burgesses.
Bridgenorth, Shropshire. 23 Edw. I.
Lord Pigot died in 1777;
 and in 1778
Admiral Pigot was elected re-elected
Thomas Whitmore, esq. re-elected
 In the corporation and freemen.——700.

Bridge-

Bridgewater, Somersetshire. 23 Edw. I.
Hon. Anne Poulett   re-elected
Benj. Allen, esq.   re-elected
                           John Acland, esq.
Stated to be in the majority of the corporation, consisting of a mayor, aldermen, and capital burgesses, in number 24. 7 Dec. 1669.———Agreed to be in those that pay scot and lot, inhabiting in the said borough. 10 Dec. 1692. 9 March, 1769.—If the mayor, aldermen, and capital burgesses, are not inhabitants, though they pay scot and lot, yet they have no right to vote. 9 Mar. 1769.—The inhabitants of the eastern and western divisions of the parish of Bridgewater have no right to vote for representatives, but the right of election is in the inhabitants of that division of the said parish which is commonly called the Borough, paying scot and lot within the said division, and in them only. 14 March, 1769.———300.

Bridport, Dorset. 23 Edw. I.
Thomas Coventry, esq.   Thomas Scott, esq.
Hon. L. Ferd. Cary   Richard Beckford, esq.
In the commonalty in general. 12 April, 1628.
Agreed to be in all the inhabitants not receiving alms. 5 May, 1715.———400.

Bristol City. 47 Edw. III.
Hen. Cruger, esq.   Sir H. Lippincott, bart. 2518
Edm. Burke, esq.   Matt. Brickdale, esq.   2771
                           H. Cruger, esq.   1271
                           S. Peach, esq.   788
                           Edmund Burke, esq. declined
                           Sir H. Lippincott died 1781.
In the freemen———5000.

Buckinghamshire.
Rt. Hon. R. Earl Verney   re-elected
Geo. Grenville, esq. succeeded
  Earl Temple in 1779
Hon. Thomas Grenville   re-elected

Buckingham Town. 33 Hen. VIII.
James Grenville, jun. esq. re-elected
Rich. Grenville, esq.   Rich. Ald. Neville, esq.
In the bailiff and twelve burgesses only. 11 Nov. 1690.
———13.

Cal-

Callington, Cornwall. 27 Eliz.
William Skrine, efq. John Morſhead, efq.
John Dyke Acland, efq. died
  in 1778
George Stratton, efq.   re-elected
  In the inhabitants 3 years houſekeepers.——100.

Calne, Wilts. 23 Edw. I.
Rt. Hon. Iſaac Barré   re-elected
John Dunning, efq.   re-elected
  In the inhabitants of the ſaid borough, having a right of common, and being ſworn at Ogborn-court. 22 Dec. 1720. —In the ancient burgeſſes of the ſaid borough only, and the right of returning burgeſſes is in the guild-ſtewards. 25 Feb. 1723.——34.

Cambridgeſhire.
Sir Samp. Gideon, bart.   Rt. Hon. Lord R. Manners
Sir J. Hynde Cotton, bart.   1741
                       Philip Yorke, efq.   1452
                       Sir Samp. Gideon, bart. 1058
  All members of colleges, halls, or corporations, having no freeholds, ſaving in right thereof; and parſons and vicars, having no other freeholds but glebe-lands, are excluded from voting. 28 May, 1724.

Cambridge Town. Edw. I.
Hon. C. Slo. Cadogan
  called to the Houſe of Peers
Benj. Keene, efq.   re-elected   96
Soame Jenyns, efq.   J. Warwood Adeane   83
                     Chris. Potter   18
  In the mayor, bailiffs, and freemen, not receiving alms. 24 Feb. 1709.——200.

Cambridge Univerſity. 1 James I.
                 James Mansfield, efq.   277
Richard Croftes, efq.   Hon. J. Townſhend,   237
The Marquis of Granby ſuc-   Lord Hyde   206
  ceeded Duke of Rutland, 1779   *R. Croftes, efq.*   150
James Mansfield, efq.   *Hon. W. Pitt*   141
  In the doctors and maſters of arts.——340.

Camel-

Camelford, Cornwall. Edw. VI.
John Amyand, esq.   James Macpherson, esq.
Francis Herne, esq. died 1776
Sir Ralph Payne   John Pardoe, jun. esq.
 Stated to be in the freemen and inhabitants paying scot and lot. 3 Aug. 1660.———19.

Canterbury City. 23 Edw. I.
Lord Newhaven	George Gipps, esq.	634
Richard Milles, esq.	Charles Robinson, esq.	617
	Lord Newhaven	460
	Sir W. H. Dashwood	150
	M. Lade	28

 In the citizens and freemen.———1000.

Cardiff.
Sir H. Mackworth, bart.   re-elected
 In the burgesses of Cardiff, Aberavon, Cowbridge, Kenfigg, Llantrissent, Lougher, Neth, and Swansey. 1000.

Cardiganshire.
Lord Lisburne   re-elected

Cardigan.
Sir Rob. Smyth, decided on.
petition in favour of
Tho. Johnes, esq.   John Campbell, esq.
 In the burgesses at large of the boroughs of Cardigan, Aberystwith, Lampeter, and Atpar only. It was resolved the burgesses of Tregaron have not a right to vote. 7 May, 1730.———1200.

Carlisle. '3 Charles I.
Flet. Norton, esq. vacated in 1775
Walter Stanhope, esq.   Earl of Surrey
Ant. Storer, esq.   William Lowther, esq.
 Agreed to be in the mayor, aldermen, bailiffs, and freemen, resident or not resident. Also, that the sons of burgesses, born after their fathers freedom, and persons serving seven years within the city, had a right to be made free. 23 Feb. 1711.———500.

Carmarthenshire.
John Vaughan, esq.   re-elected.

Car-

Carmarthen.

John Adams, efq.　　　George Phillips, efq.
In the burgeffes of the faid borough. 19 March, 1727.

Cárnarvonſhire.
T. Aſh. Smith, efq.　　　John Parry, efq.

Carnarvon.
Glynn Wynn, efq.　　　re-elected
In the burgeffes of arvon, Criccieth, Pullely, Nevis and Conway.

Caſtle Riſing, Norf.lk.　Ult. Phil. & Mary.
A. Wedderburne, efq. made his election for Oakhampton
Hon. Charles Finch
Rob. Mackreth, efq.　　　re-elected
Mr. Finch, vacated in 1777 to ſtand for Maidſtone
J. Chetwynd Talbot, efq.　　re-elected
In the free burgeffes.——50.

Cheſhire.
John Crewe, efq.　　　re-elected
Samuel Egerton, died in 1780
Sir R. Saliſbury Cotton, bart.　re-elected

Cheſter City.　34 Hen. VIII.
Hon. Tho. Grofvenor　　re-elected
Rd. Wilbraham Bootle　re-elected
Stated to lie in the freemen. 2 Dec. 1690.——1000.

Chicheſter, Suſſex.　23 Edw. I.
Hon. William Keppel　　re-elected
Rt. Hon. Tho. Conolly　Thomas Steele, efq
In the inhabitants paying ſcot and lot. 500.

Chippenham, Wilts.　23 Edw. I.
Sir Ed. Bayntun, bart.　　Henry Dawkins, efq.
Sam. Marſh, efq.　　　Giles Hudfon, efq.
In the burgeffes and freemen, more than twelve. And it was refolved, that the new charter altered not the cuftom. 2 April, 1724. 9 ibid.——150.

(Chriſ-

Christchurch, Hants. 13 Eliz.

Hon. Th. Villiers Hyde
James Harris, esq.

Sir James Harris, K. B.
re-elected, died in 1789
John Frederick, esq.

In the inhabitants paying scot and lot.——70.

Cirencester, Gloucestershire. 13 Eliz.

James Whitshed, esq. re-elected
S. Blackwell, esq. re-elected

In all the inhabitants, householders.---700.——N. B. It was resolved, in this case, that, where there is no custom or charter for the election, there the inhabitants (householders) ought to elect. 21 May, 1724.——The inmates were excluded. 4 Nov. 1690.——As also were the inhabitants of the Abbey, the Emery, and the Spiringate-lane. 8 Dec. 1709.

Clitheroe, Lancashire. 1 Eliz.

Hon. Asheton Curzon	John Parker, esq.	31
Tho. Lister, esq.	re-elected	33
	Hon. Ash Curzon	17

In such freeholders only as have estates for life, or in fee. 4 Feb. 1661.——90.

Cockermouth, Cumberland. 23 Edw. I.

Geo. Johnstone, esq. made his election for Appleby
Flet. Norton, esq. made his election for Carlisle

James Adair, esq. W. Lowther, esq.
Ralph Gowland, esq. J. Baynes Garforth, esq.

Burgage tenure.——200.

Colchester, Essex. 23 Edw. I.

Charles Gray, esq.	Sir Rob. Smyth, bar	301
If. Martin Rebow, esq.	re-elected	564
	Alex. Fordyce	121
	Robert Mayne	13

Agreed to be in the mayor, aldermen, common council, and free burgesses, not receiving alms. 6 May, 1714.---1400.

N. B. The right of making foreigners (not having a right of freedom) freemen, is in the mayor and free burgesses in common council assembled.

Corff-Castle, Dorsetshire. 14 Eliz.

John Bond, esq. re-elected
John Jenkinson, esq Henry Bankes, esq.

(As in the report) appeared to be in leſſees for years, paying ſcot and lot; and alſo in ſuch perſons as had the freehold in reverſion, upon ſuch leaſe for years. 6 April, 1699.——— Agreed to be in ſuch as have an eſtate of inheritance, or a leaſe for years, determinable upon life or lives, paying ſcot and lot. 2 March, 1699. Agreed to be in ſuch perſons as are ſeized in fee, in poſſeſſion or reverſion, of any meſſuage, tenement, or corporeal hereditament, within this borough; and in ſuch perſons as are tenants for life or lives; and, for want of ſuch freehold, in tenants for years, determinable on any life or lives, paying ſcot and lot, and in no others. 21 Jan. 1718.———140.

Cornwall.

Sir W. Lemon, bart.　　　　re-elected
Sir J. Moleſworth, bart. died
　in 1775.
Edward Eliot, eſq.　　　　re-elected

Coventry, Warwickſhire. 23 Edw. I.

Edw. Roe Yeo, eſq.	1571	Void election in Sept.	1780
Walter Waring, eſq.	1111	Election in Dec. 1780	
Tho. Green, eſq.	827	Edward Roe Yeo, eſq.	1298
Mr. Waring died in 1780,		Lord Sheffield	1295
and J. B. Holroyd was		Sir Tho. Halifax, kt.	1178
elected.		Tho. Rogers, eſq.	1177

In ſuch perſons who have ſerved ſeven years apprenticeſhip within the ſaid city to one and the ſame trade, not receiving alms. 1 May, 1708.——But perſons receiving the ſacrament or bread money, Sir Thomas White's, or Sir Thomas Wheatley's gifts, were not then diſqualified.——Members of the fullers company, being freemen, not receiving alms or weekly charity, and freemen, who have ſerved ſeven years apprenticeſhip in the city or ſuburbs, not receiving alms or weekly charity, have a right to vote. 13 March, 1711.
——In ſuch freemen as have ſerved ſeven years apprenticeſhip to one and the ſame trade, in the city or ſuburbs, and do not receive alms or weekly charity, ſuch freemen being duly ſworn and enrolled. 20 Nov. 1722.—1400.

Cricklade, Wilts. 23 Edw. I.
Arn. Nefbit, efq. died 1779
Wm. Earle, efq. died 1774
John Dewar, efq.   Paul Benfield, efq.
John Macpherfon, efq.   re-elected.
                         Samuel Petre, efq.
   Agreed to be in the freeholders, copyholders, and leafeholders for three years.—10 June, 1685.—Agreed to be in freeholders and copyholders of the borough houfes, and leafeholders for any term not under three years, only. 1 Apr. 1684.——The committee reported, that it was agreed to be in the freeholders, copyholders, and leafeholders for not lefs than three years. 20 Feb. 1695.——150.
                      Cumberland.
Sir J. Lowther, bart.   re-elected
Henry Fletcher, efq.   re-elected
            Dartmouth, Devon. 26 Edw. I.
Lord Vifc. Howe   re-elected
Richard Hopkins, efq.   Arthur Holdfworth, efq.
   In the freemen of the borough. 28 Nov. 1689.——98.
                     Denbighfhire.
Sir W. W. Wynne, bart.   re-elected
                    Denbigh Town.
Rich. Myddleton, efq.   re-elected
   In the burgeffes of Denbigh Leon, alias Holt and Ruthyn.——500.
                      Derbyfhire.
Lord Geo. Cavendifh   Lord Rich. Cavendifh
Geo. Clarke, efq. died 1774
Hon. Nath. Curzon   re-elected
             Derby Town. 23 Edw. I.
Lord Fred. Cavendifh   Lord G. A. H. Cavendifh 87
Wenman Coke, efq. made his
election for Norfolk
Dan. Parker Coke, efq.   Edward Coke, efq.   80
                              Dan. Parker Coke, efq. 7
   In the corporation, freemen, and fworn-burgeffes.—700.
               Devizes, Wilts. 23 Edw. I.
Charles Garth, efq.   re-elected, died in 1780
James Sutton, efq.   Henry Jones, efq.
                         Sir J. T. Long, bart.
   In the mayor and felect number of burgeffes only. 21 March, 1688.

Devonshire.
Sir R. W. Bampfylde, bart.
  died in 1776
J. R. *Walter, esq.* died 1779
John Rolle, esq.   re-elected
John Parker, esq.   re-elected.

Dorsetshire.
George Pitt, esq.   re-elected
Humphry Sturt, esq.   re-elected

Dorchester, Dorset.   23 Edw. I.
John Damer, esq.   Hon. George Damer
Wm. Ewer, esq.   re-elected

  In the inhabitants paying to church and poor, in respect of their personal estates; and in such persons as pay to church and poor, in respect of their real estates within the said borough. 17 and 18 May, 1720.——400.

  N. B. Part of the parish of Holy Trinity, (formerly Froome-Whitfield parish) and the tithing of Collitonrow, were voted to be no parts of the said borough.

Dover, Kent.   42 Edw. III.
John Henniker, esq.   re-elected
John Trevanian, esq.   re-elected

  In the freemen and free burgesses, inhabitants of Dover. 24 March, 1623.——The non-inhabitant freemen, as well as the inhabitant freemen, and free burgesses, have voice in the election of barons to serve in parliament. 12 March, 1770.——700.

Downton, Wilts.   23 Edw. I.
Tho. Duncombe, esq. died
  in 1779
T. Dummer, esq. died 1779
Sir Philip Hales   - Hon. Hen. Sem. Conway 23
Hon. B. Bouverie, died 1779
Robert Shafto, esq.   re-elected   24
                      Alexander Hume   8
                      J. Saunders   7

  In the inhabitants paying scot and lot.——60.

Droitwich, Worcestershire. 23 Edw. I.

Tho. Foley, esq. succeded his
father as Lord Foley, Dec.
1777   re-elected
Edward Winnington, esq.   re-elected
    In the burgesses of the corporation of Salt-springs, of Droitwich. 11 Nov. 1690.——40.

Dunwich, Suffolk. 23 Edw. I.

Sir G. W. Van Neck, bart   re-elected
Miles Barne, esq. vacated in
    Dec. 1777,
Barne Barne, esq.   re-elected
    Is not in the freemen of the said borough, commonly called outsitters, as well as in the freemen inhabiting within the said borough; but only in the freemen inhabiting within the said borough. 8 Dec. 1691.—— Is in the freemen of the said borough, commonly called outsitters, as well as in the freemen inhabiting in the said borough. 25 Nov. 1695. ...Was resolved to be only in the freemen inhabiting within the said borough, not receiving alms. 5 Feb. 1708.—•-40.

Durham County.

Sir John Eden, bart.   re-elected
Sir T. Clavering, bart.   re-elected

Durham City.   30 Char. II.
John Lampton, esq.   re-elected
John Tempest, esq.   re-elected
    In the corporation and freemen.——1200.

Eastloee, Cornwall. 13. Eliz.

John Buller, esq.   re-elected
Sir Cha. Whitworth vaca-
    ted in 1774
Tho. Graves, esq. vacated in
    1775
Will. Graves, esq.   re-elected
    In the mayor, burgesses, aldermen, and freemen.—49.

St.

St. Edmondsbury, Suffolk.
Sir Cha. Davers, bart. re-elected
Rt. Hon. A. J. Hervey, called to the House of Peers 1775
Gen. Conway re-elected
                     Lord Hervey
In 1 alderman, 12 burgesses, and 24 common council.
Essex County.
John Conyers, esq. died 1775
John Luther, esq. re-elected
Will. Harvey, esq. died 1779
T. B. Bramston, esq. re-elected
     Evesham, Worcestershire. 23 Edw. VI.
Sir John Rushout, bart. re-elected   435
H. Seymour, esq. W. Boughton Rouse   379
                 Charles Rudge   357
In the common burgesses. 22 Sept. 1669.——600.
     Exeter, Devon. 23 Edw. VI.
J. R. Walter, esq. vacated in 1776
John Baring, esq. re-elected
Sir C. W. Bampfielde, bart. re-elected
In the freeholders and freemen.——1500.
     Eye, Suffolk. 13 Eliz.
R. Phillipson, esq. re-elected
Hon. Jn. St. John   Arn. James Skelton, esq.
In the inhabitants paying scot and lot.——200.
     Flintshire.
Sir Roger Mostyn, bart. re-elected
     Flint Town.
Sir John Glynne, bart. died in 1777
Watkin Williams, esq. re-elected

In the inhabitants of the boroughs of Flint, Rhydlan, Overton, Caerwys, and Caergurley, paying scot and lot; and it was resolved that the inhabitants of Knolton, and Overton Foreign, have a right to vote in the election of a burgess for parliament for the said town of Flint. 21 May, 1728.
——The inhabitants of the several boroughs of Flint, Rhydlan, Caerwys, Caergurley, and Overton (including Knolton and Overton Foreign) renting lands or tenements for which the landlords thereof only pay scot and lot, have a

right to vote in the election of a burgefs for the borough of Flint. 5 April, 1737.——The fame have not a right. 19 March, 1741.——1.

     Fowey, Cornwall. 13 Eliz.
Philip Rafhleigh, efq.   re-elected
Lord Shuldham   re-elected
 In the prince's tenants, who are capable of being portreeves, and fuch of the inhabitants only as pay fcot and lot. 5 May, 1701.——Prince's tenants, capable of being portreeves of Fowey, are fuch tenants only as have been duly admitted upon the court-rolls of the manor, and have done their fealty. 5 March, 1770.——63.

     Gatton, Surrey. 29 Hen. VI.
Sir Wm. Mayne, made his
 election for Canterbury
Robert Scott, efq. made his
 election for Wooton-Baffet
Robert Mayne, efq.   re-elected
William Adam, efq.   Lord Newhaven
 In the inhabitants, the return made by them being adjudged good, was (by the then petitioner) infifted to be in the inhabitants not receiving alms, and in the freeholders having fuch freehold in their own occupation. 26 March, 1628. ——Was (by the then fitting member) infifted to be in the freeholders, and inhabitants paying fcot and lot ; and he was adjudged duly elected. 15 Dec. 1696.

     St. Germain's, Cornwall. 5 Eliz.
Ben. Langlois, efq.
Edward Eliot, efq. vacated
 in 1775
John Pownall, efq. vacated in Edward James Eliot, efq.
 1776
John Peachy, efq.   Dudley Long, efq.
 In the freemen.——50.

     Glamorganfhire.
Hon. G. V. Vernon   Charles Edwin, efq.

            Gloucef-

Gloucestershire.
Sir Wm. Guise, bart.   re-elected
Edward Southwell, esq. cal-
led to the House of Peers
in 1776
W. B. Chester, esq.   re-elected, died in 1780
                               James Dutton, esq.
        Gloucester.   23 Edw. I.
Charles Barrow, esq.   re-elected
G. Aug. Selwyn, esq.   John Webb, esq.
  In the freemen.—2000.
        Grampound.   7 Edw. VI.
Sir Jos. York, K. B.   Sir John Ramsden, bart.
R. A. Neville, esq.   Thomas Lucas, es.
  In the mayor, recorder, and inhabitants, paying scot and lot.—59.
        Grantham, Lincolnshire.   Edw. IV.
Lord George Sutton   George Sutton, esq.
Sir Bro. Cust, created Lord
  Brownlow, 1776
Peregrine Cust, esq.   Francis Cockayne Cust, esq.
  In the freemen of the said borough, not receiving alms or charity. 11 Jan. 1710——400.
        Great Grimsby, Lincolnshire.
Joseph Mellish, esq.   John Harrison, esq.
Evelyn Anderson, esq.   Francis Eyre, esq.
        East Grinstead, Sussex.   1 Edw. II.
Lord G. S. Germain   re-elected
Sir John Irwin, K. B.   re-elected
  Is in the inhabitants as well as burgage-holders, and the borough is an ancient borough by prescription. 7 April, 1679.——Is in the burgage-holders only, and not in the burgage-holders and inhabitants. 9 Feb. 1695.——36.
        Guildford, Surrey.   23 Edw. I.
Sir Fletcher Norton   re-elected
George Onslow   re-elected
  Is only in the freemen and freeholders, paying scot and lot, resident in the town. 24 April, 1689.——It was agreed, that one who had served seven years to a freeman, was *ipso facto* a freeman. 3 Feb. 1710.

Hamp-

Hampshire.

Sir H. P. St. John, knt. Rob. Thiftlethwaite, efq.
Sir Simon Stuart, bart. died
  in 1779
Jervoife Clarke Jervoife, efq. re-elected

Harwich, Essex. 17 Edw. III. 12 Ja. I.

John Robinfon, efq. re-elected
Edw. Harvey, efq. died 1778
Hon. G. A. North re-elected

In the mayor, aldermen, and capital burgeffes, or head-boroughs, refident within the faid borough. 6 April, 1714. —31.

Haflemere, Surrey. 27 Eliz.

T. M. Molyneux, efq. died
  1776
Peter Burrell, efq. Sir James Lowther, bart.
Sir Merrick Burrell, bart. Edward Norton, efq.

In the freeholders refident within the borough. 20 May, 1661, 9 Feb. 1698.——60.——By the word *free-holders* is meant only freeholders of meffuages, lands, or tenements, lying within the borough and manor of Haflemere, whether the fame pay rent to the lord of the faid borough and manor or not, exclufive of any lands or tenements which, are, or have been, parcel of the wafte ground of the faid borough and manor, or any meffuages or buildings which are, or fhall be, ftanding thereon. 25 April, 1755. Petition of Mr. Oglethorpe rejected, for not being figned by himfelf. 3 and 4 March, 1713.——The like relating to Wigan.

Haftings, Suffex. 42 Edw. III.

Lord Palmerfton re-elected
Rt. Hon. C. Jenkinfon John Ord, efq.

Is in the mayor, jurats, and freemen refident, and not receiving alms. 30 Jan. 1698.——200.

Haverfordweft, Pembrokefhire.

Lord Kenfington re-elected

Agreed to be in the freeholders, burgeffes, and inhabitants paying fcot and lot, and not receiving alms. 4 July, 1715. ——500.

Helfton,

Helston, Cornwall. 23 Edw. I.
Lord Caermarthen a Peer   Philip Yorke, esq.
Fr. Owen, died   Joc. Dean, esq. dead
Fr. *Cockayne Cust, esq.*   Lord Hyde
Philip Yorke, esq.   Wm. Evelyn, esq.
                     A double retura.
In the mayor and inhabitants at large. 10 Dec. 1660.—
70.—To which the house disagreed.

Herefordshire.
Thomas Foley, esq. created a
  Peer 1776
Sir George Cornewall, bart. re-elected
Rt. Hon. Thomas Harley   re-elected

Hereford City. 23 Edw. I.
John Scudamore, esq.   re-elected
Sir Rich. Symonds, bart. re-elected
In the citizens and freemen.——:200.

Hertfordshire.
Wm. Plumer, esq.   re-elected
Tho. Halfey, esq.   re-elected
On hearing the merits of a former election, it was resolved, that evidence ought not to be admitted to disqualify an elector as no freeholder, who at the election swore himself to be a freeholder. 16 Jan. 1695 ——Resolution to the contrary, concerning Bedford county. 28 June, 1715.

Hertford Town. 35 Edw. I. 21 Ja. I.
John Calvert, esq.   Thomas Dimsdale   286
Pauld Fielde, esq.   William Baker, esq.   256
                  J. Calvert   241
Is not in such persons only, as are inhabitants (householders) of the said borough, not receiving alms, and in such freemen, who, at the time of their freedom granted to them, were inhabitants of the said borough, or of the parishes thereof; but in all the freemen and inhabitants being householders, not receiving alms. 27 Jan. 1701.—Is in the inhabitants not receiving alms, and in such freemen only as at the time of their being made free were inhabitants of the said borough, or the parishes thereof. The number of freemen living out of the borough not exceeding three persons. 5 Dec. 1705.—700.

                                      Heyden,

Heyden, Yorkshire. 23 Edw. I. 1 Edw. VI.
Beilby Thomson, efq.   Chriftopher Atkinfon   118
Rt. Hon. Sir C. Saunders, di- William Chayter   92
ed in 1775
Hon. L. T. Watfon   B. Thompfon   28
Is in the burgeffes. 3 April, 1746.——150.
Heytefbury, Wilts. 27 Hen. VI.
Wm. A. Afhe, efq.   re-elected
Hon. Wm. Gordon   William Eden, efq. made his
                                 election for Woodftock
                               Francis Burton, efq.
Is in the burgage-holders.——50.
Higham Ferrers, Northamptonfhire. 2, 3, Ph, & M.
Fred. Montagu, efq.   re-elected
  In the mayor, aldermen, burgeffes, and freemen, being houfholders, and not receiving alms. 28 Jan. 1702.——100.
Hindon, Wilts. 27 Hen. VI.
Henry Dawkins efq.   Lloyd Kenyon, efq.   187
Arch. Macdonald, efq.   Nat. Wm. Wraxall, efq. 173
                               J. Saunders   23
                               S. Peach   16
  Is in the inhabitants of houfes within the faid borough, being houfekeepers and parifhioners, not receiving alms. 12 April, 1728.
Honiton, Devon. 28 Edw. I. 4 Edw. II. 16 Ch. I.
Sir Geo. Yonge, bart.   re-elected   393
Lawrence Cox, efq.   Alex. Macleod, efq.   259
                               Lawrence Cox   221
  Is in the inhabitants of the faid borough, paying fcot and lot. 3 Feb. 1710.——Is in the inhabitants, houfekeepers, commonly called potwallers, not receiving alms. 18 Dec. 1724.——450.
Horfham, Suffex. 23 Edw. I.
James Wallace, efq.   re-elected
Rt. Hon. Jere. Dyfon, died
  in 1776
Earl of Drogheda   Vifcount Lewifham, made his
                                 election for Staffordfhire
                               Sir Geo. Ofborne
  Is in all fuch perfons as have an eftate of inheritance, or for life, in burgage houfes, or burgage lands, lying within the faid borough. 16 June, 1715.——60.

Hunting-

Huntingdonshire.

L. Visc. Hinchinbroke	re-elected
Earl of Ludlow	re-elected

Huntingdon. 23 Edw. I.

Sir Geo. Wombwell, bart.	re-elected, died in 1780
Hon. Mr. W. A. Montagu	Sir Hugh Pallifer
died in 1775	
Lord Mulgrave	re-elected

In the freemen and inhabitants.——200.

Hythe, Kent. 42 Edw. III.

Sir Cha. Farnaby, bart.	re-elected	62
Wm. Evelyn, esq.	re-elected	61
	John Stevenson, esq.	44
	Rich. James, esq.	42

Is in the mayor, jurats, common-council, and freemen. 27 Jan. 1710.——50.

Ivelchester, Somersetshire. 23 Edw. I.

Nathaniel Webb, esq.	Peregrine Cust, esq.
O. Salusb. Brereton, esq.	Sam. Smith, jun. esq.

Alledged to be in the inhabitants of the said town, paying scot and lot, which the town called potwallers. 7 May, 1689.—Agreed to be in the bailiff, capital burgesses, and inhabitants not receiving alms. 28 Jan. 1702.——100.

Ipswich, Suffolk. 23 Edw. I.

Wm. Wollaston, esq.	Wm. Wollaston, esq.	347
Tho. Staunton, esq.	Tho. Staunton, esq.	341
	Jos. Grigby	253
	W. Middleton	247

Is in the bailiff, portmen, commonalty, and freemen, not receiving alms. 3 Feb. 1710.—600.—A resolution passed, that portmen are an essential constituent part of the great court for making freemen of the said borough, without some of which portmen being present, the said court cannot be held. 31 March, 1714.

St. Ives, Cornwall. 5 Mary I.

Adam Drummond, esq. died	
in 1779	
Philip Dehan, esq.	Abel Smith
Lord Newborough	William Praed, esq.

Is in the inhabitants, paying scot and lot. 8 Dec. 1702. ——183.

Kent.

Kent.

Hon. Cha. Marſham   re-elected
Tho. Knight, jun. eſq.   Filmer Honywood, eſq.

King's Lynn, Norfolk. 23 Edw. I.

Hon. Tho. Walpole   re-elected
Criſp. Molyneux, eſq.   re-elected
In the inhabitants paying ſcot and lot.——600.

Kingſton-upon-Hull, Yorkſhire. 23. Edw. III.

Rt. Hon. Lord R. Manners   re-elected   673
D. Hartley, eſq.   Wm. Wilberforce, eſq. 1126
    David Hartly, eſq.   456
In the burgeſſes and freemen.——1090.

Knareſborough. Yorkſhire.

Sir Ant. Tho. Abdy, bart.
   died in 1775
Lord G. H. *Cavendiſh*   Viſc. Duncannon
Hon. Rob. Boyle Walſing-
   ham   re-elected
Agreed to be in the burgage-holders. 17 May, 1690
1691.——50.

Lancaſhire.

Lord Stanley; became Earl
   of Derby in 1776
T. Stanley   re-elected
Sir Tho. Egerton, bart.   re-elected

Lancaſter. 23 Edw. I. Edw. VI.

Sir Geo. Warren, K. B.   Wilſon Braddyll, eſq.
Lord Rich. Cavendiſh   Abraham Rawlinſon, eſq.
In the freemen and inhabitants.——1000.

Launceſton, Cornwall. 23 Edw. I.

Rt. Hon. Hum. Morice   Lord Cranburn, ſucceeded his
    father as Earl of Saliſbury
John Buller, eſq.   in 1780
    Hon. C. G. Perceval
    Tho. Bowlby, eſq.
In the mayor, aldermen, and freemen, being inhabitants at the time they were made free, and not receiving pay of the pariſh. 17 March, 1723.——The aldermen to be elected out of the legal freemen. 24 March, 1734.

Leiceſterſhire.

Hon. T. Noel, a Peer, 1774
J. P. Hungerford, eſq.   re-elected
Sir John Palmer, bart.   Wm. Pochin, eſq.

Leicester Town.
Hon. Booth Grey   re-elected
John Darker, esq.   re-elected

Agreed to be in the freemen, not receiving alms, and in the inhabitants paying scot and lot. But persons living in the borough by certificate, not having gained a settlement, by renting 10l. per annum, or serving in an annual office, are not entitled (by paying scot and lot) to vote. 8 Feb. 1705.——1100.

Leominster, Herefordshire. 23 Edw. I.
Lord Visc. Bateman   re elected   357
T. Hill, esq. died 1776
F. Cornwall, jun. esq.   R. P. Knight, esq.   345
                    Thomas Mitton   44

Granted to be in the bailiffs, capital burgesses, and inhabitants paying scot and lot. 16 April, 1725.——400.

Leskard, Cornwall. 23 Edw. I.
Edward Gibbon, esq.   Hon. A. Tollemache
Samuel Salt, esq.   re-elected

In the corporation, and sworn free-burgesses.——1000.

Lestwithiel, Cornwall. 33 Edw. I. 4 Edw. II.
Charles Brett, esq. vacat. 1776
Thomas Potter, esq.   Tho. De Grey, jun. esq.
Lord Fairford   Hon. John St. John, made
                   his election for Newport
                   George Johnstone, esq.

Is in the mayor, and six capital burgesses, together with the seventeen assistants annually chosen, and who had a right to vote at the preceding election of a mayor. 20 Dec. 1709.

Lewes, Sussex. 23 Edw. I.
Sir Thomas Miller, bart.   Hon. Henry Pelham, esq. 95
Thomas Hay, esq.   Thomas Kempe, esq.   91
                   Thomas Hay, esq.   76

In the inhabitants, being housholders, paying scot and lot. 8 May, 1735.——400.

Lime Regis, Dorset. 23 Edw. I.
Henry Fane, esq. died 1777   Henry Harford, esq.
Hon. Henry Fane   Lionel Darell, jun. esq.
Francis Fane, esq.   Hon. Henry Fane
                   D. R. Michel, esq.
                   A double return.

Insisted to be in the mayor, burgesses and freeholders. 21 May, 1689.——Alledged to be in the mayor, capital burgesses and freemen. 28 Feb. 1727——50.

Lincolnshire.

Lord Brownlow Bertie, succeeded Duke of Ancaster
Ch. And. Pelham, efq.   re-elected
Sir John Thorold, bart.   re elected

Lincoln City. 49 Hen. III.
Lord Visc. Lumley   Sir Tho. Clarges, bart. 626
R. Vyner, jun. efq.   re-elected   616
                         Lord Lumley   339
                         T. Scroope, efq.   4

In the citizens and freemen.—1100.

Litchfield, Staffordshire. 33 Edw. I.
Geo. Anson, efq.   re-elected
Thomas Gilbert, efq.   re-elected

Is in the bailiff, magistrates, freeholders of 40s. a year, and all that hold by burgage-tenure; and such freemen as are inrolled and pay scot and lot; and also such freemen only of the taylor's company as are inrolled in the new book of constitutions (and not the old book) have a right to vote. 1. May, 1701.——Resolved to be in the bailiffs, magistrates, freeholders of 40s. per annum, and all that hold by burgage tenure; and in such freemen only as are inrolled, paying scot and lot there. 10 Dec. 1718.——600.

Liverpool, Lancashire. 23 Edw. I.
Sir Wm. Meredith, bart. Henry Rawlinson, efq.   572
Rd. Pennant, efq.   Bamb. Gascoyne, jun. efq. 608
                         Richard Pennant, efq.   462

Admitted to be in the mayor, bailiffs, and freemen not receiving alms. 5 March, 1729.——1200.

London. 49 Hen. III.
John Sawbridge, efq.   J. Kirkman, efq. died before the return

Frederick Bull, efq.   re-elected
Richard Oliver, efq.   Nath. Newnham, efq.
George Hayley, efq.   re-elected
                         George Hayley   4062
                         J. Kirkman, died before the return 3804
                         Fred. Bull   3150
                         Nath. Newnham   3036
                         J. Sawbridge   2957
                         Rich. Clarke   1771
                         J. Sawbridge, efq. elected in Nov. 1780, vice J. Kirkman

In the livery. Act of 1725.—7000.

Ludlow, Shropshire. 12 Edw. IV.
Lord Clive   re-elected
Lord Viscount Villiers   Fred. Cornwall, esq.

Is in the resiant common burgesses, as well as the twelve and twenty five. 26 Feb. 1661.———500.———It was resolved, that the sons of burgesses of Ludlow, and those that marry the daughters of burgesses, have a right to be made burgesses; and that every person, having a right to be made a burgess, ought to demand the same by petition, signed by the petitioner, according to the bye-law in 1663, and not otherwise.—1 March, 1698.

Luggershall, Wiltshire. 23 Edw. I.
Lord Melburne   re-elected
Lord George Gordon   Geo. Aug. Selwyn, esq.

Is in the freeholders or leaseholders of the said borough, determinable upon life or lives. 17 Jan. 1705.—70.

Lymington, Hants. 27 Eliz.
Henry Goodrick, esq.   Harry Burrard, esq.
Edward Morant, esq.   Thomas Dummer, esq.

Resolved to be a corporation by prescription, and that the mayor and burgesses only have a right to elect members for parliament. 29 Dec. 1691.———Is not in the mayor, burgesses, and commonalty, paying scot and lot, but only in the mayor and burgesses, exclusive of the commonalty, paying scot and lot. 18 Feb. 1695.———Is not in the mayor, burgesses, and inhabitants, not receiving alms; but in the mayor and burgesses only. 11 Jan. 1710.———So.

Maidstone, Kent. Edw. VI. 2 Eliz.
Sir Hor. Mann   re-elected   558
Lord Guernsey became Earl Clement Taylor   399
  of Aylesford in 1777
Hon. Cha. Finch   Hon. Cha. Finch   362

Agreed to be in the freemen not receiving alms or charity. Feb. 1701, 8 Dec. 1702.———700.

Malden, Essex. 2 Edw. III.
Hon. Rd. Sav. Nassau, dead   Eliab Harvey, esq.
John Strutt, esq.   re-elected

Is in such freemen as do not receive alms, and are entitled to freedom by birth, marriage or servitude; and that persons deriving their right of freedom from honorary freemen, and persons claiming their freedom by purchase, and exercising trades within the borough, have no right to vote. 20 May, 1715.

C 2   *Malm-*

[28]

Malmſbury, Wilts. 23 Edw. I.

William Strahan, eſq.
Hon. Charles James Fox

Viſc. Lewiſham, made his election for Staffordſhire
John Calvert, jun. eſq.
Viſc. Fairford

Agreed to be in the aldermen and twelve capital burgeſſes, 13 Dec. 1702.

Malton, Yorkſhire. 23 Edw. I. 16 Car.

Edmund Burke, eſq. made his election for Briſtol
Wm. Weddel, eſq.
Savile Finch, e.q.

re-elected
re-elected, vacated in 1780
Edmund Burke, eſq.

In the burgage holders.——100.

Marlborough, Wilts. 23 Edw. I.

Hon. James Brudenell
Sir J. Tylney Long, bart.

Earl of Courtown
William Woodley, eſq.

Is in the mayor and burgeſſes only. 13 May, 1771.—21.

Marlow, Bucks. 28 Edw. I. 21 Ja. I.

Wm. Clayton, eſq.
Sir J. E. Warren

re-elected
re-elected
Paul Berfield, eſq.

Is in the inhabitants only, who pay ſcot and lot. 21 Nov. 1690.——216.

St. Maw's, Cornwall. 5 Eliz.

Lord Nugent
Hugh Boſcawen, eſq.

re-elected
re-elected

In the mayor and reſident burgeſſes.——31.

St. Michael's, Cornwall. 7 Edw. VI.

James Scawen, eſq. made his election for Surry
T. Howard, eſq. ſucceeded Earl of Suffolk in 1779
Francis Hale, eſq.
John Stephenſon, eſq.

re-elected
Hon. Wm. Hanger.

In the portreeve, and lords of the manor who are capable of being portreeves, and the inhabitants of the ſaid borough, paying ſcot and lot. 20 March, 1700.—26.

Merionethſhire.

John Pugh Price, eſq. died in 1774
Ev. Lloyd Vaughan, eſq.

re-elected
H. Ar. Corbett, eſq.

Midhurſt,

Midhurst, Sussex. 4 Edw. II.
Sir H. Mackworth, bart. made
 his election for Cardiff
Cle. Tudway, esq. made his
 election for Wells
Hon. H. S. Conway   Hon. John St. John, made
John Ord, esq.   his election for Newport
                     Sir Sampson Gideon
                     Henry Drummond, esq.
     In the burgage holders.———100.
                 Middlesex.
John Glyn, esq. died in 1779
Thomas Wood, esq.   George Byng, esq.
John Wilkes, esq.   re-elected
     Milbourn Port, Somersetshire. 26 Edw. I.
Hon. T. Luttrell   J. H. Medlycott, esq.   62
C. Wolseley, esq.   John Townson, esq.   56
                     Hon. T. Luttrell   44
                     J. Hunter   36
     Is only in the capital bailiffs and their deputies, in the commonalty, stewards, and the inhabitants paying scot and lot. 8 Dec. 1702.
     Minehead, Somersetshire. 1 Eliz.
H. Fow. Luttrell, esq. va-
 cated in 1774
Tho. Pownall, esq.   Fran. Fow. Luttrell, esq.
Jn. Fow. Luttrell, esq.   re-elected
     Is in the parishioners of Minehead and Dunster, being house-keepers in the borough of Minehead, and not receiving alms. 24 Feb. 1717.---160.—The precept to be directed to the two constables, and they to make the return. 13 June, 1717.

                 Monmouthshire.
John Morgan, esq.   re-elected
John Hanbury, esq   re-elected
                 Monmouth Town. Hen. VIII.
Sir John Stepney, bart.   re-elected
     Doth not belong to the burgesses and inhabitants of Monmouth only, but the inhabitants of the borough of Newport and Aske have a right to vote. 26 Nov. 1680.——800.
                 Montgomeryshire.
Edw. Kynaston, esq. died 1772   W. Most. Owen, esq.   700
Watkin Williams, esq.   *Watk. Williams, esq.*   624

Montgomery Town.
Whitshed Keene, esq.   re-elected
Is in the burgesses of the said town only. 80.

Morpeth, Northumberland. 1 Mary.
Peter Delme, esq.   re-elected
Hon. Wm. Byron, died 1776
G. Elliot, esq. vacated 1777
J. W. Egerton, esq.   Anthony Storer, esq.
Is only in the bailiffs and free burgesses of the said borough. 9 March, 1695.——200.

Newark, Nottingham. 24 Car. II.
Sir Henry Clinton   re-elected   518
George Sutton, esq.   Lord George Sutton   510
                 Robert Forster, esq.   418
Is in the mayor, aldermen, and inhabitants within the borough, who pay, or ought to pay, scot and lot. 11 Jan. 1699.——800.

Newcastle-under-Line, Staffordshire. 27 Edw. III.
Lord Viscount Chewton   Arch. Macdonald, esq.
Sir John Wrottesley, bart.
   died 1778
Visc. Trentham   re-elected
(Before the charter) in the mayor, bailiffs, and common council; and it was resolved, that the late constitution altered not the former custom. 9 April, 1624.——Agreed to be in the mayor, burgesses, and freemen, resident within the borough. 27 Feb. 1705.——500.

Newcastle-upon-Tyne, Northumberland. 13 Edw. I.
Sir W. Blacket, died 1777
Sir M. W. Ridley, bart.   re-elected   1408
Sir J. Trevelyan, bart.   And. Rob. Bowes   1135
                 Thomas Delaval   1085
In the corporation and free burgesses.——2500.

Newport, Cornwall. 7 Edw. VI.
Rt. Hon. Hum. Morice made,
   his election for Launceston
John Frederick, esq.   Visc. Maitland
Rich. Bull, esq.   John Coghill, esq.
Two vianders, with inhabitants paying scot and lot.—62.

Newport, Hants. 23 Edw. I.
Sir Rd. Worsley, bart.   re-elected
Hans Sloane, esq.   Hon. John St. John
The mayor, 11 aldermen, and 12 burgesses; in all 24.

Newton,

Newton, Lancashire. 1 Eliz.
Ant. James Keck, esq.   Thomas Peter Leigh, esq.
Robert Atherton, esq.   Thomas Davenport, esq.
In the free burgesses.——60.
Newton, Hants. 27 Eliz.
Sir Jn. Barrington, bart. vacated, 1775
Ed. Meux Worsley, esq.   re-elected
Harcourt Powell, esq. vacated 1775
Charles Ambler, esq.   John Barrington, esq.
In the mayor and burgesses of the said borough, having borough lands within the said borough, 22 April, 1729.—12.
Norfolk.
Sir Edw. Astley, bart.   re-elected
Wenman Coke, esq. died in 1776
Tho. Wm. Coke, esq.   re-elected
Northallerton, Yorkshire. 26 Edw. I. 16 Car. I.
Daniel Lascelles, esq.   re-elected, vacated in 1780
                         Edwin Lascelles, esq.
Henry Pierse, esq.   re-elected
In the burgage-holders.——180.
Northamptonshire.
Lucey Knightley, esq.   re-elected
Thomas Powys, esq.   re-elected
Northampton Town. 2? Edw. I.
Sir G. Robinson, bart.   Visc. Althorpe
Hon. W. Tollemache   George Rodney, esq.
In the inhabitants being housholders, and not receiving alms; and the sharing in the charitable gift distributed at Christmas, is a taking of alms. 26 April, 1665.—800.
Northumberland.
Lord Algern. Percy   re-elected
Sir W. Middleton, bart. re-elected
Norwich City. 23 Edw. 1
Sir Harb. Harbord, bt.   re-elected   1382
Edward Bacon, esq.   re-elected   1199
                         John Thurlow   1103
                         W. Windham   1069
In the freeholders, and such fremen only, as are entered
in

in the books, and do not receive alms. 12 March, 1701.
———3000.

Nottinghamshire.

The Earl of Lincoln died in
1778
Hon. T. Willoughby a peer,
1774
Lord Edw. Bentinck   re-elected
Cha. Meadows, esq.   re-elected

Nottingham, Town of

Hon. Wm. Howe
Sir C. Sedley, bt. died 1778   Robert Smith, esq.   571
Abel Smith, esq. died 1779   Dan. Parker Coke, esq.   343
Robert Smith, esq.   J. Cartwright, esq.   150

Agreed to be in the mayor, freemen, and freeholders of 40s. per annum.———It was also agreed, that the eldest sons of freemen by their birth, the youngest sons of freemen, who have served seven years apprenticeship, whether in Nottingham, or elsewhere; and also such persons as served apprenticeship to any freemen of Nottingham, were well entitled to demand their freedom. 10 June, 1701.———1800.

Oakhampton. 28 Edw. I. 7 Edw. II. 16 Car. I.
Rich. Vernon, esq.   re-elected
Alex. Wedderburne, esq. vacated in 1778, now Lord Loughborough
Humphry Minchin, esq.   re-elected
         Charles Philip Jennings, esq.
         Rich. Heaviside, esq.

In the freeholders, and freemen, being made free according to the charter and bye-laws of the said borough. 24 Feb. 1710.———400.

Orford, Suffolk. 23 Edw. I.
Lord Visc. Beauchamp   re-elected
Hon. R. Seymour Conway   re-elected

In the mayor, portmen, capital burgesses, and freemen not receiving alms. 10 Feb. 1669. 29 Jan. 1708.———80.

Oxfordshire.

Rt. Hon. Lord C. Spencer   re-elected
Rt. Hon. Lord Viscount Wenman   re-elected

Oxford City. 23 Edw. I.
Hon. Peregrine Bertie   re-elected
Lord Robert Spencer   re-elected
                                 Benj. Bond Hopkins, esq.
Is stated to be in the mayor, 15 more, called the magistrates, and common council, making in all 48.——19 Feb. 18 Jac.

Oxford University. 1 James I.
Sir R. Newdigate, bart.   Sir Wm. Dolben, bart.
Francis Page, esq.   re-elected
In the doctors and actual masters.——450.

Pembrokeshire.
Hugh Owen, esq.   re-elected

Pembroke, Town of
Hugh Owen, esq.   re-elected   1089
                                 Lord Milford   912
In the mayor, bailiffs, and burgesses of the several boroughs of Pembroke, Tenby, and Whiston. 23 Feb. 1711.---500.

Penryn, Cornwall. 7 Edw. VI.
Sir G. Osborne, bart.   Sir F. Basset, bart. 118
Wm. Chaytor, esq.   John Rogers, esq.   101
                                 W. Chaytor   82
                                 P. Wentworth   44
In the mayor, portreeve, aldermen, and inhabitants paying scot and lot.——140.

Peterborough City. 1 Edw. VI.
Mat. Wyldbore, esq.   James Phipps, esq.
Rich. Devyen, esq.   re-elected
Agreed to be in the inhabitants paying scot and lot. 16 June, 1701.—The execution and return of the precept was resolved to be in the bailiff appointed by the dean and chapter. 9 April 1728.——The right of electing burgesses to parliament was resolved to be in the inhabitants within the precincts of the minster there, being housholders not receiving alms; and in the other inhabitants within the city, paying scot and lot. 13 May, 1728.——400.

Petersfield, Hants. 25 Edw. I.
Wm. Jolliffe, esq.   re-elected
Sir Abra. Hume, bart.   Samuel Jolliffe, esq.
Is in the freeholders of lands, or ancient dwelling-houses or shambles, or dwelling-houses or shambles built upon ancient

cient foundations, within the said borough. 9 May, 1727.
—150.

        Plympton, Devonshire.   23 Edw. I.

Paul Henry Ourry, esq. vacated 1775
John Durand, esq.
Sir R. Phillips, bart. now
  Ld. Milford, vacated 1779   Viscount Cranburn, succeeded his father as Earl of Salisbury in 1780
                          Hon. James Stuart
William Fullarton, esq.   Sir Ralph Payne

     In the mayor, bailiff, and freemen, and in the sons of freemen, who have a right to demand their freedom. 28 Jan. 1702.—200.

        Plymouth, Devonshire.   26 Edw. I.   20 Hen. VI.
Visc. Barrington, vacated in 1778
• *Lord Lewisham*   Sir F. L. Rogers, bart.   162
Sir Cha. Hardy, died 1780   George Darby   123
                             J. Culme   76
                             Sir G. B. *Rodney*   21

     In the mayor and commonalty. 9 June, 1660.—500.
     Resolved, that the word *commonalty* above mentioned, extends only to the freemen of the said borough. 17 Jan. 1739.

        Pontefract, Yorkshire.   23, 26 Edw. I.   Ja. I.
Sir J. Goodricke, bart.   Visc. Galway
Charles Mellish, esq.   Wm. Nedham, esq.

     Ought to be by the inhabitants (housholders) resiant there. 28 May, 1624.—Is in the persons having, within the said borough, a freehold of burgage tenure, paying a burgage rent. 6. Feb. 1770.——150.

        Poole, Dorsetshire.   36 Edw. III. 31 Hen. VI.
Sir Eyre Coote, K. B.   Joseph Gilstone, esq.
Joshua Mauger, esq.   William Morton Pitt, esq.
                            Joshua Mauger, esq.
                            John Adams, esq.

     In the out-burgesses as well as in-burgesses. 15 June, 1661. —100.—Resolved by the committee to be in the mayor, burgesses and commonalty, who pay scot and lot. 9 Feb. 1688. —To which the house disagreed.

                                                 Portsmouth,

Portsmouth, Hants. 23 Edw. I.
Sir Edward Hawke, K. B.
created a Peer in 1776
Maurice Suckling, esq, died
1778
Hon. R. Monckton   re-elected   31
Peter Taylor, esq died 1777
Sir Wm. Gordon, K. B.   re-elected   20
           Sir H. Featherstonhaugh   11
   In the mayor, aldermen and burgesses. 24 Jan. 1695.
Preston, Lancashire. 23 Edw. I. Edw. VI.
Sir H. Hoghton, bart.   re elected   487
John Burgoyne, esq.   re-elected   466
          ——— *Fenton*   208
   Is in all the inhabitants. 18 Dec. 1661.——600.
   It was determined that the words, *all the inhabitants*, did not mean only the in-burgesses of the last guild, or those admitted since by copy of court-roll, as are inhabitants of the said place, but all the inhabitants at large. 29 Nov. 1770.

Queenborough, Kent. 13 Eliz.
Sir C. Frederick, K. B.   re-elected
Sir W. Rawlinson, kt.   re-elected
   In the mayor, jurats and bailiffs only. 17 April, 1729.
——70.

Radnorshire.
Thomas Johnes, esq.   re-elected

New Radnor.
Edward Lewis, esq.   Edward Lewis, esq.
               John Lewis, esq.
               A double return.
   In the burgesses of Radnor, Ryader, Knighton, Knucklas, and Kevenlice only. 12 Nov. 1690.——600.

Reading, Berkshire. 23 Edw. I.
John Dodd, esq.   re-elected   317
Fr. Aneslcy, esq.   re-elected   350
          Hon. T. Luttrell   199
   In the freemen and inhabitants, such freemen not receiving alms, and such inhabitants paying scot and lot. 2 Dec. 1708.——Is in the inhabitants only, paying scot and lot. 30 May, 1716.——560.

                                                East

East Retford, Nottinghamshire. 9 Edw. II.
Sir Cecil Wray, bart.   Wharton Amcotts, esq.
Lord T. P. Clinton, made his
  election for Westminster
Hon. *Wm. Hanger, vacate*
  1778
Lord *J. P. Clinton*   re-elected
  The younger sons of freemen have not a right to demand their freedom of the said borough. 17 March, 1701.——
In the burgesses, resident and non-resident. 15 April, 1701.
——Persons not inhabiting in the said borough, are incapable of being made free by redemption; and the sons of freemen have a right of freedom. 28 Nov. 1702.——Is in such freemen only as have a right to their freedom by birth, as eldest sons of freemen, or by serving seven years apprenticeship, or have it by redemption, whether inhabiting or not inhabiting in the borough at the time of their being made free. 17 Jan. 1705.——Resolved to be in such freemen only as have a right to their freedom by birth, as eldest sons of freemen, or by serving seven years apprenticeship, or have it by redemption, inhabiting in the said borough at the time of their being made free. 11 Jan. 1710.——150.

Richmond, Yorkshire. 19 Eliz.
Sir Lawrence Dundas, bart. re-elected
  made his election for Edinburgh
William Norton, esq.
Thomas Dundas, esq. made
  his election for Stirlingshire
Charles Dundas, esq.   Marquis of Graham
  In such persons only as are owners of ancient burgages in the said borough, having a right of pasture in a common field, called Whitcliff pasture. 9 March, 1727.—270.

Ripon, Yorkshire. 23 Edw. I.
Wm. Aislabie, esq.   re-elected
Charles Allanson, esq. died
  1775
William Lawrence, esq.   Hon. Frederick Robinson.
In the Inhabitants.——200.

Rochester,

Rochester, Kent. 23 Edw. I.
George Finch Hatton, esq.   re-elected   331
Robert Gregory, esq.   re-elected   319
                            N. Smith   281
   In the citizens.———800.
          New Romney, Kent. 42 Edw. III.
Sir Edward Dering, bart.   re-elected
Richard Jackson, esq.   re-elected
   In the mayor, 5 jurats, and 26 freemen.———32.
          Rutlandshire.
Thomas Noel, esq.   re-elected
George B. Brudenell, esq.   re-elected
          Rye, Sussex, 42 Edw. III.
M. Onslow, esq. vacated in
 1775
Hon. T. Onslow   re-elected
Rose Fuller, esq. died 1777
William Dickenson, esq.   re-elected
   Is in the mayor, jurats and freemen, inhabiting in the said port, and paying scot and lot. 19 Dec. 1702.———100.
          Ryegate, Surrey. 23 Edw. I.
Hon. John Yorke   re-elected
Sir Charles Cocks   re-elected
   In the freeholders.———200.
          Salop, or Shropshire.
Noel Hill, esq.   re-elected
Charles Baldwyn, esq.   Richard Hill, esq.
          Saltash, Cornwall. Edw. VI.
Sir Grey Cooper, bart.   re-elected
Thomas Bradshaw, esq. died
 1778
Henry Starchey, esq.   Charles Jenkinson, esq.
                            Sir Wm. James, bart.
                            John Buller, jun.
   In the mayor, recorder, six aldermen, and twenty freeholders.
          Sandwich, Kent. 42 Edw. III.
Wm. Hey, esq. vacated in   Philip Stephens, esq.   477
 1776   Sir Rich. Sutton, bart. 366
Charles Brett, esq.   C. Brett   302
Philip Stephen, esq.
   In the freemen resiant, and non-resiant, except those who receive alms.—700.

D

New Sarum, Wilts. 23 Edw. I.
Viscount Folkestone, Earl of
Radnor in 1776.
Hon. W. Bouverie   re-elected
Wm. Hussey, esq.   re-elected

Is in the select number, i. e. the mayor and corporation, consisting of 56 persons. 1 April, 1689.

Old Sarum, Wilts. 23 Edw. I.
Thomas Pitt, esq.   re-elected
Pink. Wilkinson, esq.   re-elected

In the freeholders, being burgage-holders of the said borough. 14 Nov. 1688.——7.

Scarborough, Yorkshire. 23 Edw. III.
Sir Hugh Pallifer, bart. vacated in 1779
Hon. Charles Phipps, esq.   re-elected
Earl of Tyrconnel   re-elected

Seaford, Sussex. 42 Edw. III.
Lord Visc. Gage   John Durand, esq.   26
George Medley, esq.   John Robinson, esq.   24
                        John Molesworth   12
                        George Medley   10
                        Mr. Robinson made his election for Harwich
                        C. D'Oyley elect. in his room

Is not only in the bailiffs, jurors, and freemen, but in the popularity also. 10 Feb. 1670.

Shaftesbury, Dorsetshire. 23 Edw. I.
Hon. Wm. Mortimer, esq.   Sir G. Rumbold, bart.
George Rous, esq.   Francis Sykes, esq.
                          Hans Wintrop Mortimer, esq.
                          Sir Geo. Collier

Not only in the mayor and burgesses, but in the inhabitants paying scot and lot. 29 Feb. 1695.——300.

Shoreham, Sussex. 23 Edw. I.
Sir John Shelley, bart.   Sir Cecil Bishopp, bart.
Charles Goring, esq.   John Peachey, esq.

All the freeholders of 40s. *per annum* in the rape or hundred of Bramber, in which Shoreham is situated, have a right to vote. Act of 1771.——1500.

Shrewsbury, Shropshire. 23 Edw. I.
Rt. Hon. Lord Clive, died
John Corbet, esq.   Sir Charlt. Leighton, bart.
William Pulteney, esq.   re-elected.

In the burgesses inhabiting in the said borough, or in the suburbs thereof, paying scot and lot, and not receiving alms or charity. 20 Dec. 1709. 9 April, 1723.——Is in the mayor, aldermen, and burgesses. 27 May, 1714.——500. ——N. B. Several parishes and villages were voted to be no part of the ancient borough or suburbs. 9 April, 1723.

Somersetshire.
Rich. Hip. Coxe, esq.   re-elected
Edward Philips, esq.   Sir John Trevelyan, bart.

Southampton Town. 23 Edw. I.
Rt. Hon. Hans Stanley, died 1780.
John Fuller, esq.   re-elected   264
John Fleming, esq.   Hans Sloane, esq.   249
        John Fleming   237

In the burgesses and inhabitants. 31 Dec. 1689.—— Resolved, that the out-living burgesses, as well as the burgesses (inhabitants) paying scot and lot, had a right to vote. 17 March, 1695.——400.——Mayor and bailiffs are the returning officers. April 3 1735.

Southwark, Borough of. 23 Edw. I.
Henry Thrale, esq.   Sir Rich. Hotham, kt. 1300
Nat. Polhill, esq.   re-elected   1138
        Hen. Thrale   855

Is only in the inhabitants paying scot and lot. 10 Nov. 1702.——1500.

Staffordshire.
Sir John Wrottesley, bart.   re-elected
Sir Wm. Bagot, bart.   Viscount Lewisham

Stafford Town. 23 Edw. I.
Rich. Whitworth, esq.   Hon. Edw. Monckton 258
Hugo Meynell, esq.   Rich. Brinsley Sheridan, 247
        Rich. Whitworth   168
        Drummnd   46

In the mayor, aldermen, and burgesses resiant within the borough. 27 Nov. 1722.——400.

Stamford, Lincolnshire. 23 Edw. I.
Sir Geo. Howard, K. B.   re-elected
Henry Cecil, esq.   re-elected

In the inhabitants paying scot and lot, and not receiving alms, or public charities. 28 March, 1735.——500.

                Steyning,

Steyning, Sussex. 4 Edw. II.
Th. Ed. Freeman, esq.   Sir T. G. Shipwith, bart.
Film. Honywood, esq.   re-elected, made his election
                     for Kent
                     John Bullock, esq.

Agreed to be in the inhabitants paying scot and lot, and not receiving alms. 10 April, 1701.——Agreed to be in the constables and housholders (inhabitants) within the borough, paying scot and lot, and not receiving alms. 10 Feb. 1710.——80.

Stockbridge, Hants. 1 Eliz.
Lord Irnham
Hon. John Luttrell, vacated   re-elected   66
   in 1775
Hon. *Ja. Luttrell*   re-elected   66
                     R. Mayne   51
                     Sir *Willoughby Aston*   51

In the inhabitants paying scot and lot.——70.

Sudbury, Suffolk. 1 Eliz.
Sir Patrick Blake, bart.   re-elected
Sir Wal. Hanmer, bart.   P. C. Crespigny, esq.
                     Sir *James Marriott*
                     John Henniker, esq.

Only in the sons of freemen born after their fathers were made free, and in such as have served seven years apprenticeship, or made freemen by redemption. 6 Dec. 1703.

Suffolk.
Rowland Holt, esq.   Sir John Rous, bart.
Sir T. C. Bunbury, bart.   re-elected

Surrey.
Sir F. Vincent, bt. died 1775   Sir J. Mawbey   2419
J. Scawen, esq.   Hon. Augustus Keppel 2179
Sir *J. Mawbey, bart.*   Hon. T. Onslow   1506

Sussex.
Lord Geo. H. Lennox   re-elected
Sir T. S. Wilson   Hon. T. Pelham, esq.

Tamworth, Staffordshire. 5 Eliz.
Edw. Thurlow, esq. Lord
   Chancellor 1778
Anthony Chamier, esq.   re-elected, died in 1780
T. De Grey, jun. esq.   John Calvert, esq.
                     John Courtney, esq.

In the inhabitants paying scot and lot, and in such persons as have freeholds within the borough, whether resident in the borough, or not. 17 March, 1693.———In the inhabitants, being houſholders, paying ſcot and lot, and not receiving alms. 23 Jan. 1722.———250.

        Taviſtock, Devonſhire. 23 Edw. I.
Rt. Hon. Richard Rigby   re-elected
Hon. R. Fitzpatrick   re-elected

In the freeholders of inheritance in poſſeſſion, inhabiting within the ſaid borough. 13 March, 1695. 4 Feb. 1696. 19 Jan. 1702.—110.

        Taunton, Somerſetſhire. 23 Edw. I.
Alex. Popham, eſq.   John Roberts, eſq.
John Halliday, eſq.   re-elected

In the inhabitants within the ſaid borough, being potwallers, and not receiving alms or charity. 28 July, 1715.——300.

        Tewkeſbury, Glouceſterſhire. 12 James I.
Sir W. Codrington, bart.   re-elected
Joſeph Martin, eſq. died in 1776
James Martin, eſq.   re-elected

In the inhabitants paying ſcot and lot.—500.

        Thetford, Norfolk. 1 Edw. VI.
Hon. Ch. Fitzroy   Richard Hopkins, eſq.
C. F. Scudamore, eſq.   re-elected

In the mayor, burgeſſes (which are ten) and in the commonalty, or common council, (which are twenty) amounting in the whole to thirty-one. 7 June, 1685.

        Thirſke, Yorkſhire. 23 Edw. III. Edw. VI.
Sir T. Frankland, bart.   Sir Tho. Gaſcoigne, bart.
T. Frankland, eſq.   Beilby Thompſon, eſq.

In the burgage-holders of Old Thirſke.

        Tiverton, Devonſhire. James I.
Nat. Rider, eſq. Lord Harrowby in 1776
John Wilmot, eſq.   re-elected.
Sir John Duntz, bart.   re-elected

In the mayor, recorder, burgeſſes, and aſſiſtants.—26.

        Totneſs, Devonſhire. 23 Edw. I.
Sir Philip Jennings Clerke, bart.   re-elected
James Amyatt, eſq.   Launcelot Brown, eſq.

In the freemen not inhabiting, as well as freemen inhabiting within the ſaid borough. 4 Mar. 1695.—117.

Tregony, Cornwall. Edw. I. 5 Eliz.
Hon. G. L. Parker   John Stephenson, esq.
Sir Alexander Leith, bart. John Dawes, esq.

Agreed to be in all the inhabitants that provide for themselves, whether they live under the same roof or not. 5 March, 1695.———100.

Truro, Cornwall. 23 Edward I.
George Boscawen, esq.   Henry Rosewarne
Bamber Gascoyne, esq.   re-elected

In the mayor and select number of burgesses. 21 May, 1689.———26.

Wallingford, Berkshire. 23 Edw. I.
Sir Robert Barker, knt.   John Aubrey, esq.
John Cator, esq.   Chaloner Arcedeckne, esq.

In the mayor, aldermen, bailiffs, and eighteen assistants, together with the inhabitants of the said borough, paying scot and lot, and not receiving alms. 15 Dec. 1709.———150.

Wareham, Dorsetshire. 30 Edw. I.
Right Hon. William Gerard Thomas Farrer, esq.
  Hamilton
Christ. Doyley, esq.   John Boyd, esq.

In the mayor, magistrates, and freeholders, and all that pay scot and lot. 25 June, 1661.———Is only in the mayor and magistrates of the said borough as pay scot and lot, and in the freeholders of lands or tenements there, who have been, *bona fide*, to their own use, in the actual occupation, or in the receipts of the rents and profits of such lands or tenements, for the space of one whole year next before the election, except the same came to such freeholders by descent, devise, marriage, marriage-settlement, or promotion to some benefice in the church. 19 Jan. 1747.———150.

Warwickshire.
Sir Charles Holt, bart.   Sir Robert Lawley, bart.
T. George Shipwith, esq.   Sir George Shuckburg, bart.

Warwick Town. 23 Edw. I.
Hon. Char. Fra. Greville   re-elected   203
Hon. Rob. Fulke Greville   Robert Ladbroke, esq.   212
                           Hon. R. Greville   187

In the commonalty of the said town. 3 May, 1628.——— Is in such persons only as do pay to church and poor in the said borough. 31 Jan. 1722.———500.

Wells,

Wells City. 23 Edw. 1.
Clement Tudway, efq.   Clement Tudway   126
Robert Child, efq.   Robert Child   105
                         G. Lovell   52
Is in the mayor, mafters, and burgeffes of the faid city. 18 Feb. 1695.——*N. B.* The bye-law of 1712, for inflicting penalties on the mayor and burgeffes, declared to be arbitrary and illegal. 30 May, 1716.——Refolved to be in the mayor, mafters, and burgeffes, and in fuch perfons as are (by confent of the mayor and common-council) admitted to their freedom in any of the feven trading companies, on account of birth, fervitude, or marriage. 2 May, 1723.——The fame refolution. 18 April, 1729.——The fame again. 11 March, 1734.——500.

Wendover, Bucks. 28 Edw. I. 21 Ja. I.
John Adams efq. made his
  election for Caermarthen
Henry Drummond, *efq.*   Richard Smith, efq.
Jofeph Bullock, efq. vacated
Thomas Dummer, *efq.*   John Manfell Smith, efq.
                           Sir John Elliot
                           Richard Heavifide, *efq.*
Agreed to be in the inhabitants (houfekeepers within the borough) not receiving alms. But perfons coming by certificate to live in the borough have not a right to vote. 21 Nov. 1702.——160.

Wenlock, Shropshire. Edw. IV.
Sir H. Bridgman, bart.   re-elected
Geo. Forefter, efq.   Tho Whitmore, efq. made
                            his election for Bridgnorth
                          George Forrefter, efq.

In the burgeffes.——100.

Weobley, Herefordshire. 23 Edw. I. 16 Car. I,
J. S. Leger Douglas, efq.   re-elected
Sir Wm. Lynch, K.B vacated
  in 1780
Andrew Bayntun, *efq.*   re-elected

Agreed to be in the inhabitants of houfes of 20s. *per ann.* paying fcot and lot. 13 Jan. 1698.——Refolved to be in the inhabitants of the ancient vote-houfes of 20s. *per ann.* value and upwards, refiding in the faid houfes forty days before the day of election, and paying fcot and lot; and alfo in

the

the owners of such ancient vote-houses, paying scot and lot, who shall be resident in such houses at the time of the election. 3 March, 1736.——85.

Westbury, Wilts. 27 Hen. VI.
N. Bayly, esq. vacated 1779.
Sam. Estwick, *esq.* re-elected
Hon. T. F. Wenman John Whalley Gardiner, esq.

Resolved that the tenants of burgage-houses, by lease for years absolute, have a right to vote. 1 Dec. 1702.——Is in every tenant of any burgage tenement in fee, for life, or ninety nine years, determinable upon lives, or by copy of court-roll, paying a burgage-rent of 4d. or 2d. yearly, being resident in the borough, and not receiving alms. 1 June, 1715.——50.

Westloo, Cornwall. Edw. VI.
Wm. James, esq. re-elected
G. Ogilvy, esq. vacated 1775
John Rogers, esq. John Buller, esq.

In the mayor, aldermen, burgesses, and freemen.—53.

Westminster City. 1 Edw. VI.
Earl Percy, baron Percy 1776
Lord *Petersham,* a peer in 1779
Lord *Malden* Hon. Cha. James Fox 4878
Lord T. P. Clinton Sir G. B. Rodney, bart. 5298.
  Lord Lincoln 4257

Inhabitants paying scot and lot. The King's menial servants, having no proper houses of their own in Westminster, have no right to vote. 15 Nov. 1680.—11,000.

Westmoreland.
Sir Ja. Lowther, bart. made
his election for Cumberland
James Lowther, esq. re-elected
Sir Mic. Le Fleming, bart. re-elected

Weymouth. 12 Edw. II. and *Melcombe Regis,* 8 Edw. II. United by Elizabeth into one corporation, though two boroughs, and send four members.
Right Hon. Wellbore Ellis re-elected
W. Chafin Grove, esq. re-elected
John Purling, esq. re-elected
John Tucker, esq. died 1778
Gabriel Stewart, esq. Warren Lisle, esq. vacated in
  1780
  Gabriel Stewart
  Agreed

Agreed to be in the mayor, aldermen, bailiffs, and capital burgesses, inhabiting in the borough, and in persons seised of freeholds within the borough, and not receiving alms, 7 May, 1730.———400.

Whitchurch, Hampshire. 27 Eliz.
Rt. Hon. T. Townshend   re-elected
Lord Viscount Midleton   re-elected

In the freeholders only of lands or tenements, in right of themselves, or their wives, not split since the act of the 7th and 8th years of the reign of King William. 21 Dec, 1708.———70.

Wigan, Lancashire. 23 Edw. I. 1 Edw. VI.
Geo. Byng, esq.   Hon. Horatio Walpole   36
Beau. Hotham, esq. vacated
    in 1775
John Moreton, esq. deceased   H. Samp. Bridgeman, esq. 58
                      Sir Rich. Clayton   23

In the free burgesses.———200.

Wilton, Wilts. 23 Edw. I.
Hon. Nich. Herbert died 1775
Charles Herbert, esq.   Lord Herbert
Henry Herbert, esq.   Rt. Hon. W. G. Hamilton

Agreed to be in the mayor and burgesses, who are to do all corporate acts, and receive the sacrament. 28 Nov. 1708, 17 March, 1710.—80.

Wiltshire.
Ambrose Goddard, esq.   re-elected
Cha. Penruddocke, esq.   re-elected

Winchelsea, Sussex. 42 Edw. III.
C. Wolf. Cornwall, esq.   re-elected
Arn. Nesbitt, esq. made his
    election for Cricklade
William Nesbit, esq.   John Nesbit, esq.

Agreed to be in the mayor, jurats, and freemen. 11 Feb. 1711.—40.

Winchester City. 23 Edw. I.
Henry Penton, esq.   re-elected
Lovel Stanhope, esq.   re-elected

Stated to be in the mayor, recorder, aldermen, bailiffs, and corporation. 20 Oct. 1690.

Windsor, Berks. 5 Edw. I.
Hon. Aug. Keppell   P. Portlock Powney, esq. 174
Hon. John Montague   re-elected   214
                         Hon. A. Keppel   158
In the inhabitants who pay scot and lot. 4 Nov. 1680.
——In the mayor, bailiffs, and select number of burgesses only. 2 May, 1689.——Is not in the mayor, bailiffs and burgesses; but that all the inhabitants have the right of electing. 5 April, 1697.——300.
Woodstock, Oxfordshire. 30 Edw. I.
John Skinner, esq. vacated
   in 1777
Lord Parker   re-elected
William Eden, esq.   -   re-elected
In the mayor, aldermen, and freemen of the said borough. 16 March, 1714.—400.
Worcestershire.
Rt. Hon. W. Dowdeswell died
   in 1775
W. Lygon, esq.   re-elected
Hon. Edw. Foley   re-elected
        Worcester City. 23 Edw. I.
T. Bates Rous, esq.   re-elected   1085
John Walsh, esq.   Hon. William Ward   832
                           Sir W. Lewes   701
Agreed to be in the freemen not receiving alms. 7 Feb. 1693. In the citizens not receiving alms, and admitted to their freedom by birth or servitude, or by redemption, in order to trade within the said city. 11 Feb. 1747.—2000.
        Wotton Basset, Wiltshire. 25 Hen. VI.
Hon. Henry St. John   re-elected
Robert Scott, esq.   William Strahan, esq.
Is in the principal inhabitants.——150.
        Chipping-Wycomb, Bucks. 28 Edw. I.
Rob. Waller, esq.   re-elected
Hon. T. Fitzmaurice   Lord Mahon
Agreed to be in the mayor, bailiffs, and burgesses, not receiving alms. 28 Jan. 1702.——170.
        Yarmouth, Norfolk. 23 Edw. I.
Cha. Townshend, esq.   re-elected
Hon. Richard Walpole   re-elected
Is in the burgesses at large.——730.

Yarmouth, Hampshire. 23 Edw. I.
Jerv. Clarke, esq. vacated 1779
Rob. Kingsmill, esq.   Edward Morant, esq.
E. Worsley, esq. vacated 1775
James Worsley, esq.   Edward Rushworth, esq.
 The bye-law, made Sept. 21, 1670, for electing free-burgesses, by the mayor and five chief burgesses, was a good bye-law. 11 April, 1717.——50.

Yorkshire.
Sir Geo. Savile, bart.   re-elected
Edwin Lascelles, esq.   Henry Duncombe, esq.
 Persons whose freeholds lie in the Ainsty have a right to vote. 9 March, 1735.

York City. 23 Edw. I.
Rt. Hon. Lord J. Cavendish   re-elected
Cha. Turner, esq.   re-elected
 Is in the corporation and citizens.——1500.

WALES, by an act 27 Hen. VIII.

RECAPITULATION—The first summons for Representatives for Counties (and some Cities) was the 49th of Henry III. The first returns for shires, on record, 18th of Edward II. First returns for Cities and Boroughs, 23 Edw. I.
 147 Counties, Cities, and Boroughs, sent Representatives to Parliament at the accession of Hen. VIII.
 31 were added by Henry VIII.
 21 by Edward VI.
 14 by Mary
 31 by Elizabeth
 14 by James I.
 8 by Charles I.
 4 by Charles II.
 45 by Anne, for Scotland.

SCOTLAND.

Aberdeenshire.
Alex. Garden, esq.   re-elected

County of Air.

David Kennedy, efq.   Hugh Montgomery
                      Sir *Adam Fergusson, bart.*

Argyllshire.

Robert Campbell, efq. vacated in 1771
Adam Livingftone, efq.   Lord Frederick Campbell

Aberbrothick, Aberdeen, &c.

Hon. T. Lyon, died 1778
Adam Drummond, efq.   re-elected

Bamffshire.

R. H. Ja. Duff, Earl of Fife   re-elected

Berwickshire.

James Pringle, jun. efq. vacated 1779
Sir *John Paterson, bart.*   Hugh Scott, jun. efq.
                          Sir *John Paterson, bart.*

Bute and Caithnefsshire.

Hon. James Stuart   John Sinclair, efq.

Nairn and Cromartie Shires.

Cofmo Gordon, efq.
Mr. Gordon vacated in 1777
John Campbell, efq.   George Rofs

Craill, Kinrenny, &c.

Phil. Anftruther, efq. vacated in 1777
Hon. George Damer   Sir John Anftruther, bart.

Cupar, Perth, &c.

George Dempfter, efq.   re-elected
                         Lord Fred. Campbell

Dumbartonshire.

Sir Arch. Edmonftone, bart.   Lord Fred. Campbell
                               ——— *Elphinftone*

Culrofs, Dumferline, &c.

James Campbell

Dumfriesshire.

Sir Robert Laurie, bart.   re-elected

Edinburghshire.

H. Dundas, efq.   re-elected

Edinburgh City.

Sir Laurence Dundas   re-elected
                         Will. Miller, jun. efq.

Elginshire.
Hon. Art. Duff, vacated 1779
Lord Will. Gordon   re-elected
Fifeshire.
John Scott, esq. died 1776
J. T. Ofwald, esq. vacated 1779
Rob. Skene, esq.   re-elected
Forfarshire.
Earl of Panmure   re-elected
Glasgow, Dumbarton, &c.
Lord Fred. Campbell   John Crauford
     Wm. Fullarton, esq.
Haddingtonshire.
Sir G. Suttie, bart. vac. 1777
Well. Nesbit, esq.   Hugh Dalrymple, esq.
Invernessshire.
Hon. Simon Frafer   re-elected
Invernefs, Nairn, &c.
     Sir Hector Monro
Irvine, Air, Rothfay, &c.
     Sir J. A. Edmondstone
Kincardineshire.
Lord Adam Gordon   re-elected
Kinrofs and Clackmannan Counties.
     George Graham
Kintore, Banff, &c.
Sta. Long Morris, esq.   re-elected
     James Grant, esq.
Kirkaldy, Bruntifland, &c.
John Johnstone, esq.   John Henderson, jun. esq.
     Henry Dundas, esq.
Kirkudbright, Stewartry.
Wm. Stewart, esq.   Peter Johnston, esq.
     John Gordon, esq.
Lanerkshire.
And. Stewart, esq.   re-elected
Linlithgowshire.
Sir W. A. Cunynghame, bart. re-elected
Lauder, Haddington, &c.
Hon. J. Maitland. died 1779
Francis Charteris, esq.   re-elected
Lochmaben, Dumfries, &c.
William Douglas, jun. esq.   Sir Rob. Herries, knt.

[50]

Orkney and Zetlandshire.
Thomas Dundas, esq.   Robert Backie
                        Cha. Dundas, esq.
Peeblesshire.
Lord Advocate vacated 1775
Ad. Hay, esq. died 1775
Sir R. M. Keith, K. B.   Alex. Murray, esq.
Perthshire.
Hon. James Murray   re-elected
Renfrewshire.
John Craufurd, esq.   John Shaw Stewart, esq.
Rossshire.
Rt. Hon. J. S. Mackenzie   Hon. J. Mackenzie
Roxburghshire.
Rt. Hon. Sir G. Elliot, bt.
   died in 1777
Sir G. Elliot, his son   re-elected
                           Lord Rob. Kerr
Selkirkshire.
John Pringle, esq.   re-elected
                       ——— Selkirk, esq.
Selkirk, Lanerk, Peebles, &c.
                       Sir James Cockburn
Stirlingshire.
Thomas Dundas, esq.   re-elected
Stranrawer, Wigtown, Whiteborn, &c.
                       W. Adam
Sutherlandshire.
Hon. James Wemyss   re-elected
Wigtownshire.
Hon. Keith Stewart   re-elected
Wick, Tayn, &c.
James Grant, esq.   Hon. Charles Ross

PEERS OF SCOTLAND.

Elected in 1774.   *Elected in* 1780.
Duke of Gordon   re-elected
Earl of Galloway   re-elected
Earl of Dunmore   re-elected
Earl of Dalhousie   re-elected
Earl of Breadalbane   Duke of Athol
Earl of Englingtoun   re-elected
Earl of Abercorn   re-elected
Earl of Loudoun   re-elected

Earl of Aberdeen	re-elected
Duke of Queensberry	re-elected
Earl of Marchmont	re-elected
Earl of Roseberry	re-elected
Earl of Bute	Earl of Glencairn
Viscount Stormont	re-elected
Marquis of Lothian	re-elected
Earl of Cassilis	re-elected

ARCHBISHOPS AND BISHOPS.

Canterbury. Dr. Thomas Secker, died in August, 1768, when the Hon. Dr. Frederick Cornwallis was translated from Litchfield and Coventry

York. Dr. John Gilbert, died in 1761, and the Hon. Dr. Robert Drummond, translated from Salisbury to this see, in his room, died in 1776, and Dr. Wm. Markham translated from Chester in his room

London. Dr. Thomas Sherlock died in 1761, and was succeeded by Dr. Thomas Hayter, Bishop of Norwich, who died in 1762, when Dr. Richard Osbaldeston was translated from Carlisle, who died in 1764; and on May 22, 1764, Dr. Richard Terrick was translated to the see of London ; died April, 1777, and Dr. Robert Lowth translated from Oxford in his room

Durham. Hon. Dr. Richard Trevor, died June 9, 1771, and was succeeded by Dr. Egerton, Bishop of Litchfield and Coventry

Winchester. Dr. Benjamin Hoadley died in 1761, and Dr. John Thomas was then translated from Salisbury

Ely. Dr. Matthias Mawson died November 23, 1770, when Dr. Edmund Keene was translated from Chester to this see.

Bath and Wells. Dr. Edw. Willes died in 1773, and was succeeded by Dr. Charles Moss, Bishop of St. David's.

Lincoln. Dr. John Thomas, translated to Salisbury in 1761, and Dr. John Green consecrated in his room, died in 1779

Hereford. Right Hon. Lord James Beauclerk

Exeter. Dr. George Lavington, died in 1762, and the Hon. Dr. Fred. Keppell consecrated in his room, who died Dec. 1777, when Dr. John Ross was consecrated in his room

Carlisle. Dr. Richard Osbaldeston, translated to London in 1762,

1762, and Dr. Charles Lyttelton confecrated in his room, who died in 1769, and was fucceeded by Dr. Edmund Law

Salifbury. Dr. John Thomas, tranflated to Winchefter in 1761, vice Hoadley, deceafed, and was fucceeded by the Hon. Dr. Robert Drummond, who was in the fame year tranflated to York, and Dr. John Thomas was tranflated from Lincoln to Salifbury, who died July 20, 1766, and was fucceeded by Dr. John Hume, Bifhop of Oxford

Rochefter. Dr. Zach. Pearce, died in 1774, when Dr. John Thomas, Dean of Weftminfter, was confecrated Bifhop of Rochefter in his room

St. Afaph. Hon. Dr. Robert Drummond, tranflated in 1761 to Salifbury, and Dr. Richard Newcome tranflated from Landaff in his room, who died in June, 1769, and was fucceeded by Dr. Jonathan Shipley, Bifhop of Landaff

Norwich. Dr. Thomas Hayter, tranflated to London in 1761, and Dr. Philip Younge, Bifhop of Briftol, fucceeded him

Litchfield and Coventry. Hon. Dr. Frederick Cornwallis, tranflated to Canterbury in Auguft, 1768, and fucceeded by Dr. John Egerton, Bifhop of Bangor, who, in June, 1771, was tranflated to Durham, and the Hon. Dr. Brownlow North confecrated in his room, tranflated to Worcefter in 1774, and fucceeded by Dr. Richard Hurd

Chefter. Dr. Edmond Keene, tranflated to Ely in December 1770, and Dr. William Markham confecrated in his room. The laft tranflated to York in 1776, and Dr. Beilby Portens confecrated in his room

Worcefter. Dr. James Johnfon, died in November, 1774, fucceeded by Dr. Brownlow North, Bifhop of Litchfield and Coventry

St. David's. Dr. Anthony Ellis, died in 1761, and was fucceeded by Dr. Samuel Squire, who died May 17, 1776, when Dr. Robert Lowth was confecrated in his room; in October following he was tranflated to Oxford, and Dr. Charles Mofs confecrated Bifhop of St. David's, who was, in 1774, tranflated to Bath and Wells, and fucceeded in this fee by the Hon. Dr. James Yorke, tranflated to Gloucefter in 1779, and Dr. John Warren confecrated in his room.

Chichefter. Dr. (now Sir) William Afhburnham

Landaff. Dr. Richard Newcome, tranflated to St. Afaph in 1761, and Dr. John Ewer confecrated in his room, who,

in

in December 1768, was tranflated to Bangor, and was fucceeded by Dr. Jonathan Shipley, who, in 1769, was tranflated to St. Afaph, when the Hon. Dr. Shute Barrington was confecrated Bifhop of Landaff.

Oxford. Dr. John Hume, tranflated in July, 1766, to Salifbury, and Dr. Robert Lowth, Bifhop of St. David's, tranflated to the bifhoprick of Oxford. In May, 1777, Dr. John Butler was conecrated Bifhop of Oxford in the room of Dr. Lowth, tranflated to London.

Bangor. Dr. John Egerton, tranflated in Oct. 1768, to Litchfield and Coventry ; and in December following, Dr. John Ewer fucceeded him, who died in October, 1774, and was fucceeded by Dr. John Moore.

Peterborough. Dr. Richard Terrick, tranflated in May, 1764, to London, and Dr. Robert Lamb confecrated in his room ; Dr. Lamb died in 1768, and Dr. John Hinchliffe was then confecrated Bifhop of Peterborough.

Briftol. Dr. Philip Yonge, tranflated to Norwich in 1761, and Dr. Thomas Newton confecrated in his room.

Gloucefter. Dr. William Warburton died in 1779. Hon. Dr. James Yorke tranflated from St. David.

LORD-CHAMBERLAIN,
And his Department.

Lord Chamberlains.
Duke of Devonfhire
Nov. 22, 1762, Duke of Marlborough, vice Duke of Devonfhire
April 22, 1763, Earl Gower, vice Duke of Marlborough
July 12, 1765, Duke of Portland, vice Lord Gower
Dec. 4, 1766, Earl of Hertford

Vice-Chamberlains.
Rt. Hon. William Finch
July 12, 1765, Lord Villiers (now Earl of Jerfey) vice Finch
Feb. 13, 1770, Hon. Tho. Robinfon, vice Earl of Jerfey
Feb. 6, 1771. Lord Hinchingbroke, vice Hon. Tho. Robinfon, now Lord Grantham

Grooms of the Stole.
Earl of Rochford
Nov. 25, 1760, Earl of Bute, vice Earl of Rochford

Mar. 25, 1761, Earl of Huntingdon, vice Earl of Bute
Jan. 29, 1770, Earl of Briftol, vice Earl of Huntingdon
March   1775, The Earl of Briftol died
                 Vifcount Weymouth
Nov. 10, 1775, Earl of Afhburnham

Lords of the Bed-Chamber.

Duke of Ancafter, Duke of Manchefter (late), Marquis of Rockingham, Earls of Fauconberg, Lincoln, (now Duke of Newcaftle) Afhburnham, Hertford, Coventry, Hyndford, Northumberland, (now Duke) Effex, Oxford, Buckinghamfhire

Nov. 25, 1760, Marquis of Caernarvon, arl of March, late Earl of Eglingtoun, Vifc. Weymouth, Ld. Bruce, Vifc. Downe, Vifc. Pulteney, and Lord Robert Bertie, appointed additional Lords of the Bed-Chamber

Mar. 25, 1761, Duke of Richmond, vice late Duke of Manchefter
Mar. 25, 1761, Earl of Litchfield, vice Lord Fauconberg
Mar. 25, 1761, Earl of Pembroke, vice Lord Hyndford
Mar. 25, 1761, Earl of Oxford, vice Earl of Effex
Nov. 22, 1762, Lord Mafham, vice Lord Litchfield
Nov. 22, 1762, Lord Bolingbroke, vice Lord Downe
Feb.   1763, Earl of Pomfret, vice Lord Pembroke
Feb.   1763, Ld. Willoughby de Broke, vice Ld. Pulteney
Apr. 22, 1763, Duke of Manchefter, vice Marquis of Rockingham
Apr. 22, 1763, Earl of Denbigh, vice D. of Northumberland
June   1765, Duke of Ancafter ceafed to be a Lord of the Bed Chamber on being appointed Mafter of the Horfe to the Queen
July 12, 1765, Earl Cornwallis, vice Lord Bolingbroke
Aug. 1, 1765, Earl of Hertford difcontinued as Lord of the Bed-Chamber, on being appointed Lord Lieutenant of Ireland
Oct. 5, 1769, Earl of Jerfey
              Duke of Roxburgh, Earl of Pembroke, Lord Vifcount Bolingbroke, Marquis of Carmarthen
Feb.   1777, Earl of Fauconberg

Dec.

[55]

Dec.   1777, Earl of Winchelfea, vice Earl of Jerfey
       Earl of Aylesford, vice Marq. Carmarthen
Sept. 1780, Lord Onflow and Lord Bofton

Grooms of the Bed-Chamber.

Lieu. Gen. Campbell, (late Duke of Argyll) Lieut. Gen. Moftyn, Lieut. Gen. Waldegrave (now Earl) Major Gen. Cornwallis, Major Gen. H. S. Conway, Col. Charles Fitzroy, John Offley, efq.

Nov. 25, 1760, George Schutz, Sir James Peachy, Hon. George Monfon, Charles Ingram, Edmund Nugent, Wm. Breton, Spencer Compton (now Earl of Northampton) Geo. Pitt, Norb. Berkeley (late Lord Bottetourt) appointed additional Grooms of the Bed-Chamber

May   1, 1761, Henry Seymour, vice Lord Waldegrave
Dec.   1762, James (now Sir) Wright, vice Col. Fitzroy
Dec.   1762, Jn. Mordaunt, vice Jn. Offley
Apr. 22, 1763, Cha. Hotham (now Sir Cha. Thompfon)
       vice Colonel Monfon
Apr. 22, 1763, Aug. J. Hervey, vice Lord Northampton.
Apr.   1764. General Conway difmiffed
Feb.   1765, Adm. Keppel, vice Lord Bottetourt
Aug.   1765, Hon. Hen. Wallop, vice Henry Seymour
Apr. 26, 1771, Colonel Nugent died
March,   1775, Aug. John Hervey, vacated on the Death
       of the Earl of Briftol
March,   1775, Hon. Wm. Gordon
       Hon Col. Wn. Harcourt, Hon. H. Vernon, Sir G. Ofborne, bart. Hon. Col. H. St. John, Tho. De Grey, jun. Sir Philip Hales
       1779, Col. Lafcelles, vice Lieut. Gen. Moftyn

LORD-STEWARD's DEPARTMENT.

Lord Steward.
       Duke of Rutland
Mar. 25, 1761, Earl Talbot, vice Duke of Rutland
       Comptrollers.
       Lord Edgcumbe (late)
May 22, 1761, Earl Powis, vice late Lord Edgcumbe
Nov. 25, 1761, Lord Geo. Cavendifh, vice Lord Powis

Nov.

Nov. 22, 1762, Lord Ch. Spencer, vice Lord Geo. Cavendish
July 20, 1765, Thomas Pelham (now Lord Pelham) vice Lord Cha. Spencer
Nov. 10, 1775, Sir William Meredith, vice Lord Pelham
Dec.   1777, Lord Onflow, vice Sir W. Meredith
Nov.   1779, Sir Richard Worfley, vice Lord Onflow

Treafurers.
Lord Thomond
Nov. 25, 1761, Earl Powis, vice Lord Thomond
July 20, 1765, Lord Edgecumbe, vice Lord Powis
Nov. 27, 1766, John Shelley (now Sir) vice Lord Edgecumbe
May   1777, Earl of Carlifle, vice Sir J. Shelley
Nov.   1779, Lotd Onflow, vice Earl of Carlifle
Sept.   1780, Earl of Salifbury, vice Lord Onflow

Cofferers.
Duke of Leeds
April 3, 1761, James Grenville, vice Duke of Leeds
Nov. 25, 1761, Lord Thomond, vice James Grenville
July 20, 1765, Earl of Scarborough, vice Lord Thomond
Dec. 4, 1766, Hans Stanley, vice Lord Scarborough
            1774, Jer. Dyfon, efq. vice Hans Stanley
            1776, Hans Stanley, vice Jer. Dyfon, efq.
Jan.   1780, Lord Beauchamp, vice Hans Stanley

Maflers of the Houfhold.
John Harris
Apr. 19, 1768, Hon. Henry Fred. Thynne, vice J. Harris
Dec. 19, 1770, Sir Fra. Hen. Drake, vice H. F. Thynne

Clerks of the Board of Green Cloth.
Sir Thomas Hales, Sir Fra. Hen. Drake, Hon. John Grey, Humphry Morice
Mar. 25, 1761, Tho. Townfhend, jun. vice Sir Tho. Hales
            John Evelyn, vice Humphry Morice
Nov. 25, 1761, Hen. Bridgman (now Sir) and Simon Fanfhaw, additional Clerks
Dec.   1762, Hon. Henry Frederick Thynne, vice Tho Townfhend
April,   1764, Richard Vernon, vice Henry Bridgman
July 20, 1765, Sir Alex. Gilmour, vice Hen. Fred. Thynne
            Hon. Geo. Bridges Brudenell, vice Richard Vernon
Dec. 4, 1766, Richard Hopkins, vice John Evelyn.

April

April 19, 1768, Richard Vernon, vice Simon Fanſhaw
Dec. 19, 1770, Hon. Richard Savage Naſſau, (died in Aug.
  1780) vice Sir Francis Henry Drake
June, 1777, Sir Ralph Payne
Dec. 1777, Sir Richard Worſley, vice R. Hopkins, efq.
July, 1779, Sir Wm. Aug. Cunynghame, Bart. vice Sir R.
  Worſley
Oct. 1780, Sir William Gordon, vice
  Lovel Stanhope, efq. vice Hon. R. S. Naſſau

MASTERS OF THE HORSE.
Earl Gower
Nov. 25, 1760, Earl of Huntingdon
Mar. 25, 1761, Duke of Rutland
Aug. 1766, Earl of Hertford
Dec. 13, 1766, Duke of Ancaſter, died in Oct. 1778.
Dec. 8, 1778, Duke of Northumberland.
Jan. 1781, Duke of Montagu

CAPTAINS OF THE BAND OF
GENTLEMEN-PENSIONERS.
Lord Berkeley of Stratton
July 17, 1762, Earl of Litchfield
Dec. 8, 1772, Lord Edgcumbe

CAPTAIN OF THE YEOMEN OF THE GUARD.
Lord Viſcount Falmouth

BOARD OF WORKS.
Surveyor General.
Hon. Henry Finch
Dec. 20, 1760, Tho. Worſley, efq. vice Hon. H. Finch.
July 1777, Whitſhed Keene, efq.
  Surveyor of the Private Roads.
Dec. 20, 1760, Hon. Edw. Finch Hatton
July 27, 1771, Tho. Whateley, efq. vice Hon. E. F. Hat-
  ton, deceaſed
July, 1772, Hen. Fane, efq. vice Whateley deceaſed
  Paymaſter of the Works.
George Auguſtus Selwyn, efq.
  Surveyor of the Crown Lands.
Hon. Robert Herbert
1768, Peter Burrel, efq.
Nov. 10, 1775, Hon. John St. John

Surveyor of Gardens, Waters, &c.
Hon. Thomas Hervey
Jan. 20, 1761, George Onslow, esq. (now Lord) vice Hon. Tho. Hervey
Jan. 20, 1763, Lord Charles Spencer, vice Geo. Onslow
May 7, 1762, John Marshe Dickenson, esq. vice Lord Charles Spencer
April, 1764, Hon. Cha. Sloane Cadogan, vice Dickenson
Oct. 5, 1769, William Varey, esq. vice Cadogan

KEEPER OF THE GREAT WARDROBE.

Sir Tho. Robinson, (late Lord Grantham)
Nov. 25, 1769, Earl Gower
May 3, 1763, Lord Le Despencer
July 20, 1765, Earl of Ashburnham
Nov. 10, 1775, Lord Pelham

TREASURER OF THE CHAMBER.

Right Hon. Charles Townshend
Mar. 21, 1761, Right Hon. Sir Francis Dashwood (now Lord Le Despencer)
May 29, 1762, Rt. Hon. Sir Gilbert Elliot
April 12, 1770, Rt. Hon. George Rice, dead.
Nov. 1779, Lord Charles Spencer

MASTER OF THE JEWEL-OFFICE.

Sir Richard Lyttelton
Dec. 1762, Earl of Darlington

QUEEN'S HOUSEHOLD.

At the Establishment of the Queen's Houshold,
Lord Chamberlains.
Earl (now Duke) of Northumberland
April 21, 1763, Earl Harcourt
1768, Earl Delawar
Dec. 1777, Marquis of Carmarthen
Oct. 1780, Lord Southampton
Vice Chamberlains.
Viscount Cantalupe
1768, Hon. Charles Fitzroy, now Ld. Southampton
Masters of the Horse.
Earl Harcourt
April 21, 1763, Viscount Weymouth
May, 1765, Earl Delawar
Jan. 20, 1768, Duke of Beaufort

Nov. 1770, Earl Waldegrave
Treasurers.
Andrew Stone, esq. died in 1774, succeeded by the Earl of Guildford
Secretaries.
David Græme, esq. (now Lieut. Gen.) resigned in 1774, succeeded by Ja. Harris, esq. who was succeeded in 1780 by the Hon. G. A. North
Comptrollers.
Hon. Sewallis Shirley, died October 31, 1765, and succeeded by Gen. Græme, who resigned in 1774, and was succeeded by Ja. Harris, esq.
Attorney General.
Richard Hussey, esq.   John Morton, esq. died in 1780.
      (vacant)
Solicitor General.
Sir William Blackstone, deceased
Charles Ambler, esq. appointed in 1771

PRINCE OF WALES, &c.

Earl of Holderness, *Governor*
Dr. Markham, *Preceptor*
Leonard Smelt, esq. *Sub-Governor*
Rev. Cyril Jackson, *Sub-Preceptor*
May, 1776, Lord Bruce (now Earl of Aylesbury) *Gov.*
 Dr. Hurd, *Preceptor*
 Col. Hotham, *Sub-Governor*
 W. Arnald, D. D. *Sub-Preceptor*
June, 1776, Duke of Montagu, *Governor*
 1777, Bishop of Litchfield and Coventry, *Sub-Govern.*

LORD CHANCELLOR.

At the accession of the present King, Lord Henley was Lord Keeper
Jan. 16, 1761, Lord Henley appointed Lord-Chancellor, and, May 19, 1764, created Earl of Northington
July 30, 1766, Lord Camden appointed Lord-Chancellor
Jan. 17, 1770, Hon. Charles Yorke. Died Jan. 20, 1770
Jan. 22, 1770, Great Seal put into Commission, Sir S. S. Smythe, Hon. Henry Bathurst, and Sir Rich. Aston, Commissioners

Jan.

Jan. 23, 1771, Hon. Henry Bathurſt created Lord Apſley, (now Earl Bathurſt) and appointed Lord Chancellor reſigned in 1778
June 2, 1778, Mr. Thurlow, created Lord Thurlow, and appointed Lord-Chancellor.

LORD-PRESIDENT.

Earl Granville. Died Jan. 2, 1763. Vacant till
Sept. 9, 1763, Duke of Bedford
July 12, 1765, Earl of Winchelſea
July 30, 1766, Earl of Northington
Dec. 23, 1767, Earl Gower
Nov.   1779, Earl Bathurſt

LORD-WARDEN OF THE STANNERIES.

Lord Waldegrave, (the late)
Dec. 20, 1762, Humphry Morice, vice Lord Waldegrave

CHANCELLOR OF THE DUCHY OF LANCASTER.

Lord Kinnoul
Dec. 15, 1762, Lord Strange, vice Lord Kinnoul
June 14, 1771, Lord Hyde, (now Earl of Clarendon) vice Lord Strange

LORD PRIVY SEAL.

Earl Temple
Oct. 12, 1761, In commiſſion. E. Weſton, W. Sharpe, and Jer. Dyſon, Commiſſioners
Nov. 25, 1761, Duke of Bedford
Apr. 20, 1763, Duke of Marlborough
July 15, 1765, Duke of Newcaſtle
July 30, 1766, Earl of Chatham
Nov. 2, 1768, Earl of Briſtol
Feb. 9, 1770, Earl of Halifax
Jan. 22, 1771, Earl of Suffolk
June 12. 1771, Duke of Grafton
Nov. 10, 1775, Earl of Dartmouth

CHIEF-JUSTICES IN EYRE.

Lord Sandys, North of Trent
Earl of Breadalbane, South of Trent
Apr. 14, 1761, Duke of Leeds, N. of Trent
Nov. 5, 1765, Lord Monſon, S. of Trent
Dec. 23, 1766, Earl Cornwallis, S. of Trent
Feb. 19, 1769, Sir Fl. Norton, S. of Trent
         1774, Lord Pelham, N. of Trent

Nov. 10, 1775, Lord Lyttelton, N. of Trent, died in November, 1779
Sept.   1780, C. W. Cornwall, efq. vice Ld. Lyttelton

ATTORNEY AND SOLICITOR GENERAL.

At the Acceſſion of the preſent King,
Attorney,
Charles Pratt, (now Lord Camden)
Dec. 14, 1761, Mr. Yorke, vice Cha Pratt
Nov.   1763, Sir Fl. Norton, vice Mr. Yorke
Aug.   1765, Hon. Charles Yorke, vice Sir Fl. Norton
Aug. 6, 1766, Wm. De Grey, vice Mr. Yorke
Jan. 23, 1771, Ed. Thurlow, vice Mr. De Grey
July   1778, Alexander Wedderburne, (now Ld. Loughborough) vice Mr. Thurlow
Aug..   1780, James Wallace, efq. vice Ld. Loughborough
Solicitor.
Hon. Charles Yorke
Dec. 14, 1761, Fletcher (now Sir) Norton, vice Mr Yorke
Dec. 16, 1764, William De Grey, vice Sir Fletcher Norton
Aug.   1766, Edw. Willes, vice Mr. De Grey
Dec. 23, 1767, Jn. Dunning, vice Ed. Willes
March,   1770, Edw. Thurloe, vice Mr. Dunning
Jan. 23, 1771, Alex. Wedderburne, vice Mr. Thurlow
July, 1778. James Wallace, vice Mr. Wedderburne
Sept. 1780, James Mansfield, efq. vice Mr. Wallace

TREASURY.
Firſt Lords.
Duke of Newcaſtle
May 29, 1762, Earl of Bute
Apr. 16, 1763, George Grenville
July 12, 1765, Marquis of Rockingham
Aug. 2, 1766, Duke of Grafton
Jan. 28, 1770, Lord North
Chancellors of the Exchequer.
Hen. Bilſon Legge
Mar. 21, 1761, Lord Barrington
May 29, 1762, Sir F. Daſhwood, (now Lord Le Deſpencer)
Apr. 16, 1763, George Grenville
July 12, 1765, William Dowdeſwell
Aug. 2, 1766, [Late] Charles Townſhend
Sept. 16, 1767, Lord North

Lords of the Treasury.

James Grenville, Lord North, James Ofwald
Mar. 21. 1761, Gilbert (now Sir Gilbert) Elliot, Bart. vice James Grenville
Apr. 16, 1763, Sir John Turner, vice Elliot
Thomas Orby Hunter, vice Ofwald
James Harris, vice Dafhwood
July 12, 1765, Lord John Cavendifh, vice Sir John Turner
Tho. Townfhend, jun. vice Tho. Orb Hunter
George Onflow, vice James Harris
Aug. 2, 1766, Pryfe Campbell, vice Lord John Cavendifh
Dec. 3, 1767, Cha. Jenkinfon, vice Tho. Townfhend
Dec. 31, 1768, Jeremiah Dyfon, vice Pryfe Campbell
Feb. 6, 1770, Charles Townfhend, vice Lord North
Dec. 1772, Hon. Charles James Fox, vice C. Jenkinfon
1774, Lord Vifc. Beauchamp, and Charles Wolfran Cornwall, efqrs. vice Cha. James Fox and Jeremiah Dyfon
June 1777, Lord Weftcote, vice C. Townfhend
Dec. 1777, Lord Palmerfton, vice Lord Onflow.
Jan. 1780, Sir R. Sutton, vice Lord Vifc. Beauchamp
Oct. 1780, John Buller, fen. efq. vice C. W. Cornwall, efq.

Joint Secretaries.

James Weft and Samuel Martin
May 29, 1762, Jer. Dyfon, vice Ja. Weft
Apr. 16, 1763, Cha. Jenkinfon, vice Samuel Martin
April 1764, Tho. Whately, vice Jer. Dyfon
July 12, 1765, Cha. Lowndes and Grey (now Sir) Cooper, vice Jenkinfon and Dyfon
Aug. 2, 1766, Thomas Bradfhaw, vice Cha. Lowndes
Feb. 6, 1770, John Robinfon, vice Tho. Bradfhaw

Secretaries to the firft Lord.

May 29, 1762, Charles Jenkinfon
July 12, 1765, Edmund Burke
Aug. 2, 1766, Rd. Stonhewer, vice Burke

Secretaries to the Chancellor of the Exchequer.

John Buller
July 12, 1765, Sir Edward Winnington
Jan. 1770, William Brummell, efq.

Sol/.

Solicitors to the Treasury.
Philip Carteret Webb
July 12, 1765, Thomas Nuthall, vice Philip Carteret Webb
March, 1775, Wm. Chamberlayne, esq. vice T. Nuthall, deceased
H. V. Jones, esq.

SECRETARIES OF STATE.
Southern Department.
William Pitt, now Lord Chatham, died in 1778
Oct. 9, 1761, Earl of Egremont
Sept. 9, 1763, Earl of Sandwich
July 12, 1765, Henry Seymour Conway
May, 23, 1766, Duke of Richmond
Aug. 2, 1766, Earl of Shelburne
Oct. 21, 1768, Lord Weymouth
Dec. 19, 1770, Earl of Rochford
Nov. 10, 1775, Viscount Weymouth
Nov. 1779, Earl of Hillsborough

Northern Department.
Earl of Holderness
Mar. 25, 1761, Earl of Bute
May 29, 1762, George Grenville
Oct. 14, 1762, Earl of Halifax
July 12, 1765, Duke of Grafton
May 23, 1766, Henry Seymour Conway
Jan. 20, 1768, Lord Weymouth
Oct. 21, 1768, Earl of Rochford
Dec. 19, 1770, Earl of Sandwich
Jan. 22, 1771, Earl of Halifax
June 12, 1771, Earl of Suffolk, died in June, 1779.
Oct. 27, 1779, Viscount Stormont

For the Colonies.
Jan. 20, 1768, Earl of Hillsborough
Aug. 14, 1772, Earl of Dartmouth
Nov. 10, 1775, Lord Geo. Germain

BOARD OF TRADE
First Lord.
Earl of Halifax
Mar. 21, 1761, Lord Sandys
Mar. 1, 1763, Charles Townshend (the late)
Apr. 20, 1763, Lord Shelburne

Sept. 9, 1763, Lord Hillſborough
July 20, 1765, Lord Dartmouth
Aug. 16, 1766, Lord Hilſborough
Dec.   1766, Lord Clare
Aug. 31, 1772, Lord Dartmouth
Nov.   1775, Lord George Germain
Nov.   1779, Earl of Carliſle
     Lords of Trade.
Andrew Stone, Thomas Pelham (now Lord), Soame Jenyns,
 Wm. Gerard Hamilton, Wm. Sloper, Ed. Elliot, Ed. Bacon
Mar. 21, 1761, Hon. J. Yorke, vice Pelham
Mar. 21, 1761, Sir Edmund Thomas, vice Hamilton
Mar. 21, 1761, George Rice, vice Sloper
Oct. 23, 1761, John Roberts, vice Andrew Stone
Dec.   1762, Lord Orwell, vice J. Roberts
Apr. 20, 1763, Jeremiah Dyſon, vice John Yorke
April 20, 1763, Bamber Gaſcoigne, vice Sir Edmund Thomas
July 20, 1765, Hen. John Yorke, vice Lord Orwell
July 20, 1765, John Roberts, vice Bamber Gaſcoigne
July 20, 1765, William Fitzherbert, vice Edward Bacon
Dec.   1765, Lord Palmerſton, vice John Yorke
Sept.   1766, Hon. Tho. Robinſon (now Lord Gran-
    tham) vice Lord Palmerſton
Jan. 20, 1768, Lord Liſburne, vice Jerem. Dyſon
April 12, 1770, Lord Greville, vice Hon. Thomas Ro-
    binſon (now Lord Grantham)
April 16, 1770, William Northey, vice Lord Liſburne
Jan. 26, 1771, Thomas Whately, vice William Northey
Feb. 11, 1772, William Jollyffe, vice Wm. Fitzherbert
Aug. 15, 1772, Lord Garlies, vice Thomas Whately
Aug. 31, 1772, Lord Robert Spencer, vice John Roberts
    1774, Hon. Charles Greville and Whitſhed Keene,
    eſqrs. vice Lord Greville and Lord Garlies
June,   1777, Thomas De Grey, vice Whit. Keene
   W. Eden, vice Lord Garlies
July,   1779, Andrew Stuart and Edward Gibbon, Eſqrs.
    vice Meſſrs. Gaſcoigne and Jollyffe.
Oct.   1780, Hans Sloane and Benj. Langlois, vice Soame
    Jenyns and C. F. Greville

PAYMASTER-GENERAL OF THE FORCES.
  Right Hon. Henry Fox (afterward Lord Holland)
June 8, 1765, Right Hon. Charles Townſhend

               Aug.

Aug. 2, 1766, Right Hon. Lord North and Geo. Cooke, efq
Dec. 3, 1767, Right Hon. T. Townſhend, vice Lord North
June 5, 1768, George Cooke, efq. died
June 14, 1768, Right Hon. Richard Rigby appointed ſole paymaſter

MINT.
Warden.
John Jefferies, eſq.
Feb. —1766, Gen. Whitmore
Oct. 1, 1771, Robert Pigot, vice Whitmore
Maſter and Worker.
Hon. William Chetwynd
June 3, 1769, Charles Sloan (now Lord) Cadogan, vice Hon. Wm. Chetwynd
Comptroller.
John Buller, eſq.
Surveyor of the Meltings, &c.
Geo. A. Selwyn

POST-MASTER GENERAL.
Joint Poſt-Maſters.
Earl of Beſborough, Hon. Robert Hamden (now Lord Trevor)
Nov. 27, 1762, Earl of Egmont, vice Earl of Beſborough
Sept. 10, 1763, Lord Hyde, vice Earl of Egmont
July 20, 1765, Earl of Beſborough, vice Lord Hyde
July 20, 1765, Lord Grantham (late) vice Lord Trevor
Dec. 27, 1766, Earl of Hillſborough, Lord Le Deſpenſer
Jan. 20, 1768, Earl of Sandwich, vice Earl of Hillſborough
Dec. 19, 1770, Hon. Hen. Fred. Thynne Carteret, vice Earl of Sandwich
Lord Le Deſpencer

SECRETARY AT WAR.
Right Hon. Lord Barrington
Mar. 24, 1761, Right Hon. Charles Townſhend (late)
Feb. 27, 1763, Right Hon. Welbore Ellis
July 20, 1765, Lord Barrington
1778, Charles Jenkinſon, eſq.

ADMIRALTY.
Firſt Lord.
Lord Anſon
June 19, 1762, Lord Halifax

Oct. 16, 1762, George Grenville
April 16, 1763, Lord Sandwich
Sept. 9, 1763, Lord Egmont
Sept. 16, 1766, Sir Charles Saunders
Dec. 2, 1766, Sir Edward Hawke
Jan. 12, 1771, Lord Sandwich

Lords of the Admiralty.

Admiral Boscawen, Dr. Hay, Thomas Orby Hunter, Gilbert (now Sir Gilbert) Elliot, Admiral Forbes, Hans Stanley
Mar. 21, 1761, Lord Villiers, vice Admiral Boscawen
Thomas Pelham, vice Gilbert Elliot
Jan. 1, 1762, Lord Carysfort, vice Lord Villiers
James Harris, vice Thomas Pelham
April 16, 1763, Lord Howe, vice T. O. Hunter
Lord Digby, vice James Harris
Hon. Thomas Pitt, vice Admiral Forbes
July 2, 1765, Sir Charles Saunders, vice Lord Carysfort
Admiral Keppel, vice Dr. Hay
C. Townshend, vice Lord Howe
Sir William Meredith, vice Lord Digby
John Buller, vice Hans Stanley
Dec. 1765, Hon. John Yorke, vice Hon. Tho. Pitt
Sept. 16, 1766, Sir George Yonge, vice Sir C. Saunders, made first Lord
Lord Palmerston, vice Hon. John Yorke
Dec. 2, 1766, Sir Piercy Brett, vice Admiral Keppel
Charles Jenkinson, vice Sir W. Meredith
Mar. 19, 1768, Lord Charles Spencer, vice C. Jenkinson
Feb. 1770, Admiral Holbourne, vice Sir G. Yonge
Feb. 1770, Charles James Fox, vice Sir Piercy Brett
Lord Lisburne, vice Charles Townshend
Jan. 26, 1771, Aug. John Hervey, vice Admiral Holbourne
May 6, 1772, Thomas Bradshaw, vice Cha. J. Fox
Dec. 23, 1774, Henry Penton, vice Tho. Bradshaw, deceased
April 1775, Sir Hugh Pallifer, bart. vice Aug. John Hervey, called to the House of Peers on the death of his brother the Earl of Bristol
Dec. 1777, Lord Mulgrave, vice Lord Palmerston.
April 1779, Admiral Mann, vice Sir Hugh Pallifer
July, 1779, Bamber Gascoyne, esq. vice Ld. C. Spencer

Oct.   1780, C. F. Greville, and G. Derby, efqrs. vice J. Buller and R. Mann, efqrs.

COMMISSIONERS OF THE NAVY.

Treafurer.
Right Hon. Geo. Grenville
June 2, 1762, Lord Barrington
Aug. 9, 1765, Lord Howe
Mar. 19, 1770, Sir Gilbert Elliot, bart. died in 1777
June   1777, Welbore Ellis

Comptroller.
George Cokburne, efq.
July 31, 1770, Sir Hugh Pallifer, bart. vice George Cockburne, efq. deceafed
April   1775, Maurice Suckling, efq. vice Sir Hugh Pallifer, made a Lord of the Admiralty
July   1778, C. Middleton, vice Mr. Suckling, deceafed

Joint Surveyors.
Thomas Slade, efq. William Bately, efq.
Oct. 10, 1765, John Williams, efq. vice Wm. Bately, efq. fuperannuated
Feb. 26, 1771, John Williams (now Sir John) and Edw. Hunt, vice Sir Tho. Slade, deceafed.

Clerk of the Acts.
Daniel Devert, efq.
1766, Edmund Mafon, efq. D. Devert, efq.
July 1, 1773, G. Marſh, efq. vice E. Mafon. efq. deceafed

Comptroller of the Treafurer's Accounts.
Richard Hall, efq.
1761, Timothy Brett, efq. vice Richard Hall, efq. deceafed

Comptroller of the Victualling Accounts.
Robert Ofborn, efq.
June 26, 1771, Charles Proby, efq. vice Robert Ofborn, efq. deceafed
Oct. 24, 1771, Thomas Hanway, efq. vice Charles Proby, efq. removed to Chatham
Oct. 8, 1772, G. Marſh, efq. vice T. Hanway, efq. deceafed
1773, James Gambier, efq. vice George Marſh, efq.

Clerk of the Acts
1773, William Palmer, efq. vice James Gambier, efq. removed to Portfmouth

Comp-

Comptroller of the Store-keeper's Accounts.
George Adams, esq. [signed
1761, Hon. Wm. Bateman, vice Geo. Adams, re-
Extra Commissioners.
Hon. Wm. Bateman. None appointed in his room
Digby Dent, esq.
Timothy Brett, esq.
1761, Sir Richard Temple, bart. vice Tim. Brett, esq.
Comptroller of the Treasurer's Accounts
1762, Sir John Bentley, vice Digby Dent, esq. deceased.
This appointment discontinued, on Sir John's promotion to
a flag, and only one extra commissioner, until
May, 1779, Sir R. Temple, bart. and Edward Le Cras, esq.
They had last year but 500l. each, but now they are raised to
800l.

AT THE PORTS.
Chatham.
Thomas Cooper, esq.
1765, Thomas Hanway, esq. vice Thomas Cooper,
esq. superannuated
Oct. 24, 1771, Charles Proby, esq. vice Thomas Hanway,
esq. appointed Comptroller of the Vic-
tualling Accounts.
Portsmouth.
Richard Hughes, esq. (now Sir Rich. Hughes, bart.)
1773, James Gambier, esq. vice Sir Richard
Hughes, bart. superannuated
1778, SiSam. Hood, vice J. Gambier
Plymouth.
Fred. Rogers, esq. (now Sir F. Rogers, bart.)
Feb. 1775, Paul Henry Ourry, esq. vice Sir Fred. Rogers,
bart. superannuated
Gibraltar.
Oct. 1763, Charles Colby, esq. superannuated, and none
appointed in his room, until
June, 1779, J. A. Pownall, is said to be *Naval Officer* of
Gibraltar, with an Appointment of 200l. a year.
Halifax.
April 1775, Marriot Arbuthnot, esq.

NAVAL DEPARTMENT.
Vice-Admiral of Great Britain.
Lord Anson.
Jan,

Jan. 4, 1763, Henry Osborne, vice Lord Anson, deceased
Nov. 5, 1765, Sir E. Hawke, vice Henry Osborne, resigned
 Rear-Admiral of Great Britain.
 Sir William Rowley
Jan. 4, 1763, Sir Edward Hawke, vice Sir Wm. Rowley
Nov. 5, 1765, Sir Charles Knowles, vice Sir E. Hawke
Oct. 1770, Sir Francis Holburne, vice Sir Charles Knowles
Aug. 17, 1771, Sir George Bridges Rodney, vice Sir Fra. Holburne
 Vice-Admiral of Scotland.
 Earl Finlater
Dec. 22, 1764, John Earl of Hyndford, vice Lord Finlater
Nov. 5, 1765, Earl of March, vice Earl of Hyndford
 1776, Earl of Breadalbane, vice Lord March
 Master of Greenwich Hospital.
 Admiral Isaac Townshend
Nov. 30, 1765, Sir George Bridges Rodey, vice Admiral Townshend
June 15, 1771, Sir Francis Holburne, vice Sir George Bridges Rodney
Aug. 17, 1771, Sir Charles Hardy, vice Sir Francis Holburne deceased
Sept. 1780, Sir Hugh Pallifer, vice Sir C. Hardy, deceased

BOARD OF ORDNANCE.
 Master General.
 Lord Ligonier
May 14, 1763, Marquis of Granby, vice Earl of Ligonier
Oct. 18, 1770, Marquis of Granby died, and no Master-General was appointed till [Granby
Oct. 17, 1772, Lord Visc. Townshend, vice Marquis of
 Lieutenant General.
 Marquis of Granby
May 14, 1763, Lord Visc. Townshend, vice Marquis of Granby
Oct. 24, 1767, Right Hon. Henry Seymour Conway, vice Geo. Visc. Townshend
Oct. 22, 1772, Sir Jeffery Amherst, now Lord Amherst, vice H. S. Conway
 Surveyor.
 Charles (now Sir) Frederick

             Clerk

[70]

Clerk of the Ordnance.
William Rawlinson Earle, esq.
Dec. 18, 1772, Sir Charles Cocks Bart. vice Wm. Rawlinson Earle, who resigned

Storekeeper.
Andrew Wilkinson, esq.
Dec.   1762, Sir Edw. Winnington, vice And. Wilkinson
Sept. 7, 1765, And. Wilkinson, esq. vice Sir Edw. Winnington
July 1778. Benj. Langlois, esq. vice Mr. Wilkinson
Oct. 1780, Henry Strachey, esq. vice Mr. Langlois.

Clerk of the Deliveries.
Charles (now Sir) Cocks
Dec. 18, 1772, Benj. L'Anglois, esq. vice Sir Charles Cocks
July 1775. Henry Strachey esq. vice Mr. L' Anglois
Oct. 1780, John Kenrick, esq. vice Mr. Strachey.

Treasurer.
Francis Gashry, esq.
June 1, 1762, Charles Jenkinson, esq. vice Francis Gashry
May 14, 1763, John Rofs Mackye, esq. vice Charles Jenkinson
Oct. 1780, William Adam, esq. vice Mr. Mackye.

GOVERNORS OF FORTS, &c.
IN GREAT-BRITAIN.

Fort Augustus and Fort George, near Inverness, Sir Ch. Howard, died in Sept. 1765, and was succeeded by Gen. Studholme Hodgson

Berwick and Holy Island, Gen. John Guise, died in June, 1765, and was succeeded by Gen. Monckton, who was succeeded by Sir John Mordaunt

Blackness, Hon. Charles Hope Weir, who was succeeded by the Duke of Hamilton

Carlisle, Gen. Stanwix, lost in his passage to Ireland, and was succeeded by the Earl of Darlington

Chester, Earl Cholmondeley, died June 10, 1770, and was succeeded by his brother, Gen. Cholmondeley, who dying in 1775, was succeeded by Charles Rainford, esq.

Cinque Ports, Duke of Dorset, died Oct. 9, 1765, and succeeded by the Earl of Holderness died in 1778, and succeeded by Lord North

Dart-

Dartmouth, Arthur Holdſworth -
Dumbarton, Earl of Eglington
Edinburgh, Lieut. Gen. Humphry Bland.——At preſent,
  Earl of Loudoun
Graveſend, Lord Cadogan, who was ſucceeded by William
  Faucitt, eſq.
Guernſey, Lord Delawar, died March 14, 1766, and was ſuc-
  ceeded by Sir Rich. Lyttelton, who died Oct. 1, 1770,
  and was ſucceeded by Sir Jeffery (now ord) Amherſt
Hull, Gen. Pulteney, reſigned in July, 1766, and was ſuc-
  ceeded by Gen. Honywood
Hurſt, Sir Henry Bellenden; at preſent, Robert Sloper, eſq.
Jerſey, Gen. Huſke, who died in Jan. 1761, and was ſuc-
  ceeded by the Earl of Albemarle, who died Oct. 13, 1772,
  and was ſucceeded by Gen. Conway
Landguard, Lord George Beauclerk, died in May, 1768; then
  Gen. Armiger, and, March 19, 1770, Gen. Clavering;
  after him, the Hon. Alex. Mackay
Pendennis, Col. Arth. Owen, died in 1774, and was ſuccee-
  ded by Col. Beauclerk, who died 1775, and was ſucceeded
  by M. Gen. Robinſon
Plymouth, Gen. Waldegrave, (now Earl)
Portſmouth, Lord Tyrawley, died July, 1773, and was ſuc-
  ceeded by Gen. Harvey, who died in 1778, and was ſuc-
  ceeded by Gen. Monckton.
Scilly, Earl of Godolphin, died Jan. 17, 1766
Sheerneſs, Sir John Mordaunt; at preſent Lt. Gen. Craig
Stirling, Earl of Loudoun.——At preſent, Sir James Camp-
  bell, bart.
Tynmouth, Sir Andrew Agnew, died Aug. 14, 1771, and
  was ſucceeded by the Hon. Maj. Gen. Alex. Mackay; at
  preſent, Lord Adam Gordon
Upnor, Col. Deane, died in 1775, and ſucceeded by Lieut.
  Col. James Murray; at preſent, W. Browne, eſq.
Iſle of Wight, Earl of Portſmouth; then Lord Holmes;
  then Hans Stanley; Dec. 23, 1766, Duke of Bolton; and
  in 1770, Hans Stanley; who in 1774 had a grant of it for
  life, died Jan. 1780, now Sir Rich. Worſley, Bart.
Fort William, Gen. Kingſley, died in Nov. 1769, and was
  ſucceeded by Gen. Burgoyne, who reſigned in October,
  1779, and was ſucceeded by Major General Vaughan.

Wind-

Windsor, Earl of Cardigan, (now Duke of Montagu)
Chelsea Hospital, Sir Robert Rich, died Feb. 1, 1768, and was succeeded by Gen. Mostyn, who was succeeded by Gen. (now Sir Geo.) Howard, K. B.

LIEUTENANTS, &c. IN ENGLAND.

Bedford, Duke of Bedford. Succeeded at his death, in Jan. 1771, by the Earl of Upper Ossory

Berks, Duke of St. Albans. Succeeded, , 176 , by Lord Vere; and in July 19, 1771, Duke of St. Albans was again appointed

Bucks, Earl Temple. Succeeded, May 9, 1763, by Lord Le Despencer

Cambridge, Viscount Royston, now Earl of Hardwicke

Chester, Earl Cholmondeley. Died June 10, 1770, and was succeeded by his grandson, the present Earl Cholmondeley

Cornwall, Lord Edgcumbe

Cumberland, Earl of Egremont, Cust. Rot. Died Aug. 21, 1763, and was succeeded by Sir James Lowther, since appointed Ld. Lieut.

Derby, Duke of Devonshire. Feb. 21, 1763, Marquis of Granby appointed in his room; and June 17, 1766, Lord George Cavendish

Devon, Duke of Bedford. Succeeded at his death, in Jan. 1771, by Earl Powlett

Dorset, Earl of Shaftesbury. Died April 21, 1771, and was succeeded, June 7, following, by Lord Digby

Durham, Bishop of Durham, Cust. Rot. Earl of Darlington, Lord Lieut.

Essex, Earl of Rochford

Gloucester, Lord Chedworth. Succeeded in 1763, by Norb. Berkeley, esq. afterwards Lord Botetourt, and on July 1, 1766, the Earl of Berkeley was appointed

Hereford, Viscount Bateman

Hertford, Earl Cowper. Died Sept. 18, 1764; Oct. 19, 1764, Earl of Essex was appointed; and Mar. 1, 1771, Viscount Cranburn, now Earl of Salisbury, vice the Earl of Essex

Huntingdon, Duke of Manchester, who died May 10, 1762, and was succeeded by the present Duke of Manchester.

Kent, Duke of Dorset. Died Feb. 9, 1769. The present Duke of Dorset is now Lord Lieut.

Lancaster, Lord Strange. Died June 1, 1771, and was succeeded, July 19 following, by the Earl of Derby.
Leicester, Duke of Rutland
Lincoln, Duke of Ancaster; died in 1778, and succeeded, by the present Duke
Middlesex, Duke of Newcastle. Succeeded, 1763, by the Earl (now Duke) of Northumberland
Monmouth, T. Morgan, esq. At present, the Duke of Beaufort
Norfolk, Earl of Orford
Northampton, Earl of Halifax. Died June 8, 1771, and on July 19, 1771, Earl of Northampton appointed
Northumberland, Earl of Northumberland, (now Duke)
Nottingham, Duke of Newcastle. Succeeded, Jan. 10, 1763, by the late Duke of Kingston; Sept. 7, 1765, late Duke of Newcastle; and on Dec. 16, 1768, the present Duke of Newcastle appointed
Oxford, Duke of Marlborough
Rutland, Earl of Exeter; at present, the Earl of Winchelsea.
Salop, Earl Powis. Succeeded 176 , by the Earl of Bath, who died July 8, 1764, and was succeeded, Aug. 17, 1764, by Earl Powis, who died in 1772, and was succeeded, Oct. 9, 1772, by Lord Clive who died in 1774, and was succeeded in 1775 by his son, Lord Clive
Somerset, Earl Powlett. Died Nov. 3, 1764, and Nov. 30, 1764, Earl of Thomond appointed, who died in 1774, and was succeeded by Lord North
Southampton, Duke of Bolton. Died 1765, and was succeeded by the Marquis of Caernarvon; and on Aug. 21, 1764, the Earl of Northington was appointed; and on Jan. 23, 1771, the Marquis of Caernarvon (now Duke of Chandos) was again appointed
Stafford, Earl Gower
Suffolk, Duke of Grafton. Succeeded, Feb. 8, 1763, by Lord Maynard; and on June 3, 1769, Duke of Grafton again appointed
Surrey, Lord Onslow, died in 1776, George Lord Onslow
Sussex, Duke of Richmond, appointed Oct. 18, 1763
Warwick, Earl of Hertford
Westmoreland, Sir James Lowther
Wilts, Earl of Pembroke
Worcester, Earl of Coventry
Yorkshire, West Riding, Marquis of Rockingham. Succeeded in 1762 by the Earl of Huntingdon; and on Aug.

17, 1765, the Marq. of Rockingham was again appointed.
Ditto, North Riding, Earl of Holdernesse, Lord Lieut Marquis of Rockingham, Cuft. Rot. re-appointed Aug. 17, 1765; at present, Earl Fauconberg, lord lieutenant, vice Earl of Holdernesse

Ditto, East Riding. Earl of Holdernesse, died in 1778, Marquis of Carmarthen appointed

Tower Hamlets, Earl Cornwallis, who died in 1762. Succeeded by the late Lord Berkeley of Stratton, and on Dec. 8, 1770, the present Earl Cornwallis was appointed

OFFICERS OF STATE IN SCOTLAND.

Lord Justice General.

Marquis of Tweedale. (late)

Apr. 16, 1763, Duke of Queenfbury, vice Marquis of Tweedale, deceased

In 1778 the Duke of Queenfbury died, and Lord Stormont was appointed.

Keeper of the Great Seal.

Archibald, (late) Duke of Argyll

May, 1761, Duke of Queenfbury

April 16, 1763, James, Duke of Athol, vice Duke of Queenfbury

Jan. 28, 1764, Earl of Marchmont, vice Duke of Athol, deceased

Lord Privy Seal.

James (late) Duke of Athol

Apr. 16, 1763, Rt. Hon. J. S. Mackenzie, vice Duke of Athol

Apr. 30, 1765, Ld. F. Campbell, vice J. Stuart Mackenzie

Nov. 5, 1765, Earl of Breadalbane, vice Ld. Fred. Campbell

Aug 30, 1766, Jas. Stuart Mackenzie, vice the Earl of Breadalbane

Lord Register.

Earl of Morton (late)

1768, Lord Fred. Campbell, vice late Ld. Morton

Lord President of Police.

Earl of Marchmont

Jan. 28, 1764, Lord Cathcart, vice Earl of Marchmont

Sept. 1776, Lord March, (now Duke of Queenfbury) vice Lord Cathcart

Vice Admiral.

Earl Finlater

Dec.

Dec. 22, 1764, J. Earl of Hyndford, vice the Earl of Finlater
Aug. 30, 1766, James, Earl of March, vice the Earl of Hyndford
Sept. 1776, Earl of Breadalbane, vice Lord March
Secretary to the Order of the Thistle.
George Drummond, esq.
Apr. 13, 1765, Sir H. Erskine, vice G. Drummond, esq.
Aug. 1765, George Dempster, esq. for life, vice Sir Harry Erskine

OFFICERS OF STATE IN IRELAND.
Lord Lieutenant.
Duke of Bedford
Mar. 20, 1761, Earl of Halifax
Apr. 20, 1763, Duke of Northumberland
Apr. 30, 1765, Viscount Weymouth
Aug. 1, 1765, Earl of Hertford
Sept. 26, 1766, Earl of Bristol
Aug. 12, 1767, Lord Viscount Townshend
Oct. 9, 1772, Earl Harcourt
Dec. 18, 1776, Earl of Buckinghamshire
Oct. 13, 1780, Earl of Carlisle

Clerk of the Pells.
George Dodington (afterwards Lord Melcombe)
1763, Rt. Hon. Henry Fox (afterwards Lord Holland) for life, and also for the lives of his two sons, Stephen and Charles James, died in 1774, and succeeded by his eldest son Stephen, late Lord Holland, who also died in 1774, and was succeeded by his brother the Hon. Cha. James Fox, who resigned Oct. 1775, and was succeeded by Charles Jenkinson, esq.

Joint Vice Treasurers.
Earl of Sandwich, Rt. Hon. Welbore Ellis, Right Hon. Robert Nugent (now Lord Clare)
Dec. 1762, Rt. Hon. Rich. Rigby, vice Welbore Ellis
Feb. 19, 1763, Rt. Hon. J. Oswald, vice Earl of Sandwich
July 12, 1765, Rt. Hon. Welbore Ellis, vice Ld. Clare
Dec. 20, 1765, Right Hon. Lord George Sackville (now Germain) vice Richard Rigby
Aug. 1766, Right Hon. James Grenville, vice Lord George Sackville
Oct. 1766, Right Hon. Isaac Barré, vice Welb. Ellis
Jan. 20, 1768, Rt. Hon. Richard Rigby, vice James Oswald

June 14, 1768, Lord Clare, vice Rigby
Lord Edgcumbe, vice Isaac Barré
Feb. 2, 1770, Right Hon. Wel. Ellis, vice Jas. Grenville
Dec. 8, 1772, Right Hon. Charles Jenkinson, vice Lord Edgcumbe
Oct. 1775, Right Hon. H. Flood, vice C. Jenkinson
1777, Rt. Hon. Ch. Townshend, vice Welbore Ellis

INDEX OF OFFICES.

Admiralty — 65
Attorney and Solicitor General — 61
Bishops — 51
Board of Works — 58
Board of Trade — 63
Chancellor, Lord — 59
Chancellor of the Duchy of Lancaster — 60
Chamberlain, Lord, his Department — 53
Chief Justices in Eyre — 60
Captain of the Band of Gentlemen Pensioners — 57
Captain of the Yeomen of the Guard — 57
Commissioners of the Navy — 67
Governors of Forts — 70
Jewel Office — 58
Ireland — 76
Lieutenants of Counties — 72
Master of the Horse — 57
Mint — 65
Naval Department — 68
Ordnance — 69
Paymaster-General of the Forces — 64
Postmaster-General — 65
President, Lord — 60
Privy Seal, Lord — 60
Queen's Houshold — 58
Scotland — 74
Secretaries of State — 63
Secretary at War — 65
Steward, Lord, his Department — 55
Treasury — 61
Treasurer of the Chamber — 58
Warden, Lord, of Stanneries — 60
Wardrobe, Great — 58
Wales, Prince — 59

APPEN-

APPENDIX.

Case of the Borough of ABINGDON.—*Petitioner, Nathaniel Bayley, Esq.*—*Sitting Member, John Mayor, Esq.*

The case was, that Mr. Mayor at the time of the election was high sheriff for the county of Berks, and he returned himself duly elected, in manifest prejudice of the petitioner, who being the only candidate capable of being elected, was duly chosen, and ought to have been returned. There were two points therefore in this case: 1. Whether the high sheriff of a county may be chosen to serve in parliament for a borough within his county? 2. Whether, if he is not eligible, on such notice as was given in the present case, the votes for him are thrown away, and the other candidate who had a smaller number of legal votes duly elected, or whether it is a void election?

The counsel for the petitioner argued, that by an express clause in the writ of election, the choice of sheriffs is prohibited, and they quoted several eminent authorities, Sir Simon D'Ewes, Mr. Hakewell, Lord Chief Justice Hale, Mr. Justice Blackstone, &c. to move that it had been constantly the law of parliament to prohibit sheriffs from being chosen either for county or borough within the county. The counsel for the sitting member said that the authority of *civil* writ was unquestionable, but it was not so with political writs. They rather testify, and particularly the writs of election, the tyranny of our kings and the arbitrary power they assumed in former periods of the constitution, than afford any evidence of the law. And they shewed that there were many directions in the writ which were not complied with. If the prohibition were strictly to be adhered to, a sheriff for one county could not be chosen knight of the shire for another; but that would not be asserted in the present day; then if they are eligible for any other county, why should they not be for boroughs in their own.

The Committee decided, that neither the sitting member nor the petitioner were duly elected, and that the election was void.

Case of the city and county of the city of BRISTOL.—*Petitioners, Mathew Bricklade, Esq. certain freeholders and free burgesses of the city and county of the city of* BRISTOL.

Against

Againſt, *Henry Cruger the younger*, *Eſq.* and *Edmund Burke*, *Eſq. ſitting members*.

The petitions ſet forth that the election was holden on the 7th of October, and that *at the election* the petitioner, Mr. Bricklade, together with Robert Craggs, Lord Viſcount Clare, of the kingdom of Ireland, and Henry Cruger the younger, Eſq. and no other perſons, were candidates; that a poll was *then* demanded for each of the three candidates, proceeded upon and adjourned to the following day; that on the ſucceeding day, Lord Clare declined proceeding on the poll; and that Mr. Bricklade, the petitioner, having that day a majority of votes, ought to have been declared duly elected, and to have been returned; but that Edmund Burke, Eſq. was on the ſame day, the 8th of October, firſt named a candidate; that the ſheriffs afterwards on the 10th of October, and not before, awarded a poll to be taken for Mr. Burke, notwithſtanding the proteſtation of Mr. Bricklade, and many of the electors, to the contrary.

That, in order to influence the election, many perſons were admitted to the freedom of the city, after the date and iſſuing forth of the writ, to poll for Mr. Burke and Mr. Cruger.——That divers perſons not legally admitted to this freedom, nor having any right to vote, were admitted to poll for Mr. Burke and Mr. Cruger; and that Mr. Burke and Mr. Cruger, by themſelves, and their agents and others by their privity and direction, before and during the poll, were guilty of bribery.

From theſe allegations, it appeared that there were ſeveral queſtions in the caſe.

1. Whether a perſon may be elected who becomes a candidate on a day ſubſequent to that on which the election was appointed to be holden, and on which the poll commenced?

2. Whether perſons admitted to the freedom of the city of Briſtol after the date and iſſuing of the writ for the election of members of parliament for that city, have a right to vote at ſuch election?

3. Whether Mr. Burke and Mr. Cruger, or either of them, were guilty of bribery?

The committee proceeded to the diſcuſſion of the firſt of theſe queſtions, and after hearing the arguments of counſel pro and con. declared Mr. Burke was eligible.

They then proceeded to the remainder of the caſe. The Houſe had made no determination on the right of election in Briſtol;

Briftol; but it feemed to be taken for granted on both fides, that it is " in the freeholders, having freeholds of forty fhillings a year, and the free burgeffes." To prove that it had been the cuftom not to admit perfons made free after the tefte, feveral witneffes were called, and many arguments ftated, which were anfwered by the counfel for the fitting members; and an attempt was made to fupport the allegations of bribery: they faid that a number of gentlemen paid the fees of admiffion for the new freemen, with money raifed by fubfcription for that purpofe, but neither of the candidates had fubfcribed or paid any of that money. This charge was anfwered by an affertion that as there was no proof of bribery brought home to them, no condition had been annexed to the payment of their fees of admiffion; they were not bound to vote for the fitting members upon that account; it was therefore perfectly innocent on the part of thofe who had done it; but there had been no proof attempted of any money being paid by the fitting members for admiffion fees.

The committee declared the two fitting members to be duly elected.

Cafe of the Borough of BEDFORD.—*Petitioners, Samuel Whitbread, Efq. and John Howard, Efq. certain burgeffes, freemen and inhabitants, being freeholders of Bedford, and electors for that borough.—Sitting members, Sir William Wake, Bart. and Robert Sparrow, Efq.*

The petition of Mr. Whitbread and Mr. Howard contained a charge of bribery againft the fitting members; and the other petition alledged, that the mayor, aldermen, and other officers of the borough, had, previous to the election, got a majority of *pretended* electors under their own influence, with a defign to render the election fubfervient to the will of the corporation: that they had corruptly made offers to one or more perfons to procure them to be elected members, in confideration of a large fum of money to be paid to them; and that John Cawne, John Rofe, and Thomas Howard, the returning officers, had been guilty of corrupt, partial, and illegal practices.

The laft determination of the Houfe on the right of election in Bedford is on the 12th April, 1690. The difference between a burgefs and a freeman in Bedford is, that all the fons of a burgefs are entitled to be burgeffes, and only the eldeft fon of a freeman is entitled to be a freeman. The magiftrates are all chosen out of the burgesses. There were several questions in this case upon the construction of the last determination. 1st Point. The counsel for the petitioners contended, that the expression "being householders of Bedford," was to be applied as well to the burgesses and freemen as to the inhabitants; or, in other words, that non-resident burgesses and freemen have no right to vote. After hearing the arguments on both sides, the committee came to a resolution, " that in their opinion the words being householders of Bedford, contained in the resolution of the House of Commons, of 12 April, 1690, do not refer to the *burgesses* and *freemen*, but to the *inhabitants* only."

2d Point. The petitioners contended, that all the non-resident freemen and burgesses were *honorary* and *occasional*. On this the committee declared, " that they were clear in their opinion, that the objection of occasionality did not lie against freemen made above a year before the election." They did not determine on the point of honorary freemen.

The next point was, whether persons having received of a charity called Harpur's charity, within a year before the election, were entitled to vote; or whether they were disqualified under the words *receiving alms*. After hearing the arguments of both sides, and referring to the acts and precedents, " the committee were of opinion, that persons receiving Sir William Harpur's charity are not thereby disqualified, within the meaning of the determination of 12 April, 1690, from voting for members of parliament for Bedford."

The next point was, that thirty-six votes should be added to the poll of the petitioners, who had been rejected because they had come into the parishes where they resided in Bedford, with certificates from other parishes. This was agreed to. They then proceeded to trace bribery on the sitting members. The counsel for the sitting members objected to the votes of, 1. Persons having received Hawes's charity. 2. Persons having received Welborn's charity. 3. The master and brethren of an hospital called St. John's Hospital. 4. Freemen who had received parish relief within the year. And 5. Freemen who had an inchoate right to their freedom, but were admitted in a particular manner, different from the customary mode of admission for such freemen, and within a year before the election. On these heads the committee determined, 1. That the

the perfons receiving Hawes's charity were not difqualified. 2. That their receiving Welborn's charity were difqualified. 3. That the mafter and brethren of St. John's Hofpital were not difqualified. 4. That the word *alms*, in the refolution of 1690, refers to burgeffes and freemen as well as to inhabitants houfeholders of Bedford. And 5. That the fix perfons who tendered their votes at the laft election for Bedford, being admitted within the twelvemonth by the common council, had not a right to vote.

And finally, having corrected the polls by thefe feveral refolutions, they determined that Sir William Wake, Bart, one of the fitting members, and Samuel Whitbread, Efq. one of the petitioners, were duly elected.

Cafe of the Borough of CRICKLADE.—*Petitioners, Samuel Peach, Efq. and John Dewar, Efq.*

A vacancy having happened in the borough in the month of December after the general election, by the death of Mr. Earle, a new writ was ordered out, and Mr. Dewar and Mr. Peach were both returned by the fame indenture. Mr. Dewar's petition fet forth, that he had a great majority of legal votes; but that, notwithftanding, the returning officer, Thomas Carter, had returned Mr. Peach along with the petitioner. Mr. Peach in his petition fet forth, that on the fecond day of the election, as the returning officer, the candidates, and electors, were proceeding to the place of polling, a riot commenced, which obliged the returning officer immediately to clofe the poll, when only forty-one out of near two hundred perfons entitled to vote had given their fuffrages; and that on that account Mr. Dewar and the petitioner were returned. That the petitioner was by reafon thereof prevented from receiving the fuffrages of a large majority of the electors—That Mr. Dewar, or his agents, had, by entertainments and feafts daily given at their expence to the electors, endeavoured to procure votes, and had kept the borough in continual riot, tumult, and diffipation.

The returning officer was in the intereft of Peach, and he was attended by a barrifter retained by Peach, who dictated to him in every inftance. The counfel faid he was guided entirely by one King, a blackfmith, as to the right of the feveral voters who prefented themfelves. It was attempted to be proved, that

that Peach's friends and the returning officer had agreed, that if any disturbance should happen, and Peach be a-head, they would close the poll instantly, and make a single return. On the second day a sort of scuffle happened at the church door, between Mr. Herbert, a member of the House of Commons, and Mr. Benson, a merchant in London. Benson pushed Herbert from the door as he endeavoured to enter, on which Herbert collared him. The scuffle continuing, several of Peach's friends cried out, " a riot! a riot!" On this the counsel for the returning officer directed him to close the poll, which he did, and they left the church together, although earnestly entreated by Dewar and his friends to remain. The witnesses for Mr. Dewar swore, that there was not any thing like a riot or disturbance, sufficient to terrify any reasonable man. When the poll was closed, Mr. Herbert went to the returning officer, and intreated him to renew it, promising to give any security he should require, that he would not molest Benson, nor occasion any disturbance; and desiring, if it were thought necessary, that both Benson and he might be committed till the election should be over. But the returning officer and his counsel absolutely refused to open the poll again. On this, the electors in the interest of Mr. Dewar went and gave their voices for him before a constable; Mr. Peach's friends being apprized of this poll, but none of them came.

After hearing the arguments of the counsel, the committee, after long deliberation, resolved that the constable's poll should not be given in evidence, nor parole evidence be admitted to prove what persons polled before the constable. And, finally, they determined, that neither Mr. Peach, nor Mr. Dewar were duly returned, and that the election for the borough of Cricklade was a void election.

Second Case of the Borough of CRICKLADE.—*Petitioners, Six persons on the behalf of themselves and others, electors of the said borough.—Fourteen persons on behalf of themselves and others, electors of the said borough.—Sitting member; Samuel Peach, Esq.*

The petitions stated, that the returning officers had acted with the grossest partiality. The six electors complained, that they and many others, duly qualified, offered to give their votes for John Dewar, Esq. but were rejected by the returning

turning officer—both the petitions stated that many votes were partially admitted for Mr. Peach, which stood precisely in the same predicament with many, which he rejected, when offered for Mr. Dewar; and that he admited many for Mr. Peach who had no right to vote. There is no determination of the house, on the right of election in this borough, but the following entry stands, "22 Feb. 1695-6, Colonel Granville reports from the committee of privileges and elections, that it was *agreed*, that the right of election for Cricklade, was in the freeholders, copyholders, and leaseholders, for not less than three years." The counsel for the petitioners contended, that the boundaries of the borough extended beyond the line adopted on the part of the sitting member, and that seven houses for which votes had been tendered in favour of Dewar, and rejected on the ground of their being without, are within the boundaries. On the other side again it was urged, that the true limits of the borough excluded these seven houses. Particular evidence was gone into to ascertain the boundaries. The next part urged by the counsel for the petitioners was, that it was not necessary that the houses for which votes were claimed, should either be ancient houses, or built on ancient scites, but that a sufficient estate in any house within the borough gave a right to vote. This was denied by the other side—they said, that only ancient houses, or houses build on ancient scites, gave a right to vote. Many witnesses were called, who proved that they had never before this election heard a distinction made between new and old houses. The third point urged by the counsel for the petitioners was, "that leascholders for a term of three years or more, determinable on a life or lives, and persons having a leafe for that or a longer time granted by lessors, who have themselves leases for three or more years, but determinable on a life or lives, have a right to vote." This was admitted by the counsel for the sitting member, after having heard the evidence. It was then contended, that residence of 40 days before the election was necessary to give a person a title to vote. Witnesses were called to prove, that this was understood to be the usage. After this, they entered into evidence to prove the gross partiality of the returning officer, and to bring home a charge of bribery on the sitting member. After hearing the arguments on both sides, the committee came to

the

the following resolution: Resolved, "That it is the opinion of this committee, that the right of voting for members to serve in parliament, for the borough of Cricklade, in the county of Wilts, is, in the inhabitants possessing houses within the said borough, who are freeholders, copyholders, or leaseholders, for any term not less than three years, or for any such term, or greater term, determinable on a life or lives; such freeholder, copyholder, or leaseholder, having been in the occupation of the house, for which he may claim to vote, forty days preceeding any election."

Resolved, That it is the opinion of this committee, that the seven houses above-mentioned are within the boundary of the said borough.

By these resolutions, all the points of the petitioners were granted, and a majority was established for Mr. Dewar. The counsel for the sitting member said, they would give the committee no farther trouble. They then determined that John Dewar, Esq. was duly elected, and ought to have been returned.

Case of the Borough of DORCHESTER.—*Petitioners, Anthony Chapman, Esq. several inhabitants and electors of the borough of Dorchester.*—*Sitting Members, William Ewar, Esq. and John Damer, Esq.*

The petitions set forth, in general, that the petitioner had a majority of legal votes, and ought to have been returned, and alledged specially—that divers persons were admitted to vote, who were neither " inhabitants, nor occupiers of real estates within the borough," and had no right. The last determination of the right of election in the borough was 18th May, 1720. " Resolved, That the right of electing burgesses to serve in parliament for the borough of Dorchester, in the county of Dorset, is in the *inhabitants* of the said borough, paying to church and poor in respect of their personal estates; and in *such persons* as pay to church and poor in respect of their real estates within the said borough."— The counsel for the petitioners contended, that the last clause for the determination means only, " such as are *occupiers* of real estates within the borough; and in respect thereof, pay to church and poor."—The counsel for the sitting members contended, that it means. " *owners* of real estates within the

the borough, paying in refpect thereof to church and poor, whether fuch real eftates are in their own *occupation* or not."——The ufage fince 1720 was admitted to be in favour of out-voters.—The counfel for the petitioners contended, that the poor-rate, and church-rate, is a tax upon inhabitants or occupiers only, and not upon landlords; and the votes in Dorchefter have always been intitled, " Rates on the feveral " *occupiers* of lands, houfes, &c." In 1772, an attempt was made to alter the words in the title, and to make it run, " Rates on the feveral *owners* or occupiers, &c." but thefe words were refcinded at the veftry holden for the purpofe, and the cuftomary title reftored.—On the other fide it was contended, that the refolution in 1720 did not mention perfons *rated or rateable*, but perfons *paying* to church and poor. In Dorchefter, as in moft other places, the eftablifhed ufage is, that the owner pays the poor-rate; and when there is reafon to apprehend the occupier to be in danger of becoming chargeable to the parifh, they frequently rate the owner.—It was the fame alfo with refpect to the church-rate, for the purpofe of fupporting or repairing the edifice. Dorchefter, they faid, was a borough by prefcription, and the determination of 1720 muft be confidered as a declaration of the prefcriptive right of election. It ought not, therefore, to be inftructed with any reference to the ftatute of Queen Elizabeth.

The counfel having clofed their arguments on the meaning of the laft determination, the committee came to the following refolution:—Refolved, " That it is the opinion of this committee that, purfuant to the laft determination of the Houfe of Commons, fuch perfons as pay to the church and poor, in refpect of their real eftates within the borough of Dorchefter, in the county of Dorfet, though not inhabitants or occupiers, were intitled to vote at the laft election of burgeffes to ferve in parliament for the faid borough." The committee then decided, that the two fitting members were duly elected.

Cafe of the Borough of DERBY.—*Petitioners, Daniel Parker Coke, Efq. feveral electors of Derby.—Sitting Member, John Gifborne, Efq.*

Mr. Coke, in his petition, fet forth, that he was elected by a great majority of legal voters; but that the Mayor, by rejecting

jecting the votes of many perſons who had an undoubted right to poll, and who tendered their votes for him, and by admitting for Mr. Giſborne the votes of divers perſons who had no right, the ſitting member was returned. The other petition ſet forth, that the petitioners and divers others, having a lawful and undoubted right to the freedom of the ſaid borough, had claimed to be *admitted* previous to the election, and were, by the mayor and divers aldermen refuſed, although ſeveral perſons under the like circumſtances had been admitted. There is no determination of the right of election in Derby, by the Houſe of Commons; but the council on both ſides agreed, that every member of the corporation has a right to vote. The numbers on the poll were,

For Mr. Giſborne ———— 343
For Mr. Coke ———— 329

Majority, 14

but the counſel for the petitioner propoſed to add 42 to the poll of Mr. Coke, &c. 26, who being entitled to their freedom, had demanded admiſſion before the election, and having been refuſed, had tendered their votes at the poll, in favour of Mr. Coke; 12 under the ſame circumſtances, but who had demanded to be admitted on different occaſions.

Four who had their freedom, but whoſe votes were rejected by the Mayor. They alſo propoſed to ſtrike off 16 from the poll in the ſitting member. 5 who lived in Derby Hoſpital—3 for having received pariſh relief—3 honorary burgeſſes admitted within the year—3 who had been admitted burgeſſes under the title of ſervitude, without having ſerved a ſeven years apprenticeſhip—2 who were never admitted to their freedom.—But it was only neceſſary for the committee to hear evidence and decide concerning the votes of the 26, who claiming by antecedent titles, had demanded admiſſion to their freedom, and having been refuſed, had tendered their votes for Mr. Coke. The diſpute was about the mode of admiſſion—their pretenſions were agreed to.—The counſel for the petitioners argued, that by the expreſs proviſion of the charter, the perſons appointed to admit freemen, are the mayor and three aldermen. On the part of Mr. Giſborne, it was denied that this was the legal mode of admiſſion. The clauſe in the charter did not ſanctify ſuch a mode, and the committee on this

this point resolved, "that the clauses in the charter, which have been produced to the committee, have not so established the mode of admission of the freemen of this borough as to exclude other evidence." When this long course of evidence was gone into, to prove, in the first place, that it was usual to admit the burgesses at a common hall, and this usage was authorized by a bye-law, made on the 10th of December, 1743; but, in the year 1772, the charter having been examined by some lawyers, he construed the clause mentioned by the petitioners to mean what they had stated it, and from that period, till about the time of the election, freemen had been admitted by the mayor and aldermen. Upon this the counsel for the petitioners argued, that if the constitution was not as they had apprehended, still, as it was universally understood at that time to be the constitution of the borough, having applied to those who were at least the proper persons to administer the preliminary oaths—having been promised their admissions—put off from time to time—and at last refused by the mayor, with a view to deprive them of their votes, (he knowing them to be in the interest of Mr. Coke)—they were intitled to be put upon the poll. Of these assertions very adequate proof was brought, and their pretensions were also enquired into. On which, after hearing the arguments of counsel, the committee resolved, " that all the 27 voters in question, except William Sale, ought to be added to the poll,"—and, after this, the sitting member having said, by his counsel, he would give the committee no farther trouble, the petitioner was declared to be duly elected, and ought to have been returned.

Case of the Borough of DOWNTON.—*Petitioners,* Sir *Philip Hales, Bart. and John Cooper, Esq. certain freeholders of the borough of* DOWNTON.—*Against, Thomas Duncombe, Esq. and Thomas Dummer, Esq. sitting members.*

The petition set forth, that several persons were allowed to vote at the late election of burgesses for this place, who had no right, by which means a pretended majority was procured in favour of the sitting members, and they were returned, although the petitioners, Hales and Cooper, had a clear majority of legal votes.

There is no determination of the House of the right of election

election of this borough. Both sides considered it to be "in persons having a freehold interest in burgage tenements, holden by a certain rent, fealty, and suit of court, of the Bishop of Winchester, who is lord of the borough, and paying release on descent, and fines on alienation."

The numbers on the poll were
For Mr. Duncombe   22
Mr. Dummer   22
Mr. Cooper   11
Sir Philip Hales   10

The counsel for the petitioners objected to nineteen or twenty of the voters for the sitting members; one general objection which applied to most of them was occasionality. Mr. Duncombe was proprietor of near two thirds of the burgage tenements in Downton.—It was proved that in 1768 he had made conveyances to some of the voters; but the deeds had remained ever since in his hands; the occupiers had continued to pay their rents to him, and still considered him as their landlord. There were no entries on the court-rolls of 1768 of those conveyances, nor of the payment of the alienation fines. The conveyances to others appeared to have been made after the writ and precept had issued, some of them being brought wet to the poll. The grantees did not know where the lands lay, and one man produced at the poll a grant for which he claimed a vote, which, on examination, appeared to be made to another person; the consideration in them all was five shillings; the rent twenty shillings a year; they were by lease and release, for life, with a clause of re-entry, if the grantee should assign without the consent of the granter. These kind of votes were called *faggots*. The petitioners contended, that the votes in question were colourable, fradulent and void, both by the common law of parliament, and the statute of William III. commonly called the *Splitting Act*. Beside the general objection of occasionality, fourteen of the votes for the sitting members were impeached, for reasons drawn from the nature of burgage tenements; they defined a burgage to be " one undivided and indivisible tenement, clearly described, neither created nor capable of being created, within time of memory, which has immemorially given a right of voting." It was shewn that by the pipe-roll of 1458, the amount of all the burgages, half-burgages, and quarter-burgages in the borough, is stated to be 126 and three quarters, amounting to 6l. 6s. 2d. the rent for the whole of a burgage is one shilling, for half a burgage sixpence, and for a quarter of a burgage three-pence; a quarter of a burgage, and a half of a burgage are technical terms, and not expressive of the fourth parts or the halves of whole burgages, but of distinct and separate tenements of various extent, and apparently so called, because the quit-rents they pay to the Lord are halves or quarters of what whole burgages pay; they proved that these fourteen votes were not antient quarters of burgages carrying immemorially a right of voting, but for quarters of burgages attempted to be carved out of longer tenements.

After hearing the arguments of Counsel on both sides, resolved, That Thomas Duncombe, Esq. and Thomas Dummer, Esq. were not duly elected; and that Sir Philip Hales, Bart. and John Cooper, Esq. ought to have been returned the burgesses for the borough.

Case of the Borough of HASLEMERE.—*Petitioners, William Burke, Esq. and Henry Kelly, Esq. certain inhabitants, freeholders and legal voters of the borough of* HASLEMERE. —*Sitting members, Thomas More Molyneux, Esq. Sir Meyrick Burrell, Bart.*

The first petition stated, that the two sitting members had been guilty of undue and illegal practices—that votes had been admitted, though not legal, for the sitting members; and that the majority of legal votes were in favour of the petitioners. The other petition stated, that Haslemere is a borough by prescription, and that of late years, the practice of splitting and dividing freeholds within the said borough, for election purposes, hath prevailed to so great a degree, that if the same is not remedied, the constitution of the said borough would be subverted. It stated many illegal instances of voting in favour of the sitting members.

The last determination of the House of the right of election was on May 20, 1661. This was explained by a resolution of the House on the 24th April 1755.

The counsel for the petitioners objected to 47 out of 61 of the voters for the sitting members. To 35 as voting for tenements split within the meaning of the statute of K. William. Six as claiming their right from freeholds without the manor.

One

One his property being leasehold. Two as having no interest, but a rent reserved as a term. Three as not having freeholds.

A variety of evidence and argument was gone into on these heads, but as the committee did not come to separate resolutions on the several questions, we cannot state what the point was on which the division turned. They declared the two sitting members to be duly elected.

Case of the Borough of HINDON.—*Petitioners, James Calthorpe, Esq. and Richard Beckford, Esq. against Richard Smith, Esq. and Thomas Brand Hollis, Esq. sitting members.*

The petition set forth, that the two sitting members had, by the bribery of themselves and agents, previous to and during the election, procured themselves to be returned, although the petitioners were duly elected, and ought to have been returned.

The last determination of the house on the right of election in this borough was on the 12th April, 1728. After hearing the evidence, the committee determined, that neither the sitting members nor the petitioners had been duly elected, and that the election was void. At the same time, the chairman acquainted the house, that it appeared to the committee that the most flagrant and notorious acts of bribery and corruption had been practised; and that a very considerable majority of the electors of the borough of Hindon had been bribed and corrupted in a very gross and extraordinary manner; and that several others of the said electors had been concerned as agents for that purpose. In consequence of this the committee had resolved, " That it appeared to them that Richard Smith, Esq. by his agents, has been guilty of notorious bribery, in endeavouring to procure himself to be elected and returned a burgess, to serve in this present parliament, for the borough of Hindon, in the county of Wilts."

Similar resolutions passed respecting Mr. Hollis, Mr. Calthorpe, and Mr. Beckford.

They also resolved, that the Rev. John Nairne, of Hindon, Fasham Nairne, Esq. of Bury-street, St. James's, &c. (in all thirteen specified by name) had acted as agents; and had been accessary to, and concerned in, the notorious acts of bribery and corruption that have been practised at the last election for the said borough of Hindon.

They

They also came to a resolution, that it was the opinion of the committee, that the house should be moved for leave to bring in a bill to disfranchise the said borough of Hindon, in the county of Wilts.

The house was accordingly moved, and the previous question being put, it passed in the negative. It was then ordered, that leave be given to bring in a bill to incapacitate from voting at elections of members of parliament 190 persons, specified by name, out of 210 who had polled at the election. This bill was brought into the house, and after having passed through several stages, it was found, when referred to a committee of the whole house, that the bribery and corruption could not be proved, as the persons who had proved it before the select committee were named in the bill, and incapacitated by it; and being parties could not, without overturning the known rules of law, be receeved as witnesses. This objection was treated as of no weight by the gentlemen of the long robe; but it was strenuously supported by others, and the bill was thrown out.

Leave was then given to bring in a new bill, similar to the former, in which the names of certain persons were left out, who were intended to be made use of as witnesses. Many difficuties were also in the way of this bill. Two witnesses were committed to prison for prevarication; and two disobeyed the order for their attendance, and kept themselves concealed, on which a proclamation was made for apprehending them, with the offer of a reward, and the house was obliged to postpone the further consideration of it for that session; but the house resolved to take the report of the committee into further consideration as early as possible in the next session; and that until then no new writ should be ordered. At the same time they resolved, " That if it shall appear that any person hath procured himself to be elected, or returned a member of this house, or endeavoured so to be by bribery, or any other corrupt practices, this house will proceed with the utmost severity against such person."

An order was also made, " That the attorney-general do forthwith prosecute Richard Smith, Esq. Thomas Brand Hollis, Esq. James Calthorpe, Esq. and Richard Beckford, Esq. for the said offence.

The two persons against whom the proclamation was issued, having surrendered themselves, they were committed to Newgate.

Case of the Borough of HELLESTON, *in the county of Cornwall.—Petitioners, Philip Yorke, Esq. and Francis Cust, Esq. Richard Johns, jun. alderman, and Mathew Wills, Richard Johns, Edmund Johns, Richard Penhall, and William Rogers, freemen of Hellefton.—Sitting members, the Right Hon. Francis Godolphin Osborne, commonly called the Marquis of Carmarthen, and Francis Owen, Esq.*

Hellefton is a borough by prescription, and also by a charter of the 27th of Queen Elizabeth, confirmed by another of the 16th of Charles I. By those charters the corporation was to consist of a mayor, four aldermen, and an indefinite number of freemen. The freemen were to be selected out of the inhabitants, by the mayor, aldermen, and *commonalty*, or the major part of them: the aldermen by the mayor and aldermen out of the freemen; the mayor by the freemen out of two aldermen, to be nominated by the mayor and aldermen. The right of election of burgesses has constantly been in the mayor and commonalty, which has always been understood to mean the mayor, aldermen, and freemen only. There is no determination upon the right of election, but it has always been admitted to be as just stated. In the year 1769, two informations, in the nature of *quo warranto*, were exhibited in the Court of King's-Bench, against several persons of the borough, to shew by what authority they claimed to be freemen, having been elected without the concurrence of the commonalty. Soon after the charter of Queen Elizabeth, a bye-law had been made by the corporation, by which the right of electing freemen was restrained to the mayor and aldermen. After various trials, the Court of King's-Bench, and the House of Lords, delivered their opinion, "That the election of freemen could not be exercised by the mayor and aldermen, exclusive of the commonalty." By these and other prosecutions of the same sort, judgment of ouster was obtained against all the members of the corporation, except two aldermen and eight freemen. In 1772 a petition was presented to the king in council, from several merchants, tradesmen, freeholders, and inhabitants of Hellefton, in which two of the ten remaining corporators joined, stating the facts just mentioned, and alledging that the corporation was totally dissolved; praying therefore such relief as should be thought fit. After various hearings, a new charter was granted to the borough on

the

the 3d of September, 1774, similar to the former, with only the alteration, "that the freemen, who, notwithstanding the charter, had by the usage, been excluded from a share in the election of new freemen, should be expressly excluded by the new charter—and that by the new charter a mayor, four aldermen, and thirty-one freemen, including the mayor and aldermen, were appointed *nominatim* by this charter. Richard Johns was made an alderman, and the other seven remaining corporators (one of them having died in the interim) of the old body, were appointed among the new freemen. The charter was, on the 8th of September, delivered to the new mayor, who accepted it, and on the 9th issued notices, severally, to all the new corporators, requiring them to meet on the 12th, in order to accept the charter and the offices to which they were thereby named. All but six of the old corporators accepted the charter and their offices, and took the oaths. Each of these six severally read a protest against the charter, and refused to accept or act under it. On Sunday the 25th of September, the new corporation met for the choice of a mayor, and John Rogers, Esq. was elected. The six protesting freemen did not attend at this election.

The precept for the election of members of parliament was sent by the sheriff to Mr. Rogers, who gave notice that the election would be on the 11th of October. On the day of election, the precept being read by Mr. Rogers, all the new members of the corporation, but the six protestors, voted for the two sitting members. The six, after protesting against the legality of Rogers acting as presiding officer, gave their votes at *his* poll for Mr. Yorke and Mr. Cust. They afterwards proceeded by themselves to make an election of those two gentlemen. Richard Johns *there* acted as presiding officer, and made a return, which was delivered to the sheriff. Rogers, also, made a return of the sitting members, which he annexed to the precept, and delivered to the sheriff. Johns return was first received, but the sheriff having taken the advice of counsel, annexed the return of Rogers to the writ, and sent it by his agent to the clerk of the crown. He also sent the other return by his agent, but not annexed to the writ. The clerk of the crown said, he could not receive the last, as it was not to the writ. It was accordingly rejected, and sent back to

Cornwall,

Cornwall, but was produced by the under sheriff on the trial before the committee.

Under all the circumstances of this case, the counsel for the petitioners contended, 1. That the new charter was void, and that the only persons who had a right to elect members of parliament for Helleston, were the subsisting freemen under the old charter. 2. That if the charter was valid, still the freemen appointed by it, not having been in possession of their franchise a year before the election, they were by the statute of the 3d. of the present king, cap. 15. incapable of voting at the last election; and therefore the only competent electors, at that time, were the subsisting members of the old corporation. They argued, that if the old body existed as a corporation when the charter passed, and when it was tendered, acceptance by the majority of the old corporators was necessary to make it valid, and as they, after opposing it in all its stages, rejected it when offered for acceptance, it became by such refusal void to all intents and purposes. Acceptance is necessary to give validity to a new charter. This is an established and uncontrovertible principle of law. There were only three ways by which a corporation can cease to exist.

One forfeiture by *abuses*, or *non-uses*. 2d. Voluntary surrender. 3d. The death of all the *natural* persons members of the corporate body.

Forfeiture cannot dissolve a corporation, but by judgment of ouster against the whole. Surrender can only be by acceptance on record. But there was no pretence of surrender in this case. And there was no question, but that eight of the natural persons, members of the aggregate body, were still alive. They adduced the cases of Bewdley, Plympton, Durham, and Colchester, to prove that though some of the integral parts of the corporation were gone, yet still, as there remained several members of it, they could exercise several franchises as corporators—they could enjoy any right of common belonging to the corporation—they could accept or refuse a charter, and they could vote for members of parliament. If they could do these acts, no new charter could transfer their right from them to another corporation. But if this doctrine were not so clear, still the new corporation could not vote at the last election, having been made freemen within the year, agreeable to the statute of George III.

The

The counsel for the sitting members said, that when the new charter passed, the old corporation was totally dissolved. The six who refused the charter could not be considered as acting in a *corporate* capacity, but merely as *individuals*, and therefore their refusal did not affect the validity of the charter, and the votes of the members of the new corporation were not affected by the statute of 3 George, 1777. Every corporation aggregate consists of certain integral parts, chalked out by the hand which formed it. If it ceases to have the form given it, if any of its vital parts are lost, it no longer exists in that state in which it was endowed with its powers; it is no longer that thing on which those powers were confined; and therefore it ceases to exist. They quoted many cases to prove, that the dissolution of an integral part produced the dissolution of the corporation, and several law authorities in support of the doctrine. And that the statute of George the Third did not affect the votes of the new members, was clear from the words of that statute. The disqualification created by it, regards persons *admitted* to this freedom within the year. A man cannot be said to be admitted into what does not exist. Till those men were *made* freemen by the new charter, the corporation had no existence.

The committee determined, that Philip Yorke, Esq. and Francis Cust, Esq. the petitioners, were duly elected, and ought to have been returned. An order was accordingly made by the house for taking off the indenture of return annexed to the writ for the county of Cornwall, and annexing thereto the indenture of return expected by Richard Johns and others.

Case of the Borough of IVELCHESTER.—*Petitioners, Richard Brown, Esq. and Inigo William Jones, Esq. James Curry and John Cox, on behalf of themselves and others, being inhabitants, leaseholders, parishioners, and voters within the borough of* IVELCHESTER.—*Sitting members, Peregrine Cust, Esq. William Innes, Esq.*

The allegation in this case was principally confined to a charge of bribery; and several witnesses were called to prove that the sitting members had, by their agents, notoriously bribed and corrupted the electors; evidence was not produced, however, to destroy the majority which the sitting members had

had over the petitioners; the bribery difqualified a part, but not all of the majority; fo that the committee could not declare the petitioners to be duly elected. Their decifion was, that none of the four candidates were duly elected, and that it was a void election.

Second cafe of the Borough of IVELCHESTER.—*Petitioners, Richard Brown, Efq. and Inigo William Jones, Efq.— Sitting members, Nathaniel Webb, Efq. Owen Salifoury Brereton.*

After the petition was prefented, the parties compromifed the matter; a committee being therefore formed, the parties were called in, and the counfel for the petitioners informing them that they had no evidence to impeach the feats of the fitting members, they were immediately declared to be duly elected.

Cafe of the Borough of ST. IVES.——*Petitioners, Samuel Stephens, Efq. feveral inhabitants, electors of* ST. IVES; *William Praed, Efq. Adam Drummond, Efq.*

The petitions fet forth that the fitting members were guilty of bribery; and that the returning officer had acted partially by admitting perfons to vote, who had no vote, and rejecting others who had a right. The laft determination of the right of election was on the 8th of December, 1702.— The petitioners proved that Mr. Praed, the father of the fitting member, had advanced fums of money to the voters, for which he took their votes; that when the voters received the money, there was a condition annexed that they fhould vote for his fon and a friend; and that they were given to underftand, if they complied with this condition, the money would never be demanded of them. Mr. Praed and Mr. Drummond canvaffed together; they likewife propofed to add about forty to the poll in favour of Mr. Stephens, by proving, that though they had not been rated, and had not paid, they poffeffed rateable property, and ought to have been rated, and were therefore entitled to vote; but this the committee overruled, and refolved, "that perfons, though poffeffed of rateable property, if they have not been rated, and cannot prove mifconduct in the overfeers in not rating them, are not entitled to vote." Mr. Praed was excluded on account of the bribery

bribery, and the committee determined that Mr. Drummond was duly elected, and that the election with respect to one of the burgesses was void; and accordingly a new writ was ordered.

Case of the Borough of MILBURN PORT.—*Petitioners were, Edward Walter, Esq. and Isaac Hawkins Browne, Esq. the Hon. Temple Luttrell, and Charles Wolseley, Esq. certain inhabitants of the town and borough of* MILBURN PORT.—*(In the interest of Luttrell and Wolseley.)*

There were three returns made by different persons claiming to be returning officers, all of which had been annexed to the writ by the sheriff, and returned into the office of the clerk of the crown. Walter and Browne were returned by one, and Luttrell and Wolseley by the other two. The constitution of the borough of Milburn Port is this: it consists of nine bailiwicks, of which part were the property of Thomas Hutchins Medlycot, Esq. and part of Mr. Walter. The two principal or reigning bailiffs appoint two sub-bailiffs for the year, who are the returning officers. In the year 1773, it happened that Mr. Medlycot had the appointment of one of the sub-bailiffs, and Mr. Walter of the other; Mr. Medlycot named one Elias Oliver, and Mr. Walter nominated one Robert Baunton. In 1774, it was Mr. Medlycot's turn to nominate both the sub-bailiffs. It appeared that the court-leet for appointing sub-bailiffs had always been holden, before and since the stile was altered, on the first Tuesday after Park Monday. On the 3d of October, 1774, the precept for the election was delivered to Robert Baunton, who gave his receipt for it; and having communicated with the other sub-bailiff, they concurred in appointing the day of election to be on the 10th.

On the 4th of October, (being the first Tuesday in October, N. S.) Oliver, with Medlycot and others, entered the town-hall, and nominated the capital reigning bailiffs for the year ensuing; who again appointed John Newton, junior, and John Peckham, to be their sub-bailiffs. At the same court, Oliver was appointed a constable, and sworn into that office.

On the 10th, the election came on, and there were three polls taken: one by Baunton, who declared the majority of legal votes to be in favour of Walter and Browne; one by Oliver, and a third by Newton and Peckham. By each of the two last, Luttrell and Wolseley had the majority of votes.

"The question therefore was, whether Newton and Peckham were the legal sub-bailiffs at the time of the election? If they were so, their return only was valid: if they were not, the question would be, whether the return of Baunton, or of Oliver, was the legal return, or whether they were both void?

The evidence and the arguments of the counsel served to shew, that the court-leet holden on the 4th of October, at which Newton and Peckham were appointed, was holden a fortnight before the usual time; it has been ever until that year kept agreeable to the old stile, and not to the new; the first Tuesday of October, new stile, was on the 4th, and the first Tuesday, old stile, was on the 18th of the month, new stile; the court-leet was consequently holden a fortnight sooner than it would have been, if there had been no change of the stile, and consequently not according to the provision of the statute. The committee resolved, " that the return made by John Newton, junior, and John Peckham, of Mr. Luttrell and Mr. Wolseley, was an illegal return."

" And that the other two returns appeared to the committee to be complicated together, that they thought it their duty to go upon the merits of the election, without previously deciding between them."

The parties claimed respectively the majority of legal votes, by objecting to several of those on the poll of their opponents, and it was contended by Walter and Browne, that the last determination of the house on the right of election, was on the 8th December, 1702. On the other side it was contended, that there were only two commonalty stewards, the other seven being denominated the *assistants* or *the banage*; and proofs were adduced by both parties in support of their allegations.

There was also a mutual charge exhibited of having the votes of inhabitants fraudulently rated; it appeared that there had been great struggles between Mr. Medlycot and Mr. Walter, about the appointment of overseers of the poor. The committee therefore proposed that the following question should be argued by the counsel, viz.

" Whether persons *rateable*, and having *paid* to the rate, though that rate were made and collected by officers illegal, or doubtful, may vote as inhabitants paying scot and lot?"

and

and after hearing the arguments on both sides, they decided the question by another resolution in the affirmative.

This point of law being decided, the discussion of each particular vote turned merely on the matter of fact; one person in particular was objected to as under a conviction of felony; but this was contended on the other part to be no ground of disfranchisement.

An attempt was also made to prove that Mr. Luttrell was ineligible, because he held the office, by deputation, of *customer inwards in the port of Bristol*. No substantial proof of this fact was adduced.

After several days consideration, the committee determined on the petitions, by which they declared the honourable Temple Luttrell, and Charles Wolseley, Esq. to be duly returned, and elected burgesses to serve in parliament for the said borough; and that Edward Walter, Esq. and Isaac Hawkins Browne, Esq. were not duly elected.

Case of the Borough of MORPETH.—*Petitioners, Hon. William Byron, certain freemen and electors of the borough of Morpeth, against Francis Eyre, Esq. sitting member.*

The petitions set forth, that at the election, when Peter Delmé, Esq. Francis Eyre, Esq. Thomas Charles Bigge, Esq. and the Hon William Byron, were candidates for the borough of Morpeth, Mr. Delmé and Mr. Byron had the majority of votes at the conclusion of the poll, in the judgment of the two bailiffs who presided, and who were the proper returning officers, but that they were afterwards compelled by the violence and threats of a violent and outrageous mob, to sign a return of Mr. Eyre instead of the petitioner.

After receiving the proof of this allegation, the committee decided, "That Francis Eyre, Esq. was not duly elected, and that the Hon. William Byron ought to have been returned a burgess to serve in Parliament for the said borough."

An order was made at the same time, "That Francis Eyre, Esq. and the freemen and electors of the borough of Morpeth be at liberty to petition the house, to question the election of the Hon William Byron within fourteen days, if they thought fit."

A petition was accordingly presented by Mr. Eyre, charging Mr. Byron and Mr. Delmé directly with bribery by themselves and agents.

Cafe of the City of PETERBOROUGH.—*Petitioner,* James Phipps, *Efq.*—*Sitting Member,* Matthew Wyldbore, *Efq.*

The petition contained a charge of bribery againſt the ſitting member, and alledged that legal votes tendered for the petitioner had been rejected, and the ſuffrages of perſons not entitled to vote received for the ſitting member. The laſt determination of the houſe was on the 13th of May, 1728. The point of bribery was abandoned.

The counſel for Mr. Phipps produced evidence to ſhew, that a moſt partial rate had been made in the year 1774, for the purpoſe of garbling the election, and then they contended, that five perſons ſhould be ſtruck from the poll, being fraudulently rated for property of which they were not the occupiers. 2. That two ſhould be ſtruck off, becauſe they were not bona fide houſeholders within the precincts of the miniſter—and thirdly, they contended, that certain perſons, who had voted as inhabitants of the city, without the precincts of the miniſter, were not houſeholders, and conſequently not entitled to vote by the laſt determination. On this point the counſel for the ſitting member objected to the hearing of evidence. The counſel for the petitioner contended, that the deſcription of an inhabitant paying ſcot and lot neceſſarily implies, that the perſon ſo deſcribed ſhould be a houſeholder. After hearing the arguments on both ſides, the committee reſolved, " that the word " houſeholders" in the reſolution of the Houſe of Commons, of the 13th of May, 1728, relates to the inhabitants within the precincts of the miniſter only, and not to other the inhabitants within the ſaid city, paying ſcot and lot." The counſel for the petitioner then proceeded to ſhew that there had been great miſconduct and partiality obſerved in not rating a Thomas Felton. He had been rated immediately before, and was left out of the rate of September, 1774. After hearing arguments, the committee decided, " that the parties ſhould not go into evidence to prove that Thomas Felton ought to have been admitted upon the rate in September, 1774." But at the ſame time they reſolved, " that the council for the petitioner be permitted to proceed to offer any evidence they think proper to prove any miſconduct relative to that rate. But afterwards when they heard the ſpecies of evidence, that was to be adduced to prove the miſconduct, they reſolved, "-that th
cominitte

committee were of opinion, that the evidence which the counsel for the petitioner propofed to offer, is inconfiftent with the refolution which the committee have already come to." On this, the counfel for the petitioner faid, he would give the committee no farther trouble, and the fitting member was declared to be duly elected.

Cafe of the Borough of PONTEFRACT.—*Petitioners, the Hon. Charles James Fox, and James Hare, Efq. feveral inhabitants, houfeholders, and electors of the Borough of Pontefract.—Sitting Members, Sir John Goodricke, Bart. and Charles Mellifh, Efq.*

The only queftion in the cafe was, concerning the right of election in the borough.—Whether a refolution of 1624, or one of 1770, was to be confidered as the laft determination in the Houfe of Commons, within the meaning of the ftatute of George the Second. If the firft was that determination, Mr. Fox and Mr. Hare had an unqueftionable majority, and were duly elected; and vice verfa.

There are two journals of the year 1624. In the firft, intitled, " Originals of the Seffion of Parliament, holden at Weftminfter, 19º Februarii, 21º Jacobii, there is the following entry: 28th May, 1624. Mr. Glanvyle reporteth, for Pomfrett, two points. 1. Who, the electors?—Refolved by the committee, there being no charter, nor prefcription for choice, the election is to be made by the inhabitants, houfeholders, refiants. Refolved alfo, fo now, when the queftion—2. That the committee alfo of opinion, in refpect the poll demanded, though interrupted by Beamart, yet the poll not being purfued, the choice of Sir Jo. Jackfon, void, and a new warrant to iffue for a new choice."

In the other, intitled " Prima feffio parliamenti inchoat. apud Weftm. decimonono die Februarii, anno regni regis Jacobi, angliæ, &c. vicefimo primo, et Scotiæ, quinquagefimo feptimo,"—there is the following account of the fame report: 28th May, 1624, Mr. Glanvill reports from the committee of privileges:

Concerning Pomfret. Queftion of Sir John Jackfon.— Committee refolved, all the inhabitants, houfeholders, ought to have voice. 2. Committee refolved, upon the latter writ, no burgefs chofen, but a new writ to go. " Refolved, that the election ought to be in Pomfret, by the inhabitants, householders, resiants there.

The resolution of 1770, is as follows: 6th February, 1770, Resolved, "that the right of election for members to serve in parliament for the borough of Pontefract, in the county of York, is in persons having within the said borough a freehold of burgage tenure, paying a burgage rent."

The counsel for the petitioners argued, that if the resolution of 1624 was the last determination of the house, in 1729, when the statute of George the Second passed, no subsequent act of the house can annul it; for that statute is binding on the house, and every last determination is to be considered as incorporated with, and making part of it. And they shewed, by various quotations from the Journals, that between 1624 and 1729, there was no resolution nor determination of the house on the right. The counsel for the sitting members argued, that the resolution of 1770 was conclusive. For though the *last determination* is binding on the house, yet, where a doubt arises, whether it is the last determination, the house is the only court competent to try that question. In 1770, the house did decide that what appears on the Journals of 1624, is not a last determination within the meaning of the act of George the Second, for they refused to let it be read as such, upon a division of 161 to 32. And they shewed by various references and descriptions, that the rule appointed by the resolution of 1770 had principally obtained in all the elections since 1624.

The committee therefore confirmed the due election of the two sitting members.

Case of the Borough and County of the town of POOLE.—*Petitioners, Hon. Charles James Fox and John Williams, Esq. several inhabitants and householders (and also paying scot and bearing lot) within the borough and county of the town of Poole. Sitting members, Sir Eyre Coote, K. B. Joshua Mauger, Esq.*

The only question in the case was, "Whether the right of election is in the burgesses of the borough exclusively, or, in the inhabitants and householders within the borough, paying scot and bearing lot?" The sheriff had rejected those who tendered their votes as inhabitants, householders,

holders, and only admitted the votes of burgesses. It was admitted that the sitting members had a majority of the letter; that if the former have a right to vote, there was a great majority in favour of the petitioners.

When the Chairman desired the clerk, as usual, to read the last determination of the house on the right of election, the counsel for the petitioners denied that there was any resolution in the Journals touching the right of election in this borough, which can be considered as a determination within the meaning of the statute. The counsel for the sitting members said, that such a determination was to be found on the Journals of the 9th of February, 1688-9. This entry was that "on a petition of Thomas Chaffer, Esq. complaining that Sir Nathaniel Napper had been returned in prejudice to him, the committee reported to the House, that the matter in question was, whether the right of election be in the mayor and burgesses only, or in the mayor, burgesses, and commonalty, who pay scot and lot? That it appeared to the committee by many parliament returns, which were produced to the committee, that the right of election had anciently been in the mayor and burgesses only, except a return in the 18th year of King James the First, wherein the *commonalty* are mentioned, with the mayor, aldermen, and burgesses, in the indenture; but that indenture is sealed with the *common seal* of the mayor, aldermen, and burgesses. That Sir Nathaniel Napper had 33 burgesses, and Mr. Chaffer but 22; but of the commonalty, that Mr. Chaffer was allowed to have had the greater number; and that thereupon the committee had agreed on two resolves. 1. That it is the opinion of this committee, that the right of election of burgesses to serve in this present convention for the town and county of Poole, is in the mayor, burgesses, and commonalty of the said town and county, who pay scot and lot. And 2. That Thomas Chaffer, Esq. is duly elected." A debate arose in the house on these resolutions, and they *disagreed* with the committee. It was urged on the one side, that this could not be a determination within the meaning of the statute; and after hearing the arguments on both sides, the committee ordered the counsel to proceed, and give evidence of the right of election. The counsel for the petitioners endeavoured to prove, that the right extended to the inhabitants, from

general

general principles of law, and from the hiſtory, conſtitution, and ancient uſage of the borough. The counſel for the ſitting members brought evidence alſo to prove, that it had been almoſt the invariable uſage of the borough to confine the right of election to the burgeſſes.

The Committee agreed to this, and declared the ſitting members to be duly elected.

Caſe of the Borough of PETERSFIELD.—*Petitioner, the Hon. John Luttrell.—Sitting members, Sir Abraham Hume, Bart. William Joliffe, Eſq.*

The petition ſet forth, that Sir Abraham Hume, Bart. high ſheriff for the county of Hertford, and Mr. Joliffe, by themſelves and their agents, were guilty of notorious bribery and corruption; that the returning officer acted partially and unfairly in rejecting good and legal votes for the petitioner, and admitting bad ones for the ſitting members. The laſt determination was on the 9th May, 1727.

The counſel for the petitioner argued on the firſt point, that Sir Abraham Hume, being high ſheriff of the county of Hertford at the time of the election, was ineligible, and that notice thereof having been given to the returning officer, and the electors, the votes were thrown away; the counſel for the ſitting members argued, that the committee could not go into this point, becauſe there was no *expreſs* allegation or complaint on that ſubject, in the petition; they ſaid that the words " high ſheriff of the county of Hertford," appeared in the petition merely as an addition or deſcriptio perſonæ. The committee reſolved, that the counſel be " not permitted to argue the point of ineligibility of Sir Abraham Hume, as high ſheriff of the county of Hertford, the ſame ineligibility not being an allegation in the petition." They then proceeded to call witneſſes to prove the charge of bribery, but being prevented from aſking queſtions that tended to prove the declaration of voters not on oath, the petitioners dropt the cauſe, and the ſitting members were declared duly elected.

Caſe of the Town and Port of SEAFORD.—*Petitioners, Stephen Sayre, Eſq; and John Chetwood, Eſq.—Sitting members, William Hall, Lord Viſcount Gage; George Medley, Eſq.*

The

The petition set forth that many persons duly qualified, tendered their votes for the petitioners, but were rejected; by which means there was procured a majority for the sitting members. The last determination was 10th February, 1670-1, "that the committee were of opinion, that the bailiff, jurors, and freemen, had not only voices in election, but that the election was in the populacy. There is also an explanatory resolution on the 15th December, 1761; resolved, "that the word "populacy" (mentioned in the above determination) extended only to the inhabitants, housekeepers of the said town and port, paying scot and lot."

The counsel for the petitioners argued, that the explanatory resolution of 1761, was inconsistent with the true sense of the determination of 1670, which was the last determination of the House when the statute of 2 Geo. II. cap. 24. took place, and therefore final to all intents and purposes. The counsel for the sitting members objected to this being evidence to contradict the explanatory resolution, and after hearing arguments on both sides, the committee by a special resolution prevented them from producing evidence to call in question the said explanatory resolution. The counsel for the petitioners then proceeded to shew, that it is not necessary that persons, in order to answer the description of scot and lot-men, should actually be rated to, and pay the poor tax; 47 persons, who tendered their votes at the poll for the petitioners were rejected, because their names did not appear on the last poor rate; these would have given the petitioners a majority. A great deal of evidence was brought to prove that these people were rateable, and that they had been kept off the books, merely for the purpose of the election. On the other hand it was argued, that if their was any irregularity or injustice in the rating of the inhabitants, they ought to have had recourse to the legal means of redress.

The committee determined that the two sitting members were duly elected.

Case of the Town and County of the Town of SOUTHAMPTON.—*Petitioners, certain inhabitants of the town Southampton, in the interest of Lord Charles Montagu.*—*Sitting member John Fleming, Esq.*

The petition stated, that tho' the town of Southampton is

is governed by a mayor, and other officers, and has a sheriff of its own, and the sheriff of Hampshire has no officer to execute within the said town, yet persons having freeholds within the said town, vote in right of such freeholds, for knights of the shire, or county at large; and several other circumstances serve to shew, that the said town is still a part of the county at large; that Mr. Fleming was high sheriff of Hampshire when he was returned as a burgess for Southampton; and therefore they prayed that the committee would permit Lord Charles Montagu to take his seat instead of Mr. Fleming.

The last determination of the house on the right of election in Southampton, was on the 17th of March, 1695-6. — The sole question in this case, was the circumstance of Mr. Fleming's being high sheriff. The counsel therefore argued from the words in the writ; from the precedents on the journals, and the history of parliament; and after hearing the arguments on both sides, the committee resolved, "That it is the opinion of this committee, that John Fleming, Esq. being sheriff for Hampshire at the time of the last general election, was eligible to serve in parliament for the town of Southampton."—After this question was determined, the counsel for the petitioners said, they would prove that the sheriff of the town in making out his precept to the returning officer, had omitted the "Nolumus."

The committee would not permit them to go into this point, as it was not alledged in the petition. The sitting member was therefore confirmed in his seat.

Case of the Town of SHREWSBURY.—*Petitioners, William Pulteney, Esq. certain burgesses and others, electors of the town of Shrewsbury.—Sitting member, Charleton Leighton, Esq.*

The petitioners set forth, that at the last election Robert Lord Clive, in the kingdom of Ireland, Charleton Leighton, Esq. and the petitioner, were candidates; and that the mayor by admitting votes for the two former, which ought to have been rejected, and rejecting others for the petitioner which ought to have been admitted, had stated a majority on the poll in favour of Lord Clive and Mr. Leighton, and had returned them, although the petitioner would have had

a great

a great majority of legal votes, if juftice had been done him.
—After the petition was prefented, Lord Clive's death happened, but a new writ could not iffue while the petition was depending.—Mr. Pulteney's petition was withdrawn, and a new writ was iffued.—The only petition therefore which remained, was that of the burgeffes and electors, who only complained of Mr. Leighton's election.

The laft determination of the houfe on the right of election in Shrewfbury, was on the 9th of April, 1723.

If a clafs of men who had tendered their fuffrages, and had been rejected by the returning officer, were intitled by law to vote, it was admitted that Mr. Pulteney had a majority, and was duly elected.

The counfel for the petitioners contended, that the perfons whofe votes had been rejected, were intitled to their freedom under two immemorial cuftoms. 1. That all perfons of the age of one and twenty, and who have ferved a feven years apprenticefhip to one of the trades which form fourteen ancient companies by prefcription or incorporation, have a right to demand and be admitted to their freedom, on paying five pounds and the ufual fees.

2. That all perfons born within the borough, are, at the age of one and twenty, intitled in like manner to demand and be admitted to their freedom on the fame terms. The fact, that the rejected voters came under thefe defcriptions, was admitted—and it was proved, that they had demanded this freedom a year before the election—and that they had tendered their votes at the election—but the two cuftoms were called in queft on.—By a decifion of the Court of King's Bench, one Baxter had fued out a peremptory mandamus, and was admitted to his freedom—but the corporation after that decifion, ftill refufed to admit the perfons who claimed under the cuftoms.

The committee decided, that William Pulteney, Efq. was duly elected, and ought to have been returned.

Cafe of the Borough of SUDBURY.—*Petitioners,* Sir Walden Hanmer, Bart. *on behalf of himfelf and* Sir Patrick Blake, Bart. *(abfent in the ifland of St. Chriftopher's) certain electors for the borough of Sudbury.—Sitting members* Thomas Fonnereau, Efq. Philip Champion Crefpigny.

The petition fet forth, that a great many legal voters, who

who tendered their voices for Hanmer and Blake had been rejected, although they had been for many years in the poſſeſſion and exerciſe of their rights, to the knowledge of the mayor, and of Fonnereau, one of the ſitting members, in whoſe favour, and at whoſe requeſt, many of them had frequently polled at former elections; that many whoſe claim ſtood in the ſame predicament had been admitted to vote for the ſitting members; that others who were not legally qualified had alſo been admitted to vote for them; that the fair majority of legal votes was in favour of the petitioners; but that William Strutt, the mayor and returning officer, had acted partially and corruptly before, and during the poll, and had declared the ſitting members duly elected, and had returned them; and that money was given by the ſitting members or their agents, by way of bribe or reward to perſons who voted for them at the election.

The laſt determination of the Houſe on the right of election was 6th December, 1703. At the opening of the cauſe the counſel for the petitioners contended that the reſolution of the 6th of December, 1703, was merely explanatory of one of the 19th of January, 1702-3, in the following words, reſolved, "that the ſons of freemen, born after their fathers were made free, and thoſe that have ſerved apprenticeſhips in the borough of Sudbury, have a right to vote in the election of members to ſerve in parliament for the ſaid borough, *without any admiſſion in form to their freedom*, or taking the oath of freemen." A great number of perſons who tendered their ſuffrages for Hanmer and Blake at the election were rejected, becauſe they did not produce evidence of their admiſſions to their freedom, enrolled upon ſtamps, in the books of the corporation. The committee directed the counſel for the petitioners to produce evidence to ſhew by what right they rejected perſons claimed to vote; they then proceeded to ſhew, 1. That honorary freemen of whom a great number had polled for the ſitting members, had no right to vote. 2. That the perſons who had been rejected, becauſe they did not produce the enrollment of their admiſſion upon ſtamps, had a right to vote. And 3. That the mayor's conduct had been ſuch as merited the cenſure of the Committee and the Houſe. On the firſt point they ſtated, that till the year 1772, there had hardly been an inſtance

stance of persons admitted to their freedom without a title acquired either by birth, servitude, or redemption, but in 1772, the governing part of the corporation being in the interest of Mr. Fonnereau, made an entry in their books, importing that they had power to admit men claiming by any of the above titles, and also gratuitously or by *favour*, without any previous title or consideration in money. And the day after they admitted 170, of whom 130 had no right either by birth, servitude or redemption. On the second point, they said it had been the constant usage to permit persons having a title by birth to exercise all the rights of freemen *without any enrollment upon stamps*, and even without an entry of their admission in the books of the corporation. At the election 388 had been rejected, and it appeared that of this number 26 voted in 1734: 83 in 1747: 137 in May 1754: 187 in 1761 and 281 in 1768. The corporation had rejected them contrary to the usage. On the third point, it was said, that the lord mayor, just before the election, had a thousand copies printed of an extract from the Durham act 3 George III. cap. 15, containing the clause disqualifying freemen admitted to their freedom within the year, and mentioning the penalty of 100l. inflicted by the statute, if they shall presume to vote, *but remitting the exception in favour of persons who have an incboate title*. He had himself caused these papers to be distributed among the persons claiming to be enrolled.—By this means an alarm was spread, and proof was adduced, that many legal voters were deterred from giving their votes for the petitioners on this account.

The counsel on both sides argued upon these points, and it was clearly by an admission of these facts, that the committee at last decided that Sir William Hammer, bart. and Sir Patrick Blake, bart. were duly elected and ought to have been returned.

In order to do this it was only necessary, from the statement of the case, and the evidence produced, to come to an opinion, " that persons who derived their claims to their freedom from the antecedent title of birth, who had exercised all the rights of freemen, and that of voting for members of Parliament among the rest, for twenty years and upwards before the last election, who had demanded to be enrolled (and offered to prove that at their birth their fathers enjoyed and exercised the rights and franchises of freemen)

K   but

but were refused, had a right to vote, though they could not produce evidence of their admiffion upon stamps.

The committee feverely reprimanded the mayor for his conduct.

Cafe of the Borough of TAUNTON.---*Petitioners, Alexander Popham, Efq. and John Halliday, Efq. feveral inhabitants and electors of the Borough of Taunton.*—*Sitting Members, the Honourable Edward Stratford, Nathaniel Webb, Efq.*

The petitions, fet forth, that the mayor as returning officer, had by unneceffary adjournments protracted the poll from the 10th of October to the 18th, and that he had rejected many legal votes tendered for the petitioners, and admitted many illegal votes for the fitting members. That the petitioners were duly elected by a great majority of legal votes, and ought to have been returned. That the fitting members previous to, and during the election were guilty of bribery and corruption, by themfelves and agents.

The laft determination of the Houfe on the right of election, in Taunton, was on the 28th of July 1715. In Taunton there is a clear diftinction between *alms* and *charity*. *Alms* means parochial collection, or parifh relief. *Charity* fignifies fums arifing from the revenue of certain fpecific funds which have been eftablifhed or bequeathed for the purpofe of affifting the poor. Neither alms nor charity difqualify an elector in Taunton, unlefs they have been received within a year before the election. It was agreed that a potwaller is a perfon who furnifhes his own diet, whether he be a houfeholder, or only a lodger; and it was agreed that to be a potwaller, he muft have a refidence, and legal parochial fettlement in the borough. The counfel for the petitioners faid that the Journals of the Houfe have recognized that *apprentices* cannot be potwallers qualified to vote. The numbers on the poll, as produced by the returning officer, were as follows

For Webb, —— 260
Stratford, — 254
Halliday, — 202
Popham — 201

The counfel for the petitioners propofed to difqualify
114 as having received the town charity,
2 as having received the churchwarden's charity,
3 as Chelfea penfioners,
39 as not having fettlements in Taunton,

2 or 3 as certificate-men,
2 as apprentices,
2 as bribery agents.

144
And at the same time they said they would prove the charge of bribery. In the course of the cause it was settled that Chelsea pensioners might vote. It was agreed on both sides, that by the *lex loci* certificate-men cannot vote for this Borough. The counsel for the sitting members proposed to disqualify 31 of the petitioners votes on some clear grounds, and to recriminate the charge of bribery. After a very long investigation the committee determined that John Halliday, Esq. and Alexander Popham, Esq. were duly elected, and ought to have been returned.

The Case of the City and Liberty of WESTMINSTER.— *Petitioners, Henry Morres, Lord Viscount Mountmorres in the Kingdom of Ireland, and several other Inhabitants, Electors of the City and Liberty of Westminster.*

The petition sets forth, that at the late Election the petitioners, Lord Mountmorres, Charles Stanhope, commonly called Lord Viscount Mahon, Hugh Percy, commonly called Earl Percy, Thomas Pelham Clinton, commonly called Lord Thomas Pelham Clinton, and Humphrey Cotes, esq, being candidates, the King's menial servants, not having proper houses of their own within the city of Westminster, gave voices in the said election, contrary to an express resolution of the House. " 15th Nov. 1680, Resolved, that the King's menial servants not having proper houses of their own within the city of Westminster, have not right to give voices in the election of citizens to serve in Parliament for the said city." It also stated that divers peers and lords of parliament publickly canvassed and otherwise unduly interfered in the election, contrary to several express resolutions of the House; that during the election, after the teste and issuing out of the writ, Lord Percy and Lord Thomas Pelham Clinton by themselves or agents, were guilty of bribing, corrupting and entertaining the voters.

There is no general determination of the House, of the right of election in Westminster; but it seems to be agreed to be " In the inhabitants, householders, paying scot and lot.

The numbers on the poll stood thus:

For Earl Percy 4994
Lord Thomas Pelham Clinton 4744
Lord Mountmorres 2531
Lord Mahon 2342
Humphrey Cotes, esq. 130

It was proved that about nineteen persons under the description of the resolution of 1680, had polled for the sitting members. They were inhabitants of the Mews, and their Houses had of late, for the first time, been rated to the parish; on which account they claimed to be electors; but they acknowledged that their rates were paid by the King.—They had all been solicited for their votes by Lord Mountmorres and Lord Mahon. There was no positive proof of any direct solicitation of any peers, though there was strong presumptive proof: nor was there any evidence of bribery that came home to the sitting members.

The committee therefore declared Earl Percy and Lord Thomas Pelham Clinton to be duly elected.

Case for the City of WORCESTER.—*Petitioner, Sir Watkin Lewes, Knight.—Sitting Members, John Walsh, esq. Thomas Bates Rous, esq.*

The objects of the petitioner were I. To prove that bribery had been committed by the sitting members or their agents, and thereby to make the election void, as to them. II. To disqualify such a number of voters for the sitting members, and to add such a number to the poll for the petitioner, as to leave a majority in his favour, and entitle him to be declared duly elected. III. To induce the committee to make a special report to the House of the various matters particularly alledged in the petition against the sitting members, the corporation, the returning officer, a peer whose influence and interference was complained of, and the corrupted voters. On the first head witnesses were called, who swore to positive acts of bribery and promises by Mr. Walsh himself and by his agents. In answer to this, evidence was called on the other side, who positively contradicted the facts alledged, and in some instances the persons who were said to have given or to have received bribes persisted in denying the acts of bribery when confronted with the witnesses on the other side.—On the second point the counsel for the petitioner stated that a great number, constituting

stituting the majority of the voters had been procured by promises and by money—and in particular upwards of 300 constables were sworn in, and recieved money from the chamberlain the day before the election, who all voted for the sitting members, and many witnesses proved that offers were made to others to make them constables, if they would vote for the sitting members. To this it was anfwered, that the petitioner had given rife to apprehensions by his conduct, that the election would be riotous, and therefore the corporation had wisely increased the number of constables. 19 voters were given up by the sitting members, because their names were not to be found in the corporation books. On the third point there was nothing material infifted upon—The council for the sitting members objected to going into evidence on the improper interference of the peer, as the committee of privileges appointed annually, was the proper place for such a complaint.

The committee determined, that the two sitting members were duly elected.

Cafe of the Borough of CARDIGAN, *and its contributary Boroughs.—Petitioners, Thomas Johnes the younger, esq.—Several Burgesses of the Boroughs of Cardigan, Aberistwith, and Lampeter.—Sitting Member, Sir Robert Smyth, bart.*

The petition stated that Thomas Colby, esq. the returning officer permitted a great number of persons to poll for Sir Robert Smyth, who had no legal right to vote, and rejected the votes of divers others duly qualified, who offered to poll for Mr. Johnes, and was guilty of many other notorious acts of partiality and injuftice. The laft determination of the right of election was on the 7th of May, 1730.—Burgeffes are admitted into these boroughs without any particular qualification, and as all burgeffes, whether refident or not, have a right to vote, it has been usual, previous to an election, to admit great numbers. Above 4000 were admitted at Cardigan alone, between the beginning of the year 1774 and the laft election. Their votes, however, were not good on account of their occafionality. It had been ufual before 1765 to give to each burgess a docket of his admiffion, written on a flip of ftamped parchment, and figned by the Mayor and Town Clerk.—Since 1765, in confequence of the change then introduced in the law on this fubject, a ftamped book has been kept, in which the town clerk orders the names of the new burgesses.

At the election the mayor laid down a rule, " that he would admit every person to poll who would *say* he was a burgess of one of the four boroughs, and had polled at a former election." Mr. Johnes' managers objected to this, and insisted that none should be admitted to vote who did not produce entries of their admissions on stamps, if admitted since 1765, or stamped dockets if made free prior to that time. Notwithstanding this, however, all voters who came for Sir Robert Smyth, were admitted to vote without any investigation of their titles, but the admissions of all those who voted for Johnes were produced and inquired into. About 249 of Sir Robert's voters declared at the poll that they had no admissions to produce, and about 134 said they never had any admissions. In the course of the proceeding before the committee, it was agreed that the agents of both parties should examine the poll for Sir Robert Smyth, with the books of the corporation. In consequence of their joint examination, it was *agreed* that of the votes for the sitting members,

1. A certain number was not to be found at all in the books.
2. That the names of a certain number were in the books, but that the descriptions added to those names in the books, and on the poll were not the same.
3. That a certain number were only found in a list, written in a book called the council-book.
4. That the admissions of a certain number were entered on stamps *during* the poll.
5. That the admissions of others were entered on stamps *after* the poll.
6. And of others within a year before the election.
7. That the entries respecting a certain number in the corporation books, and on the poll, agreed both in the names and description.

The first class were given up by the counsel for the sitting member. On the second point the committee determined, " that the counsel for the petitioners should make their objections to each individual vote; and that when the description in the books should appear to differ from the description on the poll, it was incumbent on the counsel, for the sitting member to remove the objections, so as to reconcile the difference. On the third question, a deal of evidence

was

was produced, to prove that the list was vague and unauthentic. That it was made in 1741, before an election, for the purpose of serving the interest of a Mr. Lloyd, and that the names contained in it had not been shewn to be taken from presentments enrolled in the leet-books. The committee determined, "that the leet of 1741, as entered in the council book, was not admissible as evidence." On the fourth question, the committee resolved, "that the voters whose admissions were stamped during the poll, prior to their voting, are to be admitted as legal voters at this election.— The parties were to understand, that this resolution goes merely to the legality of stamping the admissions during the poll, before the voters had polled, and not to any other right whatsoever." On the fifth point, the committee resolved, "that persons, whose admissions were stamped after their votes were given, were not to be allowed as legal voters at the last election." On the sixth question, the committee resolved, "that it is not necessary by the statute of 3 George III. for freemen, whose right, in every other respect, is complete a year before an election, to have their admissions entered on stamps twelve Kalendar months before, in order to qualify them to vote at such election." On the seventh question, the council for the petitioners contended, that as there were so many persons of the same name in Wales, and as Mr. Johnes's agents were not suffered to enquire into the identity of these voters during the poll, it was now the business of the counsel for the sitting member to prove their identity. The committee, however, determined, that the onus of disproving the identity of the persons lay upon the counsel for the petitioners." In consequence of these resolutions of the committee, lists were prepared by the agents on each side, of the number of voters which were thereby disqualified, and the counsel for Sir Robert Smyth admitted, that as the poll then stood, there was a majority of fifty-eight in favour of Mr. Johnes.

Upon this, Smyth's counsel endeavoured, by evidence, to shew, that there was the greatest reason to believe, that many who had voted for Johnes, were not the persons who had really been admitted, but that they were men who had falsely personated those who were entitled to vote. On this, the committee resolved, " that as the identity of Mr. Johnes's voters had been scrutinized at the poll, it was not

in-

incumbent on his counsel to identify them before the committee.

The committee then determined, that Thomas Johnes, the younger, Esq. was duly elected, and ought to have been returned.

The Case of the Borough of NEW RADNOR, *and its Contributary Boroughs in the County of* RADNOR.———*Petitioners, Edward Lewis, esq. several Burgesses of the Borough of* NEW RADNOR, *and its Contributary Boroughs.*—*Sitting member, John Lewis, Esq.*

Both the petitions contained a general allegation, that Edward Lewis, Esq. the petitioner, had a great majority of legal votes and was duly elected.

The last determination of the House on the right of election was on the 12th of November, 1690.—The counsel for the petitioner insisted that by the word Burgesses, " Is meant all burgesses whether resident or non-resident; and that by the standing order of 1735, the counsel for the sitting member were not at liberty to go into any proof to the contrary. The counsel on the other side contended that by the standing order, the House could never intend to prohibit the explanation of ambiguous or equivocal words; they said they only meant to shew that the House must have understood in this instance, not " Burgesses at large," but " Burgesses inhabitants."—The committee were of opinion that they were not precluded by the standing order from receiving such explanation.---After having heard the arguments of the counsel, and read the various determinations of the House on the Welch boroughs, the committee resolved that out-burgesses as well as inhabitants, were intitled by the determination of the House to vote, and they therefore declared that Edward Lewis, Esq. the petitioner, was duly elected, and ought to have been returned.

Case of the County of CLACKMANNAN.—*Petitioner James Francis Erskine, Esq.*---*Sitting member Ralph Abercrombie, jun. Esq.*

The petition set forth that the sitting member was absolutely disqualified and ineligible; that the petitioner had a majority of legal votes; and that the return of the sitting member was brought about by various illegal and unwarrantable acts and proceedings.---The counsel for the petitioner argued, that the sitting member ought to have given in a *particular* of his estate to the clerk of the House,
within

within 15 days after the petition was read, according to the standing order.—It was either proved or admitted that Mr. Abercrombie had stood on the freeholders roll of Clackmannanshire even since 1759; but the petitioner objected to him on account of an alteration of circumstances—four months had elapsed and no complaint had been made to the court of session. The counsel for the sitting member contended, that now all the qualification necessary to be produced by him was his name on the roll.—That the House since the 16th of George the Second, had no jurisdiction with regard to the right of freeholders to stand on the roll, because the complaint is directed to be made to the court of session.

The committee were of opinion that they were bound by the statute of George the second; that the enrollment of the sitting member under all the circumstances of the case, was a sufficient answer to the petitioner's demand of his qualification; and that no other evidence should be called on the head of his qualification.—After this the petitioner informed them that he would not give them any further trouble—They therefore determined that the sitting member was duly elected.

Case of the County of FIFE.—*Petitioner,* John Henderson, *Esq.—Sitting Member,* James Townshend Oswald, *Esq.*

The numbers for Mr. Oswald were 61, and for the petitioner 61.—The counsel for the petitioner proposed to object to two of the votes for the sitting member, and his counsel again to one of the petitioner's.—The votes objected to by the petitioner, were those of Hugh Dalrymple, and William Melvil, Esqrs. They contended that the estate of Mr. Dalrymple was a redeemable right, not within the exception of the statute of 12 Anne, and therefore deprived of the right of voting. Mr. Melvil, they contended that he had no right to vote, as he was denuded of the title upon which he stood upon the roll; his wife in whose right he stood, having disposed her estate to her son Captain Graham.—After hearing the arguments on both sides, the committee informed the counsel that they were of opinion, that Hugh Dalrymple, Esq. of Fordell, and William Melvill, Esq. of Griegsten, had a right to vote at the last election of member to serve in parliament for the county of Fife.

Upon which the sitting member was declared to be duly elected.

Case

Case of the County of LANERK.—*Petitioner, Daniel Campbell, Esq.*—*Sitting Member, Andrew Stuart, Esq.*

The petition set forth that Mr. Stuart at the time of the election was ineligible, and that the petitioner had the majority of legal votes, and was duly elected. The counsel for the petitioner stated, that Mr. Stuart at the time of the election, held the office of joint king's remembrancer, in the court of exchequer in Scotland; which they said was an office of profit under the crown, erected since the 25th of October, 1705. The counsel for Mr. Stuart denied that he held the office at the time of his election.—On this a copy of the king's commissioner, under the union seal, bearing date the 25th of January, 1771, granting the place to Mr. Stewart, and Mr. Warrander jointly, was read. The counsel for Mr. Stewart then called several gentlemen to prove that he had resigned the office previous to the election. He had given by the hands of the solicitor-general, his resignation to the secretary of the treasury, but nothing had been done in it.

The committee resolved, " That it is the opinion of the committee, that Andrew Stuart, Esq. by the instrument of resignation executed at Edinburgh, on the 18th of October, 1774, and delivered to Mr. Cooper on the 25th of the same month, was at the time of his election divested of the office of king's remembrancer in the court of exchequer, in Scotland." This resolution of course put an end to the cause, and the sitting member was declared duly elected.

Case of the District of NORTH BERWICK, HADDINGTON, LAUDER, JEDBURGH, *and* DUNBAR.—*Petitioners,* Sir *Alexander Gilmour, Bart. Andrew Dickson, Esq. constituent Members of the Town Council of the Borough of Haddington, at Michaelmas,* 1774; *The Magistrates and Town Council of North Berwick; The Provost, Magistrates, and Council of the Borough of Dunbar.*—*Sitting Member, The* Hon. *John Maitland.*

The petitions set forth that at the election at North Berwick, the presiding borough commissions were produced in favour of persons named as delegates for the several boroughs; and David Kinloch, Esq. appeared, and claimed a vote, as having been the person duly elected delegate for the borough of Haddington; though a commission had been made out in favour of Robert Burton, Esq. provost of Haddington, and accordingly he gave his vote at the election under protest. That the delegates producing commissions from the boroughs Haddington, Lauder, and Jedburgh, voted for the Hon. John Maitland, clerk of the pipe in the court of exchequer, in Scotland; and the delegates from North Berwick and Dunbar, voted for Sir Alexander Gilmour. That Mr. Maitland was ineligible, on account of his office which had been created since the 25th of October, 1705.—That besides this, the two commissions for the boroughs of Haddington and Jedburgh, had been granted by persons who were by law incapable of electing a delegate, having no right themselves to the offices they assumed in the said borough; and that the said commissions were procured by bribery, &c. From this state of the allegations it appeared, that the two general questions in the case were 1. Whether Mr. Maitland was eligible? 2. Whether he, or Sir Alexander Gilmour had the majority of legal votes. After hearing the arguments of counsel on both sides, the committee determined on the first point, " That the Hon. John Maitland, was eligible to serve in parliament, notwithstanding his being in possession of the office of clerk of the pipe, in the exchequer of Scotland, at the time of his election."

On the second point, the counsel for the petitioners argued, that the commissions from the boroughs of Haddington and Jedburgh were illegal, because the magistrates of these boroughs had not been duly chosen.—By the 9th section of the second of George II. cap. 24. [it is enacted, " That the said statute shall be openly read at the annual election of magistrates and town-counsellors, for every borough within that part of Great Britain called Scotland." This provision was not complied with at the last annual election of magistrates for these boroughs, and therefore the election was void, and consequenly their future election of delegates. To this it was answered that this statute was merely directory, and that it never was read unless upon there quest of a member of the counsel. This point was therefore dropped; but another objection was started against the magistracy of Jedburgh, because in their last election they had departed from the *sett*, in not purging the council till some days after the election; but they were not able to prove from the usage, that there was any illegal irregularity in the proceeding.

The Committee declared the sitting member to be duly elected.

Cafe of the Diftrict of WIGTOWN, WHITEHORN, NEW-GALLOWAY, *and* STRANRAER.—*Petitioner,* Henry W. Dafhwood, *Efq.*—*Sitting Member, William Norton, Efq.*

The petition stated that the delegates for the boroughs of Wigtown, Whitehorn, and Stranraer, met at New Galloway, the prefiding borough, and that Alexander Fergufon, Efq. chofen and appointed delegate for the borough of New Galloway, abfented himfelf from the faid election, having pretended to refign the office of delegate. That John Newall, Efq. pretending to have been duly chofen delegate for the faid borough of New Galloway, upon fuch pretended refignation of the faid Alexander Fergufon, was admitted to vote, and accordingly did vote for the the fitting Member.— But the petitioner having had the votes of Wigtown and Whitehorn, and Mr. Norton the legal vote of Stranraer only, had thereby a majority of legal votes, and ought to have been returned

There were two queftions in this cafe, 1. Whether Mr. Newall was duly chofen a delegate for the borough of New Galloway, and was capable of voting: and 2. Whether a perfon, not a burgefs of any one of the boroughs compofing a diftrict, is capable of being elected a burgefs to ferve in parliament. Mr. Dafhwood was not a burgefs of either of the four boroughs, and this objection was taken to his eligibility by the counfel for the fitting member.

On the firft point it was ftated, that Mr. Fergufon was duly chofen the delegate of New Galloway, agreeable to the ftatute ; but on the morning of the day of election, a letter was prefented to the council of New Galloway, from Mr. Fergufon, in which he refigned his commiffion. The council *immediately* proceeded to the choice of another delegate, and the fame people chofe Mr. Newall.—But the ftatute fays, that two days fhould intervene between the meeting for naming the day of election, and the day of election. They urged that Mr. Fergufon could not refign, nor the council chofe another, he was *functum officio.* Upon the second point it was urged that there was not any pofitive and direct ftatute, which enjoined that the burgeffes for the royal boroughs fhould be actual burgeffes in the diftrict. It was the ufage indeed that they fhould be honorary, but honorary burgeffes can act in no corporate capacity, and are merely nominal. The committee determined that Henry Watkin Dafhwood, Efq. was duly elected.

F I N I S,

www.ingramcontent.com/pod-product-compliance
Lightning Source LLC
Chambersburg PA
CBHW032011220426
43664CB00006B/208